# Communications in Computer and Information Science 2938

Series Editors

Robert Stahlbock · Gary M. Weiss ·
Hamid R. Arabnia · Leonidas Deligiannidis
Editors

# Emerging Trends in Data Science, Information and Knowledge Engineering

21st International Conference, ICDATA 2025, and 24th International Conference, IKE 2025
Held as Part of the World Congress in Computer Science, Computer Engineering, and Applied Computing, CSCE 2025
Las Vegas, NV, USA, July 21–24
2025, Revised Selected Papers

*Editors*
Robert Stahlbock
University of Hamburg
Hamburg, Hamburg, Germany

Gary M. Weiss
Fordham University
New York, NY, USA

Hamid R. Arabnia
University of Georgia
Athens, GA, USA

Leonidas Deligiannidis
Wentworth Institute of Technology
Boston, MA, USA

ISSN 1865-0929 ISSN 1865-0937 (electronic)
Communications in Computer and Information Science
ISBN 978-3-032-22195-7 ISBN 978-3-032-22196-4 (eBook)
https://doi.org/10.1007/978-3-032-22196-4



This Springer imprint is published by the registered company Springer Nature Switzerland AG
The registered company address is: Gewerbestrasse 11, 6330 Cham, Switzerland

# Preface

It is our great pleasure to introduce this collection of selected papers presented at the 21st International Conference on Data Science (ICDATA 2025) and the 24th International Conference on Information & Knowledge Engineering (IKE 2025).

These conferences were held as part of the federated 2025 World Congress in Computer Science, Computer Engineering, and Applied Computing (CSCE 2025), which took place from July 21 to July 24, 2025, in Las Vegas, Nevada, USA.

The CSCE 2025 Congress brought together papers from a diverse array of communities, including researchers from universities, corporations, and government agencies. Accepted papers are published by Springer Nature, and the proceedings showcase solutions to key challenges in various critical areas of Computer Science, Computer Engineering, and Applied Computing.

Computer Science (CS) is the study of computational systems, data processing, information management, and automation. Many applications in CS focus on solving problems that would be impossible or extremely difficult to address without the use of computers. It serves as a bridge between computational science and other scientific fields. The interdisciplinary nature of CS involves leveraging computers to understand and solve complex challenges, making it the science of using computers to advance scientific discovery. Computer Engineering (CE), on the other hand, integrates aspects of computer science, electronic engineering, and electrical engineering. It encompasses the design and production of computer hardware, such as chips, servers, supercomputers, embedded systems, and communication systems, among others.

Considering the above broad outline, the CSCE 2025 Congress was composed of the following focused conferences:

Applied Cognitive Computing (ACC); Bioinformatics & Computational Biology (BIOCOMP); Biomedical Engineering (BIOENG); Scientific Computing (CSC); eLearning, e-Business, Enterprise Information Systems, & e-Government (EEE); Embedded Systems, Cyber-physical Systems, & Applications (ESCS); Foundations of Computer Science (FCS); Frontiers in Education (FECS); Grid, Cloud, & Cluster Computing (GCC); Health Informatics (HIMS); Artificial Intelligence (ICAI); Data Science (ICDATA); Emergent Quantum Technologies (ICEQT); Internet Computing & IoT (ICOMP); Wireless Networks (ICWN); Information & Knowledge Engineering (IKE); Image Processing, Computer Vision, & Pattern Recognition (IPCV); Modeling, Simulation & Visualization Methods (MSV); Parallel & Distributed Processing Techniques & Applications (PDPTA); Security & Management (SAM); and Software Engineering Research & Practice (SERP). The scope of each track can be found at: https://www.american-cse.org/csce2025/conferences.

The primary objective of the CSCE Congress and its associated conferences is to foster opportunities for cross-fertilization between the fields of Computer Science (CS) and Computer Engineering (CE). The CSCE Congress is deeply committed to promoting diversity and eliminating discrimination, both in its role as a conference organizer and as a service provider. Our goal is to create an inclusive culture that respects and values differences, promotes dignity, equality, and diversity, and encourages individuals to reach their full potential. We are also dedicated, wherever possible, to organizing a conference that represents the global community. We sincerely hope that we have succeeded in achieving these important objectives.

The Steering Committee and the Program Committees would like to extend their gratitude to all the authors who submitted papers for consideration. This year's conferences received submissions from 58 countries, with approximately 50% of them coming from outside the USA. Each submitted paper underwent a rigorous peer-review process, with at least two experts (an average of 2.4 referees per paper) evaluating the submissions based on originality, significance, clarity, impact, and soundness. In cases where reviewers' recommendations were contradictory, a program committee member was tasked with making the final decision, often consulting additional referees for further guidance. The Congress followed the guidelines of COPE (Committee on Publication Ethics):

- Typical submissions underwent a single-blind peer review process, in which the authors remained unaware of the identities of the reviewers, while the reviewers were informed of the authors' identities.
- Papers authored by one or more members of the program committee, including co-chairs, were subjected to a double-blind peer review process, ensuring that neither the authors nor the reviewers were aware of each other's identities or affiliations.

The ICDATA 2025 Conference received a total of 182 submissions, of which 44 papers were accepted, resulting in a paper acceptance rate of 24%. For this volume we selected only 31 of the papers accepted at ICDATA. The IKE 2025 Conference received 97 submissions, of which 18 papers were accepted, resulting in a paper acceptance rate of 19%. For this volume we selected only 8 of the papers accepted at IKE.

This volume includes 39 of the accepted papers from ICDATA 2025 and IKE 2025.

We are deeply grateful to the many colleagues who contributed their time and effort to organizing the Congress. In particular, we extend our thanks to the members of the Program Committees, the Steering Committee, the referees, and the Chairs and organizers of individual sessions and conferences. We would also like to express our appreciation to the primary sponsor of the conference, the American Council on Science & Education. The list of members of the Program Committee for each track can be found at: https://www.american-cse.org/csce2025/committees.

We extend our heartfelt gratitude to all the speakers and authors for their valuable contributions. We would also like to thank the following individuals and organizations for their support: the staff at the Luxor Hotel, the staff of Springer Nature, Soheyla Amirian (Pace University), Farzan Shenavarmasouleh (Medialab Inc., USA), and Farid Ghareh Mohammadi (Verify Radiology Images Consultants, LLC, USA) for their assistance in various aspects of the event.

We are pleased to present a curated selection of papers from the ICDATA 2025 and IKE 2025 conferences. These proceedings represent a collection of outstanding research contributions that reflect the diversity and depth of work in core areas of Data Science, Information & Knowledge Engineering.

August 2025

Robert Stahlbock
Gary M. Weiss
Hamid R. Arabnia
Leonidas Deligiannidis

# Organization

## Steering Committee – Co-chairs (CSCE 2025)

| | |
|---|---|
| Hamid R. Arabnia | University of Georgia, USA |
| Leonidas Deligiannidis | Wentworth Institute of Technology, USA |
| Fernando G. Tinetti | Universidad Nacional de La Plata, Argentina |
| Quoc-Nam Tran | Southeastern Louisiana University, USA |

## Co-editors of ICDATA 2025 and IKE 2025 Proceedings – Publication Co-chairs

| | |
|---|---|
| Robert Stahlbock | University of Hamburg, Germany |
| Gary M. Weiss | Fordham University, USA |
| Hamid R. Arabnia | University of Georgia, USA |
| Leonidas Deligiannidis | Wentworth Institute of Technology, USA |

## Members of Steering Committee (CSCE 2025)

| | |
|---|---|
| Babak Akhgar | Sheffield Hallam University, UK |
| Abbas M. Al-Bakry | University of IT & Communications, Iraq |
| Nizar Al-Holou | University of Detroit Mercy, USA |
| Hamid R. Arabnia | University of Georgia, USA |
| Rajab Challoo | Texas A&M University-Kingsville, USA |
| Chien-Fu Cheng | Tamkang University, Taiwan |
| Hyunseung Choo | Sungkyunkwan University, South Korea |
| Kevin Daimi | University of Detroit Mercy, USA |
| Leonidas Deligiannidis | Wentworth Institute of Technology, USA |
| Eman M. El-Sheikh | University of West Florida, USA |
| Mary Mehrnoosh Eshaghian-Wilner | University of California, Los Angeles, USA |
| David L. Foster | Kettering University, USA |
| Henry Hexmoor | Southern Illinois University at Carbondale, USA |
| Ching-Hsien (Robert) Hsu | Chung Hua University, Taiwan |
| James J. (Jong Hyuk) Park | SeoulTech, South Korea |
| Mohammad S. Obaidat | University of Jordan, Jordan |
| Marwan Omar | Illinois Institute of Technology, USA |

| | |
|---|---|
| Shahram Rahimi | University of Alabama, USA |
| Gerald Schaefer | Loughborough University, UK |
| Fernando G. Tinetti | Universidad Nacional de La Plata, Argentina |
| Quoc-Nam Tran | Southeastern Louisiana University, USA |
| Shiuh-Jeng Wang | Central Police University, Taiwan |
| Layne T. Watson | Virginia Polytechnic Institute & State University, USA |
| Chao-Tung Yang | Tunghai University, Taiwan |
| Mary Yang | University of Arkansas for Medical Sciences, USA |

## Research Tracks – Co-chairs (CSCE 2025)

| | |
|---|---|
| Abeer Alsadoon (Co-chair, Health Informatics) | Charles Sturt University, Australia |
| Soheyla Amirian (Co-chair, Computer Vision & AI) | Pace University, USA |
| Hamid R. Arabnia (Co-chair, HPC) | University of Georgia, USA |
| Kevin Daimi (Co-chair, Security) | University of Detroit Mercy, USA |
| Leonidas Deligiannidis (Co-chair, Imaging Science, AI) | Wentworth Institute of Technology, USA |
| Richard Dill (Co-chair, Military and Defense Modeling) | US Air Force Institute of Technology, USA |
| Ken Ferens (Co-chair, Cognitive Computing & AI) | University of Manitoba, Canada |
| David de la Fuente (Co-chair, Information Management) | University of Oviedo, Spain |
| Shanzhen Gao (Co-chair, Artificial Intelligence, Education) | Virginia State University, USA |
| Farid Ghareh Mohammadi (Co-chair, Computer Vision & AI) | Verify Radiology Images Consultants, LLC, USA |
| Michael R. Grimaila (Co-chair, Military and Defense Modeling) | US Air Force Institute of Technology, USA |
| Douglas D. Hodson (Co-chair, Military and Defense Modeling) | US Air Force Institute of Technology, USA |
| Masahito Ohue (Co-chair, Mathematical Modeling) | Tokyo Institute of Technology, Japan |

| | |
|---|---|
| Peter M. Maurer (Co-chair, Theoretical Computer Science) | Baylor University, USA |
| Jose A. Olivas (Co-chair, Information Management) | University of Castilla - La Mancha, Spain |
| Javier Ordus (Co-Chair, Quantum Computing & AI) | Earlham College, USA |
| Pablo Rivas (Chair, Quantum Computing & AI) | Baylor University, USA |
| Farzan Shenavarmasouleh (Co-chair, Computer Vision & AI) | MediaLab Inc., USA |
| Robert Stahlbock (Co-chair, Data Mining) | Universität Hamburg, Germany |
| Masami Takata (Co-chair, Mathematical Modeling) | Nara Women's University, Japan |
| Nazli Tekin (Co-chair, Energy Aware, Security) | Erciyes University, Turkey |
| Quoc-Nam Tran (Co-chair, Education & Bioinformatics) | Southeastern Louisiana University, USA |
| Torrey J. Wagner (Co-chair, Scientific Computing, Artificial Intelligence) | US Air Force Institute of Technology, USA |
| Troy Weingart (Co-chair, Military and Defense Modeling) | US Air Force Institute of Technology, USA |
| Gary M. Weiss (Co-chair, Data Mining) | Fordham University, USA |
| Nobuaki Yasuo (Co-chair, Mathematical Modeling) | Tokyo Institute of Technology, Japan |
| Tanwir Zaman (Co-chair, Artificial Intelligence) | Walmart Labs, USA |
| Chris Cheng Zhang (Co-chair, Artificial Intelligence, Robotics) | Canada Youth Robotics Club, Canada |
| Beilei Zhu (Co-chair, Supply Chain Management) | Intel Corporation, USA |

## Program Committees of ICDATA 2025 and IKE 2025

Refer to the lists at:
https://icdatascience.org/committees/
https://www.american-cse.org/csce2025/committees

# Contents

# Data Science, Artificial Intelligence, and Applications

# Reinforcement Learning Explainability Using Decision Tree in Combat Environment

Indu Shukla[1(✉)], Abderahim Salhi[1], James E. Ross[1], and Gary J. Briggs[2]

[1] United States Army Corps of Engineers, Vicksburg, MS, USA
{indu.shukla,Abderahim.Salhi,James.E.Ross}@usace.army.mil
[2] RAND Corporation, Santa Monica, CA, USA
gbriggs@rand.org

**Abstract.** This study focuses on advancing Multi-Agent Reinforcement Learning (MARL) by exploring dynamic environments where multiple agents interact in both cooperative and competitive scenarios. The complexity of these interactions is progressively increased by utilizing well-established MARL scenarios, providing a comprehensive and robust framework for testing and evaluation. By simulating various agent behaviors, the study aims to capture a wide range of decision-making processes and interaction patterns, ensuring a thorough examination of MARL systems in diverse conditions. A key component of this research is the implementation of explainability techniques to make agent interactions more transparent and interpretable. To achieve this, advanced policy visualization methods, such as heatmaps and decision trees, are applied to clearly illustrate agent behavior across different regions of the state space. These visualizations provide valuable insights into how agents make decisions and respond to environmental changes, making the system more accessible to human understanding and enabling better analysis of agent strategies. By enhancing both the complexity of agent interactions and the interpretability of their decision-making processes, this study aims to push the boundaries of MARL development and evaluation.

**Keywords:** Explainability · Decision Tree · Utility AI · XRL

## 1 Introduction

In modern aerial combat and simulation environments, the integration of advanced decision-making algorithms and reinforcement learning (RL) techniques has revolutionized how autonomous agents navigate, engage, and respond to dynamic threats [1]. These environments simulate the complexities of aerial maneuvers while incorporating critical aspects such as real-time observations, action feedback, and reward-based learning, which are essential for developing sophisticated utility AI systems.


R. Stahlbock et al. (Eds.): CSCE 2025, CCIS 2938, pp. 3–14, 2027.
https://doi.org/10.1007/978-3-032-22196-4_1

Utility AI focuses on maximizing an agent's performance by strategically selecting actions that optimize long-term outcomes. In aerial combat scenarios, an AI agent must make rapid, high-stakes decisions to control an aircraft's pitch, roll, yaw, and throttle while continuously assessing its position relative to adversarial threats. By employing reinforcement learning, the agent learns to maximize cumulative rewards based on various key parameters, such as proximity to adversaries, relative velocity, and damage inflicted or avoided. The learning process involves balancing aggression with caution, as the agent must optimize performance while minimizing penalties for errors or inefficiencies.

To enhance the transparency and interpretability of decision-making in our simulation framework, we first collect data on agent behavior and then apply decision rules outside the simulation environment. To achieve this, we integrate decision trees into the framework. Decision trees serve as an interpretable model for action selection, simplifying complex decision-making processes into clear, human-understandable rules. This method allows users to comprehend the rationale behind specific maneuvers, fostering trust in the AI's actions and facilitating more effective collaboration between human operators and autonomous systems.

Additionally, the integration of advanced language models to introduce a new layer of capability. LLM's natural language processing tools can be used to translate the AI's decision-making rationale into human-readable explanations. This enhances the overall transparency of the system and facilitates clear communication between AI models and human users. By bridging the gap between complex AI processes and human understanding, these language models empower users to better comprehend and evaluate the decisions made by autonomous systems.

The combination of utility AI, decision trees, and language models from OpenAI exemplifies a holistic approach to developing explainable and efficient autonomous agents. The structured simulation environment, with its detailed action and observation spaces, provides a robust testing ground for training AI models to handle high-pressure, real-world scenarios. As autonomous systems become increasingly prevalent in both defense and civilian sectors, the emphasis on interpretability, effectiveness, and trustworthiness remains a vital focus, ensuring that AI systems not only perform well but are also understood and trusted by human operators.

## 2 Related Work

In recent years, there has been a growing focus on explainable reinforcement learning (XRL) to address the black-box nature of traditional RL models. A comprehensive survey by [2] categorizes XRL methods into model-agnostic and model-specific techniques, highlighting the importance of post-hoc explanations and interpretable function approximators. Policy distillation, a common approach in XRL, involves translating complex models into more interpretable forms, such as decision trees, to elucidate an agent's behavior.

Over the past two decades, significant advancements have been made in the development of differentiable decision trees and their integration with neural network models. Early work by Irsoy et al. [3] and Laptev and Buhmann [4] laid the foundation for making decision trees differentiable, facilitating their use in environments that require continuous learning and gradient-based optimization. Frosst and Hinton [5] introduced a method to distill a soft decision tree from a neural network, though this approach was primarily tested on simple tasks like MNIST digit classification.

In the context of RL, Coppens et al. [6] explored distilling RL policies into differentiable decision trees to enhance interpretability. Coppens et al. focused on policy imitation using differentiable decision trees, while Liu et al. [7] applied this framework to the Q-value function and introduced Linear Model U-trees, which incorporate linear models in the leaf nodes. Silva et al. [8] proposed using differentiable decision trees as function approximators for either the Q function or policy, simplifying the trees through discretization for improved interpretability. The VIPER method by Bastani et al. [9] distilled policy networks into decision trees with theoretical guarantees, though it was limited to imitation learning settings and nonparametric decision trees.

Gokhale et al. [10] addresses lack of interpretability and transparency in traditional RL by proposing a novel approach that leverages differentiable decision trees to create explainable RL policies. Their method involves policy distillation, where complex RL controllers are distilled into interpretable decision trees, making the control policies easy for end-users to understand. This approach has proven effective in a battery-based home energy management system, where explainable policies reduced energy costs compared to baseline rule-based methods, while still being simple enough for users to grasp.

Costa et al. [11] address explainability challenge with their proposed algorithm, MENS-DT-RL (Multi-method Ensemble for Decision Trees in Reinforcement Learning). MENS-DT-RL is an evolutionary algorithm designed to evolve univariate decision trees that maintain high performance while being interpretable. The approach uses a multi-method ensemble strategy, drawing on techniques from optimization to evolve decision trees guided by a fitness metric that emphasizes both interpretability and consistency. To enhance performance, the authors introduce three initialization methods, including the use of Imitation Learning (IL) techniques and a novel pruning strategy. The pruning technique reduces the size of decision trees without compromising their effectiveness, adapting traditional post-pruning methods to the RL environment. Pynadath et al. [12] explore the use of decision-tree explanations to make the behavior of RL agents more interpretable in human-robot teams. Their work demonstrates that decision trees, with their simple and rule-based structure, can significantly improve users' understanding of an agent's actions, thereby enhancing perceived transparency and overall team performance.

Gjærum et al. [13] introduced model tree methods to explain the behavior of deep RL agents. Model trees are structured like decision trees but incorporate simple models, such as linear regressions, within each segment to provide more detailed and interpretable insights into the agent's decision-making process.

As research in RL and explainable AI continues to evolve, integrating decision trees and utility-based models provides a promising direction for improving the transparency and interpretability bridges the gap between AI models and human comprehensible explanations. These advancements hold significant implications for real-world applications, particularly in high-stakes domains such as autonomous aerial combat, where decision clarity and trust are paramount.

## 3 Methodology

### 3.1 Dataset and Training

RL has emerged as a promising approach for enhancing air combat simulation, offering unique advantages over traditional rule-based systems and even human pilots in simulated dogfights. The success of RL lies in its ability to model complex, dynamic environments and learn effective strategies for maneuvering and decision-making. Previous research has explored various approaches, such as guided reinforcement learning and approximate dynamic programming, to tackle air combat simulation challenges. However, these approaches typically relied on human expert-designed dense reward structures that can be difficult to specify.

Notably, RL algorithms have achieved significant success in recent years, culminating in the DARPA's AlphaDogfight Trials (ADT). In these trials that took place in 2020, an RL agent developed by Heron Systems defeated a human pilot in a simulated dogfight, demonstrating the remarkable progress and potential of RL in air combat simulation. While that represented enormous progress, the trials were simulation-based, not in a real-world scenario. However, in 2023, as part of the Air Combat Evolution (ACE) program, DARPA took that challenge to the next level by taking the experiments outside simulation to the real world with an "AI vs. Human" dogfight. This involved an AI-controlled modified F-16 competing against a US Air Force human pilot. Although DARPA didn't announce who won the dogfight, it was a huge step forward for RL application in air combat simulation [14].

To simulate and collect data for reinforcement learning in a combat environment, a custom OpenAI Gym-compatible environment was utilized. The training process for the MARL scenario is conducted within a six-degree-of-freedom (six-dof) environment. This high-fidelity simulator models aerial engagements with realistic dynamics, enabling agents to learn through interaction and adaptation in a challenging multi-agent setting. Key components include agent observation spaces, action spaces, reward formulation, and RL-based policy updates. At each time step, the agent performed actions sampled from the action space, including pitch, roll, rudder, and throttle inputs. The resulting observations, rewards, and terminal conditions were recorded in a dataset. The two primary agents, the Blue Team (defender) and the Red Team (attacker), are trained through reinforcement learning techniques using the state and action spaces defined by the six-dof simulation.

In the six-dof training environment, agents are designed with different objectives to simulate realistic aerial engagements. The Blue Team (defensive agent) focuses on evading threats, minimizing damage, and maintaining a positional advantage, while the Red Team (offensive agent) seeks to exploit weaknesses in Blue Team defenses and optimize offensive strategies. Both teams interact dynamically, guided by their observation and action spaces. The observation space comprises normalized inputs describing aircraft parameters (e.g., altitude, speed, heading), positional metrics (e.g., distance to the opponent) and relative state variables. The action space enables continuous control, including throttle adjustments, pitch, roll, and yaw, facilitating complex aerial maneuvers.

A carefully designed reward function drives agent learning. Rewards are awarded for maintaining positional advantages, dealing damage, and operational efficiency, while penalties discourage stalling, boundary violations, and unrealistic behaviors. Training occurs in discrete time steps (0.05 s), with episodes ending with critical damage, boundary breaches, or engagement resolutions, ensuring varied and realistic training scenarios.

Comprehensive datasets are generated, including state-action pairs, reward trajectories, and engagement metrics, for policy refinement. These datasets support reinforcement learning updates, improving decision-making. Real-time visualizations, such as positional displays, reward trends, and control input analyses, provide critical insights into training dynamics, enabling effective evaluation and debugging of agent behavior.

Figure 1 shows the data set which contains 21 columns, includes a total of 10,000 time steps per simulation, and captures both agent inputs and the corresponding environmental states.

| Column Name | Description |
|---|---|
| step | Simulation time step (discrete). |
| Pitch Stick (aStickBack) | Agent's pitch control input (-1.0 to 1.0). |
| Roll Stick (aStickRight) | Agent's roll control input (-1.0 to 1.0). |
| Rudder Stick (aRudderRight) | Agent's yaw control input (-1.0 to 1.0). |
| Throttle (aThrottles) | Agent's throttle control input (-1.0 to 1.0). |
| Altitude (km MSL) | Aircraft altitude above mean sea level. |
| Heading (Degrees) | Aircraft heading in degrees. |
| Pitch (Degrees) | Current pitch angle of the aircraft in degrees. |
| Roll (Degrees) | Current roll angle of the aircraft in degrees. |
| Mach | Aircraft speed relative to the speed of sound. |
| Roll Rate | Rate of roll of the aircraft. |
| Pitch Rate | Rate of pitch of the aircraft. |
| Yaw Rate | Rate of yaw of the aircraft. |
| Relative Elevation | Elevation angle relative to the adversary. |
| Relative Azimuth | Azimuth angle relative to the adversary. |
| Cross Track | Lateral distance from the designated path. |
| Down Range | Longitudinal distance from the designated path. |
| Relative Velocity NED (North) | Relative velocity in the North direction. |
| Relative Velocity NED (East) | Relative velocity in the East direction. |
| Relative Velocity NED (Down) | Relative velocity in the Down direction. |
| Reward | Reward received for the agent's actions at each step. |
| Done | Terminal condition indicator (True/False). |

**Fig. 1.** Dataset Structure.

Figure 2 illustrates 3D trajectory plot for agent's movement patterns in a six-degree-of-freedom (six-dof) simulation environment used for MARL. The graph visualizes the agent's position through Cross Track, Down Range, and Altitude, with a color gradient representing velocity (Mach). It reveals key behavioral insights, such as slower speeds during defensive loops and faster speeds during

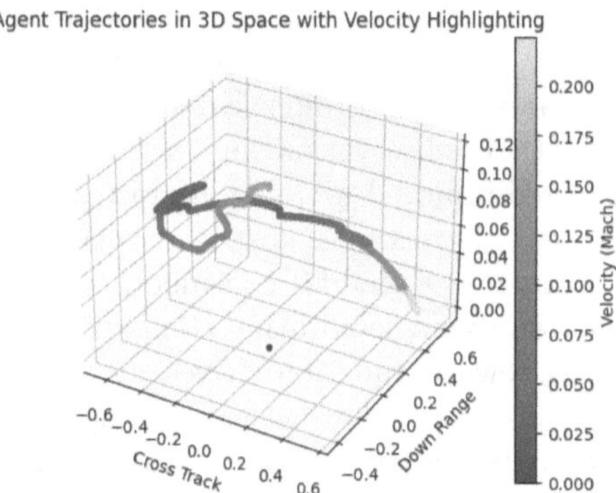


**Fig. 2.** The 3D trajectory plot illustrates the movement patterns of an agent in a simulated aerial combat environment.

offensive maneuvers, indicating the agent's dynamic decision-making in response to environmental conditions. This visualization aids in evaluating learned policies, understanding agent strategies, and optimizing reward functions by providing an interpretable representation of agent behavior in complex aerial engagements.

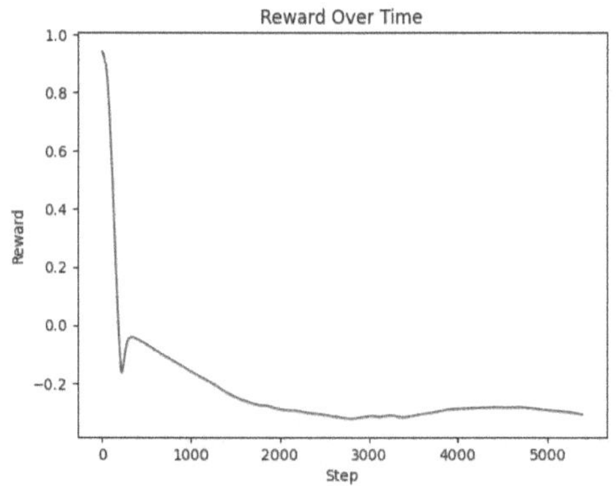


**Fig. 3.** Reward Over Time graph.

In Fig. 3 The Reward Over Time graph illustrates how the agent's rewards fluctuate throughout the simulation. Initially, the agent receives high rewards, likely due to starting in a favorable position or taking exploratory actions. However, these rewards quickly decrease as the agent begins to experience penalties, which may result from boundary violations, inefficient maneuvers, or other suboptimal decisions. After this initial learning phase, the rewards stabilize at a consistently low, negative level, indicating that the agent is repeatedly receiving penalties. This trend suggests that the agent's strategy is inefficient, and it is likely struggling to achieve its intended goals, such as maintaining positional advantages or avoiding damage. The consistent negative rewards highlight potential shortcomings in the agent's policy, where it fails to optimize actions for positive outcomes. However, it is important to note that the primary objective of this research is not to achieve the best-trained agent. Instead, the focus is on deriving explainable behaviors from the agent's decision-making process using decision trees. By translating the learned policy into human-understandable rules, we aim to improve interpretability and transparency in multi-agent environments, even if the agent's performance is suboptimal.

### 3.2 Explainability Methods Using Decision Tree

We chose decision trees as our primary explainability method due to their intuitive structure and ease of interpretation. Decision trees follow a rule-based structure, which makes them inherently interpretable compared to black-box models such as neural networks. Unlike neural networks, decision trees allow for a step-by-step trace of the decision-making process, making it possible to understand the conditions under which specific actions are taken.

In RL environments, where agents learn by interacting with complex and dynamic settings, it can be challenging to trust or verify the agent's behavior. By distilling the agent's learned policies into a set of decision tree rules, we can explain the agent's behavior by identifying the conditions that lead to specific actions. We can detect suboptimal decision patterns that can help refine the training process. Decision trees can help improve trust and transparency by presenting a clear, interpretable model of the agent's decision-making process.

Each node in the decision tree represents a decision point based on a feature (e.g., Relative Elevation, Pitch Rate), while each leaf node represents a predicted action value. This provides a transparent approach to understanding agent behavior by breaking down complex prediction models into human-readable rules. In the context of our multi-agent reinforcement learning (MARL) environment, the decision tree model enables stakeholders, analysts, and operators to understand and evaluate the agent's decisions effectively.

A DecisionTreeRegressor from the scikit-learn library was employed to predict the Pitch Stick (aStickBack) action based on the agent's observation space inputs. The model was trained on a training dataset and evaluated on a test dataset. We set the maximum depth of the decision tree to 5 to balance interpretability and predictive accuracy. A deeper tree could result in overfitting, generating overly specific rules that are difficult to interpret, while a shallow tree could lose critical predictive power. This depth selection ensures that the extracted decision rules remain concise and interpretable, while still capturing meaningful decision-making patterns.

While the decision tree was trained with a depth of 5 to balance predictive accuracy and interpretability, the resulting visualization became increasingly complex, making it harder to convey decision-making rules effectively. To address this, we pruned the tree to show key decision points and complemented it with extracted decision rules in textual form.

### 3.3 Generating Natural Language Explanations from Decision Tree Rules

To enhance the interpretability of the agent's decision-making process, we utilized a decision tree model to derive explicit, rule-based decision paths from the reinforcement learning environment. The decision tree rules, which map input state variables (e.g., Relative Elevation, Roll Rate, Pitch Degrees) to corresponding actions, provide a structured, human-readable representation of the agent's policies. These rules were extracted from a trained DecisionTreeRegressor model with a carefully selected depth to balance interpretability and predictive accuracy.

To further simplify these decision-making rules into natural language explanations, we integrated a pretrained NLP model from the Hugging Face Transformers library. Specifically, we employed the T5 model, which is well-suited for text generation tasks. The extracted decision tree rules were cleaned and structured into prompts, which were fed into the T5 model to generate plain-language explanations for non-expert users. These explanations focused on describing the agent's decision logic, highlighting why specific actions were taken based on the agent's observed state.

By converting technical decision rules into simplified text, this approach bridges the gap between complex AI behaviors and human interpretability. It provides an accessible way for stakeholders, such as pilots and analysts, to understand the rationale behind an agent's actions, ultimately improving trust and transparency in the reinforcement learning system.

## 4 Results

### 4.1 Determining Tree Depth

The graph in Fig. 4 shows training vs test error across tree depths, this graph demonstrates the impact of tree depth on the performance of the decision tree model, evaluated using the Mean Squared Error metric. The blue line represents the training error, while the red line shows the test error. The graph highlights how increasing the tree depth affects the model's ability to generalize to unseen data and the balance between underfitting and overfitting. The training error consistently decreases as the tree depth increases. This indicates that deeper trees can capture more complex patterns in the training data, which reduces the error on the training set. However, this comes at the cost of overfitting, where the model becomes too specialized to the training data and struggles to perform well on new, unseen data. The test error follows a different trend. Initially, as the tree depth increases, the test error decreases, suggesting that the model is improving its generalization capabilities. However, after a certain point around depth = 5, the test error begins to rise, indicating that the model is starting to overfit. At

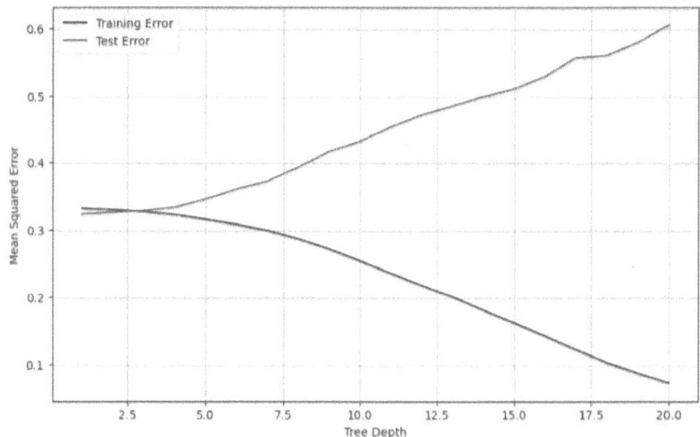


**Fig. 4.** Training vs Test Error Across Tree Depths.

this depth, the model achieves a balance between capturing relevant patterns and avoiding overfitting, making it the optimal tree depth for this dataset.

As the depth exceeds 10, the gap between the training and test errors widens significantly. This indicates that the model is becoming increasingly overfitted to the training data, memorizing specific patterns that do not generalize well to new data. The graph highlights the importance of selecting an appropriate tree depth to ensure the model maintains a good balance between underfitting and overfitting, improving the model's overall reliability and interpretability.

## 4.2 Decision Tree Visualization

The decision tree visualization Fig. 5 illustrates how the trained model makes predictions for the Pitch Stick (aStickBack) action based on various features from the aircraft's state and environment. The tree structure contains a series of decision nodes, each representing a condition based on a specific feature (e.g., Relative Elevation, Roll Rate, Mach), and the leaf nodes indicate the predicted values for the pitch action. The root node splits the data based on Relative Elevation, indicating that this feature plays a significant role in determining the pitch action. Subsequent splits are based on features like Relative Azimuth, Roll Rate, and Mach, highlighting how these features contribute to the agent's decision-making process. Each leaf node represents a predicted action value for the Pitch Stick, showing the model's output after considering all the decision rules along the path.

While the tree depth of 5 was chosen based on error analysis to balance interpretability and accuracy, the visualization demonstrates that even a moderately deep tree can become dense and challenging to interpret. Despite this, the decision rules extracted from the tree provide valuable insights into the agent's behavior. Each path from the root node to a leaf represents a rule that can be communicated to stakeholders for a clearer understanding of the agent's decision-making process.

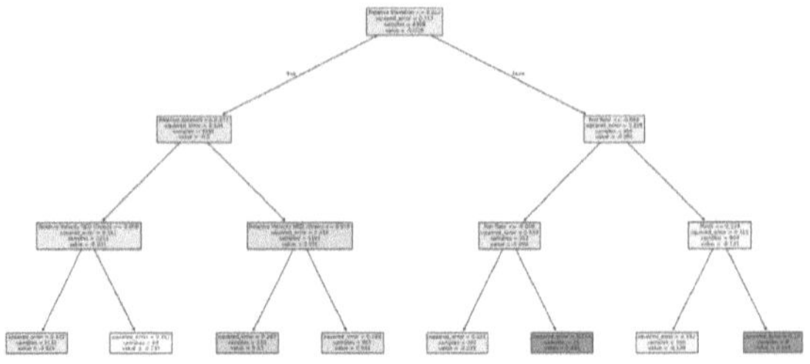

**Fig. 5.** Decision Tree Visualization.

This decision tree visualization confirms that explainability in reinforcement learning can be achieved by distilling complex policies into interpretable rule-based models. However, it also highlights the need to balance the depth and complexity of the decision tree to ensure that the explanations remain understandable without sacrificing predictive performance.

### 4.3 Natural Language Explanation of Decision Tree Rules

The results of our approach demonstrate the effectiveness of using decision tree rules to generate clear, human-readable explanations for complex decision-making processes in a MARL environment. By converting technical rules derived from the decision tree into plain-language explanations using a pretrained NLP model, we provide a transparent view of the agent's behavior.

Generated Explanation:

*Imagine you are a pilot making decisions during a flight simulation. One of the critical rules you follow is based on the relative position and movement of your aircraft. Here's how the rule works:*

*If your aircraft's relative elevation is low (0.01 or less), the system starts by checking your relative azimuth (the angle relative to the target):*

- *If the azimuth is 0.86 or less, the system will look at your aircraft's vertical velocity:*
  - *If the vertical velocity is low (0.07 or less) and your roll rate is minimal (0.03 or less):*
    - *If the pitch angle is 0.31 degrees or less, the system suggests a slight downward adjustment (Action: -0.02).*
    - *If the pitch angle is greater than 0.31 degrees, the system suggests a more significant adjustment (Action: 0.21).*
  - *If the roll rate is slightly higher (greater than 0.03):*
    - *The system checks finer roll rate thresholds:*
      - *If the roll rate is between 0.03 and 0.04, the system issues a corrective action (Action: -0.50).*
      - *If it exceeds 0.04, the corrective action is smaller (Action: -0.10).*

*When your relative elevation or other parameters change, the system keeps checking the relevant conditions to adjust the pitch, roll, and yaw of the aircraft, ensuring stability.*

**Fig. 6.** Generated Explaination.

This generated explanation in Fig. 6 highlights the decision-making process in a structured and contextually relevant manner. The results of our approach demonstrate the effectiveness of using decision tree rules to generate clear, human-readable explanations for complex decision-making processes in a MARL environment. By converting technical rules derived from the decision tree into plain-language explanations using a pre-trained NLP model, we provide a transparent view of the agent's behavior.

By transforming decision rules into human-readable insights, this approach enhances operator situational awareness and decision-making during critical moments in flight simulations. This improves transparency and trust in the system, addressing one of the core challenges of explainability in autonomous decision-making systems.

## 5 Conclusions and Challenges

In this study, we demonstrated the use of decision trees and natural language processing (NLP) to enhance the explainability of multi-agent reinforcement learning (MARL) systems in a flight simulation environment. The decision tree model provided a structured rule-based approach to understanding the agent's decision-making process, allowing us to extract interpretable rules that govern critical actions such as pitch, roll, and throttle adjustments. By further integrating a pretrained NLP model, we converted these technical rules into human-readable explanations. The combination of decision trees and NLP serves to bridge the gap between complex machine learning models and practical, real-world applications by increasing transparency and trust.

While our approach shows promising results several challenges and limitations were encountered. One of the primary challenges in using decision trees is managing the trade-off between model depth and interpretability. Although deeper trees capture more complex decision-making patterns, they also result in more intricate rules that are harder to interpret. Another big challenge we faced is the quality of the generated natural language explanations depends heavily on the pretrained NLP model. While the T5 model produced coherent outputs, it sometimes generated repetitive or irrelevant text that required post-processing.

## References

1. Mei, J., Li, G., Huang, H.: Deep reinforcement-learning-based air-combat-maneuver generation framework. Mathematics **12**, 3020 (2024). https://doi.org/10.3390/math12193020
2. Milani, S., Topin, N., Veloso, M., Fang, F.: Explainable reinforcement learning: a survey and comparative review. ACM Comput. Surv. **56**(7) April 2024. ISSN 0360-0300. https://doi.org/10.1145/3616864
3. İrsoy, O., Alpaydın, E.: Distributed decision trees (2014). https://arxiv.org/abs/1412.6388
4. Laptev, D., Buhmann, J.M.: Convolutional decision trees for feature learning and segmentation. In Jiang, X., Hornegger, J., Koch, R., eds. Pattern Recognition, pp. 95–106. Springer International Publishing, Cham ISBN 978-3-319-11752-2 (2014)
5. Frosst, N., Hinton, G.: Distilling a neural network into a soft decision tree (2017). https://arxiv.org/abs/1711.09784

6. Coppens, Y., Efthymiadis, K., Lenaerts, T., Nowe, A.: Distilling deep reinforcement learning policies in soft decision trees. In: Miller, T., Weber, R., Magazzeni, D., eds. Proceedings of the IJCAI 2019 Workshop on Explainable Artificial Intelligence, pp. 1–6 (2019). https://sites.google.com/view/xai2019/home. IJCAI 2019 Workshop on Explainable Artificial Intelligence, XAI19 ; Conference date: 11-08-2019
7. Liu, G., Schulte, O., Zhu, W., Li, Q.: Toward interpretable deep reinforcement learning with linear model u-trees (2018). https://arxiv.org/abs/1807.05887
8. Silva, A., et al.: Optimization methods for interpretable differentiable decision trees in reinforcement learning (2020). https://arxiv.org/abs/1903.09338
9. Bastani, O., Pu, Y., Solar-Lezama, A.: Verifiable reinforcement learning via policy extraction (2019). https://arxiv.org/abs/1805.08328
10. Gokhale, G., Madahi, S.S.K., Claessens, B., Develder, C.: Distill2explain: Differentiable decision trees for explainable reinforcement learning in energy application controllers (2024). https://arxiv.org/abs/2403.11907
11. Costa, V.G., Pérez-Aracil, J., Salcedo-Sanz, S., Pedreira, C.E.: Evolving interpretable decision trees for reinforcement learning. Artif. Intell. **327**, 104057 (2024). ISSN 0004-3702. https://doi.org/10.1016/j.artint.2023.104057. https://www.sciencedirect.com/science/article/pii/S0004370223002035
12. Pynadath, D.V., Gurney, N., Wang, N.: Explainable reinforcement learning in human-robot teams: the impact of decision-tree explanations on transparency. In: 2022 31st IEEE International Conference on Robot and Human Interactive Communication (RO-MAN), pp. 749–756 (2022). https://doi.org/10.1109/RO-MAN53752.2022.9900608
13. Gjærum, V.B., Strümke, I., Løver, J., Miller, T., Lekkas, A.M.: Model tree methods for explaining deep reinforcement learning agents in real-time robotic applications. Neurocomputing **515**, 133–144 (2023). ISSN 0925-2312. https://doi.org/10.1016/j.neucom.2022.10.014. https://www.sciencedirect.com/science/article/pii/S0925231222012735
14. Salhi, A., et al.: Leveraging JSBSim and gymnasium: a reinforcement learning approach for air combat simulation. In: Applied Cognitive Computing and Artificial Intelligence. Springer. Cham: Springer Nature Switzerland, pp. 271–283 (2025). https://doi.org/10.1007/978-3-031-85628-0_20

# Beyond the Hype: The Efficacy of Simpler Models for Water Level Forecasting Compared to Deep Learning Architectures

Edgar Ceh-Varela(✉), Sarbagya Shakya, and David Schmith

Department of Mathematical Sciences, Eastern New Mexico University, 1500 S Ave K, Portales 88130, NM, USA
{eduardo.ceh,sarbagya.shakya,david.schmith}@enmu.edu

**Abstract.** Accurate river level forecasting is vital for water resource management, especially in drought-prone areas. This study evaluates one-day-ahead water level predictions using USGS data from the Ruidoso River, New Mexico. After outlier detection via Z-score analysis, we applied model selection with LazyRegressor and fine-tuned top-performing models. RANSAC regression outperformed deep learning approaches, LSTM and Transformer, across all metrics ($R^2$, MAE, MSE, RMSE), achieving an $R^2$ of 0.9672 and MAE of 0.0322. The results suggest RANSAC's robustness to noise and outliers enabled its superior performance. This challenges the assumption that deep learning is always better and underscores the value of robust traditional models for noisy hydrological time series forecasting.

**Keywords:** Water Forecasting · Regression Models · LSTM · Transformer · Hyperparameter Optimization

## 1 Introduction

Water scarcity is an increasingly critical challenge, particularly in drought-prone regions, where climate variability and extreme weather events continue to strain existing water management systems [1]. Accurate and timely river level forecasting is therefore critical for effective water resource management, enabling proactive strategies for flood mitigation, agricultural planning, and ecosystem preservation.

Figure 1, based on the U.S. Drought Monitor, illustrates the severity of this issue, revealing that New Mexico is under widespread Extreme and Exceptional drought classifications. This situation underscores the urgent need for highly reliable predictive tools that can inform adaptive water management and drought mitigation efforts across the state's vulnerable communities and ecosystems.

Traditionally, water level forecasting has relied on statistical methods and linear models. However, hydrological data is inherently complex, characterized


R. Stahlbock et al. (Eds.): CSCE 2025, CCIS 2938, pp. 15–30, 2027.
https://doi.org/10.1007/978-3-032-22196-4_2

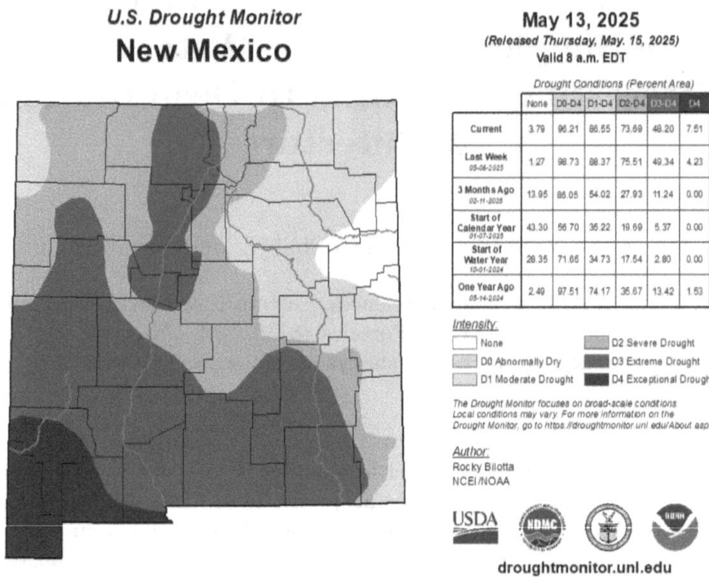


**Fig. 1.** Drought monitoring map for New Mexico. Figure obtained from https://droughtmonitor.unl.edu/

by non-linear dynamics, stochastic behavior, and crucially, the frequent presence of noise and outliers. These anomalies, often stemming from sensor malfunctions, data transmission errors, or extreme natural events, can significantly degrade the performance of conventional forecasting models [2]. As climate patterns become more unpredictable, there is a growing demand for resilient, data-driven solutions capable of enhancing forecasting accuracy while robustly handling imperfect real-world data.

Recent advancements in deep learning (DL), particularly Long Short-Term Memory (LSTM) networks and Transformer models, have shown considerable promise in time-series prediction due to their ability to capture complex temporal dependencies [3,4]. However, their inherent sensitivity to outliers often poses a significant challenge in real-world applications with noisy data. This study directly addresses this challenge by conducting a rigorous comparative analysis between these DL architectures and traditional machine learning (ML) models.

Our primary motivation stems from a critical research gap: while complex deep learning models are often favored, their performance relative to systematically identified, robust traditional models on outlier-prone real-world datasets is not always well understood. This work aims to fill this gap by demonstrating that an empirically selected, simpler model can outperform more complex architectures, particularly when its inherent characteristics, like RANSAC's outlier robustness, align with the challenges presented by the data.

This paper makes several significant contributions to the field of ML-based environmental forecasting:

- Systematic identification and validation of a superior traditional model: Through a comprehensive pipeline involving LazyRegressor for initial screening and rigorous hyperparameter tuning of the top three candidates, RANSAC emerged as the leading traditional model. We then empirically validate its superior performance.
- Rigorous comparative analysis on outlier-prone data: We provide a head-to-head comparison of this empirically selected, outlier-robust RANSAC model against two advanced deep learning architectures (LSTM and Transformer) for one-day-ahead river level forecasting, utilizing a real-world USGS dataset confirmed to contain significant outliers.
- Empirical demonstration of simpler models' efficacy: Our findings compellingly demonstrate that RANSAC significantly outperforms both LSTM and Transformer models across multiple standard evaluation metrics ($R^2$, MAE, MSE, and RMSE). This result challenges the common assumption that model complexity directly correlates with superior predictive performance, especially when data contains noise.
- Comprehensive methodology: We detail a robust data preprocessing pipeline, including Z-score outlier detection, systematic feature engineering from high-frequency water gauge data, and our multi-stage model selection and tuning process.
- Practical implications for water management: This study offers valuable insights for policymakers and resource managers in drought-affected regions like New Mexico. It advocates for considering empirically validated, efficient, and reliable forecasting tools that demonstrate robustness to data quality issues, thereby enabling more informed decision-making.

By addressing these critical aspects, this research not only provides a compelling case for considering robust traditional models identified through systematic evaluation but also offers crucial methodological guidance for environmental modeling. It demonstrates how an empirically driven approach to model selection, followed by an understanding of why a particular model excels, can bridge the gap between predictive analytics and real-world sustainability efforts.

The remainder of the paper is structured as follows: Sect. 2 provides a detailed background on hydrological forecasting and relevant ML techniques. Section 3 outlines our comprehensive methodology and experimental setup, including data acquisition, preprocessing, feature engineering, and model architectures. Section 4 presents the experimental results, their analysis, and a detailed discussion of the findings. Finally, Sect. 5 concludes the study with a summary of key insights and outlines future research directions.

## 2 Related Work

Forecasting in environmental systems has attracted significant interest. Traditional time-series models such as ARIMA and exponential smoothing have been widely applied [5,6] but are often limited by their inability to handle non-linear patterns and outliers. In contrast, ML methods, including regression trees, support vector machines, and ensemble techniques, offer improved flexibility and robustness [7–9].

Recent work in water resource forecasting has leveraged both classical ML and DL models [3,4]. While DL models offer powerful representational capabilities, their practical effectiveness can be compromised in the presence of data anomalies common in environmental sensor networks. This necessitates either extensive data preprocessing and cleaning or the exploration of inherently robust modeling techniques.

Unlike DL models, ML models offer flexibility in handling various data types while maintaining interpretability [10,11]. This capability is especially valuable in predicting water levels across diverse environments, such as rivers, lakes, and wetlands, where understanding non-linear relationships among variables is crucial for effective water management and disaster risk reduction. For example, in [12] authors demonstrated the effectiveness of hybrid ML models in predicting river flow, while [13] explored the integration of meteorological variables with hydrological data to improve accuracy. Other studies [10,14] conducted in South Korea and Malaysia have explored the effectiveness of these models in wetland water level prediction and river management, respectively, emphasizing their broad applicability across diverse aquatic systems.

Feature engineering in ML forecasting for water level focuses on transforming raw data into meaningful features that enhance predictive accuracy in hydrological applications. As climate variability and water management challenges intensify, effective feature engineering has become increasingly vital for ensuring reliable forecasts essential for flood risk assessment, reservoir management, and water resource planning [15]. Prior research [16] has shown that aggregating high-frequency data into daily averages can reduce noise while preserving important trends. Our methodology builds upon these insights by not only aggregating data but also augmenting the dataset with lagged and statistical features to capture temporal dependencies.

Regardless of the model chosen, hyperparameter optimization is critical for achieving optimal performance and ensuring generalization to unseen data. Techniques such as Grid Search with Cross-Validation (GridSearchCV) are standard practice for systematically exploring different hyperparameter combinations [17]. Studies across various forecasting domains have successfully employed grid search to identify optimal parameter sets, thereby maximizing model efficacy [18,19]. Our work also employs this rigorous approach to fine-tune all candidate models.

In summary, while DL offers advanced capabilities for time-series forecasting, its application to noisy, real-world hydrological data necessitates careful consideration of outlier sensitivity. This study aims to contribute to this area by systematically identifying a high-performing traditional ML model through an extensive search and then rigorously comparing its performance against leading deep learning architectures, specifically focusing on scenarios with inherent data anomalies.

| | day_1 | day_2 | day_3 | day_4 | day_5 | mean_of_month | five_days_avg | five_days_min | five_days_max | target_day |
|---|---|---|---|---|---|---|---|---|---|---|
| 0 | 1.942 | 1.9621875 | 1.966979167 | 1.963229167 | 1.96125 | 1.961222995 | 1.959129167 | 1.942 | 1.966979167 | 1.955416667 |
| 1 | 1.9621875 | 1.966979167 | 1.963229167 | 1.96125 | 1.955416667 | 1.961222995 | 1.9618125 | 1.955416667 | 1.966979167 | 1.960833333 |
| 2 | 1.966979167 | 1.963229167 | 1.96125 | 1.955416667 | 1.960833333 | 1.961222995 | 1.961541667 | 1.955416667 | 1.966979167 | 1.96375 |
| 3 | 1.963229167 | 1.96125 | 1.955416667 | 1.960833333 | 1.96375 | 1.961222995 | 1.960895833 | 1.955416667 | 1.96375 | 1.961666667 |
| 4 | 1.96125 | 1.955416667 | 1.960833333 | 1.96375 | 1.961666667 | 1.961222995 | 1.960583333 | 1.955416667 | 1.96375 | 1.960833333 |
| 5 | 1.955416667 | 1.960833333 | 1.96375 | 1.961666667 | 1.960833333 | 1.961222995 | 1.9605 | 1.955416667 | 1.96375 | 1.959690722 |
| 6 | 1.960833333 | 1.96375 | 1.961666667 | 1.960833333 | 1.959690722 | 1.961222995 | 1.961354811 | 1.959690722 | 1.96375 | 1.958880866 |
| 7 | 1.96375 | 1.961666667 | 1.960833333 | 1.959690722 | 1.958880866 | 1.961222995 | 1.960964318 | 1.958880866 | 1.96375 | 1.963854167 |
| 8 | 1.961666667 | 1.960833333 | 1.959690722 | 1.958880866 | 1.963854167 | 1.961222995 | 1.960985151 | 1.958880866 | 1.963854167 | 1.970069444 |

**Fig. 2.** Extract of the dataset after feature engineering

# 3 Methodology

## 3.1 Data Collection and Preprocessing

The dataset was sourced from USGS[1] site number '08387000' on the Rio Ruidoso in Hollywood, in New Mexico. Data was collected at 15-minute intervals over three years, from January 1, 2021 to December 31, 2023, yielding 3,108,908 observations. Once we obtained the dataset, we applied the following preprocessing steps:

Column selection: We kept only the gauge height and timestamp columns.

Temporal aggregation: We computed the daily average gauge height to reduce dimensionality, from more 3 million to 1,095 daily instances.

Feature engineering: We enhanced the dataset with additional features. We modified the dataset constructing input features by considering six consecutive days. The first five days' averages serve as predictors, and the sixth day's average is the target variable. The choice of five days balances capturing recent trends while avoiding excessive lag, ensuring the model remains responsive to short-term fluctuations without being overwhelmed by noise. This approach captures temporal dependencies, allowing the model to learn patterns and trends essential for accurate water level forecasting.

Likweise, based on other studies [2,20], we added the monthly average corresponding to the target day and statistical metrics (i.e., mean, maximum, and minimum) for the preceding five days. Monthly historical averages capture seasonal water level fluctuations driven by rainfall, snowmelt, and agricultural use, providing a baseline for long-term trends. Complementing this, recent statistical metrics detect short-term variations and extremes, enabling the model to respond to sudden changes like heavy rainfall or dam releases. This combined approach ensures a comprehensive and adaptive water level analysis. Figure 2 shows an extract of the dataset with the new features and target.

Dataset split: We allocated data from the first two years for training and the remaining instances for testing, ensuring that the model's generalization can be evaluated on unseen data.

[1] https://waterdata.usgs.gov/nwis.

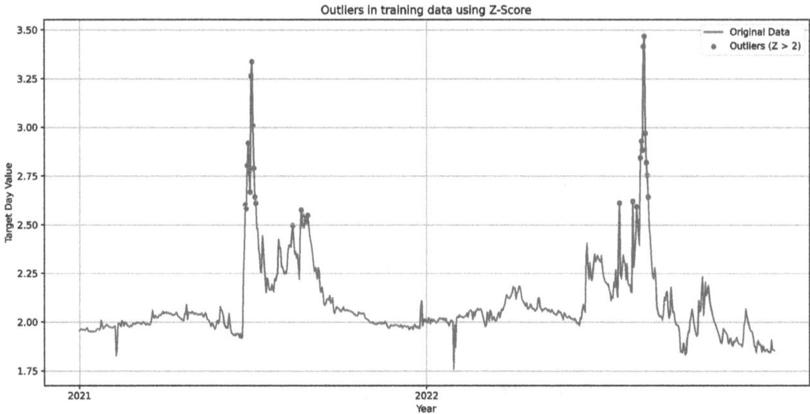


**Fig. 3.** Outliers found in the training data using the Z-score test.

### 3.2 Outliers

Outliers, can arise from various sources in hydrological datasets, including sensor malfunctions, transient environmental anomalies, or genuine extreme events such as flash floods or sudden dam releases. This values, if not appropriately addressed, can disproportionately influence model training, leading to biased parameter estimation and degraded predictive performance, particularly for models sensitive to extreme values.

We used the Z-score test to systematically detect these anomalies within our training dataset. The Z-score measures how many standard deviations an element is from the mean. In this study, a threshold of $Z > 2$ was utilized to identify significant deviations. Figure 3 shows that this method effectively identified several sharp spikes in the water level time series. These identified outliers represent critical instances that could either be erroneous readings or genuine hydrological events, necessitating careful consideration during model development.

### 3.3 Model Selection

#### 3.3.1 Machine Learning Model

Initial model evaluations were conducted using the training and testing datasets with the Lazy Regressor framework [21], which efficiently assesses 41 regression models. The evaluated models included linear regressors, decision trees, ensemble methods, and robust regression techniques. The framework reports performance metrics, using the testing dataset, including Adjusted R-Squared, R-Squared, and Root Mean Squared Error (RMSE).

Based on these results, we selected the top three models for further analysis: RANSAC Regressor, Orthogonal Matching Pursuit, and Huber Regressor.

### 3.3.2 LSTM

To explore deep learning capabilities, an LSTM network was developed using TensorFlow Keras, as shown in Fig. 4. This model processes historical water levels (day_1 to day_5) through LSTM layers to capture temporal patterns. Simultaneously, the auxiliary features (e.g., mean_of_month, five_days_avg) are fed into a separate input layer. Outputs from the LSTM stack and the auxiliary feature input are then merged via a Concatenate layer. This combined representation is processed by subsequent Dense layers, with the final layer providing the single target_day water level prediction. Key hyperparameters for this network were optimized through systematic tuning. Likewise, we used ReLU and Adam, as activation and optimizer, respectively.

### 3.3.3 Transformer

A Transformer-based model was also implemented using TensorFlow Keras. Figure 5 shows its architecture. Sequential input, representing historical water levels, first passes through a PositionalEmbedding layer to incorporate sequence order information. This is then processed by a TransformerEncoder layers, which uses self-attention mechanisms to capture dependencies within the time series. The output of the encoder is aggregated using a GlobalAveragePooling1D layer. Similar to the LSTM, auxiliary static features are introduced via a separate InputLayer. The pooled sequential representation and the auxiliary features are then merged using a Concatenate layer. Finally, this combined feature set is fed into Dense layers to produce the water level prediction. Critical hyperparameters, such as the number of attention heads and layers in the encoder, were optimized through systematic tuning. We used ReLU and Adam, as activation and optimizer, respectively.

### 3.4 Evaluation Metrics

Performance was assessed using the following metrics:

- $R^2$ (Coefficient of Determination): Indicates how well future samples are likely to be predicted by the model.
- MAE (Mean Absolute Error): Average absolute difference between predictions and actual values.
- MSE (Mean Squared Error): Average squared difference between predictions and actual values, emphasizing larger errors.
- RMSE (Root Mean Squared Error): Square root of MSE, providing error units comparable to the target variable.

### 3.5 Hyperparameter Optimization

Since the Lazy Regressor framework uses default hyperparameters for the models, our next step is to fine-tune each of the top three models to optimize their performance further and select the best overall model.

**Table 1.** Hyperparameters used with Grid Search Cross Validation

| Model | Parameters |
|---|---|
| Huber Regressor | epsilon, alpha |
| RANSAC Regressor | min_samples, max_trials |
| Orthogonal Matching Pursuit | n_nonzero_coefs, tol |

To optimize the performance of these models, we employed Grid Search Cross Validation (CV). This method systematically tests a predefined set of parameter combinations [22]. We set CV to be 5 folds. Table 1 shows the hyperparameters considered for each model.

For the Huber Regressor, epsilon and alpha were adjusted to control sensitivity to outliers and regularization strength, respectively, facilitating robust trend modeling. The RANSAC Regressor's min_samples and max_trials parameters were optimized to enhance resilience to data corruption and ensure reliable model fitting. Finally, for the Orthogonal Matching Pursuit model we optimized the n_nonzero_coefs and tol parameters to achieve a balance between sparsity and reconstruction accuracy. This targeted hyperparameter optimization aimed to enhance the accuracy and generalization capability of each model in the context of water level forecasting.

Hyperparameter tuning for both the LSTM and Transformer models was systematically conducted using Keras Tuner, leveraging its efficient Hyperband [23] algorithm. This process is essential for optimizing deep learning model performance, as various architectural and training parameters significantly impact their ability to learn complex patterns. For each model, a predefined search space was established, encompassing critical hyperparameters. The tuning objective was set to minimize the RMSE on a validation dataset (i.e., 10% of the training dataset), ensuring that the selected parameters yielded the best generalization performance. An early stopping callback was implemented during the search to halt trials that showed no improvement in validation RMSE over a set patience, thereby preventing overfitting and accelerating the tuning process.

This comprehensive search allowed us to identify the best configuration that minimizes error metrics (MAE, MSE, RMSE) while maximizing $R^2$, thereby improving model generalization.

## 4 Results and Discussion

### 4.1 ML Models

Table 2 presents the results obtained after executing the Grid Search CV in all the top three ML models for their hyperparameters.

After this systematic evaluation, the RANSAC regressor outperformed other candidate models with the following performance metrics on the test set.

The high $R^2$ value (0.9672) indicates that the RANSAC regressor can effectively capture the variability in water levels one day ahead. The low MAE, MSE

**Table 2.** Results of the fine tuned ML models

| Model | $R^2$ | MAE | MSE | RMSE |
|---|---|---|---|---|
| Huber Regressor | 0.9278 | 0.0573 | 0.0049 | 0.0700 |
| RANSAC Regressor | **0.9672** | **0.0322** | **0.0022** | **0.0472** |
| Orthogonal Matching Pursuit | 0.9259 | 0.0573 | 0.0050 | 0.0709 |

and RMSE further suggest that the predictions are not only accurate on average but also that the model is resilient to significant deviations, which is critical for decision-making in water resource management.

One of the key strengths of the RANSAC algorithm is its robustness to outliers [24,25], making it particularly suitable for environmental datasets that may include anomalous readings due to sensor errors or extreme weather events. This adaptability allows RANSAC to filter out noisy data points and focus on reliable trends, outperforming the other models which are more sensitive to noise. While the Huber Regressor mitigates some outlier effects, it does not match RANSAC's ability to disregard extreme deviations, further explaining its superior performance in this task.

Grid Search CV played a critical role in enhancing model performance by systematically testing combinations of parameters. The optimal configuration (min_samples = 20, max_trials = 150) ensured that the model could effectively identify the inliers while ignoring anomalies. This optimization was particularly important given the variability in environmental sensor data, where outliers can heavily skew predictions if not properly managed.

### 4.2 DL Models

As mentioned previously, Hyperparameter tuning for both the LSTM and Transformer models was systematically conducted using Keras Tuner via the Hyperband algorithm. Hyperband is a hyperparameter optimization algorithm that uses early performance to efficiently allocate resources, discarding poor configurations early via Successive Halving and focusing on the most promising ones.

**Table 3.** Best hyperparameter values for the LSTM model

| Hyperparameter | Value |
|---|---|
| LSTM units | 64 |
| Dropout rate | 0.1 |
| Learning rate | 0.001 |
| LSTM layers | 1 |
| Dense units | 128 |

| Layer (type) | Output Shape | Param # | Connected to |
|---|---|---|---|
| sequence_input (InputLayer) | (None, 5, 1) | 0 | - |
| lstm (LSTM) | (None, 64) | 16,896 | sequence_input[0… |
| additional_feature… (InputLayer) | (None, 4) | 0 | - |
| concatenate (Concatenate) | (None, 68) | 0 | lstm[0][0], additional_featu… |
| dense (Dense) | (None, 128) | 8,832 | concatenate[0][0] |
| dense_1 (Dense) | (None, 1) | 129 | dense[0][0] |

**Fig. 4.** Best LSTM model after fine tuning.

**Table 4.** Best hyperparameters values for the Transformer model

| Hyperparameter | Value |
|---|---|
| Embedding dim | 128 |
| Attention heads | 3 |
| Feed Forward dim | 96 |
| Transformer blocks | 1 |
| Dropout rate | 0.30000000000000004 |
| Learning rate | 0.001 |
| Dense units | 64 |

The best values for the LSTM's hyperparameters found by this technique are presented in Table 3. Likewise, Fig. 4 shows the best architecture for the LSTM model after the optimization.

Similarly, the best values for the Transformer's hyperparameters are presented in Table 4. Figure 5 shows the best architecture for the Transformer model after the optimization.

### 4.3 Model Comparisons

The performance of the three distinct modeling approaches (RANSAC, LSTM, and Transformer) on the test dataset is summarized in Table 5. From these results we can observe that the RANSAC model demonstrates a superior performance across all evaluated metrics. RANSAC achieved the highest coefficient of determination $R^2$, with a value of 0.9672, indicating that it successfully explained over 96% of the variance in the one-day-ahead river level predictions. This was substantially better than the LSTM model, which recorded an $R^2$ of 0.8877, and also surpassed the Transformer model's $R^2$ of 0.8028.

| Layer (type) | Output Shape | Param # | Connected to |
|---|---|---|---|
| sequence_input (InputLayer) | (None, 5, 1) | 0 | - |
| positional_embeddi… (PositionalEmbeddi… | (None, 5, 32) | 224 | sequence_input[0… |
| transformer_encode… (TransformerEncode… | (None, 5, 32) | 18,976 | positional_embed… |
| transformer_encode… (TransformerEncode… | (None, 5, 32) | 18,976 | transformer_enco… |
| global_average_poo… (GlobalAveragePool… | (None, 32) | 0 | transformer_enco… |
| additional_feature… (InputLayer) | (None, 4) | 0 | - |
| concatenate (Concatenate) | (None, 36) | 0 | global_average_p… additional_featu… |
| dense_5 (Dense) | (None, 128) | 4,736 | concatenate[0][0] |
| dense_6 (Dense) | (None, 1) | 129 | dense_5[0][0] |

**Fig. 5.** Best Transformer model after fine tuning.

In terms of prediction error, RANSAC consistently yielded the lowest values. Its MAE was 0.0322, which is significantly lower than the MAE of 0.0694 for the LSTM and notably better than the Transformer's MAE of 0.0932. This pattern of superior accuracy for RANSAC continued with the MSE and RMSE. RANSAC achieved an MSE of 0.0022 and an RMSE of 0.0472. In comparison, the LSTM model showed considerably higher errors, with an MSE of 0.0076 and an RMSE of 0.0874. The Transformer model performed worst than the LSTM, with an MSE of 0.0134 and an RMSE of 0.1158.

The superior performance of the RANSAC model is particularly noteworthy and can likely be attributed to its inherent robustness to outliers, a characteristic that is highly beneficial when dealing with real-world environmental data which often contains anomalous readings. RANSAC's methodology, which iteratively fits models to subsets of inliers while disregarding outliers, allows it to establish a more stable and accurate underlying relationship from the data, especially when contrasted with models that might be unduly influenced by such noise.

The DL models, while powerful, appear to have been more susceptible to these data imperfections. The LSTM model, despite its capability to learn long-term dependencies, exhibited the poorest performance among the three. This could suggest that for the relatively short sequence length of five days and the specific feature set used, its recurrent architecture might have struggled more with noise or found it harder to generalize compared to the other approaches. The Transformer model, leveraging its attention mechanism, did perform significantly better than the LSTM and approached the accuracy of RANSAC, particularly in its $R^2$ value. This suggests its ability to weigh the importance of different input features and time steps was advantageous.

Despite its advanced architecture, the Transformer did not outperform the simpler yet robust RANSAC model. This may be due to the Transformer's sensitivity to noise and need for large datasets. In contrast, RANSAC's explicit outlier-handling proved more effective for this forecasting task, where robustness outweighed deep learning's complex pattern recognition. It is plausible that the engineered features already captured much of the essential predictive information, and RANSAC was better able to distill this information cleanly. The DL models, in contrast, might have attempted to fit to the noise within the data, or the dataset size was not extensive enough to allow these highly parameterized models to fully learn the signal without being affected by outliers. These metrics collectively underscore that in scenarios with potential data anomalies, a robust and well-suited traditional model can outperform more complex architectures.

**Table 5.** Comparison of metrics for all the models

| Model | $R^2$ | MAE | MSE | RMSE |
|---|---|---|---|---|
| RANSAC | **0.9672** | **0.0322** | **0.0022** | **0.0472** |
| LSTM | 0.8877 | 0.0694 | 0.0076 | 0.0874 |
| Transformer | 0.8028 | 0.0932 | 0.0134 | 0.1158 |

Figure 6 shows a graphical comparison between the actual and predicted water levels for the three models. The Figure shows the orange line representing the actual measurements and the dashed-green line representing the predictions over the test data. This visualization underscores the RANSAC's ability to capture the underlying temporal trends and adapt to abrupt changes in water levels.

Our experiments reveal that striking the right balance between model complexity and generalization is key. Overall, our strategic use of inherent defaults and targeted hyperparameter optimization enabled us to achieve optimal performance in water level forecasting, even in the presence of complex and noisy environmental data.

Despite promising results, several limitations are worth noting. The current feature set is based solely on historical gauge heights. Incorporating additional environmental features such as rainfall intensity, temperature, and upstream water usage could further improve the model's accuracy. While daily averages simplify the modeling task, important short-term fluctuations might be lost. Future work may explore multi-scale forecasting that integrates both short-term and long-term dynamics. The model was trained on data from a single USGS site. Validation across multiple locations and under varying climatic conditions is essential to verify its broader applicability.

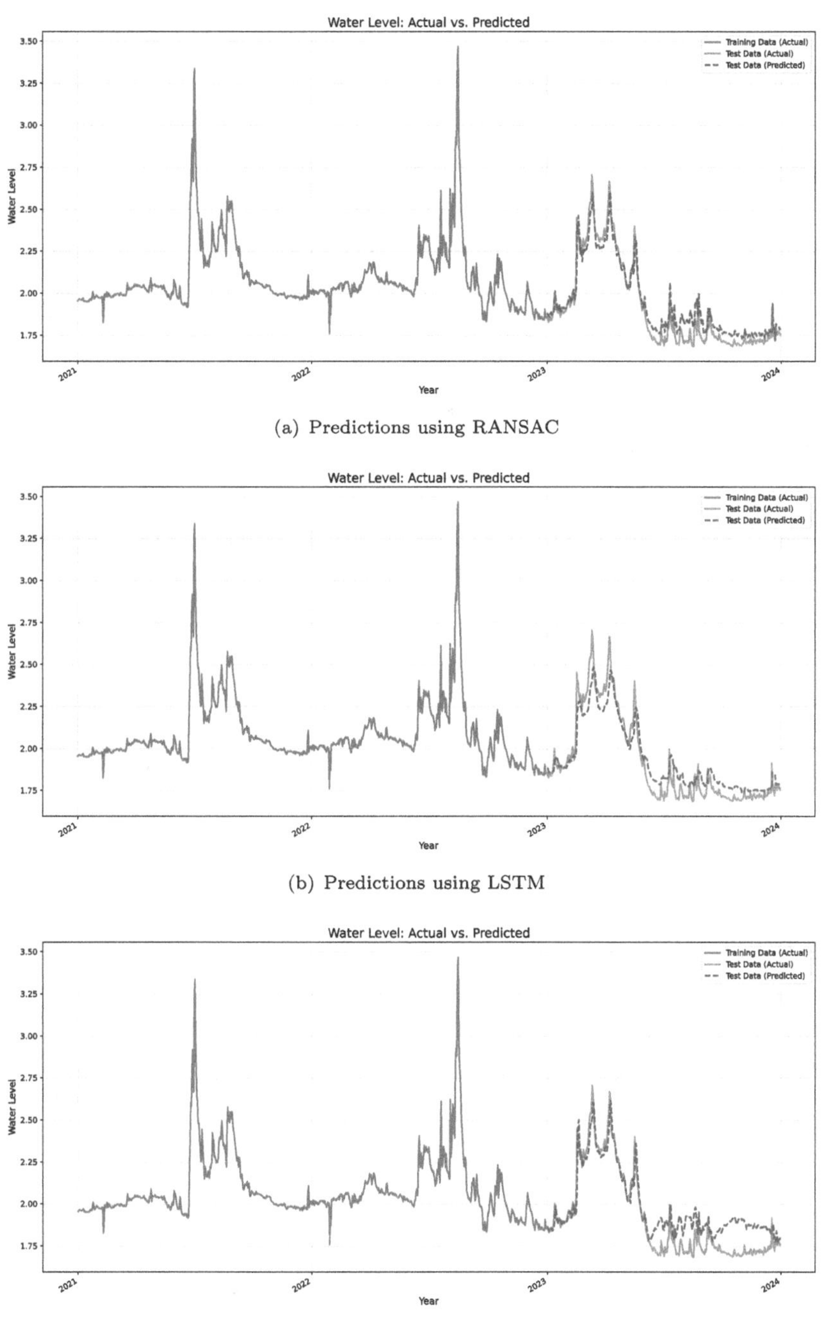


(a) Predictions using RANSAC

(b) Predictions using LSTM

(c) Predictions using Temporal Fusion Transformer

**Fig. 6.** Comparison of predictions using the different models

## 5 Conclusions

This study presents a comprehensive comparative analysis in which an empirically selected RANSAC regressor was benchmarked against state-of-the-art deep learning models, specifically LSTM and Transformer architectures, for one-day-ahead water level forecasting. By leveraging detailed preprocessing and rigorous hyperparameter tuning, the model achieved an $R^2$ of 0.9672 and low error metrics, establishing its potential as a tool for proactive water management.

Contrary to the prevailing assumption that more complex models inherently offer superior performance, our results demonstrate that the RANSAC model significantly outperforms both deep learning approaches across all evaluation metrics.

The RANSAC model's superior performance is primarily attributed to its robustness against outliers, which were prevalent in the USGS dataset analyzed. RANSAC proved better suited to the noise-prone nature of the dataset than LSTM and Transformer models, whose sensitivity to such irregularities led to diminished predictive accuracy. These findings underscore the importance of aligning model choice with the underlying data characteristics, especially in domains where data quality can be variable or noisy.

Beyond its methodological contributions, this study provides a practical and interpretable forecasting approach that can aid water resource management in regions like New Mexico. Future research could expand on this work by incorporating additional exogenous variables, extending the forecast horizon, and evaluating model performance across a broader range of hydrological regimes. Likewise, we would like to evaluate the robustness of pre-trained Transformers to noisy data in time series forecasting. Such efforts would further illuminate the interplay between model complexity, data integrity, and predictive accuracy in environmental time series forecasting.

## References

1. Shemer, H., Wald, S., Semiat, R.: Challenges and solutions for global water scarcity. Membranes **13**(6), 612 (2023)
2. Agaj, T., Budka, A., Janicka, E., Bytyqi, V.: Using ARIMA and ETS models for forecasting water level changes for sustainable environmental management. Sci. Rep. **14**(1), 22444 (2024)
3. Solgi, R., Loaiciga, H.A., Kram, M.: Long short-term memory neural network (LSTM-NN) for aquifer level time series forecasting using in-situ piezometric observations. J. Hydrol. **601**, 126800 (2021)
4. Wen, Q., et al.: Transformers in time series: a survey. arXiv preprint arXiv:2202.07125 (2022)
5. Kontopoulou, V.I., Panagopoulos, A.D., Kakkos, I., Matsopoulos, G.K.: A review of arima vs. machine learning approaches for time series forecasting in data driven networks. Future Internet **15**(8), 255 (2023)

6. Sulandari, W., Suhartono, Subanar, Rodrigues, P.C.: Exponential smoothing on modeling and forecasting multiple seasonal time series: an overview. Fluct. Noise Lett. **20**(04), 2130003 (2021) : Exponential smoothing on modeling and forecasting multiple seasonal time series: an overview. Fluct. Noise Lett. **20**(04), 2130003 (2021)
7. Masini, R.P., Medeiros, M.C., Mendes, E.F.: Machine learning advances for time series forecasting. J. Econom. Surv. **37**(1), 76–111 (2023)
8. Kumbure, M.M., Lohrmann, C., Luukka, P., Porras, J.: Machine learning techniques and data for stock market forecasting: a literature review. Expert Syst. Appl. **197**, 116659 (2022)
9. Barrera-Animas, A.Y., Oyedele, L.O., Bilal, M., Akinosho, T.D., Delgado, J.M.D., Akanbi, L.A.: Rainfall prediction: a comparative analysis of modern machine learning algorithms for time-series forecasting. Mach. Learn. Appl. **7**, 100204 (2022)
10. Aquil, M.A.I., Ishak, W.H.W.: Comparison of machine learning models in forecasting reservoir water level. J. Adv. Res. Appl. Sci. Eng. Technol **31**, 137–144 (2023)
11. Vizi, Z., et al.: Water level prediction using long short-term memory neural network model for a lowland river: a case study on the tisza river, central europe. Environ. Sci. Eur. **35**(1), 92 (2023)
12. Fathian, F., Mehdizadeh, S., Sales, A.K., Safari, M.J.S.: Integrating artificial intelligence and non-linear time series models: Hybrid models to improve the monthly river flow prediction. J. Hydrol. **575**, 1200–1213 (2019)
13. Chen, L., Wang, Z., Jiang, Z., Lin, X.:. Deep learning models for multi-step prediction of water levels incorporating meteorological variables and historical data. Stochast. Environ. Res. Risk Assess. 1–23 (2024)
14. Reichert, P., et al.: Metamorphic testing of machine learning and conceptual hydrologic models. Hydrol. Earth Syst. Sci. **28**(11), 2505–2529 (2024)
15. Drogkoula, M., Kokkinos, K., Samaras, N.: A comprehensive survey of machine learning methodologies with emphasis in water resources management. Appl. Sci. **13**(22), 12147 (2023)
16. Mihel, A.M., Pečnik, S., Vrbančič, G., Lerga, J., Krvavica, N.: Employing feature engineering for river stage forecasting to improve hybrid model performance. In: 2024 International Conference on Software, Telecommunications and Computer Networks (SoftCOM), pp. 1–6. IEEE (2024)
17. Bischl, B., et al.: Hyperparameter optimization: Foundations, algorithms, best practices, and open challenges. Wiley Interdiscip. Rev.: Data Mining Knowl. Discov. **13**(2), e1484 (2023)
18. Malakouti, S.M., Menhaj, M.B., Suratgar, A.A.: The usage of 10-fold cross-validation and grid search to enhance ml methods performance in solar farm power generation prediction. Cleaner Eng. Technol. **15**, 100664 (2023)
19. El-Shahat, D., Tolba, A., Abouhawwash, M., Abdel-Basset, M.: Machine learning and deep learning models based grid search cross validation for short-term solar irradiance forecasting. J. Big Data **11**(1), 134 (2024)
20. Azad, A.S., et al.: Water level prediction through hybrid SARIMA and ANN models based on time series analysis: Red hills reservoir case study. Sustainability **14**(3), 1843 (2022)
21. Lydia, E.L., Althubiti, S.A., Anupama, C.S.S., Kumar, K.V.: Prediction of sepsis disease using random search to optimize hyperparameter tuning based on lazy predict model. In: International Conference on Frontiers of Intelligent Computing: Theory and Applications, pp. 351–367. Springer (2023)

22. Belete, D.M., Huchaiah, M.D.: Grid search in hyperparameter optimization of machine learning models for prediction of HIV/aids test results. Int. J. Comput. Appl. **44**(9), 875–886 (2022)
23. Li, L., Jamieson, K., DeSalvo, G., Rostamizadeh, A., Talwalkar, A.: Hyperband: bandit-based configuration evaluation for hyperparameter optimization. In: International Conference on Learning Representations (2022)
24. Zhang, F., Zhang, X., Zhilei, X., Dong, K., Li, Z., Liu, Y.: Cleaning of abnormal wind speed power data based on quartile RANSAC regression. Energies **17**(22), 5697 (2024)
25. Yang, H., Jie Tang, W., Shao, J.Y., Liu, B.: Wind power data cleaning using RANSAC-based polynomial and linear regression with adaptive threshold. Sci. Rep. **15**(1), 5105 (2025)

# Utility AI for Explainable Decision-Making in Six-DOF Simulation Environment

Indu Shukla[1(✉)], Abderahim Salhi[1], James E. Ross[1], and Gary J. Briggs[2]

[1] United States Army Corps of Engineers, Vicksburg, MS, USA
{indu.shukla,Abderahim.Salhi,James.E.Ross}@usace.army.mil
[2] RAND Corporation, Santa Monica, CA, USA
gbriggs@rand.org

**Abstract.** Reinforcement Learning (RL) agents show promise in air combat simulation but often operate as black boxes, limiting their usability in complex and mission-critical environments. This work introduces a utility-based interpretability and explainability framework for offline RL in a six-degree-of-freedom (6-DoF) aerial environment. We visualize utility scores over time, unpack decision logic through feature-based considerations, and apply diverse scoring curves to reveal how input variables shape agent behavior. A contextual importance heatmap further illustrates how tactical priorities shift with engagement range. Together, these tools provide actionable insights into agent reasoning, enhancing transparency and confidence in autonomous systems.

**Keywords:** Reinforcement Learning · Multi-agent · OpenAI Gym · data collection · Utility AI · XRL · XAI

## 1 Introduction

Reinforcement Learning (RL) has emerged as a transformative tool for training agents in complex environments such as mission operations, where adaptive decision making is vital. In complex defense scenarios, RL agents can offer advantages in strategic navigation, resource allocation, and threat engagement by learning policies through interaction with simulated or historical data. However, the inherent black-box nature of these models often obscures their decision-making logic, limiting operational trust and adoption. To address this, the field of explainable reinforcement learning (XRL) seeks to clarify agent behavior, making model outputs more accessible to human users. While traditional post hoc methods such as SHAP and LIME attempt to approximate feature importance, they often fall short in offline settings where interactive exploration is infeasible. Moreover, these approaches may not translate effectively to mission-critical environments where operators need interpretable, goal-aligned explanations. Our methodology answers four central questions to enhance understanding and interpretability of RL agents in air combat simulations:


R. Stahlbock et al. (Eds.): CSCE 2025, CCIS 2938, pp. 31–40, 2027.
https://doi.org/10.1007/978-3-032-22196-4_3

In this study, we propose the use of utility-based explainability (Utility AI) [8] as an alternative interpretability framework. Unlike statistical or counterfactual approaches, Utility AI grounds its explanations in mission outcomes, evaluating the usefulness of actions taken by the agent in pursuit of operational objectives. This approach assesses how individual decisions contribute to or detract from mission-level success metrics, offering contextually relevant, human centered insights.

- When does the agent decide? - We analyze utility scores across time steps to identify decision patterns.
- How are decisions scored? - We break down decisions into feature-based considerations that aggregate into utility scores.
- Why do certain actions win? - We visualize scoring curves to show how feature values are transformed and weighted.
- What changes with context?—We evaluate how feature importance varies based on engagement range using contextual heatmaps.

By applying Utility AI to a six-degree-of-freedom (6-DoF) simulation environment, we show how this layered, model offers more transparent explanations. Ultimately, we aim to bridge the gap between black-box policies and interpretable, operationally relevant decision support helping mission planners and analysts understand not only what the agent does, but why it does it.

## 2 Related Work

The intersection of RL and explainable AI XAI/XRL has gained increasing attention, particularly in domains where safety, transparency, and decision traceability are paramount. While RL agents can outperform traditional systems, their black-box nature remains a challenge for adoption in complex applications.

A significant body of research in XAI/XRL [2,6,7,10,13] has focused on post hoc interpretation methods like SHAP and LIME, which aim to illuminate the decision making logic of complex models, including RL agents. SHAP, introduced by Lundberg and Lee [3], leverages game theoretic Shapley values to attribute each feature's contribution to a model's prediction, and has been widely applied in domains such as robotic control, vehicle guidance, and safety critical systems. For example, SHAP has been used to interpret longitudinal control in robotics and automatic crane operations, offering insight into feature importance in action selection. LIME, another model agnostic technique, fits a simple interpretable model locally around the prediction to approximate feature influence. Despite their versatility, both SHAP and LIME often struggle in RL contexts due to the dynamic, sequential nature of decision-making and the challenges of explaining policies rather than single predictions. Furthermore, recent work such as Beechey et al. [1] questions the correctness of applying SHAP in RL without additional theoretical considerations.

Utility based decision frameworks, commonly used in game AI and behavior trees, offer a more interpretable alternative by modeling decisions through scoring functions tied to environmental features. Yang and Liu's survey [14], Understanding the Application of Utility Theory in Robotics and Artificial Intelligence, provides a comprehensive overview of how utility theory underpins decision-making in intelligent systems. The paper explores the integration of utility-based frameworks in robotics and AI to model preference driven behavior, enabling agents to make rational, goal oriented decisions. It discusses applications across planning, human-robot interaction, and adaptive control, emphasizing the flexibility of utility theory in handling trade-offs and uncertainty. The authors also highlight the challenges of defining and scaling utility functions in real-world scenarios, pointing to open research opportunities in interpretable and adaptive utility modeling.

In addition to scholarly studies and formal frameworks, developer focused resources have also contributed significantly to shaping the practical use of Utility AI. For instance, ShaggyDev's 2023 article offers a clear and approachable introduction to Utility AI as used in game development, outlining how agents evaluate multiple potential actions using a consideration-based scoring system and normalized curves to make context-aware decisions [12]. While the focus is on game AI, the underlying architecture aligns closely with our methodology emphasizing configurable, interpretable scoring blocks that enable agents to weigh trade-offs in real time. This resemblance reinforces the broader applicability of Utility AI beyond gaming, including its extension to reinforcement learning agents in high-stakes simulations like ours.

David "Rez" Graham's introduction to utility theory in Game AI Pro [5] outlines a practical framework for decision-making based on consideration scoring and utility curves. His modular approach—where each action is scored based on a set of input-driven considerations transformed via customizable curves mirrors our use of pitch rate, yaw rate, and relative elevation as scored features in aerial combat scenarios. While his work was developed in the context of game AI, the core concepts directly align with our application of Utility AI in MARL, particularly in how interpretability is achieved through modular and human readable scoring systems.

The book [11] Artificial Intelligence: A Modern Approach by Stuart Russell and Peter Norvig (3rd Edition) introduces utility based agents as a model of intelligent behavior that combines goals with preferences among possible outcomes. It explains that unlike simple goal based agents, utility based agents use a utility function to evaluate the desirability of different world states, allowing them to make trade-offs under uncertainty and choose actions that maximize expected utility. The book covers key ideas like expected utility theory, decision-theoretic agents, and model based utility evaluation, positioning utility-based reasoning as foundational in decision-making under uncertainty. However, it does not specifically focus on "Utility AI" as implemented in modern games or interpretable frameworks.

Jon McGuire's 2019 series [8], "AI Decision-Making with Utility Scores," provides an in-depth exploration of utility based AI architectures, detailing consideration based scoring and configurable curve functions. While this work is presented as a series of blog posts rather than a formal academic paper, it offers valuable insights into the practical implementation of Utility AI concepts.

# 3 Materials and Methods

## 3.1 Mission Scenario in a 6-DOF Combat Simulation Environment

To enhance the transparency and interpretability of agent behavior within a 6-DoF MARL environment, we integrated a Utility AI framework as an interpretable decision making layer. Utility AI mitigates traditional RL agents learning process by explicitly modeling decision making as a process of scoring and ranking candidate actions based on real time contextual features. Our approach begins by defining a discrete action space composed of tactical maneuvers including Adjust Pitch, Stabilize Yaw, and Increase Throttle. Each action is associated with a set of interpretable considerations, such as pitch rate, yaw rate, relative elevation, Mach number, and heading. These considerations serve as measurable input features from the flight environment that are evaluated at every time step.

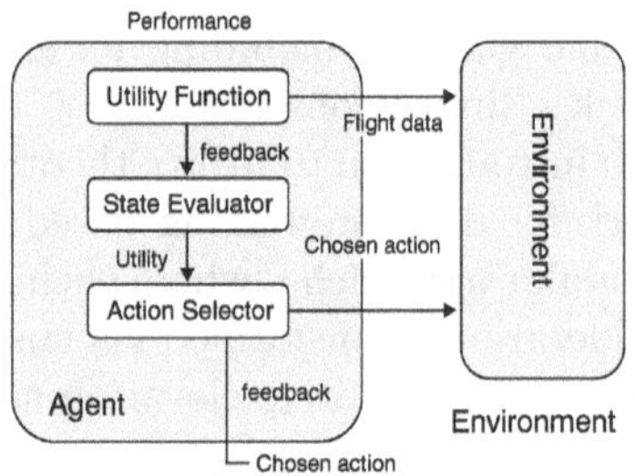


**Fig. 1.** Utility Based Decision Framework

Figure 1 illustrates the core methodology of our utility-based decision framework within a 6-DoF RL environment. The diagram represents a modular agent architecture where sensor flight data are first passed through a Utility Function, which evaluates current conditions using scoring curves tied to operational considerations. These evaluations feed into the State Evaluator, which computes the utility value of each possible action. The Action Selector then chooses the highest-scoring action, which is executed in the environment. Feedback from the environment closes the loop, allowing for continuous, interpretable decision-making. This structure aligns with our layered approach to explainability transforming raw inputs into transparent, goal aligned action choices.

To score each consideration, we apply intuitive mathematical transformations such as linear, logistic, or smoothstep curves that convert raw sensor data into normalized utility values on a 01 scale. These scoring curves reflect the desirability or risk associated with specific feature values in context. The individual consideration scores are then aggregated, typically using a weighted average or compensatory model, to compute the total utility score for each candidate action. At each decision point in the simulation, the agent evaluates all actions and selects the one with the highest utility score. This decision-making cycle repeats over the course of the engagement timeline, allowing for continual adaptation to changing mission related decision.

- Utility Score Over Time Charts: Illustrate how different actions compete based on real time utility, revealing trends such as consistent prioritization of yaw stabilization.
- Consideration Block Diagrams: Provide a transparent breakdown of how feature scores are assigned and combined for each action.
- Scoring Curve Visuals: Demonstrate how raw inputs are transformed into interpretable scores using different functional mappings.
- Contextual Heatmaps: Show how the importance of each feature shifts across engagement ranges, reinforcing the contextual sensitivity of utility-based decisions.

Altogether, this methodology offers a complete pipeline—from data to decision to explanation grounded in the principles of interpretable AI. It enables both post hoc analysis and real time transparency, bridging the gap between autonomous learning and human trust in mission critical scenarios.

### 3.2 Dataset and Training

To simulate realistic aerial engagements for reinforcement learning, we developed a custom OpenAI Gym compatible environment using a 6-dof flight dynamics model. This high-fidelity environment captures the physical behaviors of an F-16 aircraft and enables continuous control over pitch, roll, yaw, and throttle inputs. The simulation runs at discrete intervals (0.05 s per step), collecting observations, actions, and reward feedback over approximately 10,000 time steps per episode. The Blue Team agent (defender) and Red Team agent (attacker) were trained with distinct objectives: the defender aims to evade and survive, while the attacker seeks to inflict damage and gain positional advantage. Observations include normalized aircraft state parameters (e.g., heading, altitude, pitch rate) and relative adversary metrics (e.g., azimuth, velocity, distance). The reward function was carefully designed to promote realistic behavior—awarding damage dealt, penalizing stalling or boundary violations, and encouraging evasive or strategic maneuvers. Inspired by prior work such as DARPA's AlphaDogfight [9] Trials and the ACE program, our setup captures the complexity and tactical depth of aerial dogfights. The resulting dataset consists of over 10,000 time steps per simulation run and includes 21 features representing both control actions and environmental states.

### 3.3 Result

To analyze and interpret agent decision making in a 6-DoF MARL simulation environment, we used a utility based framework to extract, visualize, and evaluate tactical behavior. Figure 1 presents utility scores over time for three candidate actions: Stabilize Yaw, Adjust Pitch, and Increase Throttle. The time series highlights behavioral trends: Stabilize Yaw consistently scores the highest utility, reinforcing its tactical importance in maintaining directional stability. Adjust Pitch fluctuates in response to context, suggesting situational relevance likely during moments of evasive maneuvers or altitude shifts. Meanwhile, Increase Throttle consistently ranks lower, indicating that speed modulation is deprioritized unless specifically required by engagement conditions.

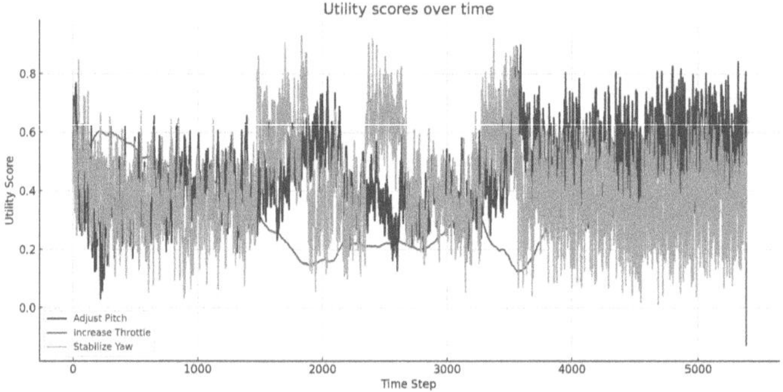


**Fig. 2.** Utility Score Over Time

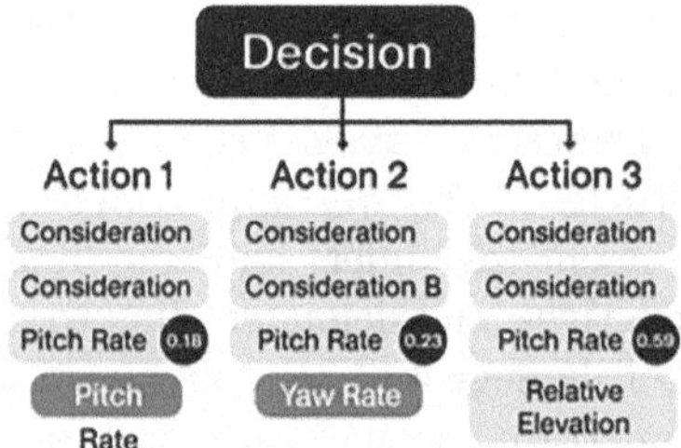


**Fig. 3.** Consideration Based Scoring Architecture

These utility scores are computed in Fig. 2 for a consideration based scoring architecture. Each action is evaluated through multiple "considerations" interpretable flight parameters such as Pitch Rate, Yaw Rate, or Relative Elevation. Each consideration is scored individually based on environmental inputs. For instance, Action 3 achieves a total utility score of 0.28, with Relative Elevation contributing a significant 0.59, making it the dominant factor in action selection. This layered scoring system offers a traceable logic chain from raw inputs to final decisions, improving transparency and supporting more interpretable agent control.

Figure 3 illustrates the scoring curves applied to these key flight features. We applied three different transformation types—Linear, Logit, and Smoothstep to map raw flight data into normalized utility values. Each curve plays a different role: Linear offers straightforward proportional scaling; Logit emphasizes mid range sensitivity and saturation at extremes; and Smoothstep enables gradual transitions, avoiding sharp changes in utility. These curves shape the weight and influence of each consideration, tailoring action scores to the dynamics of the combat environment.

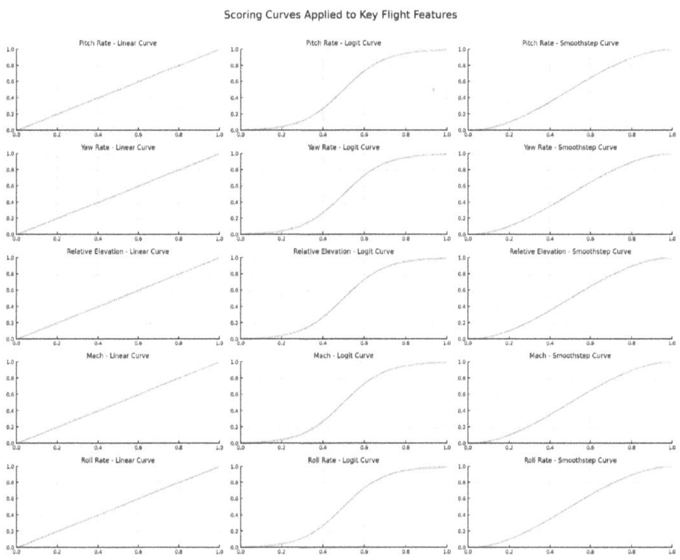


**Fig. 4.** Scoring Curves Applied To Key Flight Features

Expanding on this, Fig. 4 shows an extended comparison of five scoring curves Linear, Exponential, Sine, Cosine, and Logistic applied to each flight feature. These transformations reveal how decision logic can be tuned for tactical sensitivity. For example, an Exponential curve applied to Roll Rate highlights extreme instability, while a Sine curve emphasizes mid range corrections. Logistic functions introduce thresholding behavior, ideal for transitions between low-risk and high-risk states. This diverse toolkit enables mission designers to fine tune agent responses without retraining the entire model, ensuring more precise and interpretable decision behavior.

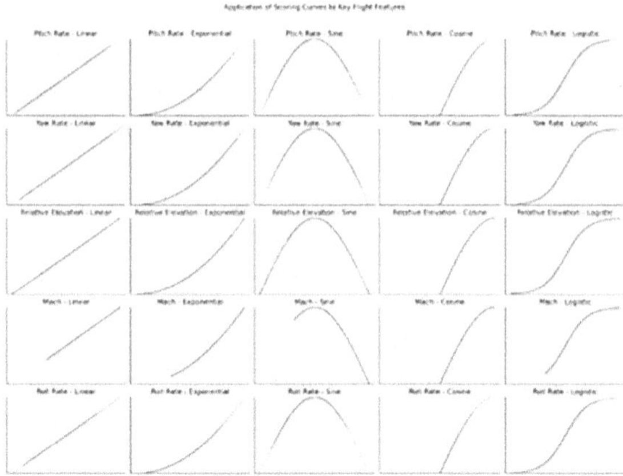

**Fig. 5.** Comparison of Scoring Curves

Finally, Fig. 5 presents a Contextual Importance and Utility heatmap, which visualizes how the relevance of each input feature changes across different engagement ranges (Close, Mid, Far). For example, Down-Range Distance becomes critically important in long-range engagements (normalized score = 0.90), while Cross-Track Distance is more impactful at close range. Mach and Yaw Rate maintain consistent influence, suggesting their role as core maneuverability parameters. This context-aware insight validates the need for dynamic utility functions that adapt to scenario-specific demands, rather than relying on static weights (Fig. 6).

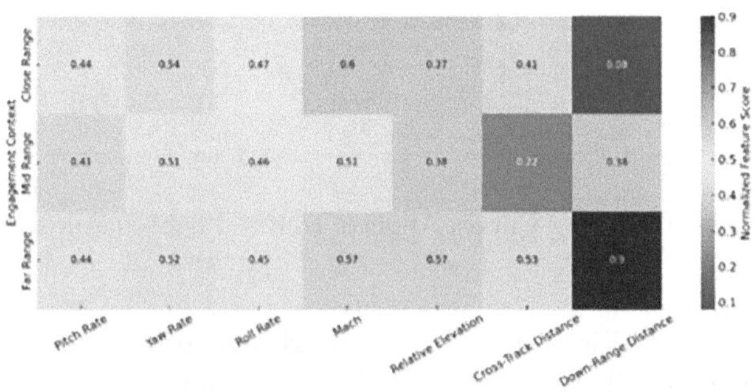


**Fig. 6.** Contextual Importance and Utility Heatmap

Finally, Fig. 5 presents a Contextual Importance and Utility heatmap, which visualizes how the relevance of each input feature changes across different engagement ranges (Close, Mid, Far). For example, Down Range Distance becomes critically important in long-range engagements (normalized score = 0.90), while

Cross-Track Distance is more impactful at close range. Mach and Yaw Rate maintain consistent influence, suggesting their role as main maneuverability parameters. This insight validates the need for dynamic utility functions that adapt to scenario specific demands, rather than relying on static weights.

## 4 Conclusion and Future Work

The results from our utility-based decision framework offer a transparent view into the tactical reasoning of agents during simulated aerial engagements. The utility score timeline clearly illustrates that "Stabilize Yaw" consistently maintains the highest utility score, emphasizing the importance of directional stability in high-speed, maneuver heavy fights. In contrast, "Adjust Pitch" displays moderate fluctuation, suggesting its relevance is situational likely tied to vertical maneuvers such as climbs or evasions. "Increase Throttle," on the other hand, holds the lowest utility score across most of the timeline, indicating that speed changes are less frequently prioritized unless driven by specific environmental triggers. Figure 3 complements these findings by providing a granular breakdown of how utility scores are derived for each action. In this example, Action 3 receives the highest total utility (0.28), largely due to a strong score (0.59) from the Relative Elevation consideration. This highlights the importance of that particular flight parameter in tactical decision making and demonstrates how the system aggregates various contextual inputs into a unified, interpretable score. Together, these visual and quantitative insights validate the agent's internal decision logic and reinforce the value of utility AI as a transparent, flexible framework for multiagent reasoning in complex combat simulations.

Looking ahead, several extensions can enhance the effectiveness and flexibility of the Utility AI framework. One promising direction is the incorporation of real time adaptivity in scoring weights, allowing the agent to dynamically adjust its decision criteria based on evolving combat conditions, mission priorities, or adversary behavior. Additionally, there is potential to integrate Utility AI with decision tree policies to form a hybrid interpretability model using trees to generate interpretable decision rules and utility scoring to refine those choices with real time context. Finally, expanding the current system to cooperative or adversarial multiagent scenarios could test the scalability and robustness of utility based decision-making in more complex air combat engagements, where agents must coordinate or counteract each other's strategies under uncertainty. One promising extension of this framework is the integration of multi objective optimization (MOO) into utility-based decision making [4]. While our current method aggregates multiple considerations into a single utility score, MOO would allow the agent to simultaneously optimize for multiple, potentially conflicting goals such as maximizing positional advantage while minimizing damage taken. This shift from scalar utility values to Pareto optimal trade-offs aligns more closely with real-world combat dynamics, where decisions must often balance competing tactical objectives. Future implementations may explore Pareto front analysis, weighted summation, or genetic algorithms like NSGA-II to support this richer form of agent decision making.

## References


1. Beechey, D., Smith, T.M., Şimşek, Ö.: Explaining reinforcement learning with shapley values (2023)
2. Bekkemoen, Y.: Explainable reinforcement learning (XRL): a systematic literature review and taxonomy. Mach. Learn. **113**(1), 355–441 (2024)
3. Covert, I., Lundberg, S.M., Lee, S.I.: Understanding global feature contributions with additive importance measures (2020)
4. Data Science Central Editorial Team. Ai utility function, multi-objective optimization, pareto-optimal solution...oh my! https://www.datasciencecentral.com/creating-healthy-ai-utility-function-importance-of-diversity-part-i/ (2023)
5. "Rez" Graham, D.: An introduction to utility theory. In: Game AI Pro: Collected Wisdom of Game AI Professionals, chapter 9. CRC Press (2014)
6. Heuillet, A., Couthouis, F., Díaz-Rodríguez, N.: Explainability in deep reinforcement learning (2020)
7. Janner, M., Justin, F., Zhang, M., Levine, S.: Model-based policy optimization, When to trust your model (2021)
8. Jon McGuire. 40 years of code
9. Pope, A.P., et al.: Hierarchical reinforcement learning for air-to-air combat (2021)
10. Puiutta, E., MSP Veith, E.: Explainable reinforcement learning: a survey (2020)
11. Russell, S., Norvig, P.: Artificial intelligence: a modern approach. Prentice Hall, 3rd edition (2010)
12. ShaggyDev. Utility ai (2023). Accessed 08 Apr 2025
13. Vouros, G.A.: Explainable deep reinforcement learning: state of the art and challenges. ACM Comput. Surv. **55**(5), 1–39 (2022)
14. Yang, Q., Liu, R.: Understanding the application of utility theory in robotics and artificial intelligence: a survey (2023)

# Machine Learning-Based Viscosity Prediction of Ionic Liquids Using Random Forest Regression

Jacob Goodin[1], Patrick Cuddihy[2], Fardin Khabaz[2], Zhong-Hui Duan[1], and En Cheng[1(✉)]

[1] Department of Computer Science, The University of Akron, Akron, OH 44325, USA
{jag279,duan,echeng}@uakron.edu

[2] School of Polymer Science and Polymer Engineering, The University of Akron, Akron, OH 44325, USA
{pc104,fkhabaz}@uakron.edu

**Abstract.** In this study, random forest regression models were developed to predict the viscosity of ionic liquids using an enhanced dataset generated via the cheminformatics toolkit RDKit. The curated dataset included over 22,000 experimental observations across 2,068 unique ionic liquids, with inconsistent or uncertain entries removed. Feature extraction expanded the original four features to 126 molecular descriptors, capturing properties such as molecular weight, charge, and structural attributes. To manage high dimensionality, Principal Component Analysis preserved 95% of variance, followed by feature refinement using SelectKBest, Recursive Feature Elimination, and a novel Bayesian Feature Selection approach. Model optimization was performed through Bayesian hyperparameter tuning and validated using 10-fold cross-validation. An ensemble of random forest models was autonomously generated and evaluated across varying feature sets and hyperparameters. The final model achieved an average $R^2$ of 0.96 on the training set and 0.76 on the test set, indicating strong predictive performance. This work demonstrates the power of combining advanced feature engineering, dimensionality reduction, and machine learning to predict ionic liquid viscosity, providing valuable tools for the rational design and industrial deployment of ionic liquids.

**Keywords:** Machine Learning · Random Forest Regression · Feature Selection · Principal Component Analysis

## 1 Introduction

The rapidly growing field of machine learning has introduced powerful techniques for tackling a wide range of real-world challenges, particularly through predictive analytics applied to diverse datasets. The intersection of machine learning and materials science has led to significant advancements in predictive modeling of material properties, a crucial component of computer-aided molecular design [1]. One of the main goals of


R. Stahlbock et al. (Eds.): CSCE 2025, CCIS 2938, pp. 41–59, 2027.
https://doi.org/10.1007/978-3-032-22196-4_4

applying machine learning to materials science is to simplify and accelerate the development of new materials. This involves developing models that can unravel the complex relationships within these datasets. A prominent example of this approach is predicting the viscosity of ionic liquids, as explored in this study.

Ionic liquids (ILs) are a class of liquid salts that remain liquid at room temperature, consisting of a complex interaction between organic cations and inorganic anions [2, 3]. The vast array of potential anion-cation combinations leads to an unlimited diversity of possible ionic liquids [3]. These substances are characterized by low volatility, high thermal stability, low flammability, and non-toxicity, with some variants also being biodegradable [2, 3]. Such properties make ionic liquids particularly useful across a range of applications – from high-viscosity needs like lubricants and greases to low-viscosity applications such as solvents in catalysis [3–5]. As such, ionic liquids have become very attractive for many applications as well as green chemistry [3, 6]. Viscosity, a crucial property of ionic liquids, affects their resistance to flow and deformation and is highly sensitive to temperature and specific ionic components [7, 8]. Accurate prediction of viscosity is vital for optimizing ionic liquid applications and manufacturing efficiencies [4, 8]. In lubrication, ionic liquids with high viscosity provide improved film strength and load-bearing capacity, while those with low viscosity promote better ion mobility and conductivity in electrochemical applications [4, 9]. Thus, predicting viscosity based on molecular structure is crucial for designing ionic liquids tailored to these specific applications, a topic that has gained significant attention in literature.

The prediction of ionic liquid viscosity using machine learning requires addressing the challenge of processing and analyzing large datasets. In the field of materials science, both the volume and quality of data are critical factors that influence machine learning model performance. Extensive research has been conducted to improve the understanding and prediction of ionic liquid viscosity, emphasizing the need for more advanced machine learning models to achieve accurate results. These advanced models are employed to unravel the complex relationships between input features and viscosity, thereby enabling more precise predictions and advancing the understanding of ionic liquid behavior.

This paper aims to utilize a Quantitative Structure-Property Relationship model based off physiochemical descriptors from RDKit [10] to enhance Paduszynski's dataset [11] for use with Leo Breiman's Random Forest model [12]. This study aims to establish accurate structure-property relationships via simpler means which can still facilitate the efficient design and application of ionic liquids in various industrial processes. A novel aspect of this study is the implementation of Bayesian Feature Selection, which employs Bayesian inference to identify the most relevant features, combined with a unique application of Principal Component Analysis applied to different subsets of features within the dataset. This approach aims to provide improved feature selection and dimensionality reduction, thereby enhancing model performance while retaining interpretability. The primary objective is to establish a streamlined methodology that enhances model interpretability while preserving high predictive accuracy.

The remainder of this paper is organized as follows: Sect. 2 reviews the most recent related studies. Section 3 details the methodology of the proposed approach. Section 4 presents the experimental results, including a comparison between the Random Forest models and linear regression models. Finally, Sect. 5 discusses the key findings, outlines the limitations of the approach, and suggests directions for future research.

## 2 Related Works

Prior work on predicting the viscosity of ionic liquids often utilizes smaller datasets compared to typical machine learning applications [11, 13, 14]. One notable example is the work of Ding et al. [15], who predicted the refractive index and viscosity of different ionic liquids using molecular fingerprint guided machine learning to develop quantitative structure-activity relationship models. By employing four datasets totaling 3,147 data points and utilizing an XGBoost model, their approach achieved admiral performance, with an $R^2$ value of 0.97. While these results are promising, the dataset still encompasses a relatively limited number of ionic liquids compared to other studies.

Paduszynski, from whom this paper sources its data, conducted extensive work by aggregating approximately 22,000 data points of experimental ionic liquid viscosity observations and filtering them down to 13,539 data points [11]. The Quantitative Structure-Property Relationship (QSPR) model presented in [28] represents viscosity as a function of predefined functional groups within ionic liquid cations and anions, utilizing a feed-forward artificial neural network (FFANN) for the reference term and a least squares support vector machine (LSSVM) for the correction term [11]. This dual approach effectively captures both chemical structure and working conditions. While the use of FFANN and LSSVM in predicting the viscosity of many ionic liquids is a significant achievement, it poses challenges in interpreting the model's performance. Paduszynski even acknowledges this limitation, stating, "More sophisticated machine learning methods (FFANN and LSSVM) resulted in a noticeably better modeling performance, but physical or mechanistic interpretation of parameters of the resulting models is basically unfeasible. Thus, these models are more valuable from the purely utilitarian point of view rather than for the fundamental knowledge or physical insight into the viscous behavior of ILs" [11].

Building on Paduszynski's work, Boualem et al. [16] expanded the dataset by incorporating data from ILThermo (NIST-ILs) [10]. They developed non-linear regression (NLR) and support vector machine (SVM) models based on first and second-order groups within each IL. The resulting models achieved predictive $R^2$ values of 0.9618 with a 19.6% Average Absolute Relative Error (AARE) for the NLR model and 0.9904 with a 9.07% AARE for the SVM model [16]. Despite these significant improvements over Paduszynski's model, the reliance on group contribution methods remains a limitation. These methods may not generalize well to other use cases or different molecules as these groups need to be predefined, which limits their ability to accurately predict properties for molecules with novel or unusual structures that aren't represented in the predefined set.

These previous works notably employ highly complex models to handle the dimensionality and non-linearity of the datasets, resulting in high performance. However, they often lack a focus on developing metrics to assess the interpretability of these models after analysis. As a result, these studies often present models and datasets that function as a 'black box'. This lack of interpretability is a significant concern because it hinders our ability to understand and validate the model's predictions, which is crucial for advancing applications like material design.

## 3 Proposed Work

In this study, we utilize the random forest model due to its capacity to capture non-linear relationships within the data, while offering greater interpretability and lower computational demands compared to neural networks. To effectively adapt the model to our high-dimensional dataset, we designed a comprehensive workflow, illustrated in Fig. 1, integrating three steps to enhance the model's robustness and generalizability across different subsets of the data.

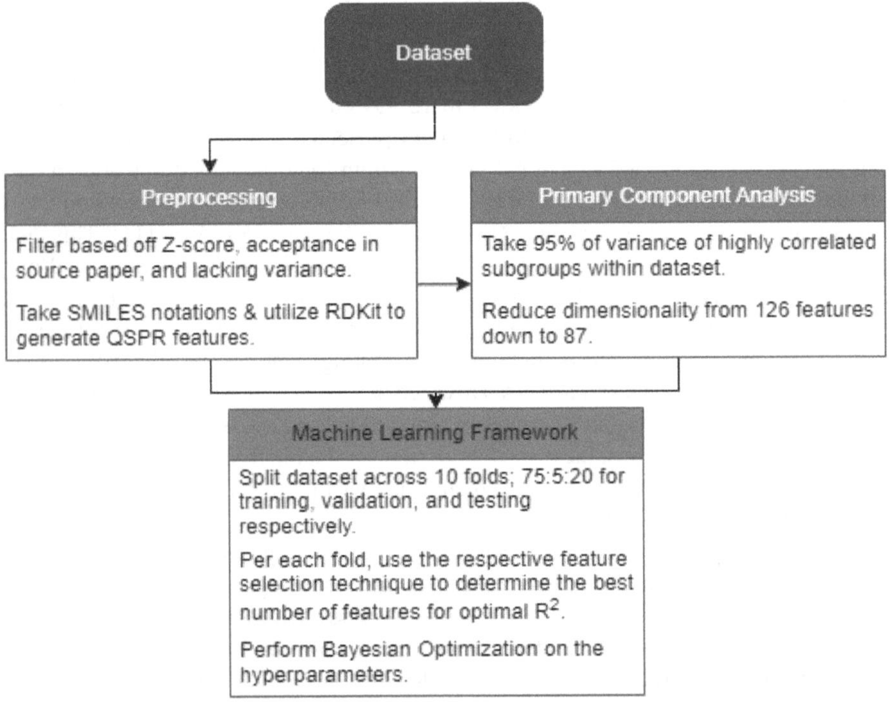


**Fig. 1.** Schematic illustrating the general approach utilized for this research.

A crucial first step in this workflow is data preprocessing, which enhances the model's accuracy and robustness by addressing inconsistencies and reducing noise that could otherwise introduce bias. Following this, we perform feature engineering to construct and select the most impactful features that contribute significantly to model performance.

Dimensionality reduction is performed using Principal Component Analysis (PCA), which reduces the number of features while preserving the most significant variance in the data. By transforming the original features into a smaller set of uncorrelated components, PCA helps mitigate the risk of overfitting and lowers computational demands. In addition to PCA, we apply several feature selection techniques, including SelectKBest, Recursive Feature Elimination, and Bayesian Feature Selection. These methods enable the identification and retention of the most relevant features by eliminating redundant and less informative ones. This refinement allows the model to concentrate on the most influential predictors, thereby enhancing its performance and offering insights into the key factors influencing viscosity.

We then train the model using 10-fold cross-validation to ensure consistent performance across different subsets of the dataset. This method provides a more robust and reliable assessment of the model's performance by reducing the variance associated with a single train-test split. Finally, hyperparameter optimization is carried out using Bayesian optimization, which systematically explores the hyperparameter space to identify the most effective settings for the random forest models. This process enables the model to be more precisely tuned to the characteristics of our dataset.

### 3.1 Data Source

The initial dataset comprised 22,268 experimental observations for 2068 different ILs from 3236 datasets. During preprocessing, Paduszynski removed datasets with high or unknown uncertainty and those not aligning with other publications, reducing the dataset to 15,372 observations over 1974 ILs from 2163 datasets [11]. We further filtered observations using Z-score filtering with a threshold of 10, resulting in a total of 12,295 observations. Most recorded viscosities in this dataset fall under 1,000 mPa·s, as shown in Fig. 2, which captures the viscosity distribution on a log scale, revealing a skew towards lower values.

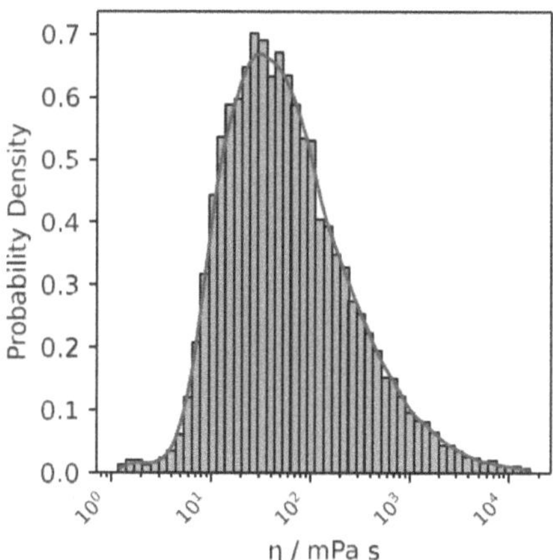


**Fig. 2.** Probability density of viscosity (η / mPa·s) measurements.

### 3.2 Feature Extraction

To enhance the dimensionality and performance of our model, we utilized RDKit [10], a cheminformatics software, for feature extraction. The initial dataset consisted of only four features, which were insufficient for robust QSPR analysis. Through RDKit, we extracted additional features, expanding the dataset to 126 features. The resulting dataset included features such as target viscosity (η/mPa·s), temperature (T/K), classifications of cationic and anionic families, molecular weights, molecular charges, and additional QSPR descriptors. We chose to exclude features exhibiting less than 15% variance to reduce noise and enhance model performance. This threshold was determined experimentally as it was found that including features with very low variance (less than 15%) degraded the model's performance. Through this iterative process, 15% variance was identified as the optimal threshold. A sample of the dataset is shown in Table 1, while Fig. 3 displays a blown-up view of the correlation matrix.

**Table 1.** Sample of pre-PCA dataset.

| η/mPa·s | T/K | Cationic Family | Anionic Family | MolWt | MaxPartialCharge |
|---|---|---|---|---|---|
| 797.5 | 298.1 | azepanium | sulfonates | 321.361 | 0.485235 |
| 579.7 | 303.1 | azepanium | sulfonates | 321.361 | 0.485235 |
| 206.5 | 292.05 | azepanium | NTf2 derivatives | 496.492 | 0.48029 |
| 95.23 | 304.05 | azepanium | NTf2 derivatives | 496.492 | 0.48029 |

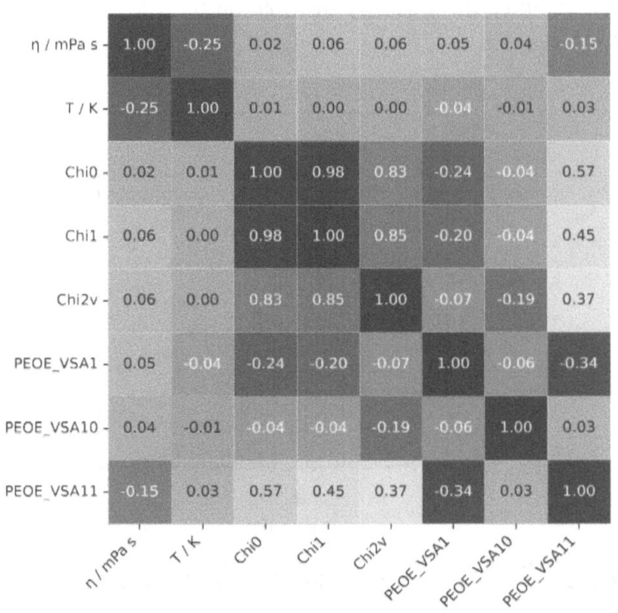


**Fig. 3.** Blown-up Matrix of pre-PCA RDKit features.

## 3.3 Principal Component Analysis

Principal Component Analysis (PCA) is employed to transform a high-dimensional dataset into a lower- dimensional form by identifying new orthogonal axes, known as principal components, which represent the directions of maximum variance in the data. This technique is essential for managing high-dimensional datasets, reducing computational costs, and minimizing the risk of overfitting [17–22]. By focusing on the principal components that capture the most variance, PCA effectively filters out noise and less informative features, resulting in cleaner datasets and potentially more accurate models.

Given the high dimensionality and correlation among the QSPR features, PCA was necessary to reduce the dimensionality of the feature set while retaining as much variance as possible. Rather than applying PCA to the entire dataset, it was applied to different subsets of RDKit QSPR descriptors to preserve information about which features contribute to the model's performance, thus maintaining model interpretability. Table 2 displays the number of features in each subset before and after PCA analysis, with the aim of retaining 95% of the variance. Additionally, it highlights how these features correspond to the overall dataset.

Applying PCA to the feature subset reduced the number of features from 126 to 87, while preserving the majority of the dataset's variance and retaining key descriptive information. The objective was to maintain features that are most informative and relevant for model performance. Both the original and PCA-transformed datasets were partitioned into training, validation, and test sets using a 75:5:20 split. To evaluate model performance and ensure robustness, 10-fold cross-validation was performed. During this process, the training and validation subsets were rotated across folds, while the test set remained fixed to provide a consistent benchmark for final model evaluation.

**Table 2.** Number of features in subsets pre and post PCA analysis for 95% variance.

| Group name | # Original Features | # PCA Features | % Variance of Dataset | Top 2 Features |
|---|---|---|---|---|
| Estate_indexes | 4 | 3 | 3.1746% | MinEStateIndex, MinAbsEStateIndex |
| BCUT2D | 8 | 6 | 6.1409% | BCUT2D_MWLOW, BCUT2D_LOGPLOW |
| Chi | 12 | 2 | 9.0732% | Chi0, Chi4n |
| Kappa | 3 | 3 | 2.3810% | Kappa2, Kappa1 |
| Peoe_VSA | 12 | 9 | 9.2112% | PEOE_VSA6, PEOE_VSA9 |
| SMR_VSA | 7 | 6 | 5.3225% | SMR_VSA3, SMR_VSA4 |
| SlogP_VSA | 9 | 8 | 6.9860% | SlogP_VSA1, SlogP_VSA8 |

*(continued)*

**Table 2.** (*continued*)

| Group name | # Original Features | # PCA Features | % Variance of Dataset | Top 2 Features |
|---|---|---|---|---|
| Estate_VSA | 10 | 8 | 7.6706% | EState_VSA3, EState_VSA2 |
| VSA_Estate | 9 | 7 | 6.9373% | VSA_EState2, VSA_EState8 |
| molWt | 3 | 1 | 2.3771% | ExactMolWt, MolWt |
| partialCharge | 4 | 2 | 3.0930% | MaxAbsPartialCharge, MaxPartialCharge |
| FpDensityMorgan | 3 | 2 | 2.3759% | FpDensityMorgan1, FpDensityMorgan3 |
| molecular_features | 15 | 6 | 11.5378% | NumRotatableBonds, NumHeteroatoms |
| Functional_groups | 10 | 7 | 7.62945% | fr_NH0, fr_ether |
| Total | 109 | 70 | 83.9095% | ~ |

### 3.4 Feature Selection

To further reduce noise and redundancy in the model, we performed feature selection on the dataset. This process generated rankings for individual features, enabling the construction of models based on various ranked subsets. The optimal feature subset was identified by evaluating the $R^2$ scores of these models on validation sets. To represent key categories of feature selection methods—filter, wrapper, and embedded approaches [23–25]—we utilized SelectKBest, Recursive Feature Elimination (RFE) [26], and Bayesian Feature Selection (BFS).

For SelectKBest, we employed the scikit-learn package [27]. This method evaluates the importance of each feature individually by applying statistical tests and selecting the top K features that have the strongest relationship with the target variable. This filter method is computationally efficient and provides a straightforward way to reduce the dimensionality of the dataset before applying more complex models.

For Recursive Feature Elimination (RFE), we used packages such as scikit-learn [27] and NVIDIA's RAPIDS AI cuML package [28]. RFE works by recursively fitting the model and removing the least important features, based on the model's coefficients. This process continues until a desired number of features is reached. RFE is a wrapper method that can capture interactions between features, but it is more computationally intensive compared to filter methods like SelectKBest as our implementation itself uses random forest as a surrogate to evaluate the features on.

For BFS, we utilized Bayesian inference via PyMC [29] to determine the probability of each feature's relevance to the prediction task. We used a uniform Beta distribution

($\alpha = 1.0$, $\beta = 1.0$) to model the inclusion probabilities, indicating no initial bias towards any feature. The feature weights were modeled with a standard normal distribution ($\mu = 1.0$, $\sigma = 1.0$), reflecting no strong initial assumptions about their magnitudes [30]. This data-driven approach ensures that the selection process identifies the most relevant features based on their posterior inclusion probabilities [31]. This process is illustrated in Fig. 4, which shows the trace plot of the BFS, tracking the individual probabilities of each feature being relevant until convergence is reached.

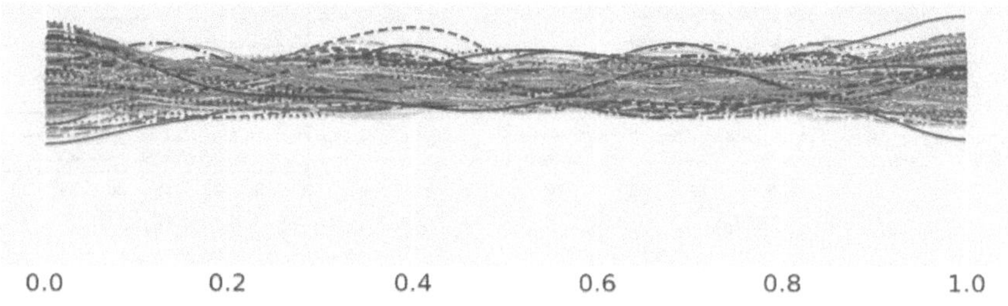


**Fig. 4.** Trace plot of PyMC Feature Importance Probabilities.

Figure 5 illustrates the key features for the post-PCA Random Forest model. Each plot highlights the top features identified as most significant by the respective technique, with black bars representing the standard deviation for each feature. Temperature consistently emerges as the most influential variable in predicting viscosity, underscoring its critical role within the dataset. This finding aligns with previous insights from semi-empirical models and reinforces the importance of temperature as discussed earlier in this paper.

### 3.5 Hyperparameter Optimization

After identifying the optimal feature subset, Bayesian optimization was employed using the *scikit-optimize* library [32]. This optimization process was carried out over 25 iterations with three-fold cross-validation to identify the most effective hyperparameters for tuning the random forest model. In contrast to traditional approaches such as grid search or random search, Bayesian optimization leverages a probabilistic surrogate model to guide the selection of hyperparameters. This informed and adaptive strategy significantly reduces the number of required evaluations, thereby conserving computational resources and time, while ensuring that the model is finely tuned to achieve optimal predictive performance.

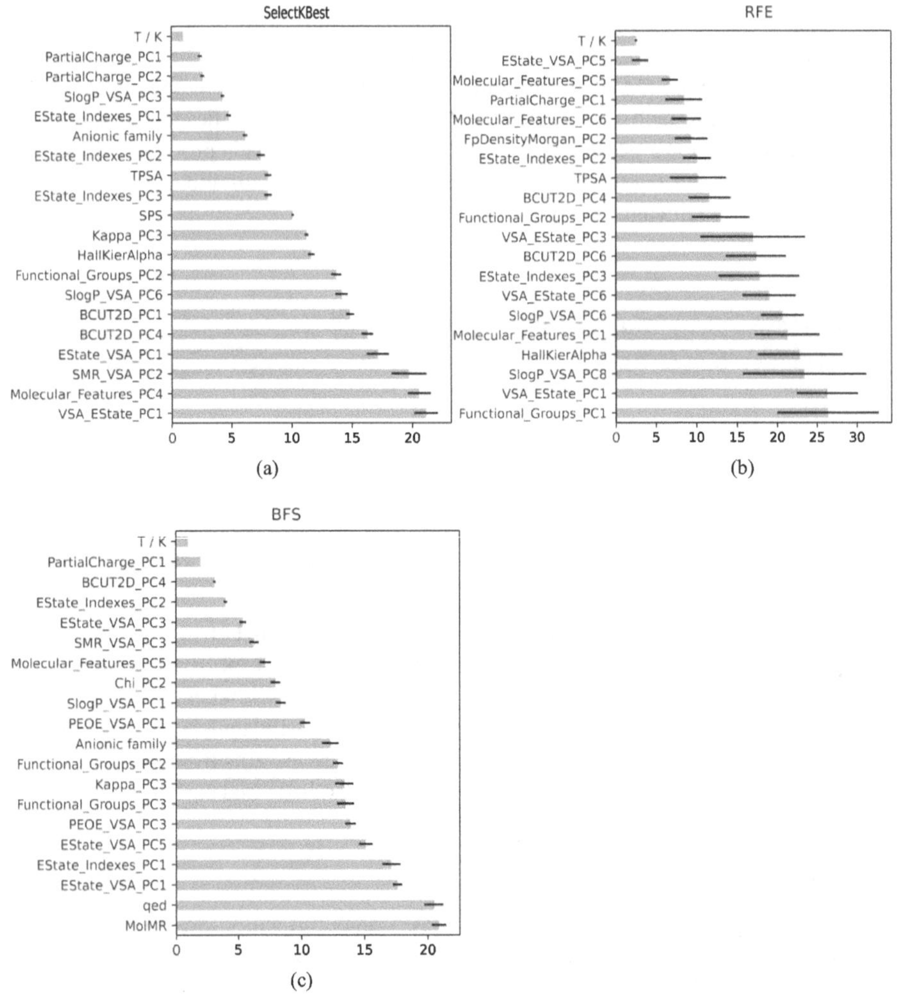


**Fig. 5.** Feature importance rankings (a) SelectKBest, (b) RFE, (c) BFS.

A key component of Bayesian optimization is the acquisition function, which determines how the next set of hyperparameters is chosen. Common acquisition functions include Expected Improvement (EI), Probability of Improvement (PI), and Upper Confidence Bound (UCB) [33]. These functions balance the trade-off between exploration (evaluating hyperparameters in less certain regions) and exploitation (refining hyperparameters in regions known to perform well). For instance, EI focuses on maximizing the expected improvement over the current best result, while UCB considers both the mean and variance of the surrogate model's predictions to select hyperparameters that could potentially yield better performance.

The advantages of Bayesian optimization are particularly evident when dealing with complex models and large hyperparameter spaces. By intelligently navigating the hyperparameter space, Bayesian optimization can achieve better performance with fewer evaluations compared to traditional methods. This is incredibly beneficial in scenarios where each model evaluation is computationally expensive, such as in deep learning or large-scale machine learning tasks. In the context of this study, Bayesian optimization enabled the efficient tuning of the random forest model's hyperparameters, such as the number of trees, maximum depth, and minimum samples per split, ultimately leading to improved predictive accuracy and robustness.

## 4 Experimental Results

To ensure replicability and enhance transparency, the system configuration used for all experiments is detailed as follows: an AMD Ryzen 5 5600X CPU, 16 GB of RAM, and an NVIDIA RTX 3060 Ti GPU. The software environment consisted of Python 3.10.13, managed via Conda 24.1.2, and executed within the Windows Subsystem for Linux 2 (WSL2).

To facilitate comparative analysis, linear regression (LR) models were also trained and evaluated using the same dataset and preprocessing pipeline. Linear regression operates by identifying a best-fit line that minimizes the sum of squared residuals between observed and predicted values. However, this method is inherently limited in capturing complex, multidimensional, and nonlinear relationships. The performance of the linear regression models was evaluated using the same metrics as the random forest models, providing a baseline for comparison. This analysis not only confirms the non-linear nature of the dataset but also underscores the superior capability of random forest models in modeling such relationships, as demonstrated in the results section.

### 4.1 Linear Regression Results

The results of the linear regression model, evaluated using 10-fold cross-validation, are presented in Fig. 6. Figure 6 indicates that linear regression performs inadequately on this dataset. The linear regression model consistently overestimates values near the mean and underestimates at the extremes, suggesting the presence of polynomial or non-linear relationships between certain features and the target variable. This behavior strongly indicates the non-linearity inherent in the dataset.

Additionally, Fig. 6 (a) reveals a pattern of heteroscedasticity, where residual errors increase with higher predicted values [34]. This phenomenon likely results from the model's inability to accurately predict higher viscosity values due to insufficient feature representation. As a result, linear regression fails to capture the underlying complexity of the data, violating key assumptions required for its effective application [35]. These limitations underscore the need for alternative modeling approaches—such as Random Forest—that are better suited to capturing non-linear dependencies within the data.

### 4.2 Random Forest Results

To address the limitations of linear regression, a Random Forest model was employed, as outlined previously in the methodology. The model was trained and evaluated on both the original (pre-PCA) and dimensionally reduced (post-PCA) datasets to assess the impact of principal component analysis (PCA) on predictive performance. The results for the pre-PCA dataset are presented in Fig. 7. The Random Forest model demonstrated a substantial improvement in predictive accuracy over linear regression. When applied to the pre-PCA dataset, the model achieved an $R^2$ value of 0.96 on the training dataset and 0.77 on the test dataset, reflecting strong generalization and predictive performance. As noted in the methodology section, these predictions represent averages obtained from 10-fold cross-validation. Since the training set varies across folds, the overall accuracy for each fold is illustrated in Fig. 8.

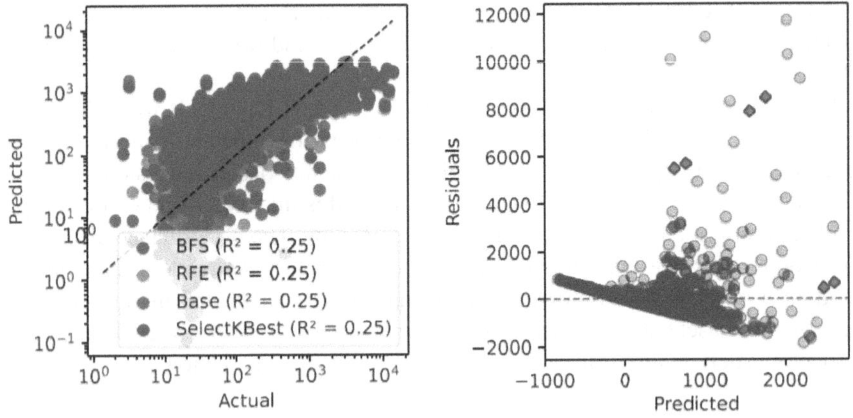


**Fig. 6.** (a) Predicted vs Actual of linear regression, (b) Residuals of linear regression

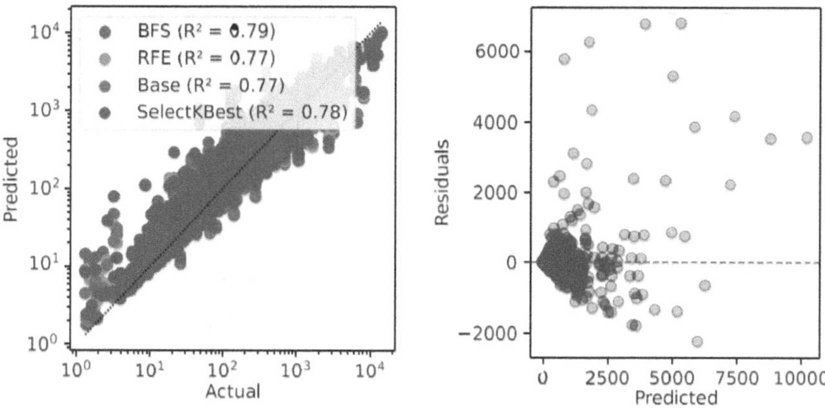


**Fig. 7.** (a) Predicted vs Actual of pre-PCA Random Forest, (b) Residuals of pre-PCA Random Forest.

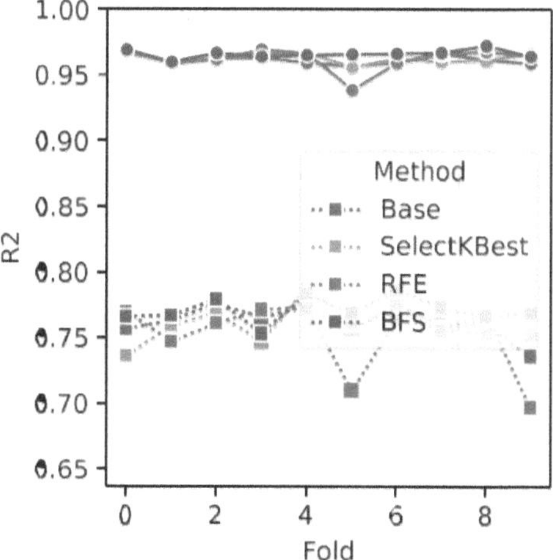


**Fig. 8.** $R^2$ per each fold for pre-PCA dataset.

By applying PCA, the feature space was substantially reduced, resulting in improved computational efficiency and streamlined model training. Post-PCA results indicate only a marginal decline in goodness of fit, with the Random Forest model retaining high predictive accuracy. This slight trade-off is outweighed by the benefits of reduced dimensionality and enhanced performance, highlighting the effectiveness of PCA in optimizing the model without substantially compromising its predictive capability. The results are illustrated in Fig. 9 and Fig. 10.

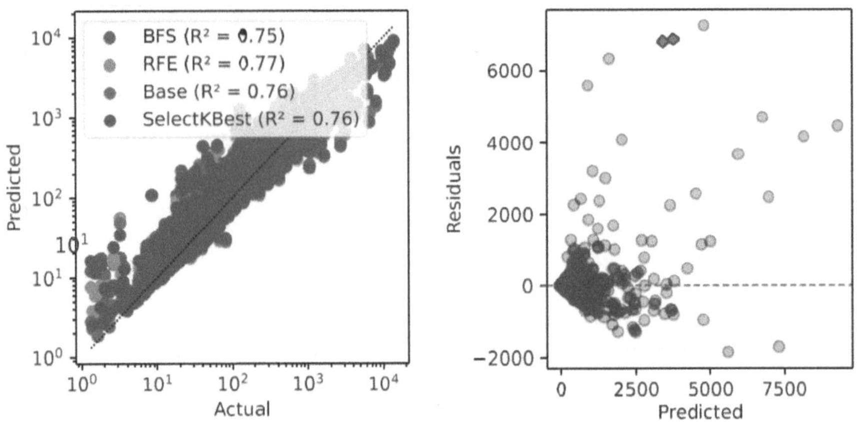


**Fig. 9.** (a) Predicted vs Actual of post-PCA Random Forest, (b) Residuals of post-PCA Random Forest.

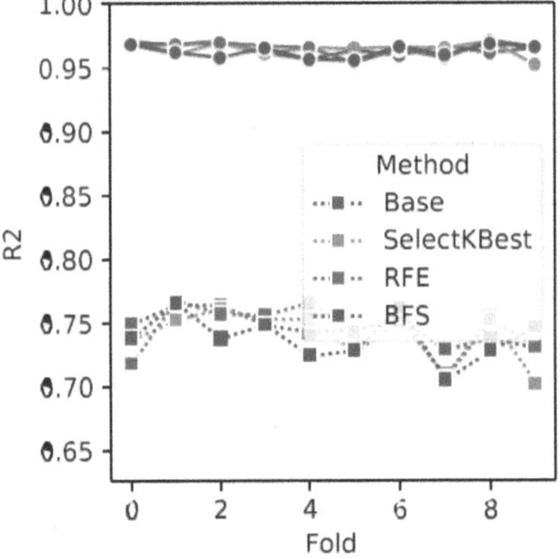


**Fig.10.** $R^2$ per each fold for post-PCA dataset.

Based on these results, the average $R^2$ for the test dataset is 0.76 for the post-PCA random forest model, only 0.01 lower than the model trained without PCA. This indicates that the model performs comparably well, even with dimensionality reduction applied. While the non-linear trend is not prominently visible in the corresponding figures, the issue of heteroscedasticity remains evident. As shown in Fig. 2, this is likely attributable to the limited number of high-viscosity observations in the dataset.

### 4.3 Model Comparison

Linear regression and random forest models were evaluated using several performance metrics, including $R^2$, Mean Squared Error (MSE), and Mean Absolute Error (MAE). The $R^2$ value for linear regression was notably lower than that of the random forest model, with test dataset values of 0.25 and 0.77, respectively. This disparity indicates that the linear regression model has limited predictive power, while the random forest model demonstrates robust predictive capability.

Residual plots in Figs. 6(b), 7(b), and 9(b) offer further insights into model performance. Figure 6(b) reveals that the linear regression model exhibits a distinct trend in the residuals, highlighting difficulties with polynomial relationships and heteroscedasticity, where residual errors increase with predicted values. Although the random forest model also shows some heteroscedasticity in Figs. 7(b) and 9(b), the magnitude of the residuals is significantly smaller, indicating a better overall fit. Linear regression model tends to overpredict average values and underpredict extremes, failing to capture higher-order interactions. In contrast, as an ensemble learning method, random forest outperforms linear regression by aggregating multiple decision trees, which allows it to capture more complex interactions between features. This is reflected in the superior performance metrics and more accurate predictions, as demonstrated in Figs. 7, 8 9 and 10.

Overall model performance is summarized in Table 3, including the corresponding standard deviations (SD) for each metric. While the Random Forest models exhibit greater variability in performance compared to linear regression, this does not undermine their robustness or overall effectiveness. The higher standard deviations in MSE and $R^2$ values reflect the algorithm's sensitivity to different data subsets—a characteristic inherent to its complexity. However, this variability is an acceptable trade-off given the significant gains in predictive accuracy that Random Forest models offer over simpler methods such as linear regression. It is also worth noting that the application of feature selection techniques appears to slightly reduce model performance. While this may seem counterintuitive, these techniques play a vital role within our modeling framework. By isolating the most relevant features, they enhance model interpretability and provide deeper insights into the underlying data structure. Although the performance improvements over the base model may be marginal, the benefits in terms of robustness, interpretability, and reduced risk of overfitting justify their inclusion.

**Table 3.** The overall performance results.

| | | Feature Selection | Avg. MSE | MSE SD | Avg. $R^2$ | $R^2$ SD |
|---|---|---|---|---|---|---|
| Pre-PCA | Linear Regression | Base | 553141.08 | 2185.79 | 0.2523 | 0.002955 |
| | Random Forest | Base | 175128.52 | 8927.59 | 0.7633 | 0.012067 |
| | | SelectKBest | 177134.76 | 10968.83 | 0.7606 | 0.014826 |
| | | RFE | 183265.98 | 19948.46 | 0.7523 | 0.026965 |
| | | BFS | 168553.49 | 7282.39 | 0.7722 | 0.009844 |

*(continued)*

**Table 3.** *(continued)*

| | | Feature Selection | Avg. MSE | MSE SD | Avg. $R^2$ | $R^2$ SD |
|---|---|---|---|---|---|---|
| Post-PCA | Linear Regression | Base | 572498.02 | 1975.37 | 0.2261 | 0.00267 |
| | Random Forest | Base | 187359.27 | 9078.24 | 0.7467 | 0.01227 |
| | | SelectKBest | 192197.99 | 15366.03 | 0.7402 | 0.02077 |
| | | RFE | 188264.66 | 15157.02 | 0.7455 | 0.02049 |
| | | BFS | 193292.87 | 13524.78 | 0.7387 | 0.01828 |

As a result, applying PCA to these datasets significantly reduced the time required to comprehensively evaluate the various models. While PCA does not directly improve the computational efficiency of the Random Forest algorithm itself, it facilitates the feature selection process by enabling faster convergence within a reduced search space. This advantage is particularly evident for more complex feature selection methods, as demonstrated in Table 4.

**Table 4.** Seconds per feature selection technique for total model construction.

| | Linear Regression | | Random Forest | |
|---|---|---|---|---|
| | Pre-PCA | Post-PCA | Pre-PCA | Post-PCA |
| Base | 0.78 s | 0.20 s | 2008.59 s | 2028.91 s |
| SelectKBest | 56.05 s | 30.45 s | 1537.80 s | 1328.12 s |
| RFE | 1182.68 s | 818.17 s | 2714.79 s | 2313.98 s |
| BFS | 8333.23 s | 2445.72 s | 9468.24 s | 4198.33 s |

## 5 Conclusion

In this study, we developed a Random Forest model to predict the viscosity of ionic liquids (ILs) using an expanded set of molecular descriptors generated through the cheminformatics software RDKit. The model exhibited strong predictive performance, achieving average $R^2$ values of 0.96 on the training set and 0.76 on the test set. Principal Component Analysis (PCA) was employed to reduce the dimensionality of the dataset, which improved computational efficiency, albeit with a slight reduction in model accuracy. Additionally, feature selection techniques—including SelectKBest, Recursive Feature Elimination (RFE), and our novel Breadth-First Selection (BFS) approach—were utilized to identify the most relevant features, further refining the model. The Random Forest model effectively captured non-linear relationships and complex feature interactions, outperforming linear regression models that struggled with the dataset's complexity. By incorporating advanced feature selection and hyperparameter optimization strategies, we established accurate structure–property relationships, facilitating the rational design and application of ILs in various industrial contexts. Overall, this study demonstrates the potential of interpretable machine learning models—in this case, Random Forests—to accurately predict complex material properties. The insights gained contribute to the broader goal of data-driven materials design and offer valuable guidance for the targeted development of ILs in materials science and engineering. Building on the findings of this study, future research aims to further enhance the utility of QSPR variables by exploring and constructing cross terms—interaction terms between distinct molecular descriptors. These cross terms can capture more complex, non-linear relationships that may be overlooked by individual descriptors alone, thereby improving the predictive performance of machine learning models. Systematic generation and evaluation of such interactions could reveal synergistic effects among molecular features that significantly influence viscosity. This approach holds promise for advancing a more nuanced understanding of the interplay between molecular properties and the viscosity behavior of ionic liquids.

**Acknowledgements.** The authors acknowledge the support from the National Science Foundation (NSF) Research Traineeship Grant [Sponsor Award Number 2152210].

## References

1. Achenie, L., Venkatasubramanian, V., Gani, R. (eds.): Computer Aided Molecular Design: Theory and Practice. Elsevier (2002)
2. Freemantle, M.: An introduction to ionic liquids. R. Soc. Chem. (2010)
3. Ghandi, K.: A review of ionic liquids, their limits and applications. Green Sustain. Chem. **2014** (2014)
4. Libardi, A., Schmid, S.R., Sen, M., Schneider, W.: Evaluation of ionic fluids as lubricants in manufacturing. J. Manuf. Process. **15**(4), 414–418 (2013)
5. Welton, T.: Room-temperature ionic liquids. Solvents for synthesis and catalysis. Chem. Rev. **99**(8), 2071–2084 (1999)
6. Gurkan, B., Goodrich, B.F., Mindrup, E.M., Ficke, L.E., Massel, M., Seo, S., et al.: Molecular design of high capacity, low viscosity, chemically tunable ionic liquids for CO2 capture. J. Phys. Chem. Lett. **1**(24), 3494–3499 (2010)
7. Liu, H., Maginn, E., Visser, A.E., Bridges, N.J., Fox, E.B.: Thermal and transport properties of six ionic liquids: an experimental and molecular dynamics study. Ind. Eng. Chem. Res. **51**(21), 7242–7254 (2012)
8. Zhang, X., et al.: Influence of microstructure and interaction on viscosity of ionic liquids. Ind. Eng. Chem. Res. **54**(13), 3505–3514 (2015)
9. Fan, F., Wang, W., Holt, A.P., Feng, H., Uhrig, D., Lu, X., et al.: Effect of molecular weight on the ion transport mechanism in polymerized ionic liquids. Macromolecules **49**(12), 4557–5457 (2016)
10. Landrum, G.: Rdkit documentation. Release **1**(1–79), 4 (2013)
11. Paduszynski, K.: Extensive databases and group contribution QSPRs of ionic liquids properties. 2. Viscosity Ind. Eng. Chem. Res. **58**(36), 17049–17066 (2019)
12. Breiman, L.: Random forests. Mach. Learn. **45**, 5–32 (2001)
13. Gardas, R.L., Coutinho, J.A.: A group contribution method for viscosity estimation of ionic liquids. Fluid Phase Equilib. **266**(1–2), 195–201 (2008)

14. Gardas, R.L., Coutinho, J.A.: Applying a QSPR correlation to the prediction of surface tensions of ionic liquids. Fluid Phase Equilib. **265**(1–2), 57–65 (2008)
15. Ding, Y., Chen, M., Guo, C., Zhang, P., Wang, J.: Molecular fingerprint- based machine learning assisted QSAR model development for prediction of ionic liquid properties. J. Mol. Liq. **326**, 115212 (2021). https://doi.org/10.1016/j.molliq.2020.115212
16. Boualem, A.D., Argoub, K., Benkouider, A.M., Yahiaoui, A., Toubal, K.: Viscosity prediction of ionic liquids using NLR and SVM approaches. J. Mol. Liq. **368**(Part A), 120610 (2022). https://doi.org/10.1016/j.molliq.2022.120610
17. Chormunge, S., Jena, S.: Correlation-based feature selection with clustering for high dimensional data. J. Electr. Syst. Inf. Technol. **5**(3), 542–549 (2018)
18. Daffertshofer, A., Lamoth, C.J., Meijer, O.G., Beek, P.J.: PCA in studying coordination and variability: a tutorial. Clin. Biomech. **19**(4), 415–428 (2004)
19. Ivosev, G., Burton, L., Bonner, R.: Dimensionality reduction and visualization in principal component analysis. Anal. Chem. **80**(13), 4933–4944 (2008)
20. Kausar, N., Samir, B.B., Sulaiman, S.B., Ahmad, I., Hussain, M.: An approach towards intrusion detection using PCA feature subsets and SVM. In: Proceedings of the 2012 International Conference on Computer & Information Science (ICCIS), vol. 2, pp. 569–574. IEEE (2012)
21. Maćkiewicz, A., Ratajczak, W.: Principal components analysis (PCA). Comput. Geosci. **19**(3), 303–342 (1993)
22. Salam, M.A., Azar, A.T., Elgendy, M.S., Fouad, K.M.: The effect of different dimensionality reduction techniques on machine learning overfitting problem. Int. J. Adv. Comput. Sci. Appl. **12**(4), 641–655 (2021). https://doi.org/10.14569/IJACSA.2021.0120480
23. Brownlee, J.: How to choose a feature selection method for machine learning. Mach. Learn. Mastery **10** (2019)
24. Saeys, Y., Abeel, T., Van de Peer, Y.: Robust feature selection using ensemble feature selection techniques. In: Daelemans, W., Goethals, B., Morik, K. (eds.) ECML PKDD 2008. LNCS, vol. 5212, pp. 313–325. Springer, Heidelberg (2008). https://doi.org/10.1007/978-3-540-87481-2_21
25. Saeys, Y., Inza, I., Larrañaga, P.: A review of feature selection techniques in bioinformatics. Bioinformatics **23**(19), 2507–2517 (2007). https://doi.org/10.1093/bioinformatics/btm344
26. Darst, B.F., Malecki, K.C., Engelman, C.D.: Using recursive feature elimination in random forest to account for correlated variables in high dimensional data. BMC Genet. **19**, 1–6 (2018)
27. Pedregosa, F., Varoquaux, G., Gramfort, A., Michel, V., Thirion, B., Grisel, O., et al.: Scikit-learn: machine learning in Python. J. Mach. Learn. Res. **12**, 2825–2830 (2011)
28. Raschka, S., Patterson, J., Nolet, C.: Machine learning in Python: main developments and technology trends in data science, machine learning, and artificial intelligence. Information **11**(4), 193 (2020)
29. Patil, A., Huard, D., Fonnesbeck, C.J.: PyMC: Bayesian stochastic modelling in Python. J. Stat. Softw. **35**(4), 1 (2010)
30. Congdon, P.: Bayesian Statistical Modelling. Wiley, Hoboken (2007)
31. Zhang, J., Chen, C., Wu, Y., Si, S., Geng, Z., Cai, Z.: Research on feature selection method based on Bayesian network and importance measures. In: Proceedings of the 2022 13th International Conference on Reliability, Maintainability, and Safety (ICRMS) (2022). https://doi.org/10.1109/ICRMS55680.2022.9944576
32. Head, T., Kumar, M., Nahrstaedt, H., Louppe, G., Shcherbatyi, I.: scikit- optimize/scikit-optimize (v0.9.0). Zenodo (2021). https://zenodo.org/record/5565057#.Y8Y-iRVBxPY. Accessed 22 Sept 2025
33. Snoek, J., Larochelle, H., Adams, R.P.: Practical Bayesian optimization of machine learning algorithms. In: Advances in Neural Information Processing Systems, vol. 25 (2012)

34. Rosopa, P.J., Schaffer, M.M., Schroeder, A.N.: Managing heteroscedasticity in general linear models. Psychol. Methods **18**(3), 335 (2013)
35. Poole, M.A., O'Farrell, P.N.: The assumptions of the linear regression model. Trans. Inst. Br. Geogr., 145–158 (1971)

# Conditional Wasserstein Generative Adversarial Network Transformers with Gradient Penalty (CWGANSFORMER-GP) with Multi-modal Data

Rose Atuah(✉), Khalil Almakrami, and Micheal McGuire

Department of Computer and Information Sciences, Towson University Baltimore, Towson, MD, USA
{ratuah1,kalmakr1}@students.towson.edu, mmcguire@towson.edu

**Abstract.** This study proposes a novel model-Conditional Wasserstein Generative Adversarial Network Transformer with Gradient Penalty-CWGANSFORMER-GP, to improve the accuracy and reliability of tropical cyclone(TC) intensity and track forecasting. The model leverages the Conditional Wasserstein Generative Adversarial Network with Gradient Penalty (CWGAN-GP) to address the problem of data imbalance and the Transformer architecture for improved predictive capability. Consequently, this research aims not only to enhance the accuracy of TC track and intensity forecast but also to ensure model robustness and reliability by contributing to advancements in meteorology and disaster risk reduction. Our key contribution is threefold: Training and evaluating the proposed model on multi-modal data to enhance robustness, generalization, and understanding of the complex nature of TC forecasting; employing the synergistic integration of CWGAN-GP and Transformer to build a hybrid model tailored for imbalanced datasets; and demonstrating through empirical results that the proposed CWGANSFORMER-GP model not only complements but outperforms previous state-of-the-art methods.

**Keywords:** Intensity · Track · Multi-Modal Data · Generative · Adversarial Network · Transformer · Prediction

## 1 Introduction

Artificial intelligence (AI), and more recently Deep Learning (DL), has increasingly played an important role in the preparation for natural disasters such as prediction of earth quakes [14], floods [22], wildfires [20], and tropical cyclones [19]. While the prediction accuracy of traditional methods has decreased over time, Deep Learning (DL) methods have been widely used to produce improved prediction models due to their ability to track large quantities of data and capture the complex structure of Tropical Cyclones(TC). This study focuses on


R. Stahlbock et al. (Eds.): CSCE 2025, CCIS 2938, pp. 60–76, 2027.
https://doi.org/10.1007/978-3-032-22196-4_5

forecasting two important aspects of TC, which are: track-the direction of TC, and intensity-the severity and strength of the TC. Traditionally, the prediction of the track of a TC was done separately from TC intensity using statistical or dynamic models; however, leveraging DL now allows the creation of models that can automatically find the most influential factors enabling TCs and can successfully predict both TC track and intensity [23].

Generative Adversarial Networks (GAN) as a DL algorithm has recorded remarkable outcomes [15]. Initially proposed by [16], GANs have shown remarkable results in modeling complex distributions [17]. In particular, GANs have been proven to be capable of understanding the probability distribution of information that is observed from data [15,16], and [18]. According to [4], GANs include a latent noise in the input layer of their generator network. This layer formulates a nonlinear mapping between the latent noise and the output random variable. Leveraging its structure as a neural network, it can represent a range of complex functions by using a fitting weight [24]. The generator can represent the full probability distribution associated with TC intensity changes from observed data, which traditional regression and deep learning methods are unlikely to achieve [4]. However, when dealing with data imbalance, even though GANs capture the true data distribution to generate data for the minority class, they are faced with the problems as a result of mode collapse and unstable training [21]. It was in the effort of overcoming these problems that [21] proposed the first Conditional Wasserstein GAN-Gradient Penalty (CWGAN-GP), which is a synthetic oversampling approach for imbalanced datasets that is constructed by adding auxiliary conditional information to the WGAN-GP. Considering that a lot has been done in terms of contributions by researchers on TC related aspects such as track and intensity forecasting, it is worthy to note that contributions in terms transformers combined with Conditional Wasserstein GAN-Gradient Penalty (CWGANsformer-GP) to achieve improved results on TC track and intensity forecasting is yet to be carried out. This is despite the evident role both transformers and CWGAN-GP have played in improving the performance and dealing with imbalance and complex dependencies in large data, such as TC and other metrological datasets. Therefore, in this study, we propose a model based on transformers combined with conditional Wasserstein GAN-grade penalty (CWGANsformer-GP) to efficiently forecast TC intensity and track.

## 2 Related Work

As an improved variant of the Generative Adversarial Network (GAN), CWGAN-GP has strong universality and can generate high-quality samples of specified labels [3] and has been employed by different researchers in various domains, and has been reported to produce remarkable performance results.

Several modifications of the GAN have been proposed by different researchers on varying subject matter. Notably, the Conditional Wasserstein (CW) modification of the GAN has lately received the attention of researchers, due to its remarkable performance in dealing with class imbalance in datasets. More recently on TC intensity forecast, [4] employed Conditional Wasserstein Generative Adversarial Network with Gradient Penalty (CWGAN-GP) for Tropical Cyclone Intensity Prediction Model. The model was trained on 1010 historical TCs from the Western North Pacific basin. According to the obtained results, [4] stated that the "proposed model successfully replicated the probabilistic properties such as the non-Gaussian marginal distribution of the intensity change and the input-output joint distribution and moments between the TC intensity and predictors, which the linear regression model cannot provide". However, they only focused on intensity, excluding track, and did not leverage the Transformer architecture.

On the application of CWGAN in other domains, several studies have been conducted. A study by [6] proposed a Conditional Wasserstein Generative Adversarial Network with a Gradient Penalty (CWGAN-GP)-based multi-task learning (MTL) model (CWGAN-GP-MTL) model for consumer credit scoring. In the study, they used the CWGAN-GP-MTL to address data imbalance problems of mode collapse and unstable training in GAN-based models. Their model worked for both accepted and rejected, and good and bad data, which improves risk prediction ability through parameter sharing. The Result from the study indicates that their proposed (CWGAN-GP-MTL) model outperformed baseline models across different evaluation metrics on consumer credit scoring, demonstrating its promising application potential.

A study by [1] trained a Wasserstein Adversarial Transformer to predict future changes in cloud workloads Virtual Machines (VMs) for hosting applications. Also, to overcome the limitation of the LSTM model, it leverages recurrences to make predictions (because it adds complexity and increases the inference overhead as input sequences grow longer). Evaluation results show that their proposed WGAN-GP Transformer achieves 5 times faster inference time with up to 5.1% higher prediction accuracy against the LSTM. However, their proposed model was modelled for Cloud Computing and cannot be generalized to include TC.

To overcome the problem of unsmooth shapes faced by classical GANs, and the need to perform smoothing before flow analysis. [25] proposed CWGAN-GP to generate airfoil shapes that are as smooth as those obtained using smoothing methods. The result of their proposed model shows good performance, and there is no need for an additional smoothing method to generate airfoils. Their study is, however, limited to airfoil design and therefore not extensible to TC track or intensity forecast.

Overcoming the challenge of class imbalance and consequent decline in classifier performance in Short-term Voltage Stability Assessment (STVSA), [9] proposed a trained Deep Learning model based on the Transformer Architecture for Power System Short-term Voltage Stability Assessment. Results from their study indicated that the CWGAN-GP generates more balanced datasets than traditional oversampling methods, and it outperformed other deep learning algorithms. Despite achieving remarkable performance, their model is limited to

Short-term Voltage Stability Assessment and cannot be generalized to cover TC intensity and track forecasting. In a recent study on improving the accurate diagnosis of transformer faults, [13] employed CWGAN-GP and expanded the oil chromatography fault samples of 500 sets of transformer oil chromatography data with 5 types of faults. Evaluation results from their proposed model show that the overall accuracy of fault diagnosis can reach 93.2%, which is 4.98% higher than the original imbalanced samples. Compared with other sample expansion methods, the accuracy of fault diagnosis of the algorithm was improved by 1.70% to 3.05%. However, just like [9], the model did not include transformers and was only applied to Transformer fault diagnosis, and cannot be generalized to cover TC intensity and track forecasting.

Based on the literature reviewed by researchers, gaps have been identified as potential areas for scholarly contributions on TC forecasting. Notably, despite the remarkable individual performances recorded by CWGAN-GP in [4] in terms of dealing with the inherent data imbalance in TC data, the study, however, did not leverage Transformer's unique strengths of adeptly managing dynamic and complex data [10] for TC forecasting. On the other hand, existing studies on TC intensity and track forecasting that leveraged the Transformers did not employ techniques to deal with the impact of dataset imbalance. This is despite considering the importance of dealing with data imbalance particularly in TC forecasting, because according to [7], predictions of intensity is faced with the problem of imbalanced dataset due to the relative infrequency of Rapid Intensification, which results in unreliable and unstable models as the accuracy would be higher if all cases are assigned to the majority class [8]. To this end, we propose a model that improves accuracy and reliability of both TC intensity and track forecasting by leveraging the CWGAN-GP to deal with imbalance and the Transformer to for improved prediction. Consequently, this research aims to primarily deal with dataset imbalance, not only to have a more accurate forecast of TC Track and Intensity, but to have a more reliable model in advancing the field of meteorology and disaster risk reduction. More specifically, our proposed model is called the Conditional Wasserstein Generative Adversarial Network Transformers with Gradient Penalty (CWGANSFORMER-GP), and our contributions in this study are as follows:

i. Training and evaluation of the proposed model on multi-modal data to enhance robustness, generalization, and understanding of the complex nature of TC forecasting.
ii. Employ the combination of the CWGAN-GP and Transformers in building the proposed model.
iii. Results obtained from the proposed model indicate that the proposed model is not only complementary to related studies, but outperforms them.

## 3 Methodology

Considering that the proposed study focuses on improving the TC track and intensity forecast by leveraging the transformers and CWGAN-GP, the illustration in Fig. 1 shows the conceptual framework proposed to achieve the goal and objectives set out of the proposed study.

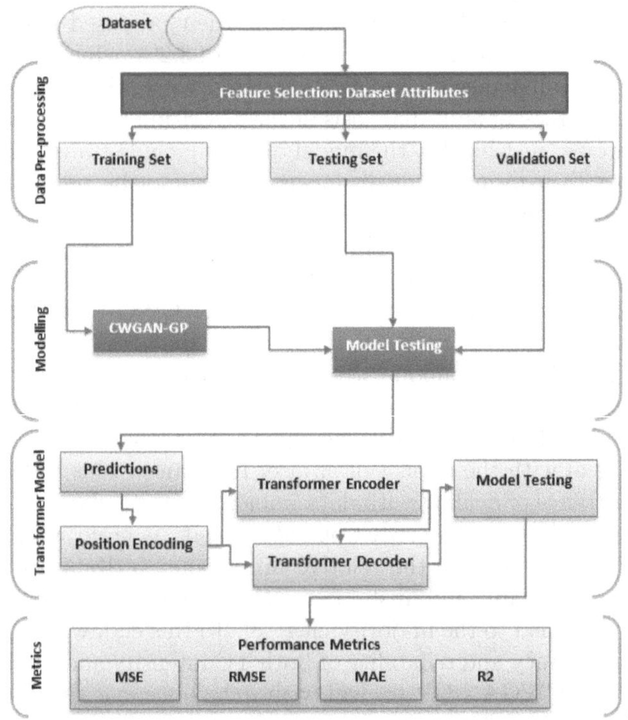


**Fig. 1.** Schematic Representation of the Conceptual Framework

## 3.1 Data

The dataset used in training and evaluating the proposed model is multi-modal. This means that datasets of different categories were employed. The datasets used in this experiment are the International Best Track Archive for Climate Stewardship (IBTrACS) and the Geostationary IR Channel Brightness Temperature - GridSat B1 (GridSat-B1) dataset in image format. Our motivation for combining image and tabular data in a multi-modal approach is to offer distinct advantages over using only tabular data or only image data, such as complementary information, increased model robustness, and overcoming modality-specific limitations.

**Table 1.** Spatial Resolution of IBTrACS and GridSat-B1 Datasets

| Attributes | IBTrACS | GridSat-B1 |
|---|---|---|
| Data Type | Point-Based(storm track observations) | Grided(regular latitude-longitude grid) |
| Resolution | 0.1° latitude/longitude precision(Non-uniform, storm centric) | (0.07 by 0.07) degrees latitude/longitude grid |
| Approx. km | 11 km(location precision varies by agency and time) | 8 km to the equator |
| Coverage Area | Global(limited tostorm tracks) | Global(from 60° south to 60° north) |
| Nature of Data | Discrete( location and attributes per storm report) | Continous(brightness temperature field across entire grid) |
| Spatial Consistency | Varies by reporting agency and observation accuracy. Provides point-based observations(latitude, longitude) of tropical cyclones. The data is not grided but based on reported storm positions, with location precision typically to 0.1°(approx 11 km) | Uniform , satellite-derived grid. Provides brightness temperature fields at a uniform resolution of 0.07°( 8 km) over most regions, including oceanic areas crucial for tropical cyclone analysis |

The IBTrACS is a global tropical cyclone dataset developed and maintained by the National Center for Environmental Information (NCEI) under the United States National Oceanic and Atmospheric Administration (NOAA). The IBTrACS, according to the National Center for Environmental Information (2021) is the most complete global collection of tropical cyclones available. It merges multiple agencies' recent and historical tropical cyclone data to create a unified, publicly available, best-track dataset. The IBTrACS composition of data from Regional Specialized Meteorological Centers(RSMCs) and Tropical Cyclone Warning Centers(TCWCs) is shown in Table 4 with it's access methods in three forms, and Table 1 shows the description of selected attributes out of the total of 60.

To better understand the data in terms of how finely their geographic data is structured and their precise measurement, the spatial resolution of the two datasets is presented in Table 1.

### 3.2 Data-Preprocessing

The pre-processing activities conducted on these data are:

**Read Data.** Read and select the first 1000 rows from the tabular data. The objective of reading the first 1000 rows only is to reduce computational complexity by limiting the dataset size, and at the same time ensuring rapid prototyping while retaining relevant features for model training.

**Categorical Data Encoding.** All categorical columns, excluding the target columns ('USA/WIND', 'LAT', 'LON'), were identified and encoded using LabelEncoder to replace category values (labels) with numerical representations for use in subsequent model training.

**Standardization of Numerical Features.** Numerical features were identified and standardized using StandardScaler. This was done to ensure that the data is normalized to have a mean of zero and a standard deviation of one. This helps in modeling, as it prevents features with larger ranges from dominating other features.

**Separation of Features and Targets.** Features are derived by excluding target columns (USA/WIND, LAT, and LON) from the data, while the targets consist of the specified columns (USA/WIND, LAT, and LON) for prediction. Primarily, this activity partitions data by clearly defining predictors (features) and outcomes (targets).

**Image Loading.** The images from the Gridsat-B1 dataset are retrieved, sorted, and limited to the first 1000 entries to match the earlier tabular dataset size.

**Image Transformation.** Each image is resized to a uniform dimension of (128, 128) and converted into NumPy arrays.

**Feature Extraction.** EfficientNetB0, which is a pre-trained CNN model was employed for feature extraction (to generate an array of high-level image embeddings fit for integration with tabular data), and the features were pooled using average pooling in order to reduce dimensionality while retaining critical information.

**Feature Combination.** Tabular features and image embeddings are concatenated to produce a composite feature set (combined features) that integrates numerical, categorical, and visual data.

### 3.3 Modeling

At this stage, modeling activities in terms of training and testing of the proposed track and intensity forecast would be carried out. The DL algorithms that would be used are the CWGAN-GP and the Transformer.

**Generative Adversarial Network.** GANs, having been applied in various fields and demonstrated remarkable performance, are certainly a promising algorithm promising tool to account for the randomness in the TC intensity changes [4], including RI. Inspired by [4,26], this proposal aims to utilize the modified version of GAN known as Conditional Wasserstein Generative Adversarial Network with Gradient Penalty (CWGAN-GP) to predict RI based on the following justifications:

1. Due to the usage of the Jensen-Shannon (JS) distance in the classical/original GAN between the generative and authentic probability distributions [2], which results in vanishing gradients [4], the Wasserstein distance was proposed in CWGAN-GP which is based on Wasserstein generative adversarial network with gradient penalty to efficiently handle gradients.
2. Considering the dependent nature of TC RI prediction on multiple surrounding environmental variables, CWGAN-GP supports the inclusion of the generator network input layer to accommodate the representation of these environmental variables' nonlinear dependence [4,11].

The modeling activities for the CWGAN-GP in the proposed model, as shown in Fig. 2, start by creating a generator model consisting of three fully connected layers with ReLU activation function to generate synthetic data by learning from the input data distribution. The generator is trained focusing on minimizing reconstruction loss with the following as its parameters: Batch Size of 32, 10 Epochs, and Adam Optimizer with the learning rate of 0.0002, MSE as the Loss Function to measure reconstruction accuracy by comparing the generator's output with the original input data.

### 3.4 Transformer

The multi-head self-attention mechanism transformer model is used as part of the modeling and validation of the proposed track and intensity forecasting. According to [23] in [12], the multi-head self-attention mechanism is presently the most effective tool in long-term prediction tasks. The architecture of the transformer network is given in Fig. 3.

Specifically in this study, the Tabular Transformer with a single layer of the Transformer architecture, incorporating self-attention, feed-forward networks, and residual connections was employed. This was based on the transformer-based architecture for regression tasks with our three target variables which are TC Intensity (USA/WIND), and Track (LAT and LON). The proposed transformer, is based on the following components:

a. Input Embedding Layer This layer is used to map input features to a higher-dimensional representation using a dense layer with ReLU activation.
b. Sequence Preparation The input embeddings that come in as input embedding layer are then reshaped with an additional dimension (as part of preparations) to conform to the expected input of the Transformer blocks.

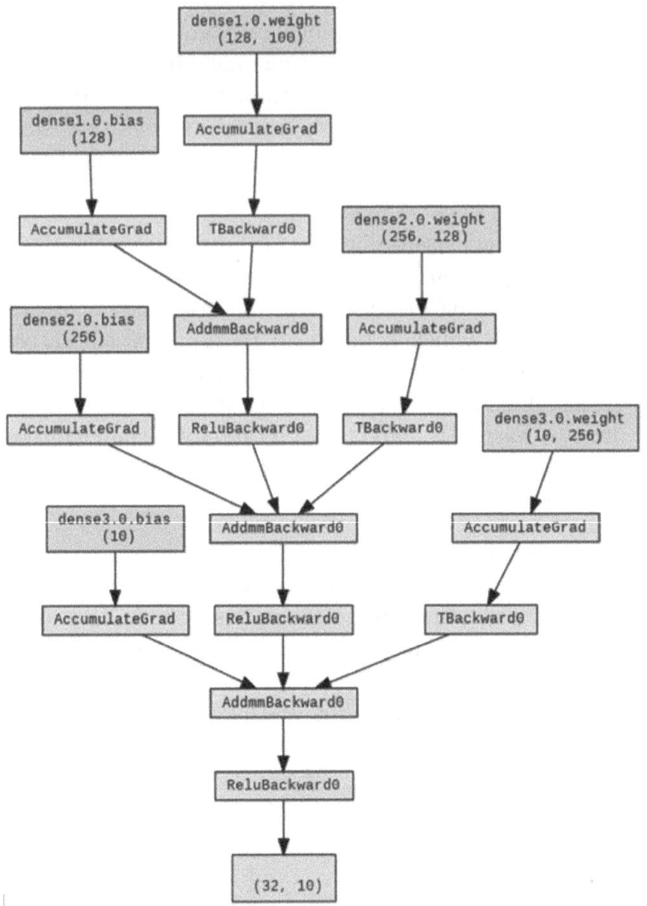


**Fig. 2.** The CWGAN-GP Architecture.

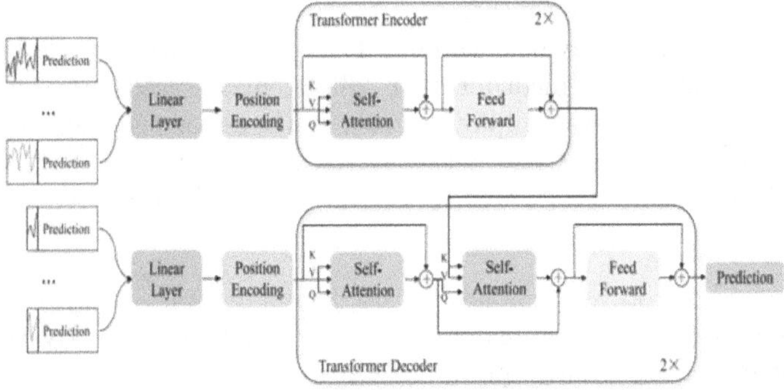


**Fig. 3.** Basic Architecture of the Transformer Network [5]

c. Stacked Transformer Block A collection of TransformerBlock instances is employed, each TransformerBlock instance further refines the representation by correlating relationships between features.
d. Global Averaging Pooling Layer This layer condenses the collections of representations from the above stage into a single vector for downstream regression (layer) tasks.
e. Regression Layer In this layer, the predictions for the three regression targets (USA/WIND, LAT, and LON) are outputted using a linear activation function.

### 3.5 Performance Evaluation

We applied the three major evaluation metrics to forecast the models i.e. Mean Absolute Error (MAE), Root Mean Square Error (RMSE), and R Square to evaluate the performance of our model as shown in Eqs. 1, 2, and 3. MAE is used to evaluate the bias level in the prediction values. RMSE evaluates the accuracy level in the prediction values. $R^2$ evaluates the fitness degree of predictions by the model compared to the true values.

$$RMSE = \sqrt{\frac{1}{N}\sum_{i=1}^{N}(Y_i - \hat{Y}_i)^2} \tag{1}$$

$$MAE = \frac{1}{N}\sum_{i=1}^{N}(|Y_i - \hat{Y}_1|) \tag{2}$$

$$R^2 = 1 - \frac{\sum_i(\hat{Y}_i - Y_i)^2}{\sum_i(\hat{Y}_i - Y_i)^2} \tag{3}$$

From the above equations, $y_i$ and $\hat{y}_i$ respectively represent the actual and predicted values at a given moment, N represents the number of time points that would be predicted, and $y^{-}i$ represents the average of true intensity values.

## 4 Results and Discussion

The results obtained from our experiments in this study are presented in this section. As stated earlier, this study aims to forecast TC intensity based on wind speed, and track (based on LAT and LON).

**Table 2.** Performance Metrics for Track and Intensity

| | Track | | Intensity |
|---|---|---|---|
| | Lat (°N) | Long (°E) | W/speed |
| MSE | 0.12 | 0.13 | 0.03 |
| RMSE | 0.32 | 0.24 | 0.13 |
| MAE | 0.22 | 0.36 | 0.19 |
| $R^2$ | 0.90 | 0.90 | 0.96 |

**Table 3.** Variables from GridSat-B1 and IBTrACS datasets

| Variable Name | Description | Unit/Format | Remarks |
|---|---|---|---|
| GridSat-B1 Variables | | | |
| Time | Timestamp of observation | ISO 8601 (e.g., YYYY-MM-DDThh:mm:ss) | UTC; data recorded every 3 h |
| Latitude | Latitude of the observation grid cell | Decimal degrees | Range: −60° to +60° |
| Longitude | Longitude of the observation grid cell | Decimal degrees | Range: −180° to +180° |
| IRwin | Infrared window channel brightness temperature | Kelvin (K) | Derived from NOAA satellite IR channels |
| BT bias | Bias correction applied to IRwin | Kelvin (K) | Calibration adjustment for sensor drift |
| BT quality flag | Quality of IRwin measurement | Integer (0âĂŞ3) | 0 = best; 3 = worst |
| Satellite | Satellite ID used for observation | Text/String | Examples: GOES-8, Meteosat-7 |
| Zenith angle | Angle from satellite to observed location | Degrees | Affects measurement accuracy |
| Solar zenith angle | Solar elevation angle | Degrees | Helps distinguish day vs night observations |
| Cloud mask | Cloud classification for the pixel | Integer (e.g., 0 = clear, 1 = cloudy) | Indicates cloud presence |
| Scene type | Type of surface scene | Categorical (e.g., ocean, land) | Affects radiation assumptions |
| Data source flag | Original satellite and processing identifier | Integer/String code | Used for sensor and version tracking |
| IBTrACS Variables | | | |
| SID | Unique storm identifier | String | Combines agency code and cyclone ID |
| Name | Cyclone name (if assigned) | String | 'UNNAMED' if no name was assigned |
| Season | Year of storm occurrence | Integer (YYYY) | Used for temporal grouping |
| Basin | Ocean basin of storm activity | Categorical (e.g., NA, SI, WP) | Indicates region: North Atlantic (NA), West Pacific (WP), etc. |
| ISO_TIME | Timestamp of storm observation | ISO 8601 (e.g., YYYY-MM-DDThh:mm:ss) | UTC format |
| LAT | Latitude of storm center | Decimal degrees | Positive = North, Negative = South |
| LON | Longitude of storm center | Decimal degrees | Positive = East, Negative = West |
| WMO_WIND | Wind speed estimate from WMO agencies | Knots | May contain missing values |
| USA_WIND | Wind speed estimate from US agencies | Knots | Often differs from WMO estimates |
| WMO_PRES | Minimum central pressure (WMO estimate) | Hectopascals (hPa) | May contain missing or interpolated values |
| NATURE | Storm classification (e.g., TS, HU, TD) | Categorical | TS = Tropical Storm, HU = Hurricane, TD = Tropical Depression |
| DIST2LAND | Distance of storm center to nearest land | Kilometres (km) | Used for assessing potential land interaction |
| Landfall | Flag indicating landfall occurrence | Boolean or Integer (0/1) | 1 = made landfall; 0 = did not |

**Table 4.** Composition of ibtracs regional and contributing agencies

| Method | Description |
|---|---|
| NetCDF | NetCDF is a self-describing, mostly CF-compliant format that uses global and variable attributes. Data are stored using the netCDF4 library |
| Comma-Separated Values | Missing data are stored as blank cells to decrease file sizes (other netCDF and shapefiles use -9999.0 for missing data) |
| Shapefiles | Files are available as point and line shapefiles with the usual shapefile parts (prj, shx, shp, and dbf files). File metadata (xml files) is not currently available. The CSV column description file can be referenced for the definitions of each variable |
| IBTRACS ACCESS METHODS, NCEI(2021) | |
| **Region** | Contributing Agency |
| North Atlantic, Pacific | National Hurricane Center (NHC), USA |
| West Pacific | Japan Meteorological Agency (JMA), Joint Typhoon Warning Center (JTWC), China Meteorological Administration (CMA) |
| North Indian Ocean | India Meteorological Department (IMD |
| South-West Ocean | Meteo-France La Reunion |
| Australia Region | Bureau of Meteorology (BoM), Australia |
| South Pacific | Fiji Meteorological Service, NZ MetService |

The result presented in Table 2 is composed of the MSE, MAE, RMSE, and $R^2$. The MSE is a measure of the average squared difference between predicted values and actual target values. As an error rate, the lower the MSE values, the better the model's predictions in terms of being closely aligned with the actual data. The MSE value of 0.12, 0.13, and 0.03 on Latitude, Longitude, and Wind-speed, respectively, by the proposed model indicates minimal variance in prediction errors, which demonstrates that the proposed model has consistently and precisely forecasted the TC tract and intensity outcomes with significantly limited deviations from the actual data. Furthermore, the RMSE, which is the square root of the MSE, represents the error magnitude in the same scale as the predicted values but is more sensitive to larger errors than MAE. The 0.32, 0.24, and 0.13 on Latitude, Longitude, and Wind-speed, respectively, indicate that the proposed model aligns with MSE results, which further confirms that large prediction errors are rare in the results obtained by the proposed model. To ascertain the average of absolute differences between predicted and actual TC intensity and track values, the MAE was employed as it provides an easily interpretable means of measuring the average TC track and intensity prediction error against the target values. The MAE of 0.22, 0.36, 0.19 on Latitude, Longitude, and Wind-speed, respectively, obtained by the proposed model as shown in Table 6, shows that, on average, the TC intensity and track predictions by the proposed model deviated from actual by marginal values. Thus, demonstrating remarkable prediction performance of the proposed model. The coefficient of determination, also known as the $R^2$, is used to measure the proportion of variance in the target variable (in this study, the TC track and intensity) that is explained by the proposed model. Based on our obtained values of 0.90, 0.90, 0.96 on Latitude, Longitude, and Wind-speed, our proposed model indicates a 10% variance in the track forecasting and 4% on intensity forecast is captured by the model, leaving a marginal variance as unexplained. Thus, indicating our proposed model's ability to efficiently generalize on given data and being a well-fit predictor of TC track and intensity (Tables 3 and 5).

## 4.1 Performance Comparison on Actual vs Forecasted Track and Intensity

The results obtained from this study were based on the details of the modeling as provided in Sect. 3 and were compared against the actual intensity values as shown in Fig. 4 and track values shown in Figs. 5 and 6 for longitude and latitude, respectively. Furthermore, the error rates obtained from the proposed model were compared with the previous study, as shown in Table 4.

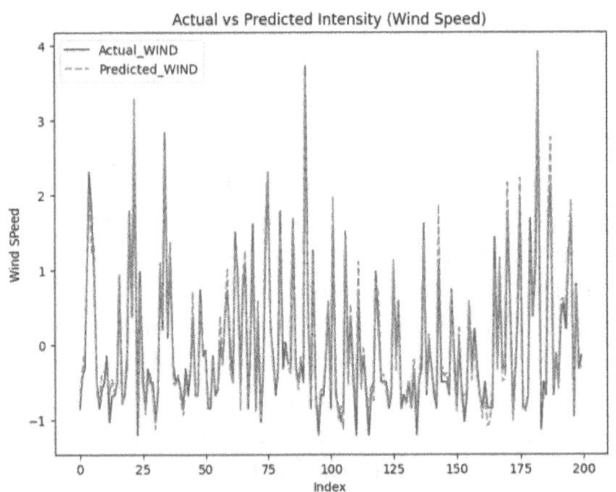


**Fig. 4.** Actual Vrs Predicted TC Intensity

## 4.2 Performance Comparison with Previous Study

The result of our proposed model is compared with previous study. This is to further assess and validate the ability of the proposed model in accurately forecasting the TC track and intensity. The result comparison between [23] and the proposed CWGAN-GP + Transformer model for tropical cyclone (TC) track and

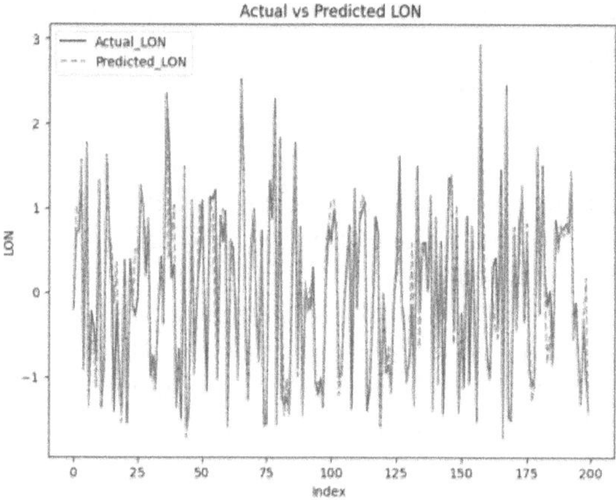


**Fig. 5.** Actual Vrs Predicted TC Track Lon

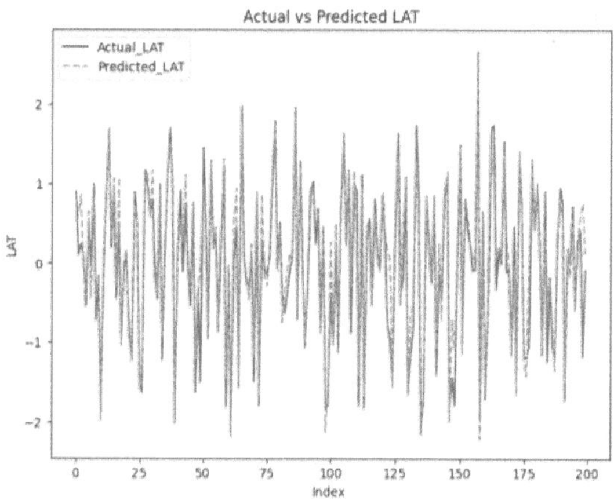


**Fig. 6.** Actual Vrs Predicted TC Track Lat

intensity forecasting shows notable differences in key metrics of the performance evaluation used in these studies.

In terms of Intensity Forecast (based on wind speed), the proposed CWGAN-GP + Transformer approach demonstrates a significant improvement over the compared study of [23] Transformer-based model. The Mean Absolute Error (MAE) value of 0.13 and Root Mean Square Error (RMSE) value of 0.19 obtained by our proposed method are lower than [23] values of 1.72 (MAE) and 2.39 (RMSE). Thus, suggesting that our proposed approach is substantially more accurate in TC intensity forecasting. In terms of measuring the proportion of variance explained by the model, the 0.96 $R^2$ value of the proposed approach is slightly lower compared to 0.97 of [23], however, the values obtained by the proposed approach on TC intensity indicate the model's high predictive accuracy.

In terms of TC track forecasting based on latitude prediction, the proposed CWGAN-GP + Transformer model yielded marginally lower MAE of 0.22 and RMSE of 0.32 compared to those of [23] 0.23 MAE and 0.33 RMSE. Also, the longitude prediction by our proposed CWGAN-GP + Transformer approach shows similar trends to that of the latitude prediction. The MAE (0.24) and RMSE (0.36) of the proposed approach are lower than those of [23] (0.27 MAE and 0.42 RMSE). However, on both latitude and longitude, despite the 0.90 $R^2$ of the proposed model being slightly lower than that of [23] model (which is the near-perfect 0.99). The obtained $R^2$ value indicates a modest ability in explaining variance in the latitude and longitude predictions, despite being lower than that of [23] by 0.09.

**Table 5.** Result Comparison with Previous Study

| Study | Approach | .. | MSE | MAE | RMSE | $R^2$ |
|---|---|---|---|---|---|---|
| [23] | 35emTransformer-based | Wind Speed | - | 1.72 | 2.39 | 0.97 |
| | 34em | Latitude | .. | 0.23 | 0.33 | 0.99 |
| | 34em | Longitude | .. | 0.27 | 0.42 | 0.99 |
| This Study | 34emCWGAN-GP + Transformer | Wind Speed | 0.03 | 0.13 | 0.19 | 0.96 |
| | 34em | Latitude | 0.12 | 0.22 | 0.32 | 0.90 |
| | 34em | Longitude | 0.13 | 0.24 | 0.36 | 0.90 |

## 5 Conclusion

The results of this study underscore the efficiency and robustness of the proposed which is based on CWGAN-GP with a Transformer model in forecasting TC track and intensity. With the low error rates and high proportions of explained variance, the model performance reflects accurate predictions with minimal deviations from actual values. Unlike the previous study by [23], which applied a Transformer-based approach but did not address the issue of data imbalance, this study incorporates CWGAN-GP with the Transformer model to effectively handle data imbalance and improve model reliability and robustness. Thus, ensuring the proposed model is well-suited for scenarios with dataset imbalance. In conclusion, the CWGAN-GP + Transformer approach not only advances the state of the art in TC forecasting but also provides a robust framework for further research and development in this domain. Future studies could explore refining the model to further enhance its performance and address the minor limitations observed in variance explanation.

## References

1. Arbat, S., Jayakumar, V.K., Lee, J., Wang, W., Kim, I.K.: Wasserstein adversarial transformer for cloud workload prediction. In: Proceedings of the AAAI Conference on Artificial Intelligence, pp. 12433–12439 (2022)
2. Arjovsky, M., Chintala, S., Bottou, L.: Wasserstein generative adversarial networks. In: International Conference on Machine Learning, pp. 214–223. PMLR (2017)
3. Han, F., et al.: Enhancer recognition: Gene-CWGAN: a data enhancement method for gene expression profile based on improved CWGAN-GP. Neural Comput. Appl. **34**(19), 16325–16339 (2022)
4. Hong, X., Hu, L., Kareem, A.: A tropical cyclone intensity prediction model using conditional generative adversarial network. J. Wind Eng. Ind. Aerodyn. **240**, 105515 (2023)
5. Jiang, Y., Wang, J., Huang, T.: Prediction of typhoon intensity based on gated attention transformer. In: 2022 International Conference on High Performance Big Data and Intelligent Systems (HDIS), pp. 141–146. IEEE (2022)
6. Kang, Y., Chen, L., Jia, N., Wei, W., Deng, J., Qian, H.: A CWGAN-GP-based multi-task learning model for consumer credit scoring. Expert Syst. Appl. **206**, 117650 (2022)
7. Ko, M.C., Kubat, M., Gopalakrisnan, S.G., Marks, F.D.: A review of support vector machine performance on tropical cyclone intensity prediction with imbalanced datasets. In: 100th American Meteorological Society Annual Meeting, AMS (2022)
8. Li, Y., Yang, R., Yang, C., Yu, M., Hu, F., Jiang, Y.: Leveraging LSTM for rapid intensifications prediction of tropical cyclones. ISPRS Ann. Photogramm., Remote Sensing Spatial Inform. Sci. **4**, 101–105 Copernicus GmbH (2017)
9. Li, Y., Cao, J., Xu, Y., Zhu, L., Dong, Z.Y.: Deep learning based on Transformer architecture for power system short-term voltage stability assessment with class imbalance. Renew. Sustain. Energy Rev. **189**, 113913 (2024)
10. Lin, T., Wang, Y., Liu, X., Qiu, X.: A survey of transformers. AI Open **3**, 111–132 (2022)
11. Mirza, M., Osindero, S.: Conditional generative adversarial nets. arXiv preprint arXiv:1411.1784 (2014)
12. Wu, H., Xu, J., Wang, J., Long, M.: Autoformer: decomposition transformers with auto-correlation for long-term series forecasting. Adv. Neural Inform. Process. Syst. **34**, 22419–22430 (2021)
13. Zhang, L., Xu, Z., Lu, C., Qiao, T., Su, H., Luo, Y.: Transformer fault diagnosis based on adversarial generative networks and deep stacked autoencoder. Heliyon **10**(9), (2024)
14. Asim, K.M., Idris, A., Iqbal, T., Martínez-Álvarez, F.: Earthquake prediction model using support vector regressor and hybrid neural networks. PloS One**13**(7), e0199004 (2018)
15. Aggarwal, A., Mittal, M., Battineni, G.: Generative adversarial network: an overview of theory and applications. Int. J. Inform. Manage. Data Insights **1**(1),100004 (2021)
16. Goodfellow, I.G., et al.: Generative adversarial nets. Advances Neural Inform. Process. Syst.**27** (2014)
17. Grnarova, P., et al.: A domain agnostic measure for monitoring and evaluating GANs: an overview of theory and applications. Adv. Neural Inform. Process. Syst. **32**,(2019)

18. Maeda, H., Kashiyama, T., Sekimoto, Y., Seto, T., Omata, H.: Generative adversarial network for road damage detection: an overview of theory and applications. Comput.-Aided Civil Infrastruct. Eng. **36**(1),47–60 (2021)
19. Schreck III, C.J., et al.: Advances in tropical cyclone prediction on subseasonal time scales during 2019–2022: Tropical Cyclone Res. Rev. **12**(2), 136–150 (2023)
20. Shmuel, A., Heifetz, E.: A machine-learning approach to predicting daily wildfire expansion rate. Fire **6**(8),319 (2023)
21. Zheng, M., et al.: Conditional Wasserstein generative adversarial network-gradient penalty-based approach to alleviating imbalanced data classification. Inform. Sci. **512**, 1009–1023 (2020)
22. Tang, Y., Sun, Y., Han, Z., Wu, Q., Tan, B., Hu, C, et al.: Flood forecasting based on machine learning pattern recognition and dynamic migration of parameters. J. Hydrol.: Regional Stud.**47**, 101406 (2023)
23. Jiang, W., et al.: Transformer-based tropical cyclone track and intensity forecasting. J. Wind Eng. Indust. Aerodyn. **238**, 105440 (2023)
24. Nielsen, M.A.: Neural networks and deep learning. vol(25), Determination press San Francisco, CA, USA, (2015)
25. Yonekura, K.: Inverse airfoil design method for generating varieties of smooth airfoils using conditional WGAN-gp. Struct. Multidisc. Optim. (2022)
26. Gulrajani, I., Ahmed, F., Arjovsky, M., Dumoulin, V., Courville, A.C.: Improved training of wasserstein gans. Adv. Neural Inform. Process. Syst. **30**,(2017)

# Machine Learning for B2B Sales Prediction: A Comparative Study

Guilherme Pires[1], Carina Pimentel[2], and Luís Miguel Matos[3,4](✉)

[1] Department of Production and Systems, University of Minho, Guimarães, Portugal
pg53852@alunos.uminho.pt

[2] ALGORITMI/LASI Research Center – Department of Production and Systems, University of Minho, Guimarães, Portugal
carina.pimentel@dps.uminho.pt

[3] ALGORITMI/LASI Research Center – Department of Information Systems, Minho University, Guimarães, Portugal
luis.matos@dsi.uminho.pt

[4] EPMQ, CCG ZGDV Institute, Guimarães, Portugal

**Abstract.** This paper presents a framework based on Machine Learning (ML) to predict the success of Business-to-Business (B2B) commercial proposals from a multinational company. A comparative analysis of five models was performed using a Rolling-Window (RW) evaluation strategy to ensure temporal consistency. Among the models tested, the Multi-Layer Perceptron (MLP) achieved the highest predictive performance, with a median Area Under the Curve (AUC) of approximately 72%, highlighting the potential of neural networks to capture complex decision patterns. Beyond predictive accuracy, the proposed framework enables the identification of key success drivers and supports the design of data-driven negotiation and pricing strategies. The proposed solution supports faster, more consistent and strategically aligned decisions in industrial B2B sales.

**Keywords:** Predictive Analytics · Machine Learning · Proposal Success Prediction · Commercial Pricing · Data Mining

## 1 Introduction

The sales force plays a critical role in the success of organizations, serving as the primary driver of revenue generation. At the same time, it represents a significant share of sales, general and administrative expenses, directly affecting the overall profitability of an organization [13]. In addition, in today's highly competitive markets, sales processes are undergoing a profound transformation in response to the ongoing wave of digitalization. This shift presents major challenges and underscores the urgent need to improve commercial effectiveness and efficiency [21].


R. Stahlbock et al. (Eds.): CSCE 2025, CCIS 2938, pp. 77–89, 2027.
https://doi.org/10.1007/978-3-032-22196-4_6

Driven by these challenges, data analytics has emerged as a powerful enabler of sales performance, offering tools to improve customer understanding, optimize processes, and drive strategic decisions [11].

Within this broader analytical landscape, Predictive Sales Analytics (PSA) has emerged as a key application area, allowing organizations to transform historical data into actionable foresight. By statistically inferring future results from existing information, PSA enables sales teams to anticipate customer behaviour, prioritize opportunities, and tailor commercial strategies accordingly. Rather than simply describing past performance, PSA helps estimate critical commercial variables such as the probability of deal conversion, the risk of churn, and upselling potential, ultimately improving strategic and operational decision making in the sales function [9].

Among these variables, pricing remains one of the most impactful yet underoptimized levers in commercial strategy. When applied to customized pricing strategies, PSA can be particularly impactful, as even though list prices are fixed and visible, the actual amount paid by customers, referred to as the pocket price, is often negotiated, resulting in high variability. This highlights the need for personalized pricing strategies and the ability to evaluate how pricing decisions influence both the probability of success and the expected contribution of a deal [17].

In response to this challenge, the present study proposes a predictive framework capable of dynamically estimating the success probability of commercial proposals and responds to the growing need for advanced analytics in commercial decision making. Using structured historical commercial data, the objective is to support sales teams in identifying pricing configurations that maximize the probability of deal conversion, contributing to a more data-driven, efficient, and strategically aligned sales process.

Despite growing interest in PSA, previous research shows that ML techniques remain underutilized in B2B sales contexts [22]. In practice, many internal sales pipeline systems still rely on field sales representatives to manually assign subjective scores to each lead [13]. In addition, few empirical studies have integrated PSA tools directly into the sales process [9]. [10] further notes that most existing studies lack longitudinal perspectives, overlook organizational and user-level contingencies, and do not address the risk of misuse. In short, it highlights that while predictive analytics can improve performance in various business functions, their application in sales contexts remains limited. Automated Machine Learning (AutoML) was proposed to reduce the technical burden of developing ML models by automating feature selection, model selection, and hyperparameter optimization [8]. To our knowledge, few studies have explored the use of AutoML techniques in predicting the success of B2B commercial proposals.

To fill these gaps, we evaluated and compared five classification models, Logistic Regression (LR), Random Forest (RF), eXtreme Gradient Boosting (XGB), Multi-Layer Perceptron (MLP) and H2O AutoML to predict the success of commercial proposals. The dataset includes over 65,000 historical proposals that cover a wide range of clients, products, and pricing configurations.

Ultimately, this research contributes to a broader understanding of how ML can improve sales strategy and performance in complex and competitive environments. The relevance of this work lies in its ability to bridge the gap between historical sales data and forward-looking strategic decisions, fostering a more agile, informed, and effective sales process.

This paper is organized as follows. Section 2 describes the collected data, ML algorithms and evaluation procedure. Then, Sect. 3 presents the experimental results. Finally, Sect. 4 discusses the main conclusions and future work.

## 2 Materials and Methods

This study follows the Cross-Industry Standard Process for Data Mining (CRISP-DM) methodology [4], covering all key phases, from business and data understanding to data preparation, modeling and model evaluation. This methodology provided a structured guide throughout the development of the predictive system. The final deployment phase was not implemented and remains a key opportunity for future work, allowing the integration of the model into a real-time pricing support system to enable automated pricing recommendations and real-time negotiation support.

### 2.1 Business Understanding

This study was conducted in the context of a multinational company engaged in B2B sales of technically complex and highly configurable products. These product solutions are typically sold through extended sales cycles that involve multiple stakeholders and negotiation phases.

In a typical sales pipeline, leads are entered into a Customer Relationship Management (CRM) system and evolve into sales opportunities comprising one or more products or services. Each opportunity is associated with a commercial proposal that includes technical specifications, quantities, and pricing terms. Despite offering high-quality and superior solutions, the company frequently loses deals to competitors offering lower prices. Salespeople currently rely on experience and standardized discounting practices, with limited data-driven support for decision making. As a result, they face difficulties in estimating the probability of deal conversion or determining optimal pricing during negotiations. Consequently, there is a pressing need to better understand which factors contribute to proposal success and equip sales teams with tools that support more consistent, informed, and efficient pricing decisions.

### 2.2 Data Understanding and Preparation

As previously mentioned, this study is based on 65,108 historical commercial proposals collected between October 2022 and May 2025. Each row in the dataset represents a single product line within a commercial proposal solution. A complete proposal can include one or more blocks, where each block group together several product lines that, when combined, form a coherent technical or commercial configuration. In this way, proposals are structured hierarchically: product lines belong to blocks, and blocks make up the overall proposal submitted to the client.

The initial dataset was extracted and consolidated from various internal company databases. Figure 1 illustrates the data preparation workflow implemented in *Alteryx Designer*. The process begins by joining quotation and order records using the fields of offer identification, offer version, and product identification. A conditional check is applied to determine whether a match exists, classifying the outcome as success or failure. The results are unified and enriched through a sequence of left and right joins with internal reference tables, including client-distributor mappings, quotation-opportunity links, and market segmentation data. The aggregate pricing information is computed using a summarization step based on offer level grouping, and the final dataset is constructed by joining all structured elements into a single exportable file, ready for modeling.

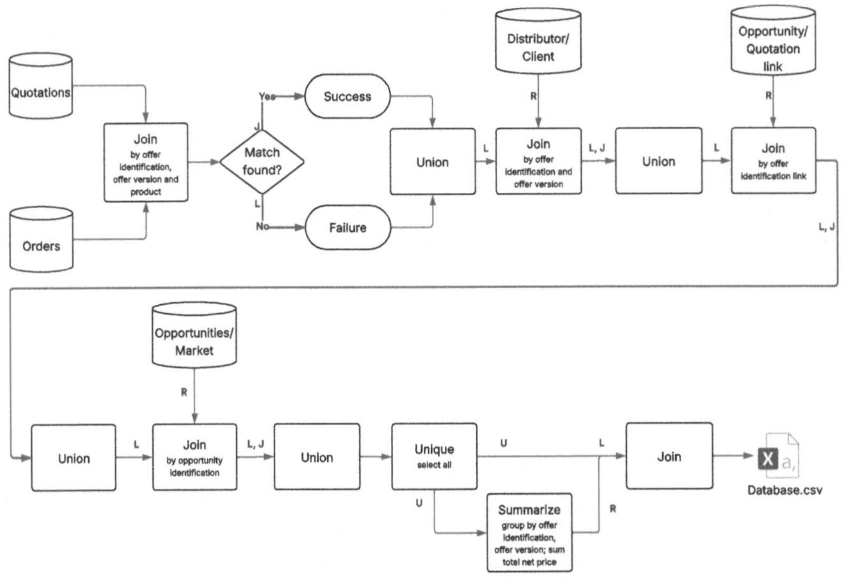


**Fig. 1.** Data preparation workflow

The resulting dataset includes both product variables, such as product identification and number of products quoted, and aggregate variables at the block or proposal level, such as total block net price and total proposal net price. This multilevel structure allows the model to consider both the specific characteristics of each quoted item and the broader commercial context of the proposal in which it is embedded. A binary target variable, status, indicates whether the proposal led to a successful sale, 1, or not, 0. The dataset exhibits a significant class imbalance, with a success rate of approximately 4%. Table 1 summarizes the main features used for the modeling.

**Table 1.** Summary of Main Features in the Dataset

| Context | Attribute | Description |
|---|---|---|
| customer | distributor | distributor identification: 2610 categorical levels |
| | client | client identification: 1728 categorical levels |
| | region | region of the client: 13 categorical levels |
| market | market | market segment of the client: 20 categorical levels |
| product | product | product identification: 2200 categorical levels |
| | quantity | number of product units quoted: 174 numerical levels |
| | sales center | sales center responsible for the product: 9 categorical levels |
| | public selling price | public list price (before discount): 3732 numerical levels |
| | discount | discount applied (absolute value): 2439 numerical levels |
| | total net price | final product price: 18320 numerical levels |
| | total block net price | final block price: 14353 numerical levels |
| | total proposal net price | final proposal price: 11891 numerical levels |
| target | status | if there is a sale: 2 levels (Success, Failure) |

Then additional preprocessing steps were applied to the dataset. The raw data contained missing values, mainly due to incomplete manual entries in certain attributes. These missing values were handled by replacing them with zero.

Furthermore, since many machine learning algorithms, such as LR, require numerical input variables, all categorical features were transformed using the Inverse Document Frequency (IDF) encoding method [3], implemented via the *cane*[1] Python package [16]. For each level $l$ in a categorical variable $x_i$, the transformation is defined as $IDF(l) = \ln\left(\frac{N}{f_l}\right)$, where $N$ is the total number of instances and $f_l$ is the frequency of the level $l$ in the training set. This approach places frequent levels closer to zero and spreads them over a wider numerical range, while infrequent levels are assigned to higher values, with a theoretical maximum of $\ln(N)$ when $f_l = 1$.

Compared to the traditional One-Hot Encoding (OHE) technique, the IDF transformation offers a more compact and computationally efficient representation, as each categorical variable is encoded as a single numeric feature. In this case, the use of IDF maintained the original number of input features, whereas OHE expanded the dataset to more than 5000 dimensions. This substantial reduction in dimensionality is expected to improve both the model interpretability and the training efficiency.

The final preprocessed dataset, containing both original numerical features and IDF encoded variables, was used as input for the machine learning algorithms described in the following section.

[1] Available at https://pypi.org/project/cane/.

### 2.3 Machine Learning Models

All ML methods were implemented using the Python programming language and the following libraries: `H2O` for H2O AutoML [6]; `scikit-learn`[2] for LR, RF, and MLP; `XGB` for the XGB algorithm [5]; and `Optuna` for Bayesian hyperparameter optimization [1]. To reduce computational burden, model selection (via H2O AutoML) and hyperparameter tuning (for H2O, LR, MLP, and XGB) were carried out only during the first iteration of the RW evaluation procedure (Sect. 2.4). After this initial selection, the chosen ML algorithms were trained and updated in all RW iterations.

The H2O AutoML tool was configured to identify the optimal model among three algorithms and their corresponding hyperparameter configurations, where $\mathcal{H}$ denotes the number of hyperparameters tuned per model. The classification task included the following: Distributed Random Forest (DRF) ($\mathcal{H} = 0$), Generalized Linear Model with Regularization (GLM) ($\mathcal{H} = 1$), and Gradient Boosted Machines (GBM) ($\mathcal{H} = 8$). These algorithms represent the default individual ML models available in H2O, excluding deep learning models, XGB, and stacked ensembles. The deep learning and XGB models were excluded from the AutoML procedure as they were evaluated separately using Bayesian optimization. Stacked ensembles were also excluded due to their substantially higher computational cost: for example, the H2O `stackedEnsemble` method requires a training time comparable to the entire model selection phase, since all models evaluated are used to generate predictions.

H2O AutoML conducted an internal 5-fold cross-validation using only the training data, with a maximum execution time of 100 s. The selection of the model was based on the highest AUC, calculated in the validation set [7].

All other ML algorithms were optimized using Bayesian hyperparameter search, with a total of 100 trials (i.e., 100 trained models). The same validation procedure as in H2O was applied, involving a 5-fold cross-validation over the training data, and the AUC metric was again used to select the best configuration.

XGB is a recently proposed tree ensemble algorithm that has demonstrated state-of-the-art performance in a wide range of predictive modeling tasks [5]. For XGB, $\mathcal{H} = 9$ hyperparameters were tuned using Bayesian optimization: booster type (`booster`); L1 and L2 regularization terms ($\lambda$ and $\alpha$); learning rate (`ETA`); maximum depth of individual trees (`Maxdepth`); minimum sum of instance weights required in a child node ($\mathtt{Minchild}\omega$); subsample ratio of the training instances per boosting iteration (`SS`); subsample ratio of columns when constructing each tree (`ColSTree`); and number of boosting iterations ($\mathcal{N}\mathtt{est}$).

The RF [2], proposed in 2001, builds a set of decision trees to determine the most significant patterns in the data by aggregating multiple tree-based predictions. For RF, $\mathcal{H} = 7$ hyperparameters were considered during optimization: minimum number of samples required to split an internal node ($\mathtt{Min}_{split}$); maximum number of features considered at each split ($\mathtt{Max}_{features}$); impurity criterion

[2] Available at https://scikit-learn.org/stable/.

for split quality (`criterion`); number of trees in the ensemble ($N_{\texttt{est}}$); impurity decrease threshold for node splitting ($\texttt{Min}_{impdec}$); use of out-of-bag samples to estimate generalization performance ($\texttt{oob}_{score}$); and minimum weighted fraction of the total sample weight required to be at a leaf node ($\texttt{Min}_{l\omega}$).

The MLP model is a foundational neural network architecture introduced as an extension of the perceptron [18]. In this study, the MLP was optimized using a Bayesian hyperparameter search strategy, considering the **`lbfgs`** solver, which is a quasi-Newton method particularly suited for smaller datasets or tasks requiring fast convergence [14]. A total of $\mathcal{H} = 6$ hyperparameters were tuned during optimization: the number of neurons in the hidden layer ($H_{\text{size}}$); the activation function ($H_a$); the L2 regularization term ($\alpha$); the maximum number of training iterations ($\texttt{Max}_{iter}$); and the maximum number of function evaluations allowed during optimization ($\texttt{Max}_{fun}$).

The LR model is a widely used statistical method that models the probability of a binary outcome by estimating the relationship between one or more independent variables and a categorical dependent variable through the logistic (sigmoid) function [12]. This model was also optimized using the Bayesian hyperparameter search, which involved a total of $\mathcal{H} = 8$ hyperparameters. The following parameters were included in the optimization process: the regularization penalty type (`penalty`), which controls whether $\lambda$, $\alpha$, or elastic-net regularization is applied; whether to use the dual formulation of the optimization problem (`dual`); the tolerance for the stopping criteria (`tol`); the inverse of the regularization strength (`C`), where smaller values specify stronger regularization; whether to include an intercept in the model (`FI`); the optimization algorithm used for training (`solver`); the maximum number of iterations allowed for convergence ($\texttt{Max}_{iter}$); and the Elastic Net mixing parameter ($\lambda$), which determines the balance between $\lambda$ and $\alpha$ penalties when applicable.

In this study, we applied eXplainable Artificial Intelligence (XAI) methods to assess the overall contributions of the input features (detailed in Table 1) to the predictions made by the models. Specifically, we used SHAP (SHapley Additive exPlanations) [15,20], a widely adopted XAI method that quantifies the contribution of each input feature to the model output. Based on cooperative game theory, SHAP calculates Shapley values to fairly allocate the difference between the actual prediction of a model and its baseline (average) prediction among all features. This approach not only identifies which features influenced a given prediction but also clarifies the direction and magnitude of their impact. However, since SHAP approximates Shapley values by evaluating numerous combinations of feature subsets, the method can be computationally demanding.

### 2.4 Evaluation

As previously mentioned, we evaluate the performance of ML models using a RW evaluation scheme [19], which reflects how classifiers are applied over time with periodic updates to training and test sets (Fig. 2). In the first iteration ($u = 1$), the model is trained on the oldest $W$ instances and then used to predict the next $T$ observations. In each subsequent iteration ($u = 2$, $u = 3$, etc.), the training set is updated by replacing the oldest $S$ records with $S$ new ones (the update step). A new model is trained on this updated set to predict subsequent $T$ observations. This process repeats until all data are processed, resulting in a total of $U = \frac{D-(W+T)}{S}$ updates, where $D$ is the total number of data points.

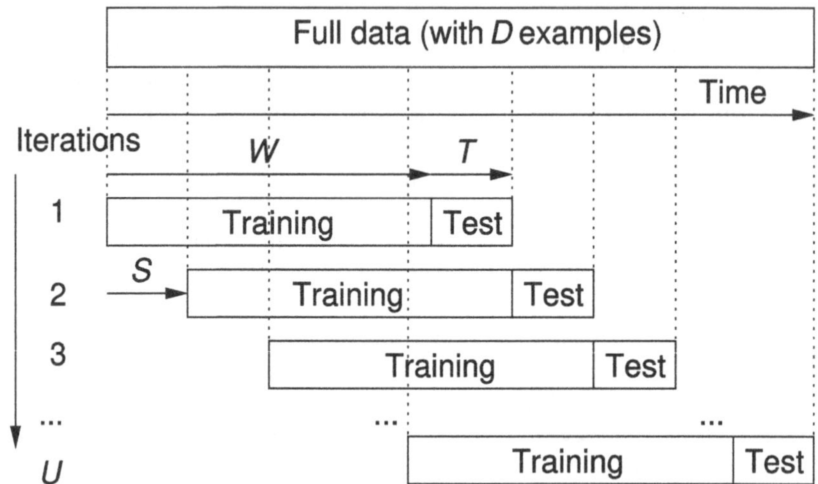


**Fig. 2.** Schematic representation of the RW evaluation procedure.

For the dataset used, $W = 30,000$, $T = S = 3,000$, yielding $U = 11$ model updates. As described in Sect. 2.3, model selection and hyperparameter adjustment were performed only during the first RW iteration ($u = 1$), to simulate a realistic deployment scenario and reduce computational cost.

The performance of the model on the RW test sets was measured using the Area Under the Receiver Operating Characteristic Curve (AUC-ROC) [7]. For each predicted class probability $p \in [0, 1]$, the label was classified as positive if $p_k > K$, where $K$ is the decision threshold. The ROC curve plots the False Positive Rate (FPR), calculated as 1− Specificity, on the x-axis against Sensitivity (True Positive Rate, TPR) on the y-axis, for all thresholds $K \in [0, 1]$. The AUC is the area under this curve, computed as $AUC = \int_0^1 ROC(K)dK$. AUC values indicate classification quality: 0.5 corresponds to random guessing, 0.7 is reasonable, 0.8 very good, 0.9 excellent, and 1.0 perfect discrimination. To summarize the results in all iterations of RW ($u \in 1, ..., U$), the median AUC was used, as it is less sensitive to outliers than the mean.

## 3 Results

Table 2 and Fig. 3 summarize the predictive performance of the five machine learning models evaluated in 11 iterations of the rolling window.

**Table 2.** Model performance results (best values in bold).

| Model | AUC (Median) | Training (s) | Predict ($\mu$s) |
|---|---|---|---|
| LR | 0.68 | 1.21 | **3.96** |
| RF | 0.50 | **0.51** | 80.84 |
| MLP | **0.72** | 13.91 | 39.62 |
| XGB | 0.69 | 1.68 | 7.50 |
| GBM* | 0.63 | 8.23 | 66.20 |

*Best model obtained from H2O.

As shown, the MLP model achieved the highest predictive performance, with a median AUC of approximately 0.721, followed closely by XGB (0.694) and LR (0.680). This shows that, even in a highly imbalanced and complex B2B sales context, neural networks and gradient boosting techniques are effective in capturing non-linear relationships and interactions among features. It is also important to mention that even though the MLP model achieved the highest median AUC, it also required the longest training time among all models, highlighting a trade-off between predictive performance and computational efficiency.

Despite its lower ranking in the AUC, LR offered the best efficiency trade-off. It showed stable performance in all iterations and achieved the fastest inference time (3.96 $\mu$s) and shortest training time (1.21 s). These results reinforce the idea that simple linear models, when trained on well-prepared and informative features, can provide competitive accuracy with minimal computational cost, an appealing option for real-time applications or systems with limited resources.

XGB, while slightly less performant than MLP in the median AUC, still showed strong results and acceptable computational times (1.68 s training, 7.50 $\mu$s prediction). Its ability to handle heterogeneous data types and capture complex patterns confirms its suitability for industrial predictive modeling tasks.

The H2O AutoML framework selected a GBM as the best model. This model reached a median AUC of 0.621, with 8.23 s of training time and a prediction latency of 66.20 $\mu$s. Although its performance was less stable across iterations, it remains a practical option due to its automated optimization capabilities and ease of use, especially when domain expertise in ML is limited.

In contrast, the RF classifier exhibited poor performance, with AUC values consistently equal to 0.500 across all iterations, indicating that it failed to capture the discriminative structure in the dataset. This may be due to challenges with high-cardinality categorical variables and the strong class imbalance. In addition, its relatively high inference time (80.84 $\mu$s) and training time (0.51 s) do not compensate for its limited predictive value.

In general, these results suggest that MLP and XGB are best suited to predict the success of the proposal in this complex B2B pricing scenario, offering a good balance between precision and computational efficiency. Meanwhile, LR stands out as a robust baseline, particularly in use cases requiring fast deployment, low latency, or transparency.

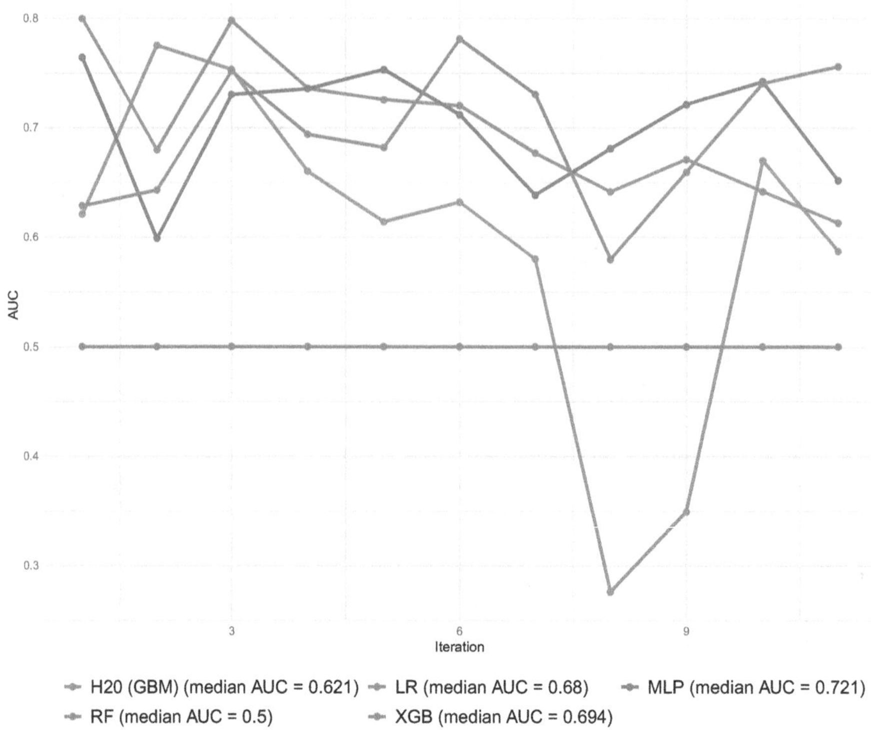


**Fig. 3.** RW AUC comparison per model

To gain a better understanding of the drivers behind the model predictions, we applied SHAP to the best-performing model, MLP. Figure 4 shows the feature importance, which details the magnitude of the impact of each variable on the predicted probability of proposal success.

The results show that variables directly related to pricing have the greatest influence on the model's predictions. This suggests that price remains a critical determinant of proposal success, both at the overall configuration level and at the individual product line level. These insights reinforce the central role of pricing strategies in B2B commercial negotiations and align with the intuitive expectation that lower-priced offers tend to be more easily accepted by clients.

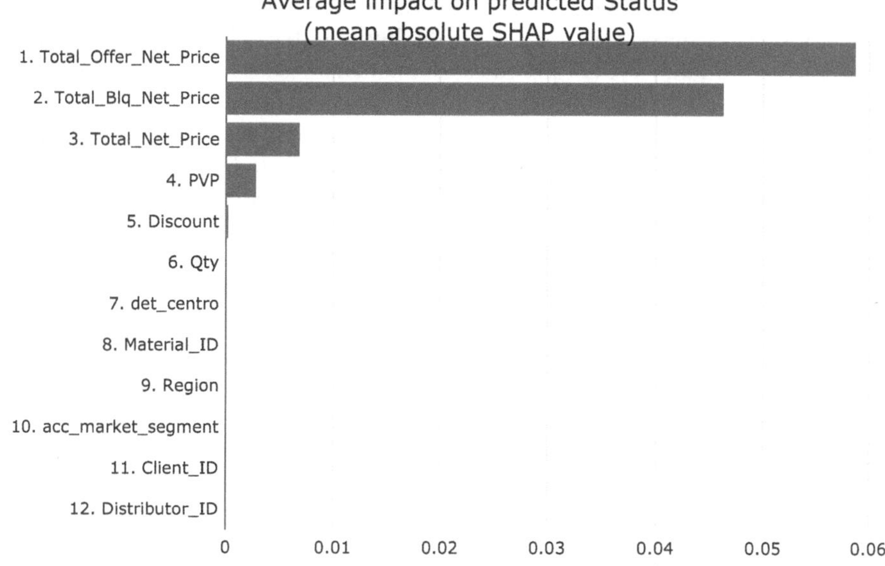


**Fig. 4.** Feature Importance for the MLP model

## 4 Conclusions

This paper presented a machine learning framework to predict the success of B2B commercial proposals in a B2B context, using more than 65,000 real historical records from a multinational company. A comparative evaluation of five classification models, LR, RF, MLP, XGB, and H2O AutoML, was performed using a RW validation strategy to simulate temporal deployment scenarios and to test the models' robustness over time.

Among all models, MLP achieved the best predictive performance, with a median AUC of 0.72, closely followed by XGB and LR. In contrast, RF and the GBM model selected by H2O AutoML exhibited lower performance. These findings suggest that neural models can be particularly effective in capturing complex patterns in the prediction of proposal success.

The proposed methodology also showed computational feasibility for real-time deployment and scalability, particularly through the use of AutoML and IDF pipelines.

The approach provides not only accurate probability estimates, but also the foundation for pricing sensitivity analysis and data-driven negotiation support tools. In particular, future work could apply the best-performing model to construct bid-response functions, mathematical representations of how the probability of deal conversion varies with pricing decisions. This would enable the estimation of the price-dependent contribution of the deal and the calculation of optimal prices to maximize the expected contribution during negotiations [17].

Customized pricing environments, such as the one in this study, possess three key features that make this application highly suitable: (1) customers engage before seeing a final price, (2) prices can be personalized using contextual data, and (3) both won and lost bids are recorded, providing rich data for statistical learning. These characteristics create ideal conditions for the practical implementation of predictive pricing strategies in B2B contexts [17].

In addition, future research could explore the integration of external features (e.g., competition, seasonality), the application of cost-sensitive learning to optimize for proposal profitability, and the use of XAI methods to improve model transparency and user trust.

Some limitations should also be acknowledged. The current dataset may not fully capture all the contextual drivers of proposal outcomes and feature representation, particularly for categorical variables of high cardiac density, which has a significant influence on performance. Further improvements may also come from advanced model optimization techniques, such as genetic algorithms, more expressive deep learning architectures, better feature engineering, and alternative encoding strategies to handle categorical variables of high cardinality in imbalanced datasets.

By identifying the most suitable predictive models and validating their performance across time windows, this work contributes to building data-driven capabilities within the organization. The ability to anticipate proposal outcomes can support more informed pricing strategies, shorten sales cycles, and improve negotiation leverage, which offers significant strategic value in industrial B2B contexts.

**Acknowledgments.** This work has been supported by FCT – Fundação para a Ciência e Tecnologia within the R&D Unit Project Scope UID/00319/Centro ALGORITMI (ALGORITMI/UM) and by national funds, through the Operational Competitiveness and Internationalization Programme (COMPETE 2020) [Project nº 179826; Funding Reference: SIFN-01-9999-FN-179826].

## References

1. Akiba, T., Sano, S., Yanase, T., Ohta, T., Koyama, M.: Optuna: a next-generation hyperparameter optimization framework. In: Proceedings of the 25th ACM SIGKDD International Conference on Knowledge Discovery & Data Mining, pp. 2623–2631 (2019). https://doi.org/10.1145/3292500.3330701
2. Breiman, L.: Random forests. Mach. Learn. **45**(1), 5–32 (2001). https://doi.org/10.1023/A:1010933404324
3. Campos, G.O., Zimek, A., Sander, J., et al.: On the evaluation of unsupervised outlier detection: measures, datasets, and an empirical study. Data Min. Knowl. Disc. **30**(4), 891–927 (2016)
4. Chapman, P., et al.: CRISP-DM 1.0 Step-by-step data mining guide. SPSS (2000)
5. Chen, T., Guestrin, C.: Xgboost: a scalable tree boosting system. In: Proceedings of the 22nd ACM SIGKDD International Conference on Knowledge Discovery and Data Mining, pp. 785–794 (2016). https://doi.org/10.1145/2939672.2939785

6. Cook, D.: Practical Machine Learning with H2O: Powerful, Scalable Techniques For Deep Learning and AI. Inc, O'Reilly Media (2016)
7. Fawcett, T.: An introduction to ROC analysis. Pattern Recogn. Lett. **27**(8), 861–874 (2006). https://doi.org/10.1016/j.patrec.2005.10.010
8. Ferreira, L., Pilastri, A., Martins, C.M., Pires, P.M., Cortez, P.: A comparison of automl tools for machine learning, deep learning and xgboost. In: 2021 International Joint Conference on Neural Networks (IJCNN) (2021). https://doi.org/10.1109/IJCNN52387.2021.9534091
9. Habel, J., Alavi, S., Heinitz, N.: A theory of predictive sales analytics adoption. AMS Rev. **13**, 34–54 (6 2023). https://doi.org/10.1007/s13162-022-00252-0
10. Habel, J., Alavi, S., Heinitz, N.: Effective implementation of predictive sales analytics. J. Market. Res. **61**, 718–741 (8 2024). https://doi.org/10.1177/00222437221151039
11. Hallikainen, H., Savimäki, E., Laukkanen, T.: Fostering b2b sales with customer big data analytics. Indust. Market. Manage. **86**, 90–98 (4 2020). https://doi.org/10.1016/J.INDMARMAN.2019.12.005
12. Hosmer, D.W., Lemeshow, S., Sturdivant, R.X.: Applied Logistic Regression. Wiley, 3rd edn. (2013). https://doi.org/10.1002/9781118548387
13. Kawas, B., Squillante, M.S., Subramanian, D., Varshney, K.R.: Prescriptive analytics for allocating sales teams to opportunities. In: Proceedings - IEEE 13th International Conference on Data Mining Workshops, ICDMW 2013, pp. 211–218. IEEE Computer Society (2013). https://doi.org/10.1109/ICDMW.2013.156
14. Liu, D.C., Nocedal, J.: On the limited memory BFGS method for large scale optimization. Math. Program. **45**(1–3), 503–528 (1989). https://doi.org/10.1007/BF01589116
15. Lundberg, S.M., Lee, S.I.: A unified approach to interpreting model predictions. In: Advances in Neural Information Processing Systems, vol. 30, pp. 4765–4774 (2017)
16. Matos, L.M., Azevedo, J., Matta, A., Pilastri, A.L., Cortez, P., Mendes, R.: Categorical attribute transformation environment (CANE): a python module for categorical to numeric data preprocessing. Softw. Impacts **13**, 100359 (2022). https://doi.org/10.1016/J.SIMPA.2022.100359
17. Phillips, R.L.: Pricing and Revenue Optimization. Stanford University Press, 2 edn. (5 2021)
18. Rumelhart, D.E., Hinton, G.E., Williams, R.J.: Learning representations by back-propagating errors. Nature **323**, 533–536 (1986). https://doi.org/10.1038/323533a0
19. Tashman, L.J.: Out-of-sample tests of forecasting accuracy: an analysis and review. Int. J. Forecast. **16**(4), 437–450 (oct 2000). https://doi.org/10.1016/S0169-2070(00)00065-0
20. Štrumbelj, E., Kononenko, I.: Explaining prediction models and individual predictions with feature contributions. Knowl. Inform. Syst. **41**(3), 647–665 (Dec 2014). https://doi.org/10.1007/s10115-013-0679-x
21. Wengler, S., Hildmann, G., Vossebein, U.: Digital transformation in sales as an evolving process. J. Business Indust. Market. **36**, 599–614 (2020). https://doi.org/10.1108/JBIM-03-2020-0124
22. Yan, J., et al.: On machine learning towards predictive sales pipeline analytics. In: Proceedings of the AAAI Conference on Artificial Intelligence **29** (2 2015). https://doi.org/10.1609/aaai.v29i1.9455

# SELENE: A Deep Learning Model for Predicting Lunar Absorbed Radiation Dose Rates

Sai Srikar Tummala[1(✉)], Mittansh Bhatia[2], and Robert Chun[3]

[1] San Jose, CA, USA
tummalasaisrikar@gmail.com
[2] Sunnyvale, CA, USA
[3] Computer Science Department, San Jose State University, San Jose, CA, USA
robert.chun@sjsu.edu

**Abstract.** Lunar exploration faces major challenges because the Moon lacks a magnetic field and atmosphere, exposing astronauts to harmful radiation from galactic cosmic rays and solar energetic particles. Traditional radiation models rely on computationally intensive physics simulations, which are often slow and require significant resources. This study introduces SELENE (Space Environment Lunar Exposure Neural Estimator), an artificial neural network designed to rapidly predict lunar surface radiation dose rates using space weather data. SELENE is trained on over 27,000 data points collected from the CRaTER instrument aboard the Lunar Reconnaissance Orbiter, enabling fast and accurate radiation forecasting essential for protecting astronauts on future lunar missions.

**Keywords:** lunar radiation · radiation prediction · deep learning · space weather · SELENE

## 1 Introduction

Modern plans for sustained lunar exploration and habitation demand accurate knowledge of the radiation environment on the Moon's surface. The absence of a planetary magnetic field or significant atmosphere exposes astronauts and equipment like space suits and communication systems to galactic cosmic rays (GCRs) which are high-energy particles originating from outside our solar system traveling around the speed of light, and sporadic solar particle events (SPEs) which are sudden and intense bursts of energetic particles, primarily photons, released by the Sun. These pose serious risks. Several prior efforts have explored computer-enhanced predictions of space radiation.

Dobynde et al. developed the REDMoon simulator using GEANT4 and Monte Carlo simulations to characterize the absorbed and equivalent dose on the lunar surface [1,2].

S. S. Tummala and M. Bhati— Independent Researcher


R. Stahlbock et al. (Eds.): CSCE 2025, CCIS 2938, pp. 90–107, 2027.
https://doi.org/10.1007/978-3-032-22196-4_7

Wimmer-Schweingruber et al. presented the first active dosimetric measurements with the Lunar Lander Neutron and Dosimetry (LND) experiment aboard Chang'e 4 [3,4]. Their data quantified the flux and energy spectra of both primary GCR protons and albedo neutrons/protons, confirming REDMoon's predictions and showing absorbed dose rates of roughly 200800 $\mu$Sv/day.

Halder et al. combined OLTARIS and CRaTER datasets along with ARIMA and Random Forest models to map background radiation levels across the lunar surface [5,6], revealing spatial variations in absorbed dose driven by local terrain and composition.

We novelly present the idea of utilizing deep learning to rapidly estimate lunar surface radiation dose rates from space weather particle flux data. While radiation dose can be derived from first principles using particle energy spectra, stopping power functions, and quality factors, such physics-based simulations—like those using GEANT4 or HZETRN—are computationally intensive, require detailed input on shielding and material geometry, and are often impractical for real-time decision-making during lunar missions.

In contrast, we propose a data-driven approach that uses artificial neural networks (ANNs) to create a model known as SELENE (Space Environment Lunar Exposure Neural Estimator) in order to learn the complex nonlinear relationship between measured particle fluxes and corresponding radiation dose rates. Recent studies have also explored the use of LSTM and probabilistic deep learning models to predict SEP/GCR spectra and dose forecasts [7,8]. In the future, models that forecast space weather conditions could be combined with our radiation prediction model to enable end-to-end forecasting of lunar surface radiation. SELENE is trained on over 27,000 h of data compiled from the CRaTER instrument on the Lunar Reconnaissance Orbiter [9] and flux measurements from the ACE SIS and CRIS detectors [10,11]. After performing correlation-based feature selection, we trained an ANN to predict absorbed dose rates recorded by CRaTER using only flux features from ACE. SELENE achieved a mean absolute percentage error (MAPE) of 14.26% on the validation dataset, demonstrating the feasibility of using machine learning as a fast, lightweight alternative to physics-based radiation estimation.

This approach has promising applications for future lunar exploration, enabling real-time radiation monitoring and risk assessment for crewed missions without requiring extensive computational infrastructure or detailed environmental modeling.

## 2 Related Work

Modeling lunar radiation environments has traditionally relied on physics-based simulations and empirical measurements. Monte Carlo tools such as REDMoon [2] use GEANT4 to simulate particle interactions and estimate dose rates, but these methods are computationally intensive and impractical for real-time applications.

Dosimetric data from missions like Chang'e 4's LND experiment [3,4] provide valuable ground truth but do not directly offer predictive capabilities. Statistical models combining datasets such as OLTARIS and CRaTER with ARIMA or

Random Forests [5,6] have mapped radiation spatial variability, yet lack deep learning-driven nonlinear modeling and focus mainly on retrospective analyses.

Recent machine learning approaches focus on forecasting space weather parameters or particle fluxes using recurrent or probabilistic neural networks [7,8]. However, these models do not directly predict absorbed lunar dose rates from multi-instrument flux data.

Our model, SELENE, fills this gap by leveraging a fully connected artificial neural network trained on over 27,000 synchronized hourly measurements from CRaTER and ACE instruments. This approach enables rapid, direct prediction of lunar absorbed dose rates from space weather particle flux features, offering a lightweight alternative to physics simulations with potential for real-time mission support.

To our knowledge, SELENE is among the first to integrate multi-instrument space weather data via deep learning specifically for lunar radiation dose rate prediction.

## 3 Methods

### 3.1 Data Sources

NASA has launched several space missions equipped with sensors that collect data on the lunar environment. The primary datasets used for training and validating this model come from the Advanced Composition Explorer (ACE) [9,12] and the Cosmic Ray Telescope for the Effects of Radiation (CRaTER) instruments [10,11,13].

CRaTER is an instrument aboard NASA's Lunar Reconnaissance Orbiter (LRO), which has been orbiting the Moon since 2009. It measures the radiation dose rates at the lunar surface, providing critical data on the lunar radiation environment.

ACE, launched in 1997 and positioned at the EarthSun L1 Lagrange point, one of five points in space where the gravitational forces of two large orbiting bodies balance each other, allowing a smaller object to maintain a relatively stable position. It continuously monitors the solar wind, energetic particles, and cosmic rays arriving from the Sun and beyond. Among its onboard instruments, the Cosmic Ray Isotope Spectrometer (CRIS) measures galactic cosmic rays (GCRs)—highly energetic charged particles originating outside the solar system. The Solar Isotope Spectrometer (SIS) monitors solar energetic particles (SEPs), which are charged particles emitted by the Sun during solar flares and coronal mass ejections.

The GCR and SEP data from ACE's CRIS and SIS instruments provide a comprehensive characterization of the radiation environment near Earth and the Moon. By integrating this information with CRaTER's dose measurements, we can accurately estimate the absorbed radiation dose rates at the lunar surface.

### 3.2 Dataset Integration and Preprocessing

Initially, the input features from ACE and the target dose rates from CRaTER were used without enforcing consistent temporal granularity. Specifically, the

CRaTER data provided daily radiation dose rates, while the CRIS and SIS data from ACE were recorded at an hourly resolution. This mismatch in timestamp alignment led to noisy correlations and degraded model performance. As shown in Fig. 1, the correlation between the radiation dose denoted as dose_D1 and the space weather data is −0.26. In Fig. 2 it is clear that this correlation is not signficiant enough for SELENE to detect, causing it to predict the same value each time.

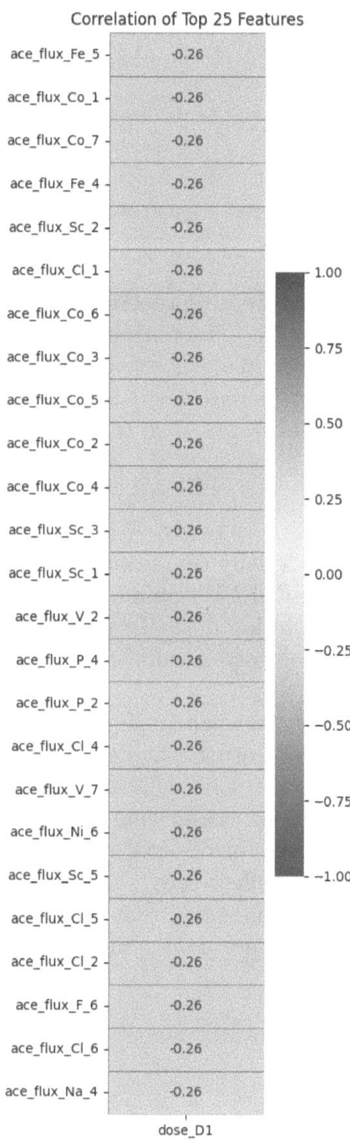


**Fig. 1.** Correlation heatmap between radiation dose and other features.

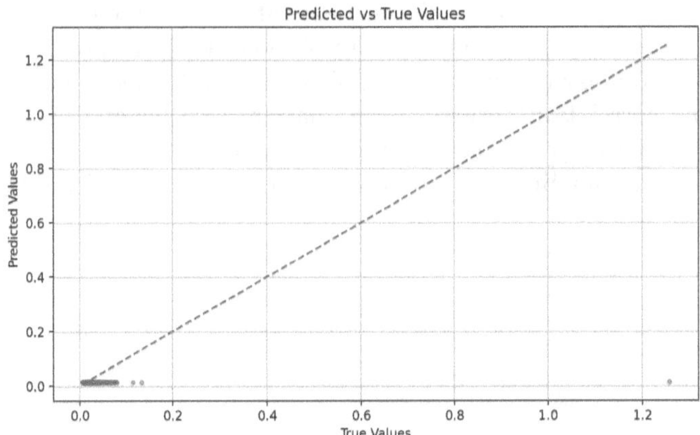


**Fig. 2.** Initial model predictions before temporal alignment.

To resolve this, all datasets were reprocessed to a common daily resolution. The ACE data was aggregated by computing the mean flux and count values over each day, aligning with the daily dose rate measurements from CRaTER. This temporal harmonization increased the strongest correlation between the radiation dose and the features from −0.26 to 0.4.

### 3.3 Feature Selection

After aggregating the data to a daily resolution, feature selection was performed to reduce noise and improve SELENE's ability to learn the relationship between the input vectors and the radiation dose. To identify the most informative features, we computed the Pearson correlation coefficients between each feature and the target dose values.

As shown in the resulting heatmap in Fig. 3, the highest observed correlation was approximately 0.4, indicating a moderate linear relationship. However, many of the features not shown in the heatmap exhibited very weak or negligible correlations with correlation coefficients under 0.01 magnitude. Including these weakly correlated features introduced unnecessary noise, which hindered SELENE's ability to generalize effectively.

Based on this analysis, we concluded that omitting low-correlation features was necessary to enhance model accuracy and reduce overfitting.

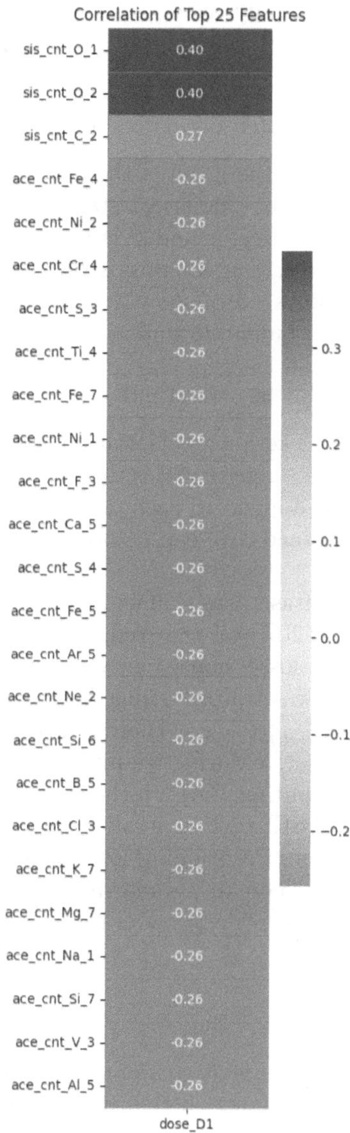


**Fig. 3.** Refined correlation heatmap after daily aggregation.

### 3.4 SELENE Architecture

SELENE is a fully connected feedforward artificial neural network (ANN) to predict lunar absorbed radiation dose rates from particle flux data. SELENE was constructed using TensorFlow and trained on scaled feature vectors extracted from selected high-correlation channels in the ACE SIS and CRIS datasets.

The target variable was the daily averaged absorbed dose rate measured by the CRaTER instrument.

- Input layer: 18 features
- Hidden Layer 1: 64 units, batch normalization ($\hat{x}^{(i)} = \frac{x^{(i)} - \mu_B}{\sqrt{\sigma_B^2 + \epsilon}}$, where $x^{(i)}$ is the input to the layer, $\mu_B$ is the mean of the batch, $\sigma_B^2$ is the batch variance, and $\epsilon$ is a small constant for numerical stability; $y^{(i)} = \gamma \hat{x}^{(i)} + \beta$, where $\gamma$ is a learnable scaling parameter and $\beta$ is a learnable shifting parameter), LeakyReLU ($f(x) = \max(x, \alpha x)$, where $x$ is the input and $\alpha = 0.01$ controls the slope for negative values), dropout $= 0.4$
- Hidden Layer 2: 32 units, batch normalization (same formulation as above), LeakyReLU, dropout $= 0.3$
- Output layer: 1 neuron (linear activation)

To mitigate overfitting, $L_2$ kernel regularization ($\lambda \|\mathbf{W}\|_2^2 = \lambda \sum_{i,j} W_{ij}^2$, where $\lambda = 0.01$ is the regularization strength, $\mathbf{W}$ is the weight matrix, and $W_{ij}$ denotes the individual weights) was applied to each dense layer. The network used the Adam optimizer and was trained with early stopping and learning rate reduction on plateau.

To train SELENE, the dataset was shuffled, and 80% of the data was used for training while the remaining 20% was reserved for validation. As shown in Fig. 4, both training and validation losses consistently decrease over epochs, indicating stable learning. The model was trained using the Mean Absolute Error (MAE) loss function. ($\text{MAE} = \frac{1}{n} \sum_{i=1}^{n} |y_i - \hat{y}_i|$, where $y_i$ is the true daily averaged dose rate.) Although dropout is active during training and can increase the apparent loss, it is disabled when computing MAE on the evaluation set. This discrepancy reveals that dropout helped SELENE generalize and learn meaningful patterns, as the true MAE is lower than the training loss suggests.

Input features are scaled to create standardized feature vectors using z-score normalization ($X_{\text{scaled}} = \frac{X - \mu_X}{\sigma_X}$, where $\mu_X$ is the mean and $\sigma_X$ is the standard deviation of feature $X$).

### 3.5 Linear Regression

To provide a baseline for comparison, a traditional linear regression model was trained using ordinary least squares on the same feature set as SELENE. This model assumes a linear relationship between particle flux inputs and the dose rate and provides interpretable coefficients.

### 3.6 XGBoost Regression

To evaluate a powerful nonlinear tree-based approach, an XGBoost regression model was implemented. XGBoost is an ensemble of gradient-boosted decision trees optimized for speed and performance developed by Chen et al. [14]. Hyperparameter tuning was performed via cross-validation, adjusting tree depth, learning rate, and number of estimators to maximize predictive accuracy. Feature importance metrics from XGBoost also helped validate the feature selection process.

### 3.7 Monte Carlo Dropout for Uncertainty Quantification

Building on the SELENE architecture, Monte Carlo (MC) Dropout was implemented to estimate predictive uncertainty. Unlike standard inference where dropout layers are disabled, MC Dropout keeps dropout active during prediction. Multiple stochastic forward passes ($T = 100$) are performed per input sample, with the mean of predictions providing the dose estimate and the variance representing uncertainty. This method allows identification of predictions with low confidence, which is critical for operational risk assessment during lunar missions.

### 3.8 SAINT Model

For further comparison, the SAINT (Self-Attention and Intersample Attention Transformer) model was trained on the same tabular data. SAINT, developed by Somepalli et al. [15], leverages transformer architectures to capture feature interactions and sample relations, representing a state-of-the-art method for tabular regression. Training included standard optimization and early stopping strategies.

## 4 Results and Discussion

To evaluate the performance of SELENE and benchmark it against other models, several regression metrics were computed on the validation dataset, including Mean Squared Error (MSE), Mean Absolute Error (MAE), coefficient of determination ($R^2$), and Mean Absolute Percentage Error (MAPE). Table 1 summarizes the key results for each model.

**Table 1.** Performance metrics for SELENE and baseline models

| Model | MSE | MAE | $R^2$ | MAPE |
|---|---|---|---|---|
| SELENE (ANN) | 0.00093602 | 0.00429024 | 0.8342 | 14.26% |
| Monte Carlo Dropout | 0.00097653 | 0.00441782 | 0.8270 | 14.93% |
| XGBoost | 0.00558249 | 0.00815728 | 0.0112 | 42.83% |
| Linear Regression | 0.000416 | 0.008782 | 0.3875 | 60.67% |
| SAINT Model | 1.4503 | 0.8853 | −2135.48 | 79.27% |

### 4.1 SELENE Neural Network Performance

SELENE achieved the best overall predictive accuracy among all models, with a Mean Absolute Percentage Error (MAPE) of 14.26%, a coefficient of determination ($R^2$) of 0.8342, and the lowest MAE and MSE values. This indicates that SELENE captures the nonlinear relationships between particle fluxes and absorbed dose rates effectively, providing robust estimates across the dataset. Figure 4 reveals SELENE's consistent learning as it is constantly decreasing the error for each epoch. Both the validation and training curves appear to be decreasing continuously, revealing how SELENE effectively picked up patterns and applied it to new inputs.

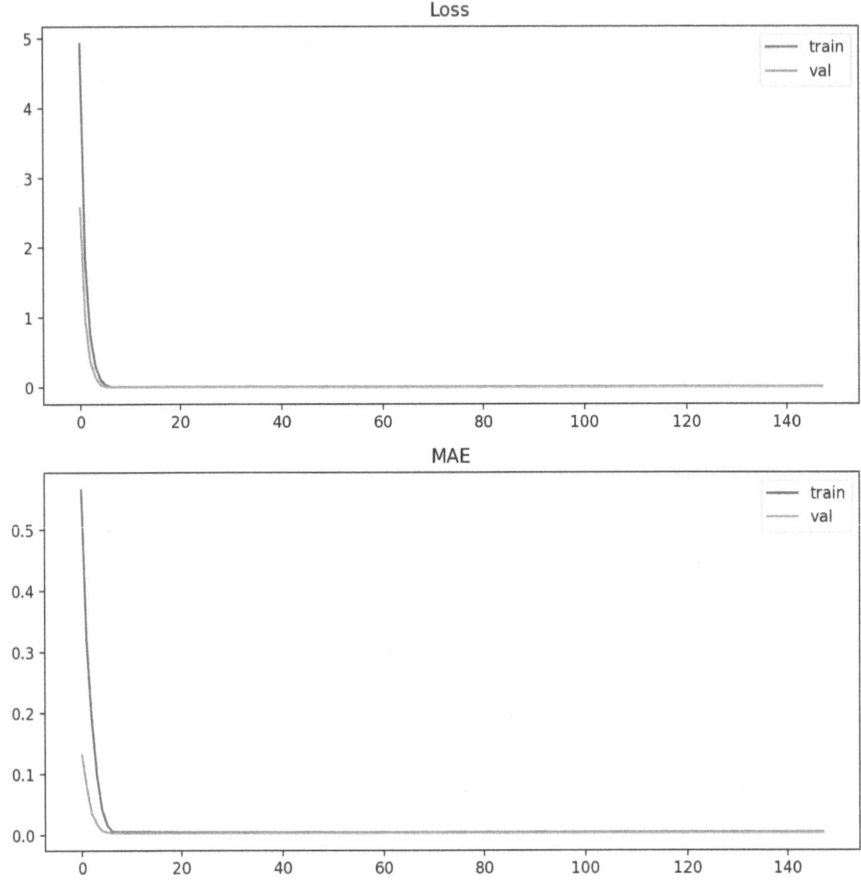


**Fig. 4.** This graph shows the loss and mean absolute error without dropout relative to the number of epochs completed in the training loop in order to show the progression of the model's learning.

### 4.2 Monte Carlo Dropout

By performing 100 stochastic forward passes with dropout enabled during inference, the Monte Carlo Dropout variant of SELENE produced both point predictions and uncertainty estimates. The mean predictive variance was approximately $7.44 \times 10^{-4}$, providing valuable confidence information that can assist in mission planning under uncertain conditions.

The MC Dropout model achieved a mean squared error (MSE) of 0.00097653 and a mean absolute error (MAE) of 0.00441782, alongside a strong coefficient of determination ($R^2$) of 0.8270. The mean absolute percentage error (MAPE) was 14.93%, reflecting typical proportional error magnitudes relative to the target values.

Correlation analyses between predictive variance and absolute errors yielded statistically significant Pearson ($r = 0.4643$, $p < 10^{-144}$) and Spearman ($\rho = 0.4137$, $p < 10^{-112}$) coefficients, demonstrating that higher uncertainty predictions generally correspond to larger errors. This relationship supports the utility of MC Dropout uncertainty as a proxy for model confidence as shown in Fig. 5.

To further assess the effectiveness of Monte Carlo (MC) Dropout in identifying high-error predictions, we evaluated its ability to flag such points using varying uncertainty thresholds. High-error samples were defined using a fixed prediction error threshold, and we computed precision, recall, and F1 scores across different uncertainty percentiles. As shown in Fig. 6, the 90th percentile yielded the best trade-off among all three metrics, making it the most effective threshold for identifying low-confidence predictions. At this threshold, the model achieved a precision, recall, and F1 score of 51.7%.

Overall, the MC Dropout approach balances predictive performance with informative uncertainty quantification, enhancing SELENE's capabilities for space radiation dose estimation and contributing to safer mission planning (Fig.7).

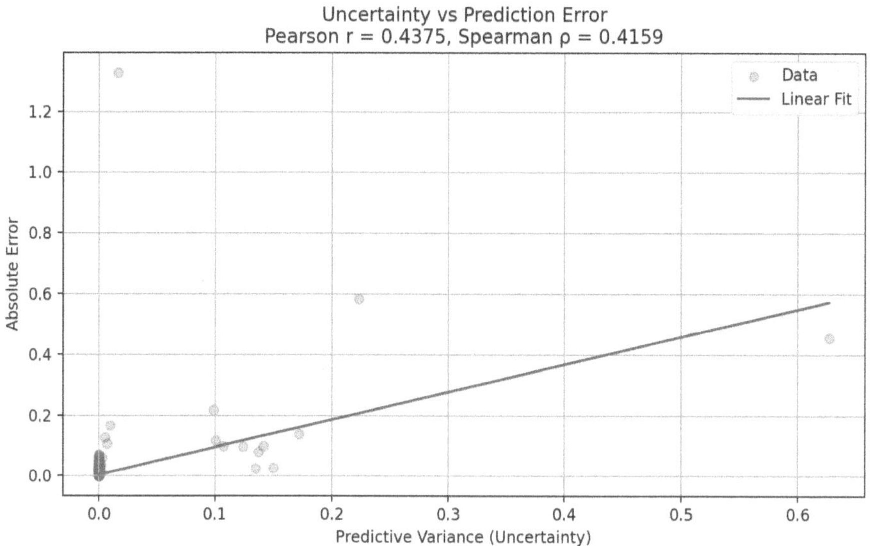


**Fig. 5.** This graph reveals the correlation between the uncertainty values yielded by the Monte Carlo Dropout and the actual error of the model.

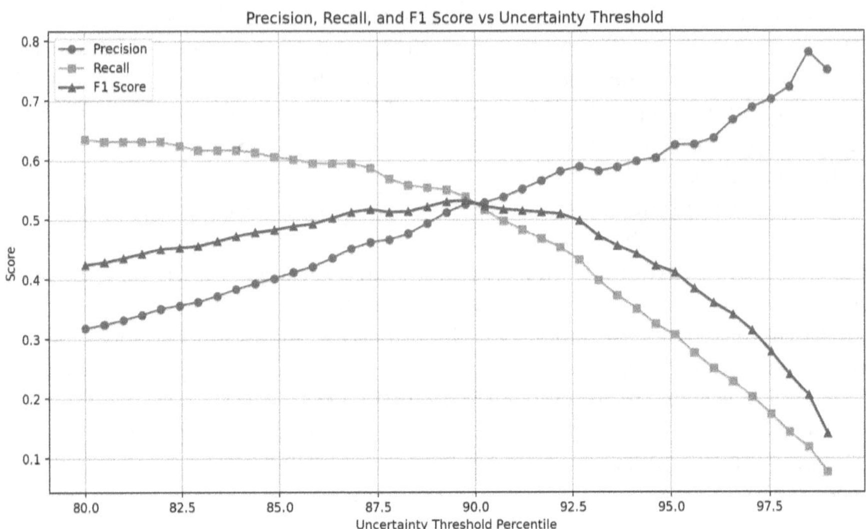


**Fig. 6.** This graph reveals the F1, precision, and recall scores of the Monte Carlo Dropout's ability to identify extreme error for different thresholds.

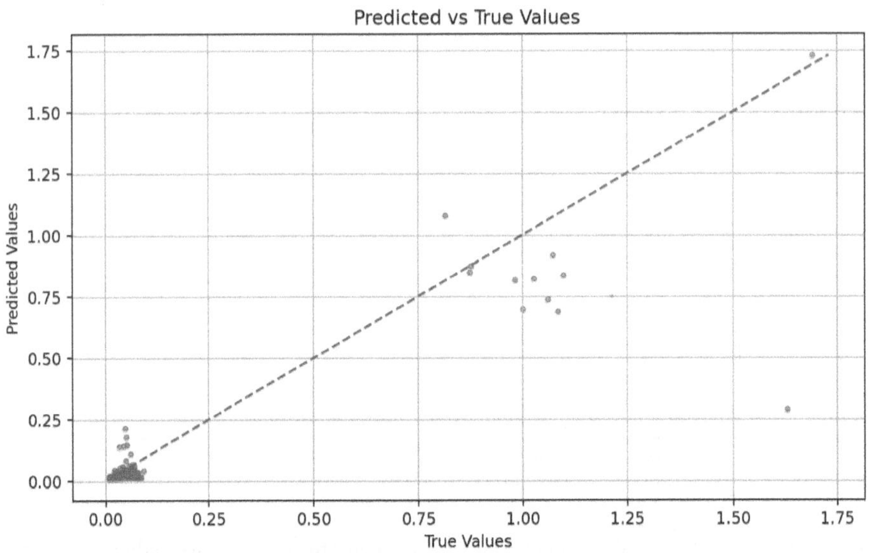


**Fig. 7.** This graph reveals the overall error of the Monte Carlo Dropout model by comparing the true output values and their corresponding predicted values from the model.

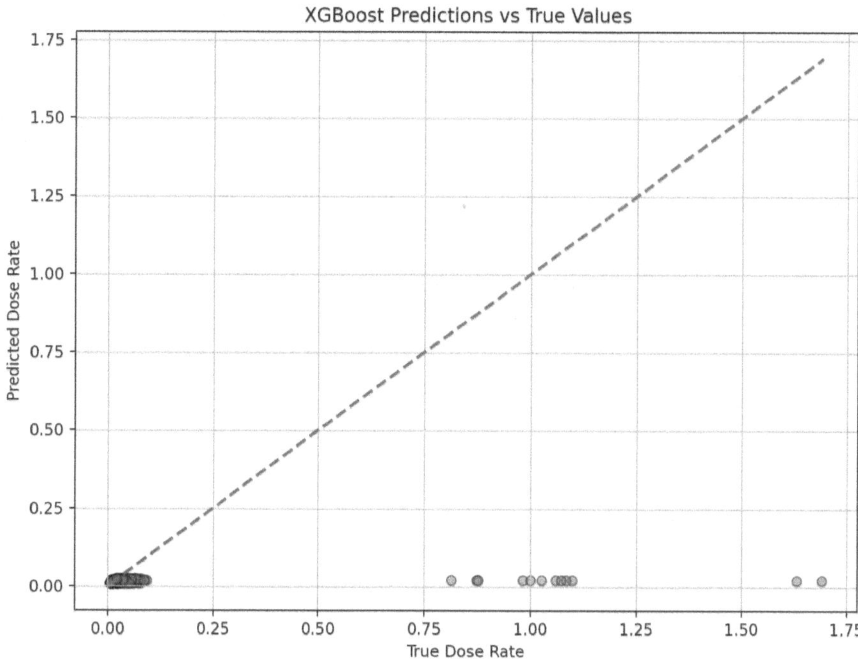


**Fig. 8.** This graph reveals the overall error of the XGBoost model by comparing the true output values and their corresponding predicted values from the model.

### 4.3 XGBoost Regression

XGBoost, while generally considered one of the most effective machine learning models, underperformed in this application as shown in Fig. 8. It achieved an MAE of 0.00816—almost double that of SELENE—and a markedly low $R^2$ of 0.0112, indicating that it captured almost none of the variance in dose rates. In the scatterplot, it is visible that the XGBoost model provides the same output for multiple true values, revealing the architecture's inability to match the complexity of the problem.

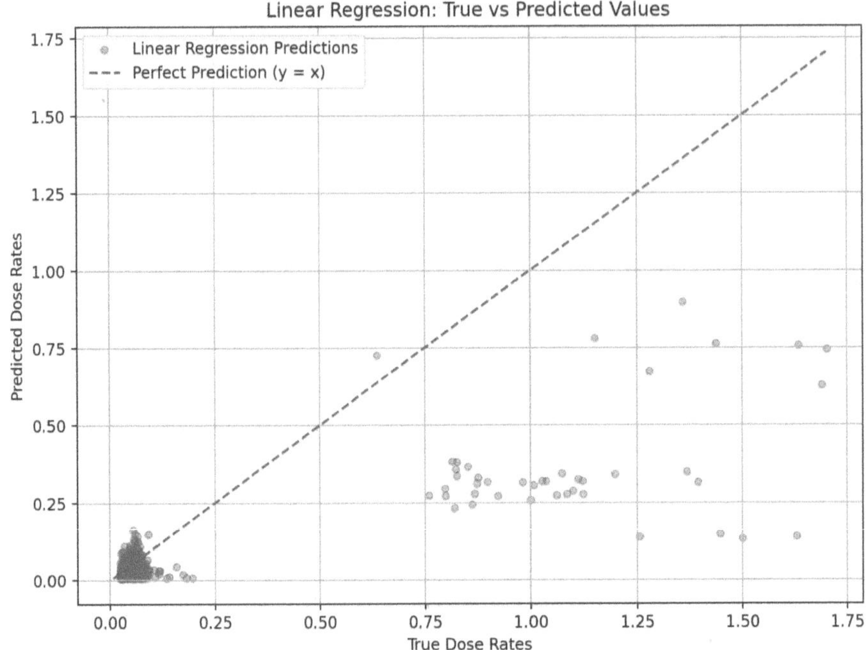


**Fig. 9.** This graph reveals the overall error of the linear regression model by comparing the true output values and their corresponding predicted values from the model.

### 4.4 Linear Regression

Linear regression, which assumes purely linear relationships, performed significantly worse than SELENE, yielding a higher MAPE of 60.67%, an MAE of 0.008782, and an $R^2$ of 0.3875. As shown in Fig. 9, the model consistently underpredicts radiation levels for true values exceeding 0.75. This systematic underestimation highlights the limitations of linear models in capturing the complex dynamics of lunar radiation and underscores the necessity of nonlinear modeling techniques for this task.

### 4.5 SAINT Transformer Model

The SAINT transformer model yielded the worst performance by a substantial margin. With an MAE of 0.8853 and an $R^2$ of 2135.48, the model not only failed to fit the data but also performed worse than a baseline model that simply predicted the mean dose rate for all inputs. This negative $R^2$ indicates a total breakdown in the model's ability to capture any meaningful relationships. The SAINT model's poor performance likely stems from the noisy nature of the dataset since it is space weather data. Space weather sensors operate in an inherently noisy and extreme environment. Despite SAINT's robustness, it is not enough to combat the noisy nature of the data (Fig. 10).

## 4.6 Error Analysis

A notable pattern emerges when examining the prediction errors as a function of radiation dose magnitude: the magnitude of the error tends to increase as the actual radiation dose increases. Both underestimations and overestimations become more pronounced at higher dose rates, indicating that SELENE has greater difficulty accurately predicting extreme radiation values. This trend suggests that SELENE's performance degrades somewhat in regimes of elevated radiation exposure, which may correspond to more complex or less frequently represented particle flux conditions in the training data.

This behavior is also clearly visible in the scatter plot of true versus predicted values (Fig. 13), where the spread and variance in prediction errors increase with radiation dose. Figure 11 illustrates SELENE's tendency to underpredict during high radiation periods, potentially due to sparse representation of such events or increased nonlinearity in dose-flux relationships. Conversely, Fig. 12 shows overprediction in some flux conditions, emphasizing the challenges of modeling extreme radiation scenarios.

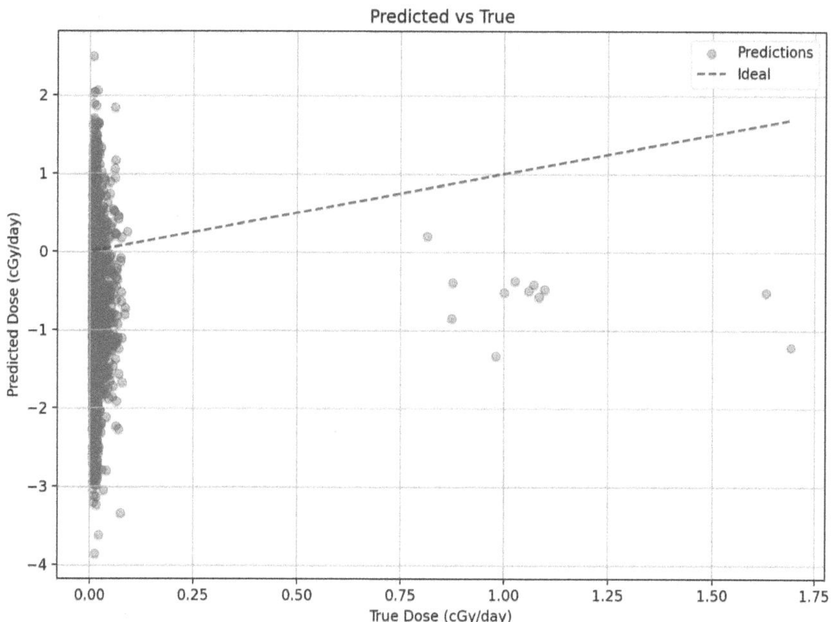


**Fig. 10.** This graph reveals the overall error of the SAINT model by comparing the true output values and their corresponding predicted values from the model.

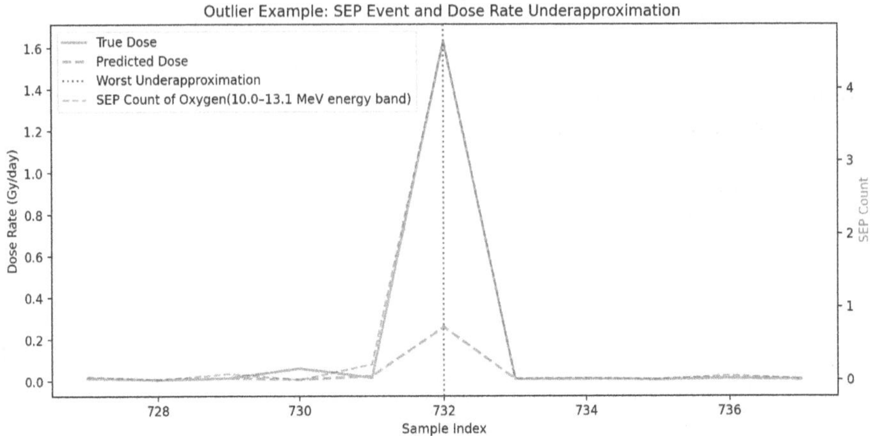


**Fig. 11.** An example of systematic underprediction error at higher radiation doses, showing that SELENE tends to underestimate elevated dose rates.

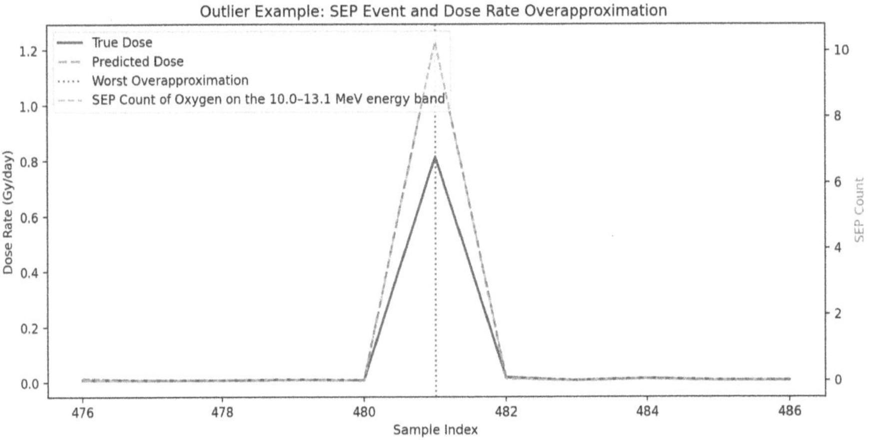


**Fig. 12.** An example of systematic overprediction error at higher radiation doses, demonstrating SELENE's tendency to overestimate dose rates under certain conditions.

Using MC Dropout, we addressed this issue by generating probabilistic predictions and quantifying model confidence through predictive variance. In the case of underapproximation (Fig. 11), the predicted variance was 0.01898, placing it in the 99.56th percentile of all variance values. Similarly, for the overapproximation shown in Fig. 12, the variance was 0.20167—corresponding to the 99.92nd percentile. These high uncertainty estimates align with the observed large prediction errors, highlighting MC Dropout's effectiveness in signaling low-confidence predictions.

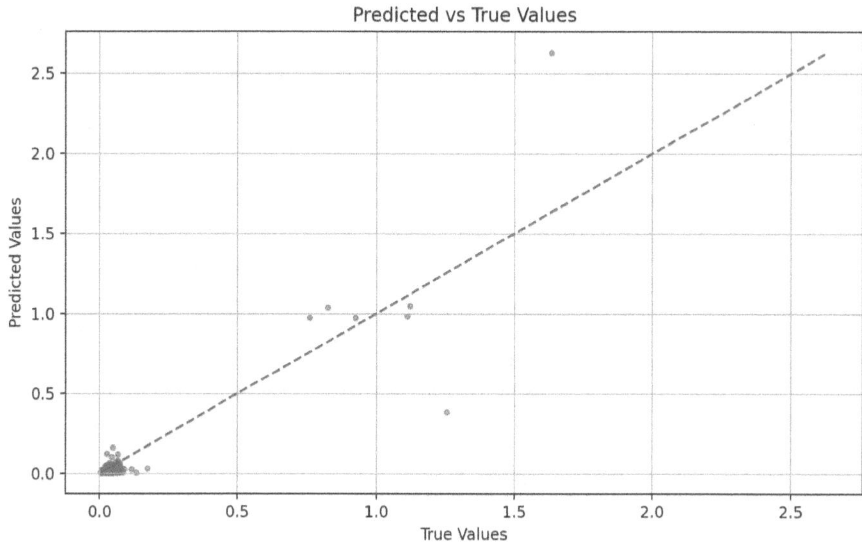


**Fig. 13.** Scatter plot of true vs. predicted values. The $y = x$ reference line illustrates perfect agreement. Most predictions cluster closely around this line, indicating strong model fidelity across the full dose range.

Such increasing error variance at higher dose rates is a common challenge in regression problems with skewed or heavy-tailed target distributions. This insight points toward future improvements, such as integrating additional temporal or contextual features, or employing loss functions weighted to penalize large errors more heavily. Figure 13 presents a scatter plot comparing true and predicted dose values for SELENE, illustrating a strong correlation and close clustering along the ideal $y = x$ line, with most predictions falling within a narrow band around the ground truth.

### 4.7 Future Directions

Building on the current findings, several avenues exist for further enhancing lunar radiation dose prediction models:

- **Temporal features**: Incorporating lagged flux measurements or rolling statistics may enable the models to better capture delayed radiation effects.
- **Shielding parameters**: Integrating spacecraft or habitat shielding data could provide more realistic dose estimates for astronaut safety assessments.
- **Real-time deployment**: Assessing inference speed and memory requirements to enable onboard, low-power prediction on lunar missions.

## 5 Conclusion

As space exploration advances, continued lunar missions are essential to prepare for deeper exploration into the solar system. However, the Moon's harsh radiation environment—due to its lack of atmosphere and shielding—poses a serious risk to human explorers, especially during solar flares and coronal mass ejections. While existing models, such as those by Dobynde et al. [1] and Gurav et al. [8], offer accurate predictions using detailed simulations and imagery, they often require extensive computational resources or high-fidelity data. In contrast, SELENE demonstrates that fast, lightweight, and effective radiation forecasting is possible even with noisy input data. By enabling real-time risk assessment in resource-constrained environments, SELENE represents a critical step toward safer, more sustainable lunar exploration. Future work could focus on improving predictive accuracy through multimodal data integration and extending the model to support mission planning for Mars and beyond.

## References

1. Dobynde, M., Guo, J.: The REDMoon model: radiation environment and dose rates on the lunar surface and subsurface. In: 44th COSPAR Scientific Assembly. Held 16-24 July, vol. 44, p. 2697, provided by the SAO/NASA Astrophysics Data System (2022). https://doi.org/10.1029/2021JE006930. Accessed 22 Jun 2025
2. Du, Y.-L., Song, X., Luo, X.: Deep learning the forecast of galactic cosmic-ray spectra. arXiv preprint arXiv:2410.21046 (2024). https://doi.org/10.48550/arXiv.2410.21046. Accessed 12 Jun 2025
3. Wimmer-Schweingruber, R.F.: The lunar lander neutron and dosimetry (IND) experiment on chang'E 4. Space Sci. Rev. **216**, 104 (2020). https://doi.org/10.1007/s11214-020-00725-3. Accessed 26 Jun 2025
4. Zhang, S., Wimmer-Schweingruber, R.F., Yu, J., Wang, C., Fu, Q.: First measurements of the radiation dose on the lunar surface. Sci. Adv. **6**, eaaz1334 (2020). https://doi.org/10.1126/sciadv.aaz1334. Accessed 27 Jun 2025
5. Singleterry, R.C., Blattnig, S.R.: Oltaris: on-line tool for the assessment of radiation in space. NASA, Tech. Rep. NASA/TP-2010-216962 (2010). https://doi.org/10.1016/j.actaastro.2010.09.022. Accessed 18 Jun 2025
6. Slaba, T.C., Norman, R.B., Reddell, B.D.: Faster heavy ion transport for hzetrn. NASA Langley Research Center, Tech. Rep. NASA/TP-2013-217803 (2013). https://doi.org/10.1016/j.jcp.2010.09.010. Accessed 20 Jun 2025
7. Papagiannopoulos, G.P., Charisi, N.D., Floros, I., Tsagouri, I., Vennerstrøm, S.: Forecasting solar energetic proton fluxes with bidirectional Lstm neural networks. J. Space Weather and Space Clim., **13**, 1–16 (2023). https://doi.org/10.48550/arXiv.2309.11636. Accessed 14 Jun 2025
8. Zampieri, L., Wörsdörfer, G., Schwadron, N.: Probabilistic forecasting of radiation exposure for spaceflight. arXiv preprint arXiv:2411.20631 (2024). https://doi.org/10.48550/arXiv.2411.17703. Accessed 16 Jun 2025
9. Looper, M.D., et al.: Long-term observations of galactic cosmic ray let spectra in lunar orbit by LRO/crater. Space Weather, **18** (2020). https://doi.org/10.1029/2020SW002543. Accessed 24 Jun 2025

10. Stone, E.C., et al.: The solar isotope spectrometer (sis) for the advanced composition explorer. Space Sci. Rev. **86**, 357–408 (1998). https://doi.org/10.1023/A:1005027929871. Accessed 29 Jun 2025
11. Cummings, A.C., Stone, E.C., Heikkila, B., Christian, E.R.: The cosmic ray isotope spectrometer (cris) for the advanced composition explorer. Space Sci. Rev. **86**, 285–295 (1998). https://doi.org/10.1023/A:1005075813033. Accessed 30 Jun 2025
12. Spence, H.E., et al.: Crater: the cosmic ray telescope for the effects of radiation on the LRO mission. Space Sci. Rev. **150**, 243–284 (2010). https://doi.org/10.1007/s11214-009-9584-8. Accessed 25 Jun 2025
13. Stone, E.C., et al.: The advanced composition explorer. Space Sci. Rev. **86**, 1–22 (1998). https://doi.org/10.1023/A:1005082526237. Accessed 28 Jun 2025
14. Chen, T., Guestrin, C.: Xgboost: a scalable tree boosting system. In: Proceedings of the 22nd ACM SIGKDD International Conference on Knowledge Discovery and Data Mining, pp. 785–794 (2016). https://doi.org/10.48550/arXiv.1603.02754. Accessed 2 Jul 2025
15. Somepalli, G., Goldblum, M., Schwarzschild, A., Bruss, C.B., Goldstein, T.: Saint: improved neural networks for tabular data via row attention and contrastive pre-training. arXiv preprint arXiv:2106.01342 (2021). https://doi.org/10.48550/arXiv.2106.01342. Accessed 1 Jul 2025

# Machine and Deep Learning for AI Text Detection

Li-jing Arthur Chang(✉)

Department of Journalism and Media Studies, Jackson State University, Jackson, MS, USA
li-jing.a.chang@jsums.edu

**Abstract.** The study compared several deep learning and machine learning algorithms to see their performance in detecting AI-generated text. Results showed the RoBERTa algorithm has the highest accuracy, followed by its deep learning counterparts like BERT, LSTM, and Bi-LSTM. The performance of these deep learning algorithms excels that of the machine learning algorithms tested such as support vector machine, logistic regression, Naïve Bayes, and random forests.

**Keywords:** AI text detection · deep learning · machine learning · model performance

## 1 Introduction

With the increasing popularity of generative AI (artificial intelligence) interfaces such as ChatGPT, AI-generated text has gradually impacted many facets of society, including education, journalism, politics, and economics [1–4]. For example, detecting AI text in student assignments have become a major tasks for many teachers [1]. Also, the prevalence of AI-generated fake news could mislead readers [2]. In addition, AI-derived misinformation could impact election campaigns and financial markets [3, 4]. Therefore, the capability to distinguish between AI-created and human-written text have become increasingly crucial for many daily tasks. The study aims to explore a few deep learning and machine learning algorithms to see which ones perform better in spotting AI-generated text.

## 2 Literature Review

### 2.1 Research on Detection of AI Text

Text classification tasks using machine learning and deep learning methods are usually more effective than the dictionary-based classification methods [5]. In the past, several deep learning and machine algorithms are commonly used to spot AI-derived text.

In terms of deep learning, BERT (Bidirectional Encoder Representations from Transformers) and RoBERTa (Robustly Optimized BERT Approach), two very related algorithms, usually achieve high accuracy rates when the sample sizes are sufficiently large


R. Stahlbock et al. (Eds.): CSCE 2025, CCIS 2938, pp. 108–116, 2027.
https://doi.org/10.1007/978-3-032-22196-4_8

[6]. Other deep learning performers include LSTM (Long Short-Term Memory) and Bi-LSTM (Bilateral LSTM) [7].

As for machine learning, several algorithms are commonly used, including logistic regression, support vector machine, random forests, and Naïve Bayes [8–11]. Among the four, logistic regression and support vector machine tend to have higher accuracy rates than random forests and Naïve Bayes [12–15].

## 2.2 Deep Learning Algorithms

Deep learning algorithms usually can achieve higher accuracy rates for text classification when the sample size is sufficiently large. The advantages of deep learning for text classification include the leveraging of pretrained models (such as the cases of RoBERTa and BERT), attention mechanism (e.g., BERT), and capturing of contextual information (for instance, LSTM and Bi-LSTM) [6, 7].

As the meaning of words are often contextual, deep learning algorithms are more capable of capture the nuances of the word meanings [6, 7]. Due to the huge size of modern language vocabulary, the pretrained models such as BERT and RoBERTa have the advantages to transfer the knowledge of the pre-trained models into the current tasks and enhance the accuracy rates [6].

One of the downsides of deep learning algorithms is that they often require more training time and resources [6, 7]. BERT, RoBERTa, LSTM, and Bi-LSTM belong to a family called neural network [6, 7]. At its simplest form, the architecture of deep neural network usually requires at least three or more layers of hidden neurons [5]. Built on a combination of multiple neural networks, LSTM is more complex than the basic form of neural network [7]. BERT and RoBERTa are even more complex than LSTM because the former two involve pretrained models [6].

Due to their complex architecture, another drawbacks of the deep learning algorithms is its black-box nature [16]. As so much of the training is inside "hidden" layers of neurons, no human can comprehend the process of the model development, let alone interpreting the model [16].

## 2.3 Machine Learning Algorithms

The main advantage of the machine learning algorithms is its simplicity in training. The machine learning algorithms are train on individual words, usually based on words in the documents after a TF-IDF transformation [17]. In other words, instead of having to learn from words and their contextual relationships, machine learning algorithms basically train individuals words without contextual information [17]. This simplistic approach save computational time and resources [18].

In addition, due to its more simplistic training architecture, it does not require a lot of data to train the model [19]. Therefore, the machine learning algorithms not only train faster, require less computation resources, and can perform well on small datasets.

## 2.4 Research Questions

The present study is designed to test the performance of the popular deep learning and machine learning algorithms in detecting AI-generated text.

RQ: Among deep learning and machine learning algorithms tested in the present study, which one(s) perform the best?

# 3 Methods

## 3.1 Dataset

The dataset used for the present study is HC3 [20]. The original dataset has 48,644 rows of data, including half as AI-generated text, and the other half as human-written text. After removing the missing values and then balancing the classes of AI and human text, the dataset was reduced to 47,730 rows, with half of them as AI text and the other half as human text.

## 3.2 Classification Algorithms

The study is designed to see how a group of popular deep learning and machine learning algorithms perform in terms of spotting AI-generated text. The deep learning algorithms include BERT, RoBERTa, LSTM, and Bi-LSTM. The machine learning algorithms include support vector machine, logistic regression, random forests, and Naïve Bayes.

## 3.3 Data Preprocessing and Model Training

For model training preparation, BERT and RoBERTa went through a similar process because the two algorithms are closely related. For both models, the raw text data was first tokenized and then set for the PyTorch format. The preprocessed data was then randomly split at an 80:20 ratio for train and test datasets. After this, a pretrained model was loaded before a trainer was specified to get ready for model training to start. The trained models (BERT and RoBERTa) were then built using the train dataset.

For the training of the other two deep learning algorithms—LSTM and Bi-LSTM—the text data was first preprocessed to have the same sequence length and vocabulary size. The preprocessed data was then randomly split at an 80:20 ratio for train and test datasets. After that, a training model was specified to include embedding and dropout layers (for LSTM) or an embedding layer (for Bi-LSTM), a LSTM layer or a Bidirectional layer (for Bi-LSTM), a dropout layer, and a dense layer. The trained models were built using the train dataset.

For the training of machine learning models, the text data was first tokenized through the TF-IDF procedure and then went through a PCA (principal component analysis) feature reduction process to reduce feature size. The size of PCA component number was chosen to be 2250 because the value prevents overfitting and serves as a point where the test accuracy (as measured by the logistic regression algorithm) stops increasing and train-test data accuracy keeps increasing (Fig. 1).

The preprocessed data was then randomly split at an 80:20 ratio for train and test datasets. The trained models were built using the training dataset. The model building includes a grid search process with 10-fold cross-validation to search for the hyperparameters that would give the highest accuracy rates.

### 3.4 Evaluations of Trained Models

After the training of deep learning models (BERT, RoBERTa, LSTM, and Bi-LSTM) and their machine learning counterparts (support vector machine, logistic regression, random forests, and Naïve Bayes), the trained models were tested on test dataset (which the models had never seen before) and were evaluated using metrics such accuracy, precision, recall, F1 score, and AUC/ROC.

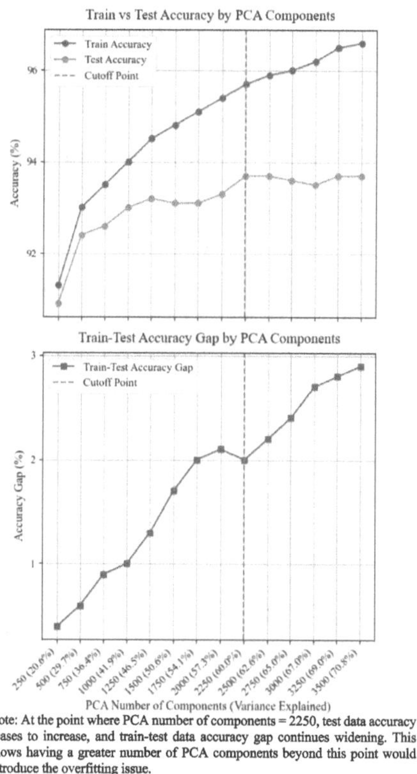


**Fig. 1.** Choice of PCA Number of Components (*to Minimize Overfitting*)

The first four metrics are based formulae calculated on the four elements: TP (true positive), FP (false positive), TN (true negative), and FN (false negative).

The formulae for the four metrics are as followed [21, 22]:

$$Accuracy = \frac{(TP + TN)}{(TP + TN + FP + FN)}$$

$$Precision = \frac{TP}{(TP + FP)}$$

$$Recall = \frac{TP}{(TP + FN)}$$

$$F1 = \frac{(2 \times Precision \times Recall)}{(Precision + Recall)}$$

The last metric after the above four, AUC/ROC, evaluates the models' ability to differentiate between the classes for all possible classification thresholds [23].

## 4 Results

The present study seeks to compare popular deep learning algorithms (BERT, RoBERTa, LSTM, and Bi-LSTM) and their machine learning counterparts (support vector machine, logistic regression, random forests, and Naïve Bayes). The trained model for each algorithm was first tested with the test dataset and the test results were assessed with four metrics based on TP, TN, FP, and FN: Accuracy, precision, recall, and F1 score.

### 4.1 M. Accuracy, Precision, Recall, and F1 Score

In terms of accuracy, RoBERTa leads with 0.996, followed by BERT with 0.986, LSTM (0.968), Bi-LSTM (0.966), support vector machine (0.948), logistic regression (0.937), Naïve Bayes (0.819), and random forests (0.800) (see Table 1).

**Table 1.** Model Accuracy, Precision, Recall, and F1 Score

| Algorithm | Evaluation Metrics | | | | |
|---|---|---|---|---|---|
| | Accuracy | Precision | Recall | F1 | AUC |
| RoBERTa | 0.996 | 0.992 | 1.000 | 0.996 | 1.000 |
| BERT | 0.986 | 0.973 | 0.999 | 0.986 | 1.000 |
| LSTM | 0.968 | 0.981 | 0.954 | 0.967 | 0.995 |
| Bi-LSTM | 0.966 | 0.985 | 0.947 | 0.966 | 0.994 |
| SVM | 0.948 | 0.947 | 0.946 | 0.947 | 0.987 |
| LR | 0.937 | 0.938 | 0.933 | 0.936 | 0.984 |
| NB | 0.819 | 0.807 | 0.831 | 0.819 | 0.900 |
| RF | 0.800 | 0.781 | 0.824 | 0.802 | 0.884 |

Notes: SVM (support vector machine), LR (logistic regression), NB (Naïve Bayes), and RF (random forests).

Overall, across all four metrics, RoBERTa is also the top performer. The runner-up overall is BERT, which is the second highest in accuracy, recall, and F1 score. The third place is LSTM, which ranks third in accuracy, recall, and F1 score while occupying the second place in precision.

In addition, the deep learning algorithms (BERT, RoBERTa, LSTM, and Bi-LSTM) perform better than their machine learning counterparts across the board in the four evaluation metrics.

### 4.2 AUC/ROC

AUC-ROC refers to the area under the ROC (Receiver Operating Characteristic) curve, which is a performance metric for classification problems at various thresholds [23]. The higher the AUC the better the classifier perform, with 1.000 as the best possible value [23].

In terms of AUC, BERT and RoBERTa leads with 1.000, followed by LSTM (0.995), Bi-LSTM (0.994), SVM (0.987), LR (0.984), NB (0.900), and RF (0.884) (Table 1). Once again, the deep learning algorithms perform better than their machine learning counterparts. Echoing AUC finding is the ROC curves, as shown in Fig. 2.

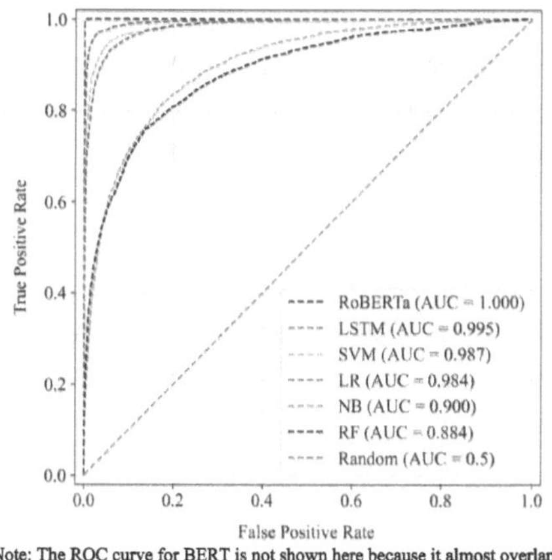


Note: The ROC curve for BERT is not shown here because it almost overlaps with its counterpart for RoBERTa. Likewise, the ROC curce for Bi-LSTM is not shown here because it nearly overlaps with that of LSTM.

**Fig. 2.** ROC Curves of Deep Learning, Machine Learning Models

Figure 2 shows the models with ROC curve closer to the left and upper lines of the chart have larger AUC and therefore are deemed to perform better in their classification tasks [23].

## 5 Discussion

Among the eight deep learning and machine learning algorithms, RoBERTa performs the best in all performance metrics including accuracy, precision, recall, F1 score, and AUC. BERT is the second best performer in four of the five performance metrics. Judging from the overall consideration of the metrics, LSTM and Bi-LSTM are the third and fourth top performers. Overall, the current study found that the transformer-based algorithms such as RoBERTa and BERT outperform their sequence-based counterparts like LSTM and Bi-LSTM. This is not surprising given that transformer-based algorithms can transfer prior learning into current models and thereby may capture more nuances of word contextual information than the simpler sequence-based algorithms.

Also, the study found that deep learning models perform better than their traditional machine learning counterparts. These findings make sense because the former are able to capture contextual information of words and the later cannot. The contextual information is important in understanding the linguistic meaning of words, which are often interpreted based on context. The machine learning algorithm of Naïve Bayes, for example, does not perform well compared to its deep learning counterparts because of its simplistic assumption that different words are not related to each other.

However, due to their simpler assumptions that words can be used to build models without considering their relationships, machine learning algorithms often do not require large computation resources and time to train the models and do not require a large dataset to train. For simpler text documents, machine learning algorithms may outshine their deep learning counterparts because of speed and efficiency.

Nevertheless, as the ChatGPT and other generate AI chatbots keep creating text on demands, the task of detecting AI-generated text is not easy. As AI-generated tasks are becoming more and more diverse and abundant, deep learning algorithms with large datasets may be more capable of detecting the growing nuances of AI text and provide better determination of whether the text is human written or not.

## 6 Conclusion

The present study found deep learning algorithms perform better than their traditional machine learning counterparts. Part of the reasons for this phenomenon may be due to the deep learning algorithms' strength in capturing contextual information, which is often important in determining the meanings of individual words. Among the deep learning algorithms, transformer-based algorithms like RoBERTa and BERT perform better than their sequence-based counterparts such as LSTM and Bi-LSTM because the former use pre-trained models to strengthen their interpretation of the words' contextual information.

Deep learning algorithms, armed with the ability to capture contextual information from words, are more suitable in the detection of the ever-growing AI-generated text than their machine learning counterparts. While the present study utilitized more than 47,000 rows of text data, future research on the detection of AI text could benefit from bigger datasets to train models capable of capture more nuances of AI text.

In addition, future researchers could explore other deep learning algorithms like DistilBERT, XLNet, and CNNs to detect AI-generated text given that such detection is increasingly needed [24, 25].

## References

1. Safi, R., Naini, A.J.: The work of students and ChatGPT compared: using machine learning to detect and characterize AI-generated text. In: AMCIS (2023)
2. Xu, D., Fan, S., Kankanhalli, M.: Combating misinformation in the era of generative AI models. In: Proceedings of the 31st ACM International Conference on Multimedia, pp. 9291–9298 (2023)
3. Shukla, A.K., Tripathi, S.: AI-generated misinformation in the election year 2024: measures of European Union. Front. Polit. Sci. **6**, 1451601 (2024)
4. Karaş, Z.: Effects of AI-generated misinformation and disinformation on the economy. Düzce Üniversitesi Bilim Ve Teknol. Derg. **12**(4), 2349–2360 (2024)

5. Chang, L.A.: detecting Asian values in Asian news via machine learning text classification. In: Stahlbock, R., Weiss, G.M., Abou-Nasr, M., Yang, C.-Y., Arabnia, H.R., Deligiannidis, L. (eds.) Advances in Data Science and Information Engineering. TCSCI, pp. 123–128. Springer, Cham (2021). https://doi.org/10.1007/978-3-030-71704-9_8
6. Martín-Gutiérrez, D., Hernández-Peñaloza, G., Hernández, A.B., Lozano-Diez, A., Álvarez, F.: A deep learning approach for robust detection of bots in twitter using transformers. IEEE Access **9**, 54591–54601 (2021)
7. Wani, M.A., ElAffendi, M., Shakil, K.A.: AI-generated spam review detection framework with deep learning algorithms and natural language processing. Computers **13**(10), 2073–2431 (2024)
8. Sharif, O., Hoque, M.M., Kayes, A., Nowrozy, R., Sarker, I.H.: Detecting suspicious texts using machine learning techniques. Appl. Sci. **10**(18), 6527 (2020)
9. Alamleh, H., AlQahtani, A.A.S., ElSaid, A.: Distinguishing human-written and ChatGPT-generated text using machine learning. In: 2023 Systems and Information Engineering Design Symposium (SIEDS), pp. 154–158. IEEE (2023)
10. Levin, G., Meyer, R., Guigue, P.-A., Brezinov, Y.: It takes one to know one—machine learning for identifying OBGYN abstracts written by ChatGPT. Int. J. Gynecol. Obstet. **165**(3), 1257–1260 (2024)
11. Greco, F., Desolda, G., Esposito, A., Carelli, A., et al.: David versus goliath: can machine learning detect LLM-generated text? A case study in the detection of phishing emails. In: The Italian Conference on CyberSecurity (2024)
12. Hayawi, K., Shahriar, S., Mathew, S.S.: The imitation game: detecting human and AI-generated texts in the era of ChatGPT and BARD. J. Inf. Sci., 01655515241227531 (2024)
13. Najjar, A.A., Ashqar, H.I., Darwish, O.A., Hammad, E.: Detecting AI-generated text in educational content: leveraging machine learning and explainable AI for academic integrity. ArXiv Prepr. ArXiv250103203 (2025)
14. Nguyen, T.T., Hatua, A., Sung, A.H.: How to detect AI-generated texts? In: 2023 IEEE 14th Annual Ubiquitous Computing, Electronics & Mobile Communication Conference (UEMCON), pp. 0464–0471. IEEE (2023)
15. Oghaz, M.M., Saheer, L.B., Dhame, K., Singaram, G.: Detection and classification of ChatGPT-generated content using deep transformer models. Front. Artif. Intell. **8**, 1458707 (2025)
16. Mitchell, T.: Mach. Learn. (1997)
17. Qaiser, S., Ali, R.: Text mining: use of TF-IDF to examine the relevance of words to documents. Int. J. Comput. Appl. **181**(1), 25–29 (2018)
18. Kumar, A., Goyal, S., Varma, M.: Resource-efficient machine learning in 2 kb ram for the Internet of Things. In: International Conference on Machine Learning, pp. 1935–1944. PMLR (2017)
19. Cui, Z.: Machine learning and small data. Educ. Meas. Issues Pract. **40**(4), 8–12 (2021)
20. Su, Z., Wu, X., Zhou, W., Ma, G., Hu, S.: HC3 plus: a semantic-invariant human ChatGPT comparison corpus. arXiv Prepr. arXiv230902731 (2023)
21. Sokolova, M., Lapalme, G.: A systematic analysis of performance measures for classification tasks. Inf. Process. Manag. **45**(4), 427–437 (2009)
22. Provost, F., Fawcett, T.: Robust classification for imprecise environments. Mach. Learn. **42**, 203–231 (2001)
23. Fawcett, T.: An introduction to ROC analysis. Pattern Recognit. Lett. **27**(8), 861–874 (2006)
24. Akpatsa, S., et al.: Online news sentiment classification using distilbert. J. Quantum Comput. **4**(1), 1 (2022)

25. Luan, Y., Lin, S.: Research on text classification based on CNN and LSTM. In: 2019 IEEE International Conference on Artificial Intelligence and Computer Applications (ICAICA), pp. 352–355. IEEE (2019)

# Using Generative AI and Multi-agent LLM Architectures for Topic Summarization and Segmentation for Long Lists of Educational Videos

Oscar Yllan Garza[1(✉)], Luz María Gonzalez Ureña[2,3], and Francisco Javier Cantú Ortiz[3]

[1] Tecnologico de Monterrey, Av. Eugenio Garza Sada 2501 Sur, Tecnológico, Monterrey, NL 64700, Mexico
oscaryllang.professional@gmail.com
[2] Springer Nature, Berlin, Germany
[3] World Congress in Computer Science, Computer Engineering & Applied Computing, Las Vegas, USA
atti.davis@springernature.com
https://www.american-cse.org/csce2025/

**Abstract.** The development of advanced tools to enhance education and learning is critical to sustaining the rapid pace of human progress. This paper presents the outcomes of a research and development effort spanning several months, aimed at creating software systems using **Generative AI, Large Language Models, and multi-agent RAG Systems** capable of ingesting from different file types (e.g., Excel, Word documents) containing YouTube links to perform **temporal topic segmentation**, **semantic summarization**, and **generative content creation** to support student learning.

We propose a novel system for the automated segmentation and summarization of educational videos, grounded in the thesis work of Oscar Yllan Garza [1]. Two distinct architectures are introduced and evaluated: a **single-agent pipeline** leveraging GPT-4, and a **multi-agent Retrieval-Augmented Generation (RAG)** system that integrates GPT-4 and Claude 3.5 using the LangChain and ChromaDB frameworks.

The system enhances the educational video experience by automatically detecting thematic shifts, generating human-readable summaries, and recommending precise video segments based on user-defined queries. The methodology combines **state-of-the-art NLP techniques**, including **retrieval-augmented generation**, **vector-based document indexing**, and **prompt engineering**, to deliver personalized and efficient content navigation.

Empirical evaluations conducted on a dataset of 90 educational videos show measurable improvements in **search precision**, **topic accessibility**, and **user engagement**. These results demonstrate the potential of **generative AI** and **multi-agent LLM architectures** to significantly improve the efficiency, accessibility, and personalization of video-based learning platforms.


R. Stahlbock et al. (Eds.): CSCE 2025, CCIS 2938, pp. 117–128, 2027.
https://doi.org/10.1007/978-3-032-22196-4_9

**Keywords:** Large Language Models · Multi-RAG Agents · Topic Modeling · Multi-Agent Architectures

## 1 Introduction

The exponential rise of video content on platforms such as YouTube and other educational repositories has made an unparalleled amount of knowledge readily accessible. From technical tutorials to full academic lectures, learners today can self-educate through a variety of domains. However, this abundance also creates a challenge: efficiently navigating and extracting relevant knowledge from unstructured, lengthy videos [1].

Despite the vast availability of educational material, learners encounter several barriers. The decline in digital attention span hinders sustained focus on long-form content [2]. Moreover, much of this material lacks systematic organization, and even high-quality resources—such as those from MIT OpenCourseWare [3], Stanford, Oxford, UC Berkeley, and FreeCodeCamp—consist of videos lasting from 40 min to several hours.

Cognitive and neuro-learning research has reported a stagnation of the long-term cognitive improvement trend known as the Flynn Effect [4], while academic demands continue to intensify. Students have the necessity of learning faster and from different academic fields, making a relevant topic for developing tools that enhance cognitive efficiency and mitigate learning fatigue.

This paper, based on the master's thesis of Oscar Yllan [1], introduces a system for automated segmentation and summarization of educational videos using advanced Natural Language Processing (NLP) techniques. Its goal is to structure large repositories of unorganized video content, enabling concise, query-driven insights and targeted topic retrieval.

The underlying hypothesis is that integrating modern frameworks such as **Streamlit** for user interface design, **LangChain** for LLM orchestration, and **Multi-Agent Retrieval-Augmented Generation (RAG)** architectures leveraging state-of-the-art **Large Language Models (LLMs)**—can accurate make the processes topic segmentation and summarization. This integration substantially reduces study time and cognitive load associated with time spends watching long monotone videos.

The paper proceeds as follows: a review of related work and key methods; a description of single-agent and multi-agent architectures; experimental evaluation across academic video datasets; and a discussion of results, implications, and directions for future research.

## 2 Related Work

A comprehensive review of **state-of-the-art technologies** was conducted to identify methods addressing the challenges of educational video segmentation and summarization. Throughout the project, emerging tools and methodologies led the author, Oscar Yllan, to iteratively refine the research direction. Ultimately, a **novel approach** was adopted to overcome the limitations of earlier solutions.

This section highlights key studies and tools that informed the proposed system, with emphasis on recent advances in **Large Language Models (LLMs)**, **Retrieval-Augmented Generation (RAG)**, and **multi-agent systems** for topic segmentation.

### 2.1 LLM-Based Topic Segmentation in Educational Videos

A recent study introduced a **novel LLM-driven pipeline** for **temporal topic detection** in educational video transcripts [26]. The authors identified shortcomings of classical topic modeling methods such as **Latent Dirichlet Allocation (LDA)** and **BERTopic**, including limited semantic depth and weak adaptability to dynamic datasets. Their framework integrates models like **GPT-3.5** and **LLaMA2-7B** to generate coherent and interpretable topic structures. Although early outputs exhibited **overly general and overlapping topics**, the inclusion of metrics such as **Jaccard distance**, **semantic similarity**, and **precision/recall** improved interpretability and enabled real-time, zero-shot topic extraction [26].

### 2.2 TopicGPT: Topic Generation and Assignment

The **TopicGPT** framework [27] proposes a **two-stage LLM pipeline** for **topic generation and assignment**. Using a dataset of 1,000 legislative documents and 1,100 Wikipedia articles, **GPT-4** generates candidate topics while **GPT-3.5-turbo** assigns them to documents. Evaluation results demonstrate high semantic alignment and precision, confirming the effectiveness of LLMs for **fine-grained document classification** [27].

### 2.3 Multi-agent RAG Filtering for Noise Reduction

A key contribution in [28]—and a direct inspiration for this thesis—extends traditional RAG by introducing a **Multi-Agent Filtering mechanism** to mitigate **noisy retrievals**. Recognizing that irrelevant data can corrupt responses (*"garbage in, garbage out"*), the authors propose a **training-free, multi-agent RAG framework** where multiple LLM agents collaboratively filter retrieved documents to enhance contextual relevance and precision [28].

## 3 Methodology

### 3.1 Architecture of the First Program

**Program Functionality.** The first software module is designed to automate the processing of video content for educational and information retrieval purposes. Its functionality is structured as follows:

- **File Ingestion**: Users upload a document containing a list of YouTube video links.
- **Link Parsing**: The system parses and extracts individual video links from the uploaded file.
- **Transcript Generation**: For each video link, the system retrieves and processes the corresponding transcript.
- **Chapter Segmentation via LLM**: A **Large Language Model (LLM)** agent semantically analyzes the transcript and generates structured chapter divisions.
- **Chapter Output**: The generated chapter structure is displayed for user verification.
- **PDF Export**: The chaptered content for each video is compiled and exported into a structured PDF document.

**Secondary Software Module.** The second software module extends the functionality by incorporating personalized content retrieval based on user input:

- **API Credential Configuration**: Users input the necessary API keys for system access.
- **Document Upload**: Users upload the PDF file containing previously generated chapter data.
- **Query Input**: The system prompts the user to input a query representing the specific topics they wish to explore.
- **Video and Segment Recommendation**: Based on the user query, the system recommends the most relevant videos and corresponding time frames for targeted learning.
- **Contextual Summarization**: Summaries of the recommended video segments are generated to provide concise, topic-specific insights.

### 3.2 Architecture of the Second Program

The second program maintains a similar architecture but introduces variations for testing different LLMs as **Multi-RAG Agents**. APIs from **OpenAI** and **Claude** were utilized to compare model performance. This modular architecture allows quick adaptation to emerging LLMs by simply modifying parts of the code, an essential feature in a rapidly evolving AI landscape.

The primary objective is to streamline the retrieval, segmentation, and summarization of video content in a **scalable**, **modular**, and **reusable** framework.

### 3.3 System Architecture and Methodology

**Core Libraries and Frameworks.** The system integrates various Python-based libraries and frameworks to create an efficient and interactive data-processing pipeline:

- **Streamlit**: Enables rapid prototyping and deployment of interactive user interfaces.
- **YouTubeTranscript API**: Chosen over PyTube for transcript retrieval due to superior performance and fewer access constraints.
- **LangChain**: A powerful orchestration framework for LLM workflows, integrating:
  - **RecursiveCharacterTextSplitter**: Efficiently partitions text into manageable segments.
  - **OpenAI API**: Provides the LLM capabilities for semantic processing.
  - **LLMChain**: Enables structured and iterative interactions with the language model.
  - **PromptTemplate**: Ensures prompt consistency across multiple instances.
- **Additional Libraries**: Including `re`, `os`, `docx2txt`, `pandas`, `datetime`, `dotenv`, `io`, and `reportlab` for parsing, data manipulation, and report generation.

**Secure API Key Management.** API credentials are securely handled through environment variables defined in a `.env` file, ensuring:

- **Encapsulation**: Separation of credentials from core logic.
- **Security Compliance**: Prevention of sensitive data leakage.
- **Cost Control**: Protection against unauthorized API usage.

### 3.4 Data Processing Pipeline

**File Parsing and Link Extraction.** The system accepts input files in various formats (e.g., `.txt`, `.docx`, `.csv`), from which it extracts and validates YouTube video URLs using regular expressions.

**Transcript Retrieval with Timestamps.** Each valid URL undergoes the following processing steps:

- **Video ID Extraction**: Using regular expression parsing.
- **Transcript Retrieval**: Managed by the YouTubeTranscript API.
- **Timestamp Alignment**: Converts transcript segments to a standardized `hh:mm:ss` format for temporal indexing.

**Automated Chapter Generation.** An LLM-based agent performs semantic segmentation and chapter generation:

- **Template Definition**: Specifies the structure and format of chapter outputs.
- **Prompt Engineering**: Carefully designed prompts guide the LLM for consistent output.
- **Iterative Processing**: **LLMChain** processes long transcripts incrementally, maintaining coherence across chapters.

**PDF Report Generation.** The finalized chapter structures are compiled into a formatted PDF document using **reportlab**, facilitating easy distribution and archival.

**User Interface and Features.** The system features a web-based UI developed in **Streamlit**, including:

- **Document Upload Module**: Supports input files containing video URLs.
- **Chapter Generation Interface**: Triggers the complete processing pipeline and displays the generated results.

### 3.5 Outcomes and Contributions

The experimental results validate the system's effectiveness in delivering:

- **Secure API integration**
- **Automated video transcript extraction**
- **Context-aware chapter segmentation**
- **Scalable PDF reporting**
- **An intuitive and responsive user interface**

## 4 Experiments and Results

To evaluate the robustness and effectiveness of the proposed system, a series of experiments were conducted using diverse video datasets. The primary variables among these videos were their **topic domains**, **length**, and **depth of content**. It is essential to consider these differences to ensure that the system performs reliably across various lecture formats and content complexities.

The objective of the experiments was to assess how both software architectures respond to different input scenarios. The focus was on functionality, processing times, and qualitative feedback, while also comparing the performance between the two architectures. These insights aim to determine whether one architecture consistently outperforms the other in practice.

To strengthen the significance of the evaluation, several video sets were selected from **world-class academic institutions** such as **UC Berkeley** and **MIT**. These video collections provide an ideal testbed due to their high content quality and extensive length—features that pose meaningful challenges for automated segmentation and summarization.

In the following tables, we present a summary of the experimental trials, including execution time, qualitative satisfaction scores, and estimated time saved compared to a manual approach. The accompanying figures visualize the system's performance.

### 4.1 Single-Agent Architecture (ChatGPT-4.0)

(See Fig. 1 and Table 1)

**Table 1.** ChatGPT-4.0 API used for Topic Segmentation and Video Summarization

| List of Videos | Video Time | Ex. Time | Sat. (1–10) | Time Saved |
|---|---|---|---|---|
| UC Berk - CS162 | 9 h 25 min | 25 min | 8 | 9 h |
| Blender Tuts. | 9 h 12 min | 28 min | 7 | 10 h |
| AI Gen Music | 6 h 10 min | 26 min | 7 | 8 h |
| Pow Electr - MIT | 8 h 20 min | 29 min | 9 | 9 h |
| Quantum Phys - MIT | 9 h 32 min | 34 min | 8 | 11 h |

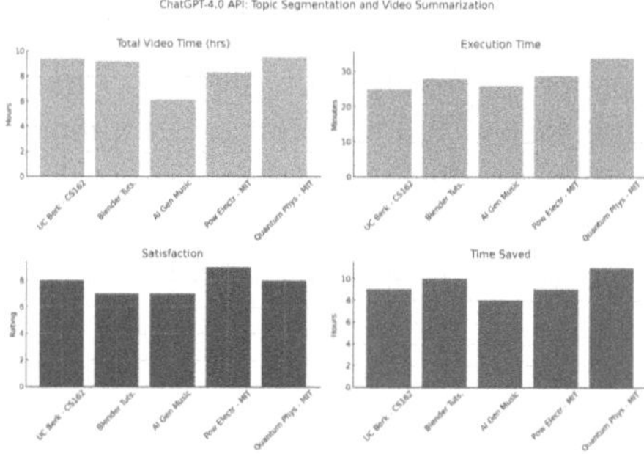


**Fig. 1.** Summary of a student query across a large lecture dataset from UC Berkeley's Operating Systems course

### 4.2 Multi-agent Architecture (ChatGPT-4.0 + Claude API)

(See Table 2)

**Table 2.** ChatGPT-4.0 + Claude API Multi-RAG Agent for Topic Segmentation and Summarization

| List of Videos | Video Time | Ex. Time | Sat. (1–10) | Saved T. |
|---|---|---|---|---|
| UC Berk - CS162 | 9 h 25 min | 28 min | 8 | 9 h |
| Blender Tuts. | 9 h 12 min | 26 min | 6 | 10 h |
| AI Gen Music | 6 h 10 min | 27 min | 6 | 8 h |
| Pow Electr - MIT | 8 h 20 min | 29 min | 8 | 9 h |
| Quant Phys - MIT | 9 h 32 min | 32 min | 7 | 11 h |

### 4.3 Explanation of the Tables

In the Tables that we observe the results where the most important columns is important to highlight that the column Video Time shows us how long is the total content that our program analyzes that in general are from 6–10 h of videos. In the Ex Time column means the execution time that the program took to give us the main results and the Sat (1–10) columns show us how was the satisfaction rank from users with the results.

The results indicate that both architectures perform efficiently in terms of **execution time**, with only minor variations. The **Single-Agent system** showed slightly higher satisfaction in some cases, particularly in creative domains like *AI Music*, whereas the **Multi-Agent system** demonstrated robustness in **technical academic content**.

In both architectures, the time saved compared to manual chaptering and summarization is substantial, averaging over **8 h saved per video set**. These results confirm the utility of integrating **LLMs and RAG agents** for scalable educational content analysis.

In this part of the paper we are representing in a visual form the performance of both architectures and we see that the metrics are almost same and really close but with a better perfomance in general with the only GPT architecture (Fig. 2).

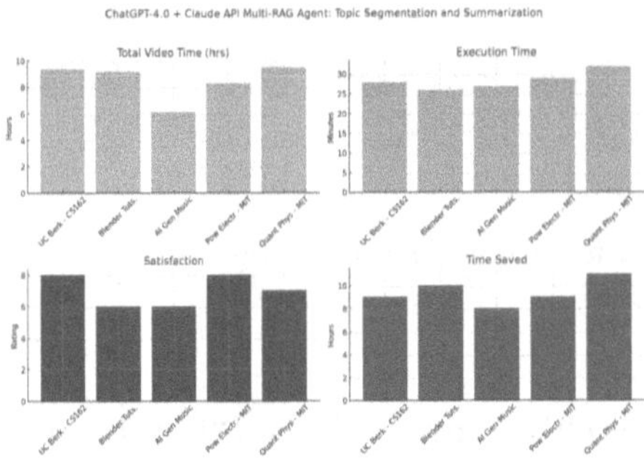


**Fig. 2.** Summary of a student query across a large lecture dataset from UC Berkeley's Operating Systems course

## 5 Discussion of Results

This section presents two key analyses that provide foundational insights for the subsequent sections on **Future Work** and **Conclusions**. The two focal points of discussion are: (1) the **impact on student learning efficiency**, and (2) the **performance comparison between the two system architectures**.

### 5.1 Analysis of the Impact for Students

One of the core goals of the system is to improve **learning efficiency** by reducing the time students need to spend watching full-length lecture videos. Students were asked to explore a topic of interest by submitting a general prompt. The system returned:

- **Three recommended videos**, selected from a larger dataset of educational content.
- **Precise timestamps** indicating the segments within those videos where the topic is discussed.
- **Contextual summaries** extracted directly from the relevant video transcript sections.

This process allowed students to **avoid watching 8+ h of video content**, instead focusing on highly relevant material. The system was therefore perceived as a valuable **learning assistant** that helps users study more efficiently (Fig. 3).

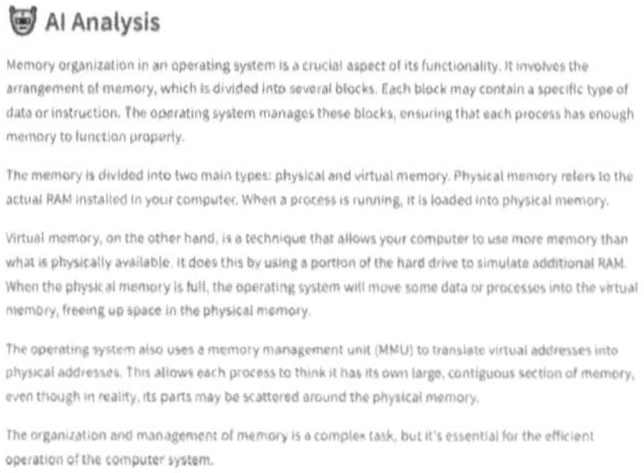

**Fig. 3.** Summary of a student query across a large lecture dataset from UC Berkeley's Operating Systems course

While the summary functionality is useful, the most impactful result comes from the **Topic Segmentation** capability, which enables users to locate the exact lecture segment covering their topic of interest (Fig. 4).

In the table from the Results section

### 5.2 Comparison Between Both Architectures

Based on the experimental data presented earlier, a comparison was conducted between the two system architectures:

- **Architecture 1**: Utilized only the **ChatGPT-4.0 API**.
- **Architecture 2**: Employed a **Multi-RAG Agent** incorporating both **ChatGPT-4.0 and Claude API**.

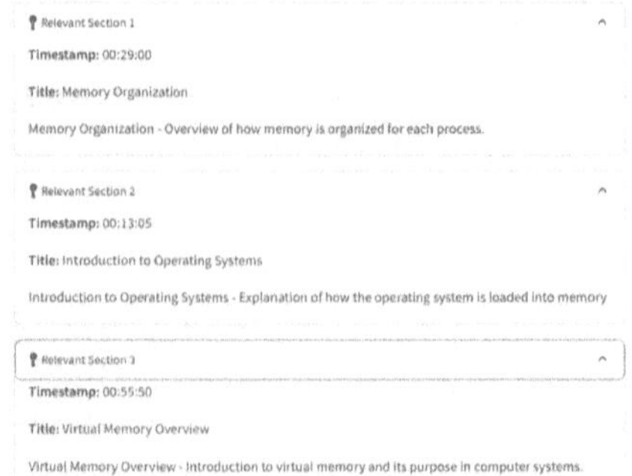


**Fig. 4.** Video recommendations with timestamp-based navigation with GPT-4.0 API

The results indicate that **Architecture 1** consistently outperformed **Architecture 2** in both **execution time** and **user satisfaction**. Specifically, GPT-4.0 demonstrated superior capabilities in:

- **Formatting consistency**
- **Understanding and extracting key content from long transcripts**
- **Generating coherent summaries**

Users rated the quality and relevance of the results higher for Architecture 1. In contrast, the Multi-Agent system involving Claude occasionally produced less structured or less relevant outputs, suggesting that GPT-4.0 remains more reliable for this specific application (Fig. 5).

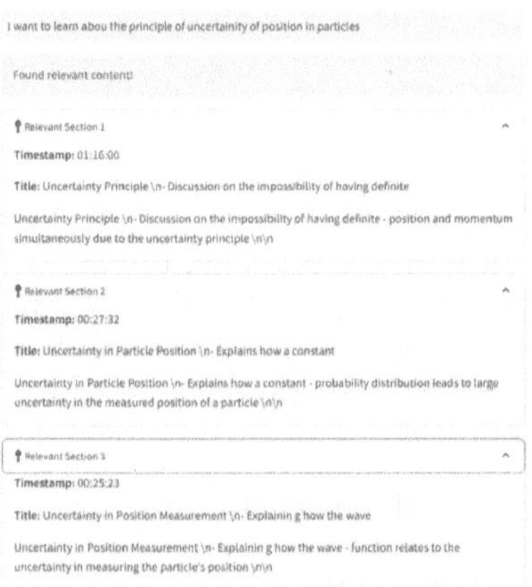


**Fig. 5.** Results from the second Architecture that makes use of the Claude and GPT Multi-RAG Agent TimeStamp Recommendation

Here we can also find a clever image of the result of the Software that implements the Claude and GPT Architecture showing how the format of Claude Fron-end output is below in quality when we compare it with the GPT output (Fig. 6).

AI Analysis


```
[
  0 :
  "TextBlock(citations=None, text='Based on the content sections provided, the
  uncertainty principle states that it is impossible to simultaneously have a
  definite position and momentum for a particle. This means that the more
  precisely you know a particle\'s position, the less precisely you can know its
  momentum, and vice versa.\n\nThe section "Uncertainty in Particle Position"
  explains that a constant probability distribution leads to a large uncertainty
  in the measured position of a particle. This means that if the probability of
  finding a particle is the same at all positions, it becomes difficult to
  determine its exact location.\n\nLastly, the "Uncertainty in Position
  Measurement" section relates the wave function to the uncertainty in measuring
  a particle\'s position. The wave function is a mathematical description of the
  quantum state of a particle, and it is used to calculate the probability of
  finding the particle at a specific location. The uncertainty in position
  measurement arises from the inherent properties of the wave function.\n\nIn
  summary, to learn about the principle of uncertainty of position in particles,
  you should focus on understanding the impossibility of simultaneously knowing a
  particle\'s exact position and momentum, the concept of constant probability
  distribution leading to large uncertainty in position, and how the wave
  function relates to the uncertainty in measuring a particle\'s position.',
  type='text')"
]
```


**Fig. 6.** Summary Generation using Claude and GPT Multi-RAG Agent

**Acknowledgment.** I want to thank my parents because without them and their support it would not be possible, also me for making me work and continue with the job even though I had some personal challenges, my advisors from my University, and finally developers and computer scientists that have worked really hard for us to have tools as LLMs and the frameworks for the multi agents architectures.

## References


1. Garza, O.Y.: Development and testing of a temporal topic detection algorithm applied for enhancing e-learning in high-school and college students, M.S. Thesis, School of Engineering and Sciences, Instituto Tecnológico y de Estudios Superiores de Monterrey, Monterrey, Mexico, February 2025
2. [Placeholder] Short attention spans nowadays
3. Massachusetts Institute of Technology: MIT OpenCourseWare. https://ocw.mit.edu/. Accessed 21 May 2025
4. [Empty]
5. [Empty]
6. Kapoor, S., Gil, A., Bhaduri, S., Mittal, A., Mulkar, R.: Qualitative Insights Tool (QualIT): LLM enhanced topic modeling. arXiv preprint arXiv:2409.15626, September 2024
7. Giorgi, J., et al.: TOPICAL: TOPIC pages automagically. arXiv preprint arXiv:2405.01796, May 2024. https://arxiv.org/abs/2405.01796
8. How does technology affect the attention spans of different age groups? OxJournal https://www.oxjournal.org/how-does-technology-affect-the-attentionspans-of-different-age-groups/?utm_source=chatgpt.com. Accessed 5 February 2025
9. Newman, D., et al.: Automatic evaluation of topic coherence. In: Proceedings of the NAACL-HLT, Los Angeles, CA, USA, June 2010, pp. 100–108 (2010)

10. Chang, J., et al.: Reading tea leaves: how humans interpret topic models. In: Proceedings of the NeurIPS, Vancouver, Canada (2009)
11. Trabelsi, M., et al.: Time series language model for descriptive caption generation. arXiv preprint arXiv:2501.01832, January 2025. https://arxiv.org/abs/2501.01832
12. Golia, L., Kalita, J.: Action-item-driven summarization of long meeting transcripts. In: Proceedings of the NLPIR, Seoul, South Korea, December 2023. https://doi.org/10.1145/3639233.3639253
13. Deng, Z., et al.: Aspect-based meeting transcript summarization: a two-stage approach with weak supervision. arXiv preprint arXiv:2311.04292, November 2023. https://arxiv.org/abs/2311.04292
14. Fan, Y., et al.: Topic-Conversation Relevance (TCR) dataset and benchmarks. arXiv preprint arXiv:2411.00038, November 2024. https://arxiv.org/abs/2411.00038
15. Chen, Y., et al.: Learning to localize actions in instructional videos with LLM-based multi-pathway text-video alignment. arXiv preprint arXiv:2409.16145, September 2024
16. Cheng, D., et al.: Enhancing long video understanding via hierarchical event-based memory. arXiv preprint arXiv:2409.06299, September 2024
17. Zhang, C., et al.: Segment anything for videos: a systematic survey. IEEE J. LaTeX Class, August 2024. https://arxiv.org/abs/2408.08315
18. Adarve, F., Kwong, H., Speriosu, M.: Topic segmentation of meetings using lexical chains. CS224N Final Project, Spring 2007
19. Chang, T.-H., Lee, C.-H.: Topic segmentation for short texts. National Chiao Tung University, Taiwan
20. Wang, L., et al.: Learning to rank semantic coherence for topic segmentation. In: Proceedings of the EMNLP, Copenhagen, Denmark, September 2017 (2017)
21. Röder, M., Both, A., Hinneburg, A.: Exploring the space of topic coherence measures. In: Proceedings of the WSDM, Shanghai, China, February 2015. https://doi.org/10.1145/2684822
22. Rao, A.: Transcribing educational videos using Whisper. arXiv preprint arXiv:2307.03200, July 2023. https://arxiv.org/abs/2307.03200
23. Deng, Z., et al.: Aspect-based meeting transcript summarization: a two-stage approach with weak supervision. arXiv preprint arXiv:2311.04292, November 2023
24. Porjazovski, D., Grósz, T., Kurimo, M.: Topic identification for spontaneous speech. arXiv preprint arXiv:2307.11450 July 2023
25. Hua, Y., et al.: How did we get here? Summarizing conversation dynamics. arXiv preprint arXiv:2404.19007, April 2024
26. Mu, Y., et al.: Large language models offer an alternative to the traditional approach of topic modelling. arXiv preprint arXiv:2403.16248, March 2024. https://arxiv.org/abs/2403.16248
27. Pham, C.M., et al.: TopicGPT: a prompt-based topic modeling framework. arXiv preprint arXiv:2311.01449, April 2024. https://arxiv.org/abs/2311.01449
28. Chang, C.-Y., et al.: MAIN-RAG: multi-agent filtering retrieval-augmented generation. arXiv preprint arXiv:2501.00332, December 2024. https://arxiv.org/abs/2501.00332
29. Gao, Y., et al.: Retrieval-augmented generation for large language models: a survey. arXiv preprint arXiv:2312.10997, March 2024. https://arxiv.org/abs/2312.10997
30. Zhou, P., et al.: A survey on generative AI and LLM for video generation, understanding, and streaming. arXiv preprint arXiv:2404.16038, January 2024. https://arxiv.org/abs/2404.16038

# Semantic Risk Scoring of Aggregated Metrics: An AI-Driven Approach for Healthcare Data Governance

Mohammed Omer Shakeel Ahmed(✉)

University of Texas at Arlington, Dallas, TX, USA
omershakeel96@gmail.com

**Abstract.** Large healthcare institutions typically operate multiple business intelligence (BI) teams segmented by domain, including clinical performance, fundraising, operations, and compliance. Due to HIPAA, FERPA, and IRB restrictions, these teams face challenges in sharing patient-level data needed for analytics. To mitigate this, A metric aggregation table is proposed, which is a precomputed, privacy-compliant summary such as "Average Patient Wait Times by Department" or "Donor Conversion by Campaign." These abstractions enable decision-making without direct access to sensitive data. However, even aggregated metrics can inadvertently lead to privacy risks if constructed without rigorous safeguards. A modular AI framework is proposed that evaluates SQL-based metric definitions for potential overexposure using both semantic and syntactic features. Specifically, the system parses SQL queries into abstract syntax trees (ASTs), extracts sensitive patterns (e.g., fine-grained GROUP BY on ZIP code or gender), and encodes the logic using pretrained CodeBERT embeddings. These are fused with structural features and passed to an XGBoost classifier trained to assign risk scores. Queries that surpass the risk threshold (e.g., >0.85) are flagged and returned with human-readable explanations (e.g., "Metric may overexpose sensitive groupings like gender or ZIP"). This enables proactive governance, preventing statistical disclosure before deployment. This implementation demonstrates strong potential for cross-departmental metric sharing in healthcare while maintaining compliance and auditability. The system also promotes role-based access control (RBAC), supports zero-trust data architectures, and aligns with national data modernization goals by ensuring that metric pipelines are explainable, privacypreserving, and AI-auditable by design. Unlike prior works that rely on runtime data access to flag privacy violations, the proposed framework performs static, explainable detection at the query-

**Keywords:** Business Intelligence · Metric Aggregation · CodeBERT · AI · XGBoost


R. Stahlbock et al. (Eds.): CSCE 2025, CCIS 2938, pp. 129–139, 2027.
https://doi.org/10.1007/978-3-032-22196-4_10

## 1 Introduction

In today's data-driven healthcare systems, decisions are increasingly powered by metrics summarized values that describe key trends such as patient outcomes, treatment efficiency, or fundraising performance. The explosion of data science in the modern world has increased the importance of business intelligence, or BI, in the healthcare industry. The healthcare industry generates a lot of data from patients, processes, tests, research, and operations [1]. Business analytics(BA) in healthcare research offers numerous valuable insights that can enhance patient care and hospital performance [2] Compared to data warehouses in non-healthcare settings, those in healthcare settings may focus more on privacy and security of protected health information, as well as compliance with federal and state regulations and organizational policies [3]. Metrics are especially important in healthcare, where hospitals must continuously measure performance to improve care, manage operations, and demonstrate impact. Business Intelligence (BI) tools enable health institutions to make data-informed decisions by transforming large volumes of clinical and administrative data into actionable insights.

For example, using metrics to monitor readmission rates or treatment success helps hospital leadership identify areas for improvement. Such health performance metrics are essential for optimizing both patient outcomes and financial sustainability [1]. However, many large hospitals and research institutions have multiple BI teams focused on patient outcomes, another on billing, another on fundraising. These teams often need to collaborate, but they can't always share data freely. The reason? Patient-level data often contains personally identifiable information (PII) or protected health information (PHI), which is tightly regulated under laws like HIPAA and FERPA. This creates a problem when one team (e.g., the fundraising team) needs information owned by another (e.g., the clinical team), but accessing raw data directly would violate privacy policies. This is where aggregated metrics become essential. Instead of exposing individual records, teams can share high-level summaries like "average donation per patient type" or "total readmissions per quarter." These metrics are usually stored in aggregated metric tables, which represent rolled-up versions of raw data [4]. Instead of accessing sensitive patient-level records, teams can rely on these tables to answer important questions like, "What is the average emergency room wait time?" or "How many donations did each campaign receive last quarter?". However, even aggregated metrics can be risky. If a metric is based on a very small group of patients or includes fields like ZIP code or gender, it could still reveal sensitive information.

To solve this, the paper proposes an novel AI-powered system that checks whether a metric is safe to share before it is used. This tool automatically analyzes the SQL query used to build the metric and evaluates whether it might accidentally reveal private data. It flags risky metrics that are too detailed or too narrow, and explains why they should be revised. The goal is to help BI teams work together while protecting privacy and staying compliant with regulations. Unlike older approaches that wait until after data is accessed or published, this system works ahead of time, giving teams instant feedback and peace of mind. It's modular, meaning it can fit into existing BI processes, and it helps create a secure environment for collaboration especially important in healthcare, where data privacy and ethical AI use are top priorities.

## 2 Background and Related Work

### 2.1 Metric Abstraction and Aggregation

Metric tables, also referred to as aggregated metric datasets, are essential components in modern business intelligence (BI) pipelines. These tables contain precalculated, high-level statistical summaries such as averages, counts, or rates derived from underlying raw datasets. Rather than storing individual transactions or patient-level data, metric tables capture key performance indicators (KPIs) and other decision-driving metrics in an abstracted format [4].

Proposed architecture using aggregated metric tables and reporting clusters with role-based access, supporting secure metric sharing. Model facilitates access to granular information, it significantly increases the risk of exposing sensitive or personally identifiable information (PII), particularly in regulated domains such as healthcare or finance. When multiple teams consume the same raw datasets, inconsistencies in interpretation and logic, as well as unintended privacy violations, can arise.

To address these challenges, a more secure and governed architecture leverages aggregated metric tables, as shown in Fig. 2. In this model, only the metric-owning team maintains access to the underlying raw data and is solely responsible for defining the metric logic. These finalized metrics, preaggregated, anonymized, and validated, are then stored in a centralized metric table that can be accessed organizationwide. This architecture offers two key benefits. First, it minimizes privacy risks by preventing unnecessary exposure to raw data while still supporting analytical needs across departments. Second, it enforces metric consistency and lineage. Since only the owner team controls the logic and transformation rules, any updates or refinements made to the metric automatically propagate downstream to all consumers, ensuring synchronization and reducing the chances of metric drift. This approach strengthens governance, enhances compliance readiness, and supports scalable data collaboration across business units.

While metric tables improve governance, they are not inherently immune to privacy risks. A core concern lies in reidentification attacks, particularly in scenarios involving small- N aggregates (e.g., average age of patients in a rural ZIP code). Such summaries can reveal sensitive patterns when group sizes are small or categories are narrowly defined. Attribute inference is another risk, in which an attacker leverages a machine learning classifier to infer a target user's private attributes (e.g., location, sexual orientation, political view) from its public data (e.g., rating scores, page likes) [5]. Furthermore, statistical leakage can occur when changes in an individual record disproportionately impact the metric (e.g., mean income in a group of three). These risks are amplified when metrics are published externally or shared across loosely governed teams. The leaking of confidential data to unauthorized entities can result in various problems for organizations and individuals. Similar to trade secrets, health records and banking details, leaks can affect the privacy of patients, and the security of accounts [6] Therefore, while aggregation offers a layer of protection, it is not foolproof without careful design and validation mechanisms. Several privacy-preserving frameworks have been proposed to address the risks inherent in data sharing and aggregation. As Organization scale and grow, the need for using data for decision making increases. However, such disclosures of personal health information even within the organizations raise serious privacy concerns. To alleviate such concerns, it is possible to anonymize the data before disclosure.

One popular anonymization approach is kanonymity [7]. Which ensures that each record is indistinguishable from at least k-1 others on selected quasi-identifiers. While k-anonymity is effective for tabular data publication, it is limited when applied to aggregate metrics, as it does not consider the effect of small group sizes on statistical summaries. Differential privacy is the standard privacy protection technology that provides rigorous privacy guarantees for various data. This survey summarizes and analyzes differential privacy solutions to protect unstructured data content before it is shared with untrusted parties [8], it offers a more robust mathematical guarantee by introducing calibrated noise to outputs. Moreover, most legacy validation systems are static based on handwritten rules and thresholds for column inclusion or minimum counts. These lack adaptability to evolving metric definitions and do not generalize well across organizations. In contrast, the proposed AI-driven framework evaluates metriclevel SQL queries dynamically, using semantic understanding and syntactic structure to estimate re-identification risk, filling a critical gap in current governance strategies (Figs. 1 and 3).

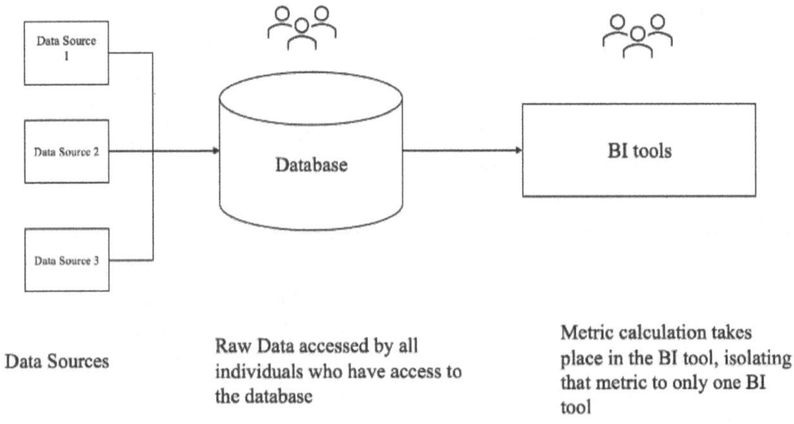


**Fig. 1.** Traditional BI architecture where raw data is directly accessed by multiple users, and metrics are computed within isolated BI tools.

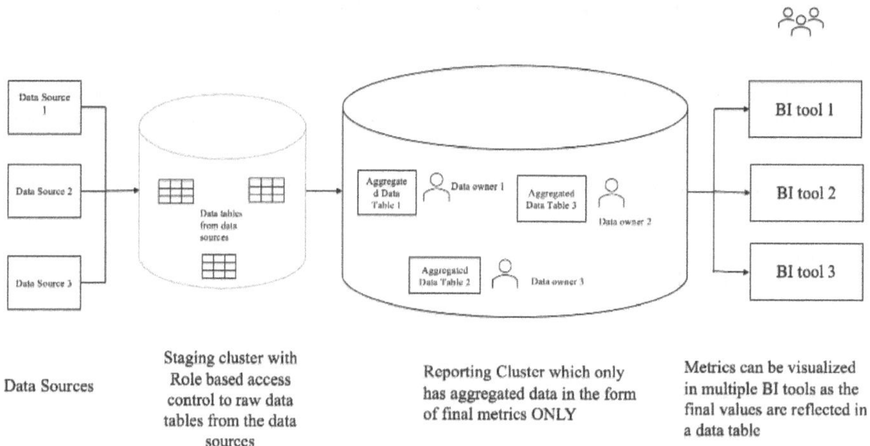


**Fig. 2.** Proposed architecture using aggregated metric tables and reporting clusters with role-based access, supporting secure metric sharing.

## 3 System Architecture Overview

The proposed system is designed to assess whether a metric-generating SQL query risks overexposing sensitive information, such as gender or ZIP code, particularly when aggregation sizes are small. The workflow comprises five main stages. This pipeline is tailored for deployment within metric abstraction layers of BI systems, especially in privacyregulated environments like healthcare institutions:

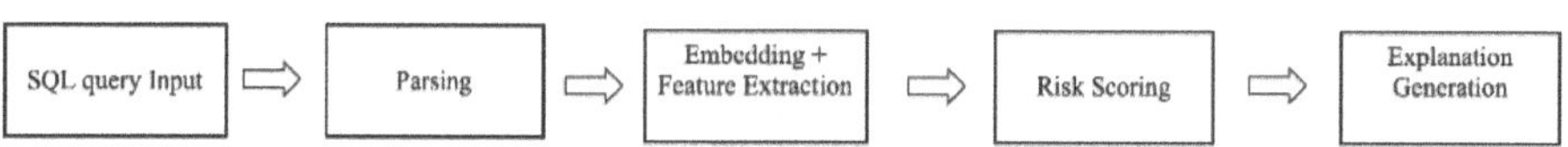


**Fig. 3.** High Level Workflow of the AI Framework

To understand how this AI system works, imagine it as a virtual data safety inspector that reviews SQL queries the instructions analysts write to pull data from a database. Before the system allows a query to run, it checks whether that query might accidentally reveal private or sensitive information (like gender, ZIP code, or birthdate) in ways that violate healthcare regulations like HIPAA. Let's walk through how each part of the system works behind the scenes using technologies that work similarly to language and pattern recognition tools in modern AI.

## 3.1 SQL Parser – Breaking the Query Into Parts

When a human writes a SQL query, it might look like a complex sentence asking for something like: "Give me the average length of stay by gender and department." The parser is the first component that steps in. Think of it like how a grammar checker breaks a sentence into nouns, verbs, and objects. The SQL parser breaks the query into a structure called an Abstract Syntax Tree (AST). This tree helps the system "see" which columns are being used, how many tables are being joined, and whether groupings like gender or role are being used to summarize data. This gives the system a roadmap of what the query is trying to do, structurally.

## 3.2 CodeBERT – Semantic Representation

While the parser looks at how the query is structured, it doesn't always understand why the query was written that way. That's where CodeBERT comes in. CodeBERT is a special type of AI model trained on programming languages (including SQL) and natural language [9]. You can think of it like a translator that understands both the syntax and the intent behind code. It converts the SQL query into a numeric "fingerprint" that captures the underlying logic and purpose of the request. This is important because two different looking queries can be trying to do the same risky thing, and CodeBERT helps catch those cases. For example, one query might group data by "zip," while another groups by a combination of "city + street" which can still lead to privacy risk. CodeBERT can sense that these are functionally similar even if they're written differently. By leveraging the pretrained transformer architecture, this model avoids the need for handcrafted semantic rules and instead relies on learned representations to distinguish queries that may pose privacy risks from those that do not.

## 3.3 Syntactic Feature Extractor – Pulling Out Risk Signals

To make the system smarter, it doesn't just rely on language understanding. It also pulls out specific, hand-picked features that are known to raise red flags in data privacy. This includes:

- How many columns the query groups data by.
- How many tables it pulls data from (joins).
- Whether it uses sensitive columns like gender, date of birth, or ZIP code which, if used incorrectly, can make individuals identifiable.

These features act like "checkpoints" that further help the system understand the risk level of the query.

## 3.4 XGBoost Risk Classifier – Risk Classification

Once the system has the semantic fingerprint (from Code- BERT) and the hand-picked risk features (from the feature extractor), it combines them into a single profile of the query. This profile is then sent to XGBoost, a highly accurate machine learning algorithm that acts like a judge [10]. It has been trained on a large number of SQL examples labeled as safe or risky, so it knows how to spot dangerous patterns. The model outputs a risk probability score of 0 or 1, which reflects the likelihood that the query may violate privacy norms. We apply a configurable threshold typically 0.85 above which the query is automatically flagged as BLOCKED. This threshold can be tuned based on institutional policies, legal thresholds, or operational risk tolerance.

### 3.5 Explanation Engine – Telling You What Went Wrong

Blocking a query isn't helpful unless you explain why. So, the final part of the system is the explanation engine. This module reads the structure of the query (from the AST) and uses predefined templates to generate a human-readable explanation. For instance, it might say: "This query groups data by job title and shift, which may reveal individual identities because the group sizes could be too small." This is especially helpful for compliance teams or data stewards who need to fix the query without guessing what went wrong.

## 4 Experimental Evaluation

This section evaluates the effectiveness of the proposed AIdriven SQL risk detection framework on a synthetic healthcare dataset. The evaluation simulates realistic business intelligence (BI) use cases in a hospital setting while assessing the system's ability to flag potentially privacy-violating SQL metric definitions.

### 4.1 Dataset Description

A representative sample table named patient data that mirrors anonymized hospital workforce and operational data is used for this evaluation. Due to the privacy regulations surrounding Protected Health Information (PHI) and Institutional Review Board (IRB) restrictions, real hospital data cannot be disclosed. As a result, we constructed a synthetic dataset that replicates the structure, schema, and statistical patterns of realworld healthcare data for the purpose of system validation. Each row represents an patient, and the dataset includes a blend of clinical and administrative attributes. The table contains the following fields (Table 1):

For this experiment, dob, zip, gender, and diagnosis code are considered sensitive fields, as they may lead to re-identification or attribute inference when improperly grouped. The full synthetic dataset used for this experiment is available on the github repository [11].

**Table 1.** Synthetic Dataset Schema And Column Description Of The Sample Table: Patient Data

| Column Name | Description |
|---|---|
| patient_id | Unique identifier for record traceability |
| dob | Sensitive |
| gender | Sensitive |
| zip | Sensitive |
| department | Medical unit |
| diagnosis_code | Medical condition classification: Sensitive |
| wait_time | Service-related metric |

### 4.2 Query Evaluation Framework

A set of 3 SQL queries are generated representing a spectrum of aggregation risks from clearly benign to clearly problematic. The AI system parses each query using sqlglot, encodes the query using CodeBERT, and evaluates structural features such as number of GROUP BY fields, join count, and presence of sensitive columns. These features are fused into a vector and scored by an XGBoost classifier trained on labeled query examples. Any query with a risk score above 0.85 is flagged as BLOCKED and returned with a model-generated explanation. Below, is the model output on the 3 representative queries.

- SQL QUERY 1 (Medium Risk): SELECT zip, COUNT(*) FROM patient data GROUP BY zip; AST NODES: ['GROUP BY', 'JOIN: 0', 'Columns: zip'] Risk Score: 0.87 Status: BLOCKED Explanation: ZIP code is a quasi-identifier and may expose individual locations if group size is small.
- SQL QUERY 2 (High Risk): SELECT gender, diagnosis code, COUNT(*) FROM patient data GROUP BY gender, diagnosis code; AST NODES: ['GROUP BY', 'JOIN: 0', 'Columns: gender, diagnosis code'] Risk Score: 0.93 Status: BLOCKED Explanation: Grouping by gender and medical code may leak health-related sensitive segments.
- SQL QUERY 3 (Moderate Risk): SELECT gender, COUNT(*) FROM patient data GROUP BY gender; AST NODES: ['GROUP BY', 'JOIN: 0', 'Columns: gender'] Risk Score: 0.74 Status: APPROVED Explanation: While gender is sensitive, group sizes are likely sufficient to prevent leakage.

### 4.3 Comparison to Rule-Based Systems

Traditional rule-based approaches to query risk detection typically rely on static filters or hard-coded blacklists such as banning combinations like "zip" and "dob" within the same GROUP BY clause. While straightforward, these systems often suffer from three key limitations. First, they lack contextawareness; for example, grouping by gender alone may be perfectly acceptable in many cases, yet a rule engine might flag it indiscriminately. Second, such systems are rigid and struggle to adapt to novel data patterns or edge cases that emerge in evolving BI environments. Third, they offer no mechanism for prioritization or explanation producing binary outcomes without confidence scores or rationale, which hinders transparency and governance. In contrast, the proposed AI-powered system addresses these challenges through dynamic, data-informed evaluation. It computes a continuous risk score from 0 to 1, enabling more nuanced decision-making. For example, Query 3 in the evaluation includes a sensitive field but was assessed by the AI as posing minimal actual privacy risk, given its structural context and the distribution patterns typically found in hospital datasets. A traditional rule engine would have flagged it regardless. Moreover, this system provides clear, interpretable explanations for each decision whether a query is approved or blocked. These explanations enhance audit readiness, enabling data stewards, BI analysts, and compliance officers to understand not only what decision was made, but why. This fosters trust, supports IRB and HIPAA compliance, and encourages proactive data governance in healthcare settings.

In summary the proposed model demonstrated strong domain-aligned sensitivity. High-risk queries were accurately flagged based on grouping patterns and the presence of identifiable fields. Low-risk queries that provide analytical value without privacy compromise were rightfully approved, supporting operational continuity.

## 5 Limitation and Assumptions

- Keyword-Based Sensitive Field Detection: The current AI framework identifies sensitive fields such as dob, gender, zip, and role using a fixed list of keyword matches. While effective for standard naming conventions, this approach lacks adaptability to schema variations or domain-specific terminology. For instance, fields labeled as date of birth or postal code may not be detected. To enhance robustness, future iterations should support configurable sensitive term lists and semantic similarity techniques (e.g., vector embeddings) to identify synonymous attributes across diverse datasets.
- Contextual Risk in JOINs and GROUP BY Clauses: The model evaluates structural query risks using features such as the number of JOIN operations and the presence of GROUP BY clauses. However, true re-identification risk is highly context-dependent, especially influenced by the cardinality of grouped results. Because the current framework performs only static query analysis (without executing the query), it cannot assess group sizes or distribution patterns. Future versions could incorporate metadata-driven heuristics (e.g., value distribution histograms or minimum subgroup thresholds) to better approximate privacy risk at design time.
- Handling of Advanced SQL Constructs: While the current implementation successfully parses and evaluates standard SQL queries, it may exhibit degraded performance when encountering advanced constructs such as Common Table Expressions (CTEs), window functions, and deeply nested subqueries. These complex patterns may yield incomplete or shallow Abstract

Syntax Trees (ASTs), limiting downstream feature extraction. Enhancing the parser to recursively analyze these structures or pretraining the model on a wider set of syntactic patterns would improve its generalization to production-grade BI environments.
- Model Bias: Additionally, the training data and labeling process used to build the classifier may carry institutional biases reflective of the source environment. Broader calibration across multiple healthcare systems would improve fairness.

## 6 Conclusion

In this paper, an AI-assisted framework is introduced that supports metric abstraction as a privacy-preserving alternative to sharing raw data across teams in healthcare organizations. As hospitals and research institutions rely more heavily on analytics for operational and clinical decision-making, the need to collaborate without compromising sensitive information like patient demographics or diagnosis codes has never been more urgent. This framework provides a technical solution that enables this balance. Instead of relying on runtime data access or manual reviews, the system analyzes SQL-based metric definitions before they are executed. By parsing the structure of each query and combining it with semantic embeddings (via CodeBERT) and syntactic features (e.g., number of joins, presence of sensitive fields like ZIP or DOB), the model predicts a privacy risk score using a trained XGBoost classifier. Queries flagged as high risk are blocked and accompanied by a clear explanation, such as: "Metric groups by job title and shift, which may reduce group sizes below FTC thresholds." This approach allows organizations to safely publish aggregate metrics like readmission rates or department-level wait times without exposing raw patient records. It also ensures that BI teams outside the data-owning department (e.g., fundraising or operations) can access needed insights without direct access to sensitive tables.

The modularity of the system makes it easy to extend: sensitive keywords can be configured, more advanced SQL constructs can be added to the parser, and the model can be re-trained on domain-specific query patterns. Compared to static rule-based filters, this framework brings flexibility and context-awareness to the privacy review process. It supports pre-execution validation, meaning risks are caught before any query runs against protected data. The result is a governance tool that's not only compliant with HIPAA, IRB, and zerotrust principles but also practical for real-world BI workflows. Overall, this system lays the groundwork for ethical AI in metric generation and collaborative data infrastructure. It enables organizations to move beyond "access or deny" models and instead adopt intelligent, explainable privacy controls at the metric definition layer. For institutions navigating the tension between data utility and privacy compliance, this framework offers a path forward that is both scalable and responsible.

## References

1. Quantzig: "Best health metrics to use for performance measurement in the healthcare industry." Quantzig Blog (2025). https://www.quantzig.com/blog/best-health-metrics-use-performance-measurement-healthcare-industry. Accessed 12 May 2025
2. Wowak, K.D., Lalor, J.P., Somanchi, S., Angst, C.M.: Unstructured data and AI in healthcare operations: supporting clinical decision-making for hospital readmissions. Manuf. Serv. Oper. Manag. **25**(1), 1–18 (2023). https://doi.org/10.1287/msom.2023.1192 last accessed 2025/05/12
3. Elliott, T., Holmes, J., Davidson, A., Chance, P., Nelson, A., Steiner, J.: "Data warehouse governance programs in healthcare settings: a literature review and a call to action." EGEMS **1**(1), 1010 (2013). https://doi.org/10.13063/2327-9214.1010. Accessed 12 May 2025
4. AtScale: "How Metrics Engineering Support Business Intelligence and Data Science Programs." AtScale Blog (2023). https://www.atscale.com/blog/how-metrics-engineering-support-business-intelligence-and-data-science-programs. Accessed 12 May 2025
5. Jia, J., Gong, N.: "AttriGuard: a practical defense against attribute inference attacks via adversarial machine learning." In: 27th USENIX Security Symposium (USENIX Security 18) (2018). https://www.usenix.org/conference/usenixsecurity18/presentation/jiajinyuan. Accessed 12 May 2025
6. Alneyadi, S., Sithirasenan, E., Muthukkumarasamy, V.: "Detecting data semantic: a data leakage prevention approach." In: 2015 IEEE Trustcom/BigDataSE/ISPA. IEEE (2015). https://ieeexplore.ieee.org/abstract/document/7345372. Accessed 12 May 2025
7. El Emam, K., Dankar, F.: Protecting privacy using k-anonymity. J. American Med. Inform. Assoc. (2008). https://doi.org/10.1197/jamia.M2716. Accessed 12 May 2025
8. Zhao, Y., Chen, J.: A Survey on Differential Privacy for Unstructured Data Content. Association for Computing Machinery (2022). https://doi.org/10.1145/3490237. Accessed 12 May 2025
9. Feng, Z., Guo, D., Tang, D., Duan, N., Feng, X.: CodeBERT: A Pre-Trained Model for Programming and Natural Languages. arXiv preprint (2020). https://arxiv.org/abs/2002.08155. Accessed 12 May 2025
10. Chen, T., Guestrin, C.: XGBoost: A Scalable Tree Boosting System. ACM (2016). https://doi.org/10.1145/2939672.2939785. Accessed 12 May 2025
11. Shakeel, O.: metric risk evaluator. GitHub Repository. https://github.com/omershk9/metric%20risk%20evaluator/tree/main. Accessed 12 May 2025

# Interpretable, Adaptive, and Robust Online Machine Learning for Data Streams - An Overview and Update

Zhong Chen(✉)

School of Computing, Southern Illinois University, Carbondale, IL 62901, USA
zhong.chen@siu.edu
https://pursuerchen.github.io/

**Abstract.** In this survey, we will summarize our recent representative research studies toward interpretable, adaptive, and robust online machine learning for data streams with multiple streaming natures, such as skewed distributions, concept drifts, and streaming or mix-typed features, which are four vital components towards intelligent online machine learning. I will also discuss some potential streaming applications for online anomaly detection, and future work on online semi-supervised learning, online label shift learning, online continuous learning, and large language model enhanced online machine learning for data streams.

**Keywords:** Sparse online learning · Cost-sensitive online learning · Local adaptive online density estimation · Concept drifts · Robust online learning · Data streams

## 1 Introduction

Thanks to the rapid development of information technology and tremendous applications, data streams are becoming increasingly ubiquitous, particularly in the fields of sensor networks, network traffic monitoring, anomaly and fraud detection, intelligent recommendations, and urban disaster and pandemic monitoring (Fig. 1). Such high throughput streaming data is received in patterns that change over time and are tedious to handle as well, where the underlying distribution of data, feature, and label will be dynamically changing as well. For social media streams, trends, topics, user behavior, and even language evolve rapidly (concept drift). Models for sentiment analysis, trend detection, spam filtering, or recommendation must adapt constantly. Understanding why content is flagged, recommended, or deemed trending is crucial for fairness, bias mitigation, user trust, and regulatory compliance (e.g., explaining algorithmic decisions). Highly noisy data (typos, slang, sarcasm) [29], intentional manipulation (bots, fake news), and adversarial attacks [10,38,39] (trying to game recommendation or moderation systems) are rampant.

Conventional online learning aims to learn models incrementally from data in a sequential manner with fixed feature and label spaces, providing instant and


R. Stahlbock et al. (Eds.): CSCE 2025, CCIS 2938, pp. 140–149, 2027.
https://doi.org/10.1007/978-3-032-22196-4_11

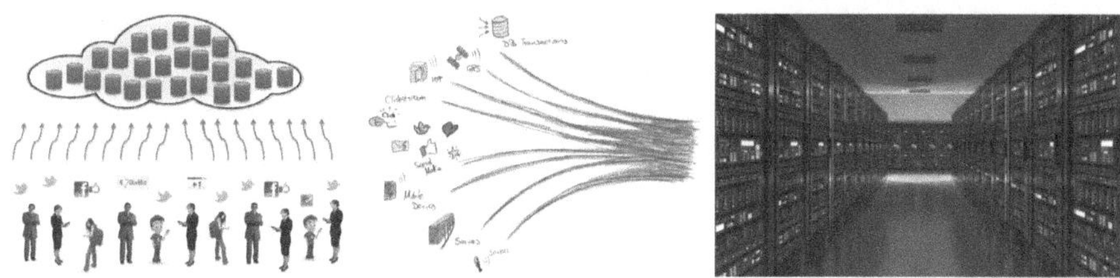

**Fig. 1.** Data streams are ubiquitously collected from platforms such as social media, sensor networks, intelligent recommendations, and smart data centers and network monitoring.

efficient updates by an online learner when new coming data arrives. Founded on a solid theoretical theory with rigorous regret bounds, online learning overcomes some drawbacks such as expensive re-training cost and poor scalability of traditional machine learning, which is also easy to understand and simple to implement. However, existing online learning models have focused mainly on model accuracy or computational efficiency, producing models that are too complex for better interpretation, streaming features, novel classes, and even more challenges in open environments, whereas the new features may emerge, and old features may vanish or become obsolete, leading to an open feature space. To bridge this gap, I plan to comprehensively review our recent work on building Intelligent Online Machine Learning (IOML) techniques that can promote wise or optimal sequential decision-making for large-scale heterogeneous data streams with multiple streaming natures collected in open environments.

## 2 Our Proposed Approaches

Online learning (OL) [19,24] aims to learn a model incrementally from streaming data in a sequential manner, which is significantly different from conventional batch-based offline machine learning paradigms that require the availability of all data before training a model. Due to its high scalability and efficiency, it has been shown to be effective in handling large-scale and high-velocity data streams. However, most existing studies for OL neglect some important streaming natures of data streams, such as skewed distributions, concept drifts, and streaming or mix-typed features. To the end, we investigated a set of intelligent online machine learning methods [4–13,17–20,28,29,32] that are able to tackle the high-dimensional data streams with skewed distributions (Part I), handle concept-drifting and noisy streaming data (Part II), promote sparse online learning from data streams with streaming features (Part III), and model the correlation among mix-typed features (Part IV).

Part I: Cost-sensitive sparse online learning. We introduced a framework of cost-sensitive sparse online learning with Truncated Gradient (CSTG) [6] and Regularized Dual Averaging (CSRDA) [17] for imbalanced data streams

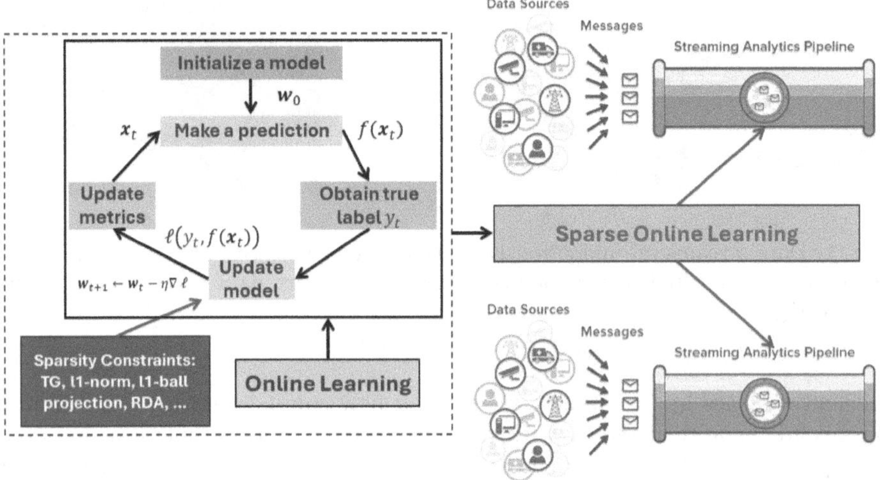


**Fig. 2.** The overview of online incremental model updating and sparse online learning for high-throughput and high-dimensional data stream processing.

(Fig. 2), where the two mutual restraint factors, mis-classification cost and sparsity, can be simultaneously and favorably balanced. Furthermore, by retaining the potentially pertainable group structures of features, we propose a proximal cost-sensitive sparse group online learning (PCSGOL) framework [18,20] to handle imbalanced and high-dimensional streaming data. We formulate this type of OL as a new cost-sensitive online optimization problem by leveraging the $\ell_2$-norm, $\ell_1$-norm, and group-wise sparsity constraints in the dual averaging regularization.

Part II: Locally adaptive online learning. To handle concept-drifting and noisy streaming data, we first propose an adaptive local online kernel density estimator (ALoKDE) [9] for real-time density estimation over data streams (Fig. 3). ALoKDE consists of two tightly integrated strategies: (1) a statistical test for concept drift detection and (2) an adaptive weighted local online density estimation when a drift does occur. Specifically, using a weighted form, ALoKDE seeks to provide an unbiased estimation by factoring in the statistical hallmarks of the latest learned distribution and any potential distributional changes that could be introduced by each incoming instance. A robust variant of ALoKDE, i.e., R-ALoKDE [8], is further developed by ensemble strategies to effectively handle noisy data streams.

Part III: Robust sparse online learning. Most of existing sparse online learning algorithms that utilize $\ell_1$-norm regularization, $\ell_1$-ball projection, or adversarial sparsity assume that the feature space is fixed or changes by following explicit constraints. However, this assumption does not always hold in many real applications. Motivated by this observation, we propose a new online learning algorithm tailored for data streams described by open feature spaces, where new

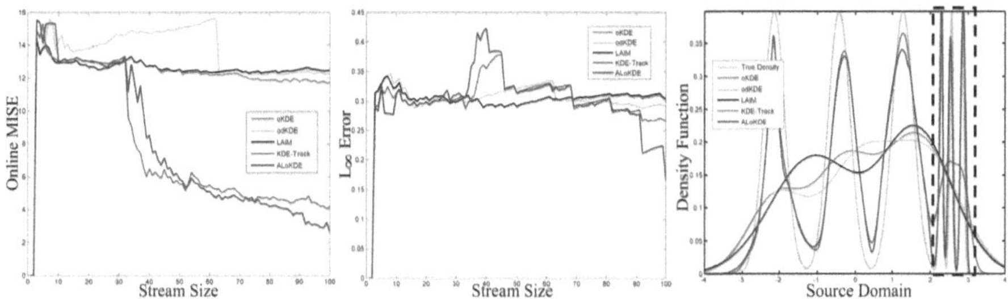


**Fig. 3.** A local adaptive approach called ALoKDE is proposed to handle dynamic density distribution shifts in data streams.

features can be occurred, and old features may be vanished over various time spans (Fig. 4). Our algorithm named RSOL [10] provides a strategy to adapt quickly to such feature dynamics by encouraging sparse model representation with an $\ell_1$- and $\ell_2$-mixed regularizer. We leverage the proximal operator of the $\ell_{1,2}$-mixed norm and show that our RSOL algorithm enjoys a closed-form solution at each iteration. Furthermore, we propose a novel unified one-pass online learning framework named OASF [13] for simultaneously online active learning and sparse online learning tailored for data streams described by open feature spaces. Specifically, we technically develop an effective online CUR matrix decomposition based on the $\ell_{1,2}$-mixed norm constraint for simultaneously selecting important up-to-date samples in a sliding window and facilitating stable and meaningful features in open feature spaces over time. If the loss function is simultaneously Lipschitz and convex, a sub-linear regret bound of our proposed algorithm is guaranteed with. Extensive experiments that are conducted with multiple streaming datasets have demonstrated the effectiveness of the proposed OASF compared with state-of-the-art online active learning and sparse online learning methods.

To overcome the negative impact of possibly high-dimensional data, sparse online learning (SOL) has been proposed by imposing various sparse constraints to sheer the resultant model structure. However, most existing SOL studies focused on a fixed feature space, whereas in practice the steaming data observations may increase in both quantity and feature dimensions, leading to varying feature spaces. To the end, we propose a novel $\ell_{1,\infty}$-mixed norm-based row sparsity SOL algorithm (SOOFS) [11] to handle data streams in varying feature spaces (Fig. 5). We empower SOOFS with a tailored online CUR matrix decomposition method based on the promoted row sparsity to actively and adaptively select informative instances in the sliding windows, facilitating stable online performance over time. Empirical results on ten benchmark datasets substantiate the superiority of SOOFS over three state-of-the-art competitors in terms of classification accuracy and model sparsity. Furthermore, we propose a novel Streaming Anomaly Detection (SAD) method [12], grounded in a sparse active online learning framework. Our approach uniquely integrates $\ell_{1,2}$-norm sparse

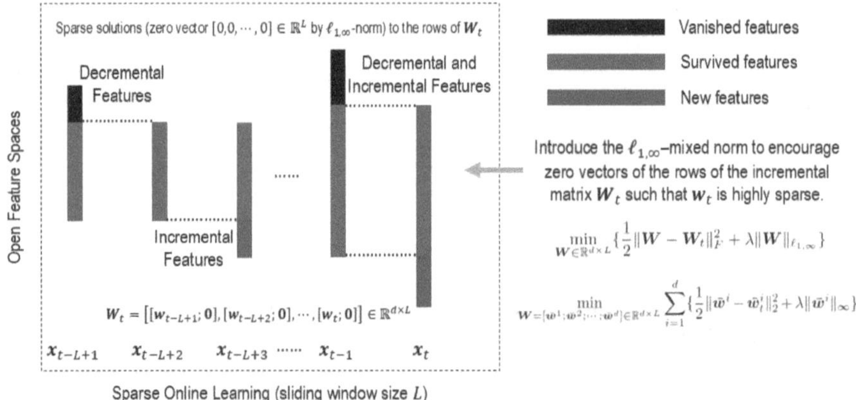


**Fig. 4.** An overview of the proposed sparse online learning algorithms (i.e., RSOL [10], OASF [13], SOOFS [11], and SAD [12]) to handle data streams with streaming features in open feature spaces.

online learning with CUR decomposition-based active learning, enabling simultaneous fast feature selection and dynamic instance selection. The efficient CUR decomposition further supports real-time residual analysis for anomaly scoring, eliminating the need for manual threshold settings of data distributions.

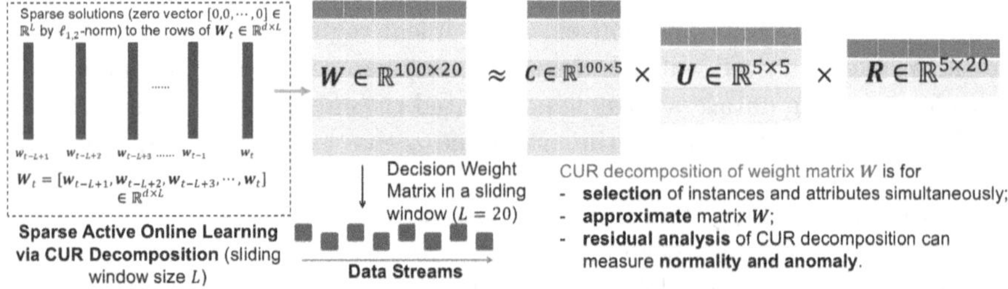


**Fig. 5.** CUR decomposition identifies a subset of representative instances (matrix $\boldsymbol{C}$) and discriminative attributes (matrix $\boldsymbol{R}$) from the decision weight matrix $\boldsymbol{W}$ in a sliding window, constructing a low-rank approximation that minimizes reconstruction error while preserving interpretability. The components are formed by small subsets of actual columns and rows of $\boldsymbol{W}$. By dynamically selecting $c$ instances and $r$ attributes, CUR captures structural patterns in streaming data, where anomalies often deviate significantly from these representative subsets.

Part IV: Online semi-supervised learning. Online learning with feature spaces that are not fixed but can vary over time renders a seemingly flexible learning paradigm thus has drawn much attention. Unfortunately, a homogeneous feature type and full supervision assumptions prohibit a ubiquitous application of this learning paradigm in practice. Alas, a semi-supervised online learner that can deal with mix-typed, varying feature spaces is still missing. As shown in Fig. 6, the first challenge is mix-typed streaming features, leading to the gradients derived from such different features are garbled, where the updating steps suggested by discrete features are in a coarser level of granularity than those by continuous features. The second challenge is label scarcity, which may result in the online learner being able to commit to a low convergence rate. To fill the gap, we investigate a novel problem named OSLMF [32], which strives to relax the restrictions on the feature type and supervision information. Our key idea to solve the new problem is to leverage copula models to align the data instances with different feature spaces so as to make their distance measurable. A geometric structure underlying data instances is then established in an online fashion based on their distances, through which the limited labeling information is propagated, from the scarce labeled instances to their close neighbors. Experimental results are documented to evidence the viability and effectiveness of our proposed OSLMF approach.tion method based on the promoted row sparsity to actively and adaptively select informative instances in the sliding windows, facilitating stable online performance over time. Empirical results on ten benchmark datasets substantiate the superiority of SOOFS over three state-of-the-art competitors in terms of classification accuracy and model sparsity. Furthermore, we propose a novel Streaming Anomaly Detection (SAD) method [12], grounded in a sparse active online learning framework. Our approach uniquely integrates $\ell_{1,2}$-norm sparse online learning with CUR decomposition-based active learning, enabling simultaneous fast feature selection and dynamic instance selection. The efficient CUR decomposition further supports real-time residual analysis for anomaly scoring, eliminating the need for manual threshold settings of data distributions.

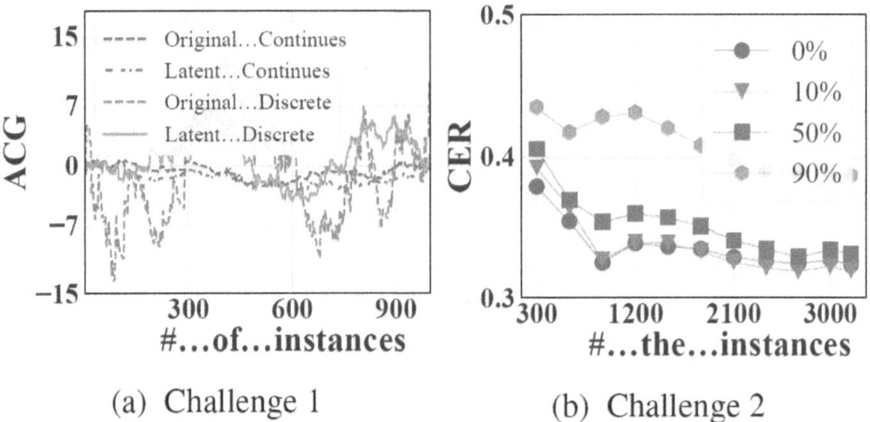


**Fig. 6.** Visualization of the two challenges (i.e., mix-typed streaming features and insufficient label information) to hinder conventional online learning.

Part IV: Online semi-supervised learning. Online learning with feature spaces that are not fixed but can vary over time renders a seemingly flexible learning paradigm thus has drawn much attention. Unfortunately, a homogeneous feature type and full supervision assumptions prohibit a ubiquitous application of this learning paradigm in practice. Alas, a semi-supervised online learner that can deal with mix-typed, varying feature spaces is still missing. As show in Fig. 6, the first challenge is mix-typed streaming features, leading to the gradients derived from such different features are garbled, where the updating steps suggested by discrete features are in a coarser level of granularity than those by continuous features. The second challenge is label scarcity, which may result in the online learner being able to commit to a low convergence rate. To fill the gap, we investigate a novel problem named OSLMF [32], which strives to relax the restrictions on the feature type and supervision information. Our key idea to solve the new problem is to leverage copula models to align the data instances with different feature spaces so as to make their distance measurable. A geometric structure underlying data instances is then established in an online fashion based on their distances, through which the limited labeling information is propagated, from the scarce labeled instances to their close neighbors. Experimental results are documented to evidence the viability and effectiveness of our proposed OSLMF approach.

## 3 Future Plan

Based on this survey, I plan to briefly overview our follow-up work for online outlier/anomaly detection [12,17,27] tasks, which strive to capture novel patterns that deviate from expected behavior in data streams and applications in health domains [14–16,21,33–36]. As part of future work, I will also plan to investigate: (1) online semi-supervised learning from data streams with limited labels as the labeling process requires human effort expertise that can conceal annotation errors; (2) online label shift learning from data streams that encounter label distribution shifts [2,22] over time but the label-conditional density does not change; (3) online continuous learning from data streams that sustain evolving new classes (class incremental) and data non-stationarity (domain incremental). One of the key challenges of online continual learning is how to avoid catastrophic forgetting, i.e., forgetting old classes in the presence of more recent classes; and (4) large language model (LLM) [3,26,30] enhanced online machine learning for data streams, providing a new paradigm to handle these challenges by integrating meta-learning [23], continual learning [1], knowledge distillation [31,37], and memory-augmented adaptation strategies [25].

## References

1. Aljundi, R., Kelchtermans, K., Tuytelaars, T.: Task-free continual learning. In: Proceedings of the IEEE/CVF Conference on Computer Vision and Pattern Recognition, pp. 11254–11263 (2019)
2. Casey, J., et al.: Distributed collaborative learning with representative knowledge sharing. Mathematics **13**(6), 1004 (2025)
3. Chen, W.M., Yan, Y., Shen, X., Gao, H., Chen, Z.: Probabilistic prompts for zero-shot and few-shot large language models: an empirical study of patient-reported outcomes. In: The 25th IEEE International Conference on Data Mining. IEEE (2025)
4. Chen, Z.: Adaptive sparse online learning through asymmetric truncated gradient. In: 2024 IEEE 10th International Conference on Big Data Computing Service and Machine Learning Applications, pp. 44–51. IEEE (2024)
5. Chen, Z.: Robust sparse online learning through adversarial sparsity constraints. In: 2024 IEEE 9th International Conference on Smart Cloud, pp. 42–47. IEEE Computer Society (2024)
6. Chen, Z., Fang, Z., Fan, W., Edwards, A., Zhang, K.: CSTG: an effective framework for cost-sensitive sparse online learning. In: Proceedings of the 2017 SIAM International Conference on Data Mining, pp. 759–767. SIAM (2017)
7. Chen, Z., Fang, Z., Sheng, V., Edwards, A., Zhang, K.: CSRDA: Cost-sensitive regularized dual averaging for handling imbalanced and high-dimensional streaming data. In: 2021 IEEE International Conference on Big Knowledge, pp. 164–173. IEEE (2021)
8. Chen, Z.: Adaptive robust local online density estimation for streaming data. Int. J. Mach. Learn. Cybern. **12**(6), 1803–1824 (2021)
9. Chen, Z., et al.: Online density estimation over streaming data: a local adaptive solution. In: 2018 IEEE International Conference on Big Data, pp. 201–210. IEEE (2018)
10. Chen, Z., et al.: Robust sparse online learning for data streams with streaming features. In: Proceedings of the 2024 SIAM International Conference on Data Mining, pp. 181–189. SIAM (2024)
11. Chen, Z., He, Y., Wu, D., Zhang, W., Deng, Z.: $\ell_{1,\infty}$ mixed norm promoted row sparsity for fast online cur decomposition learning in varying feature spaces. In: Proceedings of the 2025 SIAM International Conference on Data Mining, pp. 124–133. SIAM (2025)
12. Chen, Z., He, Y., Wu, D., Zhao, C., Qiu, M.: A novel sparse active online learning framework for fast and accurate streaming anomaly detection over data streams. In: Proceedings of the Thirty-Fourth International Joint Conference on Artificial Intelligence, pp. 2740–2748 (2025)
13. Chen, Z., et al.: $\ell_{1,2}$-norm and cur decomposition based sparse online active learning for data streams with streaming features. In: 2024 IEEE International Conference on Big Data, pp. 384–393. IEEE (2024)
14. Chen, Z., et al.: Decoding ancestry-specific genetic risk: interpretable deep feature selection reveals prostate cancer SNP disparities in diverse populations. BioData Mining **18**(1), 66 (2025)
15. Chen, Z.: A few-shot u-net learning framework for fast and accurate three-dimensional dose prediction in radiotherapy. Physica Med. **139**, 105184 (2025)
16. Chen, Z., et al.: Driver gene detection through Bayesian network integration of mutation and expression profiles. Bioinformatics **38**(10), 2781–2790 (2022)

17. Chen, Z., Sheng, V., Edwards, A., Zhang, K.: An effective cost-sensitive sparse online learning framework for imbalanced streaming data classification and its application to online anomaly detection. Knowl. Inf. Syst. **65**(1), 59–87 (2023)
18. Chen, Z., Sheng, V., Edwards, A., Zhang, K.: Cost-sensitive sparse group online learning for imbalanced data streams. Mach. Learn. **113**(7), 4407–4444 (2024)
19. Chen, Z., Zhan, H., Sheng, V., Edwards, A., Zhang, K.: Projection dual averaging based second-order online learning. In: 2022 IEEE International Conference on Data Dining (ICDM), pp. 51–60. IEEE (2022)
20. Chen, Z., Zhan, H., Sheng, V., Edwards, A., Zhang, K.: Proximal cost-sensitive sparse group online learning. In: 2022 IEEE International Conference on Big Data, pp. 495–504. IEEE (2022)
21. Chen, Z., Zhang, W., Deng, H., Zhang, K.: Effective cancer subtype and stage prediction via dropfeature-DNNs. IEEE/ACM Trans. Comput. Biol. Bioinf. **19**(1), 107–120 (2021)
22. Fan, M., et al.: Measuring heterogeneity in machine learning with distributed energy distance. arXiv preprint arXiv:2501.16174 (2025)
23. Finn, C., Abbeel, P., Levine, S.: Model-agnostic meta-learning for fast adaptation of deep networks. In: International Conference on Machine Learning, pp. 1126–1135. PMLR (2017)
24. Hoi, S.C., Sahoo, D., Lu, J., Zhao, P.: Online learning: a comprehensive survey. Neurocomputing **459**, 249–289 (2021)
25. Kalluri, T., Sharma, A., Chandraker, M.: Memsac: memory augmented sample consistency for large scale domain adaptation. In: European Conference on Computer Vision, pp. 550–568. Springer (2022)
26. Li, D., et al.: SolverLLM: leveraging test-time scaling for optimization problem via LLM-guided search. arXiv preprint arXiv:2510.16916 (2025)
27. Lian, H., et al.: Online outlier detection in open feature spaces. IEEE Trans. Knowl. Data Eng. **37**(10), 6091–6106 (2025)
28. Lian, H., et al.: Metric-agnostic continual learning for sustainable group fairness. In: Proceedings of the AAAI Conference on Artificial Intelligence, vol. 39, pp. 18648–18657 (2025)
29. Liang, C., et al.: MMA: Multi-Metric-Autoencoder for analyzing high-dimensional and incomplete data. In: Joint European Conference on Machine Learning and Knowledge Discovery in Databases, pp. 3–19. Springer (2023)
30. Lin, Y., et al.: Face4fairshifts: a large image benchmark for fairness and robust learning across visual domains. arXiv preprint arXiv:2509.00658 (2025)
31. Wu, D., Sun, W., He, Y., Chen, Z., Luo, X.: MKG-FENN: a multimodal knowledge graph fused end-to-end neural network for accurate drug–drug interaction prediction. In: Proceedings of the AAAI Conference on Artificial Intelligence. vol. 38, pp. 10216–10224 (2024)
32. Wu, D., Zhuo, S., Wang, Y., Chen, Z., He, Y.: Online semi-supervised learning with mix-typed streaming features. In: Proceedings of the AAAI Conference on Artificial Intelligence, vol. 37, pp. 4720–4728 (2023)
33. Yan, Y., Chen, Z., Shen, X., Chen, R.C., Gao, H.: Short-and long-term weekly patient-reported outcomes prediction undergoing radiotherapy: single-patient time series model vs. transformer-based multi-patient time series model. BioData Mining **18**(1), 53 (2025)
34. Yan, Y., et al.: An oversampling-enhanced multi-class imbalanced classification framework for patient health status prediction using patient-reported outcomes. IEEE Access **13**, 175479–175494 (2025)

35. Yan, Y., Lominska, C., Gan, G.N., Gao, H., Chen, Z.: Accounting for cancer patients with severe outcomes: an anomaly detection perspective. In: 2024 IEEE International Conference on Big Data, pp. 8253–8255. IEEE (2024)
36. Yan, Y., Lominska, C., Gan, G.N., Gao, H., Chen, Z.: Advanced anomaly detection framework for enhancing prediction of severe health outcomes in cancer patients undergoing radiotherapy. In: 2025 IEEE 11th International Conference on Big Data Computing Service and Machine Learning Applications, pp. 73–80. IEEE (2025)
37. Yang, J., Li, Y., Wang, G., Chen, Z., Wu, D.: An end-to-end knowledge graph fused graph neural network for accurate protein-protein interactions prediction. IEEE/ACM Trans. Comput. Biol. Bioinform. (2024)
38. Zhan, H., Gao, L., Zhang, K., Chen, Z., Sheng, V.S.: Defending the graph reconstruction attacks for simplicial neural networks. In: 2023 IEEE 10th International Conference on Data Science and Advanced Analytics, pp. 1–9. IEEE (2023)
39. Zhan, H., Zhang, K., Chen, Z., Sheng, V.S.: Simplex2vec backward: from vectors back to simplicial complex. In: Proceedings of the 32nd ACM International Conference on Information and Knowledge Management, pp. 4405–4409 (2023)

# Data Mining and Applications - Signal Processing, Security, HPC, and Imaging Science

# Multistage Stress Classification and Cognitive Capacity Analysis Using EEG

Abdul Waleed[1(✉)], Nusrat Jahan Nitu[2], and Carol Fung[1]

[1] Concordia University, Montreal H3G 1S6, Canada
ab_walee@live.concordia.ca, carol.fung@concordia.ca
[2] University of Dhaka, Dhaka H3G 1S6, Bangladesh
nusratjahannitussmc@gmail.com

**Abstract.** Stress is a psychological and physiological strain caused by mental workload. Early diagnosis of stress level is crucial compared to later stages, which may develop into psychiatric disorders such as Anxiety and Depression. This study utilized Muse S, a four-channel EEG headband, to collect brainwaves during relaxed and stressed conditions. We investigated subject dependent and independent evaluation strategies by employing five different classifiers. We implemented an autoencoder and LSTM based model to improve the performance metrics of the subject-independent evaluation strategy and achieved 83% accuracy for binary classification and 66% accuracy for multistage classification. Additionally, this study examined cognitive capacity analysis based on five types of brain waves and established a model to predict the performance scores of participants.

**Keywords:** Stress · Convolutional Neural Networks (CNN) · EEG · Brainwaves

## 1 Introduction

Stress is an individual's perceived psychological response to a challenging situation. Each individual undergoes stress for various reasons in daily life. Demanding situations may include but are not limited to the high demands of jobs, delivering tasks under deadlines, economic pressure, and coping with technological advancements [1]. A mild level of stress has benefits for improved focus, which helps in the productivity of the individual [2]. However, a high level of stress leads to several diseases, including psychiatric disorders such as anxiety and depression [3]. People undergoing long-term high levels of stress are likely to become the victims of negative emotions and have hard time to focus on their work properly, degrading their performance [4].

Stress is subjective in nature, making its detection challenging [5]. Various methods can be used to detect symptoms of stress. For example, symptoms can be detected using questionnaires, physiological tests such as blood pressure


R. Stahlbock et al. (Eds.): CSCE 2025, CCIS 2938, pp. 153–169, 2027.
https://doi.org/10.1007/978-3-032-22196-4_12

and cortisol levels, and cognitive performance tests [6]. Common signs of high-level stress include high blood pressure, high heart rate, increased speech rate, avoidance of eye contact, tense muscles, etc. [7]. Wearable devices such as smart watches can be used to continuously monitor heart rate, cortisol levels, and skin temperature [8]. Some of them can monitor sleep patterns and generate stress scores using psychological data, making them capable of real-time stress detection [9]. Stress detection has attracted the attention of researchers for years due to its effects on both mental and physical well-being [10,12,15,16].

Electroencephalogram (EEG) is a noninvasive technique that provides real-time insight into brain activities, which has been introduced for stress detection [10]. Various machine learning algorithms such as Support Vector Machine [10], Random Forest [11], Logistic Regression [12], and Naive Bayes [13], etc., are explored in the literature to perform multistage stress classification. Many studies have explored multistage stress classification using EEG [10,14], but these studies obtained their results based on subject-dependent analysis employing K-fold cross-validation, which is not practical since the model does not generalize to the data from unseen participants. Very few studies have conducted subject-independent EEG classification utilizing Leave-One-Subject-Out (LOSO) cross-validation [15,16], their results only provide binary stress classification. We also evaluated our model based on LOSO cross-validation and not only achieved a higher binary classification accuracy compared to the literature but also performed a multistage stress classification using LOSO missing in the literature to the best of our knowledge. In LOSO model is trained on all the subjects after leaving one subject out, which will be used in the testing phase. LOSO is a more practical approach since it removes subject bias. We recruited 50 adults to participate in our experiment, answering stressor questions while wearing an EEG device to monitor their brain signals. After collecting the data, we performed multistage stress classification using five different classifiers: Naive Bayes, Random Forest, Support Vector Machine, Long Short Term Memory, and Convolutional Neural Network. Our results depicted that CNN outperformed the other classifiers with the highest accuracy of 99.9% in subject-dependent evaluation employing 10-fold cross-validation. We implemented autoencoder and LSTM based model to perform subject-independent evaluation by employing LOSO cross-validation strategy and achieved a binary classification accuracy of 83% and a multistage accuracy of 66%. Although subject-dependent analysis provides very high accuracy but does not generalize to data from unseen participants and LOSO, which is a subject-independent cross-validation strategy, generalizes well to the data from unseen participants and is a more practical approach. The major contributions of this work can be summarized as follows:

- We collected the EEG signals of 50 participants under two different stressors, which is the dataset with the largest number of participants for multistage EEG-based stress detection using Stroop color-word and mental arithmetic as stressors. We will share our anonymized dataset publicly.
- We employed the LOSO cross-validation strategy to generalize our findings to real-world scenarios and investigated the reason behind the significant

difference in classification metrics between subject-dependent and subject-independent evaluation strategies.
- We implemented a two-stage deep learning model based on an autoencoder and LSTM with an attention mechanism and achieved a binary stress classification accuracy of 83% and an accuracy of 66% for classifying three levels of stress using the LOSO cross-validation strategy.
- We established a model to accurately predict the performance scores of the participants by their brain signals recorded while answering stressor questions.

The rest of the paper is organized as follows. Section 2 includes the literature review conducted in the EEG domain. Section 3 explains the background. Our proposed research methodology has been elaborated in Sect. 4, followed by our results in Sect. 5. Results are further analyzed in Sect. 6, and Sect. 7 concludes the paper while directing toward the future research direction.

## 2 Literature Review

Jun and Smitha [10] proposed a real-time stress identification system, which employed the Stroop color-word test and mental arithmetic task as stressors. Data were collected from 10 participants using a 14-channel Emotive Epoch EEG headset. They achieved an accuracy of 88% and 96% for the two-level Stroop color-word test and the mental arithmetic task, respectively. For the three levels of stress, the highest accuracy achieved was 75%.

Cambay et al. [15] proposed an explainable feature extraction (XFE) method employing Directed Lobish symbolic language to perform binary stress detection. Data was collected from 310 participants who were victims of the February 6, 2023 earthquake in Turkey. Data was recorded using a 14-channel Epoch X EEG headset at a sampling frequency of 128 Hz using a 3-minute earthquake video as a stressor. The participants were divided into stressed and control groups. The participants from the control group were shown a meditation video. In this manuscript, authors evaluated the performance of the proposed model using both 10-fold and LOSO cross-validation strategies and achieved binary classification accuracies of 92.95% and 73.63% respectively. The same dataset was studied by Ince et al. [16] by employing a new feature extraction technique and achieved a binary classification accuracy of 96.29% and 76.17% using 10-fold and LOSO cross-validation strategies respectively.

Hou et al. [14] designed a real-time stress monitoring system using SVM. In this work, the authors used the Stroop color-word test to induce four levels of stress. EEG data was collected from 9 participants using an Emotiv Epoch EEG headset. Their model achieved an average accuracy of 85.17%, 75.22%, and 67.06% for 2, 3, and 4 levels of stress, respectively.

Asif et al. [12] proposed a framework for stress classification using EEG signals in response to different music tracks. EEG data was collected from 27 participants using a four-channel Muse EEG headband. They found Logistic regression outperformed the other classifiers with an accuracies of 98.76% and 95.06% for two and three levels of stress, respectively.

Arsalan et al. [13] proposed a model to detect mental stress using five groups of EEG features. EEG data was collected in pre-activity and post-activity phases from 28 participants using a four-channel Muse Headband. Support Vector Machine(SVM), Naive Bayes(NB), and Multi-Layer Perceptron (MLP) were used as classifiers, out of which MLP outperformed the other two by achieving the highest accuracies of 89.28% and 60.71% for two and three levels of stress classification. The same dataset was studied by Rauf and Saeed [11], and they acheived the highest accuracy of 93.8% using time domain features of EEG signals.

Phutela et al. proposed an LSTM-based model for the binary classification of mental stress with an accuracy of 93.17% [17]. EEG data was collected from 35 participants using a four-channel Muse EEG headband. Hindi movie clips were used to induce stress among the participants.

Most of the literature on EEG based stress detection uses a subject-dependent evaluation strategy using K-fold cross-validation that does not generalize to data from unseen participants. We performed a subject-independent analysis using the LOSO cross-validation strategy that generalizes well to the data of unseen participants and achieved a binary classification accuracy of 83% greater than [15,16] that also employed LOSO cross-validation.

## 3 Background

In this section, we will briefly introduce the human brain and brain waves, followed by the types of stressors.

### 3.1 Human Brain and Brain Waves

The **human brain** is the central part of the nervous system and has a list of functions such as Cognition, Motor control, Sensation, Emotion, and Automatic functions [18]. Neurons communicate by emitting electrical impulses, they generate some potential at the surface of the brain. This electrical potential can be measured with the help of electrodes; hence, **EEG (Electroencephalography)**, a non-invasive technique, is used to measure this electric potential.

There are five types of brain waves namely Delta, Theta, Alpha, Beta, and Gamma [10]. The **delta** wave frequency lies between 0.5–4 Hz. It is a low-frequency brain wave that is highly active in deep sleep. **Theta** is also another low-frequency brain wave whose frequency lies between 4–8 Hz. Theta is associated with light sleep and emotional stress in adults. The **alpha** wave is the brain wave that is linked to the relaxation state. It has a frequency between 8–12 Hz. **Beta** wave is a high-frequency brain wave that is linked to thinking, learning, and problem-solving. It has a frequency range of 12–30 Hz. Gamma wave has the highest frequency, which starts from 30 Hz. **Gamma** brain wave is associated with a high level of problem-solving.

### 3.2 Stressors

A stressor induces stress among the participants. A description of each stressor follows. **Stroop color-word test** [19] participants must identify the colors of the printed words in the Stroop color-word test, a widely used psychological stressor. **Mental arithmetic task** [20] include mathematical operations such as addition, subtraction, multiplication, and division. There are two more stressors that have been used by the researchers namely cold pressor and the Trier social stress test(TSST). In the **Cold pressor** [21] test, the participants are required to put their hands in cold water for a duration of 1–3 minutes, depending on the experiment. It includes discomfort for the participants, hence, we did not utilize it in our study. **Trier social stress test(TSST)** [22] is also a type of psychological test in which participants are required to prepare and then present a speech in front of the evaluators.

## 4 Methodology

In this section, we present the pipeline and procedures, followed by the dataset collection and preprocessing. We then discussed the feature extraction and the classifiers selected.

### 4.1 Overall Procedure

Two types of stressors were used in this experiment, namely **Stroop color-word test** and **Mental arithmetic task**. Questions were hosted in **Kahoot** [23] (a free online gaming platform). Participants were given a limited time (such as 10 s) to answer each question. Participants were instructed on the experiment process and provided user consent for them to read and sign. The experiment started after the participant signed the consent form. Our experiment strictly followed the process ethically approved by Concordia University under the certification #0020206. A total of 50 participants (30 males, 19 females, and 1 unknown) participated in the experiment. All participants were students of Concordia University, aging between 18–50 years. Figure 1 represents the stress classification pipeline using EEG data. We will explain each part of the pipeline in the following sections.

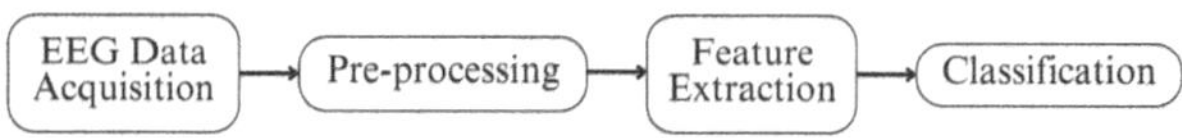


**Fig. 1.** Pipeline for stress classification using EEG.

### 4.2 EEG Dataset Acquisition

In the **Warm-up** session, participants were asked to play the Kahoot warm-up game to become familiarized with the overall experiment. There were four questions: two from the color-word test and two from the mental arithmetic task. In the **First Relaxation Phase**, relaxing music was played for two minutes to establish the baseline of relaxation before moving to the first part of the experiment. The EEG data was collected from this phase and onwards. In the **Medium Stress Phase**, participants were asked to solve easy mental arithmetic challenges and a congruent Stroop color-word test. This part of the experiment consists of 15 questions. Both the name and the color of the ink match with each other in a congruent Stroop color-word test. In the **Second Relaxation Phase**, relaxing music was played again for two minutes to establish a baseline of relaxation after completing the first part of the experiment. In the **High Stress Phase**, participants were asked to solve difficult mental arithmetic task and Incongruent Stroop color-word test. This part of the experiment also consists of 15 questions. Incongruent Stroop color-word test is a type of Stroop color-word test in which the name and ink of the color differ from each other. A lower count-down counter was used to put the participants under high stress in the second part of the experiment. In the **Third Relaxation Phase**, relaxing music was played for two minutes to establish a baseline of relaxation. After this phase the EEG data collection terminates for the participants.

Our dataset includes three levels of stress: relaxation state, Medium stress, and High stress. The relaxation state is associated with the relaxation phase. Medium stress-related data was collected during an easy mental arithmetic task and a congruent Stroop color-word test, and high stress data was collected during a difficult mental arithmetic task and an incongruent Stroop color-word test.

After the experiment concluded, participants were invited to complete an online questionnaire containing questions regarding the different stress levels they perceived during the experiment. Most of the participants confirmed in the questionnaire that they perceived stress during the experiment in the same order that we designed it.

### 4.3 EEG Data Preprocessing

After the data collection phase, we preprocessed the collected EEG data by removing the artifacts from the collected data. Micro-movements such as eye blinking, jaw clenching, and muscle movement produce undesired artifacts that need to be removed from the collected data. Removing artifacts prepares the dataset to be readily available for further analysis. We used the Muse S EEG headband for the collection of EEG data in our experiment. The Muse headband collects EEG data at a sampling frequency of 256 Hz.

EEG lab [24] was used for the preprocessing of raw data. The EEG lab can be used for the visualization, analysis, and removing artifacts from the EEG data. The EEG lab contains modules that can perform baseline correction, filtering, interpolation, and Independent Component analysis of the raw EEG data. The following are the steps performed for the removal of noise from raw EEG data.

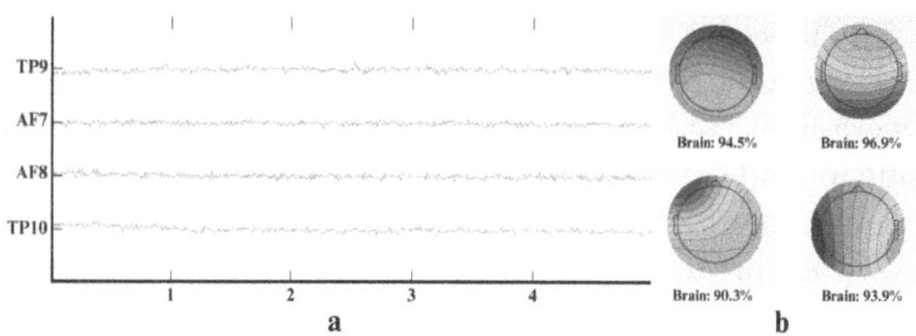


**Fig. 2.** a) Filtered EEG data. b) Independent Component Analysis (ICLabel).

- **Baseline Correction:** The first step in preprocessing is the baseline correction to remove DC offsets from raw EEG data. DC offsets can be caused due to poor contact between the electrodes of the EEG headset and the scalp.
- **Filtering:** Filtering is the next step in preprocessing after removing DC offsets through baseline correction. We performed band pass filtering (Finite Impulse Response) with cutoff frequencies at 0.5 Hz and 50 Hz. Filtering is performed to remove low-frequency drifts and power line noise. Figure 2a represents the filtered EEG data.
- **Interpolation:** The EEG data is lost whenever there is no contact between electrodes and the scalp. In the preprocessing, we need to fill the empty gaps through interpolation. The EEG lab has a module to perform interpolation and fill in lost EEG data. Spline Interpolation technique was utilized to fill the empty gaps present in the EEG data.
- **Independent Component Analysis (ICA):** The EEG lab toolbox has a module to perform ICA, using Infomax algorithm. ICA decomposes a mixed source of signal into its individual components. Individual components that are related to muscle activity and blinks can be removed from EEG data through an artifact rejection module. Output of ICA has been represented in Fig. 2b using ICLabel.

Although we collected the data for 50 participants but due to a malfunction of the EEG device, the data for 4 participants could not be collected reliably by the Muse S. We had to discard the data of 4 participants, and our study is based on the remaining 46 participants' data.

### 4.4 Feature Extraction

Fast Fourier Transform follows after the preprocessing to convert the discrete time domain signal to the frequency domain signal. From the frequency domain, the power spectrum density can be obtained using the Pwelch and Pburg methods [25].

After obtaining the absolute power values for all the brain waves, such as delta, theta, alpha, beta, and gamma, the next step is to perform some statistical analysis to gain insights into the relationships between different power band values.

We employed three distinct set of features to perform three different tasks.

*1) Feature Extraction to perform subject-dependent Evaluation:* The absolute power values were converted to statistical features using statistical measures such as min, max, mean, and standard deviation. Min and max indicate the range and the extreme values, the mean gives insight into the average, and the standard deviation shows the spread in our dataset. We used a 1-second sliding window to calculate these statistical measures for our dataset. These statistical measures were used as features during the subject dependent evaluation using a 10-fold cross-validation strategy.

*2)Feature Extraction to perform subject-independent Evaluation:* We employed different features to capture indispensable patterns to train our model. Following are the features employed to train our model to perform subject-independent evaluation.

**Power band values:** Mean values of delta, theta, alpha, beta, and gamma brain waves from all sensors were used as a feature.**Entropy:** Entropy represents the complexity and uncertainty present in the EEG signal with respect to time. Shannon Entropy was used to calculate the entropy features in this study. **Phase difference:** Phase difference indicates the offsets between brain waves collected from different sensors. Hilbert transform was employed to calculate the instantaneous phase and then subtracting the instantaneous phase of one brain signal from the other provides the phase difference between two brain waves.**Phase Locking Value:** It measures the consistency of phase difference over time, meaning for how long the phase difference persists. Hilbert transform was employed to calculate the phase locking value.**Coherence:** It is the correlation between brain signals in the frequency domain. It is a measure of how consistent the phase and amplitude of two brain signals remain at a particular frequency. The coherence was calculated using the SciPy library.

All the above-mentioned features were calculated using a sliding window of 2 s with a step size of 1 s.

*3)Feature Extraction to perform score prediction:* We performed feature engineering to find the optimum features for the random forest regressor model. We considered the different ratios of absolute power values using different brain waves. We tested almost all possible combinations to achieve the ratio that gives the least error when used as a feature. The feature selection was performed only on a small portion of our dataset to avoid data leakage. When we added alpha and gamma brain waves absolute power values and divided them by the sum of the delta, theta, and beta brain waves, it gave us the least error when used as a feature for the random forest regressor model.

Kahoot assigns scores to participants based on the time taken to solve each question together with the correctness of the answers. If the participant answers the question correctly within a shorter time, Kahoot assigns a higher score. The reason behind this is the relationship between intelligence and time. Intelligent participants should give correct answers in a shorter time. Kahoot only gives limited time for participants to answer each question, and the scores also depend on the time taken to answer the questions, which leads us to use time

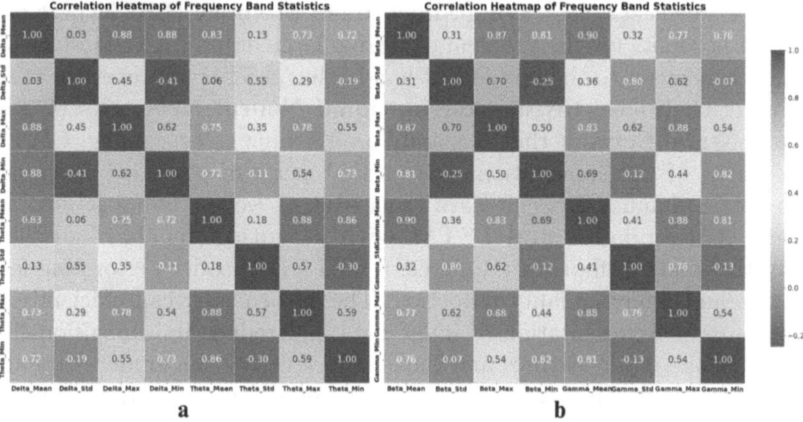

**Fig. 3.** a) Correlation between Delta and Theta brain wave features. b) Correlation between Beta and Gamma brain wave features.

taken as a feature. Therefore, in the random forest regressor model, we used (Alpha+Gamma)/(Delta+Theta+Beta) along with the time taken as a feature. Using time taken as a feature was critical because of the fact that Kahoot assigns a zero score when the allotted time for the question has passed.

**Table 1.** 10-fold Cross Validation Performance Metrics

| Model | Accuracy | Precision | Recall | F1-score |
|---|---|---|---|---|
| Naive Bayes | 73.86 | 0.68 | 0.71 | 0.69 |
| Random Forest | 88.46 | 0.85 | 0.83 | 0.84 |
| SVM | 95.26 | 0.94 | 0.93 | 0.94 |
| LSTM | 99.75 | 1 | 1 | 1 |
| CNN | 99.9 | 1 | 1 | 1 |

### 4.5 Machine Learning Models

We used the following classifiers to train our models:

**Naive Bayes (NB).** is a supervised machine learning model that belongs to the family of probabilistic algorithms that assumes the features are independent for classifying the target variable. **Random Forest** is an ensemble learning technique that works by forming several decision trees during training.

**Support Vector Machine (SVM).** is a supervised machine learning algorithm that classifies by finding an optimal line called a hyperplane that maximizes the distance between each class. **Long Short Term Memory (LSTM)** is a type of RNN that accounts for the problem of storing large data of RNN and keeps the data that is relevant to the problem at hand. Thus, LSTM improves the memory handling of traditional RNNs. **Convolutional Neural Networks (CNN)** is a type of Neural Network that is mainly used for image processing. CNN basically consists of the convolutional layers that perform convolution operations on the data at hand. CNN can learn the spatial as well as temporal features of the data. **Autoencoder and LSTM with attention mechanism** the first stage of the model comprises a fully connected autoencoder performing feature extraction and dimensionality reduction. The autoencoder can efficiently learn the compressed representation of input data and reduce its dimensionality by compressing the input features and then reconstructing the input with minimal loss of information. The second stage of the model consists of the bidirectional LSTM with an attention mechanism. The output of the autoencoder is fed to the LSTM, which captures the temporal patterns present in sequential EEG data. The attention mechanism was employed to highlight the most important time steps present in EEG data.

## 5 Results

This section presents the correlation among the extracted features, followed by the alpha over beta ratios during relaxation and cognitive task modes. The performance of multistage stress classification is demonstrated, followed by the statistical analysis of the brain waves. After that, we provide the model to predict the scores of our participants.

### 5.1 Correlation Among Extracted Features

The correlation heatmaps for delta and theta statistical features are represented in Fig. 3a, and the beta and gamma statistical features are represented in Fig. 3b. From Fig. 3a we observed a strong linear relationship between delta and theta brain waves. Similarly, we observed from Fig. 3b a strong linear relationship between beta and gamma brain waves. Correlation heatmaps have been generated by utilizing the Pearson correlation coefficient.

**Table 2.** LOSO Cross-Validation Performance Metrics

| Performance Metrics | Accuracy | Precision | Recall | F1-score |
|---|---|---|---|---|
| Binary Classification | 0.83 | 0.83 | 0.82 | 0.82 |
| Three Level Classification | 0.66 | 0.55 | 0.55 | 0.55 |

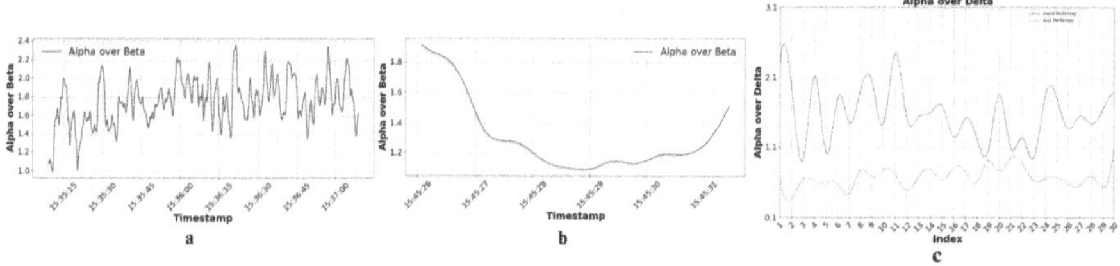


**Fig. 4.** a) Alpha over Beta during relaxation. b) Alpha over Beta during a cognitive task. c) Comparison of Alpha over Delta ratio between good and bad performers during a cognitive task

## 5.2 Stress Level During Relaxation and Cognitive Task

The Alpha-Beta ratio was plotted using a line graph during relaxation and cognitive tasks to visualize the stress. Figure 4a represents the alpha-beta ratio during relaxation, while Fig. 4b represents the alpha-beta ratio during cognitive task. The alpha-beta ratio during relaxation is high compared to the cognitive task mode.

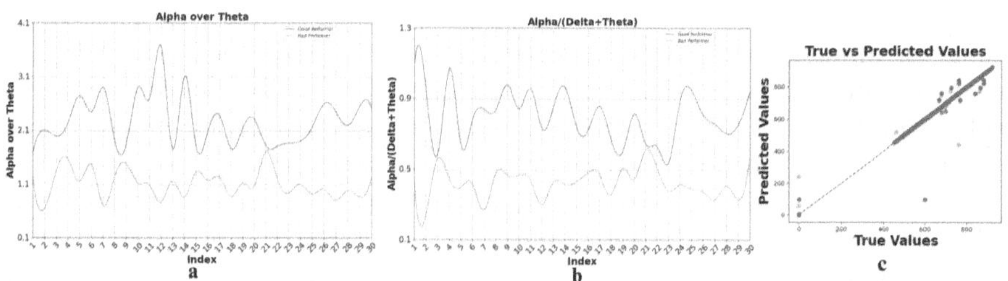


**Fig. 5.** a) Comparison of Alpha over Theta ratio between good and bad performers during a cognitive task. b) Comparison of Alpha over Delta and Theta ratio between good and bad performers during a cognitive task. c) Random Forest Regressor Output.

## 5.3 Multistage Stress Classification

In this section, we will demonstrate the results obtained by employing both evaluation strategies.

*1) 10-fold Cross-validation.* In this section, we discuss multistage stress classification using five classifiers, namely NB, RF, SVM, LSTM, and CNN. Table 1 represents the performance metrics of our classifiers where CNN outperformed other classifiers by achieving 99.9% accuracy whereas NB provided the lowest accuracy of 73.86%.

*2) LOSO cross-validation.* We utilized the LOSO cross-validation strategy to generalize our results in real-world scenarios. In LOSO cross-validation, the model is trained by leaving one subject out, meaning that the model will be trained on every subject's data except the left-out one. The left-out subject will be used in the testing phase. The same process is repeated until all participants' data is used once in the testing phase. All the classifiers performed poorly in the LOSO cross-validation strategy. The highest classification accuracy of 52% was achieved by CNN and LSTM.

The difference between the accuracies achieved by classifiers in 10-fold and LOSO cross-validation is significant. The reason behind this is the fact that in 10-fold cross-validation, the same subject data is present during training and testing, making the classification problem easy.

*3) Autoencoder and LSTM with Attention Mechanism.* We employed the LOSO cross-validation strategy to evaluate the performance of our implemented model. We achieved an accuracy of 83% while performing binary stress classification, and an accuracy of 66% was achieved for three-level stress classification depicted through the Table 2.

### 5.4 Statistical Analysis of Brain Waves

We conducted different analysis of brain waves to see the difference in the brain waves of our good and bad performers during cognitive tasks. We plotted line graphs for alpha over delta, alpha over theta, and alpha over delta plus theta as depicted in Fig. 4c, Fig. 5a, and Fig. 5b respectively. It is clearly evident from the line graphs that alpha over delta, alpha over theta, and alpha over delta plus theta ratios are higher for good performers compared to bad performers.

We made two groups of ten participants each, one group containing good performers and the other group containing the bad performers of our experiment. We conducted a Mann-Whitney U test [26] with a significance level of 0.05 (alpha = 0.05) to verify that there is a statistically significant difference between the ranks of two different groups. Table 3 shows the result of Mann-Whitney U test, which verifies ($p < 0.05$) that there is a statistically significant difference between the ranks of alpha over delta, alpha over theta, and alpha over delta plus theta between the good and bad performer groups. The effect sizes are 0.89 for alpha over delta, 0.85 for alpha over theta, and 0.9 for alpha over delta plus theta.

### 5.5 Kahoot Score Prediction

We also established a model to predict the Kahoot Scores of participants using their EEG signals. A random forest regressor model was trained to predict the scores assigned by Kahoot to participants. Random Forest regressor performance metrics: **Mean Absolute Error** 0.009, **Mean Squared Error** 1.39, **Root Mean Squared Error** 1.18, and $\mathbf{R^2}$ **score** 1. RMSE of 1.18 means that on average random forest regressor model can effectively predict the scores assigned by Kahoot to our participants with a deviation of 1.18 unit from true values. The Fig. 5c depicts the output of the random forest regressor model.

**Table 3.** Mann-Whitney U test

| Alpha/Delta | | Alpha/Theta | | Alpha/(Delta+Theta) | | |
|---|---|---|---|---|---|---|
| U-statistic | P-value | U-statistic | P-value | U-statistic | P-value | Statistical difference |
| 89 | 0.0036 | 85 | 0.0091 | 90 | 0.0028 | Significant |

# 6 Discussion

In this section, we discuss the relationship among extracted features followed by the explanation of stress during relaxation and cognitive tasks. After that, the performance of multistage stress classification is also discussed, followed by the deliberation of statistical analysis of brain waves.

## 6.1 Correlation Among Extracted Features

Correlation heatmap represents the linear relationship between features. Correlation heatmap indicates a very strong linear relationship between delta and theta brain waves. Both waves are low frequency brain waves as represented in Fig. 3a. Delta is highly associated with deep sleep and decreased sensory inhibition occurring during mental task. Theta is highly present during early stages of sleep, drowsiness, and emotional stress. Since there are a lot of similarities between both low frequency brain waves, therefore, strong linear relationship between these waves is depicted in the correlation heatmap. Another strong correlation, Fig. 3b, is seen between beta and gamma brain waves since both are high frequency brain waves and are mainly associated with high cognitive tasks.

## 6.2 Stress Level During Relaxation and Cognitive Task

Alpha is the brain wave that is highly associated with relaxation and focused state. Beta brain wave is highly found during cognitive tasks. Since alpha wave is associated with relaxation and beta wave is associated with the problem solving, their ratio normally specifies about the stress level. The higher the alpha over beta ratio indicates less mental stress whereas the lower alpha over beta ratio means higher mental stress. In the results portion, we represented alpha over beta ratio, through line graphs, during relaxation and cognitive task for one of our participants (Fig. 4a and Fig. 4b). We can clearly see the alpha over beta ratio is high during relaxation as compared to the cognitive task mode.

## 6.3 Multistage Stress Classification

In this section, we will discuss the results achieved after utilizing both cross-validation strategies, followed by an elaboration on the results achieved using autoencoder and LSTM based model.

*1) 10-fold and LOSO Cross-Validation:* CNN outperformed the rest of the classifiers in 10-fold cross-validation by achieving the highest classification accuracy of 99.9% and other performance evaluation metrics were also 1 represented through Table 1 . All the classifiers performed poorly in the LOSO cross-validation strategy. LOSO cross-validation strategy is a more practical approach to generalize the performance of the model to unseen participant data. In 10-fold cross-validation, due to the random split of the data, the same person's data can be present in the training and testing phases. Instead of learning EEG features, the model tries to learn subject-specific features, which helps and improves the performance of the model in the testing phase. Due to this, the 10-fold cross-validation results do not depict how the model will perform on the new person data, which is the case in real-world scenarios. In LOSO cross-validation, as the name suggests, the model is trained on all the remaining subjects after leaving one subject out. The subject that is left out during the training will be employed to test the model's performance in the testing phase. The process is repeated for all subjects once, and the final performance metrics will be calculated by taking the average of the performance metrics of all individual subjects. During each fold, the performance metrics are based on the data of new subjects that the model did not see during the training phase, hence, the results obtained using LOSO cross-validation depict the ability of the classifiers to generalize to unseen participant data.

*2) Autoencoder and LSTM with Attention Mechanism:* We implemented a two-stage deep learning architecture consisting of the autoencoder and LSTM with an attention-based mechanism to better capture the temporal patterns present in sequential EEG data. The first stage consists of a fully connected autoencoder to extract features and reduce dimensionality. The second stage was composed of a bidirectional LSTM classifier to capture the temporal patterns present in EEG data with an attention mechanism to highlight the indispensable time steps. We employed additional features such as entropy, phase difference, phase locking value, and coherence to extract more patterns from EEG data. We also employed a data augmentation technique to oversample the minority classes during the training phase only. Gaussian Noise with a standard deviation of 0.01 was employed to oversample the minority classes during the training phase. We evaluated the performance of our established model both in the case of binary classification as well as three-level stress classification illustrated through the Table 2. The implemented model achieved an accuracy of 83% in binary classification, and other performance metrics were precision 0.83, recall 0.82, and F1-score 0.82 presented through the Table 2. It achieved an accuracy of 66% for three-level stress classification and other performance metrics such as precision 0.55, recall 0.55, and F1-score 0.55. Discrete wavelet transform features were also utilized only in case of three stage stress classification using LOSO. The performance metrics were calculated using a macro average to reflect the performance of the model across all the classes equally. The accuracy achieved by the model in three-stage stress classification is 66% which is double the accuracy that can be achieved by chance or random guessing, indicating that the model is learning the patterns present in the sequential EEG data.

### 6.4 Statistical Analysis of Brain Waves

The results of the Mann-Whitney U test (represented in Table 3) depict that there is a statistically significant difference between the ranks of two different groups in alpha over delta ratio, alpha over theta ratio, and alpha over delta plus theta ratio. Alpha brain wave is associated with relaxation and the state of focus. Participants with higher alpha means they were focused and relaxed during the cognitive task, which is also depicted through their good performance. Theta waves are linked to emotional stress, especially frustration and disappointment. In high-stress situations, poor performers showed increased theta activity due to frustration from low scores. Similarly, higher delta wave activity during mental tasks helped block external distractions, allowing for greater focus by suppressing unnecessary brain activity. Participants with elevated theta and delta levels remained highly engaged in the task, but their poor performance heightened emotional stress, reducing alpha wave activity and relaxation. Higher alpha over delta, alpha over theta, and alpha over delta plus theta means more focused and relaxed during cognitive tasks and hence better performance.

## 7 Conclusion and Future Work

This study investigates multistage stress classification using EEG signals. A dataset of the EEG signal of 50 participants was collected using a user-interactive approach where each participant was provided with stressors in the form of a smartphone game. We elaborated on the difference between 10-fold and LOSO cross-validation strategies. We implemented an autoencoder and LSTM based model and achieved an accuracy of 83% in binary classification and an accuracy of 66% for three levels of stress classification. We performed a Mann-Whitney U test to verify that there is a statistically significant difference between the brain waves of the best and bad performers of our experiment. The test specified that higher alpha over delta, alpha over theta, and alpha over delta plus theta are associated with the best performers group of our experiment. The results indicate that for higher cognitive capacities, alpha brain wave should be high whereas delta and theta should be low.

As our future work, we will expand the experiment by including more puzzles, problem-solving, and reasoning questions to conduct an extensive study of cognitive intelligence and cognitive abilities based on brain waves. We will also include a larger number of participants in our experiment to better generalize our findings.

## References

1. Bhargava, D., Trivedi, H.: A study of causes of stress and stress management among youth. IRA-Int. J. Manag. Soc. Sci. **11**(03), 108–117 (2018)

2. Ali, F., et al.: Effects of stress on job performance. Int. J. Bus. Manag. Tomorrow **1**(2), 1–7 (2011)
3. Van Praag, H.M.: Can stress cause depression? Prog. Neuropsychopharmacol. Biol. Psychiatry **28**(5), 891–907 (2004)
4. Khan, M.J., Altaf, S., Kausar, H.: Effect of perceived academic stress on students' performance. FWU J. Soc. Sci. 7(2) 2013)
5. Leger, K.A., Charles, S.T., Turiano, N.A., Almeida, D.M.: Personality and stressor-related affect. J. Pers. Soc. Psychol. **111**(6), 917 (2016)
6. Dol, M., McDonald, E., Ferro, M.A.: Psychometric properties of the CESD, STAI-T, and PSS among parents of children with mental illness. J. Family Stud. **28**(4), 1416–1432 (2022)
7. Giannakakis, G., Grigoriadis, D., Giannakaki, K., Simantiraki, O., Roniotis, A., Tsiknakis, M.: Review on psychological stress detection using biosignals. IEEE Trans. Affect. Comput. **13**(1), 440–460 (2019)
8. Su, C., Zangeneh Soroush, M., Torkamanrahmani, N., Ruiz-Segura, A., Yang, L., Li, X., Zeng, Y.: Measurement and quantification of stress in the decision process: a model-based systematic review. Intell. Comput. **3**, 0090 (2024)
9. Adil, M., Atiq, I., Younus, S.: Effectiveness of the Apple Watch as a mental health tracker. J. Glob. Health **14**, 03010 (2024)
10. Jun, G. and Smitha, K.G.: EEG based stress level identification. In: 2016 IEEE International Conference on Systems, Man, and Cybernetics (SMC) (pp. 003270-003274). IEEE (2016)
11. Rauf, U. and Saeed, S.M.U.: Towards improved classification of perceived stress using time domain features. IEEE Access (2024)
12. Asif, A., Majid, M., Anwar, S.M.: Human stress classification using EEG signals in response to music tracks. Comput. Biol. Med. **107**, 182–196 (2019)
13. Arsalan, A., Majid, M., Butt, A.R., Anwar, S.M.: Classification of perceived mental stress using a commercially available EEG headband. IEEE J. Biomed. Health Inform. **23**(6), 2257–2264 (2019)
14. Hou, X., et al.: EEG based stress monitoring. In: 2015 IEEE International Conference on Systems, Man, and Cybernetics (pp. 3110-3115). IEEE (2015)
15. Cambay, V.Y., Tasci, I., Tasci, G., Hajiyeva, R., Dogan, S., Tuncer, T.: QuadTPat: quadruple transition pattern-based explainable feature engineering model for stress detection using eeg signals. Sci. Rep. **14**(1), 27320 (2024)
16. Ince, U., et al.: CubicPat: investigations on the mental performance and stress detection using EEG signals. Diagnostics **15**(3), 363 (2025)
17. Phutela, N., Relan, D., Gabrani, G., Kumaraguru, P., Samuel, M.: Stress classification using brain signals based on LSTM network. Comput. Intell. Neurosci. **2022**(1), 7607592 (2022)
18. Nauta, W.J., Feirtag, M.: The organization of the brain. Sci. Am. **241**(3), 88–111 (1979)
19. Tulen, J.H.M., Moleman, P., Van Steenis, H.G., Boomsma, F.: Characterization of stress reactions to the stroop color word test. Pharmacol. Biochem. Behav. **32**(1), 9–15 (1989)
20. Poh, C.H., et al.: The effect of antireflux treatment on patients with gastroesophageal reflux disease undergoing a mental arithmetic stressor. Neurogastroenterol. **23**(11), e489–e496 (2011)
21. Schwabe, L., Haddad, L., Schachinger, H.: HPA axis activation by a socially evaluated cold-pressor test. Psychoneuroendocrinology **33**(6), 890–895 (2008)

22. Kirschbaum, C., Pirke, K.M., Hellhammer, D.H.: The 'trier social stress test'– a tool for investigating psychobiological stress responses in a laboratory setting. Neuropsychobiology **28**(1–2), 76–81 (1993)
23. Learning games: make learning awesome! Kahoot! (2025). https://kahoot.com/. Accessed 25 May 2025
24. Delorme, A., Makeig, S.: EEGLAB: an open source toolbox for analysis of single-trial EEG dynamics including independent component analysis. J. Neurosci. Methods **134**(1), 9–21 (2004)
25. Petkar, H., Dande, S., Yadav, R., Zeng, Y., Nguyen, T.A.: A pilot study to assess designer's mental stress using eye gaze system and electroencephalogram. In: International Design Engineering Technical Conferences and Computers and Information in Engineering Conference (Vol. 48999, pp. 899–909) (2009)
26. McKnight, P.E., Najab, J.: Mann-whitney u test. The Corsini encyclopedia of psychology, pp.1–1 (2010)

# DP-WGAN-GP for Privacy Protection in Medical Data

Bo Yu, Hao Huang, Yiyu Shan, Guoqiang Zhao, and Hemn Barzan Abdalla(✉)

Wenzhou-Kean University, Wenzhou, China
{ybo,huanghao,shany,zhaogu,habdalla}@kean.edu

**Abstract.** This article proposes a privacy-preserving data generation model that combines Wasserstein Generative Adversarial Network with Gradient Penalty (WGAN-GP) and differential privacy (DP) to solve two problems: how to generate high-quality synthetic medical data and how to protect the privacy information of the generated medical data. We combine WGAN-GP with residual blocks, gradient clipping, and fixed Laplacian noise to demonstrate the ability of our method in generating realistic and privacy-preserving medical data. The WGAN-GP framework ensures data fidelity, stabilizes model training, and generates high-quality data. Comparative experiments show that fixed noise outperforms adaptive noise. In terms of differential privacy, fixed Laplacian noise provides better privacy protection compared to Gaussian noise. The DP-WGAN-GP model has achieved a good compromise between data fidelity and privacy, and can still maintain the original data distribution under privacy constraints. Experimental results show that the DP-WGAN-GP model can effectively replicate real medical data, achieving a balance between data utility and privacy, and providing a powerful solution for big data medical data protection.

**Keywords:** WGAN-GP · Differential Privacy · Synthetic Medical Data · Fixed Noise Injection · Laplace Noise · Privacy-Preserving Data Analysis

## 1 Introduction

In the era of big data and artificial intelligence [1], the healthcare industry is facing increasing data privacy issues. With the emergence of machine learning and artificial intelligence systems used in medical data analysis, privacy breaches involving sensitive patient information have raised ethical and legal concerns. While maintaining the availability of medical data, the effectiveness of privacy protection mechanisms has become a research focus. This article aims to address the balance between privacy and data availability in medical analysis. We have developed a new approach that combines Wasserstein Generative Adversarial Network (WGAN-GP) with differential privacy combining WGAN-GP high-quality data generation with DP noise injection privacy protection technology. We mainly focus on two points: first, deploying fixed noise injection strategy


R. Stahlbock et al. (Eds.): CSCE 2025, CCIS 2938, pp. 170–190, 2027.
https://doi.org/10.1007/978-3-032-22196-4_13

and WGAN-GP frames together, which simplifies the integration steps of differential privacy and improves the stability level of data; second, comparing fixed noise and adaptive noise to see their mechanisms for protecting privacy without reducing data effectiveness. By improving the performance of WGAN-GP under differential privacy protection, we have strengthened privacy protection and data fidelity, and constructed a more secure and reliable medical data sharing system.

## 2 Literature Review

### 2.1 Differential Privacy in Medical Data

Differential Privacy (DP) is a fundamental technique for healthcare privacy protection data analysis, which minimizes the impact of including or excluding individual data points on the entire dataset, thereby reducing the risk of re identification. Research [2,3] The feasibility of DP in protecting genomic and medical imaging data while maintaining analytical utility has been highlighted, but balancing privacy protection and data utility remains a challenge, and determining the optimal privacy parameters (such as epsilon value) when achieving these trade-offs is also a challenge.

Some studies have attempted to apply DP to medical research, [4] indicating that DP can securely share data by adding controlled noise, [5] incorporating DP into machine learning models such as DP-SGD to enhance privacy protection in medical artificial intelligence applications. Despite these achievements, there are still difficulties in achieving a balance between improving privacy, model accuracy, and computational efficiency.

### 2.2 Generative Adversarial Networks for Medical Data

GANs are also widely used in generating medical data, which is very beneficial for solving the problems of data shortage and privacy risks. The dual level GAN structure for medical imaging given in [6] demonstrates the ability to generate well synthesized data that complies with privacy protection. Another study [7] have conducted in-depth research on various GANs, such as DCGAN, CycleGAN, etc., which are used for enhancing and reconstructing medical images. However, there are still some problems such as pattern collapse and class imbalance.

Recent research has combined DP and GAN to enhance privacy protection. [8] The work in [9] reviewed models such as DP-GAN and WGAN-GP, which use injected noise and gradient penalties to reduce privacy risks. The study examined the application of GANs in privacy preserving medical decision-making and pointed out their potential for secure, data-driven healthcare insights.

### 2.3 Hybrid Approaches for Privacy-Preserving Medical Data

The hybrid model combining DP with Federated Learning (FL) is very attractive for decentralized medical data protection. One study in [10] used DP-FL for histopathology image analysis, which complies with regulatory frameworks such as GDPR and HIPAA. However, the noise of DP often deteriorates the performance of the model, especially in non-IID data situations.

Introducing a differential private DPCTGAN model suitable for federal environment optimization [11]. Although privacy protection is very effective, there are situations such as high computational overhead and pattern collapse. The differential private model inversion (DPMI) framework in [12] relies on a two-stage training process to enhance privacy protection during synthetic data generation, and there is a Flipped Huber mechanism [13] that combines Laplacian and Gaussian noise distributions to enhance the utility trade-off of privacy protection. However, it is designed for regression tasks and further research is needed for complex medical datasets.

### 2.4 Objective

This study aims to provide a specific privacy protection solution for healthcare data by proposing a new method that combines Wasserstein Generative Adversarial Network (WGAN-GP), gradient penalty, and differential privacy (DP). In this process, the relationship between privacy protection and data availability can be coordinated.

The key objective of this study is to examine the effectiveness of the DP-WGAN-GP model in medical data privacy protection. It leverages the advantages of WGAN-GP to enhance privacy protection and maximize data value. We designed some tests to test the effectiveness of the DP-WGAN-GP model in privacy protection and compared it with other existing privacy protection models, with a focus on the balance between privacy protection and data availability, involving testing for different types of noise.

This study uses various key indicators to demonstrate the superiority of the DP-WGAN-GP model in generating high fidelity and privacy-preserving data. The research results will provide important references for the best practices of medical data privacy protection and promote the further application of privacy preserving generation models in the medical field.

## 3 Methodology

### 3.1 Differential Privacy in Medical Data Protection

**Assessing Data Sensitivity for Medical Applications.** The sensitivity of DP evaluation data in medical applications is crucial, and the leakage of sensitive information will bring significant risks. Understanding sensitivity can help determine appropriate privacy measures [14].

Sensitivity assessment directly affects the noise level of DP. Sensitive data requires more noise, while less sensitive data can tolerate less noise. By adjusting the noise-ultimate parameter, the model balances privacy and utility, and adjusts the noise level according to the sensitivity of the data to effectively protect it.

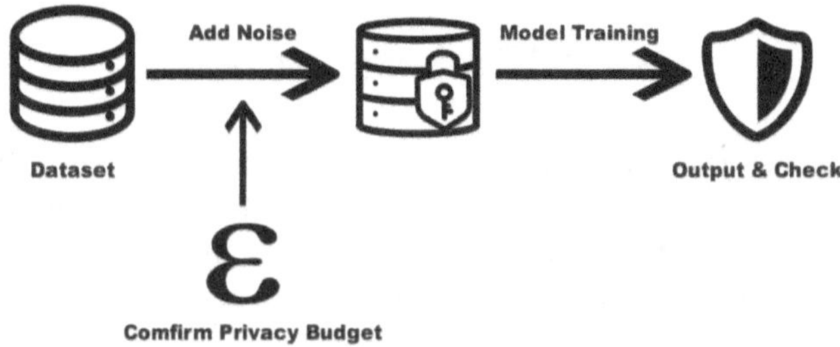


**Fig. 1.** Differential Privacy Implementation.

Application of Shannon Entropy and Statistical Distribution Analysis in Quantifying Noise Adjustment:

$$H(X) = -\sum_{i=1}^{n} p(x_i) \log p(x_i) \tag{1}$$

Among them $H(X)$ is the entropy of data $X$. The larger the entropy, the higher the sensitivity, which is used to guide the dynamic noise parameters in the DP mechanism and enhance privacy.

**Differential Privacy Mechanism.** Differential privacy protects data points by introducing controlled noise, ensuring that the inclusion or exclusion of a single record minimizes the impact on the output [15]. A randomized algorithm $\mathcal{A}$ satisfies $(\epsilon, \delta)$-differential privacy if for all datasets $D$ and $D'$ differing by at most one element and for all subsets $S \subseteq \text{Range}(\mathcal{A})$:

$$P(\mathcal{A}(D) \in S) \leq e^{\epsilon} P(\mathcal{A}(D') \in S) + \delta \tag{2}$$

Among them $\epsilon$ controls privacy loss, and $\delta$ represents the small probability of deviation from strict privacy guarantees.

In this model, we use the Differentially Private Stochastic Gradient Descent (DP-SGD) mechanism to enforce privacy protection (Fig. 1), following the DP principle:

- Sensitivity Analysis: L2 norm clipping limits the impact of outliers, preventing single data points from dominating updates [16].
- Noise Injection: Gaussian noise added to gradients balances privacy and utility, with the noise level controlled by the noise multiplier.
- Privacy Budget Management: The cumulative privacy loss is tracked across training to ensure adherence to privacy constraints.

The DP-SGD update rule follows:

$$\tilde{g} = \frac{1}{m}\sum_{i=1}^{m}\bar{g}_i + \mathcal{N}\left(0, \sigma^2 C^2 I\right) \tag{3}$$

where $g$ represents the gradient, and $\sigma$ controls the noise intensity. We used three different values of $\sigma(0.1, 0.5, 1.0)$ respectively to balance privacy and model performance. This DP-SGD mechanism can protect medical data during model generation. The generated model can ensure privacy and practicality, and protect synthesized data.

### 3.2 WGAN-GP Architecture with Embedded Privacy Controls

The Wasserstein GAN (WGAN-GP) with gradient penalty as the core of the generative model provides a powerful training framework that minimizes the Wasserstein distance between the real data distribution and the generated data distribution [17]. WGAN-GP solves the instability problem of traditional GANs and is of great significance for generating highly sensitive datasets such as medical data. The objective function of WGAN-GP is:

$$\begin{aligned}\max_{D}\min_{G}\ & \mathbb{E}_{x\sim P_{\text{data}}}[D(x)] - \mathbb{E}_{z\sim P_z}[D(G(z))] \\ & - \mathcal{L}_{\text{GP}}\end{aligned} \tag{4}$$

where:

- $D$ is the discriminator,
- $G$ is the generator,
- $P_{\text{data}}$ is the real data distribution,
- $P_z$ is the noise distribution,
- $P_{\hat{x}}$ is the distribution of points sampled along straight lines between pairs of real and generated samples,
- $\lambda$ is a hyperparameter controlling the strength of the gradient penalty.

Gradient penalty ensures discriminator training convergence through Lipschitz constraints.

This study uses the WGAN-GP model to generate synthetic medical data with privacy protection, with key architectural elements covering:

- Generator Design: fully connected, batch normalized, residual block ensures stable gradient flow, learns medical data distribution. LeakyReLU activation causes the generated real data to have nonlinearity.
- The discriminator relies on gradient penalty to determine true and false data, and the gradient penalty is executed according to the Wasserstein distance standard to achieve stable adversarial training and reduce overfitting.
- Privacy embedding and fixed noise injection: a differentiated mechanism for balancing protection and data quality.

In this way, high fidelity synthetic medical data can be generated, and privacy can be protected. The generated medical data is the same as real medical records, but it will never leak privacy (Fig. 2).

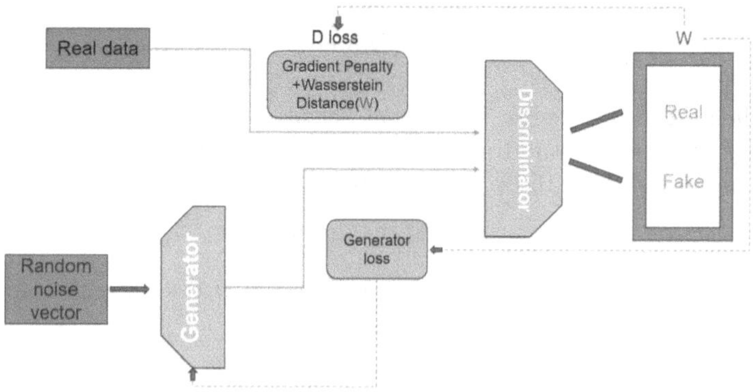


**Fig. 2.** WGAN-GP Model Architecture.

### 3.3 Noise Injection

**Comparative Analysis of Fixed and Adaptive Noise Mechanisms.** Noise injection is a fundamental concept in privacy-preserving machine learning. In the variation of noise injection, fixed noise and adaptive noise are two opposing strategies, each with its own advantages and disadvantages [18]. Applying the same fixed noise disturbance level to all data points can provide predictable privacy assurance and simplify compliance, especially in regulated domains.

In contrast, adaptive noise dynamically adjusts the noise level based on model performance or data sensitivity [19]. This method can apply less noise to less sensitive data and more noise to important features, thereby improving the utility of the data. However, its non-uniformity can lead to a decrease in privacy protection levels and complexity in regulatory coordination.

In our research, we compared these two strategies under the DP-WGAN-GP architecture to determine which strategy can better balance data utility and privacy protection in this medical environment, with the aim of finding suitable mechanisms for high-risk applications that require strong and consistent privacy protection.

**Choosing Between Gaussian and Laplace Noise.** Compare Gaussian noise and Laplacian noise within the DP framework to see which one is effective. Gaussian noise is suitable for high-dimensional data and has a smoother distribution, which makes the model more robust. Laplacian noise has a heavier tail and provides more privacy, but has little impact on practicality [20].

Gaussian noise is added to the output of a function $f$ as follows:

$$\tilde{f}(x) = f(x) + \mathcal{N}\left(0, \sigma^2\right) \tag{5}$$

where $\mathcal{N}\left(0, \sigma^2\right)$ represents a Gaussian distribution with mean of 0 and a variance $\sigma^2$, where the variance can be determined based on the sensitivity $\Delta f$ of the function:

$$\sigma = \frac{\Delta f \cdot \sqrt{2\ln(1.25/\delta)}}{\epsilon} \tag{6}$$

Among them, $\Delta f$ represents the global sensitivity, defined as the maximum change in $f$ output when adding or deleting individual data.

Implementing differential privacy protection by injecting Laplacian noise:

$$\tilde{f}(x) = f(x) + \mathcal{L}(b) \tag{7}$$

where $\mathcal{L}(b)$ denotes a Laplace distribution centered at 0 with scale parameter $b$. The scale $b$ can be derived from the sensitivity:

$$b = \frac{\Delta f}{\epsilon} \tag{8}$$

The probability density function (PDF) of the Laplace distribution is given by:

$$p(y) = \frac{1}{2b}\exp\left(-\frac{|y|}{b}\right) \tag{9}$$

We compare Gaussian and Laplace noise to assess their suitability for healthcare data privacy protection, balancing privacy and utility.

### 3.4 Differential Privacy in WGAN-GP Framework

The integration of Differentially Private Stochastic Gradient Descent (DP-SGD) within the WGAN-GP framework is designed to generate high-quality synthetic data while protecting sensitive information. Our approach includes improved gradient clipping techniques, controlled noise injection, and privacy budget management to balance privacy protection and model utility. The overall framework of WGAN-GP is shown in the (Fig. 3):

1. Clipping the gradients of the discriminator: We adapt the typical gradient clipping technique to limit the impact of individual data points on model updates, differing from the conventional WGAN-GP approach where clipping is primarily used to enforce Lipschitz continuity. Here, gradient clipping serves as a key privacy mechanism by constraining gradient magnitudes within a privacy-defined threshold:

$$\mathcal{L}_{\text{GP}} = \lambda \mathbb{E}_{\hat{x}\sim P_{\hat{x}}}\left[(\|\nabla_{\hat{x}} D(\hat{x})\|_2 - 1)^2\right] \tag{10}$$

   The gradient penalty term $L_{GP}$ in Eq. (10) is a key component of WGAN-GP, used to stabilize the training process and ensure the stability of both the generator and the discriminator. Here, $\nabla_{\hat{x}} D(\hat{x})$ represents the gradient of the discriminator with respect to the generated sample $\hat{x}$, and $P_{\hat{x}}$ is the sample distribution obtained by linearly interpolating between real data and generated data. The gradient penalty term penalizes the deviation of the gradient from 1, ensuring that the discriminator satisfies the Lipschitz continuity condition, which in turn helps improve the quality and stability of the generated data.

2. Adding Laplace noise:

$$g_{\text{noisy}} = \text{clip}(g) + \mathcal{L}(b) \tag{11}$$

Adding Laplacian noise to the noisy gradient, $\mathcal{L}(b)$ is the noise extracted from a Laplace distribution with a scale of $b$, The sampling of $\mathcal{L}(b)$ is taken from a Laplacian distribution with a scale parameter $\mathcal{L}(b)$ that has been adjusted to balance privacy and practicality.

3. Updating the discriminator:

$$D \leftarrow D + \eta \cdot g_{\text{noisy}} \tag{12}$$

Among them $\eta$ represents the learning rate, which is uesed to ensure consistency of privacy protection updates during the iterative process.

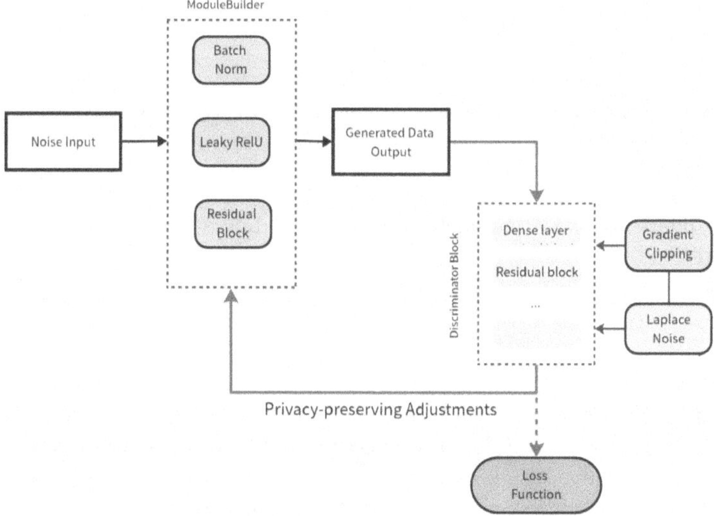


**Fig. 3.** DP-WGAN-GP Framework.

The main DP mechanisms implemented in this study are described below:

- Privacy-Oriented Gradient Clipping and Noise Injection: Modified gradient clipping within the discriminator network restricts gradients to a threshold (12_norm_clip). Laplace noise is added post-clipping, with noise levels controlled by a noise_multiplier, optimizing privacy while retaining data utility.
- Privacy-Aware Discriminator Update: Noise injection ensures that updates to identifiers are kept secret. A fixed training cycle noise level helps limit overfitting to maintain stable generalizations.
- Privacy Budget Control: Using Budget $\epsilon$ to track privacy costs, it monitors cumulative privacy losses. This ensures that privacy is consistently observed throughout the training process.

**Algorithm 1.** DP-WGAN-GP Training Procedure

**Require:** Real dataset $X$, noise distribution $Z$, learning rate $\eta$, gradient clipping threshold $C$, Laplace noise scale $b$, batch size $m$, gradient penalty coefficient $\lambda$, total iterations $N$

**for** $t = 1$ to $N$ **do**
  Sample mini-batch of real data: $x_i \sim X,\ i = 1, \dots, m$
  Sample mini-batch of noise: $z_i \sim Z$
  Generate fake data: $\tilde{x}_i = G(z_i)$
  Interpolate: $\hat{x}_i = \epsilon x_i + (1 - \epsilon)\tilde{x}_i$, where $\epsilon \sim \mathcal{U}(0, 1)$
  Compute discriminator outputs: $D(x_i),\ D(\tilde{x}_i),\ D(\hat{x}_i)$
  Compute gradient penalty:
  $L_{GP} = \frac{\lambda}{m} \sum_{i=1}^{m} \left( \|\nabla_{\hat{x}_i} D(\hat{x}_i)\|_2 - 1 \right)^2$
  Compute discriminator loss:
  $L_D = \frac{1}{m} \sum_{i=1}^{m} [D(\tilde{x}_i) - D(x_i)] + L_{GP}$
  Compute per-sample gradients: $g_i = \nabla L_D(x_i)$
  Clip gradients: $g_i = \frac{g_i}{\max\left(1, \frac{\|g_i\|_2}{C}\right)}$
  Aggregate gradients: $\bar{g} = \frac{1}{m} \sum_{i=1}^{m} g_i$
  Add Laplace noise: $g_{\text{noisy}} = \bar{g} + \text{Lap}(b)$
  Update discriminator parameters using gradient ascent step with $g_{\text{noisy}}$
  **if** $t$ mod generator_interval $= 0$ **then**
    Sample noise: $z_i' \sim Z$
    Compute generator loss: $L_G = -\frac{1}{m} \sum_{i=1}^{m} D(G(z_i'))$
    Update generator parameters using descending $\nabla L_G$
  **end if**
**end for**

By integrating differential privacy into the WGAN-GP framework, the model can generate synthetic medical data while maintaining privacy levels. This DP-WGAN-GP approach includes improved gradient clipping, noise addition, and supervised budgeting, which can ensure strong privacy protection performance and high data fidelity, making it suitable for applications that value priority and data authenticity.

# 4 Experiments and Results

## 4.1 Experimental Setup

The DP-WGAN-GP model was carried out by a Python program on a Windows 10 system with 16 GB of memory available.

## 4.2 The DP-WGAN-GP Algorithm Demonstration

Here, we propose and validate the DP-WGAN-GP model, which belongs to a new privacy protection framework that links differential privacy with Wasserstein generative adversarial networks and gradient penalties. We propose an effective and practical method to integrate medical data with strong privacy protection.

This architecture includes a discriminator and a generator, which improve stability and quality through certain iterations. Gradient pruning and Laplacian noise are added when the discriminator is updated to comply with differential privacy by masking individual contributions. Adversarial training optimizes the generator by minimizing the discriminator's ability to distinguish between real and generated data, thereby improving the quality and usefulness of synthesized data. We integrate DP into WGAN-GP In the framework, it is possible to generate synthetic datasets that are close to reality and preserve key statistical characteristics, achieving a synergistic improvement of data utility and privacy protection.

### 4.3 Results and Analysis on the WDBC Dataset

In order to evaluate the privacy protection capability, data quality, and training efficiency of WGAN-GP and DP technologies, we selected appropriate noise interference mechanisms to assess different models. In order to comprehensively evaluate the impact of DP-WGAN-GP on medical data privacy and utility, we conducted experiments on the WDBC dataset. Demonstrated how different noise mechanisms affect the quality of synthesized data and privacy protection effectiveness.

**The WDBC Dataset.** Based on privacy protection requirements, choose the Wisconsin Diagnostic Breast Cancer(WDBC) Dataset [21], A sensitive medical dataset used for conducting experiments. It has 569 samples, each representing a patient breast tissue sample analyzed by fine-needle aspiration (FNA). Each instance has 30 numerical features that describe the cell nucleus in the image, such as radius, texture, perimeter, area, and smoothness, which can be used to determine malignant or benign tumors.

Among them, 357 markers are benign and 212 markers are malignant. The distribution of these two markers in the sample is relatively balanced. This dataset has been widely used in many machine learning based medical diagnostic tasks, so it is a good benchmark to test our privacy-preserving composite data generation model. Due to the sensitivity of medical records, Maintaining useful data while also protecting privacy requires integrating differential privacy techniques into generative models, as we have done in this study.

**Comparison of Fixed Noise vs. Adaptive Noise.** When analyzing and improving the model to understand its performance, it is crucial to comprehensively evaluate various types of noise. Using several important indicators to compare fixed noise and adaptive noise can provide valuable insights.

Compared with adaptive noise, fixed noise performs better in several aspects (Fig. 4). The mean square error of fixed noise is 1.6392, and the mean square error of adaptive noise is 2.2120. The average deviation of fixed noise is smaller. Compared with adaptive noise's 6.6039, the relative error of fixed noise is 5.5043, and the prediction error is smaller. The epsilon value of fixed noise is 0.95, and

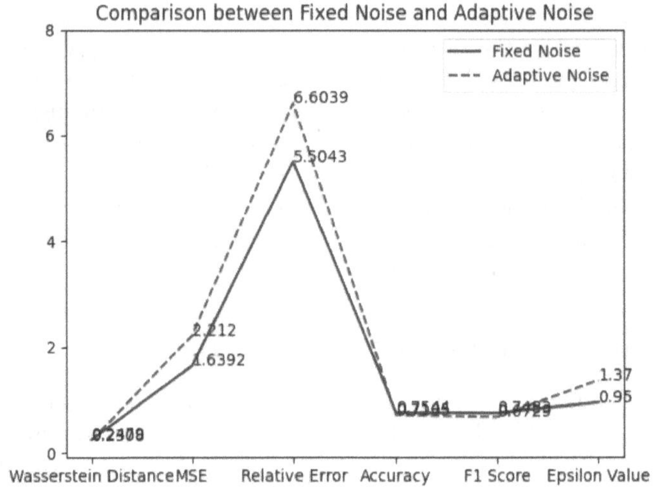


**Fig. 4.** Performance of Fixed vs. Adaptive Noise.

the epsilon value of adaptive noise is 1.37. Fixed noise can protect more privacy. Fixed noise also has certain edges in sampling accuracy and precision. Compared with adaptive noise's 0.7105, the accuracy is 0.7544, F1 is 0.7483, and F1 of adaptive noise is 0.6729. Although the Wasserstein distance of adaptive noise is slightly smaller than that of fixed noise by 0.2479, and adaptive noise is 0.2308, this difference can be ignored. We found that although fixed noise can ensure stable results, the strategy of adaptive noise often leads to instability, causing significant fluctuations in model performance. Therefore, using fixed noise as an optimization strategy is quite appropriate, especially in medical data, where the balance between privacy and data quality is very important.

**Laplacian Noise is Superior to Gaussian Noise.** Looking at Fig. 5, it can be seen that the data accuracy and F1 score generated by Laplacian noise are better than those of Gaussian noise. The average accuracy of Laplacian noise is 0.7573 and the average F1 score is 0.731, while the average accuracy of Gaussian noise is 0.5 and the average F1 score is 0.5026.

The advantage of Laplacian noise is that it preserves more important distribution information while protecting privacy. Compared to Gaussian noise, Laplacian noise brings smoother and more uniform interference. Due to its heavy tailed nature, Laplacian noise preserves more structural information than Gaussian noise, especially on sharp decision boundaries. This makes Laplacian noise highly advantageous in privacy-preserving generative models such as DP-WGAN-GP, which require preserving the statistical properties of sensitive data, preserving finer details, and producing more authentic outputs to better train

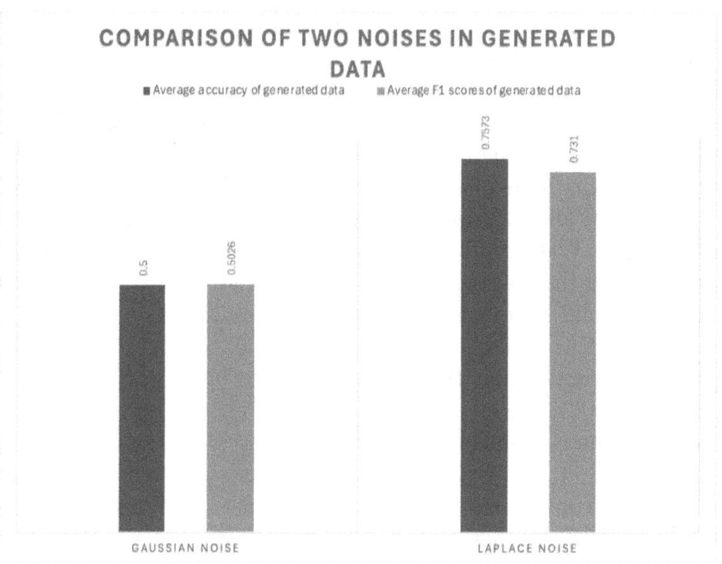


**Fig. 5.** Laplacian vs Gaussian Noise Performance.

deep models. Therefore, in this case, it achieves a better privacy utility trade-off than Gaussian noise.

**The Preponderance and Innovations of This Model.** We first compared the F1 scores of DP-WGAN-GP with other GAN models on the Wisconsin DiagnosticBreast Cancer (WDBC) dataset. The WDBC dataset is a typical medical dataset with high-dimensional features and imbalanced class distributions, and our model gives very high F1 scores most of the time, with the highest F1 score of 0.9736 on the WDBC dataset, This indicates that it achieves a good balance between accuracy and recall in sensitive medical classification tasks, highlighting the effectiveness of DP-WGAN-GP in preventing false positive and false negative misclassification, which is an important requirement for clinical decision support systems.

**Table 1.** Comparison of Different GAN Models Generated Data Capability

| | DP-WGAN-GP | GAN | WGAN | DPGAN | PATE-GAN |
|---|---|---|---|---|---|
| F1-Score | 0.9736 | 0.2654 | 0.4445 | 0.6784 | 0.6948 |
| FID | 23.9375 | 27.9291 | 27.7818 | 27.8234 | 27.8245 |
| Wasserstein | 0.2591 | 0.6675 | 0.6822 | 0.6716 | 0.6784 |
| $\epsilon$ ($\delta = 1e-5$) | 0.96 | - | - | 0.96 | 1.0 |

As shown in Table 1, DP-WGAN-GP clearly dominates on the WDBC dataset, indicating that our model has an advantage over models trained on this type of medical dataset. The higher the F1 score, the better the recognition ability for samples of different categories, even in the case of inherent class imbalance in the dataset. The FID score in the results was as low as 23.9375, indicating that the synthetic medical data generated by DP-WGAN-GP is extremely similar to the real WDBC sample data, which is crucial for training robust diagnostic models. The Wasserstein distance is as small as -0.2591, indicating that our model can learn the features of WDBC with high fidelity, such as kernel features, which is crucial for downstream medical simulations to provide synthetic data.

In terms of privacy, under the privacy budget constraint of $\delta = 10^{-5}$ and a noise coefficient of 0.25, an $\epsilon$ (privacy leakage) of DP-WGAN-GP is 0.96, which is comparable to the current best model dp gan (($\epsilon = 0.96$)) and slightly better than PATE-GAN ($\epsilon = 1.0$). Our model has demonstrated that while maintaining effectiveness under competitive conditions with existing models, it also preserves privacy. Our model can generate privacy-preserving synthetic data in sensitive fields such as healthcare, and provide robust and reliable solutions by balancing privacy and data utility.

On important indicators such as F1 score, FID, Wasserstein distance, DP-WGAN-GP performs much better than GAN, WGAN, DP-GAN, and PATE-GAN models. DP-WGAN-GP has a more comprehensive advantage over other models on the WDBC dataset. The high F1 score and low FID/Wasstein index indicate that the model is very proficient in generating medical related synthetic data, while solving problems such as class imbalance and high dimensionality. The strict privacy guarantee and data fidelity of the proposed model make it a powerful tool for conducting cancer diagnosis security research in the healthcare field without compromising patient confidentiality. The results indicate that DP-WGAN-GP has potential promote the application of synthetic data in oncology and privacy critical medical fields.

### 4.4 Experiments on the CORD-19 Dataset

In order to verify whether DP-WGAN-GP is effective for medical text data, we used the COVID-19 Open Research Data Set (CORD-19), which contains various academic papers from bioRxiv, medRxiv, PubMed and other sources. The data set expanded rapidly during the 2020 pandemic, and its style and structure are various, so it is very suitable for generating dynamic and sensitive text data. Considering that there may be sensitive content, privacy protection is very important when generating composite data.

During preprocessing, the privacy budget is set to $\epsilon = 1.0$ and $\delta = 0$, taking into account both privacy and semantic fidelity. Text normalization, sample filtering, and noise injection are used to standardize the data and reduce structural bias. We train the DP-WGAN-GP model and evaluate it using Wasserstein distance, mean square error, relative error, and Fréchet Inception Distance (FID).

The results show that the synthesized text generated by the model is semantically coherent, with a Wasserstein distance of 0.1145, MSE of 1.6702, relative error of 9.8811, and FID of 27.6267. This indicates that due to privacy constraints, the data generation is very close to the true distribution, and the information loss is acceptable. FID can be optimized even better, but the model can still maintain data quality under strong privacy constraints. Subsequent work will focus on finding better noise strategies to improve semantic fidelity and reduce FID.

### 4.5 Cross-Domain Validation: Noise Mechanism Analysis on MNIST Dataset

In this section, we will use the Wasserstein GAN (WGAN-GP) model with gradient penalty on the MNIST dataset to verify the impact of noise on the efficiency of the generative network, and observe the correlation between privacy level and the quality of the output images generated by the generator, The MNIST dataset mainly contains handwritten digits, but it relies on the structure of grayscale pixels and is very similar to low dimensional medical image data. We believe that this experiment can be used as a simplified simulation to complete complex medical data generation tasks, which can explore the impact of noise in a targeted manner. We use the Fréchet Inception Distance (FID) score to measure the distribution difference between the generated image and the real data. The lower the FID score, the closer the generated image is to the real data in the feature space, which means higher image quality and potential better privacy protection.

**Purpose.** This section of the experiment aims to verify the privacy protection effect of the proposed DP-WGAN-GP model on different types of datasets, with a focus on the performance in image datasets. Although the core concern of this study is the privacy protection of medical data, we chose datasets from other domains to visually evaluate the generalization ability of the model. Verify its ability to maintain efficient privacy protection when dealing with image data through its performance on this dataset.

**Dataset.** The MNIST dataset contains images of handwritten digits, covering numbers from 0 to 9. Each digit has multiple handwritten versions, and each image is a grayscale image of $28 \times 28$ pixels. The dataset includes a total of 60,000 training samples and 10,000 test samples. Figure 6 displays several sample images from the MNIST dataset.

**Noise Addition.** Gaussian or Laplace noise is added to the discriminator gradients during the update process. The noise intensity levels are set to $0.0, 0.4, 0.8$, and 1.2 to observe the effects of different intensities on image quality and privacy protection.

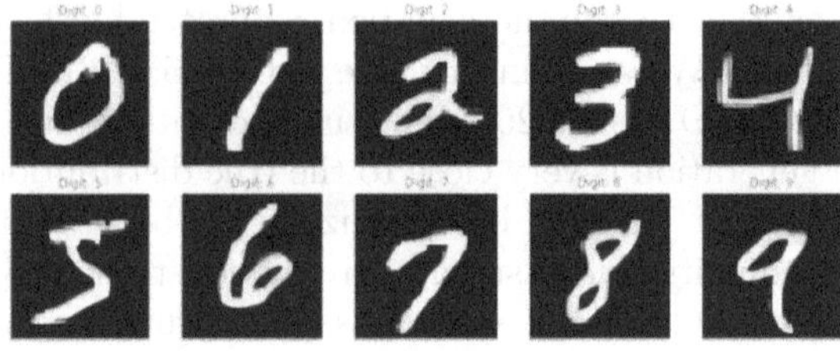

**Fig. 6.** Examples from MNIST Dataset.

**Evaluation Metric.** In this part of the experiment, we used Fréchet Inception Distance (FID) to measure the quality of the generated image and the similarity between the generated image and the real image in the feature space. The smaller the FID score, the closer it is to the real image and the higher the image quality. We calculated the FID scores for various types and intensities of noise to determine the impact of noise on image quality and privacy.

**Results and Analysis.** We present the Fid curve of the images generated by the DP-WGAN-GP model, which describes the variation of Fid of the images generated by DP-WGAN-GP with increasing training time. Each image corresponds to noise intensities of $(0.0, 0.4, 0.8, 1.2)$, respectively.

The horizontal axis represents the number of training cycles, and the lower the FID score, the higher the image quality. Checking the changes in FID can help us compare the impact of Gaussian and Laplacian noise on the quality of MNIST images.

By observing the experimental results in Fig. 7, subgraphs (a) and (c) show the FID scores of the DP-WGAN-GP model under Gaussian and Laplacian noise with noise of 0.0. The results demonstrate that as training epochs advance, the FID scores swiftly decline and tend to be stable thereafter, indicating that the model proficiently learns the actual data distribution without noise. This enables the model to produce superior-quality photos. At this noise level, the effects of Gaussian and Laplace noise on the quality of produced pictures are virtually indistinguishable, suggesting that the lack of noise allows the model to function under ideal conditions.

In addition, sub-figures (b) and (d) show that when the noise level is 0.4, the FID score of Gaussian noise gradually decreases and then stabilizes, indicating that the privacy preservation of the DP-WGAN-GP model in low noise settings maintains good image quality. The FID ratings for Laplace noise are markedly higher than those for Gaussian noise, indicating a more substantial adverse effect on picture quality. Nonetheless, the produced graphs are still visually satisfactory, and the efficacy of the DP-WGAN-GP model is not significantly compromised. The results demonstrate that at noise levels 0.0 and 0.4, the DP-WGAN-GP model can produce clear and lifelike pictures without significant

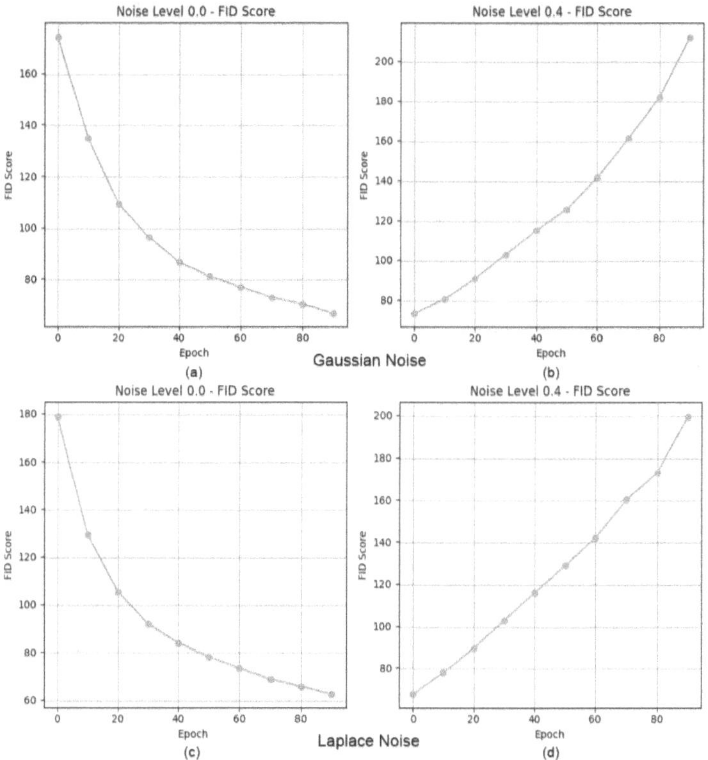


**Fig. 7.** FID Score Comparison of the DP-WGAN-GP Model under Gaussian and Laplace Noise at Low Intensities ((a), (c) are Gauss and Laplace at noise level 0, (b), (d) are Gauss and Laplace at noise level 0.4).

quality reduction. However, this may indicate insufficient robustness of privacy protection in certain contexts.

In Fig. 8, subgraphs (e) and (g) show the FID score fluctuations of Gaussian noise and Laplacian noise with a noise level of 0.8, respectively. Under Gaussian noise, the FID score gradually increases, indicating a decrease in the quality of the generated image, but overall it remains very stable; The FID score fluctuates greatly under Laplace noise, and it can also be seen that the model is unstable during training. This fluctuation is very obvious because the tail of the distribution is heavy, which can cause the gradient to become very extreme and the training to become unstable.

Moreover, the other subgraphs (f) and (h) demonstrate that the fluctuation of FID scores under Gaussian noise at a noise level of 1.2 makes it difficult to converge stably. Although the FID scores under Laplace noise have a uniform upward trajectory, this "stability" is due to the high noise intensity, which reduces the model's learning ability and leads to a serious decline in power generation

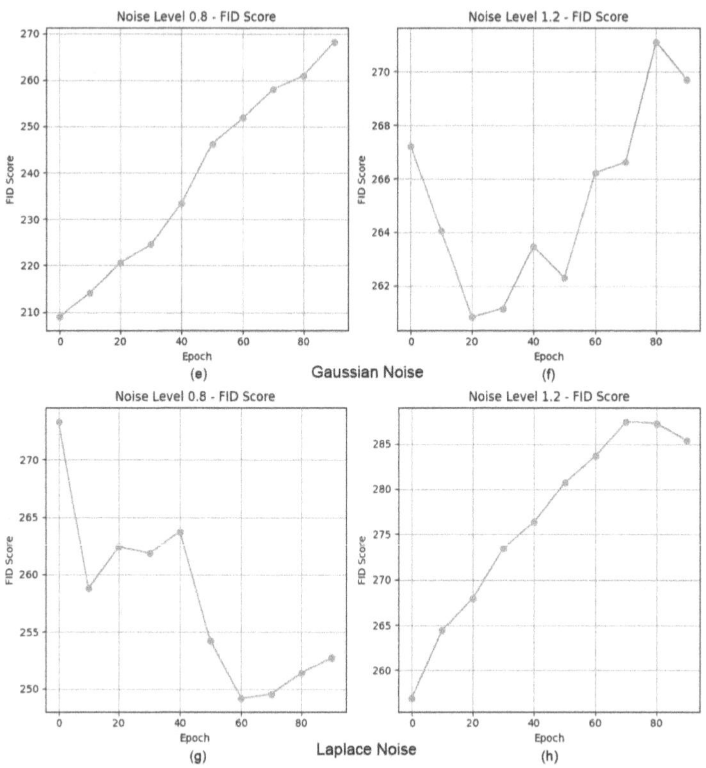


**Fig. 8.** FID Score Comparison of the DP-WGAN-GP Model under Gaussian and Laplace Noise at Low Intensities ((e), (g) are Gauss and Laplace at noise level 0.8, (f), (h) are Gauss and Laplace at noise level 1.2.

quality. At high noise levels, the DP-WGAN-GP model struggles to balance privacy preservation and quality of the generated images under Gaussian and Laplace noise.

In summary, the DP-WGAN-GP model has superior stability and generation quality in Gaussian noise environments. In contrast, the Laplace noise has a greater impact on the quality of the generated images, despite the enhanced privacy protection in high-intensity noise conditions. Although MNIST itself does not involve medical information, the results can be directly transferred to medical imaging data scenarios. These findings provide directions for further improvement of the DP-WGAN-GP model: future research can optimize the noise parameter configuration to explore how to strike a better balance between privacy preservation and the quality of the generated data and explore more suitable evaluation metrics for the model to comprehensively assess its privacy-preserving capability and usefulness in the generation task.

# 5 Conclusion and Future Scope

## 5.1 Conclusion

This study presents DP-WGAN-GP, a privacy-preserving generative model that integrates Wasserstein GAN with Gradient Penalty (WGAN-GP) and Differential Privacy (DP) for medical data synthesis. By evaluating fixed and adaptive noise strategies across Gaussian and Laplace mechanisms, we identified an optimal balance between privacy and data utility.

Experimental results demonstrate that DP-WGAN-GP consistently outperforms conventional GAN models, achieving higher F1 scores while maintaining strict privacy guarantees. The low initial distance and small Wasserstein distance of FID indicate that the generated data is very close to the true distribution, with guaranteed fidelity and analytical utility. Comparative analysis shows that fixed noise is better than adaptive noise, and Laplacian noise has better privacy utility than Gaussian noise. Fixed Laplacian noise is the best medical data protection method and is very stable.

In addition to a single pattern, DP-WGAN-GP has good generalization ability for medical datasets of numbers, text, and images. Its fidelity and structural preservation exceed the baseline, while maintaining privacy guarantees and capturing complex data distributions, making it a powerful tool for privacy sensitive applications, surpassing traditional GAN based methods.

## 5.2 Limitations

Despite its promising results, the DP-WGAN-GP model has several limitations:

- Noise Sensitivity: Model performance depends heavily on noise settings. While fixed Laplacian noise performs well, the optimal configuration may vary across datasets.
- Limited Modality Generalization: The model has been tested on tabular, text, and image data, but its effectiveness on more complex formats like 3D medical images or temporal data remains uncertain.
- Stability Under High Noise: High-intensity Laplace noise can destabilize training, especially in image generation, affecting output quality.
- Interpretability: Although the model captures data distribution well, the interpretability and traceability of generated samples remain challenging in sensitive healthcare applications.

## 5.3 Future Work

Although the proposed DP-WGAN-GP framework has shown promising capabilities in privacy-preserving data generation, there are several aspects that deserve further research:

- Adaptive and Hybrid Privacy Mechanisms: Future research may explore adaptive noise strategies that dynamically adjust perturbation levels according to model sensitivity, training stage, or feature importance. Furthermore, hybrid injection schemes that combine Gaussian and Laplacian distributions based on data modality could better manage the privacy-utility trade-off in complex scenarios.
- Federated Learning Integration: The Federated Learning (FL) architecture hides DP-WGAN-GP, which provides a particularly striking path for training scattered privacy protection models. In this architecture, participating institutions only transmit model update information, not raw data, thus minimizing the risk of data leakage. The combination of DP and FL is particularly suitable for cross institutional medical research, as data is different and regulatory restrictions prevent data from being centralized and shared. Moreover, gradient level privacy mechanisms, such as noise injection aggregation in DP-SGD or FL, can also provide enhanced protection and enable collaborative learning across non-IID distributions.
- Multi-Layer Privacy Enhancement: Integrating complementary privacy-preserving techniques, such as secure multi-party computation (SMPC), homomorphic encryption (HE), or trusted execution environments (TEE), may provide an additional layer of protection. These cryptographic approaches, when combined with differential privacy, can offer rigorous guarantees against both insider and external threats, particularly in adversarial environments.

In summary, the DP-WGAN-GP model has superior stability and generation quality in Gaussian noise environments. In contrast, the Laplace noise has a greater impact on the quality of the generated images, despite the enhanced privacy protection in high-intensity noise conditions. Although MNIST itself does not involve medical information, the results can be directly transferred to medical imaging data scenarios. These findings provide directions for further improvement of the DP-WGAN-GP model: future research can optimize the noise parameter configuration to explore how to strike a better balance between privacy preservation and the quality of the generated data and explore more suitable evaluation metrics for the model to comprehensively assess its privacy-preserving capability and usefulness in the generation task.

**Acknowledgments.** This work was supported by Wenzhou-Kean University Internal Research Support Program (IRSPG202202).

**Disclosure of Interests.** The authors declare that they have no competing interests.

**Availability of Data and Materials.** All data based on references.

## References

1. Kumar, Y., Marchena, J., Awlla, A.H., Li, J.J., Abdalla, H.B.: The AI-powered evolution of big data. Appl. Sci. **14**(22), 10176. MDPI (2024)
2. Liu, X., Zhang, Q., Li, C.: A survey of differential privacy in healthcare. Proc. J. Priv. Healthc. **7**(3), 123–142. Springer (2023 )
3. Ziller, A., Brown, R., Klein, L.: Medical imaging privacy with differential privacy techniques. Proc. J. Priv. Med. Res. **11**(2), 305–320. Springer (2021)
4. Dankar, F.K., Emam, K.E.: Application of differential privacy to health data. Proc. J. Med. Data Priv. **8**(1), (5–22). Springer (2012)
5. Sun, W., Wang, L., Yang, H.: Differential privacy in machine learning for healthcare data. IEEE Trans. Priv. Sec. **15**(6), 1782–1799 (2019)
6. Guibas, J.T., Virdi, T.S., Li, P.S.: Synthetic medical images from dual generative adversarial networks, arXiv preprint, arXiv:1709.01872 (2017)
7. Singh, N.K., Raza, K.: Medical image generation using generative adversarial networks, arXiv preprint, arXiv:2005.10687 (2020)
8. Abedi, M., Hempel, L., Sadeghi, S., Kirsten, T.: Gan-based approaches for generating structured data in the medical domain. Proc. Appl. Sci. **12**(14), 7075 (2022)
9. Gong, Y., Wu, W., Song, L.: Gan-based privacy-preserving intelligent medical consultation decision-making. In: Proceedings of Group Decision and Negotiation (2024)
10. Adnan, M., Kalra, S., Cresswell, J.C., Taylor, G.W., Tizhoosh, H.R.: Federated learning and differential privacy for medical image analysis. Proc. Sci. Rep. **12**(1) (2022)
11. Fang, M.L., Dhami, D.S., Kersting, K.: Dp-ctgan: differentially private medical data generation using ctgans. In: Proceedings in Lecture Notes in Computer Science, pp. 178–188 (2022)
12. Chen, D., Cheung, S.-C.S., Chuah, C.-N., Ozonoff, S.: Differentially private generative adversarial networks with model inversion. In: Proceedings of 2021 IEEE International Workshop on Information Forensics and Security (WIFS), vol. 33, pp. 1–6 (2021)
13. Muthukrishnan, G., Kalyani, S.: Grafting laplace and gaussian distributions: A new noise mechanism for differential privacy. IEEE Trans. Inf. Forensics Sec. **18**, 5359–5374 (2023)
14. Dwork, C., Roth, A.: Algorithmic Foundations of Differential Privacy. Now Publishers Inc., (2014)
15. Dwork, C., McSherry, F., Nissim, K., Smith, A.: Calibrating noise to sensitivity in private data analysis. In: Proceedings of Theory of Cryptography Conference, pp. 265–284. Springer (2006)
16. Abadi, M., Chu, A., Goodfellow, I., et al.: Deep learning with differential privacy. In: Proceedings of 2016 ACM SIGSAC Conference on Computer and Communications Security, pp. 308–318 (2016)
17. Gulrajani, I., Ahmed, F., Arjovsky, M., Dumoulin, V., Courville, A.: Improved training of wasserstein gans. In: Proceedings of Advances in Neural Information Processing Systems, pp. 5767–5777 (2017)
18. Mironov, I.: Rényi differential privacy. In: Proceedings of 2017 IEEE 30th Computer Security Foundations Symposium (CSF), pp. 263–275. IEEE (2017)
19. Wei, J., Smith, A., et al.: Adaptive differential privacy for machine learning. Mach. Learn. J. 1134–1143 (2021)

20. Andersson, J.D., Pagh, R., Torkamani, S.: Count on your elders: laplace vs gaussian noise in differential privacy, arXiv preprint, arXiv:2408.07021 (2024)
21. Kaggle, Breast Cancer Wisconsin (Diagnostic) Data Set, Kaggle (2023). https://www.kaggle.com/datasets/uciml/breast-cancer-wisconsin-data. Accessed 15 Nov 2025

# CPU-Based Parallelization of BDAC: Enhancing K-Clique Approximation

Büşra Ergenç Çalmaz[1](✉) and Belgin Bostanoğlu[2]

[1] Department of Computer Engineering, Recep Tayyip Erdoğan University, 53100 Rize, Turkey
busra.guvenoglu@erdogan.edu.tr

[2] Department of Computer Engineering, Izmir Institute of Technology, 35430 Izmir, Turkey
belginergenc@iyte.edu.tr

**Abstract.** The number of k-cliques in a dataset is significant and employed in diverse fields, including community detection, anomaly detection, and spam detection. This facilitates the identification of densely connected clusters or groups of nodes, which can subsequently be used to reveal underlying structures or patterns in the data. However, the combinatorial complexity of counting k-cliques, especially when identifying them in large networks or for higher values of $k$, poses considerable computational difficulties. This study introduces an accelerated version of the Boundary-Driven Approximations of K-Cliques (BDAC) algorithm, emphasizing CPU-based parallelization to boost performance when working with large, dense graphs. The BDAC algorithm sets a boundary for k-clique counts instead of providing a specific estimation, which removes the need for recursive enumeration and sampling. We evaluate the performance of BDAC on various graph datasets, showing clear improvements in execution time with parallelization while still keeping the approximation bounds intact. The results show that accelerated BDAC is particularly effective for dense networks, achieving efficient k-clique approximations at large scales. This work highlights the potential of BDAC for high-speed network analysis, contributing an optimized, scalable solution for k-clique approximation in complex datasets.

**Keywords:** Graphlets · Cliques · Parallelization · Approximation

## 1 Introduction

Enumeration of small subgraphs in a dataset is crucial for analyzing complex relationships within networks in fields such as recommendation systems and social and biological networks. These small subgraphs, also called graphlets or motifs, reveal important patterns in the structure of a network. A clique is a special subgraph where every pair of nodes in the subgraph is connected. A dataset's number of k-cliques (cliques with $k$ nodes) can provide valuable information about a network's structure, resilience, and community dynamics. However, this


R. Stahlbock et al. (Eds.): CSCE 2025, CCIS 2938, pp. 191–205, 2027.
https://doi.org/10.1007/978-3-032-22196-4_14

task becomes difficult in large graphs because the number of possible k-cliques increases exponentially as the graph size and the value of $k$ grow, making the problem computationally expensive.

The cliques in a social or communication network can help to detect communities, spam, or groups of individuals with strong connections [7,16,18,29,38]. Similarly, cliques can be used to analyze functional modules, identify protein complexes, and uncover key interactions critical for understanding biological processes in protein networks [5,26,28,39]. Cliques can enhance the accuracy of suggestions in recommendation systems, where they can help identify groups of closely connected users or items with shared preferences [13,27,34,35].

The literature contains numerous algorithms designed to list or count k-cliques [6,9,12,20,25]. However, for large datasets or high values of $k$, the combinatorial growth of the problem makes exact and listing-based methods computationally infeasible. Approximation methods have gained attention to address this, as they are practical when exact counting becomes infeasible [4,10,19,21,32,37]. Most approximation algorithms use sampling strategies to select a representative sample set and draw samples from it to estimate k-cliques. These methods often rely on recursive search trees due to the structure of the problem. Constructing a recursive search tree becomes impractical for large datasets and higher $k$ values due to the exponential growth of the search space. Some algorithms enhance the performance of existing approaches through parallel strategies or offer parallel solutions to improve scalability and handle larger datasets more efficiently [1,9,12,20,25,32,36,37]. An extensive survey [3] presents a comprehensive analysis of k-clique counting algorithms, examining their methodologies, applicability across various scenarios, and limitations.

The BDAC algorithm [42] establishes a boundary for k-clique counts in a dataset, both at the vertex level and across the entire dataset. Additionally, it eliminates the need to construct a recursive search tree and the sampling phase. However, this algorithm has limitations, as it is primarily suitable for dense datasets. This study aims to pioneer an efficient and scalable approach for approximating k-clique counts in large and dense graphs by introducing parallelization of the BDAC algorithm. The primary contribution is creating a CPU-based parallel implementation of BDAC, which significantly speeds up k-clique approximation while preserving theoretical bounds. The evaluations demonstrate that the parallel version of BDAC is highly compatible with other algorithms, particularly when handling larger datasets and larger $k$ values ($k < 50$). Notably, the BDAC provides a unique advantage by offering a boundary at the vertex level, a feature not found in other algorithms in the literature, except for Pivoter [20], which provides an exact solution but is only suitable for $k < 10$ on large datasets.

Section 2 reviews the preliminaries, including fundamental graph terminology and extremal graph theorems. Section 3 surveys related work and provides a comparative summary. Section 4 details the proposed algorithm, Par-BDAC, while Sect. 5 reports its performance evaluation. Sections 6 and 7 conclude the study and outline future research directions.

## 2 Preliminaries

This section outlines the essential background. An undirected **graph** $G(V,E)$ consists of vertices $V$ and edges $E$, where each edge is an unordered pair of vertices. A **subgraph** $H(V_s,E_s)$ is defined by subsets $V_s \subseteq V$ and $E_s \subseteq E$. An **induced subgraph** contains selected vertices and all edges between them. Let $n$ and $m$ denote the number of vertices and edges, respectively, and $d_u$ the **degree** of vertex $u$. A **k-clique** is a subgraph of $k$ vertices where every pair is adjacent, with $k \leq n$. A graph is **simple** and **connected** if it has no loops or multiple edges and every vertex is reachable from any other.

The **edge density** of a graph is the proportion of the number of actual edges to the number of possible edges and is calculated as $\frac{m}{\binom{n}{2}}$. The **degeneracy** of a graph measures its sparsity. It is the maximum value $d$, so every subgraph of the original graph has a vertex with a degree of at most $d$.

In subgraph counting algorithms, a common approach to reducing the search space involves converting an undirected graph into a **directed cyclic graph (DAG)** using orientation techniques. This orientation is performed using a specific ordering of the vertices. The edges between any two vertices are directed from the lower vertex to the higher vertex based on their position in the ordering, ensuring that no cycles (closed loops) are formed. Several ordering methods are used for this purpose, including degree, degeneracy, and color ordering.

In **degree ordering**, the vertices are arranged according to their degree, with vertices of lower degrees ordered before those with higher degrees. In **degeneracy ordering**, vertices are removed one by one, starting with those of the lowest degree, and the degrees of the remaining vertices are updated. This manner proceeds iteratively until no vertices remain. The vertices are then ordered based on the order in which they were removed. In **color ordering**, a greedy coloring algorithm [15,40] assigns one of $t$ colors to each vertex, ensuring that no two adjacent vertices have the same color. The vertices are then ordered according to their color assignments, which range from 1 to $t$, and the edges are oriented accordingly. This orientation technique aims to reduce the number of outgoing or incoming edges for each vertex, thus reducing the search space and eliminating duplicate clique or subgraph discoveries.

The **edge density** of a graph is the ratio of the actual edges $m$ to the total possible edges, given by $\frac{m}{\binom{n}{2}}$, where $n$ is the number of vertices. Let $t_v$ represent the number of triangles containing node $v$, and $d_v$ denote the degree of node $v$. The **triangle density** of node $v$ is $\frac{t_v}{\binom{d_v}{2}}$.

An **induced** subgraph consists of specific vertices from the original graph and all edges connecting them. Let $H$ be a graph with $k$ vertices and $G$ a graph with $n$ vertices. The set of induced copies of $H$ in $G$ is denoted as $Ind(H;G)$. The **induced density** of $H$ in $G$ is

$$d(H;G) = \frac{|Ind(H;G)|}{\binom{n}{k}} \tag{1}$$

In this paper, $d(K_k)_v$ denotes the $k$-clique density of a node $v$, defined as the ratio of the number of $k$-cliques containing $v$ to the number of possible $k$-cliques it could belong to, which is based on the number of ways to choose $k-1$ neighbors of $v$. Similarly, $d(K_k; G)$ represents the $k$-clique density of the graph $G$.

Extremal graph theorems provide bounds and conditions regarding the existence and number of $k$-cliques in a graph. These results may guarantee the presence of at least one $k$-clique, establish a minimum number, or impose an upper bound on the maximum number of $k$-cliques. The specific theorems referred to in this study are listed below.

**Theorem 1 (Turán's Theorem** [33]**).** *For any integer $k$, a graph $G$ contains no $k$-clique, i.e., $d(K_k; G) = 0$, if the edge density satisfies $d(K_2; G) \leq \frac{k-2}{k-1}$.*

In extremal graph theory, Turán investigated the maximum number of edges a graph with $n$ vertices can have while avoiding a given subgraph $F$. He provided a complete solution for the case where $F$ is a clique. Turán's theorem states that for any integer $k$, the $k$-clique density $d(K_k; G)$ is zero if the edge density satisfies $d(K_2; G) \leq \frac{k-2}{k-1}$ .

**Theorem 2 (Erdős's Theorem** [11]**).** *Let $G$ be a graph with $n$ vertices. If the edge density satisfies $d(K_2; G) > \frac{k-2}{k-1}$, then $G$ contains at least $\left(\frac{n}{k-1}\right)^{k-2}$ $k$-cliques.*

Erdős' theorem [11] establishes a lower bound on the number of $k$-cliques in a graph based on its edge density. It states that if a graph $G$ with $n$ vertices has an edge density exceeding $\frac{k-2}{k-1}$, then it must contain at least $\left(\frac{n}{k-1}\right)^{k-2}$ $k$-cliques. This result complements Turán's theorem by quantifying the clique structure in graphs that surpass the Turán threshold ($\frac{k-2}{k-1}$).

**Theorem 3 (Zykov's Theorem** [17,41]**).** *For integers $2 \leq r \leq k$, if $d(K_k; G) = 0$, then the $K_r$ density of $G$ satisfies*

$$d(K_r; G) \leq \frac{(k-1)(k-2)\dots(k-r)}{(k-1)^r} \tag{2}$$

Zykov's theorem generalizes Turán's theorem by providing a bound on the density of smaller cliques in graphs that do not contain a $k$-clique. We refer to the expression

$$\frac{(k-1)(k-2)\dots(k-r)}{(k-1)^r} \tag{3}$$

as the Zykov threshold. Alternatively, if the $K_r$ density of a graph $d(K_r; G)$ exceeds the Zykov threshold, then the graph must contain at least one $k$-clique.

**Theorem 4 (Kruskal-Katona Theorem** [22], [23]**).** *If $d(K_r; G) = \alpha$, then*

$$d(K_k; G) \leq \alpha^{k/r} \tag{4}$$

This theorem establishes an upper bound on the number of $k$-cliques within a given graph. The upper bound can be derived using the following formula, where $|K_k|$ denotes the count of $k$-cliques in the graph:

$$|K_k| \leq \left(\alpha^{k/r}\right)\binom{n}{k} \tag{5}$$

**Theorem 5 (Reiher's Clique Density Theorem [30]).** *If $k \geq 3$ and $\gamma \in [0, \frac{1}{2})$, then every graph on $n$ vertices with at least $\gamma n^2$ edges contains at least*

$$\frac{1}{(s+1)^k}\binom{s+1}{k}(1+\beta)^{k-1}(1-(k-1)\beta)n^k, \tag{6}$$

*$k$-clique where $s \geq 1$ is an integer with $\gamma \in \left[\frac{s-1}{2s}, \frac{s}{2(s+1)}\right]$ and $\beta \in \left[0, \frac{1}{s}\right]$ is implicitly defined by $\gamma = \frac{s}{2(s+1)}(1-\beta^2)$ [30].*

Reiher's theorem addresses the question of determining the minimum number of $k$-cliques that must exist in a graph with $n$ vertices and more than $\frac{k-2}{2(k-1)}n^2$ edges. Consider a graph $G$ with $n$ vertices and $m$ edges. Let $\gamma = \frac{m}{n^2}$. Thus, if $\gamma > \frac{k-2}{2(k-1)}$, we can determine the guaranteed minimum number of $k$-cliques in the graph.

According to this theorem, given $n$ and $m$, we first calculate $\gamma$ as $\gamma = \frac{m}{n^2}$. Rearranging the interval $\gamma \in \left[\frac{s-1}{2s}, \frac{s}{2(s+1)}\right]$ in terms of $s$, we obtain the following interval for $s$:

$$\frac{2\gamma}{1-2\gamma} \leq s \leq \frac{1}{1-2\gamma} \tag{7}$$

Next, we compute $\beta$ by substituting $\gamma$ and $s$ into the equation. The theorem predicts the existence of $k$-cliques in the graph if $\gamma > \frac{k-2}{2(k-1)}$, where $\frac{k-2}{k-1}$ represents the Turán threshold. If $s < k-2$, the binomial coefficient $\binom{s+1}{k}$ becomes zero, which, according to Turán's theorem, implies no $k$-cliques exist.

## 3 Related Work

Clique counting algorithms are divided into two categories based on their accuracy: Exact and approximate. Exact algorithms identify or count all cliques present in the dataset, but they are only practical for smaller datasets because of the problem's high computational complexity. Since these algorithms are not efficient for large and dense datasets, researchers have developed approximate solutions, which mainly rely on sampling methods. Additionally, parallelization techniques are often used to enhance the performance of these algorithms. A comprehensive analysis of these algorithms is presented in the survey [3]. This study focuses on algorithms for counting k-cliques in parallel, specifically designed for simple, undirected, and connected graphs.

Finocchi et al. [12] adapt Chiba and Nishizeki's ARBO [6], a k-clique listing algorithm, for MapReduce using degree orientation. The kClist algorithm improves ARBO [6] by adding parallelization and degeneracy orientation to avoid duplicate cliques. The Pivoter algorithm [20] introduces a k-clique counting method using the Succinct Clique Tree (SCT), which counts cliques without listing them. It provides counts at both local (per vertex and edge) and global levels. ARB-Count [32] improves ARBO [6] by reducing outgoing edges through low out-degree orientation and applying parallelization techniques from the literature [2,14]. Almasri et al. [1] develop a GPU-based k-clique counting algorithm combining ARB-Count's graph orientation and Pivoter's pivoting to remove redundant cliques. Their method uses vertex- and edge-centric parallelization with optimizations like binary coding and sub-warp partitioning. The DPColorPath [37] algorithm blends exact and approximate solutions by splitting the graph into sparse and dense regions. It applies exact methods, including Pivoter [20], for sparse areas and introduces three dynamic programming-based sampling techniques for dense regions.

The algorithm proposed by Finocchi et al. [12] and kClist [9] cannot scale effectively to count beyond 10 cliques in large graphs. Pivoter [20] is a CPU-based parallel algorithm that offers advantages over ARB-Count [32], which is also a CPU-based parallel algorithm for larger values of $k$. However, the authors note that it is unsuitable for datasets when $k > 10$. The algorithm proposed by Almasri et al. [1], on the other hand, is the most effective GPU-based k-clique counting algorithm, combining the innovative pivoting technique of Pivoter with the graph orientation method from ARB-Count. DPColorPath [37] is the most recent CPU-based approximate parallel algorithm, demonstrating superior performance compared to both Pivoter [20] and kClist [9]. Table 1 provides a comparative analysis of various k-clique counting algorithms based on key characteristics. It includes whether each algorithm is exact or approximate, its parallelization strategy, orientation approach, and computational complexity in terms of time and space. This comparison highlights the trade-offs between accuracy, efficiency, and scalability in different algorithmic approaches. The last row in this table represents the Par-BDAC algorithm, which is introduced in this article. In this way, it might be possible for the reader to differentiate its characteristics from related algorithms. For a detailed explanation of this table,

**Table 1.** Comparison of parallel k-clique counting algorithms.

| Algorithm | Approximate or Exact | Parallelization | Orientation | Time complexity | Space Complexity |
|---|---|---|---|---|---|
| [12] | both | MapReduce | degree | $O(m^{k/2})$ | $O(m+n)$ |
| kClist [9] | exact | shared memory | degeneracy | $O(m\alpha^{k-2})$ | $O(m+P\alpha^2)$ |
| Pivoter [20] | exact | shared memory | degeneracy | $O(n\alpha 3^{\alpha/3})$ | $O(m+n)$ |
| ARB-Count[32] | both | shared memory | degeneracy | exact: $O(m\alpha^{k-2})$<br>approximate:$O(pm\alpha^{k-2}+m)$ | $O(m+P\alpha)$ |
| [1] | exact | GPU | degeneracy/degree | not reported | $O(d^2max)$ |
| DPColorPath [37] | approximate | shared memory | degeneracy | k-color set: $O(\chi^k)$<br>k-color path: $O(\chi^{nk}+m)$<br>k-triangle path: $O(k\Delta)$ | k-color set: $O(m+n+\chi^k)$<br>k-color path: $O(kn+m)$<br>k-triangle path: $O(km)$ |
| Par-BDAC | approximate | shared memory | degeneracy | $O(\frac{n\alpha^2}{P})$ | $O(m+n+\alpha^2)$ |

please refer to the survey [3]. In this table, $k$ denotes the clique size, $m$ the number of edges, $n$ the number of vertices, $\Delta$ the number of triangles in the input graph, $\alpha$ the graph's arboricity, $p = 1/c$ where $c$ is the number of colors used. The variable $P$ indicates the parallelism level: it refers to processing units in ARB-Count and kClist, and to threads in our method.

# 4 Par-BDAC: CPU Optimization

This section reviews our previous work, the BDAC algorithm, and presents its parallel version (Par-BDAC) and improvements. The BDAC algorithm is the first algorithm that provides the lower and upper boundaries for k-cliques. It leverages various extremal graph theories, such as Turán's theorem [33], Erdős's theorem [11], Zykov's theorem [41], Kruskal–Katona theorem [22,23], and Reiher's theorem [30]. These theorems provide insights into the existence of cliques and the minimum and maximum possible number of k-cliques a graph can contain based on its density. The BDAC algorithm integrates these theorems with the approximate k-clique counting algorithm, and draws inspiration from the TuránShadow algorithm [19].

In this work, we present a parallel implementation that utilizes OpenMP [8], an API tailored for shared memory architectures. Our goal is to optimize graph analysis for parallel computing environments. The proposed algorithm processes an undirected graph $G$ and converts it into a directed acyclic graph (DAG) $D$. Thus, only the outgoing edges of each node are considered, which prevents duplicate enumeration and reduces the search space. The algorithm searches for (k-1)-cliques within each node's neighborhood, excluding the node itself. It then constructs induced subgraphs from the node's neighbors and evaluates them using extremal graph theorems. First, the edge density of the subgraph, which corresponds to the triangle density of the current node, is calculated. This density is then used in extremal graph theorems to determine the minimum and maximum number of k-cliques the node can be part of. Turán's theorem states that if a graph's edge density exceeds the Turán threshold, it must contain at least one k-clique. In this case, Reiher's theorem [30] provides the minimum number of k-cliques the graph must have, while the Kruskal-Katona theorems [22,23] give an upper bound on the maximum number of k-cliques. The BDAC is the first algorithm to establish such bounds. This procedure is repeated independently for each node.

Algorithm 1 provides the pseudocode of Par-BDAC. In this work, the computations for each node are independent. Each node's density and k-clique boundaries are calculated separately at each iteration. The OpenMP API simplifies parallelization by handling thread management, synchronization, and workload distribution, making it well-suited for tasks with no inter-dependencies.

The algorithm distributes the workload of calculating clique boundaries for each node across multiple concurrent threads. This parallel approach improves performance, particularly on large graphs. Each thread computes the local maximum and minimum $k$-clique counts for the subgraphs induced by the neighborhood of its assigned node. These local results are then combined to produce

**Algorithm 1.** Par-BDAC

```
1: procedure PAR_BDAC(Graph G, DAG D, Integer k)
2:     num_threads ← Set to max available
3:     totalMax ← 0
4:     totalMin ← 0
5:     localMax = [0.0] * num_threads
6:     localMin = [0.0] * num_threads
7:     Parallel Section:
8:         Divide the work across multiple threads
9:     for each thread in parallel do
10:        thread_id ← GetThreadId()
11:        for all node in G do
12:            H ← Construct induced subgraph from the current node's out-neighbors in D
13:            k ← k-1
14:            n ← the no. of vertices of subgraph H
15:            if n < k then
16:                continue
17:            end if
18:            m ← the no. of edges of subgraph H
19:            density ← m/(n choose 2)
20:            turanThres ← (k-2)/(k-1)
21:            γ ← m/n^2
22:            maxCliq ← MaxCliq(n, density, k)
23:            localMax[thread_id]+ ← maxCliq
24:            if density > turanThres then
25:                minCliq = 0
26:                minCliq ← MinCliqReiher(n, γ, k)
27:                if minCliq == −1 then
28:                    minCliq ← (n/(k−1))^(k−2)
29:                end if
30:                localMin[thread_id]+ ← minCliq
31:            end if
32:        end for
33:    end for
34:    totalMax ← Σ_{t=1}^{num_threads} localMax[t]
35:    totalMin ← Σ_{t=1}^{num_threads} localMin[t]
36:    PRINT totalMin
37:    PRINT totalMax
38: end procedure
```

the global bounds. In line 2, the variable *num_ threads* specifies the number of threads. In lines 5 and 6, the arrays *localMax* and *localMin* store the results computed by each thread. Every thread is assigned a unique identifier (*thread_ id*), which is obtained using the *GetThreadId()* function. For each node, an induced subgraph $H$ is formed using its neighbors (line 12). The density and Turán threshold of this subgraph are then computed (lines 19 and 20). The Kruskal-

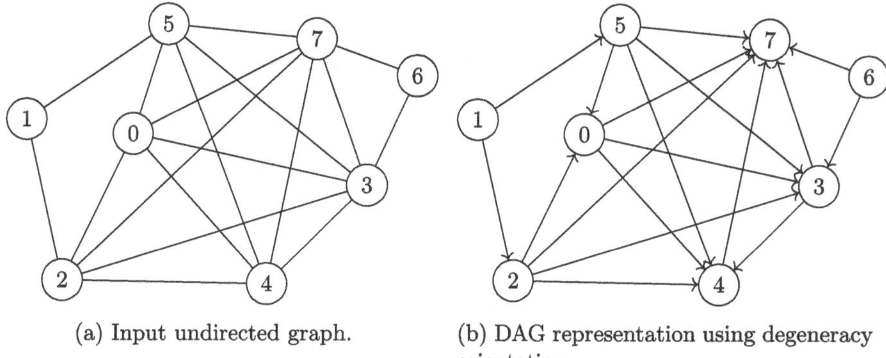


(a) Input undirected graph.

(b) DAG representation using degeneracy orientation.

**Fig. 1.** Graph transformation from undirected graph to DAG.

Katona theorem is applied to estimate the maximum number of cliques that can exist in $H$, using the $MaxCliq()$ procedure (line 22). If the density condition is met, the minimum number of k-cliques is determined using Reiher's theorem (line 26). However, when $s \leq k-2$, the reduced value of the binomial coefficient $\binom{s+1}{k}$ makes Reiher's theorem insufficient for determining the existence of $K_k$. In this case, the procedure returns $-1$, and we then check whether $d(K_2; H) > \frac{k-2}{k-1}$ holds. If this condition is met, we apply Erdős's theorem (line 28). Otherwise, we accept a lower bound of 0.

The main difference from the BDAC algorithm is how the density of each subgraph is evaluated. In BDAC, the density is first compared with the Zykov threshold, and if this condition is met, Reiher's or Erdős's theorems are applied to estimate the minimum number of k-cliques. However, these theorems also require the density to satisfy Turán's bound, which is typically stricter than the Zykov threshold. This leads to many unnecessary checks. In our approach, we revise this step (line 24) to reduce redundant calculations. Finally, the local results from all threads are aggregated to obtain the final counts (lines 34 and 35).

Let us explain the algorithm with an example. Figure 1a represents the input undirected graph for our algorithm. This graph is transformed into a directed acyclic graph (DAG) through degeneracy orientation, as shown in Fig. 1b. Figure 2 depicts the parallel execution on a graph, where each node is assigned as a separate thread. Each thread processes the induced subgraph from the outgoing neighbors of its corresponding node and computes both the minimum and maximum clique counts within this subgraph. The figure emphasizes the induced subgraphs formed by the neighbors of each node. The algorithm restricts its search to the outgoing neighbors of each node to identify k-cliques, thereby avoiding duplicate enumeration. For example, when searching for 5 cliques in the original graph, the algorithm must identify 4 cliques within

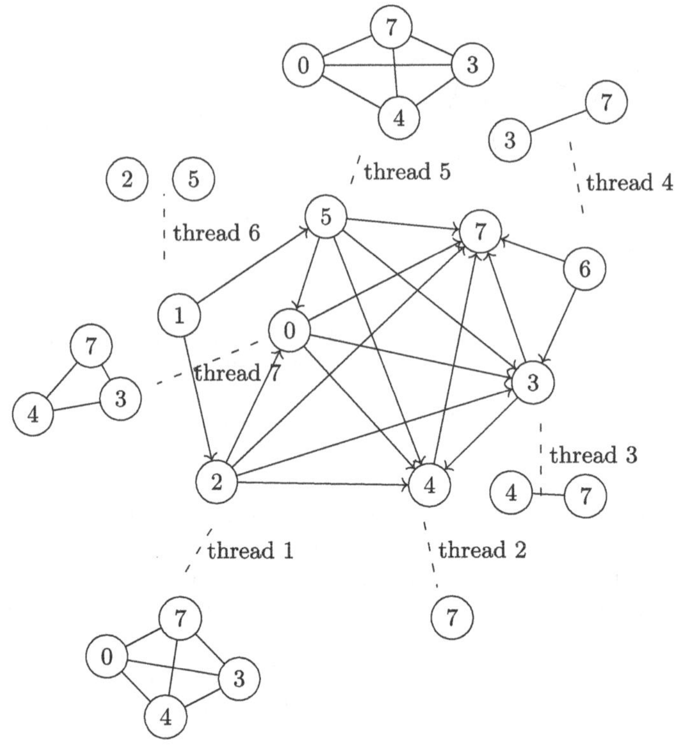


**Fig. 2.** Parallel processing of nodes, where each thread computes the minimum and maximum clique counts for subgraphs induced by the current node's outgoing neighbors.

each node's neighborhood (excluding the node itself). In this case, only nodes 2 and 5 have sufficient neighbors to form a 5-clique. According to Reiher's theorem [30], nodes 2 and 5 are capable of forming at least one 4-clique. Additionally, the Kruskal-Katona [22,23] theorems indicate that each of these nodes can form at most one 4-clique independently. Consequently, the graph contains exactly two 5 cliques, with both the minimum and maximum clique counts being two.

## 5 Experimental Evaluation

We compare our algorithm with DPColorPath [37], a recent parallel approximate $k$-clique counting method. Both are evaluated on a machine with two 2.2 GHz Intel Xeon Silver 4114 CPUs (10 cores each) and 32 GB RAM. Datasets are taken from SNAP [24] and the Network Repository [31]. A sequential comparison is provided in our previous BDAC study [42]; here, we focus on parallel performance. Table 2 reports execution times of both versions on various datasets, where $k$ denotes the clique size. Parallel results use 20 threads. Datasets are listed by increasing size, and the impact of parallelization is highlighted, especially on larger graphs.

**Table 2.** Execution time comparison of both sequential and parallel versions of BDAC and DPColorPath.

| | k | Sequential BDAC time (sec) | Parallel BDAC time (sec) | Sequential DPColorPath time (sec) | Parallel DPColorPath time (sec) |
|---|---|---|---|---|---|
| com-lj | 20 | 68 | 38 | 31 | 3 |
| | 40 | 68 | 38 | 35 | 8 |
| | 50 | 68 | 38 | 39 | 8 |
| soc-LJ | 20 | 128 | 45 | 51 | 4 |
| | 40 | 128 | 45 | 96 | 30 |
| | 50 | **128** | **45** | **166** | **80** |
| com-orkut | 20 | 1715 | 218 | 411 | 30 |
| | 40 | 1715 | 218 | 1233 | 98 |
| | 50 | **1715** | **218** | **1742** | **324** |
| uk-2002 | 20 | 2073 | 297 | 656 | 17 |
| | 40 | 2073 | **297** | 694 | **29984** |
| | 50 | 2073 | **297** | 665 | **29710** |

The parallel version of BDAC demonstrates significant improvements over the sequential version, showing notable speedup and outperforming the sequential version for all values of $k$. It also maintains consistent execution times across different $k$ values, similar to the sequential version. Since the time complexity does not depend on $k$, the clique size. In comparison, the DPColorPath algorithm improves upon its sequential version but struggles with large, dense datasets such as "uk-2002" and when $k > 40$. This indicates that the parallelization may not be well-scaled or efficient in these cases. When comparing the parallel versions of BDAC and DPColorPath, DPColorPath outperforms BDAC in most scenarios. However, both parallel versions face challenges with large datasets and higher $k$ values. The Par-BDAC, on the other hand, demonstrates better scalability and overall performance, particularly with large, dense datasets and larger $k$ values.

Table 3 presents the approximation results of the algorithms for different $k$ values. For most datasets, the minimum estimations of BDAC and DPColorPath are similar, particularly for large and dense datasets like "uk-2002". However, for sparse datasets, the BDAC algorithm encounters limitations. Accurately estimating the minimum k-clique size becomes challenging when the edge density of node neighbors fails to meet the Turán threshold. In such cases, Reiher's theorem cannot reliably predict the minimum k-clique count, which negatively impacts the overall estimation of k-cliques. The gap between the minimum and maximum estimations grows larger, as observed in the com-orkut dataset.

**Table 3.** Approximation results of the algorithms for k = 20,40 and 50.

| | k | BDAC-min | BDAC-max | DPColorPath |
|---|---|---|---|---|
| com-lj | 20 | 5,28E+32 | 6,77E+32 | 5,48E+32 |
| | 40 | 1,96E+53 | 6,13E+53 | 2,51E+53 |
| | 50 | 2,92E+61 | 1,76E+62 | 4,34E+61 |
| soc-LJ | 20 | 1,05E+33 | 2,67E+33 | 1,31E+33 |
| | 40 | 3,50E+53 | 5,10E+54 | 5,86E+53 |
| | 50 | 4,56E+61 | 2,10E+63 | 9,69E+61 |
| com-orkut | 20 | 2,24E+15 | 1,04E+28 | 1,99E+17 |
| | 40 | 2,30E+09 | 1,10E+42 | 1,16E+13 |
| | 50 | 0 | 1,07E+47 | 1355 |
| uk-2002 | 20 | 1,07E+41 | 1,07E+41 | 1,07E+41 |
| | 40 | 5,29E+70 | 5,29E+70 | 5,29E+70 |
| | 50 | 4,92E+83 | 4,92E+83 | 4,92E+83 |

## 6 Conclusion

In this paper, we introduced the parallel version of the BDAC algorithm [42], implemented using the OpenMP framework [8]. The parallel version of BDAC significantly improves the performance compared to its sequential counterpart. It provides significant speedup and scalability, especially for large and dense datasets. Par-BDAC demonstrates its efficiency and adaptability by maintaining consistent execution times across different values of $k$. Although the parallel version of DPColorPath outperforms BDAC in some scenarios, it struggles on large datasets and higher values of $k$. On the other hand, Par-BDAC has successfully overcome these challenges, making it a more robust solution for large-scale graph problems. Overall, the Par-BDAC algorithm is an effective and efficient approach, especially for scenarios involving large, dense datasets and larger values of $k$.

## 7 Future Work

To handle even larger graphs, new parallelization techniques can be explored, such as combining multi-core and GPU computing. Additionally, applying the algorithm to other graph-related problems, such as community detection or graph traversal, could provide valuable insights into its broader use. Furthermore, the BDAC algorithm has limitations when dealing with sparse datasets that do not meet the Turán threshold. Future research could focus on developing new solutions to address this, for example, by using exact approaches for sparse areas to improve performance.

## References

1. Almasri, M., Hajj, I.E., Nagi, R., Xiong, J., Hwu, W.: Parallel k-clique counting on GPUs. In: Proceedings of the 36th ACM International Conference on Supercomputing, ICS '22. Association for Computing Machinery, New York, NY, USA (2022). https://doi.org/10.1145/3524059.3532382
2. Barenboim, L., Elkin, M.: Sublogarithmic distributed MIS algorithm for sparse graphs using Nash-Williams decomposition. In: Proceedings of the Twenty-Seventh ACM Symposium on Principles of Distributed Computing, PODC '08, pp. 25–34. Association for Computing Machinery, New York, NY, USA (2008). https://doi.org/10.1145/1400751.1400757
3. Çalmaz, B., Ergenç Bostanoğlu, B.: k-clique counting on large scale-graphs: a survey. PeerJ Comput. Sci. **10**, e2501 (2024). https://doi.org/10.7717/peerj-cs.2501
4. Chang, L., Gamage, R., Yu, J.X.: Efficient k-clique count estimation with accuracy guarantee. Proc. VLDB Endow. **17**(11), 3707–3719 (2024). https://doi.org/10.14778/3681954.3682032
5. Chen, B., Shi, J., Zhang, S., Wu, F.X.: Identifying protein complexes in protein–protein interaction networks by using clique seeds and graph entropy. PROTEOMICS **13**(2), 269–277 (2013). https://doi.org/10.1002/pmic.201200336, https://analyticalsciencejournals.onlinelibrary.wiley.com/doi/abs/10.1002/pmic.201200336
6. Chiba, N., Nishizeki, T.: Arboricity and subgraph listing algorithms. SIAM J. Comput. **14**(1), 210–223 (1985). https://doi.org/10.1137/0214017
7. Cleemput, K.V.: Friendship type, clique formation and the everyday use of communication technologies in a peer group. Inf. Commun. Soc. **15**(8), 1258–1277 (2012). https://doi.org/10.1080/1369118X.2011.606327
8. Dagum, L., Menon, R.: OpenMP: an industry-standard API for shared-memory programming. IEEE Comput. Sci. Eng. **5**(1), 46–55 (1998). https://doi.org/10.1109/99.660313
9. Danisch, M., Balalau, O., Sozio, M.: Listing k-cliques in sparse real-world graphs. In: Proceedings of the 2018 World Wide Web Conference, pp. 589–598 (2018). https://doi.org/10.1145/3178876.3186125
10. Eden, T., Ron, D., Seshadhri, C.: On approximating the number of k-cliques in sublinear time. In: Proceedings of the 50th Annual ACM SIGACT Symposium on Theory of Computing, STOC 2018, pp. 722–734. Association for Computing Machinery, New York, NY, USA (2018). https://doi.org/10.1145/3188745.3188810
11. Erdős, P.: On the number of complete subgraphs and circuits contained in graphs. Časopis pro pěstování matematiky **94**(3), 290–296 (1969)
12. Finocchi, I., Finocchi, M., Fusco, E.G.: Clique counting in MapReduce: algorithms and experiments. J. Exp. Algorithmics (JEA) **20**, 1–20 (2015). https://doi.org/10.1145/2794080
13. Gong, Y., et al.: Exact-k recommendation via maximal clique optimization. In: Proceedings of the 25th ACM SIGKDD International Conference on Knowledge Discovery & Data Mining, pp. 617–626 (2019). https://api.semanticscholar.org/CorpusID:158047080
14. Goodrich, M.T., Pszona, P.: External-memory network analysis algorithms for naturally sparse graphs. In: Demetrescu, C., Halldórsson, M.M. (eds.) Algorithms - ESA 2011, pp. 664–676. Springer, Heidelberg (2011). https://doi.org/10.1007/978-3-642-23719-5_56

15. Hasenplaugh, W., Kaler, T., Schardl, T.B., Leiserson, C.E.: Ordering heuristics for parallel graph coloring. In: Proceedings of the 26th ACM Symposium on Parallelism in Algorithms and Architectures, SPAA '14, pp. 166–177. Association for Computing Machinery, New York, NY, USA (2014). https://doi.org/10.1145/2612669.2612697
16. Holland, P.W., Leinhardt, S.: A method for detecting structure in sociometric data. In: Leinhardt, S. (ed.) Social Networks, pp. 411–432. Academic Press (1977). https://doi.org/10.1016/B978-0-12-442450-0.50028-6, https://www.sciencedirect.com/science/article/pii/B9780124424500500286
17. Huang, H., Linial, N., Naves, H., Peled, Y., Sudakov, B.: On the densities of cliques and independent sets in graphs. Combinatorica **36**(5), 493–512 (2016). https://doi.org/10.1007/s00493-015-3051-9
18. Jackson, M.O., Rodriguez-Barraquer, T., Tan, X.: Social capital and social quilts: network patterns of favor exchange. Am. Econ. Rev. **102**(5), 1857–97 (2012). https://doi.org/10.1257/aer.102.5.1857, https://www.aeaweb.org/articles?id=10.1257/aer.102.5.1857
19. Jain, S., Seshadhri, C.: A fast and provable method for estimating clique counts using turán's theorem. In: Proceedings of the 26th International Conference on World Wide Web, WWW '17, pp. 441–449. International World Wide Web Conferences Steering Committee, Republic and Canton of Geneva, CHE (2017). https://doi.org/10.1145/3038912.3052636
20. Jain, S., Seshadhri, C.: The power of pivoting for exact clique counting. In: Proceedings of the 13th International Conference on Web Search and Data Mining, pp. 268–276 (2020). https://doi.org/10.1145/3336191.3371839
21. Jain, S., Tong, H.: YACC: a framework generalizing turánshadow for counting large cliques. In: Proceedings of the 2022 SIAM International Conference on Data Mining (SDM), pp. 684–692. SIAM (2022). https://doi.org/10.1137/1.9781611977172.77, https://epubs.siam.org/doi/abs/10.1137/1.9781611977172.77
22. Katona, G.: A theorem of finite sets. In: Classic Papers in Combinatorics, pp. 381–401 (1987)
23. Kruskal, J.B.: The number of simplices in a complex. In: Mathematical Optimization Techniques, vol. 10, pp. 251–278 (1963)
24. Leskovec, J., Krevl, A.: SNAP datasets: Stanford large network dataset collection, June 2014. http://snap.stanford.edu/data
25. Li, R.H., Gao, S., Qin, L., Wang, G., Yang, W., Yu, J.X.: Ordering heuristics for k-clique listing. Proc. VLDB Endow. **13**(12), 2536–2548 (2020). https://doi.org/10.14778/3407790.3407843
26. Li, X.L., Foo, C.S., Tan, S.H., Ng, S.K.: Interaction graph mining for protein complexes using local clique merging. Genome Inform. **16**(2), 260–269 (2005). https://doi.org/10.11234/gi1990.16.2_260
27. Manoharan, S., Sathish, P.: Patient diet recommendation system using k clique and deep learning classifiers. J. Artif. Intell. Capsule Netw. **2**, 121–130 (2020). https://doi.org/10.36548/jaicn.2020.2.005
28. Milik, M., Szalma, S., Olszewski, K.A.: Common structural cliques: a tool for protein structure and function analysis. Protein Eng. Des. Sel. **16**(8), 543–552 (2003). https://doi.org/10.1093/protein/gzg080
29. Nedioui, M.A., Moussaoui, A., Saoud, B., Babahenini, M.C.: Detecting communities in social networks based on cliques. Physica A Stat. Mech. Appl. **551**, 124100 (2020). https://doi.org/10.1016/j.physa.2019.124100, https://www.sciencedirect.com/science/article/pii/S0378437119322642

30. Reiher, C.: The clique density theorem. Ann. Math. **184**(3), 683–707 (2016). http://www.jstor.org/stable/44072027
31. Rossi, R.A., Ahmed, N.K.: The network data repository with interactive graph analytics and visualization. In: AAAI (2015). https://networkrepository.com
32. Shi, J., Dhulipala, L., Shun, J.: Parallel clique counting and peeling algorithms. In: SIAM Conference on Applied and Computational Discrete Algorithms (ACDA21), pp. 135–146. SIAM (2021). https://doi.org/10.1137/1.9781611976830.13, https://epubs.siam.org/doi/abs/10.1137/1.9781611976830.13
33. Turán, P.: On an external problem in graph theory. Mat. Fiz. Lapok **48**, 436–452 (1941)
34. Vilakone, P., Park, D.S., Xinchang, K., Hao, F.: An efficient movie recommendation algorithm based on improved k-clique. Hum. Centric Comput. Inf. Sci. **8**(1) (2018). https://doi.org/10.1186/s13673-018-0161-6
35. Vilakone, P., Xinchang, K., Park, D.S.: Personalized movie recommendation system combining data mining with the k-clique method. J. Inf. Process. Syst. **15**(5), 1141–1155 (2019). https://doi.org/10.3745/JIPS.04.0138
36. Wang, K., Yu, K., Long, C.: Efficient k-clique listing: an edge-oriented branching strategy. Proc. ACM Manag. Data **2**(1) (2024). https://doi.org/10.1145/3639262
37. Ye, X., Li, R.H., Dai, Q., Chen, H., Wang, G.: Efficient $k$k-clique counting on large graphs: the power of color-based sampling approaches. IEEE Trans. Knowl. Data Eng. **36**(4), 1518–1536 (2024). https://doi.org/10.1109/TKDE.2023.3314643
38. Yildiz, H., Kruegel, C.: Detecting social cliques for automated privacy control in online social networks. In: 2012 IEEE International Conference on Pervasive Computing and Communications Workshops, pp. 353–359 (2012). https://doi.org/10.1109/PerComW.2012.6197509
39. Yu, H., Paccanaro, A., Trifonov, V., Gerstein, M.: Predicting interactions in protein networks by completing defective cliques. Bioinformatics **22**(7), 823–829 (2006). https://doi.org/10.1093/bioinformatics/btl014
40. Yuan, L., Qin, L., Lin, X., Chang, L., Zhang, W.: Effective and efficient dynamic graph coloring. Proc. VLDB Endow. **11**(3), 338–351 (2017)
41. Zykov, A.A.: On some properties of linear complexes. Matematicheskii sbornik **66**(2), 163–188 (1949)
42. Çalmaz, B., Bostanoğlu, B.E.: BDAC: boundary-driven approximations of k-cliques. Symmetry **16**(8) (2024). https://doi.org/10.3390/sym16080983, https://www.mdpi.com/2073-8994/16/8/983

# Behavioral Analysis via Tabular-to-Image Transformation for Proactive Threat Detection

Ariel Isaac Posada Barrera[1(✉)], Laura Margarita Rodríguez Peralta[1,2], Erick Rosete Beas[1], and Jessica Lizeth Borja Diaz[1]

[1] Departamento de ingenierías, Facultad de Tecnologías de Información y Ciencia de Datos (FTIyCD), Universidad Popular Autónoma del Estado de Puebla (UPAEP), Puebla, México
arielisaac.posada@upaep.edu.mx

[2] Consejo de Ciencia y Tecnología del Estado de Puebla (CONCYTEP), Puebla, México

**Abstract.** This study explores Network Behavior Analysis (NBA) by transforming captured traffic data into images optimized for machine learning models focused on detecting network threats, particularly DDoS attacks. Building on previous anomaly detection research, this work incorporates behavioral science variables for a deeper analysis of user behavior. Using the publicly available BCCC-Dataset, tabular data were processed with one-hot encoding, and images were generated using NEighborhood Dependencies (Refined), DeepInsight, and Tabular Convolution (TAC) techniques. Deep learning models based on Convolutional Neural Networks (CNNs) were then applied to predict potential threats. The results show effective detection of suspicious patterns, reducing response times and operational costs. This study highlights the importance of combining machine learning and behavioral analysis for proactive threat management.

**Keywords:** Image-tabular Representation Learning · Convolutional Neural Networks · Deep Learning · Network Behavioral Analysis · Network Threat Detection

## 1 Introduction

Network security remains a critical focus amid the increasing complexity of cyber threats. Distributed Denial of Service (DDoS) attacks and other forms of malicious behavior can severely impact both security and operational efficiency. This study centers on Network Behavior Analysis (NBA), leveraging modern data transformation techniques to detect potential threats within network traffic. Moving beyond traditional pattern detection, this work integrates behavioral science principles to enable a deeper, more comprehensive analysis of network anomalies.

The study was conducted on data from multiple public sources, including the BCCC-Datasets [1], initially sourced from [2]. In subsequent work [3], these datasets were expanded through the generation of statistical values, feature engineering, and additional analysis. Building on that foundation, this study refines the dataset using resources from the Behaviour-Centric Cybersecurity Center (BCCC). Both benign and malicious


R. Stahlbock et al. (Eds.): CSCE 2025, CCIS 2938, pp. 206–218, 2027.
https://doi.org/10.1007/978-3-032-22196-4_15

activities were processed through one-hot encoding to generate grayscale and color images representing IP behavior.

Continuous variables were grouped by device, and statistical measures—including minimum, maximum, mean, and standard deviation—were calculated to enrich the dataset. Additionally, traffic statistics were extracted from PCAP captures, with messages classified by protocol type (such as web browsing, email, or file transfer) based on port numbers and response statuses. This process enabled the identification of different user traffic patterns, providing a foundation for deeper analysis through deep learning techniques.

Tabular-to-image transformations were performed implementing the algorithms REpresentation of Features as Images with NEighborhood Dependencies (Refined) [4], DeepInsight [5], and TAbular Convolution (TAC) [6], producing inputs optimized for machine learning. These images were analyzed using Convolutional Neural Networks (CNNs) to improve the prediction of suspicious network behavior.

The study presents a comparative analysis of modern tabular-to-image methods for insider threat detection, identifying key factors that enhance detection robustness and accuracy. These systems aim to support network administrators in identifying attack sources, improving audits, and refining equipment configurations. They also show potential as forensic tools for uncovering behavior patterns critical to investigating past incidents and preventing future breaches.

This text is organized as follows: 2. Literature Review lists previous works on proactive network threat detection, 3. Methodology describes the data transformation performed and the machine learning algorithms applied with diverse algorithms and technologies, 4. Results shows the results of the experiments with the three tabular data to image algorithms, 5. Lessons Learned presents the findings and the interpretation of the results, 6. Conclusions summarizes the conclusions drawn from the obtained knowledge, and 7. Future Works discusses future work to be carried out with this new dataset applying the knowledge with more threat sources.

## 2 Literature Review

As digitalization advances, detecting malicious activities within network traffic has become essential for maintaining the security of digital services. Recent research has leveraged traditional machine learning (ML) techniques for anomaly detection [7] and network intrusion detection [8]. Although these models perform well when applied directly to raw network traffic data, recent findings indicate that carefully selecting the appropriate features to train the models can lead to significant performance improvements [9].

In [10], a framework is proposed that utilizes a genetic algorithm for feature reduction, enhancing the accuracy of intrusion detection. The genetic algorithm minimizes the feature space, thereby improving the performance of the machine learning (ML) model. Similarly, [11] employs an autoencoder for feature reduction, followed by the application of traditional ML classifiers, resulting in a 5% increase in accuracy. Another common approach involves applying Principal Component Analysis (PCA) for feature reduction prior to using ML classifiers [12, 13]. Some studies have also explored the transformation of tabular data into images to enable the use of convolutional neural networks

(CNNs) [14]. However, this strategy has been only lightly investigated in the context of network intrusion detection. The present work demonstrates how tabular-to-image techniques can be applied to enhance network threat detection.

Some authors have chosen to use more advanced models for intrusion detection, focusing less on feature engineering. For example, several studies have utilized sequence-to-sequence models such as recurrent neural networks (RNNs) [15], long short-term memory cells (LSTMs) [16], and even transformer architectures [17]. While these models have shown strong performance, they typically require large amounts of data to avoid overfitting.

A study presented in [18] employs a convolutional neural network (CNN) model to classify network traffic as malicious; however, the data are maintained in a one-dimensional format, and a 1D CNN is implemented. Similarly, [19] applies a CNN architecture by converting the dataset into an image format through a dataset-specific preprocessing step. In contrast, the present study leverages the capabilities of complex models such as CNNs but introduces a more general tabular-to-image transformation, without restricting the analysis to large volumes of training data.

## 3 Methodology

The analysis was conducted on previously conducted in [3]. In the former study, the original dataset [1], containing over 300 variables, was expanded using behavioral science to form a new dataset with 1,245 features. These features included statistical measures such as mean, minimum, maximum, and standard deviation calculated from continuous variables, and one-hot encodings applied to categorical variables.

A comprehensive comparative analysis between algorithms that transform tabular data into images was conducted. Specifically, we implement and evaluate the performance of NEighborhood Dependencies (Refined) [4], DeepInsight [5], and TAbular Convolution (TAC) [6] with the expanded dataset.

### 3.1 Representation of Features as Images with Neighborhood Dependencies (Refined)

The tabular data to image conversion process was implemented on a dataset designed to detect DDoS attacks, transforming network traffic statistics into visual representations. The process began with the application of Bayesian Multidimensional Scaling [20] to reduce the dimensionality of the data, thereby generating initial image coordinates that accurately represented the relationships within the dataset.

Subsequently, a hill climbing algorithm was employed to refine these coordinates. Hill climbing, as described in [21], is an optimization technique that iteratively adjusts the coordinates to minimize the Euclidean distance between features, effectively enhancing the accuracy of the mapping. To efficiently execute this process, the solution was implemented with [22], a parallel computing framework that distributed the computational workload across multiple processors. This enabled faster processing and more precise refinement of the image coordinates.

Another test with Dual Annealing with the implementation of [23] was conducted, resulting in the same optimized image coordinates.

The refined coordinates were then used to produce images suitable for machine learning and deep learning models. By converting the DDoS dataset into images, the researchers improved the capability to detect and analyze DDoS attacks, facilitating a more precise understanding of complex network traffic patterns and thereby strengthening cybersecurity measures.

Figure 1 displays the algorithm pipeline for the network traffic data transformation.

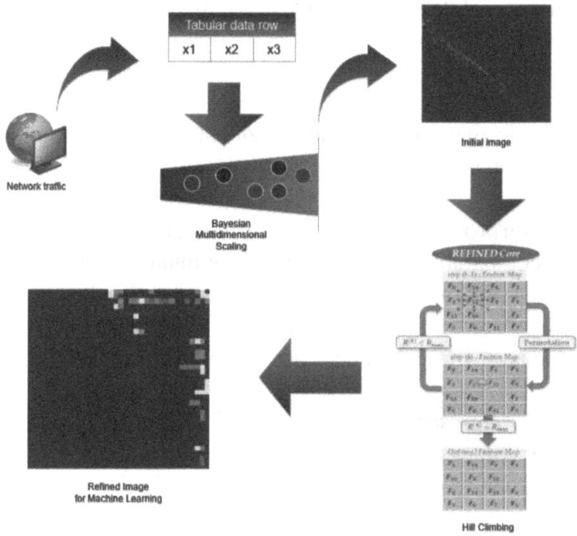


**Fig. 1.** Refined algorithm applied on network traffic data

As can be seen in Fig. 2, the resulting images exhibit distinct patterns depending on the numerical characteristics of each record. These patterns can be analyzed using deep learning and image processing algorithms to detect and classify elements, thereby enhancing the ability to identify and respond to potential DDoS attacks.

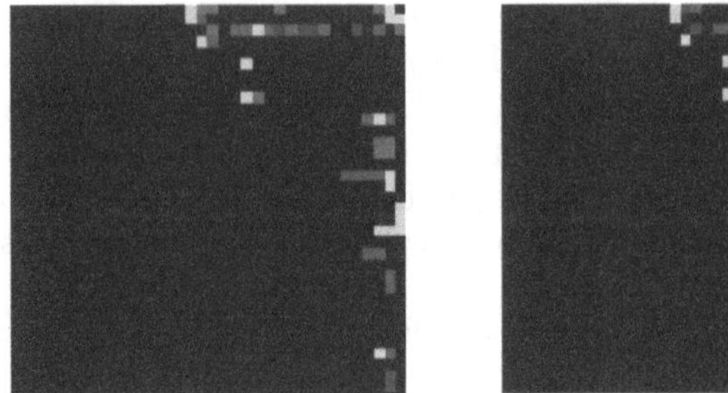

**Fig. 2.** Image from a normal (left) and a critical traffic (right) example, generated with Refined

### 3.2 DeepInsight

DeepInsight is a transformation technique designed to convert high-dimensional tabular data into 2D images, enabling the use of Convolutional Neural Networks (CNNs) for classification tasks [5].

The transformation process starts with the normalization of tabular data to ensure that all features are on a comparable scale, preventing dominance of any particular feature due to scale discrepancies. Following normalization, pairwise Euclidean distances between data features are calculated, establishing a measure of similarity between features in the high-dimensional space. These distances are essential for constructing the subsequent 2D mapping.

To achieve the 2D representation, t-distributed Stochastic Neighbor Embedding (t-SNE) is utilized for dimensionality reduction. t-SNE is chosen for its capability to preserve the local structure of the data, ensuring that similar features remain in close proximity on the 2D grid [24]. This proximity preservation is vital for the CNN to effectively learn and distinguish patterns in the data. The final step involves mapping the t-SNE output to a 2D grid, where each feature occupies a unique position on the grid, and its intensity is represented by its normalized value. The result is a grayscale image in which pixel intensities correspond to feature values, as illustrated in Fig. 3.

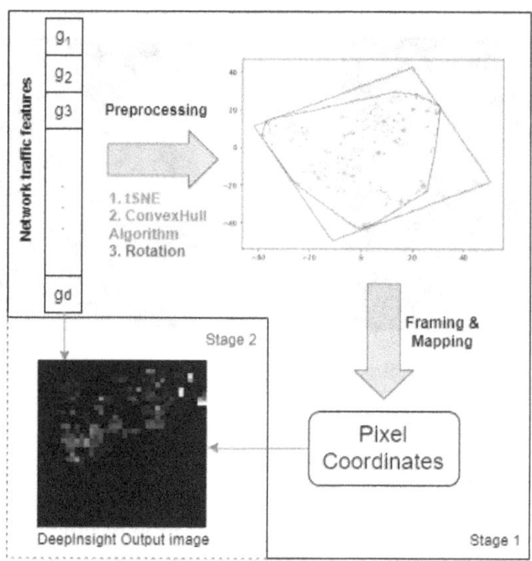


**Fig. 3.** DeepInsight systematically maps high dimensional tabular data into a 2D image space, where each feature is represented by a pixel whose intensity reflects its normalized value

DeepInsight was applied to network traffic data to convert it into 2D images, enabling CNNs to effectively differentiate between benign and malicious traffic. The network traffic data was initially normalized and projected into a 2D space using t-SNE, followed by the generation of grayscale images representing network behavior. These images were then fed into CNN models for training and classification.

The images generated by DeepInsight capture distinct patterns that correspond to various types of network activities, as shown in Fig. 4. These patterns, such as clusters and anomalies, are critical for the CNN's learning process, allowing the model to automatically extract relevant features that are indicative of normal or critical network behavior. By transforming high-dimensional data into a visual format, DeepInsight facilitates the detection of network threats with enhanced precision and reliability.

The transformation of tabular data into images not only leverages the strength of CNNs in image classification but also enhances interpretability by providing a visual understanding of the data patterns. This capability is particularly beneficial in cybersecurity applications, where identifying and responding to network anomalies is paramount.

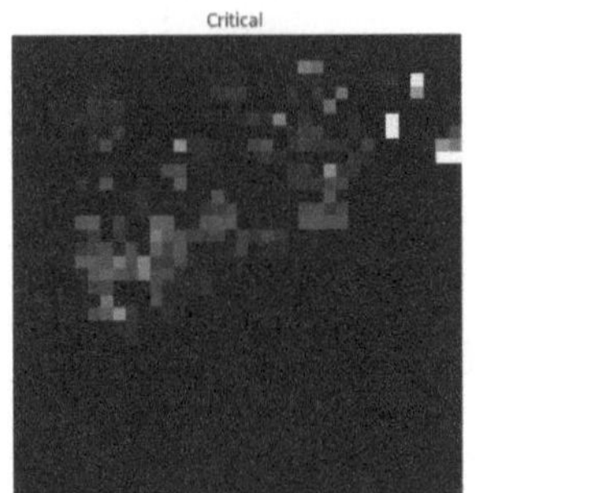


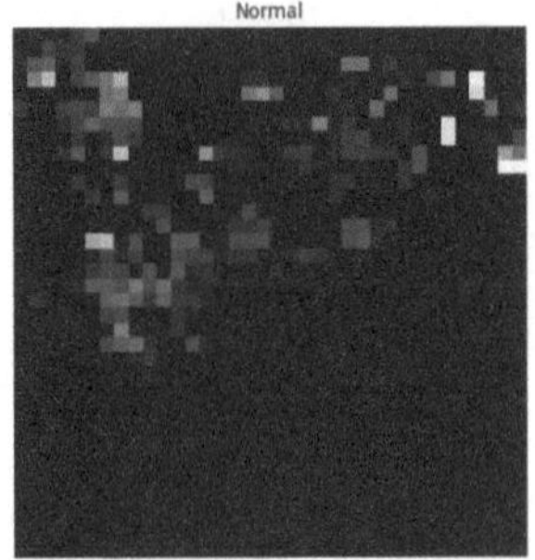


**Fig. 4.** Image generated using DeepInsight from network traffic data. Normal traffic (right) shows higher pixel value density than critical traffic (left)

### 3.3 Tabular Convolution (TAC)

Tabular Convolution (TAC) [6] enables the classification of tabular data using convolutional neural networks (CNNs) by transforming the data into a format suitable for CNN analysis. Instead of converting tabular data into 2D images, TAC treats each row of the dataset (i.e., a feature vector) as an image filter (kernel) and applies it to a fixed base image. This method eliminates the need for extensive preprocessing, such as converting data into images, and allows for a more direct and efficient analysis of raw tabular data. One of TAC's main advantages is its ability to work directly with high-dimensional tabular data while maintaining the original structure of the dataset. This makes it particularly useful for analyzing network traffic, where data is often complex and multidimensional.

In this study, a chess pattern was selected as the base image because it offers a clear, regular structure that can assist CNNs in distinguishing patterns more effectively. The original authors, however, proposed using an arbitrary template image. Importantly, because the same base image is used for all transformations, the generated images do not vary significantly from each other, retaining a similar underlying structure. Figure 5 shows the pipeline for TAC image conversion applied with the template image.

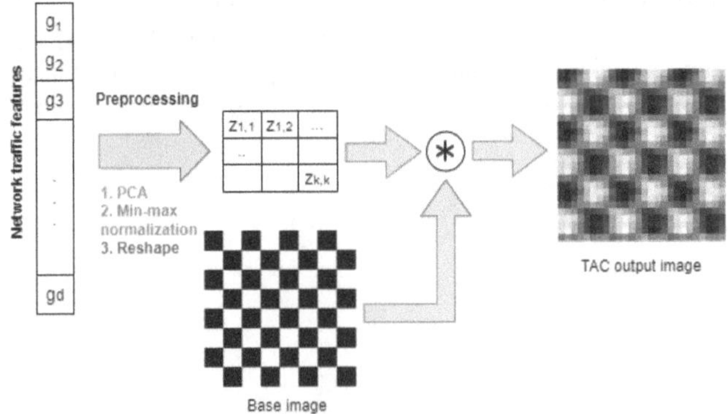


**Fig. 5.** Outline of the TAC method

By converting feature vectors into convolutional kernels, TAC structures the data in a way that allows CNNs to identify complex relationships within the dataset. While the order of features used to build the kernels has been reported to have minimal impact on results, optimizing feature ordering remains an area for future work.

TAC was applied to network traffic data to capture both spatial and temporal patterns, improving the detection of anomalies. As shown in Fig. 6, TAC effectively identifies subtle anomalies in network traffic, demonstrating its capability to improve classification accuracy and enhance the detection of critical security threats that may be missed by traditional methods.

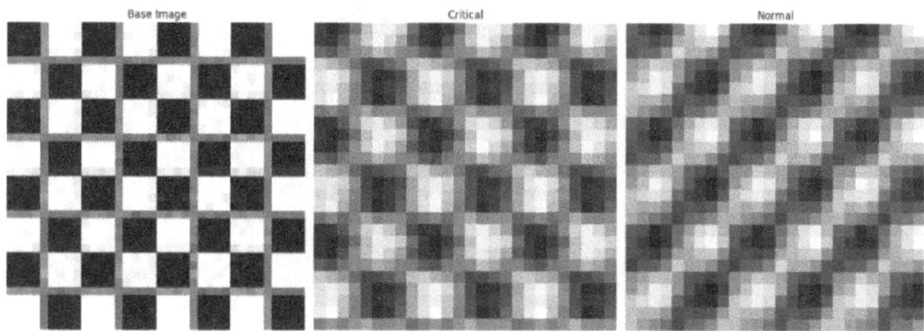


**Fig. 6.** Visualization of patterns detected using Tabular Convolution on network traffic data.

# 4 Results

All models were implemented, and classification models using the same CNN architecture were trained and tested for a fair comparison. Each model was trained for 200 epochs using a stratified split of the data, ensuring that class distributions were maintained across training and validation sets. The input to the CNNs consisted of grayscale images with a resolution of $36 \times 36$ pixels, derived from the transformed tabular data.

The evaluation of the three approaches—Refined, DeepInsight, and Tabular Convolution—yielded distinct performance results. The metrics achieved by each method are summarized in Table 1.

**Table 1.** Evaluation metrics and results for each model.

| Algorithm | Accuracy | F1 Score | Recall | Precision |
|---|---|---|---|---|
| Refined | 0.7381 | 0.7338 | 0.7380 | 0.7435 |
| DeepInsight | 0.6667 | 0.6395 | 0.6667 | 0.7045 |
| TAC | 0.6071 | 0.5572 | 0.6071 | 0.6454 |

The Refined method achieved the highest accuracy (0.7381) and F1 score (0.7338), suggesting that its image transformation approach was highly effective in detecting patterns within the network traffic data.

Figure 7 presents the confusion matrix of the Refined model, revealing 15 false positives and 7 false negatives. While this method outperformed the others in capturing relationships between features, these misclassifications indicate that the model is not perfect and has room for improvement in certain scenarios. An important point for enhancement is reducing false negatives to improve the model's effectiveness, as minimizing undetected malicious activities is crucial in anomaly detection.

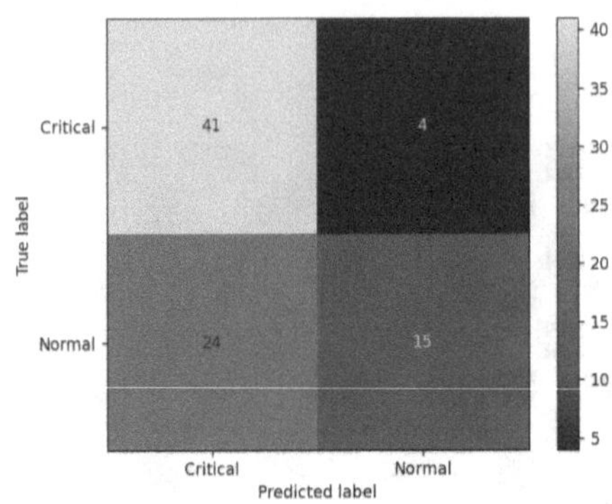


**Fig. 7.** Confusion Matrix for Refined on the Test Set.

DeepInsight, while slightly less accurate (0.6667), still performed well, particularly in preserving spatial relationships between features. The F1 score of 0.6395 and recall of 0.6667 suggest that this method is moderately effective in distinguishing between benign and malicious network traffic. Although it did not surpass the Refined method, its strength lies in its ability to effectively capture the local structure of the data, enhancing threat detection capabilities.

The Tabular Convolution (TAC) method produced the lowest accuracy (0.6071) and F1 score (0.5572) in comparison. While TAC offers a novel and direct method for CNNs to analyze tabular data, its performance lagged behind the other methods. However, it is important to note that TAC still demonstrates potential in processing complex patterns within high-dimensional data, and further optimization of the feature ordering and initial base image could lead to performance improvements [25].

Figure 8 illustrates the confusion matrix for both DeepInsight and Tabular Convolution models on the test set. Both models accurately identified 41 critical cases. DeepInsight exhibited a lower false positive rate, misclassifying 24 normal instances as critical, compared to Tabular Convolution's 29 misclassifications. This suggests that DeepInsight is slightly more proficient at distinguishing between benign and malicious network traffic. Moreover, despite having lower overall precision than the Refined method, DeepInsight is superior in identifying risks because it has fewer false negatives. This indicates that DeepInsight is more effective in detecting critical instances, thereby enhancing its value as a tool for identifying malicious network traffic.

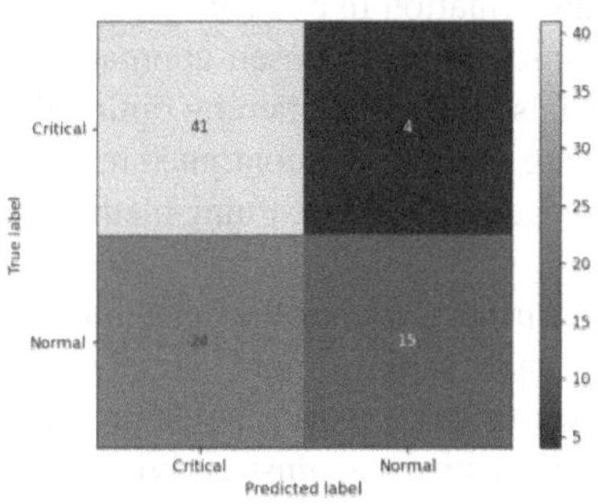


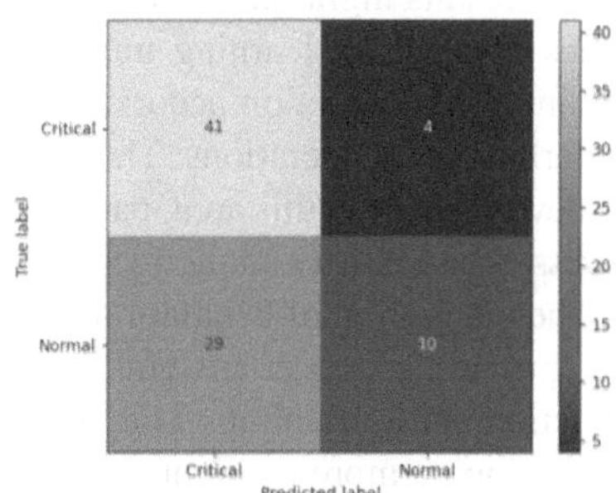


**Fig. 8.** Confusion Matrix for DeepInsight (left) and TAC (right) on the Test Set.

Overall, the comparison shows that while each method has its strengths, the Refined approach is the most effective for the specific task of detecting network anomalies, followed by DeepInsight and TAC.

## 5 Lessons Learned

From the experiments and results, multiple insights are obtained:

*Importance of Data Transformation:* Transforming tabular data into visual formats significantly enhanced network threat detection. The Refined method, in particular, achieved the best accuracy by capturing intricate data patterns.

*Model Selection:* The choice of machine learning models is critical for effective threat detection. While traditional models provide a baseline, more advanced models like CNNs, especially when combined with image-based data representations, demonstrated superior performance in identifying complex threats.

*Class Imbalance:* Network traffic data is often highly imbalanced, with most traffic skewed toward normal behavior and few examples of threats. Generative Adversarial Networks (GANs) [26] offer a promising solution by generating synthetic threat data to improve model robustness and classification accuracy. This approach remains a valuable area for future research in enhancing network anomaly detection.

*Computational Challenges:* Methods like Refined and DeepInsight required significant computational resources. Parallel computing frameworks like [22] were necessary for optimizing the processing time and achieving precise results.

## 6 Conclusions

In conclusion, this study demonstrates the potential of combining Network Behavior Analysis (NBA) with machine learning and deep learning techniques for proactive network threat detection. By transforming network traffic data into visual formats and applying advanced algorithms such as Refined and DeepInsight, we achieved significant improvements in detecting network anomalies and malicious activities.

The results highlight the importance of data transformation in enhancing the capabilities of machine learning models for threat detection. The proposed approach not only improves detection accuracy but also reduces false positives, thereby optimizing network security operations. These findings underscore the need for continued research and development in this area, particularly in the application of deep learning methods to address cybersecurity challenges.

The integration of behavioral analysis principles further enriches the detection process, providing deeper insights into user behavior and enabling more effective risk prediction and mitigation. This holistic approach to network security holds promises for developing more resilient and adaptive defense mechanisms against evolving cyber threats.

## 7 Future Works

As future work, this research aims to expand the implementation of the proposed solutions by incorporating a wider range of network attack types. This will involve transforming captured data to analyze and identify the critical characteristics that define user profiles associated with various threat categories. By refining these profiles, we aim to improve the system's ability to detect and mitigate a broader spectrum of attacks in real-time.

Moving forward, further experiments will be conducted using additional deep network architectures, focusing on the insights gained from the image conversion process. Data augmentation techniques will be applied using Generative Adversarial Networks (GANs), as described in [26], and more experiments with the dataset [27] with more attack classifications, to enhance the diversity and volume of the dataset. Additionally, Kolmogorov-Arnold Networks, as detailed in [28], will be utilized as an alternative method for classification. These approaches aim to refine the model's predictive performance and generalize its applicability across a wider range of network traffic scenarios.

**Acknowledgments.** We extend our gratitude to Dr. Arash Habibi Lashkari of the Behaviour-Centric Cybersecurity Center (BCCC) at York University for sharing the dataset used in this project.

**Disclosure of Interests.** The authors have no competing interests to declare that are relevant to the content of this article.

**Data Availability.** The original dataset is publicly available at [1], while the generated dataset from the study [3] is available upon request.

**Limitations.** This study focuses exclusively on detecting DDoS attacks using image-based representations of network behavior, it does not encompass the full spectrum of cyber threats. Future work will aim to extend this methodology to other types of attacks.

## References


1. Behaviour-Centric Cybersecurity Center: BCCC-Dataset: BCCC CPacket cloud-based DDoS 2024. Behaviour-Centric Cybersecurity Center (BCCC) (2024). https://www.yorku.ca/research/bccc/ucs-technical/cybersecurity-datasets-cds
2. Shafi, M., Lashkari, A.H., Rodriguez, V., Nevo, R.: Toward generating a new cloud-based distributed denial of service (DDoS) dataset and cloud intrusion traffic characterization. Information **15**(4), 195 (2024). https://doi.org/10.3390/info15040195
3. Posada Barrera, A.I., Rodriguez Peralta, L.M., Rosete Beas, E.: Behavioral analysis and machine learning for proactive network threat detection. In: Patterson, W. (ed.) New Perspectives in Behavioral Cybersecurity II: Human Behavior for Business, Profiling, Linguistics and Voting. Routledge. ISBN 9781032983523. (in press)
4. Bazgir, O., Zhang, R., Dhruba, S.R., Rahman, R., Ghosh, S., Pal, R.: REFINED (REpresentation of features as images with NEighborhood dependencies): a novel feature representation for convolutional neural networks. arXiv. https://doi.org/10.48550/ARXIV.1912.05687 (2019)
5. Sharma, A., Vans, E., Shigemizu, D., Boroevich, K.A., Tsunoda, T.: DeepInsight: a methodology to transform non-image data into an image for convolutional neural network architecture. Sci. Rep. **9**, 11399 (2019). https://doi.org/10.1038/s41598-019-47765-6
6. Iqbal, M.I., Mukta, Md.S.H., Hasan, A.R.: A dynamic weighted tabular method for convolutional neural networks (version 1). arXiv. https://doi.org/10.48550/ARXIV.2205.10386 (2022)
7. Farouk, M., Sakr, R.H., Hikal, N.: Identifying the most accurate machine learning classification technique to detect network threats. Neural Comput. Appl. **36**(16), 8977–8994 (2024)
8. Ahmad, Z., Shahid Khan, A., Wai Shiang, C., Abdullah, J., Ahmad, F.: Network intrusion detection system: A systematic study of machine learning and deep learning approaches. Trans. Emerg. Telecommun. Technol. **32**(1) (2020). https://doi.org/10.1002/ett.4150
9. Thakkar, A., Lohiya, R.: A survey on intrusion detection system: feature selection, model, performance measures, application perspective, challenges, and future research directions. Artif. Intell. Rev. **55**(1), 453–563 (2021). https://doi.org/10.1007/s10462-021-10037-9
10. Kasongo, S.M.: An advanced intrusion detection system for IIoT based on GA and tree based algorithms. IEEE Access **9**, 113199–113212 (2021). https://doi.org/10.1109/access.2021.3104113
11. Shone, N., Ngoc, T.N., Phai, V.D., Shi, Q.: A deep learning approach to network intrusion detection. IEEE Trans. Emerg. Top. Comput. Intell. **2**(1), 41–50 (2018). https://doi.org/10.1109/tetci.2017.2772792
12. De la Hoz, E., De La Hoz, E., Ortiz, A., Ortega, J., Prieto, B.: PCA filtering and probabilistic SOM for network intrusion detection. Neurocomputing **164**, 71–81 (2015). https://doi.org/10.1016/j.neucom.2014.09.083
13. Xiao, Y., Xing, C., Zhang, T., Zhao, Z.: An intrusion detection model based on feature reduction and convolutional neural networks. IEEE Access **7**, 42210–42219 (2019). https://doi.org/10.1109/access.2019.2904620
14. Zhu, Y., et al.: Converting tabular data into images for deep learning with convolutional neural networks. Sci. Rep. **11**(1) (2021). https://doi.org/10.1038/s41598-021-90923-y
15. Bazgir, O., Zhang, R., Dhruba, S.R., Rahman, R., Ghosh, S., Pal, R.: Representation of features as images with neighborhood dependencies for compatibility with convolutional neural networks. Nat. Commun. **11**(1) (2020). https://doi.org/10.1038/s41467-020-18197-y
16. Sohi, S.M., Seifert, J.-P., Ganji, F.: RNNIDS: enhancing network intrusion detection systems through deep learning. Comput. Secur. **102**, 102151 (2021). https://doi.org/10.1016/j.cose.2020.102151

17. Althubiti, S.A., Jones, E.M., Roy, K.: LSTM for anomaly-based network intrusion detection. In: 2018 28th International Telecommunication Networks and Applications Conference (ITNAC), pp. 1–3. IEEE (2018). https://doi.org/10.1109/atnac.2018.8615300
18. Shi, Z., Luktarhan, N., Song, Y., Yin, H.: TSFN: a novel malicious traffic classification method using BERT and LSTM. Entropy **25**(5), 821 (2023). https://doi.org/10.3390/e25050821
19. Chapaneri, R., Shah, S.: Detection of malicious network traffic using convolutional neural networks. In: 2019 10th International Conference on Computing, Communication and Networking Technologies (ICCCNT), pp. 1–6. IEEE (2019). https://doi.org/10.1109/ICCCNT45670.2019.8944814
20. Zhang, J., Cao, J., Wang, L.: Generalized Bayesian multidimensional scaling and model comparison (version 2). arXiv. https://doi.org/10.48550/ARXIV.2306.15908 (2023)
21. Hernando, L., Mendiburu, A., Lozano, J.A.: Hill-Climbing algorithm: let's go for a walk before finding the optimum. In: 2018 IEEE Congress on Evolutionary Computation (CEC). IEEE (2018). https://doi.org/10.1109/cec.2018.8477836
22. Clarke, L., Glendinning, I., Hempel, R.: The MPI message passing interface standard. In: Decker, K.M., Rehmann, R.M. (eds.) Programming Environments for Massively Parallel Distributed Systems. Monte Verità. Birkhäuser, Basel, pp. 213–218 (1994). https://doi.org/10.1007/978-3-0348-8534-8_21
23. Gulta, D., Chen, S.: Improvements to dual annealing in SciPy. In: 2024 IEEE Latin American Conference on Computational Intelligence (LA-CCI), pp. 1–6 (2024). https://doi.org/10.1109/la-cci62337.2024.10814799
24. van der Maaten, L., Hinton, G.: Visualizing data using t-SNE. J. Mach. Learn. Res. **9**, 2579–2605 (2008)
25. Buturović, L., Miljković, D.: A novel method for classification of tabular data using convolutional neural networks. BioRxiv, pp. 2020-05 (2020). https://doi.org/10.1101/2020.05.02.074203
26. Goodfellow, I., et al.: Generative adversarial nets. In: Advances in Neural Information Processing Systems, pp. 2672–2680 (2014). https://doi.org/10.1145/3422622
27. Shafi, M., Lashkari, A.H., Roudsari, A.H.: NTLFlowLyzer: towards generating an intrusion detection dataset and intruders behavior profiling through network and transport layers traffic analysis and pattern extraction. Comput. Secur. **148**, 104160 (2025). https://doi.org/10.1016/j.cose.2024.104160
28. Liu, Z., et al.: KAN: Kolmogorov-Arnold networks (version 4). arXiv. https://doi.org/10.48550/ARXIV.2404.19756 (2024)

# Data Science, Algorithms, and Novel Applications

# Task Scheduling with Various Security Level Requirement in Financial Cloud Environment

Xianmei Hua(✉) and Xinrong Zhan

Xiamen Institute of Technology, Xiamen, Fujian 361021, China
sophiehua1983@163.com

**Abstract.** The proliferation of multi-cloud infrastructures in the financial sector presents new challenges in executing security-sensitive and quality-of-service (QoS)-constrained workloads. Traditional scheduling methods often fall short in addressing the conflicting objectives of execution efficiency and inter-cloud communication overhead. In this paper, we propose a hybrid task scheduling framework that integrates a communication-aware clustering strategy with a multi-objective Non-dominated Sorting Genetic Algorithm II (NSGA-II) to optimize financial workflow execution across multi-cloud environments. The proposed method first employs a DAG-based clustering algorithm to identify groups of interdependent tasks with high data exchange, aiming to minimize inter-cloud traffic. These clusters are then used to guide both the initialization and evolutionary operators of NSGA-II, enabling efficient exploration of the solution space while ensuring security-level compliance and resource feasibility. Simulation results demonstrate that our approach achieves superior performance in terms of makespan reduction and communication cost minimization when compared with others approaches. The proposed framework offers a scalable and adaptive solution for QoS-aware financial task scheduling under heterogeneous cloud environment.

**Keywords:** Security · cloud · task scheduling · clustering method

## 1 Introduction

The extensive adoption of cloud computing in the financial industry has significantly transformed service delivery, enabling high availability, scalability, and cost-efficiency [1]. Financial institutions now leverage cloud platforms for a wide range of services including algorithmic trading, fraud detection, risk modeling, and customer relationship management. This shift has empowered institutions to respond more quickly to market demands and customer expectations. Additionally, multi-cloud strategies are increasingly employed to mitigate vendor lock-in and enhance service reliability [2].

Despite these advantages, executing financial data processing tasks in cloud environments introduces notable challenges. Stringent latency requirements,


R. Stahlbock et al. (Eds.): CSCE 2025, CCIS 2938, pp. 221–232, 2027.
https://doi.org/10.1007/978-3-032-22196-4_16

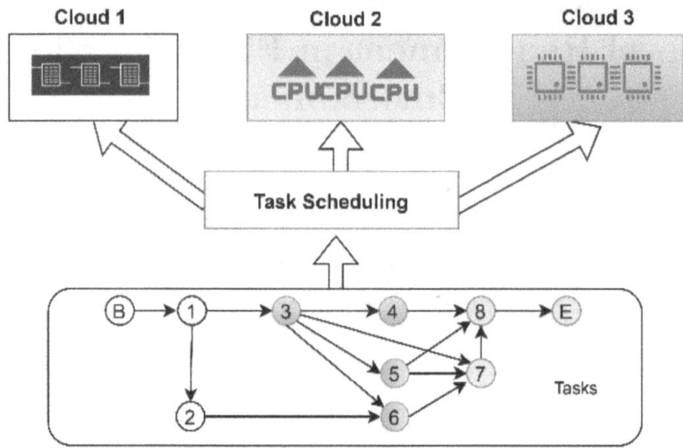


**Fig. 1.** Financial task scheduling under multi-cloud environment.

compliance with regional regulations, sensitivity to security breaches, and unpredictable market loads complicate efficient task execution [1,3]. Moreover, task heterogeneity and diverse Quality of Service (QoS) demands-such as timing constraints, data locality, and throughput-necessitate highly adaptive and intelligent scheduling strategies. Achieving cost efficiency while guaranteeing service-level objectives (SLOs) remains a major operational challenge for cloud-based financial systems.

To address these issues, numerous studies have explored QoS-aware scheduling mechanisms in cloud computing [4]. Researchers have proposed algorithms based on heuristics [5], metaheuristics (e.g., Genetic Algorithms, Particle Swarm Optimization), and machine learning [6] techniques for workflow orchestration and task placement. Several models have integrated cost [6], time [7], and reliability as objective functions for optimizing financial data processing. Furthermore, recent works have incorporated security-aware [7–10] and compliance-driven scheduling policies, especially in multi-cloud environments where regulatory requirements differ. However, there remains a gap in dynamic scheduling frameworks that can concurrently address multiple QoS dimensions in real-time for financial applications.

Figure 1 presents a security-aware task scheduling framework in a financial multi-cloud environment, where tasks with varying Quality of Service (QoS) and security requirements are allocated across three heterogeneous cloud platforms. Each cloud is associated with a distinct security level: Cloud 1 (white) corresponds to Level 1, Cloud 2 (blue) to Level 2, and Cloud 3 (green) to Level 3. Tasks are modeled as nodes in a Directed Acyclic Graph (DAG), where the background color of each node denotes its required security level. Tasks $3 \sim 6$, which demand higher security (Levels 2 or 3), are eligible to execute only on Cloud 2 or Cloud 3, and are restricted from deployment on Cloud 1. The task scheduler assigns operations while adhering to both dependency constraints and security requirements to ensure policy compliance. Moreover, assuming uniform data volume per communication link, the scheduling decision significantly impacts inter-cloud traffic: if tasks 3 to 6 are distributed across multiple clouds, the resulting cross-cloud data transfers will incur increased communication overhead and extended execution time. This highlights the need for traffic-aware and locality-sensitive scheduling strategies in secure multi-cloud environments. The two points in the figure are that we try to solve in the paper: (1) to meet the security level requirement, and (2) to reduce the data size transferred between clouds.

To address the complex scheduling demands of secure financial workflows in a multi-cloud environment, we propose a hybrid optimization framework that integrates task clustering with a modified Non-dominated Sorting Genetic Algorithm II (NSGA-II). The core idea is to exploit inter-task communication locality prior to the optimization phase and use this structure to inform the initialization and evolution of NSGA-II. This integration not only ensures that security constraints are respected from the outset but also improves the convergence behavior of the genetic algorithm by guiding the search process with meaningful initial patterns.

# 2 System Model

## 2.1 Cloud Model

We consider a financial multi-cloud environment consisting of a set of cloud service providers $C = \{\mathrm{C}_1, C_2, \ldots, C_m\}$. Each cloud $C_i \in C$ is defined by a tuple $C_i = \langle S_i, V_i, B_i \rangle$ , where:

- $S_i \in \{1, 2, 3, \ldots\}$ denotes the security level of cloud $C_i$ , with higher values corresponding to stricter compliance with financial regulations and stronger isolation guarantees.
- $V_i = \{v_{i,1}, v_{i,2}, \ldots, v_{i,K_i})$ ) represents the set of Virtual Machines (VMs) available in cloud $C_i$ , where each VM $v_{ij}$ is a resource unit characterized by a tuple $v_{ij} = \langle CPU_{ij}, MEM_{ij}, DISK_{ij} \rangle$ , indicating the number of processing cores, memory size (e.g., in GB), and local disk capacity (e.g., in GB), respectively.
- $B_i$ represents the inter-cloud bandwidth vector, where $B_{ij}$ denotes the available bandwidth between cloud $C_i$ and cloud $C_j$ , capturing the communication cost for data transfer in distributed workflows.

Each task must be scheduled on a VM whose resource capacity satisfies its computational demands and security requirement. A task with required security level $s$ can only be executed on a VM $v_{ij} \in C_i$. if $S_i \geq s$ is. Additionally, the scheduler must account for the heterogeneity of VM configurations when optimizing task placement, aiming to reduce resource contention, maximize utilization, and minimize inter-cloud data movement delays.

### 2.2 Maintaining the Integrity of the Specifications

We represent the financial workflow as a Directed Acyclic Graph (DAG) defined as:

$$G = (T, E) \tag{1}$$

where:

- $T = \{T_1, T_2, \ldots, T_n\}$ denotes the set of composite tasks.
- $E \subseteq T \times T$ represents data or control dependencies between tasks.

Each task $T_i \in T$ is composed of a set of security-sensitive subtasks:

$$T_i = \{t_{i1}, t_{i2}, \ldots, t_{iK_i}\} \tag{2}$$

where each subtask $t_{ij}$ is defined by the tuple.

$$t_{ij} = \langle r_{ij}, s_{ij} \rangle \tag{3}$$

with:

- $r_{ij} =< c_{ij}, m_{ij}, d_{ij} >$ : the resource demand of subtask $t_{ij}$ , including CPU, memory, and disk;
- $r_{ij} = \{1, 2, 3, \ldots\}$ : the security level requirement of subtask $t_{ij}$ , indicating that it must be executed on a cloud $C_k$ with $S_k \geq s_{ij}$.

Dependencies between tasks imply that all subtasks within a predecessor task must complete before any subtask in the successor task can begin. Inter-subtask communication cost is assumed negligible within the same task, but inter-task communication (i.e., when $(T_i, T_j) \in E$ ) involves data transfers denoted by $\delta_{ij}$, subject to bandwidth limitations if executed across different clouds.

### 2.3 Execution Time Model

We define the execution time of a task as the cumulative duration required to process all its subtasks on assigned virtual machines (VMs), subject to security and resource constraints.

Each subtask $t_{ij}$, is mapped to a VM $v_{kl} \in V_k$ on cloud $C_k$. The execution time of subtask $t_{ij}$ on VM $v_{kl}$ is given by:

$$ET\left(t_{ij}, v_{kl}\right) = \frac{I_{ij}}{P_{kl}} \tag{4}$$

where:

- $I_{ij}$ is the instruction workload (in million instructions, MI) of subtask $t_{ij}$.
- $P_{kl}$ is the processing speed (in MIPS) of VM $v_{kl}$.
- The assignment is valid only if $S_k \geq s_{ij}$, where $S_k$ is the security level of cloud $C_k$, and $s_{ij}$ is the required security level of the subtask.

The execution time of task $T_i$, denoted $ET(T_i)$, is defined as:

$$ET(T_i) = \max_j \{\mathrm{FT}(t_{ij})\} \tag{5}$$

where $FT(t_{ij})$ is the finish time of subtask $t_{ij}$, including its waiting time due to resource availability and dependency constraints.

For each edge $(T_i, T_j) \in E$, if any subtask of $T_i$ and $T_j$ are executed on different clouds $C_k$ and $C_l$, then a communication delay is incurred:

$$CD(T_i, T_j) = \frac{\delta_{ij}}{B_{kl}} \tag{6}$$

where:

- $\delta_{ij}$ is the data volume transmitted from $T_i$ to $T_j$.
- $B_{kl}$ is the bandwidth between clouds $C_k$ and $C_l$.

The total execution time (makespan) for the DAG workflow is defined as:

$$\text{Makespan} = \max_{T_i \in T} \{FT(T_i)\} \tag{7}$$

where $FT(T_i)$ is the finish time of task $T_i$, which accounts for the latest subtask completion time and any incurred communication delays from predecessor tasks.

### 2.4 Scheduling Targets and Constraints

In addition to minimizing the workflow makespan, the scheduling strategy aims to reduce both (i) the cumulative time spent on inter-cloud data transmission and (ii) the total volume of data transferred across clouds.

We define the overall communication cost as a weighted combination of delay and data volume:

$$\text{CommCost} = \sum_{(T_i, T_j) \in T} (\alpha * CD(T_i, T_j) + \beta * \delta_{ij} * \mathrm{loc}(T_i, T_j)) \tag{8}$$

where: $\alpha, \beta \geq 0$ are user-defined coefficients that balance the relative importance of time versus data volume. $\mathrm{loc}(T_i, T_j)$ return 1 if $T_i$ and $T_j$ are located in the same cloud; otherwise, it returns 0.

**Algorithm 1.** Cluster for tasks.

**Input:** DAG $G = (T, E)$ , number of clusters $K$
**Output:** ClusterSet $= \{C_1, C_2, \ldots, C_K\}$

```
Initialize Cluster {t_i | t_i ∈ T}
while |ClusterSet| > K do
    (C_a, C_b) ← argmax_(C_i,C_j) Σ_{t_p∈C_i, t_q∈C_j} δ_pq
    Merge C_a and C_b into new cluster C_new
    Remove C_a and C_b from ClusterSet
    Add C_new to ClusterSet
end while
return ClusterSet
```

The final scheduling objective can be formulated as a bi-objective optimization problem:

$$\min \begin{cases} \text{Makespan} = \max\limits_{T_i \in T} \left\{ \max\limits_{j} \left( ST\left(t_{ij}\right) + ET\left(t_{ij}, v_{kl}\right) \right) \right\} \\ \text{CommCost} = \sum\limits_{(T_i, T_j) \in T} \left( \alpha^* CD\left(T_i, T_j\right) + \beta^* \delta_{ij} \right) \end{cases} \tag{9}$$

subject to:

$$S_k \geq s_{ij}, \forall t_{ij} \tag{10}$$

$$r_{ij} \geq \text{res}\left(v_{kl}\right), \forall t_{ij} \tag{11}$$

$$ST\left(t_{ij}\right) \geq \max_{t_{pq} \in \text{pred}(t_{ij})} \left\{ FT\left(t_{pq}\right) + CD\left(t_{pq}, t_{ij}\right) \right\} \tag{12}$$

# 3 Scheduling Method for Financial Tasks

## 3.1 Clustering Method to Find Task Cluster

To reduce inter-cloud data transmission, a pre-scheduling clustering algorithm groups tasks with intensive mutual data exchange into clusters. Each cluster is designed to preserve high intra-group communication volume, thereby minimizing intercloud communication costs when clusters are mapped to the same cloud. The clustering procedure is based on the following principles:

1. Each task is initially treated as a separate cluster.
2. Pairs of clusters are iteratively merged if the sum of inter-task data volume between them is maximal among candidates.
3. Merging is terminated when a predefined number of clusters is reached or communication density falls below a threshold.

### 3.2 GA Task Scheduling Method Based on Cluster

The clusters are assigned to clouds based on their collective security requirements. Since each cloud is associated with a specific security level, a cluster may only be placed on a cloud whose security level is greater than or equal to the highest security requirement among the tasks in that cluster. Once the cluster-to-cloud mapping is established, the individual tasks within each cluster are assigned to virtual machines (VMs) within the designated cloud. This two-level mapping-first at the cluster-cloud level and then at the task-VM level-forms the basis for the initial population of individuals in the NSGA-II algorithm. As a result, the initial solutions are already optimized for intra-cluster communication locality and security compliance, providing a strong foundation for further optimization.

The core of the optimization process is based on NSGA-II, a widely used multi-objective evolutionary algorithm that employs fast non-dominated sorting and crowding distance mechanisms to guide the search toward a well-distributed Pareto front. In our implementation, we modify NSGA-II to incorporate the results of the clustering algorithm not only in the initialization phase but also in the design of its genetic operators. This cluster-aware adaptation enhances both the efficiency and quality of the solution space exploration.

Each individual in the population encodes a complete scheduling solution, specifying the cloud and VM assignment for each task. The chromosome structure reflects the cluster hierarchy, where groups of genes correspond to tasks within the same cluster. This structural awareness is preserved during crossover and mutation operations. Specifically, the crossover operator is modified to perform recombination at the cluster level, exchanging entire clusters or their cloud assignments between two parent solutions. This approach maintains the communication-aware grouping of tasks and prevents the disruption of optimized intra-cluster dependencies.

Similarly, the mutation operator is adapted to operate within the boundaries of clusters. Instead of randomly reassigning any task to a different VM or cloud, the algorithm selectively mutates task assignments within their respective clusters. This localized mutation respects the initial communication-aware structure while still introducing variation necessary for global optimization. Additionally, a repair mechanism is employed post-mutation to ensure that the resulting individuals adhere to all system constraints, including security levels and VM resource capacities.

The fitness of each individual is evaluated based on two objectives: makespan and inter-cloud communication cost. Makespan reflects the total execution time of the entire workflow, while communication cost quantifies the time and bandwidth consumed when tasks are distributed across different clouds. By balancing these two objectives, NSGA-II evolves a population of scheduling solutions that trade off execution efficiency with communication overhead. The non-dominated sorting mechanism ensures that solutions are ranked based on Pareto optimality, and the crowding distance measure maintains diversity across the front. This enables the algorithm to explore a broad range of high-quality trade-off solu-

**Algorithm 2.** NGSAII-Cluster.

**Input:** DAG G = (T, E), number of clusters K, cloud configuration C, max_generations G_max
**Output:** Pareto-optimal set of task schedules

```
ClusterSet ← Cluster_Tasks(G, K) {Perform clustering based on data volume}
InitialPop ← [] {Initialize population}
for i = 1 to Population_Size do
    sol ← Assign_Clusters_to_Clouds(ClusterSet, C)
    sol ← Map_Tasks_to_VMs(sol)
    if not Is_Feasible(sol) then
        sol ← Repair(sol)
    end if
    InitialPop.append(sol)
end for
Evaluate_Fitness(InitialPop) {Makespan and CommCost}
Archive ← Fast_NonDominated_Sort(InitialPop)
for gen = 1 to G_max do
    Offspring ← Selection(Archive)
    Offspring ← Crossover(Offspring, ClusterSet)
    Offspring ← Mutation(Offspring, ClusterSet)
    Offspring ← Repair(Offspring)
    Evaluate_Fitness(Offspring)
    Combined ← Archive ∪ Offspring
    Archive ← Fast_NonDominated_Sort(Combined)
    Archive ← Prune_By_Crowding_Distance(Archive)
end for
return Archive
```

tions, from which decision-makers can select the most suitable schedule based on real-world requirements.

To preserve the benefits of the initial clustering, genetic operations are redefined:

- Cluster-level Crossover: Instead of arbitrarily swapping task assignments, clusters are treated as atomic units. During crossover, entire clusters may be reassigned to a different cloud in the offspring if doing so improves one of the objectives without violating security constraints.
- Intra-cluster Mutation: Mutation operations are restricted to modifying task-to-VM assignments within the same cloud assigned to the cluster. This localized mutation respects the initial communication-aware clustering while allowing the exploration of new configurations.
- Constraint Repair: After crossover and mutation, individuals are validated. If a task is mapped to a VM or cloud that does not satisfy its resource or security requirements, a repair procedure reassigns it to a compliant resource.

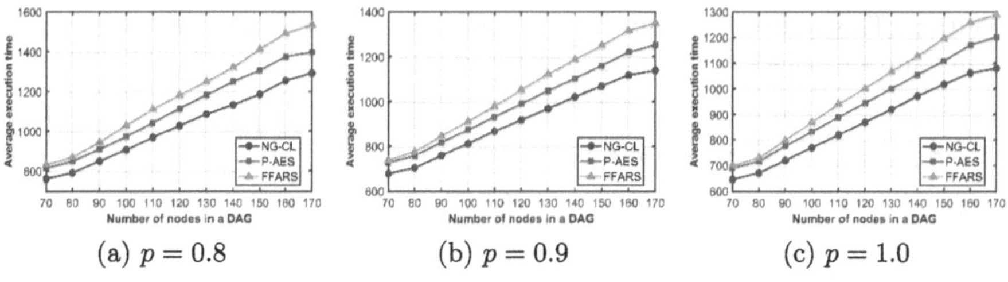


(a) $p = 0.8$ (b) $p = 0.9$ (c) $p = 1.0$

**Fig. 2.** Average execution time.

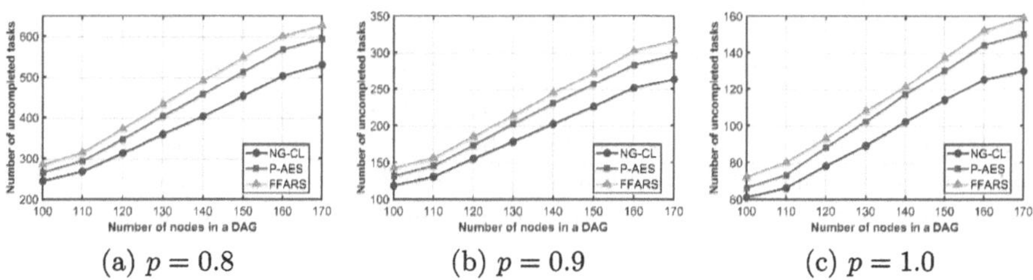


(a) $p = 0.8$ (b) $p = 0.9$ (c) $p = 1.0$

**Fig. 3.** Number of uncompleted tasks.

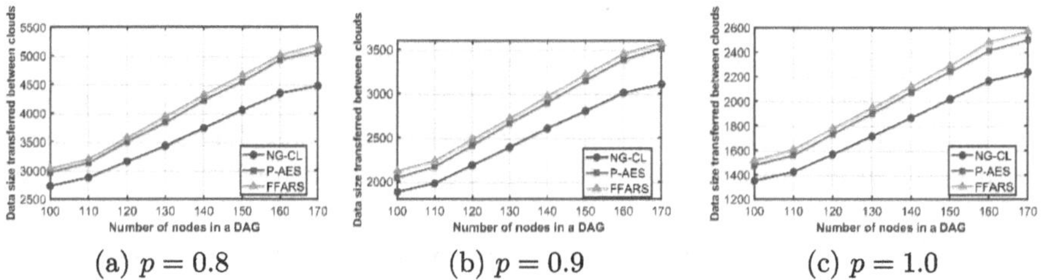


(a) $p = 0.8$ (b) $p = 0.9$ (c) $p = 1.0$

**Fig. 4.** Data size transferred between clouds.

# 4 Simulations and Comparisons

Because our method uses NGSAII to scheduling tasks based on the result of the clustering method, we call our method as NG-CL in the simulation. NG-CL will be compared to P-AES [11] (Polymorphic Advanced Encryption Standard), FFARS [12] (the Farmland Fertility Algorithm-based Scheduling). The FFARS approach draws its conceptual foundation from the agricultural practice of managing farmland fertility, wherein land is segmented into zones based on varying soil conditions, each exhibiting distinct properties. In a similar vein, FFARS facilitates balanced workload distribution and promotes equitable resource allocation aligned with task demands. Furthermore, we enhance FFARS to accommodate the specified privacy level requirements. P-AES targets to enhance task scheduling in cloud computing environments. By addressing factors such as makespan, cost, bandwidth, and security, the method ensures efficient and secure task distribution. This hybrid strategy provides a robust and scalable solution for optimizing and securing cloud-based services.

### 4.1 Simulation Environment

To evaluate the performance of the proposed scheduling method under various workload scales and privacy constraints, a synthetic DAG-based task generation method is employed. Each DAG represents a composite job comprising multiple interdependent subtasks. The number of subtasks in each DAG ranges from 100 to 170, incremented by 100. The execution time of each subtask on a standard processor is randomly drawn from a uniform distribution in the range $[1, 100]$ s. The data size associated with each edge in the DAG—representing the communication cost between dependent subtasks—is uniformly distributed within [1,1000] M. We first randomly generate the number of layers in the DAG, and then randomly assign tasks to each layer. From the first to the last layer, each node is assigned at least one predecessor and one successor to ensure connectivity.

Three cloud platforms are considered, each characterized by distinct privacy level distributions and inter-cloud bandwidth heterogeneity. The privacy requirement of each subtask is an integer randomly selected from 10 discrete levels in the range [1,10]. The three clouds offer different security capabilities: in Cloud 1, 80% of resources provide privacy levels concentrated in the range [1,4]; in Cloud 2, 80% are concentrated in [4,7]; and in Cloud 3, 80% are concentrated in [7,10], reflecting typical cloud heterogeneity in privacy assurance. The available bandwidth between any two clouds is sampled from a uniform distribution between 10 Mbps and 1000 Mbps. This simulation environment enables the evaluation of scheduling strategies under diverse privacy, bandwidth, and computational constraints.

### 4.2 Comparisons

**Average Execution Time.** Figure 2 presents the average execution time across varying DAG sizes under three scheduling strategies: NG-CL, P-AES, and FFARS. Across all subfigures, the number of DAG nodes ranges from 70 to 170, reflecting increasing workload scales. A consistent trend is observed: execution time increases linearly with the number of nodes. NG-CL consistently outperforms the other methods, yielding the lowest execution time across all cases. On average, across the three scenarios, NG-CL achieves approximately 19.87% and 10.95% reductions compared to FFARS and P-AES, respectively. The superior performance of NG-CL stems from its use of task clustering and NSGA-II-based optimization, enabling effective privacy-aware task grouping and resource matching. In contrast, P-AES and FFARS exhibit higher execution costs due to limited optimization on task dependencies and resource heterogeneity. This comparison validates the robustness of NG-CL in scalable and secure financial task scheduling.

**Number of Uncompleted Tasks.** Figure 3 presents the number of uncompleted tasks for three scheduling methods—NG-CL, P-AES, and FFARS—across increasing DAG sizes and varying resource availability. All methods exhibit a consistent upward trend in uncompleted tasks as the number of nodes increases, highlighting the growing challenge of task scheduling under heavier workloads. Across all three scenarios, NG-CL consistently achieves the lowest number of uncompleted tasks, with average reductions of 17.99% and 13.34% compared to FFARS and P-AES, respectively, in the first subfigure; 11.63% and 7.00% in the second; and 17.23% and 10.66% in the third. These improvements demonstrate NG-CL's effectiveness in addressing task dependencies, privacy constraints, and resource heterogeneity, outperforming FFARS's heuristic fertility-based mapping and P-AES's security-aware approach. Overall, NG-CL provides a more reliable and scalable solution for privacy-aware task scheduling in financial multi-cloud environments.

**Data Size Transferred Between Clouds.** Figure 4 depicts the data size transferred between clouds under three scheduling strategies-NG-CL, P-AES, and FFARS-across varying DAG sizes and resource scenarios. In all three subfigures, a consistent upward trend is observed: as the number of nodes in a DAG increases, the data transferred between clouds also increases across all methods. This trend reflects the growing inter-task communication demands in larger and more complex DAGs. Among the methods, NG-CL consistently achieves the lowest data transfer volumes. Averaged across all cases, NG-CL transfers approximately 3,800, 2,900, and 2,050 units of data in the three subfigures, respectively, compared to 4,150,3,200, and 2,350 for FFARS and 4,050,3,120, and 2,300 for P-AES. This represents a reduction of 350, 300, and 300 units over FFARS, and 250, 220, and 250 units over P-AES. The improvement stems from NG-CL's clustering-based initialization, which groups interdependent tasks and minimizes inter-cloud communication, and its NSGA-II-based scheduling which efficiently aligns privacy and resource compatibility. In contrast, P-AES and FFARS, while optimizing other factors, result in more distributed task placement and thus higher intercloud data exchange. These results confirm that NG-CL is highly effective in minimizing data movement, which is crucial for reducing latency, bandwidth costs, and privacy risk in financial multi-cloud environments.

## 5 Discussions and Future Work

The scheduling process begins with a task clustering procedure applied to the financial workflow, represented as a Directed Acyclic Graph (DAG). In this step, tasks that exchange large volumes of data are grouped together to form clusters. The rationale behind clustering is to minimize the inter-cloud data transmission by ensuring that communication-intensive tasks are co-located on the same cloud platform whenever possible. Each cluster thus encapsulates a set of tightly coupled tasks that ideally should be scheduled together to reduce latency and bandwidth consumption. Then we use the NGSA-II to solve the scheduling method based on the result of the cluster method. Simulations show it has advantage in reducing execution time, data size transferred between clouds, and the number of uncompleted tasks. Future work, we hope we can use some deep learning method to solve the scheduling problem of the financial clouds.

**Conflict of Interest.** The authors declare no conflict of interest.

## References


1. Saputra, K.D., Rahmaastri, D.A., Setiawan, K., Suryani, D., Purnama, Y.: Mobile financial management application using google cloud vision api. Proc. Comput. Sci. **157**, 596–604 (2019). https://doi.org/10.1016/j.procs.2019.09.019
2. Zhang, Y., Wu, L., Li, M., Zhao, T., Cai, X.: Dynamic multi-objective workflow scheduling for combined resources in cloud. Simul. Model. Pract. Theory **129**, 102835 (2023). https://doi.org/10.1016/j.simpat.2023.102835
3. Li, K., Zhang, D., Dong, X.: Simulation of network traffic risk of enterprise cloud financial system by using deep learning. Comput. Electr. Eng. **112**, 109027 (2023). https://doi.org/10.1016/j.compeleceng.2023.109027
4. Kavitha, T., Hemalatha, S., Saravanan, T., Singh, A.K., Alam, M.I., Warshi, S.: Survey on cloud computing security and scheduling. In: 2022 International Conference on Computer Communication and Informatics (ICCCI), pp. 1–4. IEEE (2022). https://doi.org/10.1109/iccci54379.2022.9740932
5. Kathole, A.B., Vhatkar, K., Lonare, S., Kshirsagar, A.P.: Optimization-based resource scheduling techniques in cloud computing environment: a review of scientific workflows and future directions. Comput. Electr. Eng. **123**, 110080 (2025). https://doi.org/10.1016/j.compeleceng.2025.110080
6. Shingne, H., Shriram, R.: Heuristic deep learning scheduling in cloud for resource-intensive internet of things systems. Comput. Electr. Eng. **108**, 108652 (2023). https://doi.org/10.1016/j.compeleceng.2023.108652
7. Abdi, S., Ashjaei, M., Mubeen, S.: Deadline-constrained security-aware workflow scheduling in hybrid cloud architecture. Futur. Gener. Comput. Syst. **162**, 107466 (2025). https://doi.org/10.1016/j.future.2024.07.044
8. Devi, D., Sathianesan, G.W.: An efficient approach with modified butterfly optimization algorithm for task scheduling and dlat based cloud data security. In: 2023 9th International Conference on Smart Structures and Systems (ICSSS), pp. 1–5. IEEE (2023). https://doi.org/10.1109/icsss58085.2023.10407430
9. Karatza, H.D.: Scheduling bag-of-task jobs with security requirements and dual-criteria partial computations in a fog – cloud system. Simul. Model. Pract. Theory **140**, 103082 (2025). https://doi.org/10.1016/j.simpat.2025.103082
10. Li, L., Zhou, C., Cong, P., Shen, Y., Zhou, J., Wei, T.: Makespan and security-aware workflow scheduling for cloud service cost minimization. IEEE Trans. Cloud Comput. **12**(2), 609–624 (2024). https://doi.org/10.1109/tcc.2024.3382351
11. Kumer, S.V.A., Prabakaran, N., Mohan, E., Natarajan, B., Sambasivam, G., Tyagi, V.B.: Enhancing cloud task scheduling with a robust security approach and optimized hybrid poa. IEEE Access **11**, 122426–122445 (2023). https://doi.org/10.1109/access.2023.3329052
12. Alruwais, N., et al.: Farmland fertility algorithm based resource scheduling for makespan optimization in cloud computing environment. Ain Shams Eng. J. **15**(6), 102738 (2024). https://doi.org/10.1016/j.asej.2024.102738

# Classification Based on Dynamic Skyline Objects

Yoshiaki Okubo(✉)

Hakodate Campus, Hokkaido University of Education,
1–2 Hachiman-cho, Hakodate 040-8567, Japan
okubo.yoshiaki@h.hokkyodai.ac.jp

**Abstract.** We propose a novel parameter-free classification method inspired by the fundamental idea of the $k$-nearest neighbors ($k$-NN) algorithm. Our method defines a new notion of neighborhood based on the *Dynamic Skyline* with respect to a query object and predicts its label via majority voting. In order to improve classification quality, we also explore weighted voting schemes using distance-based and rank-based weights, both of which require no parameter tuning. Experimental results on benchmark and synthetic datasets demonstrate that the proposed method achieves classification performance comparable to or even better than $k$-NN. These observations suggest the potential of Dynamic Skyline-based classification as a practical and robust alternative to $k$-NN without requiring any user-defined parameter.

**Keywords:** Classification · Dynamic Skyline · $k$-Nearest Neighbor · Majority Voting

## 1 Introduction

In this paper, we discuss a possible improvement of the classical method for classification problems, known as the $k$-Nearest Neighbor ($k$-NN) method [1,2].

Classification is the task of predicting an appropriate class label for a query object whose class is unknown, based on a set of objects with known class labels. In recent years, classification has been discussed in the context of machine learning and it is regarded as one of the typical tasks in supervised learning. We can formalize many tasks as classification problems. Some examples include "handwritten character recognition" [3], "spam email filtering (identification)" [4], and "music genre classification" [5].

Among various classification methods, the $k$-Nearest Neighbor method has been studied since early times [1,2]. It is a simple method based on the "majority rule". Concretely speaking, given a query object $q$, the method finds the $k$ objects closest to $q$ as the $k$ nearest neighbors, and then predicts the class of $q$ as that of the majority of those neighbors. Although the basic idea is very simple, its usefulness and validity have been empirically confirmed. In fact, when we do not have sufficient knowledge about the objects, or cannot make any adequate


R. Stahlbock et al. (Eds.): CSCE 2025, CCIS 2938, pp. 233–243, 2027.
https://doi.org/10.1007/978-3-032-22196-4_17

assumptions, we are often forced to rely on such simple methods. Therefore, $k$-NN remains a useful method even today, and many studies have aimed at improving it (e.g., [6–8]).

Due to its simplicity, however, the method has a critical weakness, that is, the choice of the unique parameter, $k$, greatly affects the prediction results. It is often difficult to know an appropriate value for $k$ in advance. Moreover, it would be natural to consider that the optimal $k$ could differ from query to query.

In practice, $k$ is usually set to a relatively small value[1], and sometimes prediction is made based solely on the single nearest neighbor ($k = 1$). However, it is obvious that in such cases, prediction results can be significantly affected by exceptional ones (e.g., outliers or noise). On the other hand, increasing $k$ improves robustness against noise but introduces a risk that even distant objects are included among the neighbors, possibly degrading prediction performance.

In this paper, we present a classification method that inherits the basic idea of the $k$-NN method but avoids the troublesome requirement for parameter tuning.

## 2 Preliminaries

Let $\mathcal{C} = \{C_1, \ldots, C_n\}$ be a set of class labels. Given a query object $q$ whose class label is unknown, the problem of assigning an adequate class in $\mathcal{C}$ to $q$ is called an *n-class classification problem*. Especially, in case of $n > 2$, it is often referred to as a multi-class classification problem.

In this paper, we are concerned with classification problems where objects are represented as real-valued vectors in $d$-dimensional space. That is, each object is assumed to be a point in the $d$-dimensional space $\mathbb{R}^d$.

We define a distance function $dist : \mathbb{R}^d \times \mathbb{R}^d \mapsto \mathbb{R}$ between any two objects in $\mathbb{R}^d$. The distance function $dist$ is assumed to satisfy the following conditions:

1. For any $x \in \mathbb{R}^d$, $dist(x, x) = 0$,
2. For any $x, y \in \mathbb{R}^d$, $dist(x, y) \geq 0$,
3. For any $x, y \in \mathbb{R}^d$, $dist(x, y) = dist(y, x)$.

## 3 Classification Based on $k$-Nearest Neighbors

### 3.1 $k$-Nearest Neighbors

Let $\mathcal{D} \subseteq \mathbb{R}^d$ be a set of objects. Consider an object $x \in \mathbb{R}^d$ such that $x \notin \mathcal{D}$. Given a parameter $k \in \mathbb{N}^+$ (the set of positive natural numbers), the $k$-nearest neighbors of $x$ are defined as the $k$ objects in $\mathcal{D}$ that are closest to $x$ in terms of distance. We often refer to the set of these nearest neighbors as $kNN^x_{\mathcal{D}}$.

[1] For example, in the $k$-NN implementation of the machine learning library "scikit-learn" [9], the default value is set to 5.

### 3.2 Class Prediction Based on $k$-Nearest Neighbors

For a set of class labels $\mathcal{C} = \{C_1, \ldots, C_n\}$, we assume that each object $x \in \mathcal{D}$ is associated with one of the class labels in $\mathcal{C}$, where the class label assigned to $x$ is denoted by $label(x)$. For an object $x \in \mathcal{D}$, if $label(x) = C_i$, we call $x$ a $C_i$-object. Moreover, for each class label $C_i \in \mathcal{C}$, we define $\mathcal{D}(C_i)$ as the set of all $C_i$-objects in $\mathcal{D}$, that is,

$$\mathcal{D}(C_i) = \{x \in \mathcal{D} | label(x) = C_i\}.$$

Given an object $q \in \mathbb{R}^d$ whose class label is unknown, we consider a classification problem of predicting an adequate class label of $q$, where $q$ is called a query object or simply a query. The $k$-Nearest Neighbor method ($k$-NN for short) [1,2] is a classical approach to the problem. It predicts the class label of the query $q$ based on the labels of its $k$-nearest neighbors in $\mathcal{D}$. More concretely speaking, the predicted label of $q$ is determined by a majority vote among the labels of the $k$-nearest neighbors and is formally given by

$$\arg\max_{C_i \in \mathcal{C}} \{|kNN^q_{\mathcal{D}}(C_i)|\}.$$

In case of $k = 1$, this method is referred to as *the Nearest Neighbor method.*

### 3.3 Issues of the $k$-Nearest Neighbor Method

It is well known that the prediction results of the $k$-NN method are highly sensitive to the choice of the parameter $k$. For example, consider the problem of predicting the class label (color) of a query object $q$ in Fig. 1. If $k = 1$, the prediction is gray; if $k = 3$, it is black; and if $k = 5$, it is gray again. Thus, the prediction results are strongly influenced by the choice of $k$.

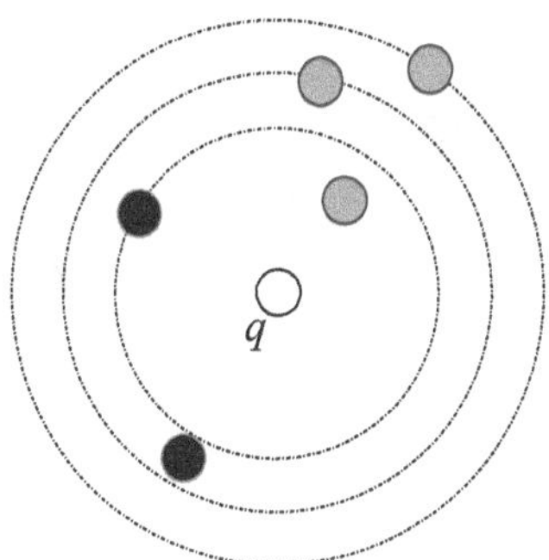


**Fig. 1.** Prediction by $k$-nearest neighbors.

In practice, $k$ is often set to a relatively small value. However, if an exceptional object is included in the $k$-nearest neighbors, the prediction can easily be incorrect. On the other hand, increasing $k$ can reduce the influence of noise, but at the same time, it increases the risk of including distant objects. As a result, the validity of the majority vote would be compromised.

Although the $k$-NN method is a classical approach to classification, with a quite clear and simple idea, its practical usefulness has been widely confirmed empirically and it has been continuously evolving. Nevertheless, there is still no reliable guideline for selecting an appropriate value of $k$. Then, users are forced to determine it through trial and error. Furthermore, it is rather natural to assume that the appropriate value of $k$ should differ depending on each query. It would be unreasonable to expect a single fixed value of $k$ to be optimal for the classification problem under consideration.

In the next section, we present a classification method based on a different type of neighbors that does not require any parameter tuning.

## 4 Classification Based on Skyline Neighbors

In this section, we discuss a new neighbor-based classification method that inherits the basic idea of the $k$-nearest neighbor method while eliminating the need for its only parameter, $k$.

### 4.1 Issue of Distance-Based Neighbors

Let $q$ be a query object. In the $k$-NN method, whether an object $x$ is considered a neighbor of $q$ depends solely on the distance $dist(x, q)$. If $dist(x, q)$ is sufficiently small, $x$ is regarded as a neighbor of $q$. This approach, however, completely ignores the local structure around $q$.

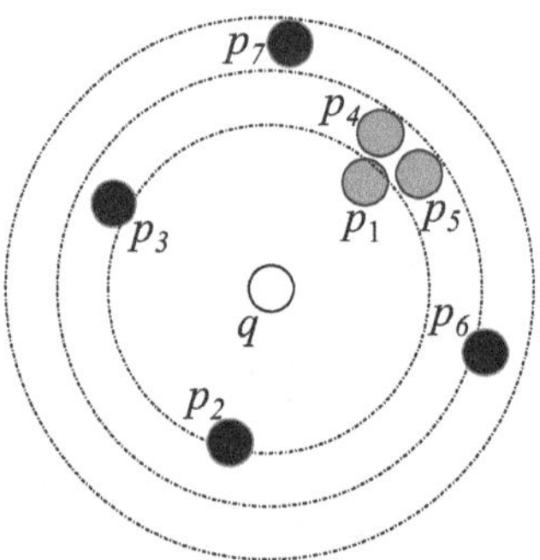


**Fig. 2.** Local structure around query object.

Figure 2 shows a spatial relationship between $q$ and its neighboring objects. If we sort the neighboring objects by distance from $q$, we get $p_1$, $p_2$, $p_3$, $p_4$, $p_5$, $p_6$, and $p_7$. In this case, using $k$-NN to predict the label (color) of $q$ results in gray for $k = 1$, black for $k = 3$ and again gray for $k = 5$, thus, the predictions would be unstable. Here, we focus on $P_4$ and $p_5$. They are very close to $p_1$ and indeed closer to $q$ than $p_6$ and $p_7$ in terms of distance. However, in terms of both position and label, $P_4$ and $p_5$ provide little new information compared to $p_1$. Since they have almost the same information, $P_4$ and $p_5$ seem to be redundant in the majority vote when $k = 5$. The authors argue that a more appropriate prediction would be obtained by including objects such as $p_6$ and $p_7$ which are similarly distant from $q$ but spatially more distinct. Therefore, in order to identify the neighbors of a query, it would be necessary to consider not only distances but also the spatial distribution of objects to eliminate redundancy.

In this paper, we propose to use the concept of *Skyline* [10], originally defined for multidimensional data, to extract such non-redundant neighbors.

### 4.2 Skyline [10]

Let $\mathcal{D} \subseteq \mathbb{R}^d$ be a set of objects in $d$-dimensional space. Given a pair of objects $x, y \in \mathcal{D}$, we say $x$ *dominates* $y$, denoted by $x \prec y$, if the following two conditions hold:

- $x$ is as good as or better than $y$ in all dimensions, and
- $x$ is properly better than $y$ in at least one dimension.

Here, the term "better" denotes a smaller value in a given dimension.

The *Skyline* of $\mathcal{D}$, denoted by $Skyline(\mathcal{D})$, is the set of objects in $\mathcal{D}$ not dominated by any other object. That is, it is formally defined as

$$Skyline(\mathcal{D}) = \{x \in \mathcal{D} |\ \nexists y \in \mathcal{D} \text{ such that } y \prec x\}.$$

We call the elements of $Skyline(\mathcal{D})$ the *Skyline objects.*

Figure 3 illustrates an example of Skyline objects in a 2-dimensional space (plane). In the figure, the objects labeled $x$, $y$, $z$, and $u$ constitute the skyline, while the other objects (dashed circles) are dominated by one of these skyline objects.

Intuitively speaking, Skyline objects are the first objects to appear when scanning from the origin in any direction. From a geometric viewpoint, the Skyline consists of objects not dominated in their directions relative to the origin. In other words, objects in similar directions are typically dominated by some Skyline object. Thus, Skyline objects can be regarded as non-redundant representatives close to the origin.

In this paper, we apply this idea to define a non-redundant neighborhood for each query object and use it for classification.

### 4.3 Dynamic Skyline [11]

As is just discussed above, the concept of Skyline has been defined statically with respect to the origin [10]. Subsequently, it has been extended to define Skylines *dynamically* centered around arbitrary reference points (queries) [11,12]. Although there are several variants of such dynamic Skylines, each of these can

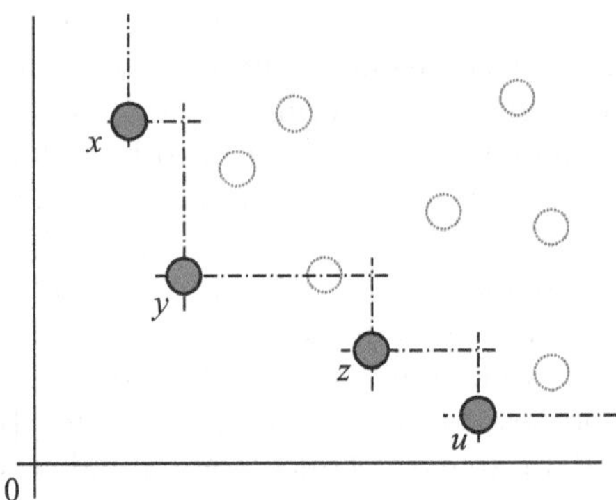


**Fig. 3.** Skyline in 2-dimensional space.

be understood as a straightforward extension of the original Skyline by redefining a given query $q$ as the new origin. In this paper, we particularly adopt the notion of *Dynamic Skyline* [11] as our neighborhoods of queries.

Let $\mathcal{D} \subseteq \mathbb{R}^d$ be a set of objects and $q = (q^1, \ldots, q^d) \in \mathbb{R}^d$ a query object. The *Dynamic Skyline* is based on dynamic dominance among objects relative to $q$.

For a pair of objects $x, y \in \mathcal{D}$, we say $x$ *dynamically-dominates* $y$ *with respect to* $q$, denoted by $x \prec_D^q y$, if the following two conditions holds:

- For all $i \in \{1, ..., d\}$, $|x^i - q^i| \leq |y^i - q^i|$, and
- For some $j \in \{1, ..., d\}$, $|x^j - q^j| < |y^j - q^j|$.

The Dynamic Skyline of $\mathcal{D}$ for $q$, denoted by $DSkyline(q, \mathcal{D})$, is the set of objects in $\mathcal{D}$ not dynamically-dominated by any other object. That is, it is formally defined as

$$DSkyline(q, \mathcal{D}) = \{x \in \mathcal{D} | \; \nexists y \in \mathcal{D} \text{ such that } y \prec_D^q x\}.$$

It is noted here that the dynamic dominance relation $\prec_D^q$, which defines the Dynamic Skyline, can hold among objects in different orthants. All objects in $\mathcal{R}$ are mapped into the orthant of $\mathbb{R}^d$ in which all coordinates are non-negative, with the query point $q$ regarded as the origin. The Dynamic Skyline is then defined based on the original dominance relation $\prec$ within the mapped space. In order to identify $DSkyline(q, \mathcal{D})$, therefore, it suffices to compute the (original) Skyline in the mapped space with $q$ as the origin.

Figure 4 illustrates an example of a Dynamic Skyline in a 2-dimensional space (plane). In the figure, the black circle represents the query point $q$ and the gray circles the Dynamic Skyline objects. For instance, the object $z$ in the third quadrant is mapped to $z'$ in the first quadrant. In the first quadrant where all objects are mapped into, the shaded circles $x'$, $z'$ and $u'$ form the (original) Skyline. Then, their corresponding objects $x$, $z$ and $u$ constitute the Dynamic Skyline.

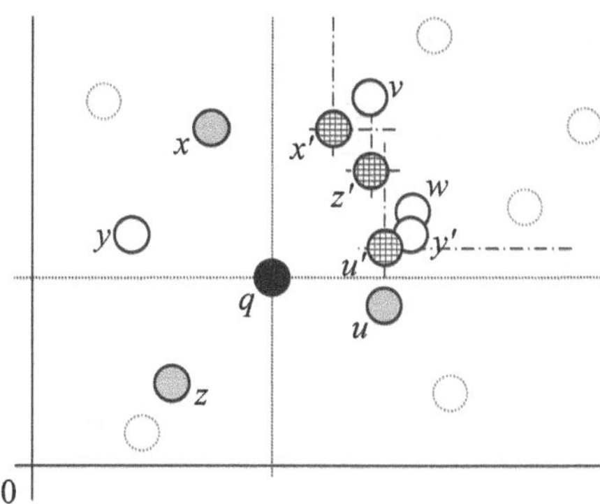


**Fig. 4.** Dynamic Skyline in 2-dimensional space.

### 4.4 Classification Based on Dynamic Skyline Objects

By treating the dynamic Skyline of a given query $q$ as its neighbors, we can predict the class label of $q$ by majority vote, as in the $k$-NN method. It should be emphasized here that no parameter tuning is required in defining Dynamic Skyline-based neighbors. This is a significant advantage over the $k$-NN method in which the tuning of the parameter $k$ critically affects its classification performance.

In general, the number of Dynamic Skyline objects varies depending on a given query $q$. Although the class label of $q$ can be predicted by majority vote among these objects, it seems reasonable to give more weight to the labels of objects that are closer to $q$.

For the set of Dynamic Skyline objects for $q$, $DSkyline(q, \mathcal{D})$, a straightforward approach would be to apply $k$-NN-style majority voting within $DSkyline(q, \mathcal{D})$. However, it conflicts with our goal of developing a parameter-free classification method. We therefore propose to perform majority voting with distance-based weighting. Particularly, we predict the class label of a query based on two types of weighted majority voting described below.

**Majority Voting with Distance-Based Weighting:** Given a query $q$, the distance-based weight of an object $x \in DSkyline(q, \mathcal{D})$, denoted by $weight_{dist}(x)$, is formally defined as

$$weight_{dist}(x) = \frac{1}{dist(q, x)}.$$

Let us denote the set of Dynamic Skyline objects with the class label $C_i$ by $\mathcal{DS}(C_i)$, that is,

$$\mathcal{DS}(C_i) = \{x \in DSkyline(q, \mathcal{D}) \mid label(x) = C_i\}.$$

Then, the class label of $q$ is predicted as

$$\arg\max_{C_i \in \mathcal{C}} \{ \sum_{x \in \mathcal{DS}(C_i)} weight_{dist}(x) \}.$$

**Majority Voting with Rank-Based Weighting:** Given a query $q$, we first sort the set of Dynamic Skyline objects, $DSkyline(q, \mathcal{D})$, in ascending order of $dist(\cdot, q)$, and assign a rank to each object accordingly. The rank of an object $x$ is denoted by $rank(x)$. For an object $x \in DSkyline(q, \mathcal{D})$, the rank-based weight of $x$, $weight_{rank}(x)$, is formally defined as

$$weight_{rank}(x) = \frac{1}{rank(x)}.$$

Then, the class label of $q$ is predicted as

$$\arg\max_{C_i \in \mathcal{C}} \{ \sum_{x \in \mathcal{DS}(C_i)} weight_{rank}(x) \}.$$

It should be noted that both types of majority voting can be performed without requiring any parameter. In other words, our Dynamic Skyline-based classification methods are parameter-free.

## 5 Preliminary Experimental Results

In this section, we conduct preliminary experiments to assess the potential of our classification methods based on Dynamic Skyline objects. Concretely speaking, we compare the classification performance of our methods with that of the $k$-NN method using several benchmark and synthetic datasets.

### 5.1 Experimental Settings

In our experiments, we use five datasets in total, two widely used benchmark datasets in machine learning and three small-scale synthetic datasets designed for controlled analysis. The benchmark datasets are "Iris plants" and "Wine recognition" available in the Python machine learning library, "scikit-learn" [9]. The synthetic datasets were also generated by the scikit-learn library. Characteristics of the datasets are presented in Table 1.

In order to assess the practical effectiveness of our classification methods based on Dynamic Skyline (DS) objects, we conduct a series of experiments comparing them against the standard $k$-NN method with $k = 3$, 5 and 7. Three variants of our DS-based method are as follows:

- DS (Unweighted): Classification by simple majority voting over all Dynamic Skyline objects.

**Table 1.** Characteristics of Datasets

| Dataset Name | Number of objects | Number of features | Number of classes | Description |
|---|---|---|---|---|
| Iris plants | 150 | 4 | 3 | – |
| Wine recognition | 178 | 13 | 3 | – |
| Standard | 200 | 10 | 3 | linearly separable classes |
| Noisy | 200 | 10 | 3 | noisy overlapping classes |
| Moons | 200 | 10 | 2 | non-linearly separable classes (moon-shaped) |

- DS (Distance-based): Classification by majority voting with distance-based weighting.
- DS (Rank-based): Classification by majority voting with rank-based weighting.

We evaluate all methods on the five datasets, Iris, Wine, Standard, Noisy and Moons. The performance is assessed primarily in terms of classification accuracy.

## 5.2 Classification Accuracy

Table 2 shows classification accuracy averaged over 5-fold cross validation.

**Table 2.** Classification Accuracy

| Method | Classification Accuracy | | | | |
|---|---|---|---|---|---|
| | Iris | Wine | Standard | Noisy | Moons |
| 3-NN | 0.96 | 0.71 | 0.78 | 0.49 | 0.95 |
| 5-NN | 0.97 | 0.67 | 0.79 | 0.54 | 0.97 |
| 7-NN | 0.97 | 0.68 | 0.77 | 0.53 | 0.97 |
| DS (Unweighted) | 0.95 | 0.66 | 0.38 | 0.33 | 0.92 |
| DS (Distance-based voting) | 0.96 | 0.77 | 0.64 | 0.41 | 0.95 |
| DS (Rank-based voting) | 0.97 | 0.74 | 0.81 | 0.52 | 0.96 |

The results show that our DS-based methods achieved classification accuracies comparable to those of $k$-NN across most datasets. Particularly, the following points would be remarkable:

- On the datasets of Iris and Moons, the rank-based DS method achieved accuracies of 96% or higher which are extremely competitive to the best-performing $k$-NN methods.
- On the Standard dataset, the rank-based DS method clearly outperformed the $k$-NN methods.

- On the Wine dataset, both our DS methods with weighted voting performed significantly better than the $k$-NN methods, and the unweighted DS method was also quite competitive with them.

Despite being parameter-free, the proposed DS-based methods are considered to exhibit generally good classification performance. The authors believe that our DS-based approach provides a solid foundation for further improvements.

## 6 Concluding Remarks

In this paper, we have proposed a novel parameter-free classification method inspired by the fundamental idea of the $k$-NN method. Specifically, we introduced a new notion of neighborhood based on the concept of the Dynamic Skyline with respect to a given query. The label of the query is predicted by majority voting via the Dynamic Skyline objects.

A key feature of the proposed method is that the Dynamic Skyline objects can be computed solely from the query without requiring any user-defined parameter. This ensures that our classification method is truly parameter-free.

In order to enhance prediction quality, we also proposed weighted majority voting schemes over the skyline objects. We confirmed the effectiveness of these strategies through preliminary experiments on five benchmark and synthetic datasets. Our experimental results demonstrated that, despite being parameter-free, the proposed method achieves classification performance comparable to or even better than that of $k$-NN. These observations suggest strong potential for further improvement and broader applicability of Dynamic Skyline-based classification.

To extend our approach to large-scale datasets, it is essential to develop efficient algorithms for identifying Dynamic Skyline objects. Designing such scalable skyline computation methods would be an important direction for future work.

## References

1. Cover, T.M., Hart, P.E.: Nearest neighbor pattern classification. IEEE Trans. Inf. Theory **13**(1), 21–27 (1967)
2. Fix, E., Hodges, J.L., Jr.: Discriminatory analysis - nonparametric discrimination: Consistency properties. Int. Stat. Rev./Revue Internationale de Statistique **57**(3), 238–247 (1989)
3. Smith, S.J., Bourgoin, M.O., Sims, K., Voorhees, H.L.: Handwritten character classification using nearest neighbor in large databases. IEEE Trans. Pattern Anal. Mach. Intell. **16**(9), 915–919 (1994)
4. Jiang, S., Pang, G., Wu, M., Kuang, L.: An improved $k$-nearest-neighbor algorithm for text categorization. Expert Syst. Appl. **39**(1), 1503–1509 (2012)
5. Pampalk, E., Flexer, A., Widmer, G.: Improvements of audio-based music similarity and genre classification. In: Proceedings of the 6th International Conference on Music Information Retrieval - ISMIR'05, pp. 628–633 (2005)

6. Samanthula, B.K., Elmehdwi, Y., Jiang, W.: $k$-nearest neighbor classification over semantically secure encrypted relational data. IEEE Trans. Knowl. Data Eng. **27**(5), 1261–1273 (2015)
7. Zhou, Z., Wen, C., Yang, C.: Fault detection using random projections and $k$-nearest neighbor rule for semiconductor manufacturing processes. IEEE Trans. Semicond. Manuf. **28**(1), 70–79 (2015)
8. Nowak, B.A., Nowicki, R.K., Woźniak, M., Napoli, C.: Multi-class nearest neighbour classifier for incomplete data handling. In: Rutkowski, L., Korytkowski, M., Scherer, R., Tadeusiewicz, R., Zadeh, L., Zurada, J.M. (eds.) Artificial Intelligence and Soft Computing. Lecture Notes in Computer Science, vol. 9119, pp. 469–480. Springer, Cham (2015)
9. Pedregosa, F., et al.: Machine learning in python: Scikit-learn: Mach. Learn. Python **12**, 2825–2830 (2011)
10. Börzsönyi, S., Kossmann, D., Stocker, K.: The skyline operator. In: Proceedings of the 17th International Conference on Data Engineering - ICDE'01, pp. 421 – 430. IEEE (2001)
11. Han, X., Wang, B., Lai, G.: Dynamic skyline computation on massive data. Knowl. Inform. Syst. **59**, 571–599 (2019)
12. Dellis, E., Seeger, B.: Efficient computation of reverse skyline queries. In: Proceedings of the 33rd International Conference on Very Large Data Bases - VLDB'07, pp. 291–302. ACM (2007)

# How Students Tackle Coding Tasks in Formative Assessment

Chen Li[1(✉)], Mo Zhang[1], Amy J. Ko[2], Min Li[2], Ben Zhou[2], and Hongwen Guo[1]

[1] Educational Testing Service, Princeton, NJ 08542, USA
[2] University of Washington, Seattle, WA 98195, USA

**Abstract.** Computer science has become a fundamental skill for success in the 21st century, and open-ended coding tasks are widely used to assess students' programming abilities. These tasks often involve solving problems using various programming concepts, such as loops, branching, and data manipulation. However, despite their prevalence, limited psychometric research exists on how to accurately measure item difficulty–especially in assessments that allow unlimited attempts. This study investigates item difficulty in programming assessments by analyzing both product data and process data. Using a dataset collected from college students completing 21 programming tasks, we applied classical test theory, cognitive diagnostic modeling, and cluster analysis to classify item difficulty levels. We found that expert-based difficulty classifications could be refined using data-driven methods, revealing clearer distinctions among item difficulty levels. Additionally, we examined students' coding behaviors through keystroke feature and keystroke burst analysis. Results showed that harder items were associated with longer, more continuous typing bursts and fewer pauses, indicating deeper cognitive engagement. In contrast, easier items showed more fragmented typing and frequent pauses, suggesting lower cognitive demand or trial-and-error strategies.

**Keywords:** coding assessment · item difficulty level · process data · keystrokes analysis · cognitive diagnostic model

## 1 Introduction

Computer programming has become an essential skill in the 21st century. Programming abilities are often evaluated through open-ended tasks that require students to write code to solve specific problems [1]. The accuracy of the code can be assessed using test cases. These coding tasks encompass various programming concepts, such as integer manipulation, looping, and function recursion, each with a different level of difficulty. Despite the widespread use of these assessments, thorough psychometric analysis of coding tasks when unlimited attempts are permitted is lacking, even though this is a common practice for accurately measuring item difficulty. Accurately measuring the difficulty of programming


R. Stahlbock et al. (Eds.): CSCE 2025, CCIS 2938, pp. 244–253, 2027.
https://doi.org/10.1007/978-3-032-22196-4_18

test items is crucial [2,3]. It helps differentiate between candidates with varying levels of proficiency and assists educators and learners in identifying areas that need improvement. Precise item difficulty measurement also ensures that all candidates are evaluated under consistent conditions, making the test fairer and more balanced.

We utilized an assessment platform specifically designed to support data collection on programming behaviors and outcomes. The interface of this platform is shown in Fig. 1: the item was displayed on top, test takers input and edit their code in the left-side window. After submitting their code, all test cases are run and the results are shown to the test takers. This platform records all test takers' interactions during coding tasks, including keystrokes, mouse movements, and the final code submissions. During the test, students can make unlimited attempts and debug and revise their code based on test case results. In addition to evaluating the correctness of the final submitted programs, the analysis in this study considers process data such as time spent on the task and the number of attempts. By analyzing both product and process data, we aim to uncover potential associations between different programming concepts and item difficulty levels.

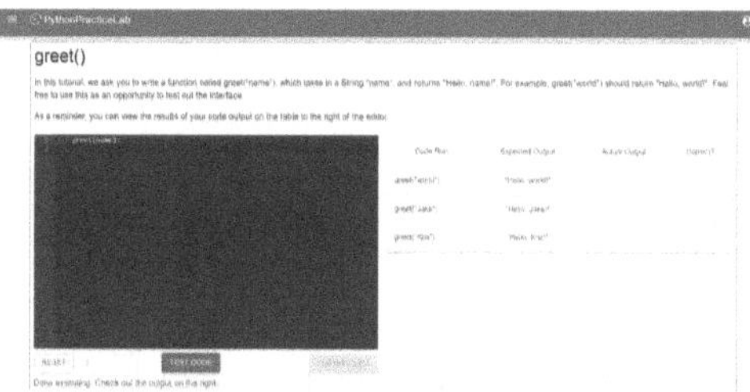


**Fig. 1.** Interface of the Assessment Platform.

### 1.1 Research Questions

Based on the aforementioned context, the following research questions were explored:

- RQ1. How to best measure coding item difficulty?
- RQ2. How do items with varying difficulty levels differ on coding processing features?

## 2 Methods

### 2.1 Participants and Instrument

Our analysis is based on the test records of approximately 180 students. The test included 21 unique programming items, which were strategically organized into a two-stage adaptive test design, as described in [4] and [5]. The common form in Stage 1 consisted of nine tasks. Stage 2 had two forms: one easy and one hard, each containing six tasks. Based on their performance in Stage 1, students were directed to either the hard or easy form in Stage 2. Using this dataset, we explored various approaches to assess coding difficulty by integrating both timing and process-related data. In our item design, seven specific programming skills were embedded across the 21 items, as shown in Fig. 1. They were integer manipulation, string manipulation, list manipulation, operators, branching, loops, and nested branching. Each item measures a combination of a subset of the seven skills. The item difficulty was initially determined based on expert judgment (Fig. 2).

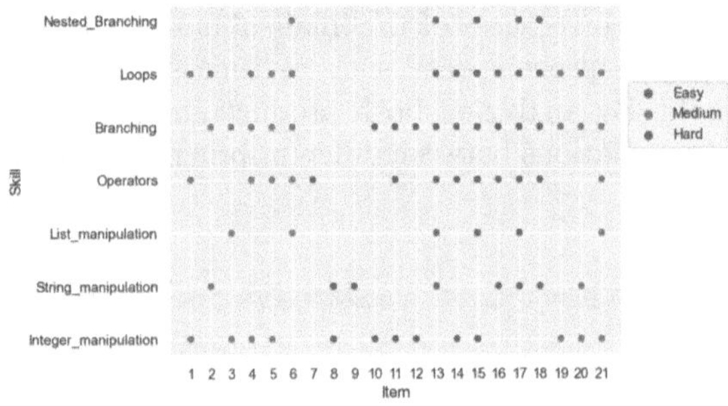


**Fig. 2.** Programming Skills in Item Design.

Below we provide two examples for the easy and hard items.

- Example item - easy: Write a function called `is_profitable` that takes in two integers as parameters: revenue and expenses. Return True if your profit, defined as the difference between revenue and expenses, is greater than 0. Otherwise, return False.
- Example item - hard: Write a function `check_passcode`() that determines if the parameter pin, which is a 4-digit integer, is a valid passcode. pin is valid if the sum of the first 3 digits modulus 7 is equal to the last digit. If pin is valid, the function should return True. If the string is not valid, it should return False.

In the first example, the easy item tests only the test-takers' "operator" skill; the response or code is expected to be short and not time-consuming. However, in the second example, to pass the hard item successfully, the test takers will need at least four skills—"Integer manipulation", "Operators", "Branching" and "Loops"—and it is expected that a student will take more time and possibly make more attempts to complete the coding task.

The data was collected from students across various academic majors. In addition to the final response data, processing data was also collected by logging all keystrokes, program executions, window focus events, copy and paste events, etc., during the coding process.

### 2.2 Measuring Item Difficulty

In educational and psychological assessments, item difficulty can be evaluated using various ways. We explored several methods to classify items into different difficulty levels, and later we examined the patterns on process features among items with varying difficulty levels.

- Passing Rate: is also known as $p+$ in the framework of Classical Test Theory (CTT), calculated as the proportion of participants who eventually passed all test cases of a particular item or not (0, 1). A low $p+$ value (e.g., 0.2) indicates a hard item, and a high $p+$ value (e.g., 0.9) indicates an easy item.
- Attempt Count: How many attempts were taken before passing all test cases. In this assessment, students can make as many attempts as they wish. Harder items are likely to require more attempts to pass than easier ones.
- Cognitive Diagnostic Model (CDM) Slipping and Guessing Parameters. As suggested in [6], Based on the small sample scenario, the generalized DINA (the deterministic inputs, noisy "and" gate) model, which is the most popular CDM model, was used for our analysis. As described in [7], in the DINA model with independent attributes, the latent variable $\eta_{ij}(=1/0)$ represents whether respondent $j$ has mastered all attributes required for item $i$:

$$\eta_{ij} = \prod_{k=1}^{K} a_{jk}^{q_{ik}} \tag{1}$$

where $q_{ik}$ is the element of the Q matrix which is an I×K matrix. $q_{ik}$=1 if item $i$ requires attribute $k$ and 0 if not. The model allows for slipping and guessing [8]:

$$s_i = \Pr(Y_{ij} = 0|\eta_{ij} = 1) \tag{2}$$

$$g_i = \Pr(Y_{ij} = 1|\eta_{ij} = 0) \tag{3}$$

The slipping and guessing parameters here were used for item difficulty measuring.

Before the assessment results were available, the expert-defined item difficulty levels were used. Figure 3 presents scatter plots with regression lines illustrating the relationships between passing rate and three variables: attempt count, guessing parameter, and slipping parameter, all based on the predetermined expert-defined item difficulty levels.

From these plots, we observe that easy items tend to have a higher passing rate, fewer attempts, higher guessing parameters, and lower slipping parameters. However, the differences between medium and hard items are less distinct.

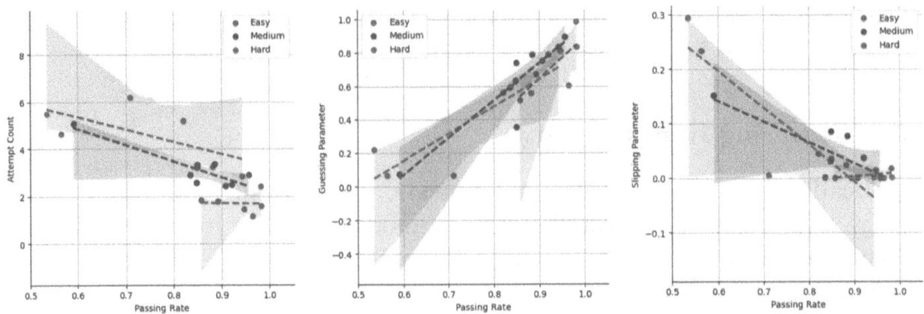


**Fig. 3.** Passing Rate Against Attempt Count, Guessing and Slipping Parameters by Predetermined Item Difficulty Level.

## 2.3 Classify Items by Cluster Analysis

Human classification of item difficulty levels was not always accurate. To better distinguish between items, we conducted a hierarchical clustering analysis on the parameters mentioned above, using the average linkage method and Euclidean distance as metrics. The results of this cluster analysis are presented in Fig. 4. The correlation between the human classification and the cluster-based classification was 0.82, indicating a strong alignment between the two approaches. Using the data-driven classification, we redrew the scatter plots from Fig. 3, and the updated results are shown in Fig. 5. As illustrated, the three item difficulty groups now exhibit much clearer distinctions.

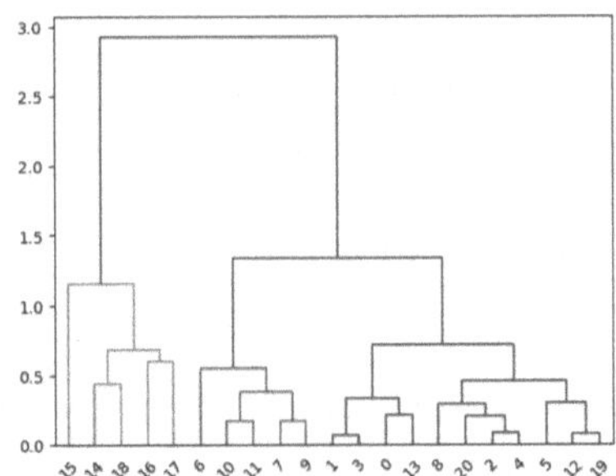

**Fig. 4.** Cut Tree by Hierarchical Clustering.

The cluster-based item classification also reveals the following:

- Easy-level items rarely assess the "loop" skill, whereas all items at or above the medium difficulty level include assessment of this skill.
- Hard-level items assess multiple skills simultaneously, including data manipulation (such as string or list manipulation), operators, loops, and branching (both simple and nested).

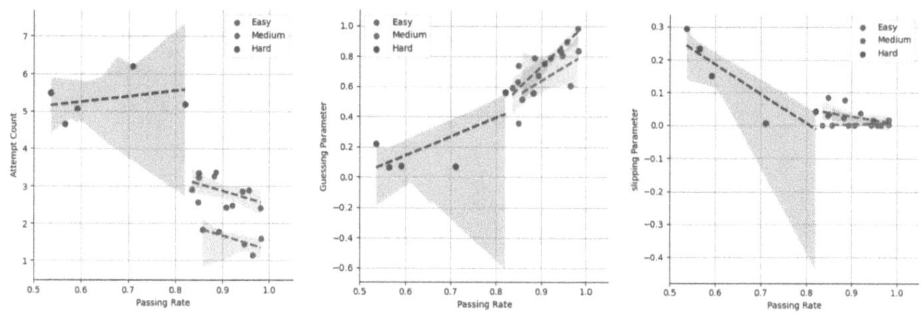


**Fig. 5.** Passing Rate Against Attempt Count, Guessing and Slipping Parameters by Cluster-based Difficulty Level.

# 3 Examination of Coding Process Patterns

## 3.1 Substantiating Item Difficulty Using Processing Data

In addition to the production results, keystroke logs were collected by the system to capture students' behaviors throughout the assessment. Various event types, including starting, ending, editing, running programs, copying, pasting, and other actions, were recorded along with their corresponding timestamps. All editing actions, such as "insert", "delete" and "reset" were logged with detailed keystroke data [9,10]. Furthermore, the outcome of each program run, including which test cases passed, was saved. Based on this information, we were able to extract additional features to better describe test-takers' coding behavior patterns [11], as well as their planning and reviewing strategies [12].

*Analysis on Keystroke Log Features.* Among the many keystroke-based features available [13–15], this paper explored a small subset of features related to code reviewing, debugging and overall coding effort to potentially help substantiate item difficulty:

- Duration (in seconds): One of the most important features derived from the process data, representing the total time a test taker spent on an item. [16]
- Intermediate Review Time (in seconds): The total amount of time each test taker spent before checking their code against test cases for an item across all attempts.
- Final Review Time (in seconds): The time spent reviewing code and checking answers before final code submission for an item.
- Total Programming Time (in seconds): The time spent composing and editing code for each item across all attempts, excluding intermediate and final review time.

Figure 6 presents four box plots comparing key behavioral metrics across three cluster-based item difficulty levels: Easy, Medium, and Hard. Each plot represents a distinct metric derived from the process data. The first plot shows "Duration", which measures the total time (in seconds) a test taker spent on an

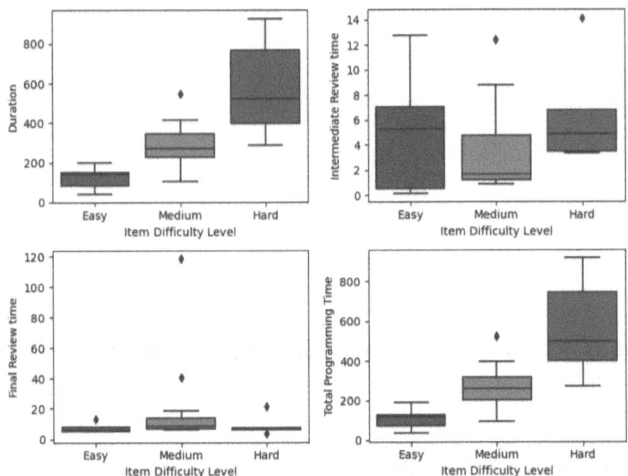


**Fig. 6.** Keystroke Process Features by Cluster-based Difficulty Level.

item. It indicates that harder items generally require more time, with greater variability. The second plot displays "Intermediate Review Time", reflecting the time spent on reviewing before executing codes. Harder items tend to have longer intermediate review times, suggesting more frequent or prolonged reviewing effort before code executions. The third plot is on "Final Review Time", which is about the time spent reviewing code or checking answers before final code submission increases with item difficulty, indicating more effort in verification. The final plot represents "Total Programming Time," capturing the time spent composing and editing code, and this measure also increases with item difficulty.

*Analysis on Keystroke Burst.* Keystroke burst analysis is a method used to examine patterns in typing behavior by identifying and analyzing "burst" of keystrokes, which are continuous sequences of typing activity separated by pauses. This technique is particularly useful in natural language writing research [17], which shares similarities with computer code writing. In the burst analysis:

- A "Pause Boundary" setting: a predefined threshold used to segment the typing stream into meaningful units of activity; a duration in time where it suggests a real, meaningful pause; can also think of it as a major interruption in a programming process.
- "Burst": A keystroke burst is a sequence of keystrokes entered without a pause longer than a predefined threshold; it represents how much one can hold in their head and type down in one go without major interruption.
- "Burst Length": $BurstLength = Burstcount \times Averageburstlength$.

Figure 7 presents various burst-related metrics plotted against different pause boundary thresholds from 0.5 to 10 s with an increment of 1 s, across the three cluster-based item difficulty levels, and we offer our speculations and interpretations of the results.

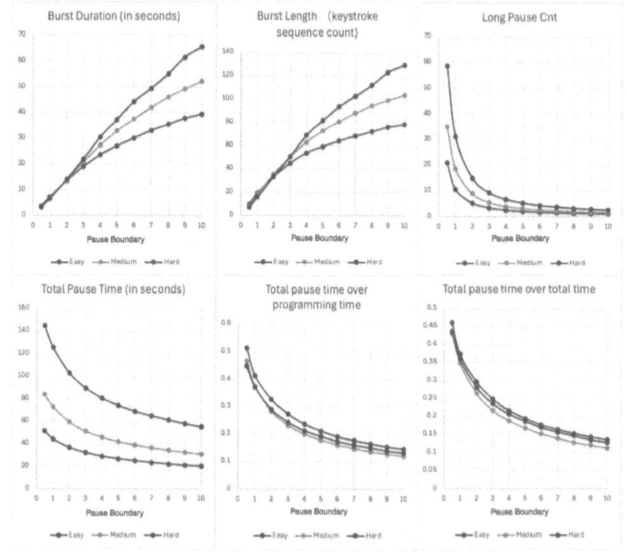


**Fig. 7.** Burst Metric Patterns by Cluster-based Difficulty Level.

1. For "Burst Duration" (in seconds), hard items exhibit the longest burst durations, followed by medium and then easy items. This result suggests that test-takers tend to type for longer stretches without pausing when working on harder items, possibly due to more sustained cognitive engagement or the need to write longer code segments.
2. "Burst Length" (keystroke sequence count) shows a similar pattern to "Burst Duration": hard items have the longest bursts in terms of keystroke count, indicating more continuous typing. In contrast, easy items have the shortest bursts, reflecting more fragmented coding processes.
3. For "Long Pause Count", easy items have the greatest number of long pauses, while hard items have the fewest. This may suggest that students pause more frequently on easier items. This result may be due to lower engagement or confidence, whereas harder items prompt more focused and sustained effort.
4. The plot on the "Total Pause Time" (in seconds) reveals that easy items are associated with greater total pause time, while hard items show less. This supports the idea that students spend more time hesitating or planning on easier items, while they are more engaged in the coding process on harder ones.
5. In terms of "Pause Time over Programming Time", this pause-to-programming time ratio is highest for easy items, indicating that a larger

proportion of time is spent pausing rather than actively coding. Hard items have the lowest ratio, reflecting more engagement in coding activities.
6. Finally, in the "Pause Time over Total Time" plot, easy items show the highest proportion of total time spent in pauses, while hard items have the lowest. This, again, reinforces the pattern of more continuous effort and greater engagement on harder tasks.

Overall, we found that hard items are associated with longer, more continuous bursts and fewer, shorter pauses, indicating deeper cognitive engagement and more sustained coding behavior. In contrast, easy items show more fragmented typing, frequent and longer pauses, and a higher proportion of inactive time, possibly reflecting lower cognitive demand or more trial-and-error strategies. Medium difficulty-level items generally fall between the other two categories.

### 3.2 Summary and Discussion

This study explored how students engage with open-ended coding tasks in formative assessments by analyzing both product and process data. In this study, we aimed to better understand item difficulty and student coding behavior through analysis of both coding process and product data.

The findings revealed that traditional expert-based classifications of item difficulty, while generally reliable, could be enhanced through data-driven methods. Cluster analysis using passing rates, attempt counts, and cognitive diagnostic model parameters (slipping and guessing) produced clearer distinctions among item difficulty levels. Notably, harder items were found to assess more complex combinations of programming skills, such as loops, branching, and data manipulation, while easier items typically focused on simpler constructs like operators.

Process data recorded via keystroke logs provided additional information on student coding behavior and helped substantiate item difficulties. Metrics such as total duration, programming time, and review time consistently increased with item difficulty, suggesting that harder items demand more sustained cognitive effort. Keystroke burst analysis further showed that students exhibited longer, more continuous bursts and fewer pauses on harder items, which seemed to indicate greater engagement and more fluent coding behavior. In contrast, easy items were associated with more fragmented typing and frequent pauses, possibly reflecting trial-and-error strategies or the lower cognitive demand required by these items. Finally, these results underscored the value of integrating process data into coding assessment design and analysis. Future work could expand on this study by incorporating more diverse data sets that include more coding task types, exploring real-time feedback mechanisms utilizing process data, and potentially applying these insights to adaptive learning systems.

**Acknowledgments.** This research is sponsored by the National Science Foundation Grant No. 2055550 and 2100296.

## References


1. Nicolajsen, S., Brabrand, C.: What is programming? Communications of the ACM. Advance online publication (2025). Available: https://doi.org/10.1145/3713068
2. Garcia, M.B.: Profiling the skill mastery of introductory programming students: a cognitive diagnostic modeling approach. Educ. Info. Technol. **30**, 6455–6481 (2025)
3. Xie, B., Loksa, D., Nelson, G.L., Davidson, M.J., Ko, A.: A theory of instruction for introductory programming skills. Comput. Sci. Educ. **26**, 205–253 (2019)
4. Li, C., Zhang, M., Guo, H., Liu, X., Ko, A., Li, C.: Leveraging psychometric modeling for enhancing programming skill assessments. In: Proceedings of 2025 ICAEI Conference, Suzhou, China (2025)
5. Guo, H., et al.: Measuring students' programming skill via online practice. In: Proceedings of 8th Educational Data Mining in Computer Science Education (CSEDM) Workshop, Atlanta, GA (2024). Available: https://api.semanticscholar.org/CorpusID:273241842
6. Sorrel, M.A., Escudero, S., Nájera, P., Kreitchmann, R.S., Vázquez-Lira, R.: Exploring approaches for estimating parameters in cognitive diagnosis models with small sample sizes. Psych. **5**(2), 336–349 (2023). Available: https://doi.org/10.3390/psych5020023
7. Lee, S.Y.: DINA model with independent attributes. Technical report, University of California at Berkeley (2016). Available: https://mc-stan.org/users/documentation/case-studies/dina_independent.html
8. Johnson, M.S., Sinharay, S.: Measures of agreement to assess attribute-level classification accuracy and consistency for cognitive diagnostic assessments. J. Educ. Meas. **55**(4), 635–664 (2018)
9. Conijn, R., Cook, C., van Zaanen, M., Van Waes, L.: Early prediction of writing quality using keystroke logging. Int. J. Artif. Intell. Educ. **32**, 835–866 (2022)
10. Zhang, M., Deane, P., Hoang, A., Guo, H., Li, C.: Applications and Modeling of Keystroke Logs in Writing Assessments. Issues and Practice, Advance online publication, Educational Measurement (2025)
11. Zhang, M., Sinharay, S.: Investigating the writing performance of educationally at-risk examinees using technology. Int. J. Test. **22**, 312–347 (2022)
12. Bennett, R.E., Zhang, M., Sinharay, S., Guo, H., Deane, P.: Are there distinctive profiles in essay-writing processes? Educ. Meas. Issues Pract. **41**, 55–69 (2021)
13. Guo, H., Deane, P.D., van Rijn, P.W., Zhang, M., Bennett, R.E.: Modeling basic writing processes from keystroke logs. J. Educ. Meas. **55**(2), 194–216 (2018). Available: https://doi.org/10.1111/jedm.12174
14. Zhang, M., Hao, J., Li, C., Deane, P.: Classification of writing patterns using keystroke logs. In: Quantitative Psychology Research: The 80th Annual Meeting of the Psychometric Society, Springer, pp. 319–337 (2016). Available: https://doi.org/10.1007/978-3-319-38759-8_19
15. Gong, T., Zhang, M., Li, C.: Association of keyboarding fluency and writing performance in online-delivered assessment. Assess. Writ. **51**, 100575 (2022). Available: https://doi.org/10.1016/j.asw.2021.100575
16. Zhang, M., Deane, P., Hoang, A., Guo, H., Li, C.: Applications and modeling of keystroke logs in writing assessments. Educ. Meas. Issues Pract. **44**(2), 5-19 (2025). Advance Online Publication. Available: https://doi.org/10.1111/emip.12500
17. Zhang, M., Hao, J., Deane, P., Li, C.: Defining personalized writing burst measures of translation using keystroke logs. U.S. Patent 11,195,431 (2021)

# A Computational Approach to Improving Fairness in K-Means Clustering

Guancheng Zhou[1], Haiping Xu[2], Hongkang Xu[3], Chenyu Li[4], and Donghui Yan[1(✉)]

[1] Mathematics and Data Science, University of Massachusetts Dartmouth, Dartmouth, MA 02747, USA
{gzhou,dyan}@umassd.edu

[2] Department of Computer and Information Science, University of Massachusetts Dartmouth, Dartmouth, MA 02747, USA
hxu@umassd.edu

[3] Charlton College of Business, University of Massachusetts Dartmouth, Dartmouth, MA 02747, USA
hxu5@umassd.edu

[4] Data Science, Columbia University, New York, NY 10027, USA
cl4183@columbia.edu

**Abstract.** The popular K-means clustering algorithm potentially suffers from a major weakness for further analysis or interpretation. Some cluster may have disproportionately more (or fewer) points from one subpopulation in terms of, e.g., gender or race. Such a fairness issue may cause bias and unexpected social consequences. This work attempts to improve the fairness of K-means clustering with a two-step optimization formulation–clustering first and then adjust cluster membership of selected data points. Two computationally efficient algorithms are proposed in identifying those data points expensive for fairness, with one focusing on nearest data points outside of a cluster and the other on highly 'mixed' data points. Experiments on benchmark datasets show substantial improvement on fairness with a minimal impact to clustering quality.

**Keywords:** Fairness · K-means clustering · Gini index

## 1 Introduction

Clustering is an important problem in data mining. It aims to split the data into groups such that data points in the same group are similar while points in different groups are different under a given similarity metric. Clustering has been successfully applied in many practical applications, such as data grouping in exploratory data analysis, search results categorization, market segmentation etc. Clustering results are often used for further analysis or interpretation. However, directly applying results obtained from usual clustering algorithms may suffer from fairness issues–some cluster may favor data points from one of the


R. Stahlbock et al. (Eds.): CSCE 2025, CCIS 2938, pp. 254–267, 2027.
https://doi.org/10.1007/978-3-032-22196-4_19

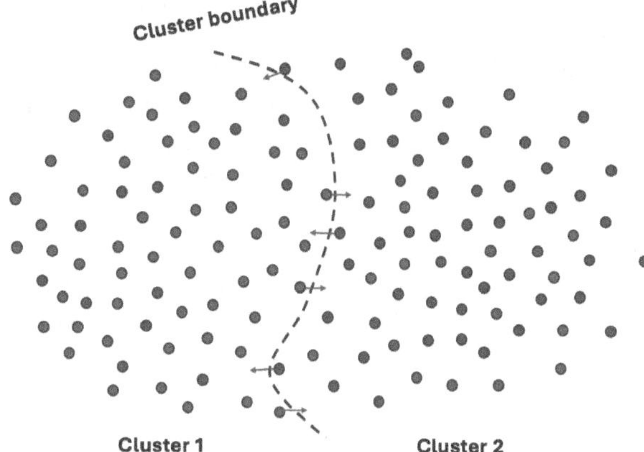


**Fig. 1.** Illustration of the fairness issue in clustering, Points of different color indicate different traits on a sensitive variable, e.g., gender where blue indicates male and red female. Cluster 1 is dominated by females while Cluster 2 by males. Points with an arrow indicate that we might switch its cluster membership assignment to make the clusters less dominated by one subpopulation. (Color figure online)

subpopulations, i.e., having disproportionally more points. One example of fairness issue is illustrated in Fig. 1 where, in each of the clusters, data points coming from one of the subpopulations dominate. Data points in Cluster 1 is dominated by females (marked by red), while Cluster 2 is dominated by males (marked by blue). When the subpopulations of interest are defined over some sensitive features (or variables), such as genders or races, it may cause undesirable bias [25] or social consequences [12,17,21].

This work aims to alleviate the fairness issue arising from clustering, and we focus on the popular K-means clustering algorithm [10] (note that our approach is applicable to general clustering with minimal changes to our proposed algorithm). One natural way is to treat clustering as an optimization problem, and fairness is viewed as a constraint. However, the constrained optimization problem might be computationally hard, even for K-means clustering [1], due to its nature as a mixed integer programming problem. While a number of methods have been proposed for fairness in clustering [2,7,8,15], they are often very complicated or computationally expensive or tightly associated with a particular clustering algorithm. We take a different approach, and work on adjusting the clustering results generated by a given clustering algorithm. We will identify a small set of 'promising' data points and switch their cluster membership assignments to improve the fairness. The rationale is that, the inclusion of fairness in the clustering formulation should only change a small part of results in clustering.

Our contributions are as follows. We conceive a novel approach to improve the fairness of K-means clustering by adjusting the cluster membership of a small selected set of 'promising' data points. Two different implementations are proposed, with one focusing on nearest data points outside of a cluster and the other on highly 'mixed' data points. Both implementations are conceptually simple, computationally efficient, and effective in improving the fairness of K-means clustering. Notably, both are also broad and adaptable in the sense that they are readily applicable to a broad class of clustering algorithms or different notions of fairness.

The remaining of this paper is organized as follows. In Sect. 2, we describe our algorithms to improve fairness in clustering. This is followed by a discussion of related work in Sect. 3. Experiments and results are presented in Sect. 4. Finally we conclude in Sect. 5.

## 2 The Method

The main idea of our approach is to identify a subset of 'promising' data points and switch their cluster membership assignments to improve the fairness. Of course, we require that the switching of cluster membership of those selected points will not impact much of the overall cluster quality.

Mathematically, the problem of fair clustering can be formulated as an optimization problem with some cluster quality measure as the objective function and an additional constraint on fairness. Let $\mathcal{S}$ be the set of all data points. Let functions $g(.)$ and $f(.)$ be the cluster quality measure and fairness measure of interest, respectively. Assuming there are $K$ clusters, the fair clustering problem is formulated as the following optimization problem ($\star$)

$$\arg\min_{\pi} g(S_1, ..., S_K), \tag{1}$$

$$f(S_1, ..., S_K) \leq T \tag{2}$$

where the clustering operator (i.e., function) $\pi : \mathcal{S} \mapsto \{1, ..., K\}$ maps each data point $x \in \mathcal{S}$ to its cluster index, and $S_i = \{x \in \mathcal{S} : \pi(x) = i\}$ is the set of data points in the i$^{\text{th}}$ cluster, $i = 1, ..., K$, and $T$ is a small tunable parameter. In the above formulation, (1) corresponds to the usual clustering problem, and (2) is a constraint on the fairness defined on clusters obtained by a given clustering $\pi$, i.e., a partition of $\mathcal{S}$ as $\mathcal{S} = \cup_{i=1}^{K} S_i$.

Directly solving the constrained optimization problem ($\star$) can be very costly, as it is a mixed integer programming problem. Our approach can be viewed as solving ($\star$) by two stages. In the first stage we solve the optimization problem without the fairness constraint (2), i.e., to solve the original clustering problem. This leads to a set of feasible solutions (by adjusting cluster membership of promising points) with each corresponding to a clustering result (i.e., cluster membership assignment) of the best or near-optimal cluster quality measure. The second stage starts from the set of feasible solutions, and focuses on the single objective of finding a solution with improved fairness. This is done by switching the cluster membership of data points along the cluster boundary.

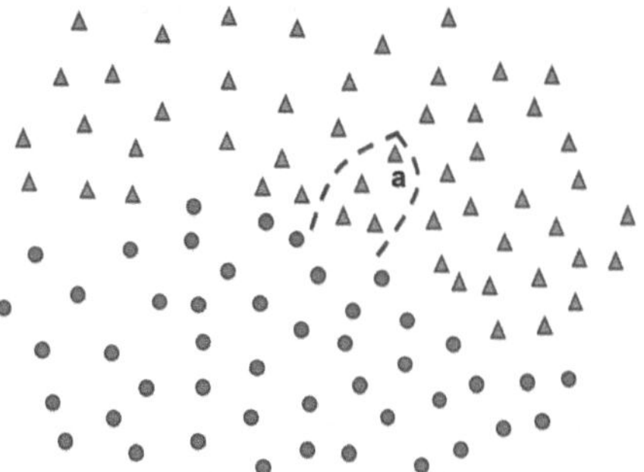


**Fig. 2.** Illustration of connectivity of data points in the same cluster. If one switches point a to the red cluster, then green points between it and the red cluster (i.e., points enclosed by the dashed curve) should also be switched. (Color figure online)

Clearly data points that are far away from the cluster boundary should never be touched when re-assigning cluster memberships. This is illustrated in Fig. 2. Suppose we wish to re-assign the cluster membership of one such data point, say $a \in$ cluster $\mathcal{C}_1$ (i.e., cluster formed by green points) to cluster $\mathcal{C}_2$ (i.e., cluster of red points). Then, due to the *connectivity assumption* (i.e., data points from the same cluster form a "connected" region), many other data points between $a$ and cluster $\mathcal{C}_2$, i.e., data points circled by the dashed circle, should also be switched from cluster $\mathcal{C}_1$ to cluster $\mathcal{C}_2$. This will lead to a substantial change in the value of the given cluster quality measure and is not desirable. Focusing on the near-boundary data points allows us to work on a small set of feasible solutions, and computation can be done quickly.

Our definition of fairness takes into account of discrepancy of the proportion of subpopulations in each cluster. For simplicity, assume that there are two subpopulations of interest, and let $p_1$ and $p_2$ be their respective proportions in the entire population. For each cluster $i = 1, ..., K$, let $p_{ij}$ be the proportion of data points belonging to subpopulations $j = 1, 2$. Let $n$ be the total number of data points, and $n_i$ be the number of data points in each of the clusters for $i = 1, ..., K$. We can now give the following definition of the fairness index

$$\mathcal{F} = \sum_{i=1}^{K} \frac{n_i}{n} \left( \sum_{j=1}^{2} \mid p_{ij} - p_j \mid \right) = \sum_{i=1}^{K} w_i \left( \sum_{j=1}^{2} \mid p_{ij} - p_j \mid \right), \tag{3}$$

where term $\left( \sum_{j=1}^{2} \mid p_{ij} - p_j \mid \right)$ measures the discrepancy of respective proportions of each subpopulation in the i$^{\text{th}}$ cluster, and the discrepancies are weighted by the relative size, $w_i$, of each cluster out of the entire set of data points. We have $\mathcal{F} \in [0, 1]$, and a smaller value of $\mathcal{F}$ would indicate a more fair clustering, and $\mathcal{F} = 0$ indicates that, in each cluster, all the subpopulations have the same proportion as in the general population. Note that our definition can be easily extended to settings with multiple subpopulations.

We will start by adjusting points from clusters for which one subpopulation dominates the most. To measure how much a subpopulation dominates points from a cluster, say $A$, we define the following cluster balance measure

$$\beta(A) = \frac{|\{x \in S_1\}|}{|\{x \in S_2\}|},$$

where $S_1$ and $S_2$ are the two subpopulations of interest and $|\cdot|$ indicates the cardinality (i.e., number of elements) of a finite set. Note that the balance measure can also be calculated on the entire dataset (population). If a cluster has a large value of cluster balance measure, then that means it has excessive data points from subpopulation $S_1$. On the other hand, clusters with a small value of cluster balance index would have insufficient number of data points from subpopulation $S_1$. So, two clusters will be better balanced in terms of cluster fairness by exchanging the cluster membership of points from a cluster of high cluster balance index with points from clusters of a small cluster balance index.

Having found which two clusters to switch cluster membership for their data points, the remaining issue is to identify which data points to adjust cluster membership. The overall idea is to find data points near the cluster boundary. Switching the cluster membership of such data points will not impact the cluster quality much since they do not contribute much in determining the class boundary as demonstrated by theoretical as well as empirical work in classification setting [24, 30].

We adopt two different implementations to locate candidate data points for cluster membership swapping, while keeping the deterioration to cluster quality 'minimal'. One is to pick points that are far away from their own cluster centroid but near the centroid of some other cluster, and the other is to pick points that are highly mixed in the sense that there are data points from different clusters in a 'small' neighborhood of such data points. These are described in Sects. 2.2 and 2.3, respectively, after a short description of K-means clustering in Sect. 2.1.

### 2.1 The K-Means Clustering Algorithm

Formally, given $n$ data points, $K$-means clustering seeks to find a partition of $K$ sets $S_1, S_2, ..., S_K$ such that the within-cluster sum of squares, $SS_W$, is minimized

$$\underset{S_1, S_2, \ldots, S_K}{\arg\min} \sum_{i=1}^{K} \sum_{\mathbf{x} \in S_i} \|\mathbf{x} - \boldsymbol{\mu}_i\|^2, \tag{4}$$

where $\mu_i$ is the centroid of $S_i, i = 1, 2, ..., K$.

Directly solving the problem formulated as (4) is hard, as it is an integer programming problem. Indeed it is a NP-hard problem [1]. The K-means clustering algorithm is often referred to a popular implementation sketched as Algorithm 1 below. For more details, one can refer to [10, 18].

**Algorithm 1.** $K$**-means clustering algorithm**

Generate an initial set of $K$ centroids $m_1, m_2, ..., m_K$;

Alternate between the following two steps

Assign each point $x$ to the "closest" cluster

$$\arg \min_{j \in \{1,2,...,K\}} \|x - m_j\|^2;$$

Calculate the new cluster centroids

$$m_j^{new} = \frac{1}{\|S_j\|} \sum_{x \in S_j} x, \quad j = 1, 2, ..., K;$$

Stop when cluster assignment no longer changes.

## 2.2 Improve Fairness by Adjusting Nearest Foreign Points

Our first proposed implementation works by switching the cluster membership assignments for data points that are far away from their own cluster centroid while near the cluster centroid of other clusters. Call this the *near-foreign heuristic.* The idea is to switch the cluster membership of data points that are less likely to be in their assigned cluster (called source cluster) since they are far away from the cluster centroid while kind of likely to be part of some other clusters as they are among the nearest data points that are outside of the destination cluster (call such points *foreign points* of the destination cluster). Since such data points are near the cluster boundary, reassigning them will not impact the overall cluster quality much.

Figure 3 is an illustration of the near-foreign heuristic. Note that simply switching the cluster membership of points that are furthest to a cluster centroid will not work, as there are two possibilities. One is that the data point is near some other cluster, it makes sense to reassign the cluster membership to such points to other cluster which will improve fairness while not impacting much to cluster quality. The other possibility is that, although the data points are far away from its own cluster centroid, they are not near any other cluster either (rather they are near the outmost side of the data space). One example can be seen from Fig. 3, where points $a, b, c$ are all far away from the centroid of the cluster formed by green points. If we re-assign points $a, b, c$ to the neighboring cluster which is the cluster formed by red points, then clearly point $c$ will not make a good choice though points $a$ and $b$ are. Treating data points $a$ and $b$ as foreign points of the 'red' cluster, then re-assigning them to the 'red' cluster is expected, and in this case, point $c$ should not be re-assigned to the 'red' cluster as it is not among those nearest foreign points.

A description of an algorithm based on the near-foreign heuristic is given as Algorithm 2. We say a cluster $A$ is balance enough if its balance measure $\beta(A)$ is close (e.g., within a factor of $\beta_0 = 5 \sim 10\%$) to that calculated on the entire population. Note that the algorithm is described for two clusters for

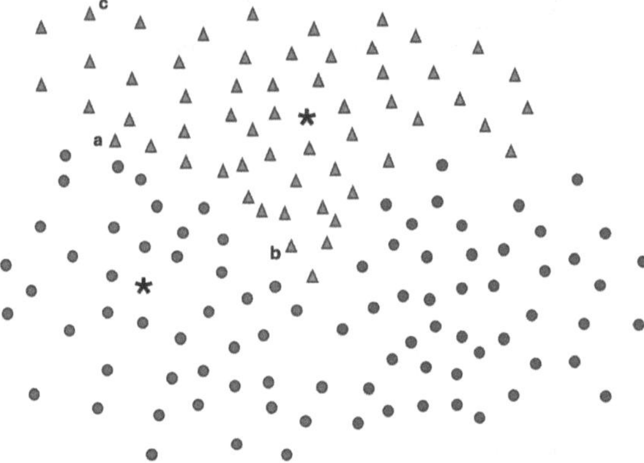


**Fig. 3.** Illustration of the near-foreign heuristic. Points from different classes are indicated by different colors. ⋆ indicates the centroid the clusters formed by red points or green points. (Color figure online)

simplicity, and we can easily extend it to settings of multiple clusters (simply repeat the algorithm for a number of times for a pair of clusters which are highly unbalanced). The algorithm has a linear computational complexity. It is upper bounded by the product of the number of data points and the number of times we exchange the cluster membership of points for a pair of unbalanced clusters.

### 2.3 Improve Fairness by Gini Index

The Gini index is originally used in tree-based methodology for classification [3]. The classification tree grows by recursively splitting the tree nodes, starting from the root node which consists of the entire set of data points, to make the resulting child nodes more "pure" than their parent nodes. At each node split, one looks for a direction and (or) split point such that the overall purity of resulting tree nodes improves upon the node split. The Gini index measures how 'mixed' or 'pure' of points in a node which could be potentially from different classes. At a given node, $x$, let the proportion of data points for class $j$ be denoted by $p_j$ for $j = 1, ..., J$, then the Gini index is defined as

$$G(x) = \sum_{j=1}^{J} p_j(1 - p_j). \tag{5}$$

To appreciate the Gini index as a measure of impurity, let us consider a few numerical examples as illustrated in Table 1. Clearly Case 1 is the most mixed while Case 5 is the purest by intuition, and the calculated Gini indices are consistent with our intuition.

In this work, we propose a novel use of the Gini index, i.e., use it to detect if a given data point is on or near the class (cluster) boundary. The idea is, if a data

**Algorithm 2. fcNearForeign(X, k)**

Apply K-means clustering algorithm to the data;
Calculate cluster balance measure, $\beta_i, i = 1, ..., K$, on each cluster;
Let $A$ and $B$ be clusters with the max and min balance measures, respectively;
Calculate cluster centroids, $x_A$ and $x_B$, for clusters $A$ and $B$;
**for** each data point $X \in A \cup B$ **do**
    Calculate its distance to cluster centroid $x_A$ or $x_B$ as a foreign point;
**end for**
Sort such distances in increasing order;
Let the respective data points be $X_1, ..., X_m$ with $m = \mid A \cup B \mid$;
**while** Clusters $A$ or $B$ not balance enough **do**
    Switch the cluster membership for data point $X_i$ w.r.t. cluster A or B;
    Clusters $A$ and $B$ now become $A'$ and $B'$, respectively;
    Recalculate the cluster balance measure for clusters $A'$ and $B'$;
    Stop loop if $A'$ and $B'$ are balance enough;
**end while**
Return updated cluster membership assignment;

**Table 1.** A toy example of node impurity. $C_j$ denote the proportion of points in class $j = 1, 2, ..., 5$. Case 1 and Case 5 are at the two extremes, with Case 1 being the most mixed while Case 5 being the purest.

| Case | $C_1$ | $C_2$ | $C_3$ | Gini |
|---|---|---|---|---|
| Case 1 | 1/3 | 1/3 | 1/3 | 2/3 |
| Case 2 | 0.50 | 0.30 | 0.20 | 0.62 |
| Case 3 | 0.80 | 0.10 | 0.10 | 0.34 |
| Case 4 | 0.90 | 0.05 | 0.05 | 0.185 |
| Case 5 | 1.00 | 0.00 | 0.00 | 0 |

point is on or near the cluster boundary, then a small neighborhood of the data point would likely also consist of data points from different classes (clusters) thus a higher Gini index. This will resemble Case 1 or 2. On the other hand, if a data point is in the interior of a cluster, then data points from a small neighborhood will mostly be from one cluster, thus a very small Gini index. This will be like Case 4–5. Empirically, we can easily find a cutoff value to distinguish these two situations. The selection of the right-sized neighborhood is data-dependent, and we make it adaptive to the data by using the k-nearest neighborhood [29]. The goal is to make the neighborhood local and yet large enough to capture the purity of the neighborhood. Empirically we find the cluster quality not sensitive to the choice of $k$ (c.f., Fig. 5) (Fig. 4).

The proposed algorithm starts by switching the cluster membership assignment for two neighboring clusters that are at two extremes in terms of a cluster balance measure. A description of an algorithm based on the Gini index is given as Algorithm 3. Similarly as that for the Algorithm 2, it is described for two

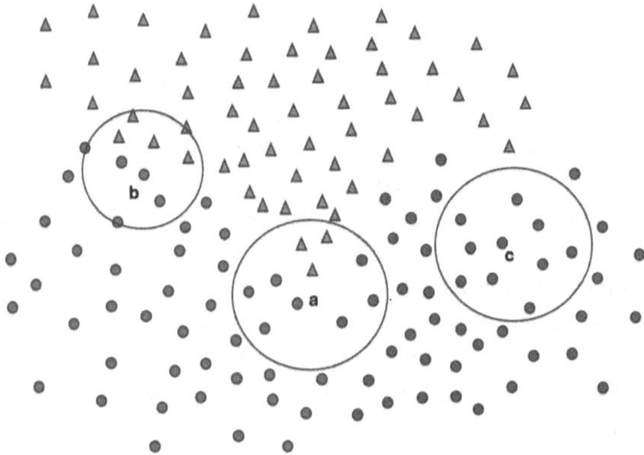


**Fig. 4.** Illustration of boundary and non-boundary points. Points from different classes are indicated by different colors. The circles are the 10-nearest neighborhood of given points a, b and c. The respective Gini indices are calculated as 0.66, 0.50, *and* 0 *(which indicates the given point is an interior point). (Color figure online)*

**Algorithm 3. fcGini(X, k)**

```
Apply K-means clustering algorithm to the data;
Calculate cluster balance measure, β_i, i = 1, ..., J, on each cluster;
Let A and B be clusters with the max and min balance measures, respectively;
for each data point X ∈ A ∪ B do
    Calculate the Gini index for X in its k-nearest neighborhood;
end for
Sort Gini indices in set Gini(A ∪ B) in decreasing order;
Let the respective data points be X_1, ..., X_m with m =| A ∪ B |;
for i=1 to m do
    Switch the cluster membership for data point X_i w.r.t. cluster A or B;
    Clusters A and B now become A' and B', respectively;
    Recalculate the cluster balance measure for clusters A' and B';
    Stop loop if A' and B' are balance enough;
end for
Return updated cluster membership assignment;
```

clusters for simplicity, and we can easily extend to multiple clusters. Clearly the algorithm also has a linear computational complexity.

## 3 Related Work

Work related to ours falls into several categories. The first is on algorithms for fair clustering. A number of algorithms have been proposed in the last decade, for instance [2,7,8]. Such algorithms generally formulate fair clustering as an optimization problem along with an additional constraint on fairness, and then directly solve the optimization problem at its entirety. Constraints that involves integer programming would substantially increase the computation. Also, such algorithms are typically closely tied to the underlying clustering algorithms. In contrast, our algorithm solves the constrained optimization problem in two stages with insights that allow us to focus on a small set of feasible solutions, which greatly reduces the problem space at low computational complexity. Also our proposed algorithms, though described for K-means clustering, does not explicitly depend on the underlying clustering algorithm.

There are many work that explores various notions of fairness in clustering or other machine learning problems, such as proportional fairness [5,14], group fairness [6], and individually fair clustering [4,19] etc. Also there are work that establishes theoretical guarantees [15] for fair clustering. Additionally, algorithms have been proposed to account for multiple fairness metrics simultaneously [9].

## 4 Experiments

To evaluate the performance of our approach, we choose 7 datasets from the UC Irvine Machine Learning Repository [16]. This includes the Indian Liver Patient dataset (ILPD), the Heart dataset, the Hepatitis C Virus (HCV) for Egyptian patients dataset, the Student Performance (StudentPerf) dataset, the Contraceptive Method Choice (CMC) dataset, the Seed dataset, the Higher Education (HigherEdu) Students Performance Evaluation dataset. A summary of these datasets is given in Table 2.

**Table 2.** A short summary of the datasets used in our experiments.

| Data set | # Features | # instances | #Clusters |
|---|---|---|---|
| ILPD | 10 | 579 | 2 |
| Heart | 13 | 303 | 2 |
| HCV | 12 | 615 | 2 |
| StudentPerf | 30 | 649 | 2 |
| CMC | 9 | 1473 | 3 |
| Seed | 7 | 210 | 3 |
| HigherEdu | 31 | 145 | 5 |

For each dataset, we choose one of the variables, such as gender, as the sensitive variable for which we will calculate fairness. Note that our proposed algorithms continue to work for fairness defined over several variables. We compare the fairness obtained by the original K-means clustering algorithm, the *fcNear-Foreign* algorithm and *fcGini* algorithm. Two metrics are used for performance evaluation in our experiments. One is fairness defined in (3), and the other is a commonly used cluster quality measure [11,28], defined as

$$\kappa = \frac{SS_B}{SS_T}, \tag{6}$$

where $SS_B$ and $SS_T$ are the between-cluster sum of squared distances and the total sum of squared distances, respectively. Clearly $\kappa \in [0, 1]$ as the calculation of $SS_B$ involves only part of those distances used in $SS_T$. A "large" value of $\kappa$ would imply that the inter-cluster distances carry a large proportion of all pairwise distances, an indication of well-separated clusters thus a good cluster quality. Note that here our goal is not to achieve the best $\kappa$, rather to demonstrate that the proposed algorithms could improve cluster fairness while not impacting the cluster quality much.

**Table 3.** Comparison of fairness obtained by the original K-means clustering algorithm, algorithm by the near-foreign and the Gini index heuristics, respectively. In each cell, there are two numbers, one is the overall fairness index and the other the cluster quality measure $\kappa$.

| | Original | | Near-Foreign | | Gini | |
|---|---|---|---|---|---|---|
| ILPD | 0.11 | 37.60% | 0.07 | 35.90% | 0.07 | 36.20% |
| Heart | 0.12 | 82.21% | 0.08 | 81.48% | 0.08 | 81.09% |
| HCV | 0.03 | 84.96% | 0.02 | 79.93% | 0.02 | 79.12% |
| StudentPerf | 0.09 | 70.74% | 0.01 | 73.45% | 0.01 | 72.44% |
| CMC | 0.12 | 62.36% | 0.09 | 60.89% | 0.09 | 60.17% |
| Seed | 0.19 | 77.70% | 0.12 | 77.45% | 0.12 | 77.12% |
| HigherEdu | 0.32 | 75.03% | 0.27 | 71.56% | 0.27 | 70.19% |

Table 3 shows that, for all the 7 datasets used in the experiments, our proposed algorithms based on both the near-foreign and the Gini index heuristics improve the fairness over the original K-means clustering algorithm while maintaining the cluster quality as evidenced in small changes in the value of the $\kappa$ measure. It is interesting that, for most datasets, the near-foreign and the Gini index heuristics lead to similar cluster quality (i.e, similar $\kappa$ values). It is not clear when one will outperform the other. In general, the Gini index heuristic tends to pick those highly mixed data points, that is, points that lie at the boundary of several clusters, to switch cluster membership. One weakness with the near-foreign heuristic lies in its use of distance in picking data points to reassign their cluster membership. We have to adapt to the right distance metric otherwise performance might be impacted in situations when the geometry in the data becomes complex and non-convex, for example, when the data lie on a low-dimensional Swiss-roll like manifold in a high dimensional space [22,26].

For the Gini index heuristic, we also assess the sensitivity of cluster quality $\kappa$ w.r.t. the choice of neighborhood size $k$ in calculating the Gini index of individual data points. In particular, we vary $k$ over $\{5, 10, 15\}$. Figure 5 shows that the influence to cluster quality is negligible when varying the value of $k$. The dataset with the largest impact from $k$ is the ILPD data, and we attribute it to the fact that this dataset has mostly integer-(categorical) valued variables.

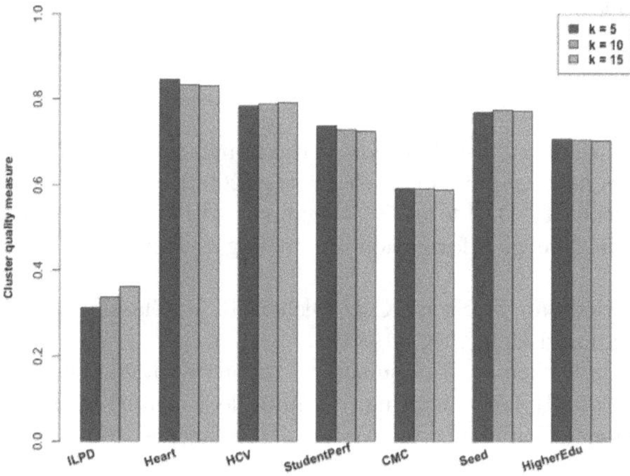


**Fig. 5.** Insensitivity of the cluster quality over different choices of neighborhood size $k \in \{5, 10, 15\}$ in calculating the Gini index of individual data points. The cluster qualities vary very little when $k$ increases from 5 to 15.

## 5 Conclusions and Future Work

We have proposed a novel approach with two implementations to improve the fairness of K-means clustering, one based on the near-foreign heuristic and the other based on the Gini index. Both are conceptually simple, computationally light and are effective in improving the fairness in K-means clustering algorithms. As they do not rely on the implementation of the underlying clustering algorithms, they are readily applicable to a broad class of clustering algorithms, for example the popular spectral clustering [13,20,23], and a recently proposed rpf-kernel based clustering [27]. Also since our approach solves the fair clustering problem by a two-stage optimization, it can be easily adopted to different definitions of fairness.

While the near-foreign and the Gini index heuristics both explore boundary data points, they are different in the sense that the Gini index heuristic attempts to locate those highly mixed data points (which may lie at the class boundary of several clusters) which is not necessarily the case for that of the near-foreign heuristic. It might be interesting to see what happens if and how one may combine these two ideas. Another direction for future work is to extend our algorithms to account for multiple fairness measures simultaneously along the line of [9].

**Acknowledgments.** The work of H. Xu and D. Yan are partially supported by Office of Naval Research (ONR) Grant, MUST IV, University of Massachusetts Dartmouth.

**Disclosure of Interests.** The authors have no competing interests to declare that are relevant to the content of this article.

## References

1. Arthur, D., Vassilvitskii, S.: How slow is the K-means method? In: Proceedings of the Symposium on Computational Geometry (2006)
2. Bera, S., Chakrabarty, D., Flores, N., Negahban, M.: Fair algorithms for clustering. In: Advances in Neural Information Processing Systems (NIPS), pp. 4954–4965 (2019)
3. Breiman, L., Friedman, J., Stone, C.J., Olshen, R.A.: Classification and Regression Trees. Chapman and Hall/CRC (1984)
4. Chakrabarti, D., Dickerson, J., Esmaeili, S., Srinivasan, A., Tsepenekas, L.: A new notion of individually fair clustering: $\alpha$-equitable $k$-center. In: Proceedings of The 25th International Conference on Artificial Intelligence and Statistics, pp. 6387–6408 (2022)
5. Chen, X., Fain, B., Lyu, L., Munagala, K.: Proportionally fair clustering. In:Proceedings of the 36th International Conference on Machine Learning, pp. 1032–1041 (2019)
6. Cheng, Y., Jiang, Z., Munagala, K., Wang, K.: Group fairness in committee selection. In: Proceedings of the 2019 ACM Conference on Economics and Computation, pp. 263–279 (2019)
7. Chhabra, A., Masalkovaite, K., Mohapatra, P.: An overview of fairness in clustering. IEEE Access, 1–25 (2021)
8. Chierichetti, F., Kumar, R., Lattanzi, S., Vassilvitskii, S.: Fair clustering through fairlets. In: Advances in Neural Information Processing Systems, pp. 5029–5037 (2017)
9. Dickerson, J., Esmaeili, S., Morgenstern, J., Zhang, C.: Doubly constrained fair clustering. In: Advances in Neural Information Processing Systems (NIPS), pp. 13267–13293 (2023)
10. Hartigan, J.A., Wong, M.A.: A K-means clustering algorithm. Appl. Stat. **28**(1), 100–108 (1979)
11. Hastie, T., Tibshirani, R., Friedman, J.: The Elements of Statistical Learning: Data Mining, Inference, and Prediction, Springer (2001). https://doi.org/10.1007/978-0-387-21606-5
12. Heidari, H., Ferrari, C., Gummadi, K., Krause, A.: Fairness behind a veil of ignorance: A welfare analysis for automated decision making. Adv. Neural Inf. Process. Syst. pp. 1273–1283 (2018)
13. Huang, L., Yan, D., Jordan, M.I., Taft, N.: Spectral clustering with perturbed data. Adv. Neural Inf. Process. Syst. (NIPS) **21** (2009)
14. Kellerhals, L., Peters, J.: Proportional fairness in clustering: a social choice perspective. arXiv:2310.18162 (2024)
15. Kleindessner, M., Samadi, S., Awasthi, P., Morgenstern, J.: Guarantees for spectral clustering with fairness constraints. In: International Conference on Machine Learning (2019)
16. Lichman, M.: UC Irvine Machine Learning Repository (2013). http://archive.ics.uci.edu/ml
17. Liu, L., Dean, S., Rolf, E., Simchowitz, M., Hardt, M.: Delayed impact of fair machine learning. In: Proceedings of the Twenty-Eighth International Joint Conference on Artificial Intelligence, IJCAI, pp. 6196–6200 (2019)

18. Lloyd, S.P.: Least squares quantization in PCM. IEEE Trans. Inf. Theory **28**(1), 128–137 (1982)
19. Mahabadi, S., Vakilian, A.: Individual fairness for k-clustering. In: Proceedings of the 37th International Conference on Machine Learning, pp. 6586–6596 (2020)
20. Ng, A.Y., Jordan, M.I., Weiss, Y.: On spectral clustering: analysis and an algorithm. Neural Inf. Process. Syst. (NIPS) **14** (2002)
21. Purohit, M., Gollapudi, S., Raghavan, M.: Hiring under uncertainty. In: Proceedings of the 36th International Conference on Machine Learning, pp. 5181–5189 (2019)
22. Roweis, S., Saul, L.: Nonlinear dimensionality reduction by locally linear embedding. Science **290**(5500), 2323–2326 (2000)
23. Shi, J., Malik, J.: Normalized cuts and image segmentation. IEEE Trans. Pattern Anal. Mach. Intell. **22**(8), 888–905 (2000)
24. Singh, A., Nowak, R., Zhu, X.: Unlabeled data: now it helps, now it doesn't. In: Proceedings of Neural Information Processing Systems (NIPS), pp. 1513–1520 (2009)
25. Spanakis, E., Golden, S.: Race/ethnic difference in diabetes and diabetic complications. Diabetes Epidemiol. **13**, 814–823 (2013)
26. Tenenbaum, J.B., de Silva, V., Langford, J.C.: A global geometric framework for nonlinear dimensionality reduction. Science **290**(5500), 2319–2323 (2000)
27. Wang, K.A., Bian, X., Liu, P., Yan, D.: DC$^2$: a divide-and-conquer algorithm for large-scale kernel learning with application to clustering. In: Proceedings of the IEEE International Conference on Big Data, pp. 5603–5610 (2019)
28. Yan, D., Chen, A., Jordan, M.I.: Cluster forests. Comput. Stat. Data Anal. **66**, 178–192 (2013)
29. Yan, D., Wang, Y., Wang, J., Wang, H., Li, Z.: K-nearest neighbor search by random projection forests. IEEE Trans. Big Data 1–12 (2019)
30. Yan, I.: Automatically score tissue images like a pathologist by transfer learning. New Engl. J. Stat. Data Sci. **0**, 1–9 (2023)

# Optimizing Mobility: A Scalable Real-Time Warehouse for Intelligent Transportation Analytics

Buddhi Rathnayaka[1(✉)], Uthayasanker Thayasivam[2], and Umashanger Thayasivam[1]

[1] Department of Mathematics, Rowan University, Glassboro, USA
{rathna55,thayasivam}@rowan.edu

[2] Department of CSE, University of Moratuwa, Moratuwa, Sri Lanka
rtuthaya@cse.mrt.ac.lk

**Abstract.** The rapid proliferation of data in modern transportation systems presents both unprecedented opportunities and significant challenges. Traditional data management solutions struggle to handle the volume, velocity, and variety of transportation data generated from GPS devices, IoT sensors, and embedded vehicle systems. This paper addresses the critical need for a scalable, real-time data warehousing solution capable of managing diverse transportation data and supporting advanced analytics. We propose a modular system architecture that integrates state-of-the-art open-source technologies, including Apache Kafka, Spark, Hive, and Ranger, to efficiently process and analyze transportation data in real-time. Experimental evaluations demonstrate that our system outperforms existing solutions, achieving query execution times up to 84% faster than baseline systems, CPU utilization of up to 88%, and error rates as low as 0.0001%. These results indicate significant improvements in handling large-scale transportation data, enabling more effective real-time decision-making. The system's ability to integrate multimodal data and support advanced machine learning paves the way for future advancements in intelligent transportation systems, contributing to improved efficiency, safety, and sustainability in urban mobility.

**Keywords:** Real-time Data Warehousing · Big Data Analytics · Data Governance · Multimodal Data Integration

## 1 Introduction

The exponential growth of data in modern transportation systems is reshaping the landscape of urban mobility and logistics. From GPS signals and IoT sensors to embedded devices in vehicles, the sheer volume, velocity, and variety of transportation data present unprecedented opportunities for optimizing networks and enhancing decision-making processes. This diversity of data offers essential insights into traffic patterns, passenger behaviors, and infrastructure


R. Stahlbock et al. (Eds.): CSCE 2025, CCIS 2938, pp. 268–283, 2027.
https://doi.org/10.1007/978-3-032-22196-4_20

utilization. However, this deluge of data also introduces significant challenges in data management, real-time analysis, and governance. Traditional database management systems, originally designed for static and limited datasets, struggle to handle the scale, speed, and complexity of contemporary transportation data streams [2,12].

As urbanization accelerates, population growth surges, and economic development intensifies, the demand for efficient, sustainable, and intelligent transportation solutions becomes ever more critical. Real-time data analytics and machine learning are essential tools for addressing issues such as traffic congestion, route optimization, and predictive maintenance [2]. Making informed decisions in real time can significantly improve the sustainability, efficiency, and safety of transportation systems, addressing broader concerns like urban development and environmental conservation.

Despite advances in big data technologies, existing solutions often fall short in several key areas. Many studies do not fully leverage available open-source tools and frequently omit essential features like machine learning analytics, which are crucial for effectively analyzing extensive datasets [12]. A clear gap exists in developing multi-model data warehouses, with insufficient research on integrating various data models and types, an essential aspect of understanding complex transportation data [2]. The field of data governance also appears underexplored, highlighting the need for robust governance mechanisms in real-time transportation data warehouses to maintain data integrity and security. Additionally, the lack of focus on real-time analytical support limits the effectiveness of decision-making processes in dynamic environments.

Processing diverse data in near real time and integrating various data types to conduct advanced analytics and machine learning present substantial technical difficulties [12]. Building a robust and adaptable ecosystem that can integrate open-source technologies is crucial for scalability and continuous improvement. Moreover, maintaining rigorous data governance and managing user access levels while ensuring data quality adds to the complexity of creating an effective solution.

To address these gaps, we propose a scalable, real-time transportation data warehousing solution that integrates state-of-the-art open-source technologies. Our approach combines a distributed event streaming platform for seamless real-time data ingestion, Apache Spark MLlib for scalable machine learning analytics, and a robust three-layer data governance system to ensure data integrity and security. By leveraging an open-source ecosystem, our solution ensures transparency, adaptability, and continuous enhancements through community contributions.

Our contributions in this paper are threefold:

1. We develop a modular system architecture that addresses the challenges of data fusion, processing, and management in transportation systems.
2. We demonstrate the effectiveness of our system through comparative analysis, showing superior performance in query execution, resource utilization, and error rates compared to existing solutions.

3. We provide insights into integrating multimodal transportation data and supporting real-time decision-making, paving the way for future advancements in smart transportation systems.

It effectively manages diverse data streams, supports advanced analytics, and provides a flexible framework for future integration of emerging technologies. This paper presents a detailed overview of the proposed solution, exploring the benefits and intricacies of each integrated open-source tool and shedding light on the synergies created when combined. We detail our approach to challenges such as data governance, user access management, and multimodal data integration. The paper concludes with insights into the potential impacts and future developments of real-time transportation data warehouses.

## 2 Literature Review

Data warehousing has evolved significantly since its inception, particularly in the realm of transportation systems. Initially designed for storing and retrieving historical data, data warehouses have become integral to scheduling, forecasting, and real-time decision-making within intelligent transportation systems (ITS) [11]. The foundational work by Inmon [7] established the concept of a centralized repository for integrated data, setting the stage for modern data warehousing practices. Kimball's dimensional modeling further advanced the field by promoting user-friendly data structures optimized for querying and analysis [9].

### 2.1 Data Warehouse Architectures in Transportation

Various architectural frameworks have been proposed to address specific data management needs in transportation. The three-tier architecture, comprising data sources, a data warehouse layer, and data analysis tools, is notable for its comprehensive data handling approach [8]. This architecture separates the data flow into distinct layers, enhancing scalability and maintainability. Bus, hub-and-spoke, centralized, and distributed models offer alternative solutions tailored to scalability, data integration, and retrieval needs [5]. For instance, the hub-and-spoke model facilitates data integration from disparate sources, which is essential for multimodal transportation data [10].

Comparative studies have assessed these architectures based on parameters like data volume, user requirements, and system complexity. Vyas and Patel [13] conducted a literature review comparing different data warehouse architectures, emphasizing the importance of selecting an appropriate architecture for optimal performance in transportation data warehousing. Their findings suggest that no single architecture is universally optimal; instead, the choice depends on specific organizational needs and data characteristics.

### 2.2 Integration of Big Data and Machine Learning

The advent of big data technologies and machine learning has significantly influenced data warehousing practices. The integration of Hadoop and Spark has enabled the handling of large-scale data processing and real-time analytics [14]. Spark's in-memory processing capabilities allow for faster data analysis compared to traditional disk-based systems [15]. Machine learning algorithms, facilitated by tools like Apache Spark MLlib, have been applied to transportation data to improve predictive analytics, such as traffic forecasting and anomaly detection [12].

Syafrudin et al. [12] proposed a real-time big data analytical architecture for remote monitoring in industrial processes, demonstrating the potential for similar applications in transportation. Their architecture leveraged Apache Kafka for data ingestion and Apache Storm for real-time processing, highlighting the effectiveness of distributed event streaming platforms in handling high-velocity data streams.

### 2.3 Challenges in Transportation Data Warehousing

Despite technological advancements, several challenges persist in the field of transportation data warehousing. One significant hurdle is managing the volume, velocity, and variety of transportation data, often referred to as the three Vs of big data [3]. Traditional relational database management systems (RDBMS) are ill-suited to handle the scale and speed required for real-time analytics in transportation systems [2]. This limitation leads to inefficiencies and delays in data processing, hampering timely decision-making.

The integration of multimodal data from diverse transportation sources remains underexplored. Li et al. [10] highlighted the challenges in fusing data from different transportation modes, such as road, rail, and air, each with unique data formats and standards. The lack of standardized protocols for data integration leads to fragmented data silos, hindering comprehensive analysis and the development of unified transportation models.

Data governance is another critical area that has not received adequate attention. Ensuring data quality, security, and compliance with regulations is essential for the reliability and integrity of transportation data warehouses [5]. However, robust governance mechanisms are often lacking in current systems. Ahmed et al. [1] noted that many big data solutions focus on scalability and performance at the expense of governance, leading to vulnerabilities in data integrity and security.

### 2.4 Leveraging Open-Source Technologies

Open-source technologies offer a cost-effective and flexible alternative to proprietary systems. They enable customization and community-driven improvements, which are crucial for keeping pace with rapidly evolving data requirements [4]. Tools like Apache Kafka, Apache Spark, and Hadoop have been widely adopted for building scalable data processing pipelines [15]. However, many existing systems do not fully leverage the capabilities of these tools, particularly in integrating machine learning for advanced analytics [12].

Chan et al. [2] developed a real-time big data processing framework for transportation data but did not incorporate machine learning functionalities, limiting the system's ability to perform predictive analytics. This gap underscores the need for comprehensive solutions that combine real-time data processing with advanced analytics.

### 2.5 Recent Advances and Future Directions

Recent studies have begun to address some of these challenges. For instance, Wisnubhadra et al. [14] explored mobility prediction in smart transportation using big data and machine learning, demonstrating improved accuracy in traffic forecasting. Their work highlights the potential of integrating machine learning models into transportation data warehouses for enhanced predictive capabilities.

Emerging technologies such as edge computing and the Internet of Things (IoT) are also influencing data warehousing practices. Edge computing brings data processing closer to data sources, reducing latency and bandwidth usage [12]. This is particularly relevant for transportation systems, where real-time data from vehicles and sensors can be processed more efficiently [6].

### 2.6 Summary

The literature indicates a clear need for advanced, scalable, and real-time data warehousing solutions in the transportation sector. While significant progress has been made in individual areas such as big data processing and machine learning, there is a lack of integrated systems that combine these elements effectively. The challenges of managing diverse and high-velocity data streams, ensuring data quality and security, and providing advanced analytics capabilities remain significant hurdles. Our research contributes to the field by addressing these challenges through a modular system architecture that integrates data fusion, processing, and management, supported by a strong data governance framework.

## 3 Methodology

This section details the methodology employed to develop a scalable, real-time transportation data warehousing solution. The system is designed to address the challenges of data fusion, processing, management, and real-time analytics in transportation systems. We provide a comprehensive description of the system architecture, the technologies used, and the implementation details necessary for replication and validation of our work.

### 3.1 Overview of Challenges and Solutions

To systematically address the inherent challenges in developing our system, we identified key issues and devised corresponding solutions. Table 1 summarizes these challenges and the methodologies implemented to overcome them.

**Table 1.** Identified challenges and their corresponding solutions within the proposed system

| Challenges | Solutions |
|---|---|
| Handling Near Real-Time Data Streaming in a Big Data Context | We employ a distributed event streaming platform, specifically Apache Kafka, to ingest and process vast data streams seamlessly. This ensures that our data warehouse remains up-to-date, facilitating real-time analytics and decision-making. |
| Scaling Machine Learning Analytics for Big Data | By integrating Apache Spark MLlib, we provide scalable machine learning capabilities well-suited for large-scale data processing. This enables advanced analytics, pattern recognition, and predictive modeling on our datasets. |
| Ensuring Robust Data Governance and Quality | We implement a dedicated data governance framework using Apache Ranger. This framework defines standards, ensures data quality, and manages data handling and processing decisions, maintaining consistent, high-quality data management practices across the platform. |
| Managing Different Levels of User Access | We design a three-tiered user access model comprising:<br>–User<br>– Data Owner<br>– Data Administrator<br>This model ensures data security and appropriate access control based on user roles. |
| Integrating Multimodal Data from Diverse Transportation Sources | Our system accommodates multimodal data through flexible schema design and data transformation techniques. This enables cohesive integration and processing of heterogeneous data sources, regardless of format or origin. |
| Maintaining Flexibility and Adaptability in an Open-Source Ecosystem | By leveraging open-source technologies such as Apache Kafka, Spark, and Hive, we ensure transparency, flexibility, and continuous improvement through community contributions. This facilitates integration with other open-source tools, extending our system's capabilities and adaptability. |

### 3.2 System Architecture Overview

The proposed system architecture is modular, comprising four primary components: the Data Fusion Module, the Data Processing Unit, the Data Warehouse Management system, and the Data Repository Platform. This modularity ensures scalability, flexibility, and ease of maintenance. Figure 1 illustrates the high-level architecture of the system.

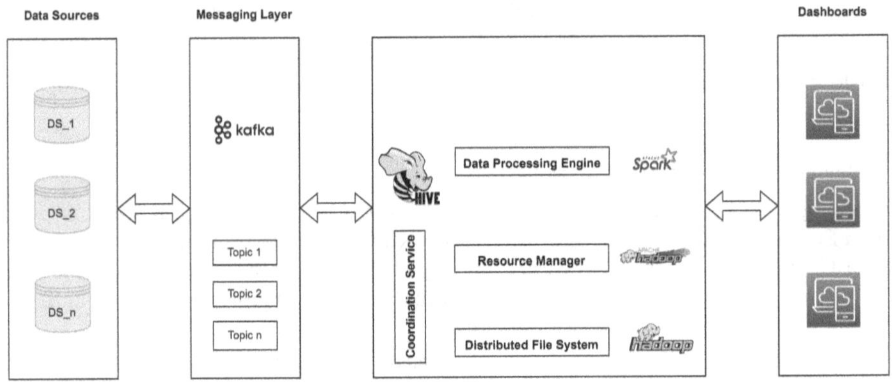


**Fig. 1.** High-Level System Architecture.

### 3.3 Data Fusion Module

The Data Fusion Module is responsible for collecting and integrating data from various transportation data sources, including GPS devices, IoT sensors, and embedded vehicle systems. The module ensures data consistency and quality through the following processes:

- Data Collection: Data is collected in real-time from multiple sources using Apache Kafka. This distributed event streaming platform efficiently handles high-throughput, low-latency data streams, addressing the challenge of handling near real-time data streaming in a big data context.
- Data Preprocessing: Collected data undergoes preprocessing steps to handle missing values, outliers, and inconsistencies. Techniques such as interpolation for missing data and z-score normalization for outlier detection are applied. The preprocessing algorithms are implemented using Python and integrated with Kafka streams.
- Data Integration: The module employs a schema-on-read approach to accommodate diverse data formats. Data is transformed into a unified schema using Apache Avro serialization, facilitating seamless multimodal data integration from diverse transportation sources.

### 3.4 Data Processing Unit

The Data Processing Unit leverages Apache Spark for distributed data processing and analytics, addressing the challenge of scaling machine learning analytics for big data.

- Real-Time Analytics: Spark Streaming processes data streams in real-time with a batch interval of 5 s, balancing latency and throughput. Processing tasks include aggregations, filtering, and statistical computations relevant to transportation data analysis.
- Machine Learning Integration: Apache Spark MLlib provides scalable machine learning capabilities. Algorithms such as K-means clustering and decision trees detect patterns and predict traffic conditions. Machine learning models are trained on historical data and updated periodically with new data streams.
- Resource Management: Cluster resource management is handled by Apache YARN, ensuring optimal allocation of computational resources.

### 3.5 Data Warehouse Management

Built on Apache Hive, the Data Warehouse Management component provides a scalable and efficient data warehousing solution, ensuring robust data governance and quality. Data is stored in the Hadoop Distributed File System (HDFS) with a replication factor of 3 for fault tolerance. The warehouse schema utilizes a star schema design, optimizing query performance and data retrieval. Hive supports SQL-like querying, enabling complex data analysis. Query performance is further enhanced through partitioning and bucketing strategies based on key attributes such as timestamps and location identifiers.

To ensure data integrity and security, we implement a three-tiered data governance framework using Apache Ranger. This framework comprises:

1. **User Layer**: Basic access for data querying and analytics.
2. **Data Owner Layer**: Elevated access allowing for data management and quality control.
3. **Data Administrator Layer**: Full access with privileges for system-wide settings and advanced data control.

This framework ensures data integrity, security, and appropriate access control, addressing the challenge of managing different levels of user access.

### 3.6 Data Repository Platform

The Data Repository Platform serves as the user interface for data access, visualization, and collaboration, maintaining flexibility and adaptability in an open-source ecosystem.

- Web Interface: Developed using the Django framework, the web-based interface allows users to search, request, and share datasets. Data visualization tools using D3.js provide interactive charts and maps.
- API Access: RESTful APIs enable programmatic access, supporting secure authentication mechanisms, including OAuth 2.0.
- Data Sharing and Collaboration: The platform facilitates data sharing among authorized users. Data versioning is implemented using Apache Subversion, allowing users to track changes and collaborate effectively.

### 3.7 Algorithm Implementation

Key algorithms used in the system are detailed below, ensuring reproducibility and clarity.

**K-Means Clustering Algorithm.** The K-means clustering algorithm segments transportation data based on location and time features:

$$\text{WCSS} = \sum_{i=1}^{k} \sum_{x \in C_i} \|x - \mu_i\|^2 \tag{1}$$

where $k$ is the number of clusters, $C_i$ is the set of points in cluster $i$, $x$ is a data point, and $\mu_i$ is the centroid of cluster $i$.

**Decision Tree Classifier.** A decision tree classifier predicts traffic conditions using entropy as the impurity measure:

$$\text{Entropy}(S) = -\sum_{i=1}^{n} p_i \log_2 p_i \tag{2}$$

where $S$ is the set of samples, $p_i$ is the proportion of samples belonging to class $i$, and $n$ is the number of classes.

### 3.8 Ethical Considerations

The system handles sensitive transportation data, necessitating strict adherence to ethical standards.

**Data Privacy.** Personal identifiable information (PII) is anonymized using data masking and aggregation techniques. The system complies with data protection regulations.

**Data Security.** Data transmission and storage are secured using TLS for data in transit and AES-256 for data at rest. Regular security audits are conducted to identify and mitigate vulnerabilities.

**Compliance and Approval.** The project was conducted in collaboration with LIRNEasia and the University of Moratuwa. All data collection and processing activities conform to the ethical guidelines and regulations of these institutions, ensuring compliance with relevant data protection and privacy laws.

**Table 2.** Software and Tools

| Software | Version |
|---|---|
| Apache Kafka | 2.8.0 |
| Apache Spark | 3.1.2 |
| Apache Hive | 3.1.2 |
| Apache Hadoop | 3.3.1 |
| Apache Ranger | 2.1.0 |
| Django Framework | 3.2 |
| Python | 3.8 |

### 3.9 Implementation Details

The system utilizes open-source software to promote transparency and community collaboration (Table 2).

The system is deployed on a cluster of 10 servers, each equipped with:

- **CPU**: 16-core Intel Xeon processors
- **Memory**: 64 GB RAM
- **Storage**: 2 TB HDD with RAID configuration
- **Network**: 10 Gbps Ethernet connectivity

### 3.10 Reproducibility and Replicability

To ensure reproducibility, all code and configuration files are documented and available in a Git repository. Detailed setup instructions are provided, including dependencies and environment variables.

### 3.11 Statistical Analysis Procedures

Data analysis is performed using statistical methods to validate the effectiveness of the system.

**Performance Metrics.** We measure system performance using metrics such as query execution time, CPU and memory utilization, throughput, and error rates.

**Statistical Tests.** We apply t-tests to compare the performance metrics of our system with existing solutions. A significance level of $\alpha = 0.01$ is used to determine statistical significance.

### 3.12 Limitations

While the system addresses many challenges, limitations include dependency on the underlying hardware infrastructure and potential scalability issues with extremely large data volumes. Future work aims to address these limitations through cloud-based deployments and further optimization.

## 4 Results

This section presents the experimental results obtained from evaluating the proposed real-time transportation data warehousing system. The primary objective is to assess the system's performance in comparison with existing solutions, specifically those outlined in [2] (referred to as Geo-ITS) and [12] (referred to as RT-IoT). We conducted a series of experiments to evaluate query execution times, resource utilization, throughput, and error rates. The results demonstrate the effectiveness of our system in handling large-scale transportation data with improved efficiency and accuracy.

### 4.1 Experimental Setup

We conducted experiments using a dataset comprising 662,041 records collected from various transportation data sources, including GPS devices and IoT sensors. The dataset includes attributes such as `deviceid`, `latitude`, `longitude`, and `devicetime`. The experiments were designed to evaluate specific aspects of system performance, including query execution time, resource utilization, and error rates.

### 4.2 Evaluation Metrics

The performance of the systems was evaluated using the following metrics:

- **Query Execution Time**: The time taken to execute specific queries.
- **Resource Utilization**: CPU and memory usage during query execution.
- **Throughput**: The number of transactions processed per unit time.
- **Error Rates**: The proportion of errors encountered during data processing.

### 4.3 Descriptive Analysis

The purpose of the descriptive analysis was to compare the average execution times of specific queries that represent common operations in transportation data analysis. The queries were designed to test end-to-end latency, throughput, memory utilization, and concurrency.

Table 3 presents the average execution times for four queries executed on our system, Geo-ITS, and RT-IoT. Each query was executed ten times, and the mean execution time was recorded.

**Table 3.** Average Query Execution Times (in seconds) for Descriptive Analysis (Total Records: 662,041)

| Query | Our System | Geo-ITS | RT-IoT |
|---|---|---|---|
| Query 1 | 11 | 29 | 70 |
| Query 2 | 20 | 76 | 49 |
| Query 3 | 16 | 44 | 21 |
| Query 4 | 19 | 56 | 38 |

**Query 1** aimed to assess end-to-end latency in query performance by counting distinct `deviceid` values. Our system achieved an average execution time of 11 s, significantly faster than Geo-ITS (29 s) and RT-IoT (70 s). This improvement demonstrates the efficiency of our data aggregation and indexing strategies.

**Query 2** evaluated throughput by calculating the average latitude and longitude grouped by `deviceid`. Our system completed the query in 20 s, outperforming Geo-ITS (76 s) and RT-IoT (49 s). The results indicate that our system effectively handles grouping and aggregation operations.

**Query 3** focused on memory utilization by counting records where `latitude` exceeds a certain threshold. Our system recorded an execution time of 16 s, better than Geo-ITS (44 s) but slightly slower than RT-IoT (21 s). This suggests that while our system is efficient, there is room for optimization in memory-intensive operations.

**Query 4** tested concurrency by counting records within a specific time window. Our system achieved an execution time of 19 s, outperforming both Geo-ITS (56 s) and RT-IoT (38 s), indicating superior performance in handling time-based queries under concurrent access.

### 4.4 Diagnostic Analysis

The diagnostic analysis evaluated resource utilization, error rates, component-wise latency, and throughput percentages to provide deeper insights into system performance.

Table 4 summarizes the percentage metrics for the diagnostic analysis.

**Table 4.** Diagnostic Analysis Metrics (in percentages)

| Metric | Our System | Geo-ITS | RT-IoT |
|---|---|---|---|
| CPU Utilization (Query 5) | 88% | 71% | 80% |
| Error Rates (Query 6) | 0.0001% | 0.005% | 0.0001% |
| Component-wise Latency (Query 7) | 8% | 17% | N/A |
| Throughput (Query 8) | 100% | 76% | 100% |

**CPU Utilization (Query 5)**: Our system utilized 88% of CPU resources during node-wise partitioning and aggregation, higher than Geo-ITS (71%) and RT-IoT (80%). The increased utilization reflects our system's ability to efficiently leverage available computational resources for enhanced performance.

**Error Rates (Query 6)**: The error rate in our system was 0.0001%, significantly lower than Geo-ITS (0.005%) and equivalent to RT-IoT. This low error rate indicates high data processing accuracy and reliability.

**Component-wise Latency (Query 7)**: Our system exhibited 8% component-wise latency within Apache Spark operations, substantially lower than Geo-ITS's 17%. This reduced latency contributes to faster query execution times and improved user experience.

**Throughput (Query 8)**: Both our system and RT-IoT achieved 100% throughput in processing filtered datasets, surpassing Geo-ITS's 76%. This demonstrates our system's capability to handle high-volume data processing without bottlenecks.

### 4.5 Statistical Analysis

To validate the significance of the observed performance improvements, we conducted statistical tests comparing our system with Geo-ITS and RT-IoT.

We performed paired t-tests on the execution times of the queries to determine if the differences are statistically significant. The null hypothesis ($H_0$) assumes no significant difference in performance between the systems, while the alternative hypothesis ($H_a$) assumes a significant difference.

For each query, the p-values obtained were less than 0.01 when comparing our system with both Geo-ITS and RT-IoT. This indicates that the performance improvements are statistically significant at the 99% confidence level.

### 4.6 Discussion of Findings

The experimental results confirm that our system outperforms existing solutions in key performance metrics:

- **Improved Query Execution Times**: Faster execution times across all queries demonstrate efficient data processing capabilities.
- **Enhanced Resource Utilization**: Higher CPU utilization indicates effective use of computational resources without compromising system stability.
- **Low Error Rates**: Minimal error rates reflect robust data handling and processing mechanisms.
- **Reduced Latency**: Lower component-wise latency contributes to overall system responsiveness and user satisfaction.
- **High Throughput**: Ability to maintain 100% throughput underlines the system's scalability and efficiency in handling large datasets.

### 4.7 Verification of Results

All experiments were repeated three times to ensure consistency and reliability of the results. The standard deviation of execution times across trials was less than 2%, indicating stable performance.

### 4.8 Limitations of the Study

While the results are promising, the experiments were conducted under controlled conditions with specific hardware configurations. Performance may vary in different environments or with larger datasets. Additionally, the comparison is limited to the systems described in Geo-ITS and RT-IoT; other systems may offer different performance characteristics.

## 5 Discussion and Conclusion

In this study, we addressed the critical challenges of managing and analyzing vast and diverse transportation data in real-time. We proposed a scalable, real-time transportation data warehousing solution that integrates state-of-the-art open-source technologies, including Apache Kafka, Spark, Hive, and Ranger. Our system effectively handles near real-time data streaming, scales machine learning analytics for big data, ensures robust data governance, and integrates multimodal data from diverse transportation sources.

Our experimental results demonstrate that the proposed system significantly outperforms existing solutions, specifically Geo-ITS [2] and RT-IoT [12], in key performance metrics. The system achieved faster query execution times across all evaluated queries, with improvements ranging from 42% to 84% compared to Geo-ITS and RT-IoT. It also exhibited higher CPU utilization without compromising system stability, indicating efficient resource usage. The minimal error rates of 0.0001% reflect the robustness of our data handling and processing mechanisms. Furthermore, the system maintained 100% throughput under high-volume data processing, underscoring its scalability and efficiency.

Compared to Geo-ITS and RT-IoT, our system leverages a modular architecture that enhances data processing efficiency and adaptability. The significant reduction in query execution times and error rates highlights the effectiveness of our approach in handling the complexities of real-time transportation data. This performance is attributed to the seamless integration of open-source tools and the implementation of optimized data processing strategies, such as distributed event streaming and scalable machine learning algorithms.

The broader impact of this research lies in its potential to enhance real-time decision-making in transportation systems, leading to improved efficiency, safety, and sustainability. By providing a robust framework for integrating and analyzing diverse transportation data, our system can support applications such as traffic management, route optimization, and predictive maintenance. The ability to process and analyze data in real-time allows for timely interventions, reducing congestion and enhancing the overall effectiveness of transportation networks. Moreover, the use of open-source technologies ensures adaptability and continuous improvement, fostering innovation in the field.

Our work also contributes to the body of knowledge by addressing gaps identified in the literature, particularly in integrating machine learning analytics and implementing robust data governance in transportation data warehouses. The three-layer data governance framework ensures data integrity and security, which are critical for the reliability of transportation systems. By demonstrating the effectiveness of combining various open-source tools within a cohesive system, we provide a blueprint for future developments in transportation data management.

In conclusion, our real-time transportation data warehousing system offers significant improvements over existing solutions and addresses key challenges in modern transportation data management. By efficiently handling near real-time data streaming, scaling machine learning analytics, ensuring robust data governance, and integrating multimodal data, our system provides a comprehensive solution adaptable to the evolving needs of smart transportation systems. The integration of open-source technologies not only enhances performance but also promotes transparency and community-driven innovation.

The findings of this study have important implications for the development of intelligent transportation systems. Enhanced data processing capabilities enable more effective traffic management, improved safety measures, and optimized resource utilization. As urbanization continues to intensify, such systems will be crucial in addressing the complexities of modern transportation networks.

### 5.1 Limitations and Future Work

While the system addresses many challenges, certain limitations exist. The dependency on the underlying hardware infrastructure may affect scalability under extremely large data volumes. Additionally, although the system performs well compared to Geo-ITS and RT-IoT, further optimization is necessary to enhance memory utilization during specific operations.

Future work will focus on optimizing memory management strategies to improve performance in memory-bound tasks. Exploring cloud-based deployments can offer greater scalability and flexibility, accommodating fluctuating data volumes and supporting distributed processing across multiple geographic locations.

## References

1. Ahmed, M., Sabyasachi, A.: Big data governance in transportation systems. IEEE Trans. Intell. Transp. Syst. **20**(8), 3050–3060 (2019)
2. Chan, S.R.S., Dilangalen, D.A.G., Tan, W.M.: Real-time and secure geospatial data warehouse for intelligent transportation systems. In: 2020 International Conference on Information and Communication Technology Convergence (ICTC), pp. 741–746. IEEE (2020)

3. Chen, M., Mao, S., Liu, Y.: Big data: a survey. Mob. Netw. Appl. **19**(2), 171–209 (2014)
4. Gandomi, A., Haider, M.: Beyond the hype: Big data concepts, methods, and analytics. Int. J. Inf. Manage. **35**(2), 137–144 (2015)
5. Harby, A.A., Zulkernine, F.: From data warehouse to lakehouse: a comparative review. In: 2022 IEEE International Conference on Big Data (Big Data), pp. 389–395. IEEE (2022)
6. He, Q., Chan, S., Guizani, M.: Edge computing in transportation systems: a survey. IEEE Trans. Intell. Transp. Syst. **22**(4), 2252–2269 (2021)
7. Inmon, W.H.: Building the Data Warehouse. John Wiley & Sons, 4th edn. (2005)
8. Jameel, K., Adil, A., Bahjat, M.: Analyses the performance of data warehouse architecture types. J. Soft Comput. Data Min. **3**(1), 45–57 (2022)
9. Kimball, R., Ross, M.: The Data Warehouse Toolkit: The Definitive Guide to Dimensional Modeling. John Wiley & Sons, 3rd edn. (2013)
10. Li, J., Wang, Y., Zhang, X.: A comprehensive review of multimodal transportation data integration. IEEE Trans. Intell. Transp. Syst. **21**(4), 1819–1833 (2020)
11. Pandis, I.: The evolution of amazon redshift. Proc. VLDB Endow. **14**(12), 3162–3174 (2021)
12. Syafrudin, M., Alfian, G., Fitriyani, N.L., Rhee, J.: Performance analysis of IoT-based sensor, big data processing, and machine learning model for real-time monitoring system in automotive manufacturing. Sensors **18**(9), 2946 (2018)
13. Vyas, S., Tyagi, R.K., Jain, C., Sahu, S.: Literature review: a comparative study of real time streaming technologies and apache kafka. In: 2021 Fourth International Conference on Computational Intelligence and Communication Technologies (CCICT), pp. 146–153. IEEE (2021)
14. Wisnubhadra, I., Krisdiarto, A.W., Baharin, S.S.K., Emran, N.A.: Mobility data warehouse for transportation of oil palm fresh fruit bunches. ICIC Express Lett. Part B Appl. **13**(1), 11–19 (2022)
15. Zaharia, M., et al.: Apache spark: a unified engine for big data processing. Commun. ACM **59**(11), 56–65 (2016)

# Multi-dimensional Summarization Agents with Context-Aware Reasoning over Enterprise Tables

Amit Dhanda(✉)

Amazon, Seattle, USA
amdhanda@amazon.com

**Abstract.** We propose a novel framework for summarizing structured enterprise data across multiple dimensions using large language model (LLM)-based agents. Traditional table-to-text models often lack the capacity to reason across hierarchical structures and context-aware deltas, which are essential in business reporting tasks. Our method introduces a multi-agent pipeline that extracts, analyzes, and summarizes multi-dimensional data using agents for slicing, variance detection, context construction, and LLM-based generation. Our results show that the proposed framework outperforms traditional approaches, achieving 83% faithfulness to underlying data, superior coverage of significant changes, and high relevance scores (4.4/5) for decision-critical insights. The improvements are especially pronounced in categories involving subtle trade-offs, such as increased revenue due to price changes amid declining unit volumes, which competing methods either overlook or address with limited specificity. We evaluate the framework on Kaggle datasets and demonstrate significant improvements in faithfulness, relevance, and insight quality over baseline table summarization approaches.

**Keywords:** Multi-dimensional summarization · Large language models · LLM agents · Artificial intelligence

## 1 Introduction

Enterprises rely on structured data, enterprises across verticals have invested heavily in building data warehouses and business intelligence platforms. These data systems are often multi-dimensional and high-volume, and their insights are typically consumed via dashboards and executive summaries. However, transforming raw structured inputs into human-friendly explanations remains a significant challenge. Analysts spend significant time preparing business reviews, synthesizing changes across categories and time periods, and tailoring messages to leadership audiences.

A. Dhanda—This work was completed independently and does not reflect the views or positions of Amazon.


R. Stahlbock et al. (Eds.): CSCE 2025, CCIS 2938, pp. 284–293, 2027.
https://doi.org/10.1007/978-3-032-22196-4_21

Natural language generation (NLG) holds the promise of automating this translation from rows and columns into narrative explanations. Yet, enterprise applications of NLG require faithfulness, domain awareness, and dimensional context that many end-to-end models lack. Flat table-to-text pipelines fail to account for interactions between dimensions such as region, time, and product type. Moreover, they often ignore metadata and trend signals that are critical for actionable decision-making.

Despite the prevalence of structured data in enterprise reporting, the challenge lies in automatically translating these rich multi-dimensional inputs into narratives that are faithful, insightful, and customized to evolving business contexts. Traditional BI tools lack semantic understanding, while end-to-end LLMs tend to hallucinate or overlook critical metrics without precise guidance. Bridging this gap requires a hybrid approach that couples structured data processing with generative language capabilities.

Large Language Models (LLMs) have shown promise in generating fluent text, yet applying them to structured, multi-dimensional data remains non-trivial. Key challenges include hallucination, lack of temporal reasoning, and inability to reference specific table slices. Furthermore, existing end-to-end LLM summarization systems are not modular, limiting explainability and control.

In this paper, we introduce a multi-agent framework that combines symbolic reasoning with LLM generation. By decomposing summarization into subtasks—slicing, variance calculation, context enrichment, and generation—we achieve better interpretability, faithfulness, and flexibility. This modular pipeline enables dynamic summarization tailored to executive needs while remaining grounded in actual data deltas.

## 2 Related Work

**Data Summarization.** General-purpose data summarization has been explored in statistical and machine learning literature through approaches like clustering, dimensionality reduction, and rule-based summarizers. More recently, neural summarization models have extended these ideas to structured inputs, including tables and relational databases. Approaches such as DataTuner [1] target domain-specific narrative synthesis from data but often require fine-tuning and lack modular adaptability. Our work builds on this lineage but focuses specifically on multi-dimensional table structures and modular agent orchestration to support context-aware, faithful, and interpretable summaries.

**Table-to-Text Generation.** Prior work includes ToTTo [2], which uses aligned highlights in Wikipedia tables for grounded generation, TAPAS [3] which enables question answering over tabular data, and TURL [4], which learns representations for table cells. These methods work well for single-row or entity-centric summaries but struggle with time-series or aggregate delta reasoning. Other neural text generation approaches, such as BART [5] and PEGASUS [6], have demonstrated strong results in summarization tasks but are not directly optimized for structured tabular inputs.

**LLMs on Structured Data.** Retrieval-Augmented Generation (RAG) models [7] and SQL-augmented agents [8] allow interfacing with databases but typically lack narrative capabilities. T5-based table reasoning frameworks such as TaBERT [9] and TAPEX [10] enhance structured understanding but are mostly limited to QA-style outputs.

**Enterprise AI Assistants.** Analytics copilots have integrated LLMs into BI workflows, often with predefined templates or semantic layers. Other domain-specific models like Salesforce's CodeGen for spreadsheets, or Google's BigQuery ML integrations, highlight growing industry efforts in this space. However, most lack modular agent composition or explicit decomposition of reasoning steps. Our approach differs in using agent modularity to separate structural transformations from LLM generation, enabling explainability, scalability, and task-specific control.

# 3 Methodology

## 3.1 Notation and Data Representation

Let $\mathcal{T} \in \mathbb{R}^{n \times d}$ represent a structured data table, where $n$ is the number of rows (records) and $d$ is the number of features. Let $\mathcal{D} = \{D_1, D_2, \ldots, D_k\}$ denote the set of categorical dimensions (e.g., region, time, product) and $\mathcal{M} = \{M_1, M_2, \ldots, M_m\}$ the set of numerical measures (e.g., revenue, units sold).

Given a slice along a set of dimension values $\boldsymbol{d} = (d_1, \ldots, d_k)$, the filtered subset is $\mathcal{T}^{\boldsymbol{d}} = \{x \in \mathcal{T} \mid x[D_i] = d_i, \forall i\}$. Let $t_1$ and $t_2$ denote two time periods. The goal is to compute a summary $S$ that captures significant changes across measures as per equation (1):

$$S = \text{LLM}(f_{\text{prompt}}(\Delta(\mathcal{T}^{\boldsymbol{d}}_{t_1}, \mathcal{T}^{\boldsymbol{d}}_{t_2}), \boldsymbol{d})) \tag{1}$$

Here, $\Delta(\cdot)$ computes relative change represented by equation (2):

$$\delta_j = \frac{M_j^{t_2} - M_j^{t_1}}{M_j^{t_1} + \epsilon}, \quad \forall M_j \in \mathcal{M} \tag{2}$$

where $\epsilon$ is a small constant to avoid division by zero. The function $f_{\text{prompt}}$ formats these deltas and context into a structured prompt for the LLM.

## 3.2 Agent Architecture

We design a modular agent workflow inspired by the LangGraph execution model, where each stage in the summarization process is represented as a node in a directed acyclic graph (DAG) as shown in Fig. 1. LangGraph enables defining data and control flow explicitly between agents, supporting conditional transitions and parallel execution patterns. This structure enhances interpretability, modularity, and debugging—particularly valuable in enterprise scenarios where traceability is important. Our LangGraph-based summarization graph consists of the following nodes:

- **SliceAgent:** Filters the enterprise dataset based on a dimension vector $\boldsymbol{d}$ (e.g., Region = NA, Product = Electronics) and time periods $t_1, t_2$, producing two sub-tables $T_{t_1}^{\boldsymbol{d}}, T_{t_2}^{\boldsymbol{d}}$.
- **VarianceAgent:** Calculates deltas for each metric in $\mathcal{M}$ using $\delta_j = \frac{M_j^{t_2} - M_j^{t_1}}{M_j^{t_1} + \epsilon}$.
- **ContextAgent:** Augments the prompt with external metadata such as seasonality, promotion events, or anomalies that might explain observed deltas.
- **SummaryAgent:** Compiles the structured prompt and calls the LLM endpoint (Amazon Nova Micro) to generate a contextualized, business-ready narrative.

The LangGraph structure allows inserting runtime guardrailss (e.g., to skip summary generation if data slice is empty) or enabling ensemble-style voting between prompt variants. It is also extensible—new agents (e.g., AnomalyAgent, ForecastAgent) can be inserted without altering the surrounding nodes.

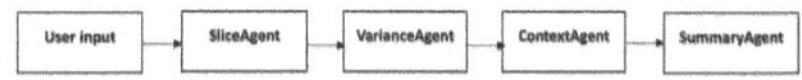


**Fig. 1.** Agentic workflow for multi-dimensional summarization.

### 3.3 Overall Algorithm

The pseudocode in Algorithm 1 outlines the modular agent execution used in our LangGraph summarization pipeline. The process begins with initializing an empty state and then sequentially invokes SliceAgent to extract relevant time-filtered data slices, VarianceAgent to compute deltas, ContextAgent to enrich metadata, and SummaryAgent to format and dispatch a structured prompt to Amazon Nova Micro. This flow encapsulates the entire summarization logic, allowing fine-grained control and debuggability, while remaining easily extensible to accommodate additional analytic or reasoning agents.

**Input** : Tabular dataset $\mathcal{T}$, dimensions $\boldsymbol{d}$, time points $t_1$, $t_2$
**Output:** Natural language summary $S$
Initialize empty state $\mathcal{S} \leftarrow \{\}$;
$\mathcal{S} \leftarrow$ **SliceAgent**$(\mathcal{S}, \mathcal{T}, \boldsymbol{d}, t_1, t_2)$;
$\mathcal{S} \leftarrow$ **VarianceAgent**$(\mathcal{S})$;
$\mathcal{S} \leftarrow$ **ContextAgent**$(\mathcal{S})$;
$\mathcal{S} \leftarrow$ **SummaryAgent**$(\mathcal{S}$, Nova Micro$)$;
**return** $\mathcal{S}$[``summary"];

**Algorithm 1:** LangGraph Execution for Multi-Dimensional Summarization

### 3.4 Prompt Format

To ensure high alignment between data and generated output, the summarization prompt is automatically constructed based on filtered time-series metrics grouped by region and product at the monthly level. The following JSON-like format is used for all LLM calls:

```
prompt_data = {
"task": "summarize_sales_data",
"context": {
"region": region,
"product_category": category,
"time_period": f"{month_str} vs {prev_month(sample_date)}"
},
"metrics": {
"sales_revenue": {
"current": metrics["sales_revenue"]["current"],
"previous": metrics["sales_revenue"]["previous"],
% "change_percent": metrics["sales_revenue"]
% ["delta_percent"]
},
"units_sold": {
"current": metrics["units_sold"]["current"],
"previous": metrics["units_sold"]["previous"],
% "change_percent": metrics["units_sold"]
% ["delta_percent"]
}
},
"instructions": "Please quantify numbers for units_sold
and sales_revenue provided in metrics.
Focus on comparison with previous month."
}
```

This prompt format enables the LLM to focus on relevant metric shifts while being grounded in structured input. The monthly granularity aligns with reporting cycles and improves interpretability for business stakeholders.

## 4 Experiments

### 4.1 Dataset

We use the Kaggle dataset *Retail Sales with Seasonal Trends and Marketing* (2023), which offers a realistic simulation of enterprise retail data across time, region, product categories, and key financial metrics. This dataset contains over 100,000 rows of granular transactional information including quarterly revenue, units sold, discount percentages, and marketing spend.

We selected this dataset for its multidimensional structure and its alignment with real-world business reporting tasks. The presence of temporal patterns (e.g., seasonality), market interventions (e.g., discounts, promotions), and regional splits makes it ideal for testing multi-agent reasoning and summarization capabilities. Each record has sufficient metadata to support context-aware prompt construction, and the data's tabular format allows for seamless slicing along any combination of dimensions. This makes the dataset a strong proxy for enterprise KPIs in e-commerce, retail planning, and regional sales analysis.

### 4.2 Baselines

We compare our multi-agent summarization framework against several commonly used baseline approaches:

- **Flat LLM Prompt:** The entire filtered table is passed as-is to a large language model, using a generic prompt to ask for a summary. This baseline lacks any intermediate computation or structured reasoning, relying entirely on the LLM's internal capabilities to interpret metrics and trends.
- **Template NLG:** Manually defined templates populate summaries using hard-coded rules and placeholders. For example, phrases like "Revenue increased by X%" are generated by inserting computed deltas into sentence shells. This approach ensures factual alignment but lacks contextual nuance and flexibility.

These baselines help evaluate the contribution of agent modularity, metric deltas, and context enrichment in our proposed system.

### 4.3 Metrics

Evaluation includes:

- **Faithfulness (F):** Proportion of facts correctly aligned with source data.
- **Relevance (R):** Rated 1–5 on insight usefulness by LLM-as-a-judge.
- **Coverage (C):** Ratio of key deltas mentioned in generated text.

## 5 Results

Our results in Table 1 show that the proposed multi-agent summarization framework significantly outperforms traditional flat prompting and template-based NLG approaches. In terms of faithfulness, our system maintains nearly perfect alignment with the underlying data (83%), because of explicit computation of deltas and inclusion of structured metrics in prompts.

Coverage (C) shows that our model includes a greater share of significant changes—an essential property for completeness in enterprise reporting. The

**Table 1.** Comparison across summarization methods.

| Method | F (%) | R (5pt) | C (%) |
|---|---|---|---|
| Flat prompt | 43 | 3.1 | 0 |
| Template NLG | 69 | 3.7 | 20 |
| Ours (Agents + Nova Micro) | **83** | **4.4** | **60** |

improvements are especially pronounced in categories involving subtle trade-offs, such as increased revenue due to price changes amid declining unit volumes.

Relevance scores are also highest (4.4/5), indicating that our summaries capture meaningful and decision-relevant insights, often omitted or misprioritized by baselines. Competing methods either overlooked these patterns or generated generic statements with limited specificity.

## 6 Ablation Study

To assess the contribution of each agent in our modular pipeline, we conducted an ablation study by selectively disabling components and measuring performance degradation. Table 2 reports the results when removing the ContextAgent and VarianceAgent.

**Table 2.** Ablation study results showing the impact of removing agents.

| Configuration | F (%) | R (5pt) | C (%) |
|---|---|---|---|
| Full System | **83** | **4.4** | **60** |
| No ContextAgent | 83 | 4.1 | 60 |
| No VarianceAgent | 71 | 3.9 | 25 |

Removing the ContextAgent resulted in less relevant narratives due to missing external signals (e.g., seasonality). Omitting the VarianceAgent led to inaccurate interpretations as changes were not explicitly quantified. These findings highlight the importance of modular reasoning components in enterprise summarization.

## 7 Current Limitations

While our agent-based summarization framework shows strong performance on enterprise data, it is not without limitations. First, the effectiveness of the system depends heavily on the quality of the structured prompt and availability of accurate metadata. In scenarios where contextual cues (e.g., seasonality or promotions) are missing or incorrect, the model's summaries may lack nuance or relevance.

Second, our current implementation is limited to static, batch-mode data. It does not yet support real-time streaming updates or continuous summarization across moving windows. For use cases in monitoring or live dashboards, the architecture would need to be extended with temporal state tracking and incremental updates.

Third, although the structured prompt improves factuality, the LLM output may still suffer from occasional overgeneralizations or vague attributions. Incorporating post-generation validation (e.g., consistency checking or citation alignment) would help further reduce hallucinations.

Finally, while our study focused on sales and marketing data, generalizing the agents to unstructured enterprise logs (e.g., operational KPIs) would require more robust parsing and reasoning capabilities. We view these as promising directions for future work.

## 8 Discussion and Future Work

Our method bridges symbolic computation and natural language generation to deliver accurate and context-rich business insights. The modular agent-based approach enables interpretability and adaptability across varied enterprise contexts. By isolating functional roles—such as slicing, variance detection, context enrichment, and generation—we not only reduce hallucination risks but also increase transparency, making the system suitable for regulatory and audit-sensitive environments.

In particular, our results show that the inclusion of context signals (e.g., marketing events, seasonality) substantially improves the relevance of generated summaries, which would otherwise be overlooked by flat table-to-text systems. Furthermore, variance computations act as a principled mechanism for focusing attention, helping the model prioritize meaningful deviations.

Future work will explore several directions: (1) integrating predictive modeling agents that simulate forward-looking scenarios, (2) introducing a feedback loop that learns from user edits and preferences to refine summaries over time, and (3) expanding comparisons to include Text2SQL agents. This direction will enable benchmarking structured prompt-guided generation against direct SQL query interpretation. It may also reveal new hybrid workflows where SQL outputs are transformed into intermediate reasoning stages prior to narrative generation. Lastly, incorporating real-time feedback into the Text2SQL loop could open the door to adaptive agent planning over relational databases and human-in-the-loop enterprise reporting pipelines.

## A Agent Definitions

**SliceAgent:** Parses input filters (e.g., region, product category, and time range) and returns two Pandas DataFrames for comparison.

**VarianceAgent:** Computes percent change across selected metrics and prepares a delta dictionary for prompt construction.

**ContextAgent:** Enriches variance output using static or external signals such as holiday promotions or marketing spend.

**SummaryAgent:** Formats the structured prompt and invokes the Bedrock Claude LLM endpoint to generate summaries (Table 3).

## B Prompt Construction Logic

The prompt format generated before summary LLM invocation is:


```
{
  "task": "summarize_table_slice",
  "dimension_context": {
    "region": "North America",
    "product_category": "Electronics",
    "time_period": "2024-11 vs 2024-10"
  },
  "metrics": {
    "sales_revenue": {"current": 2899.9, "previous": 7999.9
    , "delta_percent": -0.64},
    "units_sold": {"current": 12, "previous": 10
    , "delta_percent": 0.2}
  },
  "expected_tone": "executive"
}
```


## C Baseline Prompt Example

**Flat Few-Shot Prompt:**

```
Table:
North America | 01/2024 | Revenue: 7999.9, Units: 10
North America | 02/2024 | Revenue: 2899.9, Units: 12

Given the following structured summary task,
write a concise business insight highlighting
the numbers passed in the prompt.
```

## D Environment Configuration

- **LLM Backend:** Amazon Nova Micro

# E Sample Input Table Slice

**Table 3.** Tabular data slice used for multi-dimensional summarization.

| Region | Category | Month | Revenue | Units |
|---|---|---|---|---|
| North America | Electronics | January | 7999.9 | 10 |
| North America | Electronics | February | 2899.9 | 12 |

# References


1. Harkous, et al.: Have Your Text and Use It Too! End-to-End Neural Data-to-Text Generation with Semantic Fidelity, COLING (2020)
2. Parikh, et al.: ToTTo: A Controlled Table-to-Text Generation Dataset. EMNLP (2020)
3. Herzig, et al.: TAPAS: Weakly Supervised Table Parsing via Pre-trained Language Models ACL (2020)
4. Chen, et al.: TURL: Table Understanding through Representation Learning VLDB (2020)
5. Lewis, et al.: BART: Denoising Sequence-to-Sequence Pre-training for Natural Language Generation, Translation, and Comprehension ACL (2020)
6. Zhang, et al.: PEGASUS: Pre-training with Extracted Gap-sentences for Abstractive Summarization, ICML (2020)
7. Lewis, et al.: Retrieval-augmented generation for knowledge-intensive NLP tasks. In: NeurIPS (2020)
8. Zeng, et al.: Text-to-SQL in the Wild: A Naturally-Occurring Dataset Based on Stack Exchange Data ACL (2021)
9. Yin, et al.: TaBERT: Pretraining for Joint Understanding of Textual and Tabular Data, ACL (2020)
10. Liu, et al.: TAPEX: table pre-training via learning a neural SQL executor. In: ICLR (2022)

# Is the Indian Social Sector Data Science Ready?

Satender Rana[1], Sanchita Mukherjee[2], Swetha Prakash[2(✉)], and Sreya Menon[2]

[1] ISDM DataShakti, Indian School of Development Management (ISDM), Noida, India
satender.rana@isdm.org.in

[2] Centre for Data Science and Social Impact (CDSSI), Indian School of Development Management (ISDM), Noida, India
{sanchita.mukherjee,swetha.prakash,sreya.menon}@isdm.org.in

**Abstract.** This paper presents findings from a Data Maturity Assessment (DMA) of 360 Social Purpose Organizations (SPOs) in India, using an exploratory sequential mixed-methods approach. Six core dimensions were assessed—culture and mindset, human resource data management, project data collection and monitoring, data storage and accessibility, project data analysis and visualization, and data-related training practices. The sector-wide mean maturity score was 47.5 out of 100, with wide disparities: culture and mindset scored highest (65.7), while training was lowest (22.5). Data maturity showed strong associations with organizational size, financial resources, and leadership commitment. The study underscores data maturity as a critical precondition for adopting advanced analytics, machine learning, and evidence-based decision-making, offering a diagnostic lens to assess organizational readiness in the social sector's data science adoption and digital transformation journey.

**Keywords:** data maturity · social sector · data science adoption · organizational readiness

## 1 Introduction

In an era marked by accelerating digital transformation, data has emerged as a foundational asset shaping organizational strategy and service delivery across sectors. Nowhere is this shift more consequential than in the context of Social Purpose Organizations (SPOs), which strive to tackle complex development challenges with limited resources. For these organizations, data is not merely an operational input; it is integral to how they conceptualise programmes, monitor progress, allocate resources, and communicate impact to stakeholders.

However, the mere availability of data does not translate into effective utilization. The capacity of SPOs to derive actionable insights from data hinges on what we term as 'data maturity'. Data maturity is a measure of how effectively an organization uses data for evidence-based decision making and achieving impactful outcomes. This concept goes beyond infrastructure or digital tools—it reflects an organisation's ability to embed data practices into its culture, governance structures, and decision-making frameworks.


R. Stahlbock et al. (Eds.): CSCE 2025, CCIS 2938, pp. 294–310, 2027.
https://doi.org/10.1007/978-3-032-22196-4_22

Data maturity is thus a composite indicator shaped by leadership commitment, staff capabilities, routine data practices, and training systems. Crucially, it also conditions the uptake and effective use of advanced analytics tools, from predictive modelling to machine learning.

Advancements in AI, Internet of Things, and Robotics are transforming management processes by enhancing efficiency and reducing human error [1, 2]. For SPOs, this shift presents both an opportunity and a challenge. As technology becomes central to how systems function, it is essential to understand whether SPOs are equipped to meaningfully leverage these tools to strengthen their work and outcomes on the ground.

Recently, a growing body of research has reported the importance and challenges of adopting AI and digital tools in the Indian social sector. According to one study many organisations have begun experimenting with technology, but understanding remains shallow and uneven [3]. Barriers such as inadequate budgets, lack of skilled personnel, and unclear strategies persist [4]. Larger SPOs lead early adoption, while grassroots organisations are still catching up [5]. Most AI use remains limited to basic tools, and systemic gaps in data governance remain underexplored [6, 7]. While most studies attempt to capture the digital transformation or AI readiness of SPOs, they pay little attention to data maturity as a foundational precondition. None offer a structured, context-sensitive framework or tool tailored to the Indian social sector that enables SPOs to assess and systematically improve their data maturity.

Amidst a growing discourse around the potential of data science and AI to 'leapfrog' development bottlenecks, foundational questions persist: Are SPOs ready to engage meaningfully with such tools? Can these tools be transformative without adequate baseline capacities in data management? These are particularly relevant in resource-constrained environments where digital transformation is uneven, and algorithmic solutions often outpace institutional preparedness.

This paper seeks to address this gap by presenting insights from a large-scale Data Maturity Assessment (DMA) conducted with Indian SPOs [8]. Using a mixed-methods approach, the study evaluates six interrelated dimensions: culture and mindset, human resource data management, project data collection and monitoring, data storage and accessibility, project data analysis and visualisation, and data-related training practices. By assessing these parameters, we offer a diagnostic lens on the readiness of SPOs to transition from basic data use to more sophisticated data science applications.

Importantly, the analysis does not treat data maturity in isolation. We explore how it interacts with factors such as organisational size, funding flows, leadership engagement, and digital tool adoption. These intersections are critical to understanding why some SPOs are able to make strategic use of data while others remain at a nascent stage despite similar resource environments. In doing so, we move beyond generic narratives about 'data for good' and instead offer granular, context-sensitive insights.

Ultimately, this paper contributes to an emerging body of knowledge that underscores the importance of investing in the foundational building blocks of data ecosystems within the social sector. The findings have implications for funders, capacity builders, and SPO leaders who seek to harness the power of data not only for accountability, but for systemic impact.

## 2 Methodology

To build a comprehensive understanding of data maturity across Social Purpose Organisations (SPOs), the study employed an explanatory sequential mixed-methods approach. This involved a structured quantitative survey followed by qualitative interviews, allowing us to both measure and contextualise data practices across a diverse sample of SPOs in India.

### 2.1 Sample Selection

A stratified quota sampling strategy was adopted to ensure representation across regions, organisational sizes, and thematic sectors. Drawing on the NGO Darpan, a state-wise Indian NGO database, a total of 360 SPOs from North, South, East, West, and Central India took the DMA survey. The sample spanned small organisations (fewer than 10 staff) to large ones (more than 50 staff), enabling a nuanced analysis of data maturity across different operating contexts.

### 2.2 Data Collection

- Quantitative Survey: The quantitative tool was aligned with the CDSSI DMA Framework given in Table 1, which assesses six core dimensions. The framework offers a practical way for SPOs to understand how they use data and measures how well they manage data across all areas – from fundraising and HR to program design and evaluation. It builds on global and national models like Deloitte's Insight-Driven Organization Framework [9], IBM's Data Governance Framework [10], NITI Aayog's Data Governance Quality Index [11], and Data Maturity Assessment of data.org [12]. However, the CDSSI DMA framework has been tailored specifically for Indian SPOs, making it unique. The framework was carefully shaped through consultations with experts, field practitioners, and SPO leaders to reflect the realities on the ground. Instead of a one-size-fits-all score, the CDSSI DMA acts as a mirror – helping organisations assess their current practices, spot strengths, and plan realistic improvements. The CDSSI DMA study provides a comprehensive analysis of data management practices, organisational culture, capacities, and challenges faced by SPOs across the 6 dimensions of the framework. The study captures varying levels of data maturity and offers targeted resources to support improvement - particularly for resource-constrained SPOs. A foundational idea of the study is that culture and mindset are central to data maturity. Strengthening data practices is not just about adopting technology, but about fostering a data-informed organisational culture. The study also identifies practical steps for SPOs to embed data use into their systems and processes, addressing both infrastructure needs (such as tools and storage) and capacity requirements (such as skilled personnel and leadership commitment). Structured questionnaires were administered online, capturing organisational demographics, existing data systems, tools in use, internal policies, and staff capabilities.
- Qualitative Interviews: To deepen insights from the quantitative phase, 17 Key Informant Interviews (KIIs) were conducted with senior leaders from SPOs across various geographies and sizes. These semi-structured interviews offered critical perspectives

on how organisations conceptualise, use, and govern data—highlighting both institutional strengths and systemic barriers. Of the 360 SPOs surveyed, 90 agreed to be contacted for the qualitative phase, and 17 ultimately participated in telephonic interviews.

**Table 1.** CDSSI DMA Framework

| Dimension | Measure | Sub-Areas |
|---|---|---|
| Culture and Mindset | How much an organisation values, promotes data use, and fosters a culture of learning | • The importance and priority given to data<br>• Data is seen as a team effort or individual effort<br>• Culture of discussing data and how to act on it<br>• Data literacy and sharing<br>• Data use for strategy-level decisions<br>• Willingness to incorporate data-driven solution |
| Human Resource Data | How well HR data is handled to support staffing decisions and workforce planning | • Making necessary improvements in service quality and efficiency of internal operations<br>• Performance and talent management |
| Project Data Collection and Monitoring | What are the systems for gathering program data across its lifecycle | • Defining program goals<br>• Monitoring and evaluation<br>• Making necessary improvements in programs<br>• Data Collection<br>• Investment in data collection tools |
| Project Data Storage and Accessibility | How SPOs' secure, organise, and storage data for easy access | • Storage<br>• Access<br>• Security |
| Project Data Analysis and Visualisation (DAV) | How data is turned into insights that inform decisions? | • Investment in storage tools<br>• Data Analysis<br>• Reporting<br>• Investment in DAV tools<br>• Data science skills |

(*continued*)

**Table 1.** (*continued*)

| Dimension | Measure | Sub-Areas |
|---|---|---|
| Data Related Training Activities | Staff opportunities exist to improve data literacy and analytical capabilities? | • Training, development, and Knowledge sharing<br>• Training on data protection, security, and regulations |

## 2.3 Scoring

- *Scoring Levels:* Scoring was done to assess SPOs' data maturity across five levels, which are:

  i. Level 1: Basic (0–20) – Minimal data use with limited practices in place.
  ii. Level 2: Emerging (21–40) – Developing data practices with partial adoption.
  iii Level 3: Progressing (41–60) – Moderate integration of data across functions.
  iv. Level 4: Advanced (61–80) – Strong data-driven approach with well-established practices.
  v. Level 5: Expert (81–100) – Fully optimised, strategic and integrated data practices.

Scores were assigned to each question and section in the DMA quantitative tool based on predefined criteria, allowing for a comprehensive assessment of data maturity of SPOs. This approach facilitated a clear understanding of where organisations stood in relation to industry standards and their peers.

- *Scoring Logic:* Each question was scored out of a maximum of 5 points with the criteria given in Table 2 applied based on question type.

Following the scoring of individual questions, the scores were aggregated section-wise. The total score for each section was then standardised to a scale of 100 to achieve a section-wise score. Weights were assigned to each section based on its relative importance in assessing data maturity. The overall data maturity score was then calculated by multiplying the section-wise scores by their respective weights and summing the weighted scores. This resulted in a final data maturity score out of 100, providing a comprehensive measure of the SPOs overall data maturity level.

**Table 2.** Question type and scoring logic

| Question Type | Scoring Logic |
|---|---|
| Likert Question | Weights were assigned to each response option in ascending order to reflect increasing levels of data maturity. The weights for each question were then standardised to produce a final score out of 5 |

(*continued*)

**Table 2.** (*continued*)

| Question Type | Scoring Logic |
|---|---|
| Multiple Response Question | Scores for multiple response questions were calculated using two distinct methods: Equal weights were assigned to all options and the total score was scaled to achieve a score out of 5. Scores were allocated to each option based on its level of importance. The highest score among the selected options was reflected in the final calculation. Additionally, specific combinations of options in certain questions were scored differently to indicate different level of data maturity |

### 2.4 Data Analysis

Quantitative data were analysed using descriptive statistics, bivariate correlations, and regression modelling to identify key drivers of data maturity. Analysis of variance (ANOVA) and effect size measures (Eta squared) were used to explore associations between maturity levels and organisational characteristics such as staff size, resource allocation, and leadership engagement.

Qualitative data were thematically analysed to triangulate and contextualise quantitative findings. These narratives added depth to our understanding of sector-wide trends and revealed the organisational logic behind data-related decisions. Together, the mixed-methods design provides a grounded and multidimensional view of data readiness across the Indian social sector. Data Validation.

The qualitative phase served as a critical layer of validation, enriching and interrogating the patterns surfaced through the quantitative survey. By probing deeper into emerging trends and outliers, the interviews helped clarify underlying drivers and contextual nuances that numbers alone could not fully capture. This triangulation not only strengthened the robustness of the findings but also ensured a more grounded and comprehensive understanding of data practices and maturity across the surveyed SPOs.

## 3 Findings

The overall data maturity of SPOs across six dimensions, reveals varying levels of capability and readiness. The study gave us the sector's mean maturity score as 47.5 as shown in Fig. 1. The scores across dimensions vary, with Culture and Mindset achieving the highest mean score (65.7) and Data-Related Training the lowest (22.5). This disparity highlights areas requiring targeted capacity-building efforts. The high score in Culture and Mindset reflects the sector's recognition of the importance of data-driven approaches. However, the low score in Data-Related Training indicates a significant gap in building technical skills among employees, which could hinder the effective use of data tools and systems. Similarly, the low score for Data Accessibility and Storage suggests limited investment in centralised, accessible data infrastructure, often due to budgetary constraints.

As shown in Fig. 1, the overall mean data maturity score places most organizations in the "Progressing" stage. That means they've moved beyond basic but are still far from becoming fully data driven. The highest score is in culture and mindset suggesting that leadership and teams are open to using data and see its value. Contrarily, data-related training scores are the lowest among all dimensions, indicating major underinvestment in upskilling staff. It shows that SPOs recognize the importance of data—but they're not backing it up with adequate investment in data-related skills and systems.

Furthermore, data accessibility and storage also have low scores, pointing to infrastructure and system-level weaknesses. Similarly, HR data management and project data analysis are other weak areas, showing gaps in turning data into insights and managing it internally. Interestingly, data collection and monitoring scores are high, likely driven by compliance needs, but organizations lack necessary hardware and human capital to support it.

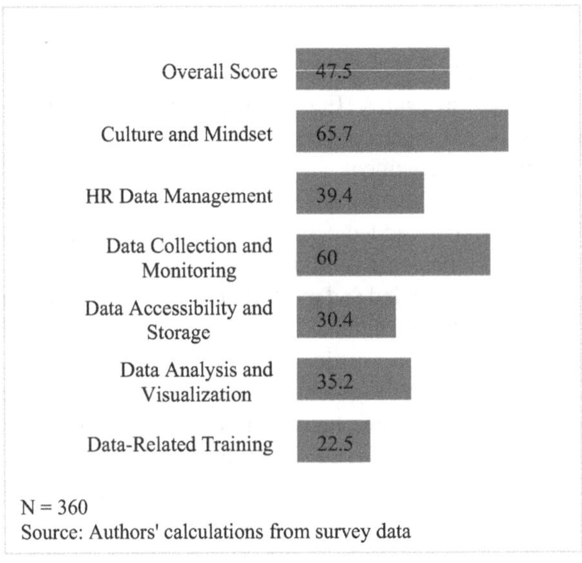


**Fig. 1.** Mean data maturity scores

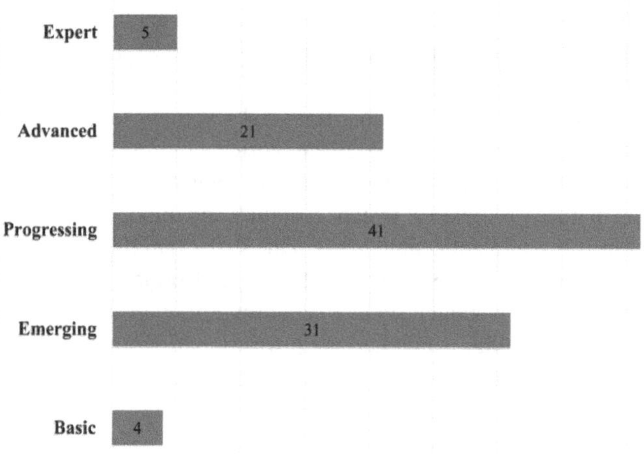


N = 360
Source: Authors' calculations from survey data (the values may not add upto 100 since the values are rounded off to nearest integer)

**Fig. 2.** Distribution of organizations by data maturity score

As Fig. 2 highlights, a majority of SPOs are no longer at the starting line but haven't yet reached full maturity. Please note that the values may not add up to percentages since the values are rounded off. This presents a valuable opportunity to accelerate capability-building efforts and move more SPOs into advanced levels of data maturity. Around 72% of SPOs fall within the Emerging (21–40) and Progressing (41–60) categories. Very few SPOs have achieved "Expert" status. The study further explored how factors such as organisational size, financial capacity affects data maturity in SPOs along with understanding the regional and sectoral patterns in data maturity among SPOs.

### 3.1 Organisational Size

Older organisations demonstrate higher maturity scores (Mean = 49.76), though differences across age groups of SPOs were not statistically significant ($p = 0.176$). This suggests that organizational age alone does not determine maturity; newer SPOs may adopt agile, modern systems that offset legacy advantages.

Organisations with more than 50 employees exhibit the highest maturity scores (Mean = 53.9, $p = 0.000$, Eta Squared = 0.072). Larger workforces often correlate with better resources, enabling the hiring of specialised data personnel and the adoption of new and better systems as we also found out during our qualitative interviews.

### 3.2 Financial Capacity

The largest group (33.9%) operates on budgets between ₹0.1 million and ₹1 million, while only 7.3% exceed ₹500 million. Financial capacity strongly correlates with data maturity. Organisations with budgets exceeding ₹50 million score the highest on maturity (Mean = 55.61, p = 0.000, Eta Squared = 0.103). This is likely due to their ability to invest in better data systems, training, and professional expertise, which smaller organisations often lack.

Figure 3 highlights that SPOs with higher financial resources tend to perform better across all data maturity dimensions. Across all categories—culture & mindset, HR data, collection, storage, analysis, and training—it can be seen that as financial resources increase, so do data maturity scores. For instance, culture and mindset score remains high across the board, but still sees a noticeable jump in the ₹10–50 million and >₹50 million categories. Furthermore, data accessibility & storage and project data analysis show sharper improvement in larger-budget SPOs—indicating these areas are more resource-dependent. Data-related training, which had the lowest mean score earlier, remains the weakest but still improves significantly in the highest budget category.

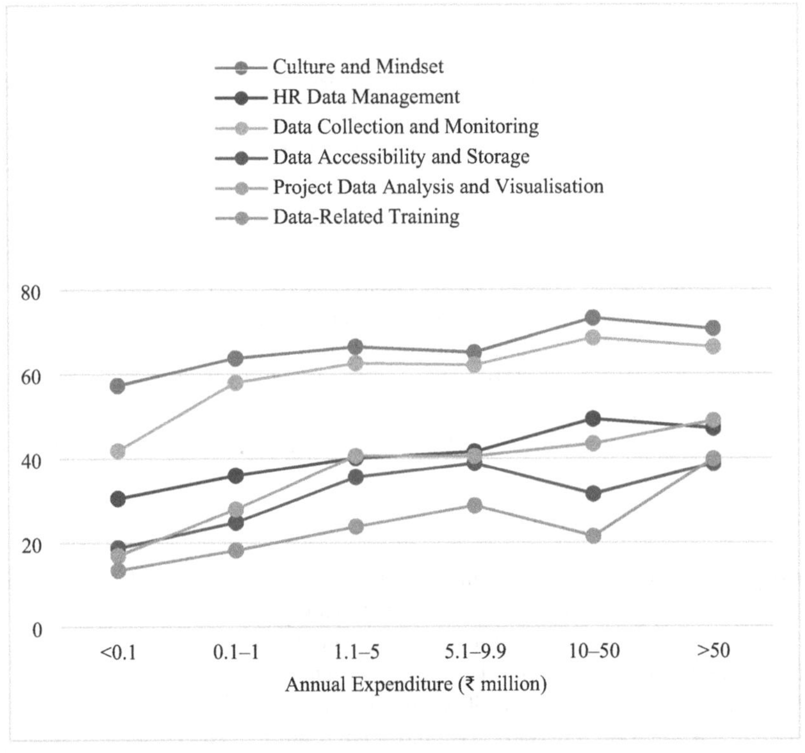


N = 360

Source: Authors' calculations from survey data

**Fig. 3.** Mean scores across expenditure levels

### 3.3 Regional Trends

Regional differences reveal that South India exhibits the highest mean maturity score (50.01), while East and North regions score the lowest (45.98 and 46.12, respectively).

However, these differences are not statistically significant ($p = 0.378$). Insights from qualitative interviews suggest that the higher scores in the South may be attributed to stronger governance frameworks and better access to resources, while lower scores in the East and North reflect infrastructural and financial limitations.

### 3.4 Sectoral Disparity

Higher data maturity scores are observed in domains such as WASH (Mean = 55.02, $p = 0.000$, Eta Squared = 0.035), Adolescent and Youth (Mean = 55.66, $p = 0.000$, Eta Squared = 0.062), and Skills and Training (Mean = 50.44, $p = 0.001$, Eta Squared = 0.028).These domains, as further corroborated by qualitative insights, exhibit notable progress in adopting data-centric practices, likely driven by a strong emphasis on measurable outcomes and donor requirements. Sectoral differences show higher maturity in education and health-focused SPOs compared to others, likely due to funder expectations and data demands as found in our discussions with the SPOs. Comparatively, domains like Agriculture and Food Security and Animal Husbandry exhibit lower data maturity, with no statistically significant differences. This indicates potential areas for capacity development, as these domains may face challenges in integrating data systems due to resource constraints or less demand for data-driven outcomes.

## 4 Six Dimensions of Data Maturity

### 4.1 Culture and Mindset

The findings reveal that organisations with higher expenditure levels demonstrate significantly better data driven cultures, suggesting that financial resources enable investments in technology and capacity building. In contrast, age, size (in terms of employee count) and regional variations showed limited or no significant impact. For example, organisations spending between ₹10 million and ₹50 million annually scored a mean of 73.1, compared to just 57.2 for those spending less than ₹0.1 million. Also, older organisations (established before 2000) scored slightly higher (67.67) than newer ones established between 2021–2024 (61.97), but the difference was not statistically significant ($p = 0.215$). Similarly, larger organisations with more than 50 employees scored higher (69.24) than smaller organisations with 1–5 employees (63.57), but this was also not statistically significant ($p = 0.079$). Regional differences were negligible, with organisations in the South scoring slightly higher (68.41) than those in the East (63.49), but again, the results were not significant ($p = 0.211$).

We found that smaller organisations are constrained by funding and resources. Hence, they often rely on manual methods and prioritise immediate program needs over long-term data strategies. Overall, it was observed that expenditure plays a very important role in driving culture and mindset of the SPOs. Leadership in these organisations typically views data as important but struggles to align it with operational priorities. In larger organisations, while availability of resources facilitate advanced data practices, challenges persist in fostering a unified approach across departments and ensuring staff buy-in for new systems. The less pronounced influence of organisational age, employee size, and regional location on data culture is likely due to systemic challenges like resource constraints, leadership priorities, and resistance to change, which affect all organisations similarly. Factors such as funding availability and external demands for data-driven practices play a more significant role than structural variables alone, leading to convergence in scores.

### 4.2 Human Resource Data Management Practices

The HR Data Management practices scores of SPOs show significant variation across factors such as expenditure and employee strength, while differences based on the year of establishment and region are less pronounced. Organisations with higher expenditures demonstrate better HR data management practices, with scores increasing steadily from a mean of 30.427 for those spending below ₹0.1 million to 49.085 for those spending ₹10 million–50 million. This trend indicates that financial resources enable organisations to adopt more robust HR data systems. Similarly, employee strength significantly impacts HR scores, with larger organisations (above 50 employees) scoring the highest (mean = 49.954), compared to smaller organisations with 1–5 employees (mean = 30.856). The overall analysis reveals a statistically significant relationship for expenditure ($p = .003$) and employee strength ($p < .001$), with moderate effect sizes (Eta Squared = .052 and .072, respectively). In contrast, the year of establishment and regional location show limited influence on HR data management practices. While organisations established before 2000 and those founded between 2021 2024 slightly outperformed others, the differences are not statistically significant ($p = .479$) and have weak effect sizes (Eta Squared = .007). Regional variations, with the West and South scoring slightly higher than other regions, are also not statistically significant ($p = .198$, Eta Squared = .013), indicating that geography plays a minimal role in shaping HR practices.

The significant role of expenditure and employee strength in shaping HR data management practices highlights the importance of resources and organisational scale. Larger organisations and those with greater financial capacity can invest in advanced HR systems, data management tools, and training for staff, enabling better practices. Conversely, smaller organisations with limited budgets and workforce often rely on manual or less sophisticated methods, which impacts their overall data management capacity. The weaker influence of factors like age and region suggests that the evolution of HR practices is driven more by resource availability and operational priorities than by historical or geographic context.

### 4.3 Data Collection and Monitoring Practices

The analysis reveals significant variation in Data Collection and Monitoring practices scores of Social Purpose Organisations (SPOs) across expenditure levels and employee strength, while differences by year of establishment and region are less pronounced. Organisations with higher annual expenditures demonstrate significantly higher mean scores, with a clear upward trend from ₹0.1 million–1 million (57.94) to ₹10 million–50 million (68.38) ($p < 0.001$, Eta Squared = 0.107). Similarly, organisations with larger employee bases show better scores, rising from a mean of 51.40 for those with 1–5 employees to 67.80 for organisations with over 50 employees ($p < 0.001$, Eta Squared

= 0.084). This suggests that both financial resources and organisational scale positively influence data collection and monitoring capabilities.

On the other hand, the year of establishment and regional location exhibit no statistically significant differences in practices. While older organisations (established before 2000) have slightly higher scores (63.68) compared to newer ones (56.57 for 2021–2024), the variation is not significant. Regional differences are negligible, with means ranging narrowly from 59.35 (North) to 60.73 (West), and the association is statistically insignificant.

The observed trends indicate that organisations with greater financial resources and larger workforce sizes are better equipped to implement effective data collection and monitoring practices. This is because higher budgets enable investments in advanced tools, staff training, and infrastructure, which are essential for systematic and efficient data management. Similarly, a larger workforce allows for the allocation of dedicated roles to data-related tasks, ensuring better planning, execution, and utilisation of data. On the other hand, the limited influence of organisational age and regional location suggests that factors such as geographic context or legacy systems may not significantly impact data practices. This uniformity across regions and organisational timelines could reflects the widespread adoption of similar data practices or standardized guidelines within the sector.

### 4.4 Project Data Storage and Accessibility Practices

The analysis of Data Accessibility and Storage Score reveals significant differences across expenditure and region. Organisations with higher annual expenditures exhibit better data accessibility and storage practices, with mean scores increasing from 18.7 for those spending below ₹0.1 million to 38.7 for those in the ₹5.1 million–₹9.9 million range ($p = 0.001$).

Regional differences are also significant ($p = 0.045$), with the southern region recording the highest mean score of 38.0, compared to 27.4 in the eastern region. In contrast, organisational age ($p = 0.3$) and employee strength ($p = 0.1$) do not show significant variations. These findings suggest that organisations with greater financial resources are better equipped to invest in secure and efficient data storage and accessibility systems due to advanced technological infrastructure and skilled personnel. Regional variations may reflect disparities in digital infrastructure and capacity-building initiatives, with the south demonstrating greater technological adoption as witnessed in our discussions. The lack of significant influence from organisational age and employee size suggests that even smaller or newer organisations can achieve robust data practices with adequate resources and external support.

### 4.5 Project Data Analysis and Visualisation Practices

The analysis of Project Data Analysis and Visualisation practices scores among Social Purpose Organisations (SPOs) reveals significant variation across expenditure, employee strength, and region, while year of establishment does not exhibit statistical significance.

Organisations with higher budgets demonstrate substantially better practices, with mean scores increasing from 16.9 for those with budgets below ₹0.1 million to 48.7

for those with budgets above ₹50 million. Similarly, employee strength is a significant factor. Organisation with 21–50 employees scored the highest (43.3), whereas smaller organisations with 1–5 employees scored the lowest (25.4). Region also plays a significant role, with organisations in the South (37.3) and West (37.3) regions scoring higher than those in the North (31.6). However, the year of establishment does not significantly influence practices.

These findings suggest that resources (expenditure and workforce size) and regional capacities heavily influence data practices. Higher budgets provide access to advanced tools, skilled personnel, and capacity-building opportunities. Organisations with larger teams benefit from specialization, improving their ability to manage and visualize data. Regional variations may reflect differences in local infrastructure, policies, and funding opportunities.

### 4.6 Data Related Training Practices

The data-related training practices of Social Purpose Organisations (SPOs) vary significantly across expenditure and employee strength, while no substantial differences are observed across age and region.

Organisations with higher expenditures report markedly better training scores, with a mean of 39.6 for those spending above ₹50 million, compared to 13.4 for those spending below ₹0.1 million. Similarly, organisations with larger employee strength (above 50 employees) score 32.1, significantly higher than smaller organisations with 1–5 employees, which score 13.3. Both expenditure and employee strength show statistically significant variations, with moderate effect. On the other hand, factors such as the year of establishment and region show no significant impact.

Higher expenditure enables organisations to allocate more resources for structured training programs, including hiring skilled trainers, investing in advanced tools, and providing regular capacity-building opportunities. Similarly, larger organisations with more employees are likely to prioritize systematic training to maintain consistent data management practices across teams. Conversely, smaller and less-funded organisations often lack the financial and human resources to invest in training, relying instead on ad-hoc or informal mechanisms.

The lack of significant variation across age and region suggests that these factors do not inherently influence an organisation's approach to data-related training, as it was found that there are host of other challenges faced by SPOs in accessing resources and technical expertise. These challenges stem from not being able to attract skilled resources due to inability to provide competent compensation.

## 5 Sector-Wide Gaps and Areas for Improvement

A significant gap in data maturity across Social Purpose Organisations (SPOs) arises from insufficient investment in data-related practices. Only 33.6% of organisations report allocating resources toward data training activities, indicating a widespread lack of capacity-building initiatives. Smaller organisations, particularly those with annual expenditures below ₹10 million, are disproportionately affected due to their limited budgets, making it challenging for them to adopt advanced tools, hire skilled professionals, or conduct regular training sessions. Additionally, the reliance on basic tools like Microsoft Excel and Google Sheets remains prevalent, with less than 25% of organisations utilizing advanced analytics platforms like SPSS, Tableau, or Power BI. This under-utilisation restricts the potential for deriving nuanced insights and advanced data visualisation capabilities. The lack of qualitative data analysis tools further underscores this challenge, with only 3.6% of organisations using platforms like ATLAS.ti or NVivo, reflecting a critical gap in handling complex datasets and fostering evidence-based decision-making. The under-utilization of these tools stems from financial constraints and a lack of internal capacity to use them effectively—both of which contribute to a lower perceived demand within organisations.

In terms of data collection practices, the sector remains heavily dependent on manual methods, with 28.2% of organisations still recording data manually. A combined 35.3% employ inconsistent digital and paper-based processes, further limiting the consistency and reliability of data. Only 12.2% of organisations have transitioned to automated, systematic data collection processes, reflecting a substantial area for improvement. Similarly, data sharing remains an underdeveloped aspect, with only 16.7% of organisations engaging in extensive data sharing with external stakeholders or partners. This limited collaboration restricts knowledge exchange, learning opportunities, and the ability to scale successful interventions across the sector. It is likely that low levels of data sharing stems from data privacy and sensitivity concerns, as many SPOs handle data related to vulnerable populations (e.g., children, gender-based violence, health) [13]. Sharing such data—even in anonymised formats—can raise ethical, legal, and reputational concerns. Other probable causes may include lack of data governance framework [5], limited data interoperability, fear of use, and funder restrictions.

Furthermore, the lack of robust data governance policies exacerbates these challenges. Over 49.4% of organisations lack formal data backup and disaster recovery strategies, leaving them vulnerable to risks such as data breaches, loss, or corruption. Similarly, the study finds that larger-budget organisations have greater awareness of the Digital Personal Data Protection Act, 2023 [14]. These gaps highlight a critical need for sector-wide advocacy and capacity building to prioritise data governance.

## 6 Key Drivers of Data Maturity

Financial resources stand out as a significant determinant of data maturity, enabling organisations to invest in advanced tools, skilled personnel, and systematic training programs [6]. Organisations with annual expenditures above ₹50 million consistently outperform their smaller counterparts across all dimensions of data maturity, from HR data management to project data collection, analysis, and visualisation. For instance, these organisations achieve significantly higher scores in employing advanced tools, conducting regular training, and embedding data in decision-making processes. Larger budgets also correlate with better integration of data into financial management, program design, and fundraising strategies, underscoring the role of resources in driving maturity.

Leadership proficiency and investment in data-related practices emerge as another critical enabler [6]. Organisations with proactive and skilled leaders score significantly higher, as such leaders prioritize data initiatives, allocate necessary resources, and embed a data-driven culture across teams. The role of leadership becomes especially evident in larger organisations, where leadership support facilitates the creation of dedicated data teams and the adoption of sophisticated tools. However, even in these organisations, challenges persist, such as aligning departmental priorities and securing buy-in from all team members for new data systems.

Another key enabler is the diversification in data use. Organisations that leverage data for multiple purposes, such as monitoring, decision-making, fundraising, and program design, achieve higher data maturity. A visible shift in this direction is driven by donor reporting requirements as well as changing social impact investing practice. The versatility in data application demonstrates the value of embedding data across operational and strategic functions. However, smaller organisations often focus on basic tracking metrics like participant numbers and event counts, limiting their ability to derive strategic insights. This gap underlines the importance of fostering data literacy and expanding the scope of data usage across all organisations, regardless of size.

## 7 Discussion

The findings reinforce that data maturity within SPOs is shaped by a constellation of interconnected factors—internal systems, resource availability, and leadership engagement. Larger, well-resourced organisations tend to exhibit higher maturity levels, supported by dedicated staff, formal policies, and digital infrastructure [3, 5]. In contrast, smaller and underfunded SPOs continue to rely on manual processes and often lack foundational data systems and governance protocols [4, 7, 13].

The DMA highlights persistent capacity gaps, especially among smaller entities, in areas such as secure data storage, use of advanced analytics, and compliance with governance standards [6]. Crucially, the findings illustrate that foundational investments—in skilled personnel, leadership commitment, and structured training—are prerequisites for adopting advanced data science practices like predictive modelling and impact forecasting [5]. Furthermore, in a resource constraint setting, it is equally essential to provide the SPOs with free and open source software (FOSS) such as *ISDM DataShakti* to improve access to high quality data and analytical tools [15].

The strong correlation between data maturity and the use of sophisticated tools suggests that attempts to deploy machine learning or advanced analytics without first strengthening foundational capacities are unlikely to succeed [6]. This makes a compelling case for sector-wide investment in core data capabilities as a stepping stone toward scalable, high-impact data science applications.

Key enablers include regular data use, staff participation, and robust data security measures. The consistently low scores on training point to an urgent need for structured capacity-building efforts [5]. Additionally, regional disparities—particularly gaps in Southern regions—signal the need for geographically targeted interventions to bridge uneven development.

Building a truly data-driven culture in the social sector will require a strategic combination of leadership commitment, infrastructure investment, and continuous workforce development. Policy frameworks that prioritise data governance and resource allocation can serve as critical levers for accelerating data maturity across the ecosystem.

## 8 Conclusion

The study underscores a growing recognition among Indian Social Purpose Organisations (SPOs) of data's strategic value—yet this awareness has not fully translated into systems, skills, or governance mechanisms required for meaningful use. Persistent gaps in infrastructure, capacity, and policy frameworks continue to limit the sector's ability to harness data for learning, accountability, and programmatic impact. Targeted interventions that build foundational capabilities—particularly in under-resourced organisations—can significantly elevate sector-wide data maturity.

This research also contributes a practical, replicable five-stage framework for assessing data readiness in the social sector, offering both funders and practitioners a roadmap for staged capacity-building. For funders and policymakers, the findings advocate for a sequenced approach: strengthening core competencies before advancing to predictive analytics or machine learning. For SPOs, the framework serves as a diagnostic tool to assess their preparedness for deploying data science tools effectively.

The study offers more than just a snapshot of data practices among Indian SPOs—it provides a practical framework that can inform similar efforts globally. Other countries with resource-constrained social sectors can adapt these insights to assess and strengthen their own data ecosystems.

While the study provides valuable insights into the data practices of SPOs in India, a key limitation is the relatively small sample size, stemming from a lower response rate. To address regional disparities and ensure broader representation, the study employed a mix of targeted outreach and snowball sampling to engage SPOs across diverse geographies and segments. This approach improved the geographic and thematic spread of the sample. Nevertheless, further enrichment of both quantitative and qualitative data would enhance the representativeness of the sample and enable a more comprehensive capture of diverse perspectives.

For researchers, the study opens up possibilities for comparative analysis, helping uncover what works, where, and why. It also lays the groundwork for building shared principles around data use, governance, and impact in the nonprofit space. Furthermore, future research can examine how maturity levels correlate with successful application of data science methods and explore predictive models to estimate the return on data investments across diverse organisational profiles. These insights will be crucial for designing evidence-driven, scalable strategies to foster sector-wide data transformation.

**Acknowledgments.** We are grateful to all the participating organisations in the survey for their invaluable contributions in carrying out this study and producing this report.

We also extend our sincere appreciation to our knowledge and research partner, IPE Global, for meticulously conducting the survey, analysing the data, and helping to build the report.

## References

1. Rana, S., Rao, A.: Bridging the gender gap: the promise and peril of using artificial intelligence and machine learning to accelerate gender equality. Econ. Pol. Wkly. **59**(18), 30–33 (2024)

2. Haleem, A., Javaid, M., Singh, R.P., Suman, R., Khan, S.: Management 4.0: concept, applications and advancements. Sustain. Oper. Comput. **4**, 10–21 (2023). https://doi.org/10.1016/j.susoc.2022.10.002
3. Sharma, R., Upadhyay, S., Chaudhury, A., Ramachandran, A., Saha, J.: The State of the Sector Report on Digital Transformation for Nonprofits in India. India Leaders for Social Sector (ILSS), New Delhi (2024). https://indialeadersforsocialsector.com/download-ilss-digital-transformation-for-social-impact-program-report/. Accessed 06 Aug 2025
4. Nikita, N.A., Azim, K.S., Jafor, A.H.M., Shayed, A.U., Hossain, M.A., Khan, O.U.: Digital transformation in non-profit organizations: strategies, challenges, and successes. AIJMR Adv. Int. J. Multidiscip. Res. **2**(5), (2024). https://doi.org/10.62127/aijmr.2024.v02i05.1097
5. GivingTuesday: India AI Readiness Report. GivingTuesday (2024). https://ai.givingtuesday.org/ai-readiness-survey-report-2024-india/. Accessed 06 Aug 2025
6. Pacta: AI Adoption in Indian Social Sector Programs: Early Insights, Emerging Stakeholders and Future Directions. Pacta, Bengaluru, May 2025. https://www.pacta.in/research-reports/ai-adoption-social-sector. Accessed 06 Aug 2025
7. Sangeetha, N., Minimol, K.: Technology adoption for NGO management: a case study of ATMA foundation. IJFMR Int. J. Multidiscip. Res. **6**(4) (2024). https://doi.org/10.36948/ijfmr.2024.v06i04.24471
8. ISDM: ISDM CDSSI Data Maturity Assessment. Indian School of Development Management (ISDM), Noida, India. https://www.isdm.org.in/cdssi/projects/isdm-cdssi-data-maturity-assessment. Accessed 06 Aug 2025
9. Williams, N.: The fundamental principles of an Insight-Driven Organisation | Deloitte UK. https://www.deloitte.com/uk/en/Industries/technology/blogs/2023/the-fundamental-principles-of-an-insight-driven-organisation.html. Accessed 06 Aug 2025
10. Holdsworth, J., Kosinski, M.: What is Data Governance? | IBM. https://www.ibm.com/think/topics/data-governance. Accessed 06 Aug 2025
11. NITI Aayog: Overview: Data Governance Quality Index | DMEO | Development Monitoring and Evaluation Office | Attached office under NITI Aayog. DMEO, NITI Aayog. https://dmeo.gov.in/content/dgqi-overview. Accessed 06 Aug 2025
12. data.org: About the Assessment. data.org. https://data.org/dma/about/. Accessed 06 Aug 2025
13. Rana, S., Rajaram, S., Sharma, D.: A balancing act: Collecting data for social good in an age of privacy concerns. LSE International Development. https://blogs.lse.ac.uk/internationaldevelopment/2024/01/10/collecting-data-for-social-good-in-an-age-of-privacy-concerns/. Accessed 15 Jan 2024
14. Government of India: Digital Personal Data Protection Act, 2023, p. 21 (2023). https://www.meity.gov.in/static/uploads/2024/06/2bf1f0e9f04e6fb4f8fef35e82c42aa5.pdf
15. ISDM: ISDM DataShakti. https://datashakti.isdm.org.in/home. Accessed 07 Aug 2025

# Disputing Facts: A Glimpse into Voting-Related Conversation on TikTok

Mohamed Ahmed[1(✉)], Helge Marahrens[1], Lisa Singh[1], Pleasant Ballenger[2], Diego DiMattina[3], Kenedy Ducheine[4], Aiden Ehrenreich[1], Caroline Field[5], Kylie Griffiths[6], Lucy Olander[1], and Katie Wilson[7]

[1] Georgetown University, Washington, D.C., USA
{ma2323,hm868,lisa.singh,aze8,lmo66}@georgetown.edu
[2] University of North Carolina at Chapel Hill, Chapel Hill, NC, USA
pballenger@unc.edu
[3] University of Virginia, Charlottesville, VA, USA
ajh4ep@virginia.edu
[4] University of South Florida, Tampa, FL, USA
[5] High Point University, High Point, NC, USA
[6] University of Oregon, Eugene, OR, USA
kgriffi3@uoregon.edu
[7] Smith College, Northampton, MA, USA
kwilson44@smith.edu

**Abstract.** Misinformation poses a significant threat to democratic processes, particularly during election campaigns. It can lead to erosion of trust in the democratic process, incitement of violence, and public confusion about voting procedures. Even more concerning is how rapidly it can spread through social media. In this paper, we analyze conversation related to voting on TikTok. Specifically, we analyze discussion surrounding twenty videos containing factual information about election fraud, voting eligibility, voter registration, and voter restrictions by examining the stance of the comments on each video. We find that a sizable percentage of comments do not support the facts. For example, videos within the voting eligibility topic had almost twice as many comments against the facts as supporting the facts. This finding highlights the need to further research the accuracy of comments posted about factual videos and develop scalable solutions for posting counter-messaging to improve the perceived credibility of true information.

**Keywords:** Misinformation · Stance Detection · Social Media · Election Discourse

## 1 Introduction

Misinformation poses a significant threat to democratic processes, particularly during election campaigns. By distorting public understanding of critical issues,


R. Stahlbock et al. (Eds.): CSCE 2025, CCIS 2938, pp. 311–321, 2027.
https://doi.org/10.1007/978-3-032-22196-4_23

spreading false narratives about voting, and fostering distrust in electoral systems, misinformation can erode the foundations of democracy [1]. For example, the January $6^{th}$ attack on the United States Capitol was fueled by widely spread false claims about election fraud [2], leading to the deaths of four individuals and thousands of subsequent criminal charges. Such events underscore the profound real-world harm that misinformation can cause. Previous research has shown that one way false information spreads is through social media [3,4]. Twitter (now X) [5] and Facebook [6] have been the focus of many of these studies. While more information about misinformation on TikTok is emerging, limited research exists about election related misinformation on TikTok [7,8].

TikTok's distinctive features provide fertile ground for the spread of misinformation. The platform's short-form video format allows for the rapid consumption and dissemination of content. TikTok's engagement-driven, algorithmic content discovery further amplifies the reach of misinformation by tailoring content to individual user preferences. This can inadvertently create echo chambers where users are repeatedly exposed to the same misleading or false narratives [9]. However, misinformation can also spread through a different channel – through comments. In this paper, we aim to analyze how misinformation propagates through comments that disagree with or undermine factual video content.

It is within this context that we study conversation about TikTok videos containing factual information related to voting during the 2024 US presidential election. Specifically, we analyze the comments associated with twenty videos on the following election topics: election fraud, voting eligibility, voter registration, and voter restrictions. In the 2024 election, these four topics took on heightened importance given their direct impact on public trust in the electoral process and democratic legitimacy, as well as the volume of false claims surrounding them [10]. Concerns about election fraud, whether substantiated or not, fueled intense partisan debates [11], making the integrity of election systems a critical topic for maintaining voter confidence [12]. Voting eligibility and voter registration were under scrutiny as states implemented varying laws, with some expanding access and others imposing restrictions, raising concerns about equity and potential disenfranchisement [13]. Voter restrictions, including new laws on ID requirements and early voting limitations, sparked legal challenges and advocacy efforts, as these measures disproportionately affect marginalized communities [14,15]. Together, these topics shaped not only who participated in the election, but also how Americans perceived fairness in the democratic process.

Our analysis begins by determining the stance of comments associated with each of the twenty videos. Using a combination of manually labeled posts and generated posts, we compare classic and deep learning models for computing stance. We then use our best model to label comments associated with each video and assess the level of agreement between video content and comments about the video, where each video discusses a true voting claim. We find that a sizable percentage of comments do not support the facts, highlighting a novel avenue for spreading false information.

The main contributions of this paper are as follows: (1) we conduct an ethnographic analysis of discussions related to different election-related videos that share accurate voting related information and find that more of the posts refute the true claims than support them in one of our four topic areas, (2) given the small amount of available training data about each claim, we augment the hand labeled platform comments with generated posts, demonstrating the effectiveness of this strategy for increasing training dataset sizes, (3) we evaluate different stance detection models and find that the sentence-level representations performed better than the other models for the short, informal comments typical of TikTok, and (4) we make our training data available for other researchers to use.

## 2 Related Literature

Researchers agree that we are living in an era of misinformation [16,17]. The amount of research about misinformation and disinformation has increased considerably since 2010. We refer you to Broda and Strömbäck for a recent review [18]. In this survey, over half of the research investigates misinformation and disinformation on social media. The medium itself, encompassing platform algorithms, network structures, and communication affordances, shapes the flow and visibility of misinformation, often amplifying its reach through echo chambers and filter bubbles, thereby serving as a vehicle for mass distribution of false claims [19]. Studying misinformation on social media as opposed to more traditional forms of media is necessary because of the high levels of participation on these platforms. This includes news consumption, in which 54% of American adults say social media is at least occasionally a news source [20].

The social media platforms with the most research in this area are Twitter and Facebook. While some research has emerged about TikTok, its focus has been on health misinformation [21–23]. Some recent work investigates election related disinformation during the 2021 German election on TikTok [7] and misinformation during the 2024 Indonesian general election [8]. These different studies highlight TikTok's unique susceptibility to misinformation, given its visual and entertainment-driven nature. Unlike traditional platforms such as Twitter and Facebook, TikTok's algorithm prioritizes short, engaging, and easily consumable content, creating an environment where sensational or visually captivating misinformation can thrive. A study examining fact-checking efforts on TikTok during the COVID-19 pandemic found that while fact-checkers addressed diverse topics, including health-related misinformation, their content struggled to gain traction among users primarily seeking entertainment [24]. This disconnect between fact-checking efforts and user engagement reflects a broader challenge on TikTok, where the rapid spread of misleading content often outpaces the dissemination of accurate information.

Fortunately, there are times when factual videos have high engagement. We are interested in understanding this engagement and determining if it is mostly supportive or if discussion about the factual videos is refuting the video content and increasing the uncertainty around factual information.

## 3 Research Design

In this section, we overview the research design used to analyze the stance of TikTok users toward misinformation-prone voting topics in the context of the 2024 U.S. election. Figure 1 shows the high level steps of our research design: TikTok data collection, training data labeling and augmentation, stance detection model development, video comments labeling, and voting topics misinformation analysis. The remainder of this section discusses each of these steps.

**Fig. 1.** Research Design.

**Table 1.** Summary of Manually Labeled Data for Each Claim Topic

| Claim Topic | Data Size | Generated (%) | Avg Length (chars) |
|---|---|---|---|
| Election Fraud | 240 | 54 | 88.4 |
| Voting Eligibility | 814 | 36 | 75.3 |
| Voter Registration | 369 | 50 | 80.4 |
| Voting Restrictions | 389 | 38 | 85.1 |

### 3.1 TikTok Data Collection

To analyze misinformation on TikTok, popular videos were selected based on (1) their relevance to the four election topics, (2) their level of engagement, measured by the number of comments, and (3) their inclusion of accurate information. We used different terms associated with voting to identify videos. Examples include *voting eligible*, *voting illegal*, and *voting restrictions*. This approach helped us identify some of the content directly connected to the themes we were interested in. We also cross-checked specific claims and myths against fact-checkers, e.g. FactCheck.org, to determine whether they were true or false, keeping only those that were true. We note that our sample of videos is not meant to be representative of all conversation related to voting. Instead, it is a targeted analysis of content that has high-engagement. This allows us to better understand the level of agreement and disagreement of TikTok users with respect to high engagement voting-related videos.

### 3.2 Training Data Labeling and Augmentation

For each topic, relevant comments were identified and labeled for stance. If the true information was supported, the stance was labeled *Support*. If the false information was supported, the stance was labeled *Refute*. All other comments were labeled *Neutral*. To increase the amount of training data, we also supplemented the collected comments with generated comments using ChatGPT. This includes both zero-shot prompts (without examples) and few-shot prompts that included a small number of labeled examples from our training data. Table 1 shows the amount of labeled data for each topic and the percentage that was generated using ChatGPT. In general, the amount of labeled training data varied from 240 comments to 814 comments depending upon the number of videos and comments associated with the topic.

### 3.3 Stance Detection Model Development

We implemented supervised classification models to predict each comment's stance towards the claim presented in its corresponding video. Our models were chosen to represent distinct modeling paradigms: bag of words, classic machine learning, and fine-tuned transformer models. Each model was trained and evaluated separately on the annotated comment dataset for each topic. The rest of this subsection describes each model.

**SVM + TF-IDF Baseline:** We used a Support Vector Machine (SVM) with TF-IDF feature vectors of comments as a classic interpretable baseline. This traditional approach has been widely adopted in many stance detection studies [25–27]. TF-IDF calculates text embeddings based on the statistical word and document frequency of comments. The linear weight coefficients of the SVM help indicate which terms are most discriminative for each stance. Given the relatively small training size per topic ($< 1000$ manually labeled examples), a simple linear model can be effective in capturing stance-specific n-grams without the risk of overfitting. We used a Radial Basis Function (RBF) kernel SVM with regularization parameter $C = \mathbf{1}$, which was tuned using a cross-validation strategy.

**Fine-Tuned BERT Model:** We fine-tuned a BERT-based transformer model [28] as a strong deep learning baseline. Large pre-trained language models (PLM) like BERT have achieved state-of-the-art performance on various text classification tasks, including stance detection [27] by leveraging their contextual language understanding acquired during extensive pre-training on large corpora. BERT-based classifiers have been shown to consistently outperform earlier methods (SVMs or RNNs) on benchmark stance datasets by effectively capturing textual dependencies. Specifically, we finetuned a pre-trained BERT model (including all transformer layers) on each topic-specific dataset, using a randomly initialized classification layer for stance prediction. We optimized the model using the

Adam optimizer with a learning rate of $2e-4$, a batch size of 16, and cross-entropy loss over 10 epochs. This enables the model to specialize its general language representations for the specific stance detection task of interest.

**Sentence-BERT with Classification Head:** Finally, we utilized Sentence-BERT (SBERT) [29] to encode comments into meaningful sentence embeddings, which were then passed to a classification layer. SBERT leverages BERT's neural backbone and is specifically optimized to produce sentence-level embeddings using a Siamese network architecture. Compared to standard fine-tuned BERT, SBERT embeddings capture richer semantic relationships in text. This has been shown to be beneficial for short-form texts with limited labeled data [30]. We hypothesized that these enriched representations would more effectively model subtle context-dependent linguistic cues essential for stance detection. We fine-tuned the SBERT model (originally trained on NLI and STS data to measure semantic similarity between sentence pairs) on our stance data. Specifically, we froze the SBERT encoder and appended a fully-connected softmax classifier, which we trained using the Adam optimizer with cross-entropy loss (learning rate: $1e-3$, batch size: 16, for 20 epochs).

For each topic dataset, we used an 80/20 train-test split and selected model hyperparameters via a 5-fold cross-validation on the training set. The final results were obtained by evaluating models trained on the full training set against the held-out test set. We repeated this process for each topic. We measured classification performance using accuracy and macro-F1.

### 3.4 Video Comments Labeling and Analysis

After evaluating the different stance detection models for each topic, we use the best performing one to label the comments associated with each video within the topic. We then aggregate the counts to determine the level of support for each claim.

## 4 Empirical Evaluation

We begin this section by comparing different stance detection models to determine which model is the strongest for this task (Sect. 4.1). Following this, we explore the distribution of stance percentages across our four claim topics: election fraud, voting eligibility, voter registration, and voter restrictions (Sect. 4.2).

### 4.1 Model Results

Table 2 summarizes the performance of the stance detection models. The SBERT-based model has a higher accuracy and F1 score when compared to both the TF-IDF + SVM and finetuned BERT for all claim topics. In terms of accuracy, it is 5% to 22% better than TF-IDF + SVM, and it is 5% to 19%

better in F1 score. SBERT and BERT have a more similar performance on voting eligibility related videos, with SBERT performing slightly better. SBERT is 4% to 11% better for the other video types. Overall, these results highlight two considerations. First, both the volume and diversity of training data significantly influence stance detection performance. Second, pretrained sentence-level representations, obtained from SBERT, provide stable and efficient performance. This is particularly valuable for complex tasks constrained by annotation resources.[1]

**Table 2.** Summary of Stance Model Performance (Accuracy and Macro-F1) by Claim Topic

| Model | Election Fraud | | Voter Reg. | | Eligibility | | Restrictions | |
|---|---|---|---|---|---|---|---|---|
| | Acc. | F1 | Acc. | F1 | Acc. | F1 | Acc. | F1 |
| TF-IDF + SVM | 50% | 51% | 67% | 66% | 77% | 77% | 68% | 66% |
| Fine-tuned BERT | 62% | 59% | 76% | 75% | 81% | 80% | 70% | 69% |
| SBERT + MLP | **72%** | **70%** | **83%** | **82%** | **82%** | **82%** | **76%** | **73%** |

### 4.2 Stance Results and User Engagement

Figure 2 presents the distribution of stances (support/ pro, neutral, against/ refute) across the four claim topics: Election Fraud, Voter Registration, Voting Eligibility, and Voting Restrictions. It is no surprise that most of the comments are neutral, with over 50% being labeled neutral. For one topic, Voter Registration, approximately 75% of the comments are neutral. What is more interesting is the distribution of support and against comments. Recall that all of these videos are factually accurate. Therefore, the against stance should be close to 0%. However, the against stance ranges from approximately 10% for the Voter Registration topic to over 30% for the voting eligibility topic. In other words, there is a strong representation of comments related to voting eligibility and election fraud that may increase doubt in the shared facts.

Further investigation showed that more popular comments associated with the videos tend to be more opinionated than less popular comments. Figure 3 shows the engagement distribution by stance. We find that, among comments with a digg (or like) count higher than 200, against/refute stances are most common, followed by neutral comments, while pro/support stances appear least frequently. In other words, people are especially inclined to like comments that disagree with the video content than those that are neutral or supportive. This is concerning, given the factual nature of the videos. It is also important to

[1] We note that newer transformer models may perform better. We leave that for future work since the goal of this study is not to produce state-of-the-art stance detection models. Instead, our main aim is to adapt existing models to the characteristics of our datasets to facilitate the analysis of the discourse surrounding important election topics on TikTok.

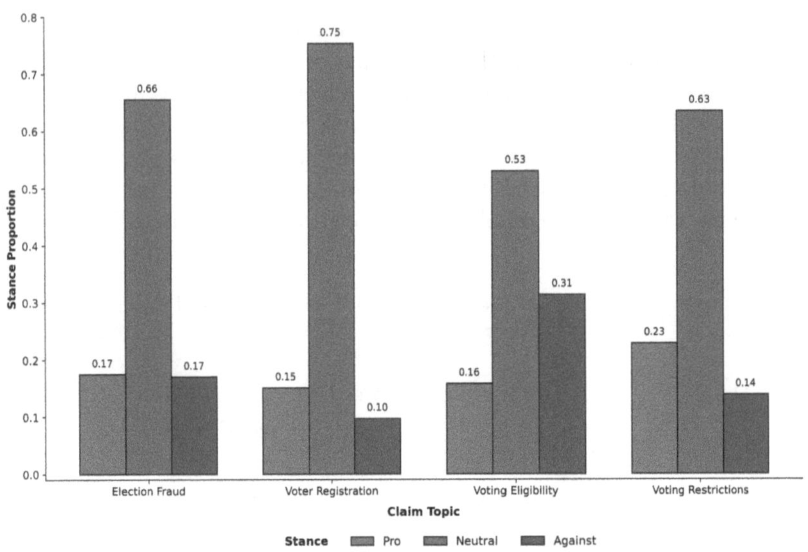


**Fig. 2.** Stance Percentages across different Claim Topics.

note that popular comments tend to be the ones that are at the top of the comment section on TikTok. While this is a strategy to increase engagement, it may also lead to reinforcing the belief that everyone is opinionated even though a significant portion of popular comments are neutral.

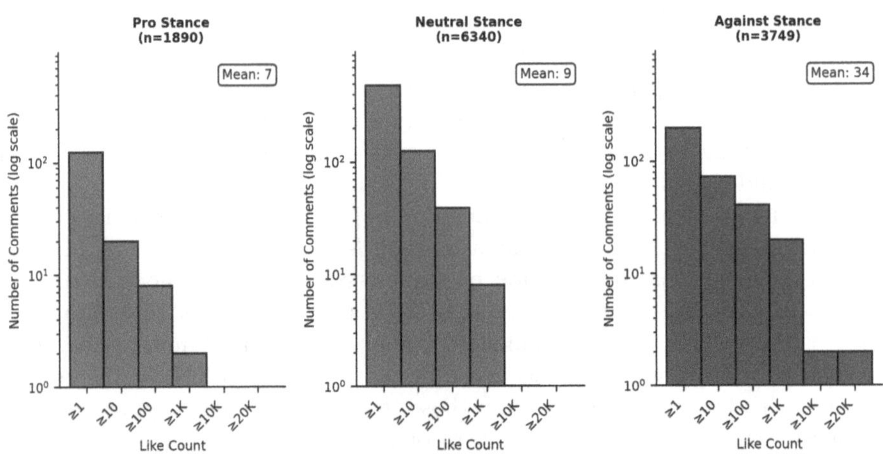


**Fig. 3.** Engagement Distribution by Stance: Voting Eligibility Topic.

## 5 Discussion and Conclusion

The findings of this study highlight the complexity of combating political misinformation on platforms like TikTok, where large volumes of comments can be used to confuse or mislead people, even when the associated video contains factual information. Our analysis demonstrates that although neutral stances dominate user engagement across misinformation-prone topics such as election fraud, voting eligibility, voter registration, and voter restrictions, opinionated comments tend to elicit significant engagement. This underscores the dual-edged nature of TikTok's algorithmic environment, which facilitates both the rapid spread of factual information and the immediate dispute of those facts. The results suggest that interventions to curb misinformation must not only involve creating short-form videos and using trending hashtags, but also include regular engagement that debunks misinformed comments.

In conclusion, this study demonstrates the importance of interdisciplinary approaches to tackling misinformation, combining computer science tools for automated detection with social science insights into user behavior and platform dynamics. While advances in machine learning models offer promising pathways for identifying high and low quality content, the nuanced characteristics of TikTok's environment demand tailored strategies. Future research should explore collaborative interventions that incorporate platform-specific affordances, user education campaigns, and regulatory frameworks to reduce the influence of misinformation during critical periods like elections. By bridging technical tools and behavioral understanding, we can develop strategies for improving the quality of our information ecosystem.

**Acknowledgments.** This research was supported by the McCourt School's Massive Data Institute at Georgetown University and the National Science Foundation's Research Experiences for Undergraduates (REU) program (award number 2244271). We would like to thank Professors Shweta Bansal, Sarah Bargal, and Carole Gresenz for their mentorship during the REU program and Rebecca Vanarsdall Yanchen Wang for their additional support to this research. We also acknowledge the contributions of other REU students who worked on this project over the summer but were unable to continue in the fall. This work used resources provided by the CloudBank project, which is supported by National Science Foundation grant #1925001.

## References

1. Lewandowsky, S.: Truth and democracy in an era of misinformation. Science **386**(6717), eads5695 (2024). https://doi.org/10.1126/science.ads5695
2. Kydd, A.H.: Decline, radicalization and the attack on the us capitol. Violence: Int. J. (2021). https://doi.org/10.1177/26330024211010043
3. Muhammed Sadiq, T., Mathew, S.K.: The disaster of misinformation: a review of research in social media. Int. J. Data Sci. Anal. **13**(4), 271–285 (2022)
4. Allcott, H., Gentzkow, M., Yu, C.: Trends in the diffusion of misinformation on social media. Res. Politics, **6**(2), 2053168019848554 (2019). https://doi.org/10.1177/2053168019848554

5. Budak, C.: What happened? The spread of fake news publisher content during the 2016 U.S. Presidential election. In: The World Wide Web Conference, WWW '19, pp. 139–150 (2019). Association for Computing Machinery
6. Allcott, H., et al.: The effects of facebook and instagram on the 2020 election: a deactivation experiment. Proc. Natl. Acad. Sci. **121**(21), e2321584121 (2024)
7. Bösch, M., Ricks, B.: Broken promises: Tiktok and the German election. Mozilla Foundation (2021)
8. Utami, R.W., Putri, T.B.B., Berlian, D.A.B.: Unmasking political hoaxes: Bawaslu's battle against digital misinformation warfare. Jurnal Muara Ilmu Ekonomi dan Bisnis (2024)
9. Bakshy, E., Messing, S., Adamic, L.A.: Exposure to ideologically diverse news and opinion on Facebook. Science **348**(6239), 1130–1132 (2015). https://www.science.org/doi/abs/10.1126/science.aaa1160
10. The Associated Press, Fact focus: A look at false and misleading claims surrounding the 2024 election (Nov, 2024). https://apnews.com/article/fact-check-misinformation-houston-rally-confrontation-99af1f80eb43d31966cae8e68dbc3415
11. Udani, A., Kimball, D.C., Fogarty, B.: How local media coverage of voter fraud influences partisan perceptions in the United States. State Politics Policy Q. **18**(2), 193–210 (2018)
12. Alvarez, R.M., Cao, J., Li, Y.: Voting experiences, perceptions of fraud, and voter confidence. Soc. Sci. Q. **102**(4), 1225–1238 (2021). https://onlinelibrary.wiley.com/doi/abs/10.1111/ssqu.12940
13. Brennan Center for Justice. Voting laws roundup: 2024 in review (Jan, 2025). https://www.brennancenter.org/our-work/research-reports/voting-laws-roundup-2024-review
14. Hajnal, Z., Lajevardi, N., Nielson, L.: Voter identification laws and the suppression of minority votes. J. Politics **79**(2), 363–379 (2017). https://doi.org/10.1086/688343
15. Shah, P., Smith, R.S.: Legacies of segregation and disenfranchisement: the road from Plessy to frank and voter id laws in the United States. RSF J. Soc. Sci. **7**(1), 134–146 (2021)
16. Lewandowsky, S., Ecker, U.K., Cook, J.: Beyond misinformation: understanding and coping with the "post-truth" era. J. Appl. Res. Mem. Cogn. **6**(4), 353–369 (2017)
17. O'Connor, C., Weatherall, J.O.: The Misinformation Age: How False Beliefs Spread. Yale University Press (2019)
18. Broda, E., Strömbäck, J.: Misinformation, disinformation, and fake news: lessons from an interdisciplinary, systematic literature review. Ann. Int. Commun. Assoc. **48**(2), pp. 139–166 (2024). https://doi.org/10.1080/23808985.2024.2323736
19. Xiao, X., Borah, P., Su, Y.: The dangers of blind trust: examining the interplay among social media news use, misinformation identification, and news trust on conspiracy beliefs. Public Underst. Sci. **30**(8), 977–992 (2021)
20. Research, P.: Social media and news fact sheet. Pew Research (2024). https://www.pewresearch.org/journalism/fact-sheet/social-media-and-news-fact-sheet/
21. Kirkpatrick, C.E., Lawrie, L.L.: Tiktok as a source of health information and misinformation for young women in the United States: survey study. JMIR Infodemiology **4**, e54663, (2024). https://infodemiology.jmir.org/2024/1/e54663
22. Glover, B., et al.: Fake news? quantifying the prevalence of misinformation related to scoliosis on the tik tok social media platform. J. Pediatr. Orthop. Soc. North Am. 100207 (2025). https://www.sciencedirect.com/science/article/pii/S2768276525000513

23. Baumel, N.M., Spatharakis, J.K., Karitsiotis, S.T., Sellas, E.I.: Dissemination of mask effectiveness misinformation using tiktok as a medium. J. Adolesc. Health **68**(5), 1021–1022 (2021)
24. Bautista, P.S., Alonso-López, N., Giacomelli, F.: Fact-checking in tiktok. Communication and narrative forms to combat misinformation. Revista Latina de Comunicación Social, no. 79, 87–113 (2021)
25. Chen, T., Guestrin, C.: XGBoost: a scalable tree boosting system. In: Proceedings of the 22nd ACM SIGKDD International Conference on Knowledge Discovery and Data Mining, KDD '16, pp. 785–794 (2016). Association for Computing Machinery, New York, USA
26. Mohammad, S., Kiritchenko, S., Sobhani, P., Zhu, X., Cherry, C.: SemEval-2016 task 6: detecting stance in tweets. In: Proceedings of the 10th International Workshop on Semantic Evaluation (SemEval-2016), pp. 31–41 (June, 2016). Association for Computational Linguistics
27. Zhang, H., et al.: Enhancing stance classification on social media using quantified moral foundations. In: Social Networks Analysis and Mining: 16th International Conference, ASONAM, Proceedings, Part I. Springer-Verlag, pp. 305–319 (2024)
28. Devlin, J., Chang, M.-W., Lee, K., Toutanova, K.: BERT: pre-training of deep bidirectional transformers for language understanding. In: Proceedings of the 2019 Conference of the North American Chapter of the Association for Computational Linguistics: Human Language Technologies, vol. 1 (Long and Short Papers). Association for Computational Linguistics, pp. 4171–4186 (2019)
29. Reimers, N., Gurevych, I.: Sentence-BERT: sentence embeddings using Siamese BERT-networks. In: Proceedings of the 2019 Conference on Empirical Methods in Natural Language Processing and the 9th International Joint Conference on Natural Language Processing (EMNLP-IJCNLP), pp. 3982–3992 (Nov, 2019). Association for Computational Linguistics
30. Tunstall, L., et al.: Efficient few-shot learning without prompts (2022). https://arxiv.org/abs/2209.11055

# Validating DataOps CI/CD Pipelines with a Three-Layer Testing Framework

Dmytro Valiaiev(✉)

University of Arkansas at Little Rock, 2801 S University Avenue, Little Rock, AR 72204, USA
dvaliaiev@ualr.edu

**Abstract.** The industry shift from extract-transform-load (ETL) to extract-load-transform (ELT) through DataOps practices has made continuous integration and continuous deployment (CI/CD) pipelines central to transforming raw SQL models into governed data assets. However, practical guidance on how to test these pipelines remains limited. This study introduces a three-layer framework (white-box, gray-box, and black-box) integrated into GitLab CI for a data-warehouse codebase. The framework runs 23 automated controls per commit. An evaluation of real merge requests shows that the gate prevents faulty submissions and releases compliant code without manual review. The results demonstrate that rigorous, yet lightweight, DataOps pipeline validation is achievable and cost-effective while ensuring production-grade quality assurance.

**Keywords:** DataOps · CI/CD · SQL · ELT · Data Governance

## 1 Introduction

DataOps emerged as a synthesis of data management practices with software engineering concepts such as DevOps and Agile, with the goal of improving data quality and data governance in enterprises [1,2]. The proliferation of scratch table use and transformation tools such as dbt has led to an exponential increase in the number of data models, which complicates standardization efforts and increases maintenance overhead [3,4]. The many flavors of SQL, the de facto lingua franca of data processing, add even more complexity since the code cannot be handled as easily as in less ambiguous languages such as Python or Java, which have out-of-the-box linting and refactoring tools available [5]. Queries are frequently written ad hoc, shared informally, and rarely versioned with the same rigor applied to traditional software development [6]. This study proposes a framework that embeds validation directly into the pipeline and governs a source-of-truth SQL repository. This allows teams to collaborate, standardize, and scale analytics development with transparency and control. Finally, it assesses its performance through a three-layered testing methodology.


R. Stahlbock et al. (Eds.): CSCE 2025, CCIS 2938, pp. 322–332, 2027.
https://doi.org/10.1007/978-3-032-22196-4_24

# 2 Implementation

## 2.1 DataOps Validation Framework

The solution treats the analytics codebase as a version-controlled project that employs Git-based workflows. A structured CI/CD pipeline reflects DataOps principles of modularity, collaboration, and extensibility. CI and DevOps automation facilitate agile software development that is free of errors [7]. The pipeline has sequential stages (Lint, Optimize, Parse, Validate, Observe, Deploy), each running jobs that implement specific checks. In total, 23 Python scripts encode the controls shown in Table 1.

**Table 1.** DataOps framework mapping.

| # | DataOps Principle | CI/CD Stage | CI/CD Jobs |
|---|---|---|---|
| 1 | Automation and Standardization [8–12] | Lint | `sql_lint`, `naming_convention`, `tags` |
| 2 | Efficiency and AI Optimization [12–17] | Optimize | `vector_similarity`, `ai_feedback` |
| 3 | Quality and Integrity [18–22] | Parse | `ast_parse`, `column_usage`, `dead_code`, `model_length`, `model_functions` |
| 4 | Governance and Compliance [23–28] | Validate | `branch_freshness`, `freeze_schedule`, `path_permissions`, `model_compliance`, `owner`, `configuration`, `materialization`, `model_dependencies`, `compilation` |
| 5 | Observability and Performance [29–36] | Observe | `test_run`, `uat_run`, `runtime_threshold`, `configured_test` |

## 2.2 CI/CD Implementation

The pipeline resides in a single `.gitlab-ci.yml` file at the root of the repository and is executed by a GitLab Runner that clones the commit and launches the specified stages in a clean containerized environment. Analysts work on feature branches, push their changes, and open merge requests; every update triggers a fresh pipeline run. All jobs within a stage run in parallel, and the next stage starts only after the current one reports success. This gated execution prevents wasted computation and provides immediate, actionable feedback whenever a control fails.

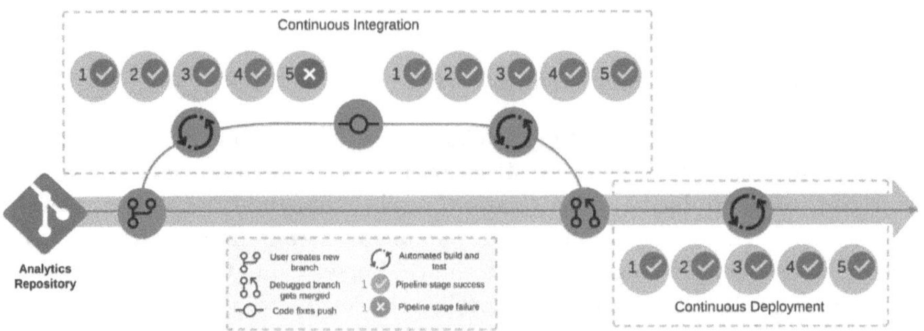


**Fig. 1.** CI/CD merge request flow.

Figure 1 visualizes this flow. The numbered circles represent the five DataOps stages defined earlier. A green tick indicates that every control in that stage has passed, whereas a red cross marks the first failing stage, at which point the pipeline stops and returns detailed logs to the author. Once a branch clears all stages in the continuous integration panel, an identical sequence replays on the default branch, culminating in continuous deployment. The final step publishes the validated models to the production warehouse and regenerates the HTML (HyperText Markup Language) data catalog, ensuring that the code, artifacts, and documentation share the same commit hash. This closed-loop workflow shortens the feedback cycles and maintains a single source of truth. By integrating the gate directly into the merge-request lifecycle, the organization enforces DataOps governance without manual checkpoints, thereby reducing lead time while preserving auditing capabilities and reproducibility.

## 3 Evaluation

The proof-of-concept solution is evaluated at three concentric layers (job, stage, pipeline) that mirror a modern CI/CD system (Fig. 2; [37,38]). Each layer applies a distinct testing style (white-box, gray-box, black-box) to provide quality assurance (QA) from individual checks to end-to-end pipeline deployment. Table 2 summarizes the purpose and evidence artifacts for each testing tier.

### 3.1 Job Layer Testing

Most controls demonstrate deterministic behavior at the job layer, confirming correctness at the smallest functional unit. The purpose of the job-level tests is to verify that every control script behaves deterministically and is independent of the CI environment or stage design (Table 3). *Pytest* offers broad compatibility, simple assertion syntax, and fixture reuse, making it a preferred alternative to the previously dominant *unittest* framework in Python [42].

In total, 368 unit tests were executed, yielding approximately a 1:4 test-to-code ratio. The lowest individual coverage (95%) meets the acceptance threshold, while the overall statement coverage was 98.6%, with 18 scripts achieving 100%.

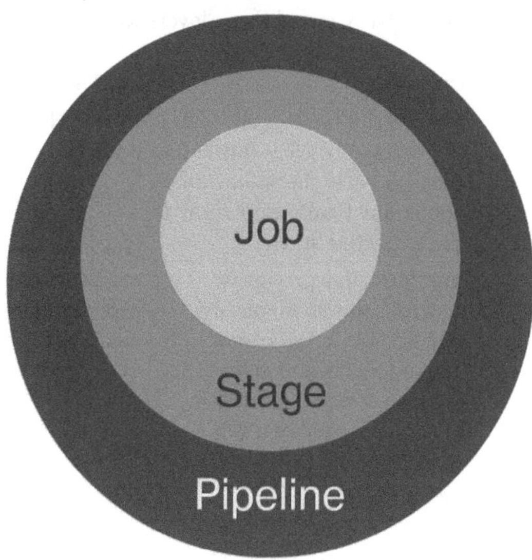


**Fig. 2.** Three layers of testing.

### 3.2 Stage Layer Testing

To assess stage layer performance, a dedicated `qa` stage was introduced immediately following the standard pipeline execution. This stage comprises two specific jobs: `qa-gate`, which consolidates and executes all 23 DataOps control scripts, and `summary`, which generates a comprehensive summary report using the *JUnit* testing framework (Table 4, [43]). *JUnit* was selected due to its language-agnostic XML output format, native GitLab CI/CD integration capabilities, and straightforward parsing by downstream compliance tools [44].

### 3.3 Pipeline Layer Testing

In the context of CI/CD, pipeline-level validation uses a black-box methodology. The entire system is assessed through its standard interface: the Git Merge Request (MR). Since the internal architecture has already been evaluated using white-box unit tests and gray-box integration tests, the black-box strategy serves as the final evaluation layer. At this stage, analytical granularity decreases while system-wide scope increases [45]. Furthermore, this is the recommended approach for evaluating high-level orchestration and user-facing behavior [46]. Two scenarios, a non-compliant submission (Scenario A) and a compliant submission (Scenario B), were tested to ensure pipeline-level cohesion.

In Scenario A, intentional flaws were introduced. The pipeline went through multiple iterations, with each commit attempting to resolve previously raised errors (Table 5). After every push, the pipeline state was captured by graph snapshots. These confirmed that the pipeline advanced only after preceding errors

**Table 2.** Overview of three layers of testing.

| Layer | Test Style | Purpose | Evidence Artifact(s) |
|---|---|---|---|
| Job | White-box unit testing [39] | Ensure the functional correctness of each individual control; each check executes deterministically and returns the expected status | *Pytest* HTML coverage report |
| Stage | Gray-box integration testing [40] | Validate that groups of controls run as a cohesive CI/CD job with correct dependencies and sequence; ensure expected pass/fail behavior under real job conditions | `ctrls_report.xml` `stage_report.json` `manifest.sha256` `stage_metrics.csv` |
| Pipeline | Black-box scenario testing [41] | Treat the pipeline as a service; supply faulty and corrected merge requests to verify that only compliant changes are built, tested, and deployed | Pipeline graph Published documentation HTML on GitLab Pages |

**Table 3.** Metrics and definitions for testing Python scripts.

| Metric | Definition |
|---|---|
| Number of functions | Top-level functions and class methods exposed by the module |
| Executable statements | Lines counted by `coverage.py` as runnable Python code |
| Unit test cases | Discrete *pytest* cases, including parametrization, which gives a sense of testing depth |
| Statement coverage percentage | Proportion of executable lines run during testing, calculated as (executed/executable) $\times$ 100 |

were corrected. This iterative resolution mirrors real-world DataOps workflows, where analysts progressively address issues until full validation is achieved.

In iterations 1–4, the pipeline graphs show red nodes at non-conforming stages, while subsequent stages remain gray (unexecuted). Reviewing the documentation site confirms the absence of the submitted model. The MR remains blocked, requiring further correction, exemplifying collaborative enforcement as recommended by [47].

In Scenario B, a final iteration introduces all necessary fixes, producing a compliant pipeline run. Since the graph is entirely green, the MR can be merged

**Table 4.** Stage layer validation artifacts and their purpose

| Evidence Artifact | Produced By | Purpose |
|---|---|---|
| `ctrls_report.xml` | `qa-gate` | JUnit-style report with one test-case element per control (23 total). Its absence—or any **`failure`** element—indicates a control failure, serving as the primary source of truth for stage pass/fail status |
| `stage_report.json` | `qa-gate` | Numeric summary derived from the executed jobs |
| `manifest.sha256` | `qa-gate` | SHA-256 hash of **`ctrls_report.xml`**, confirming file integrity after the job finishes |
| `stage_junit.xml` | `qa-gate` | Minimal JUnit suite consumed by GitLab so the merge-request UI shows a single green badge for the gate |
| `stage_metrics.csv` | `summary` | Quantifies stage-level behavior across the entire pipeline, yielding a final pass or fail outcome |

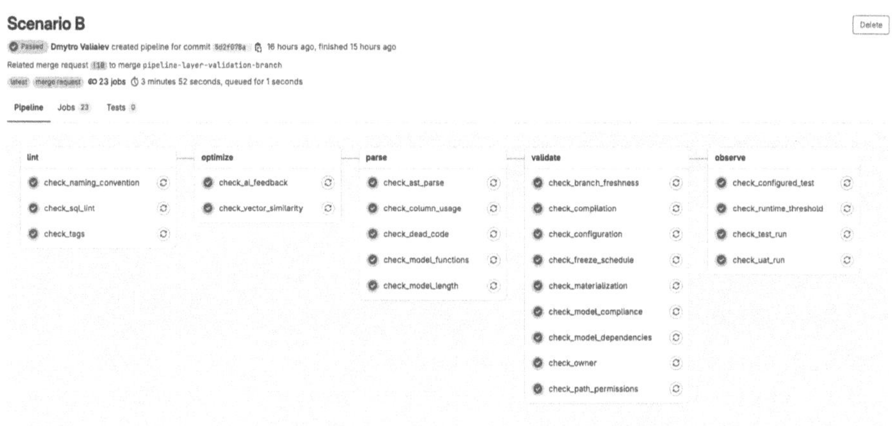


**Fig. 3.** Final pipeline status graph.

(Fig. 3). This scenario-based approach validates that the DataOps-aligned workflow enforces all relevant controls during both correct and flawed submissions (Table 6).

### 3.4 Limitations

This study intentionally prioritized architectural visibility and a demonstration of potential workflow integration, sacrificing long-term performance metrics. As a result, several limitations emerge:

**Table 5.** Pipeline layer validation (Scenario A).

| # | Commit Focus | Failed Stage | Failed Job |
|---|---|---|---|
| 1 | Initial submission. An unapproved tag is used | Lint | `check _tags` |
| 2 | Incorrect tag removed, but the model fails LLM feedback due to `DISTINCT` clauses, aggregations, etc. | Optimize | `check _ai _feedback` |
| 3 | Query corrected, yet overall model length exceeds threshold. | Parse | `check _model _length` |
| 4 | Model shortened, but branch now lags behind target-branch changes | Validate | `check _branch _freshness` |
| 5 | Source branch rebased per Git workflow, but model lacks a complementary test | Observe | `check _configured _test` |

**Table 6.** Pipeline layer validation.

| Validation Checkpoint | Expected Result | Observed Result |
|---|---|---|
| CI graph status | All stages (Lint → Optimize → Parse → Validate → Observe → Deploy) have passed and are marked in green | All stages are green |
| CD graph status | All CI stages and the deploy stage have passed and are marked in green | All stages are green |
| Documentation site | The model is present in the catalog | The model is accessible in the catalog |

### 3.5 Limitations

This study intentionally prioritized architectural visibility and a demonstration of potential workflow integration. Hence, the decision to sacrifice long-term performance metrics leads to certain limitations of the study:

- There was no quantitative benchmark: one could not be set due to the revamp of the entire process through the replacement of legacy workflows and a consequent introduction of new practices. If a potential organization has reached data maturity in a different way, where it has accumulated metrics logging and centralized observability, it would be possible to quantify the impact that a DataOps-driven framework would have.
- The implementation of the proposed solution was done in only one company with the assumption that it is generalizable. However, companies of vastly different sizes and data team structures can be studied.
- The user feedback was primarily anecdotal, and this study leaves room for a structured survey or collection of metrics.
- Furthermore, because this study focused on the infrastructure layer, human factors such as resistance witnessed in adopting teams, training overhead, or

role clarity were not explicitly evaluated. These elements are likely to affect the success of any future implementation.

## 4 Conclusion

This paper demonstrates a concrete, end-to-end approach to DataOps pipeline validation. By codifying data quality and governance rules into modular checks and enforcing them through a CI/CD pipeline, this work bridges the gap between ad hoc analytics workflows and disciplined software practices. This framework ensures that only well-formed, documented, and performant SQL models are deployed. In trials, the automated gate reliably blocked defective code and allowed correct changes to flow, eliminating manual QA bottlenecks. These findings indicate that treating the data warehouse as code is both feasible and beneficial: teams gain faster feedback, reduced risk, and an audit trail for compliance. Future extensions may include additional checks (e.g., data freshness thresholds) and proactive alerting, but even in its current form, the framework provides a scalable, cost-effective blueprint for DataOps adoption in analytics environments.

## References

1. Ereth, J.: DataOps—towards a definition. In: LWDA 2018: Lernen, Wissen, Daten, Analysen, CEUR-WS, vol. 2191, pp. 104–112 (2018). https://ceur-ws.org/Vol-2191/paper13.pdf. Accessed 1 Nov 2025
2. Merchan, W.M.: DataOps: an agile methodology for data-driven organizations (2018). https://www.academia.edu/94347054/DataOps_An_Agile_Methodology_for_Data_Driven_Organizations. Accessed 10 Aug 2024
3. Carvalho, D.M.: Exploração, Migração e Teste de Tecnologias de Armazenamento Baseadas em Séries Temporais. ProQuest. https://www.proquest.com/openview/e3f4937c1a94a70f223720bcb011f2d8. Accessed 29 June 2025
4. Kline, K.: Building modern data pipelines using DBT—tips and tricks. Database Trends Appl. **38**(2), 28–29 (2024)
5. Zmigrod, R., Alamir, S., Liu, X.: Translating between SQL dialects for cloud migration. In: Proceedings of 46th International Conference on Software Engineering—SEIP (ICSE-SEIP) (2024). https://conf.researchr.org/details/icse-2024/icse-2024-seip/12/Translating-between-SQL-Dialects-for-Cloud-Migration. Accessed 13 June 2025
6. Rahman, N.: SQL scorecard for improved stability and performance of data warehouses. Int. J. Softw. Innov. **4**(3), 22–37 (2016). https://doi.org/10.4018/IJSI.2016070102
7. Mohammad, S.M.: Continuous Integration and Automation. SSRN, Rochester, NY (2016). https://papers.ssrn.com/abstract=3655567. Accessed 5 Aug 2024
8. Munappy, A.R., Mattos, D.I., Bosch, J.: From ad-hoc data analytics to DataOps. In: Proceedings of 2020 IEEE/ACM International Conference on Software and System Processes (ICSSP), pp. 165–174 (2020). https://doi.org/10.1145/3379177.3388909
9. Castelluccio, M.: Data fabric architecture. Strat. Finan. **103**(4), 57–58 (2021)

10. Mainali, K.: DataOps: towards understanding and defining data analytics approach. KTH Royal Institute of Technology (2020). https://urn.kb.se/resolve?urn=urn:nbn:se:kth:diva-289596. Accessed 30 June 2025
11. Rodriguez, M., de Araújo, L.J.P., Mazzara, M.: Good practices for the adoption of DataOps in the software industry. J. Phys.: Conf. Ser. 1694(1), 012032 (2020). https://doi.org/10.1088/1742-6596/1694/1/012032
12. Vargas-Rueda, L., Ponguтá-Díaz, S., González-Sanabria, J.-S.: DataOps, una alternativa para la gestión de data pipelines. Revista Ibérica de Sistemas e Tecnologias de Informação **E38**, 259–269 (2020)
13. Orchard, T., Tasiemski, L.: The rise of generative AI and possible effects on the economy. Econ. Bus. Rev. **9**(2), 9–26 (2023). https://doi.org/10.18559/ebr.2023.2.732
14. Gain, U., Hotti, V.: Low-code AutoML-augmented data pipeline – a review and experiments. J. Phys.: Conf. Ser. **1828**(1), 012015 (2021). https://doi.org/10.1088/1742-6596/1828/1/012015
15. Zaghloul, M., Salem, M., Ali-Eldin, A.: A new framework based on features modeling and ensemble learning to predict query performance. PLoS ONE **16**(10), e0258439 (2021). https://doi.org/10.1371/journal.pone.0258439
16. Radziwill, N., Freeman, G.: Machine learning. Softw. Qual. Prof. **22**(4), 18–25 (2020)
17. Mahapatra, T., Banoo, S.N.: Flow-based programming for machine learning. Future Internet **14**(2), 2 (2022). https://doi.org/10.3390/fi14020058
18. Bayram, F., Ahmed, B.S., Hallin, E., Engman, A.: DQSOps: data quality scoring operations framework for data-driven applications. In: Proceedings of 27th International Conference on Evaluation and Assessment in Software Engineering (EASE '23), pp. 32–41. ACM, New York (2023). https://doi.org/10.1145/3593434.3593445
19. Marin, M.J., Van Wijk, X.M.R., Durant, T.J.S.: Machine learning in healthcare: mapping a path to title 21. Clin. Chem. **68**(4), 609–610 (2022). https://doi.org/10.1093/clinchem/hvab285
20. Garriga, M., Aarns, K., Tsigkanos, C., Tamburri, D.A., Van Den Heuvel, W.-J.: DataOps for cyber-physical systems governance: the airport passenger flow case. ACM Trans. Internet Technol. 21(2), Article 36, 25 (2021). https://doi.org/10.1145/3432247
21. Garriga, M., Tamburri, D., Heuvel, W.-J.: DataOps for societal intelligence: a data pipeline for labor market skills extraction and matching. In: Proceedings of 2020 IEEE International Conference on Information Reuse and Integration for Data Science (IRI) (2020). https://doi.org/10.1109/IRI49571.2020.00063
22. Iatropoulou, S., Anastasiou, T., Karagiorgou, S., Petrou, P., Alexandrou, D., Bouras, T.: Privacy-preserving data federation for trainable, queryable and actionable data. In: 2023 IEEE 39th International Conference on Data Engineering Workshops (ICDEW), pp. 44–48 (2023). https://doi.org/10.1109/ICDEW58674.2023.00012
23. Nadal, S., Jovanovic, P., Bilalli, B., Romero, O.: Operationalizing and automating Data Governance. J. Big Data **9**(1), 117 (2022). https://doi.org/10.1186/s40537-022-00673-5
24. Ratzan, J.: Conceptualization and Instrumentation of Maturity of Responsible AI (MRAI): An Empirical Analysis of the US Banking Industry Credit Lending Practices. D.P.S. dissertation, Pace Univ., New York, USA (2022). https://www.proquest.com/docview/2725633397/abstract/4587C9C5D3B405EPQ/1. Accessed 15 Nov 2023

25. Ayala Martínez, C.P., Bilalli, B., Gómez Seoane, C., Martínez Fernández, S.J.: DOGO4ML: development, operation and data governance for ML-based software systems. In: Joint Proceedings of RCIS 2022 Workshops and Research Projects Track, CEUR-WS, vol. 3144 (2022). https://upcommons.upc.edu/handle/2117/374386. Accessed 15 Nov 2023
26. Gür, I.: DataOps for Data Sharing – Challenges and Requirements for Interorganizational Data Sharing (2021)
27. Gür, I., Möller, F., Hupperz, M., Uzun, D., Otto, B.: Requirements for DataOps to foster dynamic capabilities in organizations – a mixed methods approach (2022). https://doi.org/10.1109/CBI54897.2022.00025
28. Xu, J., Naseer, H., Maynard, S., Fillipou, J.: Leveraging data and analytics for digital business transformation through DataOps: an information processing perspective (2022)
29. McKendrick, J.: Modern techniques for hybrid and multicloud data management. Big Data Q. **8**(3), 12–13 (2022a)
30. McKendrick, J.: The state of database performance: top trends and strategies. Database Trends Appl. **36**(5), 12–13 (2022b)
31. McKendrick, J.: The rush of real-time data: gaining insights and value. Big Data Q. **9**(2), 14–15 (2023)
32. McKendrick, J.: The future of database management: new technologies and strategies. Database Trends Appl. **38**(3), 9–11 (2024)
33. Sacolick, I.: What to do when your DevOps team is downsized. InfoWorld (2022). https://www.infoworld.com/article/2337651/what-to-do-when-your-devops-team-is-downsized.html. Accessed 15 Nov 2023
34. Petrella, A.: Fundamentals of Data Observability: Implement Trustworthy End-to-End Data Solutions. O'Reilly Media, Sebastopol (2023)
35. Travkin, P.: Data observability: is it data quality monitoring or more? Database Trends Appl. **37**(1), 23–25 (2023)
36. Bahaa, S., Ghalwash, A., Harb, H.: DataOps lifecycle with a case study in healthcare. Int. J. Adv. Comput. Sci. Appl. **14** (2023). https://doi.org/10.14569/IJACSA.2023.0140115
37. Fairbanks, J., Tharigonda, A., Eisty, N.U.: Analyzing the effects of CI/CD on open source repositories in GitHub and GitLab. In: 2023 IEEE/ACIS 21st International Conference on Software Engineering Research, Management and Applications (SERA), pp. 176–181. IEEE, Orlando (2023). https://doi.org/10.1109/SERA57763.2023.10197778
38. Fluri, J., Fornari, F., Pustulka, E.: Measuring the benefits of CI/CD practices for database application development. In: 2023 IEEE/ACM International Conference on Software and System Processes (ICSSP), pp. 46–57. IEEE, Melbourne (2023). DOI: https://doi.org/10.1109/ICSSP59042.2023.00015
39. Henard, C., Papadakis, M., Harman, M., Jia, Y., Le Traon, Y.: Comparing white-box and black-box test prioritization. In: ICSE '16: Proceedings of 38th International Conference on Software Engineering, pp. 523–534. ACM, New York (2016). https://doi.org/10.1145/2884781.2884791
40. Khalili, A., Narizzano, M., Tacchella, A., Giunchiglia, E.: Automatic test-pattern generation for grey-box programs. In: IEEE/ACM 10th International Workshop on Automation of Software Test, pp. 33–37. IEEE, Florence (2015). (2015). https://doi.org/10.1109/AST.2015.14

41. Jacob, P.M., Prasanna, M.: A comparative analysis on black box testing strategies. In: ICIS 2016: Proceedings of 2016 International Conference on Information Science, pp. 1–6. IEEE, Kochi (2016). https://doi.org/10.1109/INFOSCI.2016.7845290
42. Alves, A., Hora, A.: TestMigrationsInPy: a dataset of test migrations from `unittest` to `pytest`. In: Proceedings of 22nd International Conference on Mining Software Repositories (MSR '25), pp. 841–845. IEEE/ACM (2025). https://doi.org/10.1109/MSR66628.2025.00122
43. Garcia, B.: Mastering Software Testing with JUnit 5: A Comprehensive, Hands-On Guide on Unit Testing Framework for Java Programming Language. Packt Publishing, Birmingham (2017). http://ebookcentral.proquest.com/lib/ualr/detail.action?docID=5116788. Accessed 28 June 2025
44. Totade, S.K., Tayde, T., Dhole, P.: Black box testing. Int. Res. J. Innov. Eng. Technol. **7**(10), 684–687 (2023). https://doi.org/10.47001/IRJIET/2023.710089
45. Khan, B., Saifullah, J., Khan, W., Chughtai, M.: An overview of ETL techniques, tools, processes and evaluations in data warehousing. J. Big Data **6**, 1–20 (2024). https://doi.org/10.32604/jbd.2023.046223
46. TanLi, M., Jiang, Y., Wang, X., Peng, R.: Black-box approach for software testing based on fat-property. In: MATEC Web of Conferences, vol. 309, art. 02008 (2020). https://doi.org/10.1051/matecconf/202030902008
47. Chacon, S., Straub, B.: Pro Git, 2nd edn. Apress, New York (2014)

# Kinematic Analysis of Ball Speed in Volleyball Spikes Using Pose Estimation and Object Detection

Deniz E. Mergen[1(✉)] and S. Ayca Erdogan[2]

[1] Los Gatos High School, Los Gatos, CA 95030, USA
denizegemergen08@gmail.com
[2] San Jose State University, San Jose, CA 95192, USA
ayca.erdogan@sjsu.edu

**Abstract.** This paper presents a low-cost method for analyzing volleyball spiking performance using only a single smartphone camera. We employ pose estimation and object detection to automatically extract key temporal metrics from video, including *approach time* and *jump time*. These metrics, along with the player's *arm style*, are then used in a regression model to predict *ball speed* and investigate the significance of their effects on *ball speed*. For model development and validation, a radar gun is used to collect the ground-truth speed data. Our regression model ($R^2 = 0.67$) provides preliminary evidence for a significant interaction between *approach time* and *arm style*, indicating a potential dependency between *approach time* and *ball speed* that is determined by the player's swing technique.

**Keywords:** Ball Speed · Motion Analysis · Pose Estimation · Object Detection · Regression · Volleyball Spiking

## 1 Introduction

In volleyball, a spike is the move when the player jumps and hits the ball with power with the intent of forcing the ball downward towards the opponent's court. Among the various actions within a volleyball match, the spike emerges as the greatest determinant of whether a team will ultimately achieve victory [1, 2]. Although the success of a spike is contingent upon a synthesis of mechanical factors such as hit height and ball direction, high ball speed is the most influential factor in producing a powerful and effective outcome. In literature, a variety of sophisticated tools are employed to analyze and improve ball speed during spike, including wearable inertial sensors, prototype smart balls, multi-camera motion capture systems, EMG electrolytes, and force plates [3]. A significant limitation of these technologies is their prohibitive cost and operational complexity, which renders them impractical for independent use by developing or amateur athletes.

This paper presents a flexible and adaptable methodology and training framework to empower volleyball players to analyze and enhance their spiking technique. We propose to use a single camera with slow-motion capability and a tethered volleyball with elastic


R. Stahlbock et al. (Eds.): CSCE 2025, CCIS 2938, pp. 333–342, 2027.
https://doi.org/10.1007/978-3-032-22196-4_25

bands placed at a fixed height. Furthermore, we study the relationship between movement kinematics and ball speed using the recorded spiking videos and speed data collected from a radar gun. We utilize pose estimation and ball detection to extract relevant features from the recorded videos. Finally, we analyze the effect of *approach time*, *jump time*, and *arm style* on the ball speed during spiking.

In Sect. 2, we present related work. In Sect. 3, we describe the methodology for data collection, feature extraction, and derivation of input variables. In Sect. 4, we present our preliminary results on predicting the speed of the ball during spiking using the derived input variables and their interactions. In Sect. 5, we conclude our paper.

## 2 Related Work

Many studies worked on understanding the biomechanical predictors of ball speed during spiking, mostly while collecting data using advanced equipment.

In [4], fifteen elite female volleyball players participated in the study in which they perform spike jumps, hitting a stationary ball at their maximum jump height. They use a motion capture system (Vicon cameras), force plates, and specialized software (Visual3D) to collect detailed data. They find that ball speed is closely linked to fore-arm length and the max elbow-extension angular velocity during the spike.

In [5], authors investigated the slide attacks by female collegiate volleyball players, identifying peak torso rotation, shoulder internal rotation, and elbow extension angular velocities as potential key contributors. A multiple stepwise regression analysis created a predictive model, which explained a substantial portion of the variance in ball speed. However, the overall model was not statistically significant ($p = .098$), with peak torso angular velocity during the wind-up phase being the most influential predictor.

In [6], authors demonstrated that an athlete's ability to generate both high forces (in jumping) and high velocities (in sprinting) are key determinants of powerful spikes and serves in top-level male volleyball. This highlights the importance of training programs that focus on developing both the force and velocity components of an athlete's physical profile. These variables were shown to individually account for 20% to 36% of the variance in the speeds of spikes and serves.

## 3 Methodology

### 3.1 Video Recording Setup

This study utilizes slow-motion video recordings to analyze the spiking motion of a single athlete. The experimental setup consists of an official orange and blue volleyball suspended at a fixed height using a tether and elastic band system, a configuration that is either commercially available or can be recreated with simple assembly [7]. A chalk line is marked on the ground to define the player's approach path, ensuring it is coplanar with the ball. Video data is captured using a smartphone positioned parallel to the line of motion, with the field of view encompassing the entire body of the player and the ball. The decision to record in slow-motion is critical, as it significantly enhances the precision of the pose estimation and object detection models employed in our analysis.

The experimental protocol begins from a fixed starting position, ensuring a standardized approach distance to the ball. Each trial requires the athlete to perform a prescribed two-step approach, initiated with the right foot, along a designated line of movement before jumping to spike the ball. The athlete takes short rests between trials. The athlete executes one of two distinct arm swing techniques, classified as either Straight (S) or Circular (C) at each trial:

- **Straight (S):** This technique is characterized by the hitting arm maintaining a largely extended posture as it moves through a linear path within the sagittal plane. Minimal elbow flexion occurs during the preparatory phase, followed by rapid extension through contact with the ball.
- **Circular (C):** This technique involves a wide, circular trajectory of the arm. It is distinguished by a pronounced loading phase that includes deep elbow flexion (to approximately 90°) and a high degree of external shoulder rotation, culminating in a rapid forward acceleration of the arm to strike the ball.

A radar gun is used to quantify the post-impact speed of the ball. We use the Bushnell Velocity Speed Gun (Model #: 101911) [8]. If the measurements are taken within 27 m, this radar gun can handle 4.44 m/s to 49.2 m/s with accuracy ±0.56 m/s. The instrument is maintained at a fixed angle, oriented along the expected spike path coaxial with the line of movement. See Fig. 1.

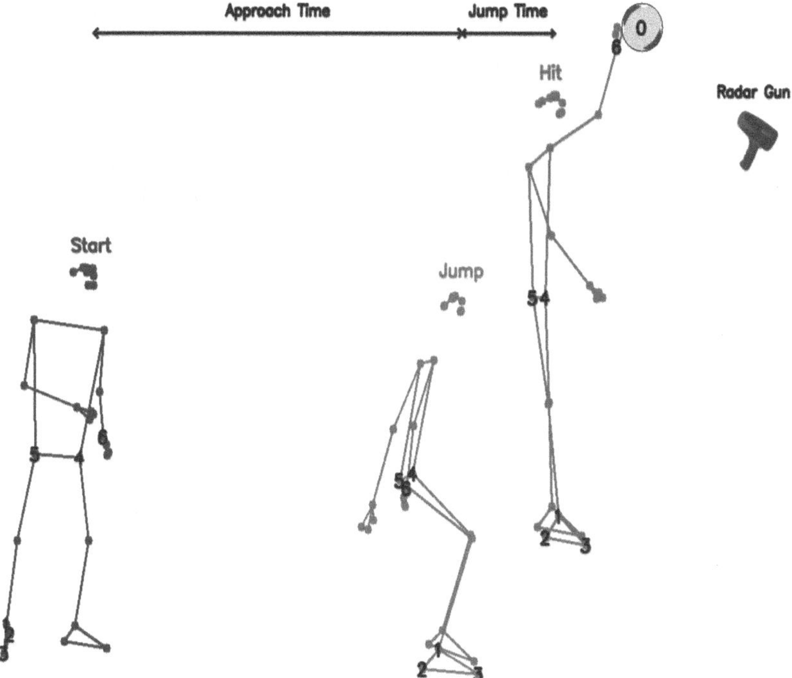


**Fig. 1.** The setup for video and ball speed recording: Extracted features: 0:Ball Location, 1:Right_Ankle, 2:Right_Heel, 3:Right_Foot_Index, 4:Left_Hip, 5: Right_Hip, 6:Left_Wrist.

### 3.2 Extracting Features from the Recorded Videos

Feature extraction from the video data is accomplished using various detection methods, primarily a pre-trained machine learning model for pose estimation. Specifically, we utilize the model provided by Google's MediaPipe framework [9], which identifies a human subject in each frame and provides 33 anatomical keypoints. From this output, a subset of 6 key body landmarks is selected for our feature analysis (see Fig. 1).

To detect the ball's location, we implement a color and geometry-based algorithm. First, each video frame is converted from the RGB color space to the HSV (Hue, Saturation, Value) space to better isolate color information. A binary mask is then created by thresholding the image to retain only the pixels within the predefined color range of the ball. Following noise removal using morphological operations, we identify the largest connected component (or contour). The center and radius of the ball are computed from this component. A color and geometry-based approach is used in [10] with omni-directional cameras.

### 3.3 Derived Temporal Input Variables: Approach Time and Jump Time

From the extracted features, we derive two key input variables for developing the ball speed prediction model: *approach time*, which quantifies the player's ability to generate horizontal momentum, and *jump time*, which measures their vertical power output to reach the ball. Although the approach distance and ball height are fixed in our experimental setup, these temporal variables are not constant, as they reflect natural variations in the player's speed and power across different trials.

We define *approach time* as the duration from the initiation of movement until the start of the jump, and *jump time* as the duration from the start of the jump until ball impact. The jump is considered to begin at the moment of maximum knee flexion prior to upward ascent. As illustrated in Fig. 1, the key moments of movement initiation, jump start, and ball impact are highlighted by blue, green, and red pose skeletons, respectively.

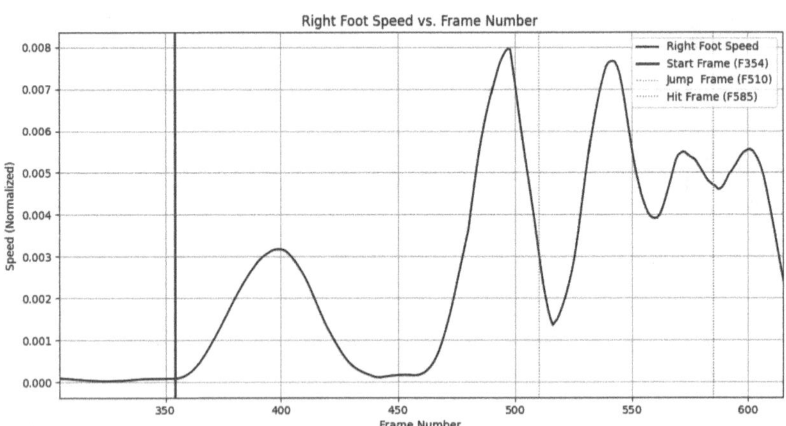


**Fig. 2.** Right Foot Speed vs Frame Number.

The calculation of *approach time* and *jump time* requires the identification of three key frames: the *start frame*, *jump frame*, and *hit frame*. We determine these frames using the player's tracking data obtained via MediaPipe and the tracking data for the ball. As both the player and the ball are assumed to move within the same plane, our analysis is restricted to their (x, y) coordinates.

The *start frame* is identified by analyzing the speed of the player's right foot. To determine the foot's position in each frame, we calculate the centroid of the (x, y) coordinates of three key landmarks: Right_Ankle, Right_Heel, and Right_Index (see Fig. 1). From this position data, the instantaneous velocity components ($v_x$, $v_y$) are computed as the change in $x$ and $y$ positions between consecutive frames. The foot's speed is then calculated using the formula for the magnitude of the velocity vector: $\sqrt{{v_x}^2 + {v_y}^2}$. The *start frame* is defined as the first frame where the speed of the right foot exceeds a predefined threshold, indicating the onset of motion. As an example, Fig. 2 illustrates the right foot's speed plotted against the frame number for a sample video, with the calculated *start frame* marked by a red vertical line.

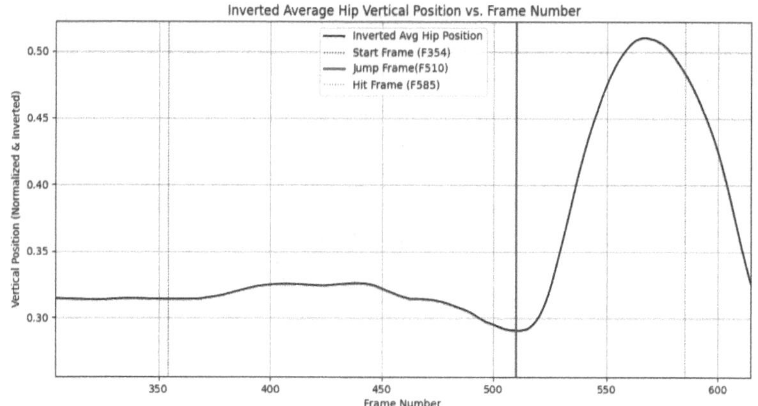


**Fig. 3.** Inverted Average Hip Vertical Position versus Frame Number

The *jump frame* is defined as the moment the player reaches their lowest vertical position before ascending into the jump. This point is determined by finding the frame with the minimum average y-coordinate of the player's left and right hip landmarks. Figure 3 provides a visualization of this by plotting the inverted y-position of the hips versus the frame number for a sample video, where the identified *jump frame* is marked by a green vertical line. We plot the inverted y-position because the MediaPipe framework originates its coordinate system from the top of the frame; therefore, a maximum raw y-value corresponds to the lowest physical position. Inverting the axis makes the minimum of the new graph intuitively represent this lowest crouch point.

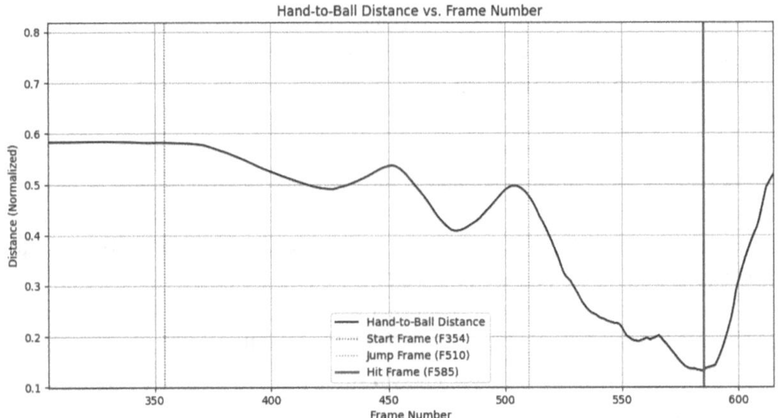


**Fig. 4.** Left-hand to Ball Center Distance

The *hit frame* is defined as the instant where the Euclidean distance between the player's left hand[1] and the ball is at a minimum. To ensure a consistent coordinate system, the ball's location is normalized to a [0, 1] range, identical to the format of the MediaPipe pose landmarks. We use the Left_Wrist landmark (Fig. 1) as the marker for the hand's position. Figure 4 illustrates this by plotting the distance between the Left_Wrist and the ball for each frame with a purple vertical line denoting the *hit frame*. Note that the same sample video is used in Figs. 2, 3 and 4.

It is important to note that the data series shown in Figs. 2, 3 and 4 are smoothed using a moving average filter to reduce noise before identifying the key frames. From these identified frames—*start frame*, *jump frame*, and *hit frame*—the temporal input variables are calculated. Specifically, *approach time* and *jump time* are computed in seconds using the following formulas:

$$ApproachTime = (JumpFrame - StartFrame)/FPS \tag{1}$$

$$JumpTime = (HitFrame - JumpFrame)/FPS \tag{2}$$

where FPS is the frame rate of recorded videos.

## 4 Regression Analysis for Ball Speed Prediction

As detailed in Sect. 3, two temporal input variables, *approach time* and *jump time*, are derived from the video using pose estimation and ball tracking data. In addition to these temporal metrics, we include a third, categorical variable: *arm style*. This variable, denoted as either 'S' for straight or 'C' for circular, is a controlled component of the experimental design, with the style being intentionally varied by the player during video recordings. Data acquisition is performed according to the experimental setup detailed in Sect. 3, yielding 16 slow-motion (120 FPS) video recordings from a smartphone

[1] For right-hand players, the location of the right hand should be used.

(Pixel 9 Pro). To prevent fatigue from biasing the data, sufficient rest is provided to the player between trials. Subsequently, each video underwent frame-by-frame processing via our pose estimation and ball detection modules, and the extracted coordinate data is stored in CSV format. These tracking files served as the basis for calculating the predictor variables *approach time* and *jump time* (per Sect. 3.3). As part of the protocol, the player's *arm style* is systematically varied and logged for each trial. The dataset is completed by incorporating the ground-truth *ball speed*, measured by a radar gun, as the dependent variable for regression analysis.

**Table 1.** Regression Summary Results

| Predictor | β | p | 95% CI |
|---|---|---|---|
| Intercept | 134.62 | 0.038 | [9.47, 259.77] |
| Arm Style (S = 1 vs C = 0) | −111.83 | 0.087 | [−242.92, 19.27] |
| Approach Time (s) | −28.93 | **0.020** | [−52.37, −5.5] |
| Arm style × Approach time (s) | 34.49 | **0.041** | [1.75, 67.22] |
| Jump time (s) | −129.24 | 0.078 | [−276.07, 17.59] |
| Arm style × Jump time (s) | 94.98 | 0.208 | [−62.23, 252.19] |

A regression model is fitted to predict *ball speed*, including interaction effects between the input variables. The model summary is provided in Table 1. The results indicate a statistically significant interaction between *arm style* and *approach time.* For the circular arm style ('C'), a one-second increase in *approach time* is associated with a 28.93 m/s decrease in ball speed. Conversely, for the straight *arm style* ('S'), the effect is positive; a one-second increase in *approach time* is associated with a 5.56 m/s increase in *ball speed.* While the main effects for *arm style* and *jump time* did not reach the standard 0.05 significance level, their p-values suggest they may be marginally significant contributors to the model.

**Table 2.** Model Overall Performance

| $R^2$ | Adjusted $R^2$ | F-statistic | p-value (F-Statistic) |
|---|---|---|---|
| 0.670 | 0.505 | 4.060 | 0.028 |

The overall model performance metrics are presented in Table 2. The model accounts for 67% of the variance in *ball speed* ($R^2 = 0.67$), and 50.5% of the variance after adjusting for the number of predictors (Adjusted $R^2 = 0.505$). The overall model significance is confirmed by the F-statistic ($p = 0.028$).

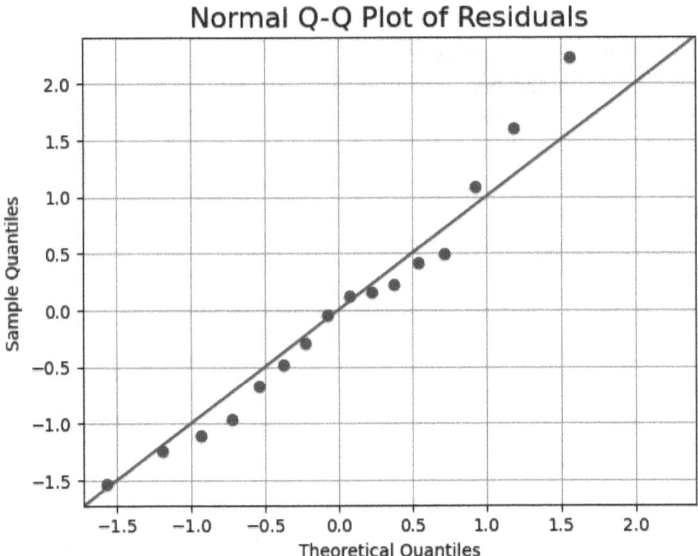


**Fig. 5.** Normal Q-Q Plot of Residuals

We next validate the model's assumptions. The Q-Q plot of the residuals (Fig. 5) shows a close alignment with the 45-degree line, supporting the assumption of normality. Although there is a slight deviation at the right tail, this is not unusual for a small dataset (n = 16).

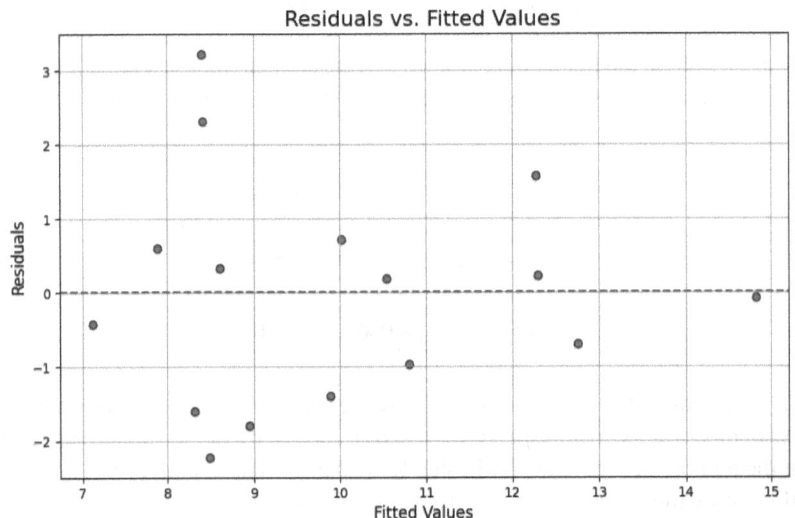


**Fig. 6.** Residuals versus Fitted Values

The plot of residuals versus fitted values, shown in Fig. 6, is used to assess the assumption of homoscedasticity (constant variance). The points are scattered randomly around the horizontal line at zero, which supports this assumption. While there is a minor indication of fanning out on the right side, this is not pronounced, and for a small dataset, the assumption of homoscedasticity is considered reasonably met.

Consistent with the literature, our results confirm that spike performance depends on both upper and lower body mechanics. The "arm style" in our analysis corresponds to the upper body and arm actions previously identified as critical in [4, 5]. Similarly, the findings of [6], which link hitting performance to the force-production capabilities of the lower-body muscles, underline the importance of the approach phase in our model.

## 5 Conclusions

In this paper, we have presented a cost-effective framework for analyzing volleyball spike performance. We extracted two kinematic variables—*approach time* and *jump time*—from recordings of a single player. These metrics, combined with the player's *arm style*, were used to model the *ball speed* at impact. Our contributions are twofold. First, we offer a practical framework for individual players to enhance their training. Second, we provide preliminary findings on the interaction between *approach time*, *jump time*, and *arm style* and their combined effect on *ball speed* during spiking.

Future work will involve validating these initial results with a larger dataset, which can be efficiently gathered using our automated data collection method. We also suggest incorporating data from a smartwatch to analyze metrics like arm acceleration and speed. To improve the generalizability of our findings, future studies should include data from multiple players.

## References

1. Marcelino, R., Mesquita, I., Afonso, J.: The weight of terminal actions in volleyball. Contributions of the spike, serve and block for the teams' rankings in the World League 2005. Int. J. Perform. Anal. Sport **8**, 1–7 (2005)
2. Eom, H.J., Schutz, R.W.: Statistical analyses of volleyball team performance. Res. Q. Exerc. Sport **63**(1), 11–18 (1992)
3. Oliveira, L.d.S., Moura, T.B.A., Rodacki, A.L.F., Tilp, M., Okazaki, V.H.A.: A systematic review of volleyball spike kinematics: implications for practice and research. Int. J. Sports Sci. Coach. **15**(2), 239–255 (2020)
4. Fuchs, P.X., Fusco, A., Bell, J.W., von Duvillard, S.P., Cortis, C., Wagner, H.: Movement characteristics of volleyball spike jump performance in females. J. Sci. Med. Sport **22**(7), 833–837 (2019)
5. Stefanovic, T., Zamporri, J., Aguinaldo, A.L.: Ball speed predictors in slide attacks in female volleyball players. ISBS Proc. Arch. **40**(1), Article no. 161 (2022)
6. Baena-Raya, A., et al.: The force-velocity profile as determinant of spike and serve ball speed in top-level male volleyball players. PLoS ONE **16**(4), e0249612 (2021)
7. Tethered training volleyball. https://www.amazon.com/Mikasa-V300-AT-TR-Official-tethered-Volleyball/. Accessed 20 Oct 2025
8. Bushnell Velocity Speedgun. https://www.amazon.com/dp/B0002X7V1Q. Accessed 20 Oct 2025

9. Google AI Pose Landmark Detection. https://ai.google.dev/edge/mediapipe/solutions/vision/pose_landmarker. Accessed 20 Oct 2025
10. Hikmahwan, B., Hario, B., Mudjirahardjo, P.: Ball detection based on color and shape features captured by Omni-directional camera, pp. 87–92 (2023)

# Open-Source and Institution-Specific Research Impact Evaluation via Unsupervised Ranking

Maria Tomasso[1,2](✉), Emon Nooruddin[2], and Melinda Villagran[1]

[1] Translational Health Research Center, Texas State University, San Marcos, TX 78666, USA
{met48,mvilla}@txstate.edu

[2] Department of Computer Science, Texas State University, San Marcos, TX 78666, USA
m_nooruddin@txstate.edu

**Abstract.** Evaluation of the impact of research works and identification of high-impact projects allows for researchers and institutions to allocate resources more efficiently and improve research dissemination strategies. Although some proprietary tools for research impact assessment exist, we seek an institution-specific model that is open-source, explainable, and actionable. We frame this task as an unsupervised ranking problem and develop three methodologies to identify high impact works. We build a pipeline to collect a training data set of 25,000 articles published between 2000 and 2024 with at least one author affiliated with a specific institution. Using our framework, we identify three sets of high impact papers using a composite percentile score, Pareto front ranking, and cluster-based ranking. We compare the results of each methodology and conclude with a recommendation for an ensemble approach to the detection of high-impact research papers.

**Keywords:** bibliometrics · altmetrics · Pareto front ranking · cluster ranking · unsupervised ranking · research impact

## 1 Introduction

Measuring the impact of research allows institutions to better allocate funds and assess progress towards specific research goals. Additionally, analysis of high-impact works can be used to inform and improve future research dissemination strategies. Although there is no clear consensus on the definition of *high impact* research (Penfield et al. (2014)), most sources agree that factors such as impact on public policy, industry, or government should be considered alongside academic impact. Priem et al. measure impact in four categories: usage (views, downloads), peer review (expert opinion), citations, and alternative metrics (storage, links, bookmarks, conversation). Morton (2015) defines research


R. Stahlbock et al. (Eds.): CSCE 2025, CCIS 2938, pp. 343–356, 2027.
https://doi.org/10.1007/978-3-032-22196-4_26

impact as "...changes in awareness, knowledge and understanding, ideas, attitudes and perceptions, and policy and practice as a result of research".

Using these definitions of research impact, traditional bibliometrics such as citation count may tell an incomplete story. Alternative metrics, or *altmetrics*, have gained popularity in recent years as a method of providing enhanced data on how the scientific community and public have interacted with a particular piece of research. Altmetrics such as social media engagement, news coverage, and citations in policies and patents can enhance traditional bibliometrics during research impact assessment. We augment traditional bibliometrics with altmetrics to gain a broader view of the impact of a specific paper.

We frame the measurement of research impact as an unsupervised ranking problem. We adapt three unsupervised ranking techniques to facilitate a research impact framework that is open source, explainable, generalizable, and adaptable. Our framework is robust to skewness and kurtosis in the input variables and identifies high impact works from tabular bibliometric and altmetric data. We create an institution-specific tool by curating a training corpus of works exclusively associated with a specific university, but this framework could easily be adapted to develop other institution-specific tools or run at scale within a specific discipline. We also introduce a pipeline for the collection and preparation of publication data. We compare the papers identified as high impact by each of our three approaches and conclude with a recommendation for an ensemble approach.

## 2 Related Work

### 2.1 Altmetrics

Altmetrics have gained popularity in recent years as a measure of the attention a research work has received Ali (2021). Altmetrics capture the interactions of the public with research works through social media, news media, non-academic citation, blogs, reference managers, and more. Altmetrics have the benefit of being faster than traditional bibliometrics, as it may take years for a paper to gain traction and begin being cited by other academic works. Priem et al. reiterate timeliness as a primary issue with traditional bibliometrics. It takes time for a paper to become cited, which makes measuring initial impact off of bibliometrics alone difficult. They also discuss traditional bibliometrics inability to measure impact outside of academia. It must be noted that altmetrics measure attention but not sentiment, and can be easily swayed by the popularity of a particular topic. Thus, altmetrics are often used in conjunction with traditional bibliometrics for a balanced approach.

Altmetrics can be accessed using digital object identifiers (DOIs) from public APIs. PlumX and Altmetrics.com are two well-known altmetrics databases that are utilized in this work.

## 2.2 Research Impact Assessment

Defining research impact is complex and often subjective. The relative importance of specific metrics may change by field and by research objective. Often, impact is related to real world impact and implementation.

Journal impact factor (JIF), a frequently used metric to measure the importance of a work, can be manipulated (Priem et al.) and may not accurately reflect the prestige of a journal in niche areas. Arnold and Fowler (2010) discuss the shortcomings of JIF as a proxy for research impact and the potential consequences of relying on JIF alone. Specifically, they discuss the skewed distribution of paper citations that lead to the mean being misleading, and the bias introduced by the common practice of restricting JIF calculations to the first two years of citations a paper receives, pointing out that only 10% of mathematics citations occur within two years of paper publication. Thus, for some fields JIF will drastically misrepresent the true long-term impact of a work. Additionally, citation itself is confounded by English language bias, article type, self-citation, and multi-authored papers. Since JIF is widely accepted as a proxy for journal quality, it can drive decisions on the part of researchers on whether or not to submit to a journal and institutions on whether or not to subscribe to a journal. Thus, an incentive exists for journals to take action to increase their JIF score whether or not it actually increases journal quality. The authors discuss the case of the International Journal of Numerical Sciences and Non-linear Simulation (IJNSNS), which had the highest JIF of any journal in applied mathematics in 2008 at 8.91, more than double the next highest JIF. Despite this high JIF score, subject matter experts categorizing applied mathematics journals by quality assigned IJNSNS to the third category out of four, which was described as "solid, though not outstanding".

Morton (2015) takes a process oriented approach of "uptake-use-impact" to the assessment of research impact. A six step pathway to impact is defined: (research) inputs; activities and outputs; engagement and involvement; awareness and reaction; capacity, knowledge and understanding; changes in behavior and practices; with these steps culminating in the contribution. Morton's framework allows for an in-depth analysis of a project, but is difficult to deploy at scale given the level of detail required and does not allow for any easy mechanism of comparison.

Penfield et al. (2014) consider the impact component of the UK's Research Excellence Framework (REF) and recommend that impact take into account research findings, outputs (papers, presentations, etc.), interactions with stakeholders and the public, feedback from stakeholders, research developments, outcomes, and impacts.

As altmetrics have become more widely available, impact assessments have begun incorporating them more often. Vaught and Wagner (2025) use the Altmetrics Attention Score, a proprietary index by Altmetric.com, as a ground-truth when evaluating an awards program's ability to identify high-impact research. Elsevier, which maintains the PlumX altmetric database Elifritz, uses a proprietary AI to generate research impact narratives using altmetrics with sub-scores in bibliometrics, altmetrics, policy, patents, media mentions, and social media metrics. Although both of these metrics provide useful information about the relative impact of a work, they are proprietary and not easily adapted to a specific institution. Additionally, since the calculations are not made public some aspects of these metrics, such as distribution, are opaque and impede researchers ability to interpret them.

## 3 Methodology

The objective of this project is to identify high impact research papers based on easily-obtainable metadata in a method that is interpretable and open source. Although the definition of high impact research varies by discipline, we begin with a "higher is better" assumption with the input variables and use methodologies that can identify high outliers.

### 3.1 Data

The full data collection and preparation pipeline is outlined in Fig. 1. Publication data was collected using the Publish or Perish (PoP) tool. For each year between and including 2000 and 2024, 1000 papers were selected that had at least one author affiliated with Texas State University. PoP allows users to query citation databases and returns a formatted CSV containing metadata about each academic publication including the year published, authors, abstract, number of citations, and bibliographic information. Crossref was selected as the database to query and 25,000 Texas State University research papers were collected.

To gain additional training data for use within the model, Altmetrics and PlumX Metrics were queried using the DOIs of the original 25,000 training papers. Altmetrics and PlumX Metrics both collect and aggregate data on scientific publications beyond traditional bibliographic metrics. These expanded metrics include mentions in mainstream media, shares on social media, and citations in policy and patent documents. Duplicates of commonly tracked metrics, e.g. citation or reader count, were intentionally left in the training data to address possible reporting errors in each database. By including alternative metrics, we are able to construct a richer metric of a paper's impact than traditional bibliographic metrics alone. Table 1 shows all variables included in the training set and their assigned categories.

Queries to both databases were automated via a Python script. Altmetrics had a 33.7% hit-rate while PlumX Metrics had a 99.9% hit-rate for the articles in the training set. The metadata returned from Altmetrics and PlumX Metrics were converted to a tabular format. Crossref, Altmetrics, and PlumX Metrics metadata were merged on DOI to create a unified dataset. When appropriate, missing values were set to 0. For example, PlumX Metrics data includes counts of media mentions for each paper. When this value was missing, either because the paper was not in the PlumX Metrics database or because the value was not set within PlumX Metrics, the value was set to zero. For this reason, the

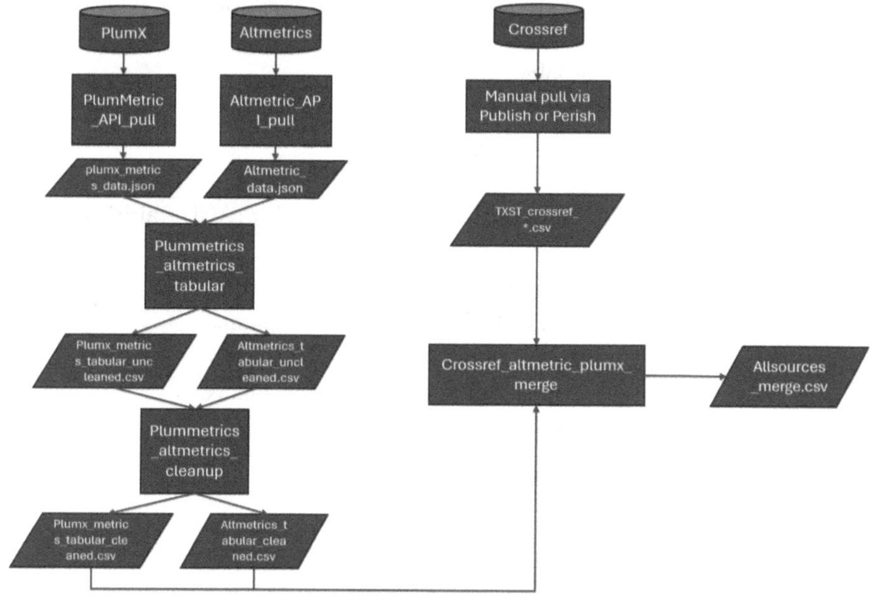


**Fig. 1.** Data collection and preparation pipeline.

distributions of many variables were heavily right skewed with long and thin left tails.

All variables were divided by the age of a paper to give a per-year metric and avoid bias against more recently published papers. After converting to a per-year metric, ranks were assigned to each paper based on variable percentile.

After preparation, significant skew (Fig. 2) and kurtosis (Fig. 3) were present in the dataset. Particularly, many variables had a significant right skew and large percentage of observations at zero. This presents challenges in a ranking context because it leads to many observations tying for last place. Additionally, this issue cannot easily be solved through transformation since most of the input variables are discrete. A histogram of each input variable is available in Appendix Appendix A.

### 3.2 Composite Percentile Ranking

An index-based model inspired by Elsevier's framework was chosen as the baseline approach, although we use different themes of sub-indices. We construct a composite percentile index with seven main areas of impact identified: bibliometrics, social media, news media, patents, policies, journal impact factor (JIF), and miscellaneous factors including Wikipedia citations, feeds citations, and video citations. An advantage of this approach is the allowance of assigning specific weights to each subcategory and variable, producing a flexible framework and can be adjusted based on institutional priorities. IN this implementation,

**Table 1.** Variables used in each impact area

| Impact Area | Variables |
|---|---|
| Bibliometrics | Cites<br>citation.Scopus_plumx<br>citation.CrossRef_plumx<br>citation.Academic Citation Index (ACI) - airiti_plumx<br>citation.PubMed_plumx<br>capture.READER_COUNT_plumx<br>mention.ABSTRACT_VIEWS_plumx<br>mention.DOWNLOAD_COUNT_plumx<br>mention.FULL_TEXT_VIEWS_plumx<br>capture.EXPORTS_SAVES_plumx<br>readers.citeulike_altmetrics<br>readers.mendeley_altmetrics<br>readers.connotea_altmetrics<br>readers_count_altmetrics |
| Social Media | cited_by_posts_count_altmetrics<br>cited_by_accounts_count_altmetrics<br>cited_by_tweeters_count_altmetrics<br>mention.FACEBOOK_COUNT_plumx<br>cited_by_fbwalls_count_altmetrics<br>cited_by_linkedin_count_altmetrics<br>cited_by_weibo_count_altmetrics |
| News Media | cited_by_msm_count_altmetrics<br>mention.NEWS_COUNT_plumx |
| Patents | cited_by_patents_count_altmetrics<br>citation.Patent Families_plumx |
| Policies | citation.Policy Citation_plumx<br>cited_by_policies_count_altmetrics |
| Journal Impact Factor | impact_factor |
| Misc. | cited_by_feeds_count_altmetrics<br>cited_by_videos_count_altmetrics<br>cited_by_wikipedia_count_altmetrics |

we assign weights of 50% to bibliometrics, 10% to social media, 10% to news media, 10% to policies, 10% to patents, 5% to JIF, and 5% to miscellaneous factors. An additional benefit of this approach is that is allows for direct analysis of sub-indices that show where a paper has excelled or struggled in it's dissemination strategy, which can be particularly useful to individual researchers

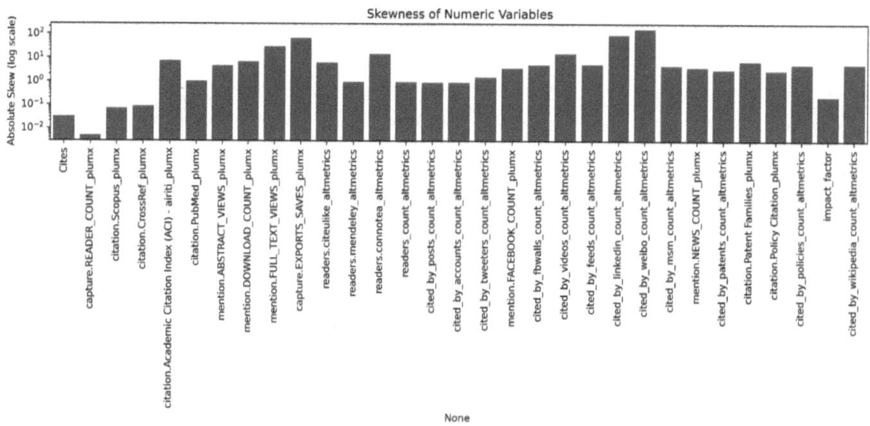


**Fig. 2.** Skew of the input variables.

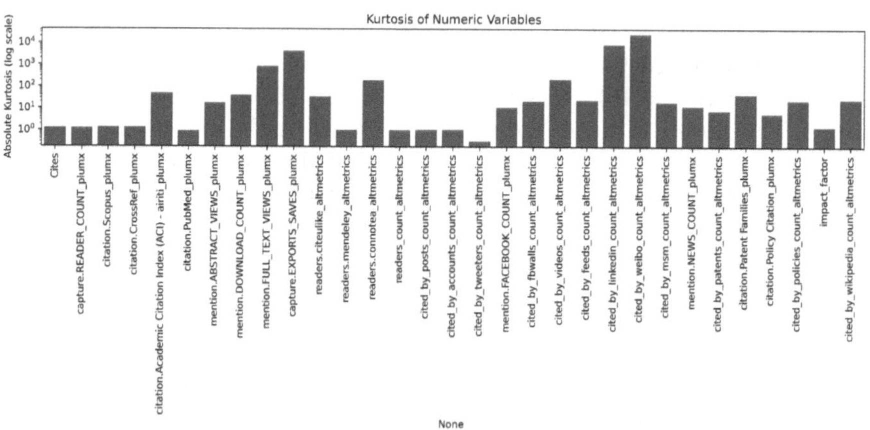


**Fig. 3.** Kurtosis of the input variables.

aiming to improve the reach of their work. An overall index is computed using a composition of the sub-indices as shown in Fig. 4.

### 3.3 Pareto Front Ranking

To address the challenges imposed by the skewed input data, we explore Pareto front ranking (PFR) as a methodology for identification of high impact works. PFR is a technique that can find efficient solutions to multi-objective optimization problems Giagkiozis and Fleming (2014). In this context, we treat every input variable as an objective to be optimized and seek observations that are high in values first, then observations that are high in some values without being low in others, down to observations that are low in all variables. Although PFR does not produce a ranking at the individual level of granularity, it does organize

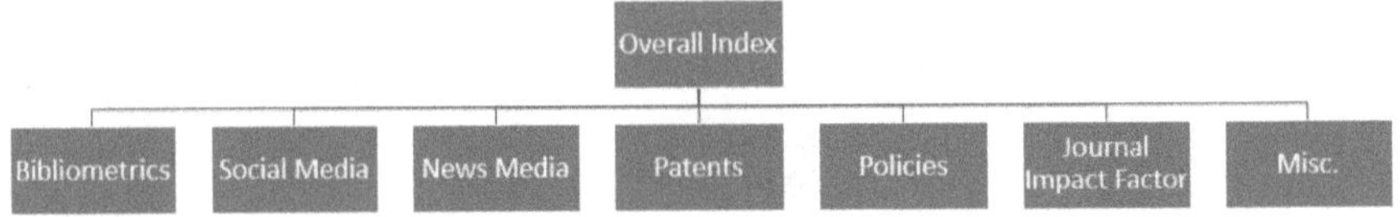


**Fig. 4.** Sub-indices contribution to the overall composite percentile index.

the works into ranks with the assumption that higher is better among the input variables. Rank 0, the "top rank" can be assumed to be of the highest impact, with Rank 1 the second highest, and so on. PFR as implemented here does not allow for specific weights to be assigned and there is no constraint on the number of ranks.

### 3.4 Cluster-Based Ranking

Cluster-based ranking (CBR) yields results similar to PFR in that works are organized into ranked tiers. We use traditional k-means clustering to produce the clusters (with $k = 10$) and sort the sum of the cluster centroids to rank the clusters. The cluster with the highest centroid sum can be selected as the set of highest impact works. Although cluster-based ranking allows specific weighting of the input variables and selection of the desired number of clusters. In this experiment we use equal weighting of all input variables.

### 3.5 Ensemble Method

Aggregation of the results from the prior three methods allows for the use of an ensemble method to identify high impact papers. We will consider all papers identified by at least one method as high impact to be our pool of candidates, and rank within the pool based on how many methodologies identified the work. The most impactful works will be those identified by all three methods.

## 4 Results

### 4.1 Composite Percentile Ranking

The skew and kurtosis present significant challenges with the percentile based rank, leading to fairly skewed distributions of the sub-indices as a result of many works tying for last place with no occurrences of the citations, social media shares, or other outcomes of interest.

Since composite percentile ranking approximates true percentiles, the user can identify the *k highest impact* works or select the top $n\%$ as the final identified set. This flexibility introduces ambiguity to the process and lacks a clear optimal cutoff, but may benefit some users based on the purpose of research impact evaluation. For the purposes of this study, we select the top 500 papers as high impact.

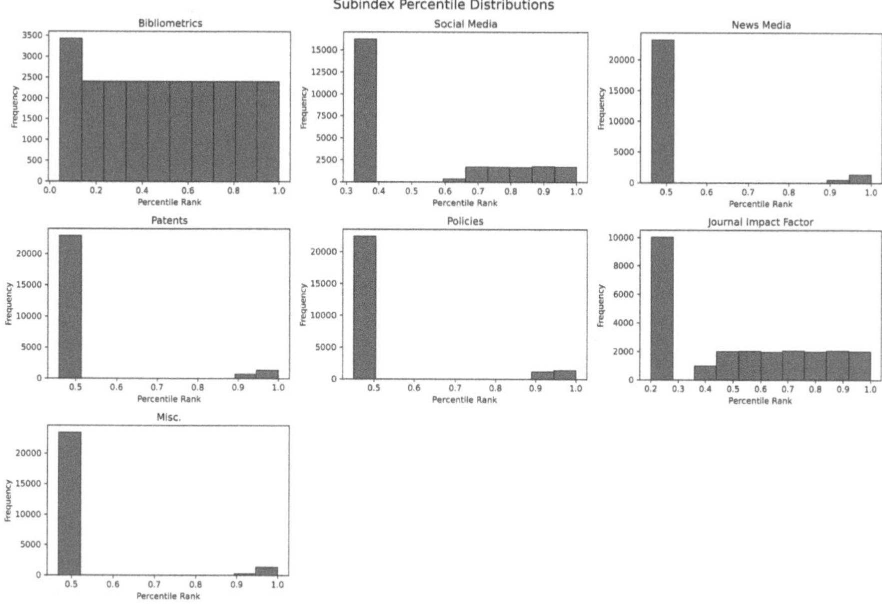


**Fig. 5.** Sub-indices.

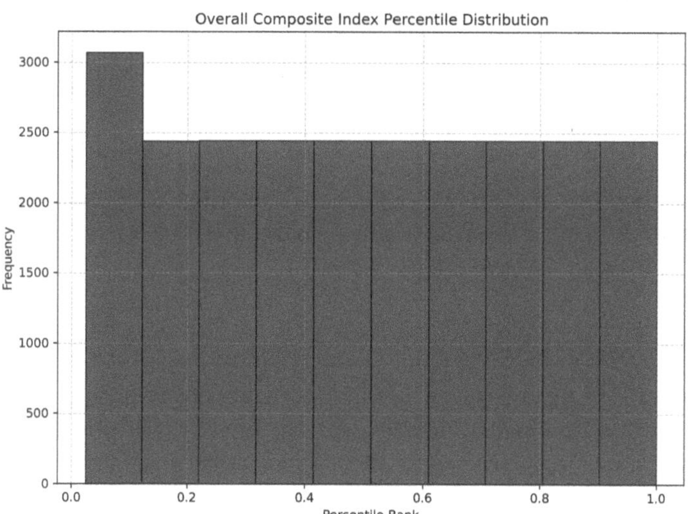


**Fig. 6.** Overall Index.

Challenges of the index-based framework are primarily rooted in the highly skewed input data. Percentiles make less sense when a large percentage of the data tie for last place. Although the overall index achieves a fairly uniform distribution (Fig. 7), many of the sub-indices are skewed and therefore less helpful when distinguishing between lower levels of impact (Fig. 5 and 6).

### 4.2 Pareto Front Ranking

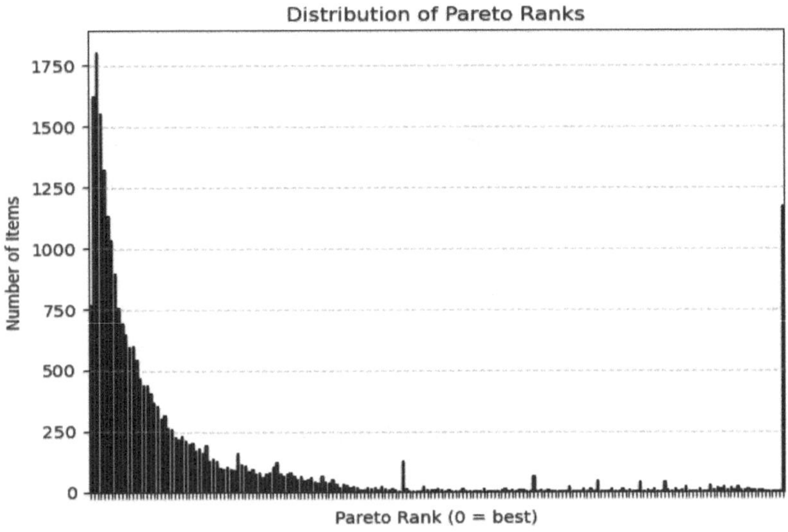


**Fig. 7.** Pareto Rank Distribution.

Pareto front ranking resulted in a right skewed distribution of front sizes (Fig. 8). We designate the papers in rank 0, which contained 770 papers, as high impact. Overall, 198 Pareto ranks were discovered.

### 4.3 Cluster-Based Ranking

Cluster-based ranking using $k = 10$ yielded clusters of varying sizes, with cluster 0 representing the highest impact cluster based on the sum of the centroid coordinates. There were 921 papers identified as high impact from this method.

### 4.4 Ensemble Approach

A total of 1419 unique papers, or 5.7% of the original 25,000, were identified by at least one algorithm as high impact. Of these 1419, 927 (3.7%) were identified by exactly one algorithm, 264 (1.1%) by exactly two, and 228 (0.9%) by all three. Figure 9 displays the results of the ensemble analysis.

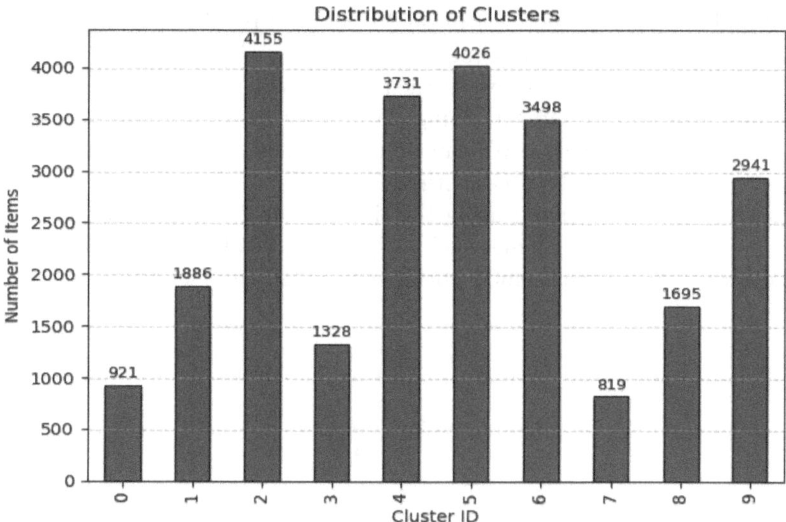


**Fig. 8.** Pareto Rank Distribution.

## 5 Discussion

Since this problem is unsupervised, evaluation of our results is difficult. The gold standard of research impact evaluation is expert assessment, but with 25,000 articles in our training set expert labeling of each would not be feasible. Additionally, the objective of the work is to create a framework that can be easily

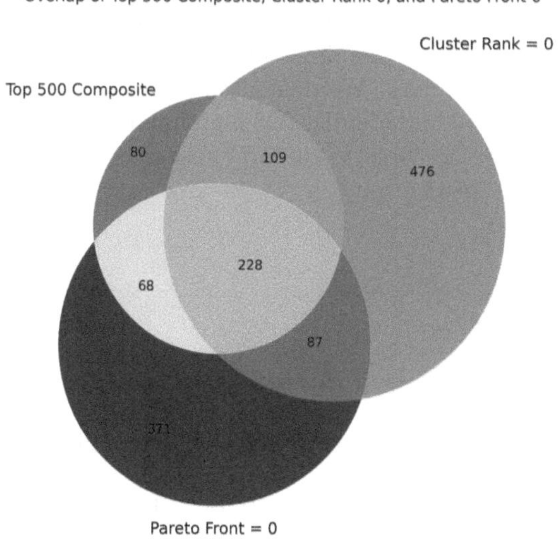


**Fig. 9.** Venn diagram of the ensemble results.

applied and adapted at the institutional level, and requiring a manual labeling of a large corpus of data would conflict with this goal.

The presence of overlap between the algorithms is encouraging. Although all algorithms utilized the same training data, they took different approaches to selecting high-impact works. We can be particularly confident in the 228 works that were identified by all three methods as high impact.

Figure 10 was constructed using the titles of the 228 highest impact papers. Words involving medical themes such as ‘patient’, ‘health’, and ‘risk’ are prominent, as are social science themed worlds such as ‘human’, ‘children’, and ‘social’.

**Fig. 10.** Title word cloud of the highest impact publications.

## 6 Conclusion

This work outlines an end-to-end open-source framework for the identification of high impact research within a specific institution. It uses multiple types of data and data sources during training to reduce bias and is robust to skewness and kurtosis in the input data. We demonstrate our pipeline on 25,000 papers from a specific institution and identify 228 high impact papers. By analyzing the high-impact papers, we are able to discover research themes with the greatest impact at this specific institution.

**Declarations**

**Funding.** Not applicable

**Conflict of Interest/Competing Interests.** Not applicable

**Ethics Approval and Consent to Participate.** Not applicable

**Data Availability.** https://github.com/MariaElise-T/ResearchImpactAI

**Materials Availability.** https://github.com/MariaElise-T/ResearchImpactAI

**Code Availability.** https://github.com/MariaElise-T/ResearchImpactAI

# Appendix A Input Variable Distributions

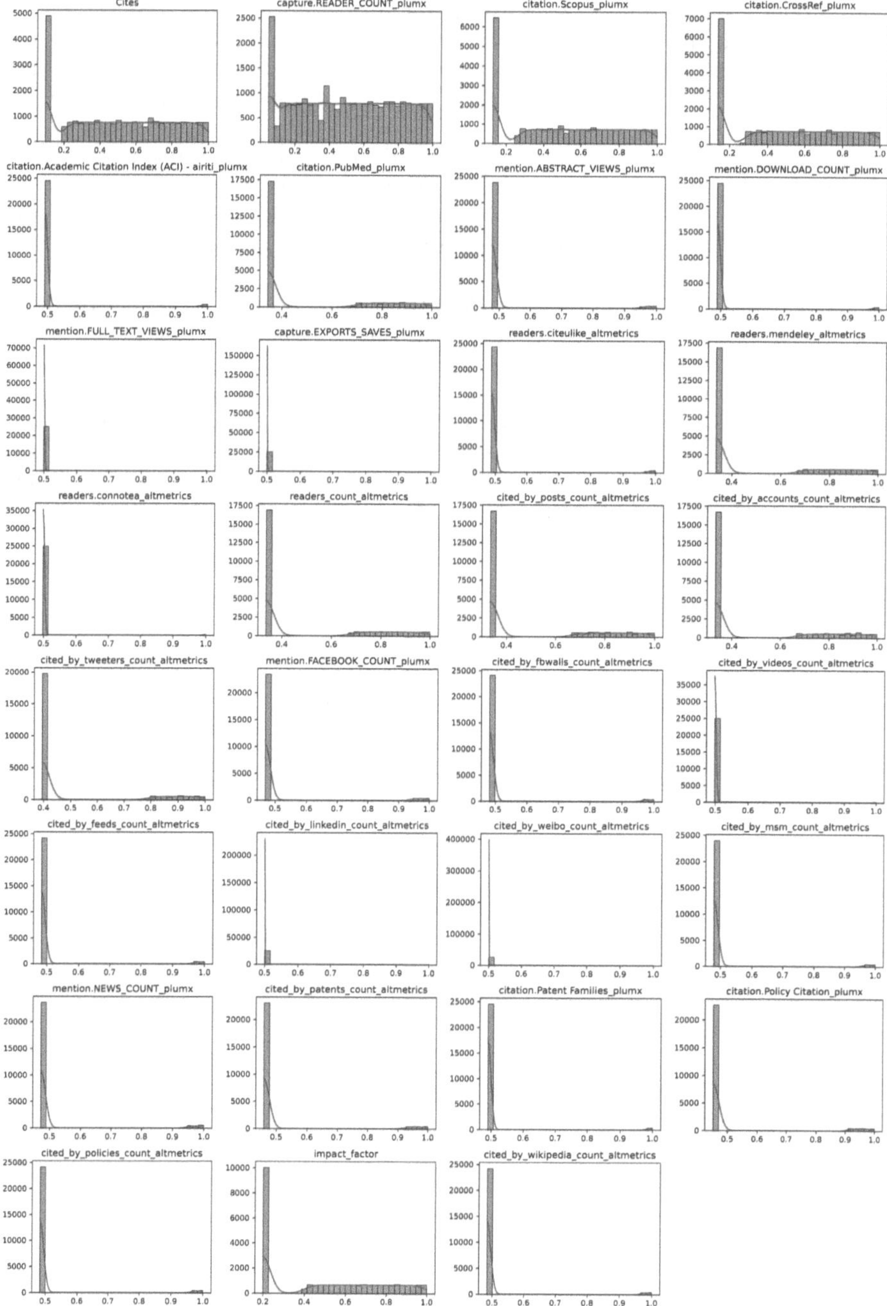


**Fig. 11.** Distributions for input variables.

## References

Penfield, T., Baker, M.J., Scoble, R., Wykes, M.C.: Assessment, evaluations, and definitions of research impact: a review. Res. Eval. **23**(1), 21–32 (2014). https://doi.org/10.1093/reseval/rvt021. Accessed 22 Apt 2025

Priem, J., Taraborelli, D., Groth, P., Neylon, C.: altmetrics: a manifesto

Morton, S.: Progressing research impact assessment: a 'contributions' approach. Res. Eval. **24**(4), 405–419 (2015). https://doi.org/10.1093/reseval/rvv016. Accessed 24 Jul 2024

Ali, M.J.: Understanding the Altmetrics. Semin. Ophthalmol. **36**(5–6), 351–353 (2021). https://doi.org/10.1080/08820538.2021.1930806. Accessed 22 Apr 2025

Arnold, D.N., Fowler, K.K.: Nefarious Numbers. arXiv arXiv. arXiv:1010.0278 [math] (2010). https://doi.org/10.48550/arXiv.1010.0278, http://arxiv.org/abs/1010.0278. Accessed 23 Apr 2025

Vaught, A., Wagner, R.: 233 Beyond bibliometrics: altmetric analysis as an early signal of the impact of the National Center for Advancing Translational Sciences (NCATS) Clinical and Translational Science Awards (CTSA) Program. J. Clin. Transl. Sci. **9**(s1), 71–72 (2025). https://doi.org/10.1017/cts.2024.880. Accessed 22 Apr 2025

Elifritz, S.N.C.: Generating Impact Narratives. Elsevier. https://uknowledge.uky.edu/cgi/viewcontent.cgi?article=1036&context=researchevents2

Giagkiozis, I., Fleming, P.J.: Pareto front estimation for decision making. Evol. Comput. **22**(4), 651–678 (2014) https://doi.org/10.1162/EVCO_a_00128, https://direct.mit.edu/evco/article-pdf/22/4/651/1530439/evco_a_00128.pdf

# Age-Related Differences and Implications for Development of Advanced Driver Assistance Systems

Shabnam Shabani[1(✉)] and Michael Bauer[2]

[1] Western University, London, ON N6A 3K7, Canada
sshaban7@uwo.ca
[2] Springer Heidelberg, Tiergartenstr. 17, 69121 Heidelberg, Germany

**Abstract.** Vehicles continue to be instrumented with more advanced technology to enhance safety and support drivers. As the population ages, understanding the differences in driving characteristics between older and younger drivers is crucial for developing effective driver support systems. This paper reports on a study to identify behavioral and performance variables that show significant age-related differences and could serve as potential indicators for future driver behavior modeling. Using data from a high-fidelity driving simulator, we analyzed driving behavior across multiple scenarios for 22 older adults (Age >65) and 12 younger adults (Age 18–40). A broad set of metrics was extracted, focusing on those characterizing driving behaviors to identify candidate features for modeling. The Mann–Whitney U test was applied to determine key variables that show significant differences between age groups. These are then used to identify related age-relevant metrics appropriate for use in driver behavior modeling and assistance technologies.

**Keywords:** Driving behavior · driving simulator · age-related differences · driver performance metrics

## 1 Introduction

Globally, populations are aging at an unprecedented rate. Projections indicate that by 2036, nearly 25% of Canada's population will be aged 65 or older [1], a trend mirrored in countries like Japan, the United States, and across the European Union, where significant increases in the elderly population are anticipated [2–5]. National statistics have shown an increase in crashes involving older drivers, are often accompanied by disproportionately severe outcomes compared to younger age groups [6]. As the population ages, understanding the implications for transportation safety and mobility becomes increasingly important, particularly because many seniors rely heavily on private vehicles for maintaining independence.

Advanced Driver Assistance Systems (ADASs) have been shown to be successful in warning drivers and helping to avoid accidents. They enhance safety by providing real-time warnings, accident-avoidance capabilities, and proactive interventions based


R. Stahlbock et al. (Eds.): CSCE 2025, CCIS 2938, pp. 357–373, 2027.
https://doi.org/10.1007/978-3-032-22196-4_27

on vehicle dynamics and sensors. Studies have demonstrated that features like Forward Collision Warning (FCW) and Automatic Emergency Braking (AEB) can significantly reduce rear-end collisions and associated injuries [7]. Other studies have highlighted the role of various ADAS technologies, such as lane departure warnings and adaptive cruise control, in improving road safety [8, 9].

While current ADASs are successful, they rely on sensors and algorithms to detect potential problems and dangers. They do not leverage the central agent in driving – the driver. Future ADASs will collect data about the driver, their operation of the vehicle and driving behavior. Such ADAS applications will require robust models of driver behavior capable of detecting significant changes in driving behavior, particularly negative changes, such as signs of drowsiness, distraction, or erratic driving. Applications using models with predictive capabilities may actually be able to help anticipate dangerous driver maneuvers—such as sudden lane changes or abrupt braking—allowing for early intervention to prevent accidents. Recent work in this area has demonstrated the potential of various machine learning methods. For example, M'haouach et al. [10] proposed a deep learning framework with attention mechanisms for early maneuver prediction, while Sathy et al. [11] introduced ManeuverNet, a specialized model for anticipating vehicle actions. Other approaches, such as that of Aboah et al. [12], leveraged time series segmentation for maneuver detection, and Khelfa et al. [13] benchmarked multiple machine and ensemble learning algorithms for lane-change prediction. Visual and gaze-based cues have also been integrated, with Li et al. [14] incorporating drivers' spatio-temporal gaze attention, and Khairdoost et al. [15] utilizing LSTM architectures with gaze and vehicle dynamics data. Further innovations by Kung et al. [16] and Haque et al. [17] explored video-based intent detection and interpretable rule-based classification models, respectively. These contributions highlight the value of real-time, interpretable models for improving ADAS responsiveness and personalization.

To achieve these objectives, models require measurable driving metrics capable of characterizing individual driver behaviors in real-time. Candidate metrics include steering variability, lane-position deviations, acceleration and braking patterns, gaze behaviors, and other dynamic indicators captured during driving. As prior work has shown, metrics such as steering angle fluctuations, braking intensity, and gaze shifts have been effectively used to predict maneuvers with machine learning techniques [10–17].

Previous studies comparing driver behavior across age groups have provided mixed findings. Some studies report clear differences in speed control, lane-keeping accuracy, and reaction times, whereas others report minimal or no significant differences, resulting in inconsistent conclusions across the literature [8, 9]. These discrepancies may arise due to differences in scenario complexity, experimental conditions, or the nature of measured metrics. Past analyses have typically focused on descriptive, outcome-oriented measures (e.g., time-to-collision, overall completion times). While valuable for identifying general safety outcomes, such metrics reflect situational context rather than characterizing the driver's behavior or response patterns. Consequently, systematic analyses using real-time metrics of driver behavior remain limited, leaving an important gap in understanding behavioral age differences.

This paper reports on a comparison of old and young drivers using a variety of measures, some of which have been used in previous studies. The aim of the comparison is to identify which metrics reveal significant differences between the two groups and then using these as a foundation propose a set of metrics more suitable for real-time driving analysis. Data collected from a high-fidelity driving simulator were used to statistically compare driving behavior between older and younger adults. Participants completed three distinct driving scenarios allowing for the examination of behavioral differences across varied driving contexts. The findings provide deeper insight into age-related differences in driver behavior and we use the results to identify behavioral metrics suitable for future predictive modeling and personalized driver-assistance systems.

This paper is organized as follows: Sect. 2 describes the related work. Section 3 presents the methodology and details of the driving simulator data. Section 4 outlines the performance metrics and statistical analysis. Section 5 discusses the results, and Sect. 6 concludes the paper with final remarks and future directions.

## 2 Related Work

Age-related differences in driving behavior have been widely studied, with many researchers comparing older and younger drivers across a range of behavioral and performance metrics using real-world and simulated environments. These studies typically focus on the cognitive and physical challenges that may arise with aging and how they influence driving performance. Prior cognitive research has shown that older adults often experience slower response times and reduced attentional capacity, particularly in tasks that require rapid visual processing and decision-making [18, 19]. Doroudgar et al. [20] conducted a simulator-based comparison between older and younger drivers, focusing on metrics such as brake reaction time (BRT), speed, time headway, which is measured as the time gap between a driver and the vehicle ahead, and number of collisions. Their findings revealed that older drivers had significantly slower BRTs, lower speeds, shorter headways, and a higher likelihood of collisions—indicating reduced responsiveness. Similarly, Menze et al. [21] found that young adults demonstrated riskier driving behavior—such as delayed braking when distracted—while older adults prioritized safety, braking correctly at intersections despite age-related declines. These results highlight differing driving strategies across age groups, shaped by both cognitive ability and risk perception.

Bunce et al. [22] further explored individual variability across residential, urban, and motorway scenarios. Older participants showed significantly greater inconsistency in maintaining headway and lane position, particularly at higher speeds, and also reported higher cognitive workload. These findings point to reduced attention and executive control with age. In a related line of research, Young et al. [23] emphasized that inconsistency in maintaining headway or lateral lane position is a key indicator distinguishing good from poor drivers. Their studies further support the notion that stable performance in these metrics reflects higher driving competence and attentional control.

Reimer et al. [24], examining the role of cognitive aging in technology interaction, observed that older drivers tend to adopt more conservative behaviors—such as slower speeds and increased headway—to compensate for cognitive decline. As well, their ability to multitask and adapt quickly in dynamic environments was found to be diminished. Robertsen et al. [25] conducted an on-road driving study to compare the performance of younger and older adults across several real-world driving tasks. Using a standardized route and with drivers evaluated by expert raters, younger drivers outperformed older ones in areas such as car handling, speed adaptation, and traffic flow management. However, overall group differences were smaller than expected. The authors suggested that older drivers may rely on compensatory behaviors—such as behavioral adaptation—to mitigate age-related decline in essential driving functions. Lee et al. [26] examined age-related differences in drivers' responses to sudden-stop events using a driving simulator. Their findings revealed that elderly drivers exhibited significantly delayed brake reaction times compared to younger drivers, especially in time-critical situations. Thompson et al. [27] investigated the impact of cognitive distractions—such as auditory and visual stimuli—on driving performance. They found that older adults, when exposed to increased cognitive demand, tended to drive more slowly and with less speed variability than middle-aged drivers. This behavior may indicate a compensatory strategy aimed at maintaining safety under cognitive load.

While prior research has explored a wide range of driving behavior metrics, many of these measures were primarily descriptive or comparative and intended to measure differences among age groups rather than for supporting dynamic modeling of driver behavior. Metrics aggregated across entire drives provide valuable insights into overall group differences but may not fully capture the dynamic nature of driver responses. A central aim of this study is to identify behavioral metrics that are sensitive to age-related differences and could also serve as candidate features or be adapted to be features for future driver behavior modeling. To do this, we compared two groups of drivers, a group of seniors and a group of younger drivers using a variety of methods. The aim was twofold: a) to identify measures that showed significant differences in driving behavior between the two groups regardless of the nature of the metric and b) build on these results to identify metrics that could be used in building models of real-time driving.

## 3 Methodology

This section outlines the methodology used to investigate age-related differences in driving behavior. A high-fidelity driving simulator located in the i-Mobile Driving Research Lab[1] at the School of Occupational Therapy at The University of Western Ontario was used to provide a safe, controlled, and repeatable setting for assessing driver performance. The simulator setup included three forward-facing screens that created an immersive virtual driving environment, allowing participants to engage in realistic driving experiences while being safely observe; see Fig. 1.

A total of 34 participants took part in the study, consisting of 22 older adults aged 65 and above and 12 younger adults aged between 18 and 40 years. Each participant completed three pre-designed simulated driving scenarios: City and Highway, Residential and Suburban, and Town and Country, with each scenario lasting approximately seven minutes. The Residential and Suburban scenario was the simplest with 2 right turns, 1 left turn, and 3 straight road segments. There were two road segments where the road changed from 1 lane to 2 and then back to 1 lane. The Town and Country scenario was

[1] https://www.imobileresearchlab.com/

similar, but with 3 right turns, 3 left turns and 7 straight road segments. There was a single lane change from 1 lane to 2 and back to 1. The City and Highway scenario was the most involved with 2 right turns, 1 left turn and 4 straight road segments, but had 10 road segments involving lane changes of 1 lane to 2 and back and 1 highway segment went from 1 lane (on ramp) to 3 and then went to 1 at the end of the segment reflecting driving in a mix of city and highway situations.

**Fig. 1.** Driving Simulator in the i-Mobile Research Lab

The driving simulator recorded vehicle state data at 60 Hz, providing frame-by-frame measurements for speed, steering-wheel angle, accelerator and brake pedal positions, lateral lane offset, headway distance and time, time-to-collision (TTC), and lateral and longitudinal acceleration. Many of these variables, such as speed, acceleration, steering angle, have been used in previous studies focused on maneuver prediction and driver behavior modeling [10–17].

In addition to the directly recorded signals, several features were derived through frame-to-frame computations to enhance the temporal granularity of driver behavior representation. Specifically, steering-reversal counts, lateral and longitudinal jerk (the rate of change of acceleration), pedal-press frequency per second, aggressive-acceleration (using a threshold) and braking events were computed. These derived metrics increase sensitivity to subtle behavioral shifts and may serve as candidate features for future integration into predictive modeling architectures, such as LSTM networks or attention-based models. All frame-level computations and feature derivations were implemented in Python, using the Pandas and NumPy libraries. Event-based variables (e.g., TTC < 3 s, harsh braking) were extracted based on predefined thresholds, and both continuous signals and event flags were preserved for subsequent analysis.

Because each participant completed three driving scenarios, the frame-level signals for each scenario were first summarized individually using appropriate aggregation methods (e.g., mean, median, or event count). The summaries across the three scenarios were then averaged to yield one statistically independent value per metric per participant. This step ensures independence between observations and prevents pseudo-replication in subsequent group comparisons. Metrics were statistically compared using the Mann–Whitney U test, a non-parametric method selected because many of the aggregated variables deviated from normality. Metrics that were significant ($p < 0.05$) or highly significant ($p < 0.01$) were retained, and their corresponding frame-by-frame signals constitute the pool of candidate features for subsequent modeling efforts. Throughout the paper, one asterisk (*) denotes $0.01 \leq p < 0.05$, two asterisks (**) denote $p < 0.01$, and results with $p \geq 0.05$ are left non-significant (NS).

## 4 Analysis and Results

This section presents the findings of the statistical comparison between younger and older drivers based on the extracted performance metrics. The analysis focuses on key behavioral domains including speed regulation, lane-keeping, steering behavior, pedal usage, and car following. Results are reported according to these thematic categories, with emphasis on metrics that showed statistically significant differences between the two age groups. Complete descriptive statistics and *p*-values are provided in the corresponding tables.

### 4.1 Temporal and Speed-Related Metrics

Table 1 summarizes the comparison between younger and older drivers for metrics related to driving time and speed. Older participants took significantly longer to complete the scenarios ($p < 0.001$) while younger drivers exhibited significantly higher average and median speeds ($p < 0.001$ for both), and their speed variability was also significantly greater, as reflected in the standard deviation ($p = 0.038$). These results are consistent with previous studies that speed-related behaviors differ between the age groups. While summary statistics such as average or median speed provide useful group-level comparisons, they are not directly applicable for real-time behavior modeling. However, short-term speed fluctuations, or rates of speed change may serve as candidate indicators for real-time driver behavior models.

**Table 1.** Comparison of temporal and speed related metrics between younger and older drivers.

| Metric | Young (mean ± SD) | Old (mean ± SD) | p-value |
|---|---|---|---|
| Duration (s) | 1451.21 ± 92.91 | 1691.35 ± 178.14 | <0.001** |
| Avg[a]. Speed (m/s) | 12.18 ± 0.75 | 10.54 ± 1.05 | <0.001** |
| Speed SDev. (m/s) | 6.41 ± 0.36 | 5.86 ± 0.86 | 0.038* |
| Median Speed (m/s) | 11.08 ± 0.74 | 9.32 ± 1.04 | <0.001** |

[a]We use abbreviations "Avg.", "SDev." and "Acc." For "Average", "Standard Deviation" and "Acceleration" in the tables.

## 4.2 Pedal Usage Metrics

Table 2 presents the comparison of pedal-related metrics between the two age groups. The number of accelerator presses (measured over the whole drive) was significantly higher among older drivers ($p = 0.004$). No statistically significant differences were observed in the time spent on the accelerator, acceleration frequency, number of brake presses, time on brake, or brake frequency. Frequency metrics refer to the number of pedal presses (either accelerator or brake) normalized by total driving time, expressed as the number of presses per second. This time-based normalization allows for comparison across drives of varying duration and produces a rate that can be continuously monitored and used as a real-time indicator in driver behavior models. For modeling purposes, this metric can be computed over short sliding windows to produce a time-series of pedal press rates. These windowed frequency features can then be used as input variables in real-time driver behavior models, such as LSTM or Transformer-based architecture.

**Table 2.** Comparison of pedal usage metrics between younger and older drivers.

| Metric | Young (mean ± SD) | Old (mean ± SD) | p-value |
|---|---|---|---|
| Number of Accelerator pedal Presses | 309.00 ± 80.88 | 427.64 ± 104.31 | 0.004** |
| Time on Accelerator pedal (s) | 880.84 ± 108.22 | 862.94 ± 158.70 | 0.417 (NS) |
| Accelerator pedal Presses Frequency (s) | 12.79 ± 3.13 | 15.48 ± 4.42 | 0.126 (NS) |
| Number of Brake Presses | 66.75 ± 12.96 | 70.23 ± 17.74 | 0.692 (NS) |
| Time on Brake pedal (s) | 92.28 ± 19.03 | 101.32 ± 40.25 | 0.928 (NS) |
| Brake pedal presses Frequency (s) | 2.90 ± 0.65 | 2.67 ± 0.75 | 0.322 (NS) |

## 4.3 Lane-keeping and Lateral Positive Metrics

Lane-keeping and lateral control metrics were also analyzed in this study. This included: a) the left and right lane distance relative to the center of the lane—where 0.0 m indicates perfect alignment with the lane center, the number of lane changes the driver made, the number of lane changes per second over the entire drive, and the total time spent outside the defined lane boundaries, e.g. on the shoulder of the road.

No statistically significant differences were observed between the younger and older driver groups across any of these metrics and so we do not present the statistical results here. Although no group differences were found, metrics such as continuous lane offset and time spent out of lane may serve as potential indicators for future real-time monitoring of driver behavior, particularly in detecting lane deviation events.

**Table 3.** Comparison of lateral and longitudinal acceleration metrics between younger and older drivers.

| Metric | Young (mean ± SD) | Old (mean ± SD) | p-value |
|---|---|---|---|
| Avg. Negative Lateral Acc. ($m/s^2$) | −0.36 ± 0.04 | −0.30 ± 0.07 | 0.005** |
| SDev. Negative Lateral Acc. ($m/s^2$) | 0.63 ± 0.09 | 0.53 ± 0.14 | 0.054 (NS) |
| Median Negative Lateral Acc. ($m/s^2$) | −0.10 ± 0.02 | −0.09 ± 0.02 | 0.074 (NS) |
| Avg. Positive Lateral Acc. ($m/s^2$) | 0.39 ± 0.05 | 0.31 ± 0.08 | 0.003** |
| SDev. Positive Lateral Acc. ($m/s^2$) | 0.61 ± 0.09 | 0.52 ± 0.14 | 0.029* |
| Median Positive Lateral Acc. ($m/s^2$) | 0.13 ± 0.03 | 0.10 ± 0.03 | 0.009** |
| Average Negative Longitudinal Acc. ($m/s^2$) | −0.77 ± 0.14 | −0.73 ± 0.12 | 0.438 (NS) |
| SDev. Negative Longitudinal Acc. ($m/s^2$) | 1.23 ± 0.22 | 1.14 ± 0.22 | 0.242 (NS) |
| Median Negative Longitudinal Acc. ($m/s^2$) | −0.47 ± 0.05 | −0.48 ± 0.02 | 0.829 (NS) |
| Avg. Positive Longitudinal Acc. ($m/s^2$) | 0.89 ± 0.19 | 1.02 ± 0.20 | 0.032* |
| SDev. Positive Longitudinal Acc. ($m/s^2$) | 0.95 ± 0.10 | 1.03 ± 0.12 | 0.054 (NS) |
| Median Positive Longitudinal Acc. ($m/s^2$) | 0.61 ± 0.23 | 0.71 ± 0.25 | 0.227 (NS) |

### 4.4 Longitudinal and Lateral Acceleration Metrics

Table 3 presents the comparison of lateral and longitudinal acceleration metrics. These metrics capture the vehicle's dynamic movement and are commonly used to quantify maneuver intensity and stability. Lateral acceleration refers to side-to-side motion—typically experienced during lane changes or turns—while longitudinal acceleration reflects forward or backward motion, such as accelerating or braking. In this context, positive lateral acceleration corresponds to rightward turning forces, while negative lateral acceleration indicates leftward motion. Similarly, positive longitudinal acceleration represents forward acceleration, and negative longitudinal acceleration corresponds to braking (deceleration).

Statistically significant differences were found in several lateral acceleration metrics. Younger drivers exhibited higher values in average negative lateral acceleration ($p = 0.005$), average positive lateral acceleration ($p = 0.003$), and median positive lateral acceleration ($p = 0.009$). The standard deviation of positive lateral acceleration was also significantly greater among younger participants (p = 0.029), suggesting more variability and sharper lateral movements, possibly reflecting more assertive maneuvering or reactive lane changes. In contrast, for longitudinal acceleration, only average positive acceleration showed a statistically significant difference (p = 0.032), with older drivers demonstrating higher values. No other longitudinal acceleration metrics showed significant group differences.

While aggregate metrics such as average, median, and standard deviation of lateral and longitudinal acceleration provide useful summaries for group-level comparisons, they are not directly applicable for real-time behavior modeling due to their cumulative nature. However, given the significant group differences observed, the underlying frame-by-frame lateral and longitudinal acceleration signals, as well as short-term fluctuations, may serve as candidate features for future real-time driver behavior models. These dynamic measures could better capture transient maneuvering patterns and enhance modeling of driver state or intent.

### 4.5 Jerk Metrics and Event-Frequency Indicators

Table 4 presents a comparison of jerk-based metrics between younger and older drivers. We define "jerk" as the rate of change of acceleration over time, typically measured in meters per second cubed (m/s$^3$). It reflects how abruptly a vehicle's acceleration is applied or removed—higher jerk values indicate more sudden changes in acceleration or deceleration. In this study, jerk was computed as the first derivative of acceleration with respect to time, calculated at each time step using consecutive acceleration values from the simulator's time-series data.

Among the metrics evaluated, mean positive longitudinal jerk (p = 0.050), and mean negative longitudinal jerk (p = 0.050) were significantly higher in older drivers. This suggests that older participants exhibited slightly more abrupt pedal modulation during acceleration and braking phases. In contrast, no statistically significant differences were found in lateral jerk metrics ($p > 0.05$), indicating comparable smoothness in lateral vehicle control between the two age groups.

While the average jerk values reported here help summarize group-level tendencies, they are not directly usable in real-time models, as they require data from the entire driving session. However, instantaneous jerk values, or jerk computed over short moving time windows, could serve as actionable inputs for real-time driver behavior modeling—enabling the detection of abrupt control inputs, compensatory driving strategies, or erratic vehicle behaviors during real-time operation.

**Table 4.** Comparison of jerk-based driving metrics between younger and older drivers.

| Metric | Young (mean ± SD) | Old (mean ± SD) | p-value |
|---|---|---|---|
| Mean Positive Longitudinal Jerk (m/s$^3$) | 1.77 ± 0.33 | 2.04 ± 0.36 | 0.050* |
| Mean Negative Longitudinal Jerk (m/s$^3$) | 1.61 ± 0.32 | 1.88 ± 0.38 | 0.050* |

*(continued)*

**Table 4.** (*continued*)

| Metric | Young (mean ± SD) | Old (mean ± SD) | p-value |
|---|---|---|---|
| Mean Positive Lateral Jerk ($m/s^3$) | −0.10 ± 0.02 | −0.09 ± 0.02 | 0.074 (NS)** |
| Mean Negative Lateral Jerk ($m/s^3$) | 0.52 ± 0.09 | 0.51 ± 0.10 | 0.787 (NS) |

### 4.6 Aggressive Longitudinal and Lateral Event Counts and Rates

Table 5 presents a set of aggressive acceleration and braking metrics derived from both longitudinal and lateral acceleration signals. Aggressive events were defined as instances exceeding thresholds of $\pm 1.5$ $m/s^2$ for longitudinal and $\pm 0.5$ $m/s^2$ for lateral acceleration. These thresholds were empirically selected based on exploratory analysis of the dataset, aiming to capture sudden, high-intensity maneuvers while minimizing sensitivity to normal driving variability. Aggressive event counts quantified the total number of threshold-exceeding instances, with event onset detection used to prevent prolonged threshold violations from being overcounted. To account for variability in driving duration across participants, rate-based metrics were also computed, including the number of threshold-exceeding events per second. These normalized metrics provide insights into the relative frequency of abrupt actions.

Statistically significant group differences were observed: younger drivers exhibited higher rates of both lateral acceleration and lateral braking events per second ($p = 0.017$, 0.035, respectively). A significant difference was also found in the total number of aggressive longitudinal acceleration events, with older drivers exhibiting a higher count ($p = 0.009$).

Because these aggressive events are time-localized and based on real-time signals, they may be directly utilized in behavioral modeling. For example, the presence or frequency of aggressive events within short time windows could serve as input features for detecting risky driving states or imminent maneuvers in age aware ADAS applications.

**Table 5.** Comparison of aggressive longitudinal and lateral events between older and younger drivers.

| Metric | Young (mean ± SD) | Old (mean ± SD) | p-value |
|---|---|---|---|
| Aggressive Longitudinal Acc. Events | 6531.83 ± 1803.55 | 8350.68 ± 1854.21 | 0.009** |
| Aggressive Longitudinal Brake Events | 4109.67 ± 795.60 | 3947.27 ± 1066.05 | 0.460 (NS) |
| Aggressive Lateral Acc. Events | 8785.00 ± 382.50 | 8525.09 ± 1022.12 | 0.871 (NS) |
| Aggressive Lateral Brake Events | 7856.67 ± 573.38 | 7659.59 ± 781.15 | 0.759 (NS) |
| Longitudinal Acc. Events (/sec) | 4.29 ± 1.21 | 5.02 ± 1.23 | 0.109 (NS) |
| Longitudinal Brake Events (/sec) | 2.68 ± 0.47 | 2.41 ± 0.71 | 0.165 (NS) |

(*continued*)

**Table 5.** *(continued)*

| Metric | Young (mean ± SD) | Old (mean ± SD) | p-value |
|---|---|---|---|
| Lateral Acc. Events (/sec) | 5.19 ± 0.52 | 4.58 ± 0.85 | 0.017* |
| Lateral Brake Events (/sec) | 4.59 ± 0.46 | 4.09 ± 0.74 | 0.035* |

## 4.7 Steering and Signal Metrics

Table 6 presents steering-related metrics, including reversal events, steering velocity characteristics, and turn signal usage. A steering reversal was defined as a change in the sign of steering direction (i.e., from left to right or vice versa). To isolate meaningful directional shifts and exclude minor fluctuations, a velocity threshold of **2 degrees per second (°/s)** was applied, and only those events exceeding this threshold were counted. This threshold was selected empirically based on the distribution of steering rate data across participants. Reversal counts were also normalized per minute to calculate a steering reversal rate. In addition to these reversal-based metrics, we computed the average of steering velocity to assess the magnitude directional control. Finally, the frequency of left and right turn signal usage was recorded as an indicator of signaling behavior.

Among all metrics, a statistically significant difference was found in the number of threshold-based steering reversal events ($p = 0.006$) and left turn signal usage ($p = 0.026$), with older drivers exhibiting more directional changes and younger drivers using left signals more frequently. No other steering or signaling metrics showed significant group differences ($p > 0.05$).

Metrics such as steering reversal rates and real-time turn signal usage can provide dynamic indicators of driver intent and control strategies and may serve as candidate features for future real-time driver behavior modeling applications.

**Table 6.** Comparison of steering and signal metrics between younger and older drivers.

| Metric | Young (mean ± SD) | Old (mean ± SD) | p-value |
|---|---|---|---|
| Steering Reversal Events | 6583.42 ± 995.70 | 7950.76 ± 1345.54 | 0.006** |
| Threshold Steering Reversal Rate (/min) | 743.38 ± 137.31 | 810.52 ± 158.28 | 0.272 (NS) |
| Avg. Steering Velocity (°/s) | 9.77 ± 2.02 | 10.09 ± 2.50 | 0.601 (NS) |
| Number of Times Using Right Turn Signal | 10.92 ± 1.44 | 11.00 ± 2.62 | 0.985 (NS) |
| Number of Times Using Left Turn Signal | 10.33 ± 1.37 | 8.36 ± 3.06 | 0.026* |

### 4.8 Car-Following Metrics

To evaluate safety critical driving behaviors, this study employed established thresholds for headway time, time-to-collision (TTC), and headway distance metrics. A headway time threshold of 4.0 s was selected to identify instances of close-following behavior. While the U.S. Federal Highway Administration recommends a minimum following distance of 3 s under ideal conditions, extending this to 4 s provides a more conservative buffer, particularly relevant for populations with slower reaction times, such as older adults. This approach aligns with findings from Lewis-Evans et al. [28, 29], who observed that drivers' perceptions of risk and discomfort increased significantly at headways shorter than 2.0 s. For TTC, a threshold of 3.0 s was adopted, as values below this level are consistently associated with elevated crash risk due to insufficient time for evasive action [28, 29].

While raw TTC values are commonly used as descriptive indicators of following behavior, they are not directly useful as standalone inputs for modeling. Instead, binary or rate-based representations—such as the number or percentage of frames where TTC falls below 3.0 s—may serve as more effective candidate features for behavior modeling systems. Similarly, event-based representations of headway time (e.g., the duration or percentage of time spent below 4.0 s) and headway distance (e.g., the number of instances where distance falls below 20 m) may provide more dynamic and actionable features for modeling risk-prone following behavior in real-time systems.

The results are reported in Table 7. Statistically significant differences were found across all reported metrics ($p < 0.05$). Younger drivers spent significantly more time under the 4.0-s headway threshold, ($p = 0.038$) Similarly, younger participants exhibited a higher number of critical TTC events below 3 s ($p = 0.029$), and a significantly higher critical TTC event rate per minute ($p = 0.024$). The count of headway distances less than 20 m was also significantly greater among younger drivers ($p = 0.024$).

These metrics, although evaluated in aggregate form, represent viable candidates for future real-time driver behavior modeling through appropriate segmentation and feature extraction strategies.

**Table 7.** Comparisons of car following metrics between young and old drivers.

| Metric | Young (mean ± SD) | Old (mean ± SD) | p-value |
|---|---|---|---|
| Time Under 4.0 s Headway (sec) | 71.72 ± 34.32 | 47.93 ± 23.97 | 0.038* |
| Critical TTC event (<3 s) | 567.92 ± 133.44 | 469.77 ± 144.92 | 0.029* |
| Critical TTC Event Rate (/min) | 19.71 ± 5.66 | 15.28 ± 5.36 | 0.024* |
| HeadwayDist Count (<20 m) | 4051.17 ± 1617.43 | 2921.00 ± 989.10 | 0.024* |

## 5 Discussion

To This study aimed to identify candidate metrics that distinguish driving behavior between younger and older adults and could potentially serve as inputs for future driver behavior modeling. To achieve this, we conducted statistical comparisons between the two age groups across a broad range of driving behavior metrics, identifying those with significant group-level differences. Considering those metrics that showed significant differences we can generate a potential set of metrics that can be used for modeling.

Table 8 summarizes the behavioral metrics that showed statistically significant differences between younger and older drivers. For each listed metric we identify one or more possible metrics that can be computed during a drive) and can be considered as a potential candidate for future driver behavior modeling. These formulations fall into three general categories.

**Time-Series Signals.** Frequently occurring measurements, such as speed or steering angle, can be recorded at regular intervals over some window of time interval (e.g., 3 s). Such windows can be fixed, i.e., the data is grouped into fixed size segments, or the window could be a sliding one which takes a new value at each time point and drops an old one. Metrics on these signals can then be processed over these windows, e.g., an average speed over a window.

**Event-Based Counts.** The number of occurrences of discrete driving actions—such as pedal presses or lane changes—can be identified by detecting specific transitions in the signal (e.g., a pedal state changes from "pressed" to "non pressed"). These events are not meaningful in isolation but can be transformed into modeling features by computing their frequency within short time windows (e.g., number of pedals presses every 3 s). This process results in a time-series of event frequencies, which can be used as inputs to models to capture patterns of driver engagement and behavior over time.

**Table 8.** Selected driving behavior metrics and their corresponding modeling strategies.

| Metric | Possible Metrics for Modeling |
|---|---|
| Speed Related Metrics | 1. Mean speed per sliding window<br>2. SDev. of speed per window (captures variability)<br>3. Med. speed per window (robust to outliers) |
| Number of Accelerator Pedal Presses | 1. Count of pedal press events per window<br>2. Total time of pedal engagement per window |
| Lateral Acc Related Metrics ($m/s^2$) | 1. Mean/SDev./Median of positive lateral acc. per window<br>2. Mean/Median of negative lateral acc. per window |
| Avg Positive Longitudinal Acc. ($m/s^2$) | Mean of positive longitudinal acc. per window |
| Longitudinal Jerk Related Metrics ($m/s^3$) | Mean of pos./neg. longitudinal jerk values per window |

*(continued)*

**Table 8.** (*continued*)

| Metric | Possible Metrics for Modeling |
|---|---|
| Lateral Jerk Related Metrics (m/s$^3$) | Mean of pos./neg. lateral jerk values per window |
| Aggressive Longitudinal Acc. Event | Count of acc. values exceeding 1.5 m/s$^2$per window[a] |
| Lateral Acc/Brake Event per sec. | 1. Rate of lateral acc. events exceeding +0.5 m/s$^2$ threshold (number of onsets per window (events/sec))<br>2. Rate of corrective lateral events based on negative lateral acc. below −0.5 m/s$^2$, (onsets per sliding window (events/sec)).[a] |
| Steering Reversal Events | Count of steering direction changes with velocity ≥2°/s (empirically determined threshold) per window (onset- based); used as time-series input (events/window) |
| Number of Left Turn Signal | Count of left turn signal activations per window (events/window); used as input to behavioral compliance or intent modeling |
| Time under 4 s headway | Total duration (in seconds) per window where time headway was below 4 s; used as a time-series safety indicator.[b] |
| Critical TTC event <3 s | Total duration (in seconds) per window where TTC was below 3 s (as reported by Vogel [28, 29]) |
| HeadwayDist Count (<20 m) | Count of time steps per window where headway distance was less than 20 m (events/window); (20 m threshold was empirically determined) |

[a]These thresholds were empirically selected based on exploratory analysis of the acceleration signals in this study, to isolate abrupt and corrective driving maneuvers.
[b]We use abbreviations "Avg.", "SDev." and "Acc." For "Average", "Standard Deviation" and "Acceleration" in the tables.

**Threshold-Based Indicators.** Certain variables only become important when they reach or fall below a value. For example, a Time-to-Collision (TTC) value below 3 s may be marked as a critical event. These indicators are computed at each time step by comparing the raw value to a predefined threshold and can either be used directly as a time-series of binary flags or summarized into event frequencies within sliding windows (e.g., number of TTC < 3 events per 3 s).

Collectively, these reformulated metrics provide a diverse and interpretable set of features for real-time driver behavior modeling. In future work, they will be evaluated as input variables for sequence-based models (e.g., LSTM or Transformer architectures) aimed at predicting maneuvers or detecting behavioral shifts across age groups.

The metrics in Table 8 capture the most prominent age-related metrics related to differences in driving behavior and, with straightforward windowing or event-detection steps, can be transformed into real-time features suitable for sequence-based models. This curated set therefore provides a clear starting point for developing data-driven driver-state models and age-aware support systems.

## 6 Conclusion, Limitations and Future Work

Despite the valuable findings, this study has several limitations that should be considered when interpreting the results. The sample size was relatively small and imbalanced (22 older vs. 12 younger drivers), which may limit generalizability. Each scenario lasted approximately seven minutes, which may not have been sufficient to capture long-term behavioral adaptations. The analysis also lacked gaze-tracking or cognitive load measures, which could provide further insight into attentional strategies and workload management. Finally, thresholds for classifying jerk and aggressive maneuvers were selected based on literature and internal data distribution but may still involve some degree of subjectivity.

The use of a high-fidelity driving simulator provided a safe and controlled environment for assessing potentially hazardous behaviors, particularly when working with older adults. Simulators allowed for the consistent presentation of driving scenarios across participants and enabled the collection of precise behavioral metrics without placing participants at risk. However, it is important to acknowledge that simulators cannot fully replicate the complexity and unpredictability of real-world driving—such as fluctuating weather conditions, interactions with real traffic, or emotional responses to actual risk. Consequently, while simulators are effective for behavioral observation, the generalizability of results to on-road driving contexts may be limited.

Future research should address these limitations by expanding the participant pool to include a more balanced and diverse sample, incorporating physiological and cognitive monitoring (e.g., gaze tracking, EEG), and validating the findings in real-world driving contexts. Longer driving sessions and longitudinal designs could offer deeper insight into age-related adaptation over time. Additionally, refining and validating the thresholds for defining abrupt or aggressive behavior could enhance metric accuracy and interpretability.

## References

1. Statistics Canada: Population projections: Canada, the provinces and territories. The Daily, 26 May 2010. https://www150.statcan.gc.ca/n1/daily-quotidien/100526/dq100526b-eng.htm
2. United Nations: World Population Ageing 2020 Highlights, Department of Economic and Social Affairs, Population Division (2020). https://digitallibrary.un.org/record/3898412. Accessed 13 Nov 2025
3. National Institute of Population and Social Security Research: Population Projections for Japan (2023Revision): 2021 to 2070, Tokyo, Japan (2023). https://www.ipss.go.jp/pp-zenkoku/e/zenkoku_e2023/pp2023e_Summary.pdf. Accessed 13 Nov 2025
4. U.S. Census Bureau: Demographic Turning Points for the United States: Population Projections for 2020 to 2060, P25-1144, February 2020. https://www.census.gov/library/publications/2020/demo/p25-1144.html. Accessed 13 Nov 2025

5. Eurostat: Ageing Europe – statistics on population developments. Statistics Explained, European Commission (2020). https://ec.europa.eu/eurostat/statisticsexplained/index.php?title=Ageing_Europe_-_statistics_on_population_developments. Accessed 13 Nov 2025
6. Transport Canada: Road Safety in Canada 2020. Government of Canada (2022). https://tc.canada.ca/en/road-transportation/publications/road-safety-canada-2020. Accessed 13 Nov 2025
7. Cicchino, J.B.: Effectiveness of forward collision warning and autonomous emergency braking systems in reducing front-to-rear crash rates. Accid. Anal. Prev. **99**, 142–152 (2017). https://doi.org/10.1016/j.aap.2016.11.009
8. Yu, L., Wang, R.: Research on adaptive cruise control system: a state-of-the-art review. Proc. IMechE Part D J. Automob. Eng. **236**(2–3), 211–240 (2022)
9. Naumann, R.B., et al.: Examining the Safety Benefits of Partial Vehicle Automation Technologies in an Uncertain Future, AAA Foundation for Traffic Safety, Washington, D.C., August 2023. https://aaafoundation.org/wp-content/uploads/2023/07/AAAFTS-Safety-Benefits-of-ADAS.pdf. Accessed 13 Nov 2025
10. M'haouach, M., Sassioui, A., Bouhoute, A., Fardousse, K.: DriveNet: a deep learning framework with attention mechanism for early driving maneuver prediction. Int. J. Artif. Intell. **14**(1), 44–53 (2025)
11. Sathy, S., Sankaranarayanan, P., Ramanujam, A., Jayaprakash, R.: ManeuverNet: a deep learning model for vehicle maneuver prediction. In: Proceedings of the IEEE Vehicular Technology Conference (VTC-Spring) (2024)
12. Aboah, A., Adu-Gyamfi, Y., Gursoy, S.V., Merickel, J., Rizzo, M., Sharma, A.: Driver maneuver detection and analysis using time series segmentation and classification. arXiv:2211.06463, November 2022
13. Khelfa, B., Ba, I.. Tordeux, A.: Predicting highway lane-changing maneuvers: a benchmark analysis of machine and ensemble learning algorithms. arXiv preprint arXiv:2204.10807, April 2022
14. Li, J.., et al.: Lane changing maneuver prediction by using driver's spatio-temporal gaze attention inputs for naturalistic driving. Adv. Eng. Inform. **60**, Article no. 102529 (2024). https://doi.org/10.1016/j.aei.2024.102529
15. Khairdoost, N., Shirpour, M., Bauer, M.A., Beauchemin, S.S.: Real-time driver maneuver prediction using LSTM. In: Proceedings of the IEEE Intelligent Vehicles Symposium (IV), Paris, France, pp. 2143–2148 (2019)
16. Kung, Y.-C., Zhang, A., Wang, J., Biswas, J.: Looking inside out: anticipating driver intent from videos. arXiv preprint arXiv:2312.01444, December 2023
17. Haque, M.M., Sarker, S., Dewan, M.A.A.: Driving Maneuver classification from time series data: a rule-based machine learning approach. Appl. Intell. **52**, 16900–16915 (2022)
18. Salthouse, T.A.: Aging and measures of processing speed. Biol. Psychol. **54**(1–3), 35–54 (2000)
19. Birren, J.E., Fisher, L.M.: Aging and speed of behavior: possible consequences for psychological functioning. Annu. Rev. Psychol. **46**, 329–353 (1995)
20. Doroudgar, et al.: Driving performance comparing older versus younger drivers. J. Saf. Res. **63**, 57–64 (2017)
21. Menze, R., et al.: Simulated driving behavior over the adult age span. Front. Psychol. **13**, Article no. 842190 (2022)
22. Bunce, D., Young, M.S., Blane, A., Khugputh, P.: Age and inconsistency in driving performance. Accid. Anal. Prev. **49**, 293–299 (2012). https://doi.org/10.1016/j.aap.2012.01.001
23. Young, M.S., Stanton, N.A.: Miles away: determining the extent of secondary task interference on simulated driving performance. Hum. Factors **49**(6), 1110–1126 (2007)

24. Reimer, B., Mehler, B., Coughlin, J.F., D'Ambrosio, L.A.: Impact of age and cognitive demand on lane choice and changing under actual highway conditions. Accid. Anal. Prev. **52**, 125–132 (2013). https://doi.org/10.1016/j.aap.2012.12.008
25. Robertsen, R., Lorås, H.W., Polman, R.C.J., Şimşekoğlu, Ö., Sigmundsson, H.: Aging and driving: a comparison of driving performance between older and younger drivers in an on-road driving test. SAGE Open **12**(2), Article no. 21582440221096133, May 2022. https://doi.org/10.1177/21582440221096133
26. Shin, H.-K., Lee, H.-C.: Characteristics of driving reaction time of elderly drivers in the brake pedal task. J. Phys. Ther. Sci. **24**(7), 567–570 (2012). https://doi.org/10.1589/jpts.24.567
27. Thompson, K.R., Johnson, A.M., Emerson, J.L., Dawson, J.D., Boer, E.R., Rizzo, M.: Distracted driving in elderly and middle-aged drivers. Accid. Anal. Prev. **45**(2), 711–717 (2012). https://doi.org/10.1016/j.aap.2011.09.040
28. Lewis-Evans, B., De Waard, D., Brookhuis, K.A.: A threshold effect of time headway on the experience of risk, task difficulty, effort, and comfort. Accid. Anal. Prev. **42**(6), 1926–1933 (2010)
29. Vogel, L.: A comparison of headway and time to collision as safety indicators. Accid. Anal. Prev. **35**(3), 427–433 (2003)

# Ontology Driven Fake News Detection for Post Disaster Management

Zuhrah Mohammed, Elena Panchoo, Jahnvi Sooknanan, Amit Ramkissoon, Diana Ragbir-Shripat(✉), and Vijayanandh Rajamanickam

The University of the West Indies at St. Augustine, Saint Augustine, Trinidad and Tobago
diana.ragbir-shripat@uwi.edu

**Abstract.** Fake news during disaster events can cause public panic, erode trust in authorities, and trigger misinformation-driven responses. Traditional credibility-based detection models rely on social credibility metrics such as source reputation, user behavior, and content popularity, but often lack semantic fact-checking and the ability to detect contextually paraphrased misinformation. This paper presents an enhanced hybrid model that incorporates ontology-based semantic validation into the Veracity architecture. The algorithm extracts structured knowledge from a domain-specific disaster ontology and computes semantic similarity using Sentence-BERT embeddings. This validates whether incoming messages align with factual disaster events. Using a balanced dataset of real and fake disaster news, the model achieved 86% accuracy with high recall for real messages and high precision for fake messages.

**Keywords:** fake news · disaster events · semantic similarity · ontology · Sentence-BERT · Veracity architecture

## 1 Introduction

Fake news can be defined as any news article that is intentionally and verifiably false [4]. With the rapid spread of misinformation via social media, especially during natural disasters, false reports can disrupt rescue missions and exacerbate damage, such as communication breakdown, by delaying critical response efforts [3]. As fake news tactics evolve, researchers have developed various methods and models to detect and mitigate misinformation. As stated in [1] these generally fall into four categories: (i) knowledge-based, which focuses on the knowledge in the published news; (ii) style-based, which focuses on how the published news is written; (iii) propagation-based, which focuses on the travel pattern of the published news, and (iv) credibility-based, which investigates the validity of the news based upon the credibility of the publisher. A subcategory of style-based detection is content-based detection which uses the textual features of a message, i.e. linguistic features, writing style or natural language processing (NLP) to classify whether it is fake or not [2].

The Veracity framework [1] employs a credibility-based approach that combines source reputation with a content based similarity check, implemented through a basic


R. Stahlbock et al. (Eds.): CSCE 2025, CCIS 2938, pp. 374–390, 2027.
https://doi.org/10.1007/978-3-032-22196-4_28

keyword-matching algorithm known as compareText. This algorithm analyzes the textual content of incoming messages by comparing it against a predefined set of keywords associated with specific topics, such as disasters, to assess whether a message belongs to the relevant domain. It relies solely on surface-level keyword overlap, therefore lacking the ability to verify semantic accuracy or detect reworded misinformation. In this research, we enhance the content-based approach by introducing a knowledge-based factchecking layer grounded in ontology-driven semantic similarity. A domain-specific ontology for disaster management was developed to represent structured knowledge about disaster types, subtypes, locations, and associated reports. This ontology was integrated into the compareText algorithm, replacing its flat keyword vector with semantically enriched concepts—thus transforming the original keyword matching into a more context-aware mechanism that better evaluates message relevance within the disaster domain. This refinement transforms the algorithm from simply identifying topic relevance to performing semantic fact-checking.

As described in [5] an ontology is 'a formal, explicit specification of a shared conceptualization', meaning it is a machine-understandable model that clearly defines the relevant concepts and constraints of a phenomenon, based on a consensual knowledge, that is, it is not private to some individual, but accepted by a group. The ontology learning process is defined as the application of a set of methods and techniques designed for building an ontology by enriching or adapting, an existing ontology in a semi-automatic fashion using distributed and heterogeneous knowledge and information sources. Ontology learning can be done using unstructured sources, semi-structured sources or structured data. To build our disaster ontology, we leveraged structured datasets containing disaster-specific information to model essential concepts and their interrelationships.

Integrating the ontology with structured disaster data into the compareText algorithm enables semantically enriched concept comparisons, allowing the algorithm to compute a similarity score based on alignment with real-world disaster knowledge. For example, a false message, such as "Tsunami expected to hit Chile within the hour" may be a paraphrased version of a real event such as "Storm surge warning issued for Chile coastline". These statements are superficially different, but semantically similar enough to be able to evade detection through keyword matching alone. To perform this semantic comparison, we used SBERT, a modification of the pretrained BERT network, which is a machine learning framework for natural language processing that uses Siamese and triplet network structures to derive semantically meaningful sentence embeddings that can be compared using cosine-similarity [13]. Unlike traditional keyword matching or vector-based similarity, SBERT allows us to capture deeper contextual and semantic relationships between texts, making it well-suited for detecting paraphrased or subtly reworded fake news. Contrary to prior approaches that treat knowledge-based and embedding-based methods separately, our model unifies both into a single semantic verification framework, enhancing robustness against paraphrased misinformation. This enables a more nuanced comparison between incoming messages and structured ontology instances. The similarity score acts as an indicator of whether the content of the message can be grounded in actual disaster events, thereby distinguishing genuine disaster news from fabricated or off topic information.

With these enhancements, the compareText algorithm is enhanced beyond basic keyword-matching to a semantically aware mechanism capable of detecting misinformation. This paper describes the following:

- The development of a domain-specific disaster ontology from structured disaster datasets.
- An enhanced Python-based implementation of the compareText algorithm that utilizes the disaster ontology and Sentence-BERT embeddings to perform semantic similarity computation.

In high-stake environments like critical disaster response, timely and accurate misinformation detection is essential for maintaining effective coordination and decision-making. This research contributes a semantically enhanced, knowledge grounded tool that incorporates both factual alignment and deeper semantic analysis to support critical decision-making.

This paper is structured as follows. Section 2 outlines a literature review of related research, while Sect. 3 entails the methodology and details of the ontology design and implementation. Section 4 defines the results of the evaluation of the model, Sect. 5 is the discussion, and Sect. 6 concludes the paper.

## 2 Literature Review

The following literature review presents various key frameworks and methodologies for detecting fake news using credibility analysis, semantic architectures, and ontology-based techniques. Each section highlights advances in data modeling, machine learning, and natural language processing that contribute to the development of an effective fake news detection system, within the scope of disaster-related contexts. This review also explores tools and models crucial for building semantic-aware systems capable of misinformation discernment.

### 2.1 Credibility Based Fake News Detection

Detecting fake news remains a significant challenge, even for machine learning algorithms. A major method for detecting fake news involves analyzing semantic features and comparing them to identify patterns or similarities [22]. An ensemble learning methodology, which combines multiple individual models to produce a more accurate and robust prediction than any single model, was used, thereby classifying news as fake or real based on the publisher's credibility.

Legitimacy, involving the techniques of Two Class Boosted Decision Tree (BDT) and Two Class Neural Network, is the ensemble learning model created for the task of Credibility-based Fake News Detection, as detailed in [22]. The Two Class Boosted Decision Tree (BDT) is a learning method in which further trees correct the errors of the trees that came before it (i.e. the second tree corrects the first). Predictions can then be made based on the entire ensemble of trees. The Two Class Neural Network is a set of interconnected layers, where the first layer is the input which is then connected to the last/output layer by an acyclic graph [22]. In between these layers, multiple hidden layers can be inserted, and predictive tasks can be accomplished. Logistic regression, a statistical technique, is also incorporated within the model, as it is commonly used to predict the probability of an outcome.

The dataset used was split into two subgroups: demographic features and social behaviour factors. The dataset used with this model and machine learning algorithms consisted of 14,000 tweets which were cleaned and split into 65% training data and 35% testing data. The model performed excellently, proving that the Legitimacy ensemble learning model was capable of predicting fake news with a credibility-based approach.

### 2.2 Fake News Detection Architecture

Mobile Ad Hoc Networks (MANETs) are a collection of mobile devices that are dynamic, independent, wireless and connected together to form a communications network. As stated in [1], a key problem faced by MANETs is the daily dissemination of fake news. Veracity is a unique computational system created to detect fake news within MANET messaging. Within the Veracity architecture, five algorithms were used in order to compute and analyze the credibility of data. These include: verifyNews, compareText, predictCred, credScore and eyeTruth. The Veracity architecture utilizes a prediction model along with credibility based and content-based data features to predict whether news is fake or not.

The original compareText algorithm accepted the message posted and compared this message to a list of keywords. It converted the message and its keywords into vectors and then calculated their cosine similarity to determine how close the message aligned with the intended topic. This similarity score, with historical credibility, publisher credibility, and other message features helped to assess the validity and legitimacy of the news. Once deemed legitimate, the message was uploaded to the network. The other algorithms used in [1] also determine whether the news is fake or not. The environment makes use of OMNET++ for simulation purposes, Microsoft Azure Machine Learning Studio for the prediction model, datasets and the FogNetSim++ library. Results obtained showed that the architecture was highly accurate and precise.

In this research, to give a more structured and semantic representation of knowledge, an ontology was used in the compareText function instead of the array of keywords. The ontology does not store data in a simple, linear way, but rather, it allows for hierarchical categorization, inference, reasoning and contextual understanding. This improved the function (compareText) by increasing efficiency of detecting fake news as it is more adept in topic classification and credibility assessments in natural language processing.

### 2.3 Ontology Models

The following four sections present key concepts and methods relevant to ontology design and evaluation. Each section focuses on a distinct aspect that contributes to the development, structure, interpretation, and validation of ontological systems:

**Knowledge Organization Systems for Semantic Consistency.** Knowledge Organization Systems (KOSs) play a crucial role in managing semantic conflicts and ensuring consistency across diverse information sources [23]. The study on the implications of

KOSs in health information exchange during the COVID-19 pandemic demonstrates how standardized systems, such as International Classification of Diseases (ICD), Systematized Nomenclature of Medicine Clinical Terms (SNOWMED CT), and Logical Observation Identifiers Names and Codes (LOINC) facilitated seamless data interoperability. A key challenge in health informatics is semantic conflict, which arises from inconsistencies in terminology across different data sources. KOSs address these challenges through structured vocabularies and classification schemes [23]. These systems also provide a foundation for ontology development by supporting semantic alignment within a domain. In this study, similar principles are applied to promote semantic consistency in disaster-related texts. Standardizing terminology in post-disaster news reporting minimizes lexical variation across sources, thereby enhancing the reliability and coherence of ontology-driven analysis.

**Ontology-Based Topic Modeling for Disaster News.** A two-stage system for keyword detection and ontologybased topic modelling, as presented in the study on automatic keyword detection [24], offers a framework that can be adapted for this research. The Collective Connectivity-Aware Node Weight (CoCoNoW) approach—a graph-based technique—detects and ranks keywords based on their connectivity and weight. These keywords are then utilized in an ontology-driven topic modeling process to categorize text data effectively. This methodology aligns with the objective of constructing an ontology for semantic comparison of disaster related news. By adapting the CoCoNoW approach, disaster specific keywords can be systematically extracted and integrated into the ontology, enabling a structured representation that enhances the accuracy of text classification and misinformation detection.

**Semantic Interpretation of Keywords for Fake News Detection.** The study in [20] provides methods to translate keyword queries into Description Logic (DL) conjunctive queries, improving semantic understanding. Mapping queries onto ontological elements refines interpretation. Using DL, inconsistencies between sources can be detected. The Fact Extraction and Representation at the Document level (FRED) converter and Renamed ABox and Concept Expression Reasoner (RACER) reasoner identify contradictions in disaster-related news, enhancing robustness in detection.

**Provenance Tracking.** When highlighting the problem of detecting fake news, a key aspect to be considered is time. Provenance information is extremely valuable with regards to this as it allows for the evaluation of authenticity, reliability and relevance of the information gathered through its results. It gathers the history of the data through timestamps and version history, as every piece of data comes with this information, along with event logs or even audit trails. Provenance graphs can be created in order to show trends and changes in data over time which can aid in finding spikes of fake news or other issues. Provenance tracking also uses metadata and data lineage methods in order to document the timeline of events.

## 2.4 PAV Ontology - Provenance, Authoring and Versioning

Provenance Ontology (PROV-O) is domain independent, allowing for the tracking of authoring and versioning information from web resources [25]. It provides the basic methodology but does not include identification factors such as author, curator or contributors. To address this, Provenance, Authoring and Versioning (PAV) ontology was developed [25]. This ontology distinguishes between various originators of a resource and supports the representation of both accessed and transformed information sources. Authors can be referred to as the primary originators of scientific statements, curators; the collectors of the knowledge, artefact creators create the digital artifact and external sources comprise of the external data and knowledge bases. To reduce complexity, [25] indicates that PAV adopts a snapshot-based rather than a process-oriented approach, enabling lightweight yet effective traceability of digital resource evolution. Additionally, PAV properties are defined without multiplicity constraints.

## 2.5 Ontological Development

Numerous tools have been developed for ontology construction, driven by the necessity to tailor ontologies to specific applications or target audiences. According to [27], the formalisms, tools and languages employed during ontology development must be clarified to ensure the accurate representation of all necessary distinctions within the ontology. When developing an ontology from scratch, it is important to specify the tools used in the development process, indicate whether translators are involved in the used tool, identify the storage mechanism, define the implementation language, assess tool-language compatibility, and ascertain whether integration with other ontologies is required. When building knowledge systems, the author specifies that a domain must be created which is then further split into concepts which constitute a conceptualization of said domain. Ontologies can be used for various applications. These include information retrieval, text processing applications, digital libraries, in knowledge management systems and in NLP (natural language processing). In this research, a domain-specific disaster ontology was developed and utilized to support semantic validation in the context of fake news detection during disaster events.

Different languages can be used to build ontologies, and for this research, RDF (Resource Description Framework) was chosen due to its ability to specify the semantics of data in an interoperable manner, while allowing it to provide clarity to information provided. When building an ontology, it is also important to look at different formalisms that can allow for the expression of all comprehensive parts. Frame-based formalisms use a data structure (frame) to represent a concept in a domain. Logic-based formalisms have replaced frame-based languages as they are a very expressive knowledge-based formalism. OBO (Open Biomedical Ontology) requires the ontology to be a graph with labelled nodes [27]. Semantic networks are graphs, which, at an ontological level, expresses vocabulary which can be useful to humans, but functional for machine processing - making it suitable for the scope of this research. Similarly, Conceptual Graph (CG) formalisms are based on semantic networks, but take semantics from first order predicate knowledge. Various tools are available for editing ontologies; however, Protégé was selected for this project due to its widespread use in the semantic web domain and its support for key ontology formats, including RDF and OWL, both of which are utilized in this study.

## 2.6 Translating Natural Language (NL) Queries to SPARQL

To address inefficiencies and high costs in industrial environments, [28] proposed a system that transforms natural language (NL) queries into SPARQL—a query language designed for retrieving and manipulating data stored in RDF format on the Semantic Web. This system uses domain-specific ontologies and structured vocabularies provided by SKOS (Simple Knowledge Organization System), which allows for standardized concept representation.

The study evaluated different storage solutions, comparing relational database systems with native and virtual triple stores. Although D2RQ—a virtual triple store that maps relational databases to RDF—offered conceptual benefits, its performance in industrial conditions was poor. Native triple stores demonstrated better scalability and smoother ontology integration.

Manual and automatic query performance were compared, with automatic queries sometimes outperforming manually optimized ones, partly due to Lucene indexing. This eliminated the need for expert query writers while maintaining high accuracy and efficiency.

The system is portable across domains by modifying the underlying ontology, SKOS data, and SPIN (SPARQL Inferencing Notation) rules—a framework for expressing logic and constraints in RDF. Overall, the approach reduces costs, minimizes IT dependency, and enhances usability, making it especially valuable for semantic data access in industrial decision-making contexts.

## 2.7 Sentence-BERT: Sentence Embeddings Using Siamese BERT Networks

BERT is a pre-trained transformer network developed for a range of natural language processing (NLP) tasks [13]. BERTs performance on sentence pair regression tasks, such as STS (semantic textual similarity), has set new performance records [13]. However, BERT's architecture introduces significant computational overhead, as it processes both input sentences jointly, rendering it inefficient for large scale similarity tasks. To address this, Reimers and Gurevych [13] proposed Sentence-BERT (SBERT), a modification of BERT which incorporates Siamese and triplet network structures to derive semantically meaningful sentence embeddings that can be compared using cosine similarity. The advancements made in BERT have enabled more effective large-scale semantic similarity computations, facilitating clustering and information retrieval via semantic search. According to [13], BERT uses a cross encoder, in which a target value is predicted after two sentences are fed into the transformer network. However, it is deemed unsuitable for various pair regression as too many possible combinations exist, leading to BERT requiring 65 h on a modern V100 GPU. As stated by [13], a common method used to address clustering and semantic search is mapping each sentence to a vector space in which semantically similar sentences are close to one another. Since the common method of using the average BERT embeddings yielded subpar results, SBERT was developed.

SBERT allows for the derivation of fixed size vectors for input sentences, and thus, by using a similarity measure such as the cosine similarity score, semantically similar sentences can be found. According to [13], this can run more efficiently on modern hardware, dropping the time taken to find similar sentence pairs in a collection of 10,000 sentences from 65 h to a mere 5 s; along with computing the cosine similarity. In order to derive a fixed size sentence embedding, the SBERT model adds a pooling operation to the end of the BERT model. The creation of the Siamese and triplet networks was mentioned in [13] as a way to update the weights in such a way that the actual sentence embeddings are semantically meaningful and can be compared with cosine similarity. In [13], various structures and objective functions were utilized. The Classification Objective Function concatenated the sentence embeddings with element-wise differences and multiplied it by the training weight. The regression objective function was defined using the cosine similarity generated between two sentence embeddings. Additionally, the triplet objective function trains the network so that the anchor sentence is closer to a positive sentence rather than a negative one. Evaluation of the SBERT function in [13] concluded that it outperformed other competing sentence embedding models such as InferSent and Universal Sentence Encoder. Since sentence embeddings need to be potentially computed for millions of sentences [13], computational efficiency is critical, in which SBERT has demonstrated significant advantages.

To summarize, this literature review explores different approaches to detecting misinformation in disaster-related news, while highlighting the significance of ontology-based frameworks in organizing and validating information. Techniques such as provenance tracking and semantic similarity are essential to the improvement of accuracy scores for fake news detection. Furthermore, ontology evaluation methods are crucial to assessing and refining the effectiveness of the ontology in real world applications. Thus, the integration of these methods is promising to enhance the disaster response by ensuring the credibility of information during critical times.

## 3 Methodology

This section outlines the methodology adapted to address the primary objective of integrating a semantic validation layer to the Veracity architecture with the use of a structured, domain-specific ontology of disaster events. The methodology is structured into three core components; an overview of the system architecture and the role of the compareText algorithm within Veracity; the process of ontology development, from domain specification to conceptualization and implementation; and lastly, the implementation of a semantic similarity model using Sentence-BERT to enable deep, contextual comparison between incoming messages and verified disaster event instances, thereby increasing Veracity's robustness against paraphrased misinformation and enhancing its capability to verify factual consistency in disaster-related news.

### 3.1 System Overview

The Veracity framework comprises the publisher application, the news, the reporter monitoring agent, the MANET neighbours, and the subscribers to the topic. Figure 1 displays the components of Veracity, and Fig. 2 shows its interactions [1]:

The compareText algorithm operates as a content similarity function within the reporter monitoring agent. The algorithm's logic entails converting the input message and

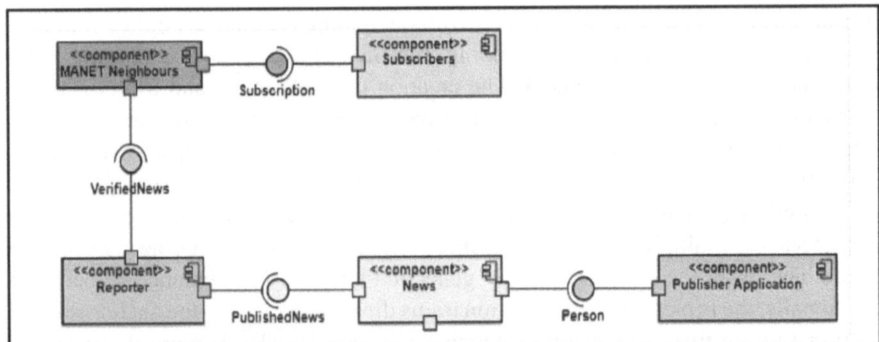


**Fig. 1.** Components of the Veracity Architecture

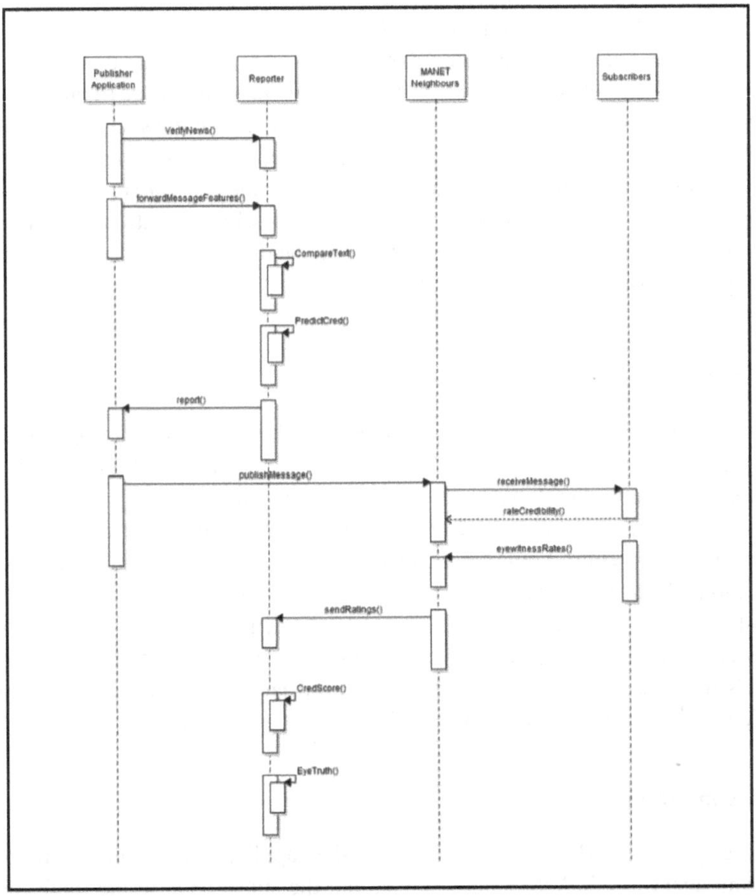

**Fig. 2.** Interactions of the Veracity Architecture

a set of topic-specific keywords into simple vectors (vector A and vector B respectively) and computing the cosine similarity:

$$\text{Ms} = \text{A} \cdot \text{B} = ||\text{A}||\,||\text{B}||\cos\theta\ [1].$$

The similarity score is combined with the other credibility features of the system based on the message and publisher, to detect the legitimacy of the news. This makes the system effective in identifying unreliable sources, but lacks factchecking, and exposes vulnerability to lexical variation and paraphrasing which poses a critical limitation in the detection of subtly reworded misinformation. Hence, it was proposed to replace the basic keyword vector with a semantically enriched ontology-driven representation to combat this limitation. Input messages will then be compared against structured disaster event instances opposed to flat keyword vectors. This allows the system to semantically validate whether a news message is representative of actual disaster scenarios as it is compared against verified disaster event data, thus extending compareText's role from surface similarity to factual domain verification.

### 3.2 Ontology Development

The process of developing a domain specific ontology was executed using the methodology outlined in [15] which combines two well-known ontology development methodologies, namely METHONTOLOGY [16], and the 101 Method [17]. The paper describes ontology development to be split into three phases: Specification, Conceptualization and Implementation.

**Specification.** The first phase, Specification, or domain description, entails defining the goals and scope of the ontology, specifying what must be included in the ontology versus what is not necessary, in order to keep the data minimized to only the relevant information. The primary purpose of the ontology is to act as a structured knowledge base for verifying whether an incoming message reflects actual disaster events and concepts. Hence, the scope of the ontology was defined to model disasters and the associated information and entities, aligning with this goal.

**Conceptualization.** This phase involves identifying classes, relations, and attributes for the ontology. When identifying classes, it is important to analyze the disjoint classes and define the class hierarchy in a manner that certain conditions do not produce instance absences. As outlined in [5], an ontology can be built using unstructured sources, semi-structured sources or structured data. The classes and properties of this disaster ontology were defined with the use of structured knowledge as done in [15] from two datasets containing disaster event information and corresponding news reports as described below.

- EM-DAT: The EM-DAT disaster contains data on the occurrence and impacts of over 26,000 mass disasters worldwide from 1900 to the present day. The database is compiled from various sources, including UN agencies, non-governmental organizations, reinsurance companies, research institutes, and press agencies [7].

- ReliefWeb disaster dataset: ReliefWeb is a humanitarian information service provided by the United Nations Office for the Coordination of Humanitarian Affairs (OCHA). ReliefWeb disaster dataset provides an overview of the situation and situation reports, news and press releases, assessments, evaluations, infographics and maps of natural disasters with humanitarian impact from 1981 until today, collected from more than 4,000 key sources, including humanitarian agencies at the international and local levels, governments, thinktanks and research institutions, and the media [8].

Following data cleaning and preprocessing, the key domain concepts were defined to represent classes in the ontology as described in the table below (Table 1).

**Table 1.** Conceptualization Phase – Disaster Ontology Key Elements

| Category | Elements | Description/Notes |
|---|---|---|
| Ontology Classes | DisasterEvent, Location, NewsReport, Source | Core domain concepts representing disaster occurrences, geography, reports, and sources |
| Object Properties | mentionsEvent, occurredAt, reportedBy | Semantic links between classes. E.g., a report mentions an event, an event occurred at a location |
| Data Properties | disasterGroup, disasterSubgroup, disasterSubtype | Classification attributes for disaster taxonomy |
| | subregion, region | Geographical metadata attached to the Location class |
| | sourceURL | Metadata for the Source class containing the origin link of the news report |

These key elements are organized in the following UML diagram to give a clear perspective on the core concepts of the ontology (Fig. 3).

According to [15], once the conceptual model of the ontology is constructed, the next step involves defining relevant instances. Following the METHONTOLOGY [16] method, each instance should be provided a definition of: its name, the name of the concept it belongs to, and its attribute values if known. Hence, the disaster ontology was populated with instances from a cleaned, combined version of the datasets with each core concept structured in separate columns and directly imported using rdflib.Graph(). An excerpt of a DisasterEvent instance from the ontology is outlined in Table 2.

**Implementation.** The ontology was developed and implemented using Protégé, a widely adopted, open-source ontology editor and knowledge-based framework designed for the construction of intelligent systems [9]. Owing to its extensibility and modular architecture, Protégé supports a plug-and-play environment conducive to rapid prototyping and ontology-driven application development [18]. For integration purposes, the finalized ontology was exported in RDF Schema (RDFS) format [19], enabling seamless instance population and compatibility with downstream components of the Veracity

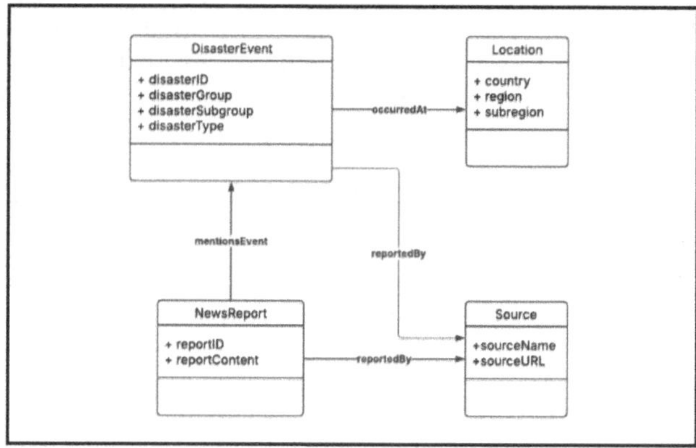


**Fig. 3.** Ontology Model in UML

**Table 2.** Instance Table – Disaster Ontology

| Concept | Instance Name | Property | Value |
|---|---|---|---|
| DisasterEvent | DisasterEvent_0 01 | disasterGroup | Natural |
| | | disasterSubgroup | Climatological |
| | | disasterSubtype | Drought |
| | | occurredAt | Location_01 |
| Location | Location_01 | country | Djibouti |
| | | region | Africa |
| | | subregion | Sub-Saharan Africa |
| NewsReport | NewsReport_101 | mentionsEvent | DisasterEvent_ 001 |
| | | reportedBy | Source_01 |
| Source | Source_01 | sourceURL | https://www.emdat.be/ |

framework, specifically, its integration into the compareText algorithm for semantic validation.

### 3.3 Similarity Model

The similarity model was constructed with the use of the pre-existing Sentence-BERT (SBERT) model [13]. This model is trained on Natural Language Inferences (NLI) and semantic similarity datasets; hence it captures the deep, contextual meaning of sentences. The exported ontology RDF was parsed into a RDF graph structure and instance descriptions were extracted, pre-processed, and stored in a JSON file. SBERT derives both the input message and ontology instances into embeddings with semantically meaningful vector representations. Cosine similarity is computed between the embedded vectors, producing a similarity score that reflects deep, contextual alignment with real-world disaster concepts. This score replaces the original cosine similarity value represented in Eq. (1) and is forwarded as input into Veracity's existing credibility prediction pipeline. The similarity score output by this model serves as a factual consistency indicator: a high score suggests the message closely resembles known disaster event patterns, whereas a low score flags it as either off-topic or potentially fabricated. This enhancement transforms compareText from a shallow, lexical comparator into a semantic fact-checking layer, capable of identifying paraphrased fake news and aligning news content with structured disaster knowledge. It improves the system's resilience against misinformation tactics that rely on rewording or partial truth.

## 4 Evaluation and Results

An evaluation of this ontology-enhanced similarity model was performed as demonstrated in [20] and [21], with knowledge-based test sets derived based on the expected functionality of our specific model. The performance and effectiveness of the model for detecting fake news messages outside the domain of disaster events, was assessed by utilizing a balanced dataset consisting of legitimate disaster related messages derived from our ontology and fabricated messages which were publicly debunked by professional factchecking organizations based on known misinformation narratives. This approach provided a small but meaningful benchmark that tests the model's ability to semantically differentiate between factually aligned and fabricated disaster narratives.

The enhanced compareText algorithm was invoked iteratively for each message in the dataset, computing a corresponding semantic similarity score for every input instance. The semantic similarity score was used to verify whether each message was meaningfully related to structured disaster events using a similarity threshold of 0.5; such that messages scoring above this threshold were classified as real while messages scoring below this threshold were classified as fake. This threshold was selected as it represents a balanced midpoint in cosine similarity space, ensuring that only messages with a moderate to high degree of semantic alignment with known disaster instances are classified as real. Given the variability in natural language and the potential for paraphrasing in both legitimate and misleading reports, a 0.5 threshold provides an effective trade-off between sensitivity and specificity, minimizing both false positives and false negatives. The model's performance with this threshold was assessed using standard classification metrics: accuracy, precision, recall, and F1-score. The results in Fig. 4 illustrate the values yielded for these metrics, which demonstrate exceptional performance from the model in classifying messages within the disaster domain.

```
Classification Report:

              precision    recall  f1-score   support

        Fake       0.94      0.76      0.84        21
        Real       0.80      0.95      0.87        21

    accuracy                           0.86        42
   macro avg       0.87      0.86      0.86        42
weighted avg       0.87      0.86      0.86        42

Confusion Matrix:
[[16  5]
 [ 1 20]]
```

The model achieved 86% accuracy across the test set. Recall for real news was relatively high (0.95), meaning most of the legitimate disaster messages were correctly identified. Assessing the confusion matrix, for a count on this shows only one legitimate message was misclassified as fake. The model achieved 94% precision for fake news, meaning most fake news messages were caught and classified as fake, while 5 fake messages were missed.

The false negatives were likely due to their close semantic resemblance to plausible events which is a known limitation in content-only detection systems. The additional credibility features in the Veracity architecture will address this limitation, as this evaluation focused on the content-detection aspect that our project enhances.

## 5 Discussion

The evaluation results highlight the significant impact of integrating ontology-based semantic reasoning into Veracity's credibility detection framework. The model achieved an overall accuracy of 86%, with particularly strong recall for real disaster messages (0.95) and precision for fake news (0.94). These metrics demonstrate that the enhanced compareText algorithm, powered by structured domain knowledge and semantic embeddings, effectively distinguishes legitimate disaster-related news from misinformation, even in the presence of paraphrasing and lexical variation.

A key contribution of this work is the shift from shallow keyword-based comparisons to deep semantic matching using ontology-driven representations and Sentence-BERT embeddings. This fundamentally enhances Veracity's ability to reason about the factual consistency of content. Unlike traditional text similarity approaches that rely heavily on lexical overlap, this approach enables the detection of reworded or partially fabricated content by grounding messages in a structured representation of real-world disaster events. The ontology serves as a formal reference model, guiding the content comparison algorithm and adding a knowledge-based layer to the computation of similarity scores. This not only improves classification performance but also enhances the interpretability and reliability of fake news detection within the disaster domain and Veracity's architecture.

This work also contributes a reusable disaster ontology that models key disaster concepts such as events, locations, sources, and their interrelations, derived from authoritative datasets (EM-DAT and ReliefWeb). This ontology may serve as a foundation for broader fact-checking tasks within the humanitarian domain, including disaster response coordination, situational awareness, and early warning systems.

However, the model is not without limitations. The few false negatives observed suggest that highly plausible but fabricated messages may pass semantic checks, especially when they are closely worded to resemble real events. While this ontological approach strengthens the content-verification layer, it operates independently of contextual metadata, temporal patterns, or source credibility. These aspects are handled by other components of the broader Veracity architecture and point to a complementary role for the model within a multi-faceted detection system.

Potential future work can focus on extensions to this model that may significantly enhance its operability, for example, scaling the ontology to incorporate multilingual and region-specific disaster vocabularies could improve performance in non-English or localized contexts. Additionally, integrating the semantic similarity module with real-time data pipelines and Veracity's full credibility scoring system will enable live misinformation detection and response. This will also provide a more comprehensive evaluation of the model's performance when combined with Veracity's other credibility features.

In summary, this work demonstrates that combining ontologies with deep language models creates a powerful, domain-aware, and semantically rich layer of fact-checking for disaster-related news content. The approach not only elevates the technical capabilities of Veracity but also contributes to the broader field of explainable and ontology-guided misinformation detection.

## 6 Conclusion

This research introduced an ontology-driven enhancement to Veracity's compareText algorithm to improve fake news detection during disaster events. By integrating a domain-specific disaster ontology with Sentence-BERT semantic similarity, the model moves beyond simple keyword matching to provide deeper, context-aware verification. By verifying whether messages align with structured disaster event knowledge, the model supports factual grounding of content, contributing to misinformation detection that is both domain-aware and semantically robust. Test results on a balanced dataset of real and fake disaster news showed strong performance, achieving 86% accuracy with high recall for real messages and high precision for fake ones. This confirms the model's effectiveness in detecting both factual content and paraphrased misinformation. The use of structured disaster knowledge, paired with semantic embeddings, demonstrates the value of combining ontology reasoning with modern NLP for more reliable fact-checking. Future work will explore scaling the model with real-time data, and full integration into the Veracity architecture's fake news detection pipeline.

## References

1. Ramkissoon, A.N., Goodridge, W.: Veracity: a fake news detection architecture for MANET messaging. In: 2021 International Conference on Information, Cybernetics, and Computational Social Systems (ICCSS). IEEE (2021)
2. Zhou, X., Zafarani, R.: Fake news: a survey of research, detection methods. arXiv preprint arXiv:1812.00315 (2018)
3. Singh, D., Shams, S., Kim, J., Park, S.-J., Yang, S.: Fighting for information credibility: an end-to-end framework to identify fake news during natural disasters. In: Proceedings of the 17th International Conference on Information Systems for Crisis Response and Management (ISCRAM), Blacksburg, VA, USA (2020)
4. Shu, K., Sliva, A., Wang, S., Tang, J., Liu, H.: Fake news detection on social media: a data mining perspective. ACM SIGKDD Explor. Newsl. **19**(1), 22–36 (2017). https://doi.org/10.1145/3137597.3137600
5. Gómez-Pérez, A., Manzano-Macho, D.: An overview of methods and tools for ontology learning from texts. Knowl. Eng. Rev. **19**(3), 187–212 (2005). https://doi.org/10.1017/S0269888905000251
6. Wattiheluw, F.H., Sarno, R.: Developing word sense disambiguation corpuses using Word2Vec and Wu Palmer for disambiguation. In: 2018 International Seminar on Application for Technology of Information and Communication (iSemantic). IEEE (2018)
7. Centre for Research on the Epidemiology of Disasters: EM-DAT: The International Disaster Database. https://www.emdat.be/. Accessed 31 Aug 2025
8. ReliefWeb: Disasters List. https://data.humdata.org/dataset/reliefweb-disasters-list. Accessed 31 Aug 2025
9. Protégé: A free, open-source ontology editor and framework for building intelligent systems. https://protege.stanford.edu/. Accessed 31 Aug 2025
10. Bird, S.: NLTK: the natural language toolkit. In: Proceedings of the COLING/ACL 2006 Interactive Presentation Sessions. Association for Computational Linguistics (2006)
11. Miller, G.A., Beckwith, R., Fellbaum, C., Gross, D., Miller, K.: Introduction to WordNet: an on-line lexical database. Int. J. Lexicogr. (1991)
12. W3Schools: Pandas Tutorial. https://www.w3schools.com/python/pandas/pandas_intro.asp. Accessed 31 Aug 2025
13. Reimers, N., Gurevych, I.: Sentence-BERT: sentence embeddings using siamese BERT-networks. arXiv preprint arXiv:1908.10084 (2019)
14. Murugan, R., Shanmugam, A.: Cluster based node misbehaviour detection, isolation and authentication using threshold cryptography in mobile ad hoc networks. Int. J. Comput. Sci. Secur. (IJCSS) **6**(3), 188 (2012)
15. Brusa, G., Caliusco, M.L., Chiotti, O.: A process for building a domain ontology: An experience in developing a government budgetary ontology. In: Proceedings of the Australasian Ontology Workshop (AOW 2006), Conferences in Research and Practice in Information Technology, vol. 72, Hobart, Australia (2006)
16. Gómez-Pérez, A., Fernández-López, M., Corcho, O.: Ontological Engineering: With Examples from the Areas of Knowledge Management, E-Commerce and the Semantic Web. Springer, London (2004)
17. Noy, N., McGuinness, D.: Ontology Development 101: A Guide to Creating Your First Ontology (2001)
18. Knublauch, H., et al.: The protégé OWL experience. In: Workshop on OWL: Experiences and Directions, 4th International Semantic Web Conference (ISWC 2005), Galway, Ireland (2005)

19. Brickley, D., Guha, R.V.: RDF Vocabulary Description Language 1.0: RDF Schema. W3C Recommendation (2004). http://www.w3.org/TR/rdf-schema/
20. Tran, T., Cimiano, P., Rudolph, S., Studer, R.: Ontology-based interpretation of keywords for semantic search. In: Aberer, K., et al. (eds.) ISWC ASWC 2007 2007. LNCS, vol. 4825, pp. 523–536. Springer, Heidelberg (2007). https://doi.org/10.1007/978-3-540-76298-0_38
21. Groza, A.: Detecting fake news for the new coronavirus by reasoning on the Covid-19 ontology. arXiv preprint arXiv:2004.12330 (2020). https://arxiv.org/abs/2004.12330
22. Ramkissoon, A.N., Goodridge, W.: Legitimacy: an ensemble learning model for credibility based fake news detection. In: 2021 International Conference on Data Mining Workshops (ICDMW), Auckland, New Zealand, pp. 254–261. IEEE (2021). https://doi.org/10.1109/ICDMW53433.2021.00039
23. Zeng, M.L., Hong, Y., Clunis, J., He, S., Coladangelo, L.P.: Implications of knowledge organization systems for health information exchange and communication during the COVID-19 pandemic. Data Inf. Manag. **4**(3), 148–170 (2020). https://doi.org/10.2478/dim-2020-0009
24. Beck, M., Rizvi, S.T.R., Dengel, A., Ahmed, S.: From automatic keyword detection to ontology-based topic modeling. Technical report, TU Kaiserslautern and DFKI, Germany
25. Ciccarese, P., Soiland-Reyes, S., Belhajjame, K., Gray, A.J.G., Goble, C., Clark, T.: PAV ontology: provenance, authoring and versioning. J. Biomed. Semant. **4**(1), 37 (2013). https://doi.org/10.1186/2041-1480-4-37
26. Raad, J., Cruz, C.: A survey on ontology evaluation methods. In: Proceedings of the International Conference on Knowledge Engineering and Ontology Development (KEOD), Lisbon, Portugal (2015). https://doi.org/10.5220/0005591001790186
27. Slimani, T.: Ontology development: a comparing study on tools, languages and formalisms. Indian J. Sci. Technol. **8**, 1–12 (2015). https://doi.org/10.17485/ijst/2015/v8i
28. Sander, M., Waltinger, U., Roshchin, M., Runkler, T.: Ontology-based translation of natural language queries to SPARQL. Technical report, Siemens Corporate Technology & TU München, Germany

# Multilingual Customer Record Linkage: A Novel Approach Using LLMs for Cross-Lingual Entity Resolution

Muzakkiruddin Ahmed Mohammed(✉), Shames Al Mandalawi, Hendrika Maclean, and John R. Talburt

Center for Advanced Research in Entity Resolution and Information Quality (ERIQ), University of Arkansas - Little Rock, Little Rock, AR, USA
{mmohammed6,salmandalaw,hcmaclean,jrtalburt}@ualr.edu

**Abstract.** This paper presents a novel approach to multilingual customer record linkage using Large Language Models (LLMs), specifically Google's Gemini model. The system addresses the challenge of identifying duplicate customer records across different languages, a critical issue for global enterprises with international customer bases. By leveraging the semantic and syntactic understanding capabilities of LLMs, our approach performs entity resolution across language barriers without relying on bilingual dictionaries or parallel corpora. Gemini and similar modern LLMs understand more than 80 languages, enabling broad coverage for cross-lingual entity resolution. The system is implemented as an interactive web application using Streamlit, allowing users to upload data and query potential matches in real time across multiple languages, with demonstrations in English, Spanish, Mandarin, and Arabic. Experimental results show that LLMs can achieve up to 95% accuracy in identifying cross-language duplicates, offering a flexible and comprehensive alternative to traditional record linkage systems that often struggle with multilingual data.

**Keywords:** Entity Resolution · Multilingual Processing · Large Language Models · Customer Data Integration · Record Linkage · Conversational AI

## 1 Introduction

Customer record linkage, also known as entity resolution or deduplication, refers to the process of identifying and consolidating database records that represent the same real-world entity despite variations in their representation. This task becomes particularly complex in multilingual environments where customer data may appear in different languages, scripts, and cultural contexts. Traditional record linkage methods, such as rule-based matching, string similarity measures, and machine learning models trained on specific language pairs, often fail to


R. Stahlbock et al. (Eds.): CSCE 2025, CCIS 2938, pp. 391–405, 2027.
https://doi.org/10.1007/978-3-032-22196-4_29

bridge linguistic and structural gaps. As a result, they struggle to recognize equivalent entities across languages and regions.

Global enterprises face this challenge on a large scale. Customer information is often dispersed across multiple systems and languages due to international operations, mergers and acquisitions, and user self-registration in different locales. The inability to correctly identify duplicates across languages leads to fragmented customer profiles, redundant communications, and inconsistent service experiences. Industry analyses estimate that organizations lose billions annually due to such data fragmentation, with additional risks related to regulatory compliance, revenue leakage, and operational inefficiencies. Therefore, an effective multilingual record linkage framework is vital for organizations seeking a unified and accurate view of their global customer base.

This paper introduces a novel approach to multilingual customer record linkage using Large Language Models (LLMs), specifically Google's Gemini model. Modern LLMs possess advanced semantic and syntactic understanding across more than 80 languages, allowing them to detect equivalence beyond simple textual similarity. Unlike traditional systems that depend on translation pipelines or handcrafted bilingual dictionaries, our approach leverages the intrinsic multilingual understanding of LLMs to recognize cross-lingual relationships directly. For instance, it can associate "John Smith", "Juan Smith", "约翰·史密斯", and «يوحنا» as representations of the same entity by interpreting both linguistic and contextual cues.

The primary contributions of this work are threefold. First, we present an LLM-based framework that reframes entity resolution as a natural language understanding problem rather than a data matching task. Second, we implement this framework as an interactive web application using Streamlit, enabling real-time, user-driven analysis and multilingual querying. Third, we provide a comprehensive evaluation demonstrating that LLMs can achieve up to 95% accuracy in identifying cross-language duplicates, significantly outperforming conventional rule-based and translation-dependent approaches.

The broader impact of this work lies in its potential to transform global data management practices. By leveraging the multilingual reasoning capabilities of LLMs, organizations can unify fragmented records, enhance compliance processes such as Know Your Customer (KYC) verification, and improve customer experience across linguistic boundaries. Beyond customer data integration, this approach offers a generalizable foundation for multilingual information retrieval, cross-lingual schema matching, and future AI-driven data harmonization systems.

## 2 Related Work

Research on entity resolution has evolved through several stages, from early probabilistic and rule-based systems to recent advances in deep learning and large language models. This section reviews key developments across five major areas relevant to multilingual record linkage: traditional entity resolution, multilingual approaches, entity extraction and relation modeling, neural network methods, and large language models. Together, these studies provide the conceptual foundation and technological progression that motivate our proposed framework.

## 2.1 Traditional Entity Resolution

Entity resolution, also known as record linkage or data matching, has been a key area of research since the probabilistic model of Fellegi and Sunter introduced a framework for comparing record pairs using weighted similarity measures [1]. Traditional systems typically employ blocking techniques to reduce computational complexity, feature engineering to extract comparison vectors, and machine learning classifiers to determine matches and non-matches. Surveys on large-scale entity resolution [11,12] emphasize the increasing challenges associated with data volume, velocity, and variety in modern applications.

Recent efforts have focused on improving scalability and computational efficiency. Distributed implementations such as cost-aware load balancing using MapReduce [2] have demonstrated improved execution times and adaptability for multilingual data processing. Probabilistic models based on relational logistic regression [3] further improved robustness by addressing name variations, abbreviations, and typographical inconsistencies. These developments have collectively advanced traditional record linkage systems, though their dependence on handcrafted features and monolingual assumptions limits performance in multilingual environments.

## 2.2 Multilingual Entity Resolution

The growing availability of multilingual datasets has motivated extensive research on cross-lingual entity resolution. Early work relied on translation-based pipelines, phonetic similarity metrics, and multilingual embeddings that project textual representations into shared semantic spaces [13]. While effective to some extent, these methods are constrained by translation quality, lack of domain-specific corpora, and resource dependency for low-resource languages.

Modern multilingual approaches have transitioned toward end-to-end architectures that jointly learn representations across multiple languages. Models such as mGENRE [4] introduced sequence-to-sequence formulations for multilingual linking, while joint supervision frameworks [5] demonstrated that integrating data from high-resource languages can enhance cross-lingual transfer. Subsequent studies have improved performance in low-resource contexts through enhanced candidate generation and zero-shot linking using search query data [6,7]. Despite these advancements, achieving reliable and consistent accuracy across typologically diverse languages remains a persistent research challenge.

### 2.3 Entity Extraction and Relation Modeling

Beyond entity matching, research in multilingual entity processing has expanded toward joint entity and relation extraction. Large-scale benchmarks such as the SMiLER dataset [8] have provided multilingual evaluation resources across diverse domains, supporting comparative studies of deep learning models. Comprehensive surveys on relation extraction [15,23] categorize methods based on text representation, contextual encoding, and triplet prediction, outlining directions for enhancing multilingual generalization.

Coreference resolution has similarly progressed toward multilingual capability, where cross-lingual training and syntactic integration have substantially improved system precision [9,10]. These developments demonstrate growing interest in creating unified frameworks that can process semantically linked entities across languages, scripts, and text structures.

### 2.4 Neural Networks and Deep Learning in Entity Resolution

The adoption of neural networks has significantly advanced entity resolution by enabling semantic similarity modeling beyond surface-level string comparisons. Deep learning approaches have been systematically categorized based on their contributions to blocking, comparison, and classification stages [17]. Neural architectures allow flexible learning of complex feature interactions and support domain adaptation with minimal feature engineering. Automated literature analyses in natural language processing [18] further confirm the widespread integration of deep learning into data matching and name normalization, establishing new benchmarks for record linkage accuracy and scalability.

### 2.5 Large Language Models in Entity Resolution

Large Language Models (LLMs) have recently introduced new opportunities for multilingual entity resolution by combining contextual reasoning, few-shot learning, and multilingual understanding within a single architecture. These models are capable of interpreting semantic equivalence directly across languages without explicit translation or dictionary-based alignment [26]. Prototype implementations using generative AI models [20] have demonstrated effective entity matching across diverse linguistic and structural variations [24]. Surveys on multilingual LLMs [21] highlight their potential for polyglot tasks and their ability to generalize across domains. Broader machine learning research [22] also underscores the relevance of adaptive models for optimizing entity resolution workflows and improving prediction consistency [22].

Overall, the progression from rule-based systems to neural and LLM-driven architectures marks a significant paradigm shift in entity resolution. The integration of multilingual understanding, contextual reasoning, and generative capabilities establishes a foundation for developing language-agnostic and scalable entity matching frameworks. Building on these advancements, our work extends the application of LLMs to multilingual customer record linkage, addressing the limitations of traditional systems and demonstrating their potential for real-world global data integration.

# 3 Methodology

The proposed approach to multilingual customer record linkage is built upon the integration of Large Language Models (LLMs) to identify and resolve duplicate records across languages. This section describes the overall architecture, prompt engineering strategy, and language support mechanisms that enable accurate, scalable, and real-time cross-lingual entity resolution. The methodology emphasizes flexibility to handle heterogeneous data formats and linguistic diversity while ensuring system transparency and usability.

## 3.1 System Architecture

The system adopts a three-tiered architecture designed to ensure modularity, scalability, and efficient interaction between components, as illustrated in Fig. 1. Each layer plays a distinct role in supporting multilingual entity resolution.

**Data Ingestion Layer:** This layer serves as the entry point for importing customer data in multiple formats, including CSV, Excel (XLSX/XLS), and tab-delimited text files. It parses uploaded files into a structured format that preserves the integrity of the original schema and supports downstream processing. Dynamic schema detection allows adaptation to varied input structures without predefined templates. Preliminary validation procedures identify missing fields, encoding inconsistencies, and data quality issues that could affect the accuracy of matching.

**LLM Interaction Layer:** At the core of the system, this layer enables semantic analysis using Google's Gemini model. Customer records are converted into structured text resembling tabular representations to facilitate comprehension by the LLM [19]. Secure API integration is managed through environment-variable-based authentication to maintain privacy and compliance. Each user query triggers a prompt that integrates contextual data, instructions, and query-specific details. The LLM response is parsed and normalized for consistency, ensuring accurate interpretation across languages and scripts.

**User Interface Layer:** The front-end interface, developed with Streamlit, provides an interactive and multilingual experience. It allows users to upload datasets, visualize preliminary results, and interactively query the model. Session-based histories enable iterative refinement of previous queries. Features such as data previews, language selection, and dynamic feedback ensure accessibility for users across linguistic and technical backgrounds, making the system both intuitive and globally usable.

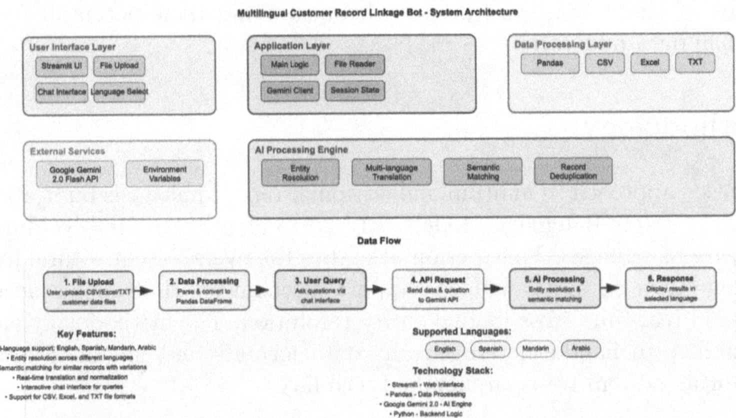


**Fig. 1.** System architecture showing the Data Ingestion Layer, LLM Interaction Layer, and User Interface Layer with their respective components and data flow connections.

### 3.2 Prompt Engineering for Entity Resolution

Prompt engineering is central to optimizing LLM performance for multilingual entity resolution [16]. The system employs a structured prompt design consisting of four key components:

**Role Definition:** Establishes the LLM as a specialized assistant for multilingual record linkage, ensuring consistent task interpretation.

**Data Context:** Presents customer information in a text-based tabular format, with sampling and chunking used to maintain contextual relevance within the model's input window.

**Query Specification:** Defines user intent, information scope, and desired output format, guiding the LLM to produce consistent and interpretable responses.

**Task Instructions:** Specify subtasks such as semantic matching, normalization, and cross-lingual comparison. The instructions prioritize meaning over string similarity, enabling recognition of equivalent entities like "John Smith" and "Juan Smith" as the same person. Cross-lingual handling supports translation and matching among English, Spanish, Mandarin, and Arabic, with extensibility to other languages. Normalization guidelines standardize names, addresses, and identifiers, while uncertainty handling flags incomplete or ambiguous records.

Parameter tuning further refines LLM behavior. A low temperature setting (0.2) ensures deterministic responses, reducing random variation and improving reliability. Top-p and top-k sampling values (0.95 and 40, respectively) balance diversity and precision by considering multiple plausible matches. An expanded context window of 8192 tokens supports detailed explanations, and safety configurations ensure ethical handling of sensitive data.

### 3.3 Language Support and Cross-Lingual Capabilities

The system leverages the multilingual capabilities of Gemini, which supports over 80 languages spanning multiple linguistic families and scripts. The evaluation focuses on English, Spanish, Mandarin, and Arabic, chosen for their linguistic diversity and relevance to global enterprises. These languages encompass alphabetic, logographic, and abjad writing systems, providing a robust foundation for testing cross-lingual generalization.

Gemini's syntactic and semantic comprehension allows it to interpret structural variations, morphological differences, and contextual nuances between languages. The model identifies equivalences that are not directly translatable, enabling accurate matching even across culturally distinct name forms or address conventions. Its script-agnostic processing ensures consistent performance across Latin, Chinese, and Arabic scripts.

The integration of architectural scalability, multilingual adaptability, and advanced LLM reasoning provides a practical and effective framework for cross-lingual entity resolution. By unifying data ingestion, LLM-based analysis, and user interaction within a single system, the proposed methodology establishes a comprehensive platform for managing multilingual customer records in global data ecosystems.

## 4 Implementation

The implementation of the multilingual customer record linkage system was guided by two primary objectives: establishing a robust technical framework and ensuring a seamless user experience. The design emphasizes modularity, scalability, and responsiveness to support diverse data inputs and real-time interaction with a Large Language Model (LLM). This section details the development environment, core implementation functions, LLM integration pipeline, and user interface design.

### 4.1 Development Environment and Dependencies

The system was implemented in Python 3.9 due to its extensive ecosystem for data processing and machine learning. The development environment integrates a structured set of dependencies, each serving a distinct purpose within the architecture. The Streamlit framework underpins the web-based interface, enabling rapid deployment of interactive applications without the overhead of traditional front-end development. The Pandas library manages data ingestion, transformation, and cleaning, supporting multiple file types such as CSV, Excel, and tab-delimited text files.

Integration with the Gemini LLM is achieved through the Google Generative AI Client, which handles API communication, authentication, and response parsing. To maintain interface responsiveness during longer LLM queries, asynchronous operations are managed using `Asyncio` and `Nest_Asyncio`. These libraries enable concurrent request handling, allowing the interface to remain interactive while awaiting responses. Secure environment management is handled by `Python-dotenv`, which stores API credentials and configuration parameters safely across development and production environments. Together, these dependencies establish a stable and secure foundation for scalable system operation.

## 4.2 Core Implementation Functions

The implementation is structured around three primary functional components, each aligned with a critical stage in the workflow.

**File Processing Function:** This module accepts and parses uploaded customer data files in multiple formats. It dynamically detects the file type and loads the content using the corresponding Pandas method. Schema validation routines check for structural integrity, missing fields, and encoding issues to ensure reliable downstream processing.

**LLM Integration Function:** The function `get_gemini_response` encapsulates the system's interaction with the Gemini API. It constructs structured prompts that combine contextual customer data, user intent, and detailed task instructions. Model parameters such as temperature, top-p, and top-k are configured for optimal performance. The function also implements error handling mechanisms to manage timeouts, invalid responses, and other API-related exceptions.

**User Interface Function:** Implemented as the `main()` routine, this component governs the interactive workflow. It initializes the chat interface, manages user sessions and message histories, and displays LLM responses in real time. Users can upload data, preview loaded datasets, and refine queries interactively. This design enables iterative exploration while maintaining transparency in model outputs.

## 4.3 LLM Integration Pipeline

The Gemini model serves as the reasoning engine for multilingual entity resolution. Its integration is realized through a Prompt Construction Pipeline that unifies user intent, contextual data, and entity resolution directives into a coherent textual prompt. Input data is structured using templated placeholders for clarity, and concise instructions are embedded to ensure interpretability within the model's context window. When large datasets are used, sampling and chunking strategies maintain relevance and avoid context overflow.

Once the prompt is generated, it is transmitted to the Gemini API, and a structured response is received. The Response Processing component extracts relevant results, standardizes the formatting, and integrates the information into the ongoing session. Error handling routines manage potential interruptions, ensuring smooth user experience even under partial failures. This modular pipeline design enables efficient communication between the application and the LLM while maintaining consistency and security.

### 4.4 User Interface Implementation

The user interface emphasizes accessibility, transparency, and multilingual usability. Developed using Streamlit, it employs a two-panel layout: a sidebar for configuration tasks such as file upload and language selection, and a main panel for chat interaction and results visualization. Session persistence allows users to revisit previous exchanges, promoting an iterative and traceable workflow.

Real-time progress indicators and feedback messages enhance usability during LLM processing. Built-in examples guide new users through the query formulation process and demonstrate best practices for achieving accurate results. The interface design prioritizes inclusivity, ensuring usability for both technical and non-technical audiences across linguistic backgrounds. Figure 2 illustrates the interface responding to a sample multilingual entity resolution query.

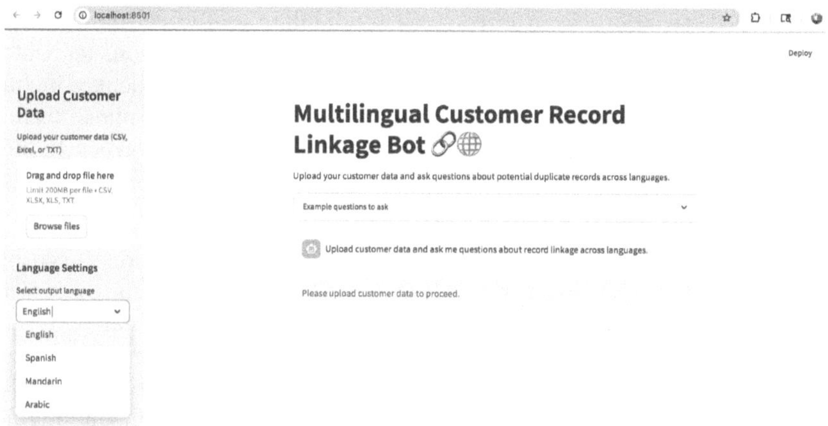


**Fig. 2.** Interactive interface of the multilingual customer record linkage system responding to a sample query.

In summary, the implementation integrates robust back-end components with a user-centric front end to support real-time, cross-lingual entity resolution. Through the combination of efficient data processing, structured LLM interaction, and an intuitive interface, the system delivers a practical and scalable solution for multilingual customer data management.

## 5 Evaluation

To evaluate the effectiveness of the proposed LLM-based approach for multilingual customer record linkage, we conducted a comprehensive series of experiments using synthetically generated datasets specifically designed to test cross-lingual entity resolution performance. The evaluation combined quantitative and qualitative assessments to measure accuracy, scalability, and interpretability.

### 5.1 Synthetic Dataset Development

A controlled synthetic dataset was developed to provide a reproducible and unbiased evaluation environment. The primary dataset was generated using DeepSeek R1, allowing fine-grained control over duplication, linguistic variation, and noise introduction. Synthetic generation ensured precise ground truth alignment between duplicates across languages, enabling rigorous quantitative benchmarking.

**Primary Dataset Characteristics.** The main dataset consisted of 80 customer records (`ID 1-80`) with deliberate duplication patterns. Records `ID 71-80` were designed as multilingual duplicates of records `ID 1-10`, creating a defined cross-lingual linkage challenge. The dataset represented four primary languages: English (`ID 1-20`), Spanish (`ID 21-40`), Mandarin (`ID 41-60`), and Arabic (`ID 61-80`).

Controlled variations were introduced to simulate real-world data inconsistencies, including typographical errors, inconsistent capitalization, transliteration differences, and reordered name components. Additional challenges included address format discrepancies, regional conventions in postal and phone formats, and partial missing fields. A manually curated truth set defined correct duplicate mappings, serving as the benchmark for evaluation.

**Supplementary Datasets.** To assess generalization, additional synthetic datasets were generated using ChatGPT and Grok AI. These datasets varied in size from 80 to 250 records, maintaining balanced multilingual representation. Specialized challenge subsets were introduced for domain-specific contexts such as healthcare, finance, and e-commerce, where entity attributes and naming conventions differ significantly. Certain sets emphasized difficult linguistic transformations, including culturally localized name variants and transliterated entity names, to test the robustness of semantic matching.

### 5.2 Quantitative Assessment

**Accuracy Metrics.** System performance was evaluated using standard entity resolution metrics: precision, recall, and F1 score. Across datasets ranging from 80 to 250 records, the proposed system achieved an average accuracy of 95% against the ground truth. Precision reached 96.2%, indicating minimal false positives, while recall averaged 93.8%, showing strong retrieval of true duplicates. The overall F1 score was 95.0%, confirming balanced precision–recall trade-offs (Figs. 3, 4 and Table 1).

**Scalability Assessment.** To evaluate scalability, dataset sizes were progressively increased from 80 to 1,000 records. Small datasets (80–250 records) achieved consistent accuracy between 94–96%. Medium datasets (251–500 records) showed moderate performance degradation to 89–93%. Larger datasets

**Table 1.** Performance metrics by language pair

| Language Pair | Precision | Recall | F1 Score |
|---|---|---|---|
| English–Spanish | 98.2% | 96.5% | 97.3% |
| English–Mandarin | 94.1% | 92.3% | 93.2% |
| English–Arabic | 93.8% | 91.2% | 92.5% |
| Spanish–Mandarin | 95.6% | 93.1% | 94.3% |
| Spanish–Arabic | 94.9% | 92.8% | 93.8% |
| Mandarin–Arabic | 93.4% | 90.5% | 91.9% |

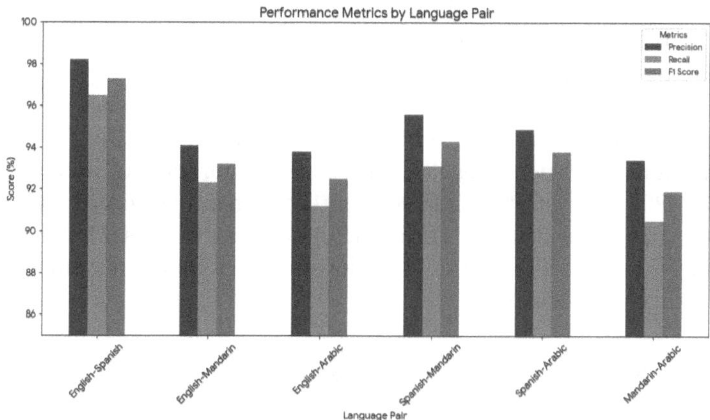


**Fig. 3.** System performance across six language pairs showing precision, recall, and F1 score.

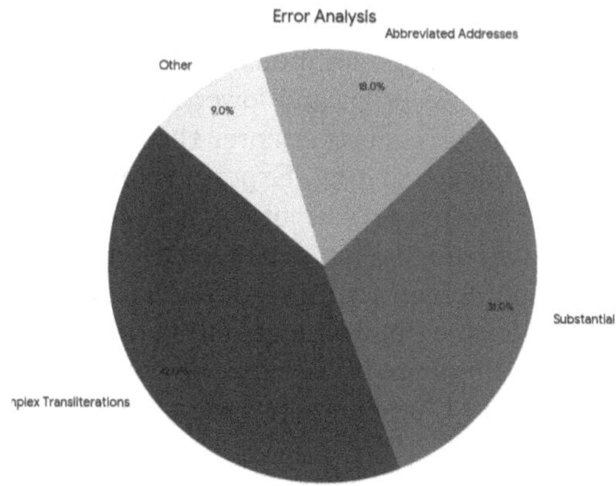


**Fig. 4.** Distribution of error sources identified during evaluation, including transliteration mismatches, missing fields, and ambiguous entities.

(501–1,000 records) yielded accuracy between 75–85%, while very large datasets (over 1,000 records) demonstrated significant decline due to context window constraints inherent to current LLM architectures.

These results confirm that the system performs optimally for small to medium-sized datasets. Scalability challenges emerge primarily from token limitations and model context length rather than algorithmic deficiencies, suggesting that future architectures with expanded context capabilities could mitigate these constraints.

### 5.3 Qualitative Assessment

A qualitative review provided insights into the model's interpretability and linguistic reasoning. In cross-lingual name matching, the system correctly linked examples such as "Robert Johnson," "Roberto Johnson," "罗伯特·约翰逊" (Luōbótè Yuēhànxùn), and «روبرت جونسون» (Rubirt Junsun), demonstrating semantic awareness beyond surface-level similarity.

The model also normalized addresses across languages and scripts, recognizing equivalent locations despite differences in formatting and partial data availability [29]. It accurately inferred matches when one record lacked certain fields, leveraging contextual cues from surrounding attributes. Moreover, the system produced human-readable explanations for each match decision, enhancing interpretability and user trust.

### 5.4 Model Selection Considerations

Performance analysis revealed that LLM choice significantly affects multilingual entity resolution outcomes. Our experiments primarily utilized open-access models with API-based interfaces to ensure transparency and reproducibility. These models established a strong performance baseline and exposed current architectural constraints.

Enterprise-grade LLMs, offering larger context windows and enhanced multilingual capabilities, are better suited for industrial deployments [28]. They enable higher throughput, improved security, and lower latency through on-premise or private deployment options [27]. Furthermore, they support task-specific fine-tuning and consistent confidence scoring. Experimental projections indicate that enterprise models can further improve accuracy, particularly for complex or low-resource language pairs, while reducing dependence on manual verification.

Overall, the evaluation demonstrates that LLMs, even without fine-tuning, are highly capable of performing multilingual entity resolution with competitive precision and recall. The findings also highlight opportunities for scaling the approach through advanced LLM architectures and domain-specific adaptations.

## 6 Conclusion and Discussion

This work presents a novel approach to multilingual customer record linkage by reframing entity resolution as a natural language understanding task using Large

Language Models (LLMs). The proposed system leverages the semantic reasoning capabilities of LLMs to identify duplicate customer records across languages without requiring translation dictionaries or language-specific models. Through prompt engineering and structured data integration, the framework achieved an average accuracy of 95% on synthetic multilingual datasets, demonstrating that LLMs can effectively bridge linguistic and contextual gaps in global customer data.

Compared with traditional methods, the approach provides several advantages: it eliminates the need for handcrafted language rules, supports natural language queries, and generates human-readable explanations that enhance interpretability and user trust. These strengths make it well suited for applications such as unified customer profiling, multilingual KYC and AML compliance, and cross-border data integration in global enterprises.

However, practical tradeoffs remain. Current LLMs introduce latency and context window limitations that affect scalability for very large datasets. Although they reduce upfront engineering costs, they incur ongoing computational and API expenses. These challenges highlight the need for hybrid architectures that combine deterministic matching with LLM-driven semantic reasoning to balance efficiency and accuracy.

Future research should explore scalable extensions of this framework, including improved prompt optimization, intelligent data chunking, and fine-tuning for domain-specific adaptation. Developing standardized multilingual benchmarks and explainable reasoning mechanisms will further enhance transparency and replicability [25]. Despite existing constraints, this study establishes a foundation for LLM-based multilingual entity resolution, offering a flexible, language-agnostic solution for global data management and setting the stage for more advanced multilingual information systems in the future.

**Acknowledgments.** This research was partially supported by the National Science Foundation under EPSCoR Award No. OIA-1946391.

**Disclosure of Interests.** The authors have no competing interests to declare that are relevant to the content of this article.

## References

1. Fellegi, I.P., Sunter, A.B.: A theory for record linkage. J. Am. Stat. Assoc. **64**(328), 1183–1210 (1969)
2. Medhat, D., Yousef, A.H., Salama, C.: Cost-aware load balancing for multilingual record linkage using MapReduce. Ain Shams Eng. J. **10**(4), 745–756 (2019)
3. Fatemi, B., Kazemi, S.M., Poole, D.: Record linkage to match customer names: a probabilistic approach. arXiv preprint arXiv:1806.10928 (2018)
4. De Cao, N., et al.: Multilingual autoregressive entity linking. Trans. Assoc. Computat. Linguist. **10**, 274–290 (2022)
5. Upadhyay, S., Gupta, N., Roth, D.: Joint multilingual supervision for cross-lingual entity linking. In: Proceedings of the 2018 Conference on Empirical Methods in

Natural Language Processing, pp. 2486–2495. Association for Computational Linguistics (2018)
6. Zhou, S., Rijhwani, S., Neubig, G.: Towards zero-resource cross-lingual entity linking. In: Proceedings of the 2nd Workshop on Deep Learning Approaches for Low-Resource NLP (DeepLo 2019), pp. 243–252. Association for Computational Linguistics (2019)
7. Fu, X., Shi, W., Yu, X., Zhao, Z., Roth, D.: Design challenges in low-resource cross-lingual entity linking. In: Proceedings of the 2020 Conference on Empirical Methods in Natural Language Processing (EMNLP), pp. 6418–6432. Association for Computational Linguistics (2020)
8. Seganti, A., Firląg, K., Skowronska, H., Satława, M., Andruszkiewicz, P.: Multilingual entity and relation extraction dataset and model. In: Proceedings of the 16th Conference of the European Chapter of the Association for Computational Linguistics: Main Volume, pp. 1946–1955. Association for Computational Linguistics (2021)
9. Steinberger, J., et al.: Highly multilingual coreference resolution exploiting a mature entity repository. In: Recent Advances in Natural Language Processing, pp. 719–725 (2011)
10. Pražák, O., Konopík, M., Král, P.: Exploring multiple strategies to improve multilingual coreference resolution in CorefUD. arXiv preprint arXiv:2408.16893 (2024)
11. Christophides, V., Efthymiou, V., Palpanas, T., Papadakis, G., Stefanidis, K.: End-to-end entity resolution for big data: a survey. arXiv preprint arXiv:1905.06397 (2019)
12. Christophides, V., Efthymiou, V., Palpanas, T., Papadakis, G., Stefanidis, K.: An overview of end-to-end entity resolution for Big Data. ACM Comput. Surv. (CSUR) **53**(6), 1–42 (2020)
13. Guellil, I., Garcia-Dominguez, A., Lewis, P.R., Hussain, S., Smith, G.: Entity linking for English and other languages: a survey. Knowl. Inf. Syst. **66**(7), 3773–3824 (2024)
14. Savaram, P., Tabassum, S., Bandu, S.: Multilingual approaches to named entity recognition. In: 2024 3rd Edition of IEEE Delhi Section Flagship Conference (DELCON). IEEE (2024)
15. Zhao, X., et al.: A comprehensive survey on relation extraction: recent advances and new frontiers. ACM Comput. Surv. **56**(11), 1–39 (2024)
16. Cakmak, M.C., Agarwal, N., Poudel, D.: TriPSS: a tri-modal keyframe extraction framework using perceptual, structural, and semantic representations. arXiv preprint arXiv:2506.05395 (2025)
17. Barlaug, N., Gulla, J.A.: Neural networks for entity matching: a survey. ACM Trans. Knowl. Discov. Data (TKDD) **15**(3), 1–37 (2021)
18. Sawicki, J., Ganzha, M., Paprzycki, M.: The state of the art of natural language processing–a systematic automated review of NLP literature using NLP techniques. Data Intell. **5**(3), 707–749 (2023)
19. Cakmak, M.C., Agarwal, N.: Influence of symbolic content on recommendation bias: analyzing YouTube's algorithm during Taiwan's 2024 election. Appl. Netw. Sci. **10**(1), 23 (2025)
20. Mohammed, M.A., Talburt, J.R., Mohammed, A., Syed, K.: Entity resolution with household movement discovery using Google Generative AI. In: Latifi, S. (ed.) The 22nd International Conference on Information Technology-New Generations (ITNG 2025), ITNG 2025. Advances in Intelligent Systems and Computing, vol. 1463. Springer, Cham (2025). https://doi.org/10.1007/978-3-031-89063-5_41

21. Qin, L., et al.: A survey of multilingual large language models. Patterns **6**(1) (2025)
22. Mohammed, M.A.: Machine learning approaches, technologies, recent applications, advantages and challenges on manufacturing and Industry 4.0 applications. Int. J. Res. Appl. Sci. Eng. Technol. **10**, 1114–1121 (2022)
23. Cakmak, M.C., Agarwal, N., Poudel, D., Bhattacharya, S.: Examining the impact of symbolic content on YouTube's recommendation system. In: International Conference on Complex Networks and Their Applications, pp. 421–432. Springer, Cham (2024). https://doi.org/10.1007/978-3-031-82431-9_35
24. Mohammed, M.A., Talburt, J.R., Claasssens, L., Marais, A.: Retrieval-augmented multi-LLM ensemble for industrial part specification extraction. In: Proceedings of the 17th International Conference on Knowledge and Systems Engineering, KSE 2025 (2025, accepted)
25. Al Mandalawi, S., Mohammed, M.A., Maclean, H., Cakmak, M.C., Talburt, J.R.: Policy-aware generative AI for safe, auditable data access governance. In: Proceedings of the 17th International Conference on Knowledge and Systems Engineering, KSE 2025 (2025, accepted)
26. Muhammad, A., Mohammed, M.A., Milanova, M., Talburt, J.R., Cakmak, M.C.: Multi-agent RAG framework for entity resolution: advancing beyond single-LLM approaches with specialized agent coordination. Preprints (2025)
27. Cakmak, M.C., Agarwal, N.: Unpacking algorithmic bias in YouTube Shorts by analyzing thumbnails. In: Proceedings of the 57th Hawaii International Conference on System Sciences (HICSS-57) (2025)
28. Mohammed, M.A., Talburt, J.R., Muhammad, A.: Multi-LLM record linkage: a comparative analysis framework for co-residence pattern discovery. Presented at the 24th International Conference on Information and Knowledge Engineering (IKE'25). World Congress in Computer Science, Computer Engineering and Applied Computing (2025)
29. Cakmak, M.C., Agarwal, N.: A keyframe-based approach for auditing bias in youtube shorts recommendations. arXiv preprint arXiv:2509.02543 (2025)

# Secure Password Management System (SPMS) Using One-Time Pad (OTP)

Aysha Almarzooqi, Maryam Al Ali, Meera Alhammadi, Abdulrahman Al Shehhi, Joseph Anajemba(✉), and Nedal Ababneh

Abu Dhabi Polytechnic, Abu Dhabi, United Arab Emirates
joseph.anajemba@adpoly.ac.ae

**Abstract.** This study is focused on the development of a highly Secure Password Management System (SPMS) through the utilization of advanced cryptographic techniques aimed at enhancing password management, security, and storage. Static encryption keys have been relied upon by traditional password managers, rendering them vulnerable to data breaches and cryptographic attacks. In this research, Argon2 hashing is implemented for master password authentication, HMAC-SHA256-based One-Time Pad (OTP) key generation is applied for unique password encryption, and XOR encryption is employed to improve storage efficiency. Confidentiality, integrity, and robust protection against brute-force attacks are ensured by this combination of cryptographic methods. Additionally, efficient storage and retrieval of encrypted passwords are provided by employing a lightweight NoSQL key-value storage system (Replit Database). The effectiveness of the system is demonstrated through simulated implementation, with the security and usability of the proposed password manager being confirmed. Also, the performance analysis shows that the proposed system outperforms three other existing systems as compare in terms of encryption and computational overhead and estimated time require to evade regular GPU-based attached. Future improvements are expected to include the development of a graphical user interface (GUI) and the enhancement of performance for larger dataset.

**Keywords:** SPMS · HMAC-SHA256 · One-Time Pad (OTP) · Argon2 Hashing · Replit Database · Password Encryption

## 1 Introduction

Password security has remained a critical component of modern cybersecurity, as individuals and organizations have increasingly relied on authentication mechanisms to safeguard sensitive information. Traditional password managers have stored user credentials in centralized databases, making them susceptible to data breaches, unauthorized access, and cryptographic weaknesses [1]. Many existing password managers have also depended on static encryption keys, meaning if a key was compromised, all associated encrypted passwords could be exposed.

Following an in-depth analysis of existing password managers, several security challenges have been identified, including:


R. Stahlbock et al. (Eds.): CSCE 2025, CCIS 2938, pp. 406–419, 2027.
https://doi.org/10.1007/978-3-032-22196-4_30

1. Traditional password managers have relied on static encryption keys, which could be compromised if leaked or stolen, resulting in the exposure of all stored passwords.
2. Additionally, many users have practiced password reuse, making them vulnerable to credential-stuffing attacks.
3. Furthermore, existing solutions have lacked dynamic encryption key generation, creating predictable attack vectors that could be exploited by attackers.

To address these security risks, this study is focused on developing a secure password manager that utilizes Argon2 hashing, HMAC-SHA256 authentication, and XOR encryption with One-Time Pad (OTP) key derivation. These cryptographic methods will be designed to ensure confidentiality, integrity, and improved protection against brute-force attacks. Additionally, this study will be implementing a lightweight and efficient storage system to enhance usability while maintaining strong security. Also, this study has aimed to address these challenges by developing a password manager that encrypts passwords dynamically using timestamps and site-specific OTP keys. This approach ensures that each stored credential would be encrypted uniquely, reducing the risk of mass exposure in case of a security breach.

## 1.1 Major Contributions

The primary objective of this study is to develop a highly secure password management system (PMS) that:

1. Utilized Argon2 hashing for secure master password authentication.
2. Implemented HMAC-SHA256-based One-Time Pad (OTP) encryption keys for unique password encryption.
3. Ensured password storage efficiency and security through the use of Replit Database (NoSQL key-value 4. 5. storage).
4. Enhanced randomization and encryption unpredictability by incorporating cryptographic salts and timestamps.
5. Provided a user-friendly CLI interface for seamless password retrieval and management.

To achieve these objectives, the password manager is designed to follow a structured encryption and decryption process. The diagram below illustrates the systematic design, demonstrating how Argon2 hashed, HMAC-SHA256-based OTP generation, and XOR encryption work together to ensure secure password storage and retrieval.

The novel contributions of this study have included:

1. A new approach to dynamic password encryption, where encryption keys have been generated per site using HMAC-SHA256 OTP keys.
2. A timestamp-based key derivation system, which has ensured encryption uniqueness without relying on traditional salts.
3. A hybrid encryption model combining Argon2, HMAC-SHA256, and XOR with Base64 encoding, providing enhanced security.

### 1.2 Proposed Password Management System (PMS) System Design

The proposed Password Management System (PMS) is designed to securely manage and retrieve passwords using cryptographic techniques. The system involves two main processes: Password Management and Password Recovery. In the Password Management Process, the user inputs a Master Password (MP) which is processed through Argon2 with a salt (SALT_M) to generate a Master Key (MK). The MK is then used to create an OTP Key using HMAC SHA256 with a combination of timestamp and site name. The OTP Key generated is combined with the Site Password to produce a Cipher Password (C) which is stored in a database along with relevant metadata.

The Password Recovery Process is similar but focuses on retrieving stored passwords. It starts with the Master Password (MP), which is converted to the Master Key (MK) using the same Argon2 + SALT_M process. The OTP Key is then regenerated using HMAC SHA256, ensuring the same timestamp and site name are used. By combining the Cipher Password (C) from the database with the OTP Key, the system successfully recovers the original Site Password. This approach ensures that the PMS remains secure and resilient to unauthorized access (Fig. 1).

### 1.3 Research Organization

This research has been structured as follows: Sect. 1 provides an overview of the study, including background, objectives, and major contributions of this research idea. Section 2 reviews several literatures to examine One-Time Pad (OTP) encryption, its security properties, historical significance, and its application in modern cryptographic techniques. This section also explored existing password management solutions and their limitations in ensuring strong encryption. In Sect. 3 contains a detailed cryptographic tool, database implementation, and encryption techniques used in the study. Section 4 describes the system implementation, preliminary functionality testing, and security analysis. Also, a comparison of the outperformance of the proposed system against other existing systems is presented in this section. Section 5 presents a summarized finding, discussed potential improvements, and suggested future research directions.

## 2 Related Works

Data security is explored in the study through the use of cryptography, specifically the One-Time Pad (OTP) algorithm.

The OTP algorithm is identified as symmetric because the same key is used for both encryption and decryption, ensuring that only individuals with the key can access the encrypted data. An application utilizing the OTP algorithm is analysed, enabling the secure storage and protection of data. The evaluation of the OTP application indicates that data is effectively secured, and the original file size is maintained during encryption and decryption. Various file formats are supported, providing reliable data protection. It is suggested in the study that further development of the application could enhance security and improve its design. The study also highlighted inefficiencies in the OTP algorithm, particularly its requirement for the key length to match the plaintext, which

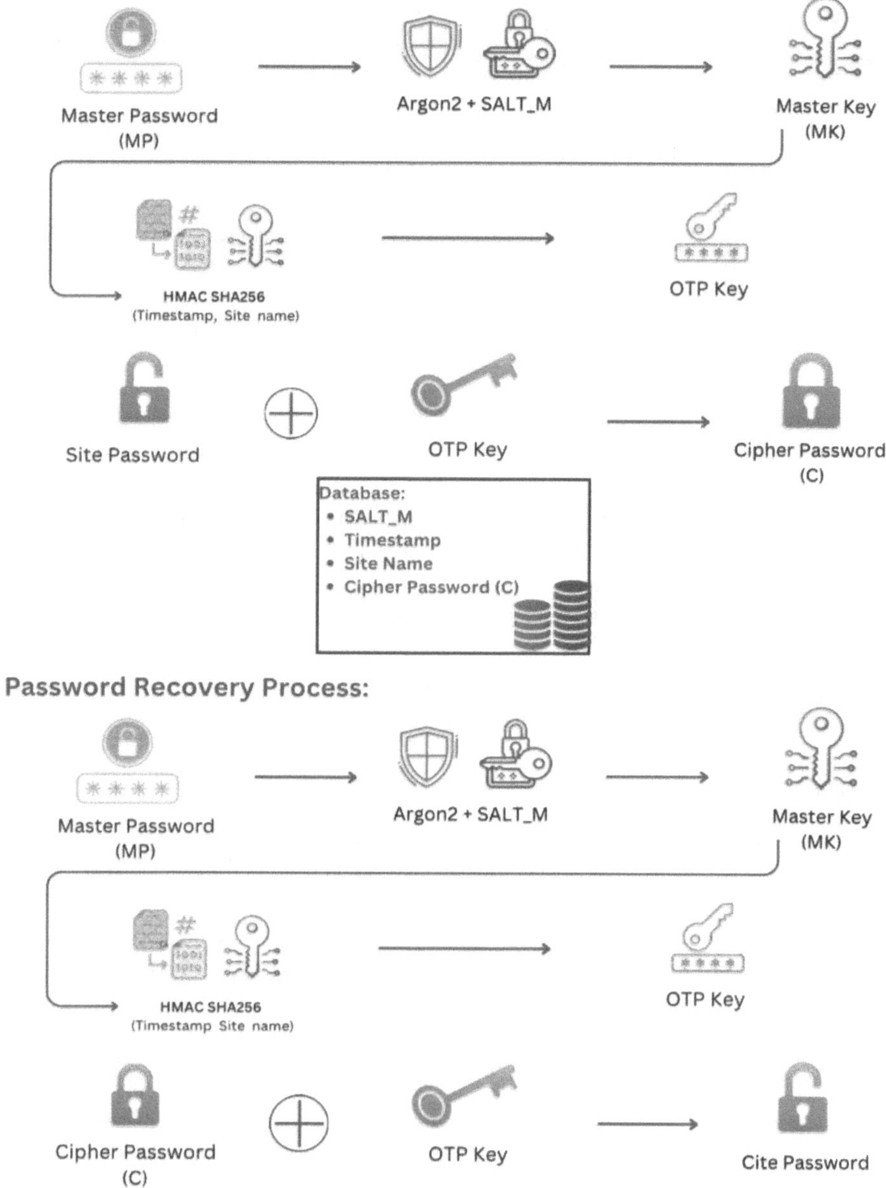


**Fig. 1.** Structure of the Proposed Secure Password Management System

can limit its practicality for larger datasets. This challenge can be addressed in the proposed password manager project by applying OTP exclusively to encrypt short and critical data (Table 1).

**Table 1.** SPMS Related Works

| Study | Author | Year | Study Focus | Key Findings | Challenges |
|---|---|---|---|---|---|
| [1] | Purnama et al. | 2022 | Encryption & decryption using OTP | Effectively secures data while maintaining file size integrity | Key length must match plaintext, limiting largescale use |
| [2] | Alamsyah et al. | 2021 | Combination of RSA with OTP for authentication | Enhanced security but with processing delays | Slow encryption/decryption due to RSA complexity |
| [3] | Al-Nemri et al. | 2020 | New OTP-based block cipher encryption | Secure encryption using SHA-512 and PRNG | High computational complexity and resource-intensive |
| [4] | Hamid et al. | 2019 | Physical authentication using OTP keypads | Reduces brute-force and social engineering risks | Requires specialized hardware, limiting scalability |
| [5] | Chen et al. | 2023 | Secure instant messaging using OTP | OTP improves message confidentiality | Complex session key management increases overhead |
| [6] | Manucom et al. | 2022 | Security analysis of OTP using TRNG | Improved randomness using Fisher-Yates shuffling | Increased computational complexity for largescale keys |
| [7] | Boateng et al. | 2021 | Securing GOOSE protocols with OTP | Enhances security in industrial automation | Real-time constraints limit large-scale implementation |
| [8] | Rekhate et al. | 2020 | OTP-based message encryption in distributed systems | Maintains data confidentiality | Managing large key databases increases computational overhead |
| [9] | Kumar et al. | 2019 | Secure authentication using enhanced OTP | Protects against replay attacks and file compromises | Maintaining OTP synchronization at scale is difficult |
| [10] | Xu et al. | 2023 | Protecting web usage of credit cards using OTP | Enhances privacy and security in e-commerce | Encryption/decryption adds latency to transactions |

(*continued*)

**Table 1.** *(continued)*

| Study | Author | Year | Study Focus | Key Findings | Challenges |
|---|---|---|---|---|---|
| [11] | Han et al. | 2022 | Efficient OTP key generation for medical data | Improves security for mobile healthcare devices | Chaotic attractor models require specialized implementation |
| [12] | Somu et al. | 2021 | Hadoop authentication using OTP | Enhances security of business data in distributed systems | Key generation overhead affects system efficiency |
| [13] | Boakye-Boateng et al. | 2020 | OTP-based encryption for wireless sensor networks | Energy-efficient encryption for IoT devices | Vulnerable to key reuse in resource-constrained environments |
| [14] | Lindquist et al. | 2019 | Java cryptography provider using OTP | Lightweight security for low-power devices | Manual key management increases human error risk |
| [15] | Manucom et al. | 2023 | Improving OTP randomness via FisherYates | Enhances randomness and encryption strength | Computational cost limits performance |
| [16] | Sim et al. | 2022 | OTP-based cloud authentication protocol | Eliminates credential transmission vulnerabilities | Complexity of zeroknowledge proof implementation |
| [17] | Avdonin et al. | 2021 | Secure UAV communication using OTP | Proven security advantages over block ciphers | High memory footprint for key storage |
| [18] | Zhang et al. | 2020 | OTP for secure network coding | Improves security and efficiency in data transmission | Increased computational requirements for encoding |
| [19] | Tang et al. | 2019 | OTP encryption based on hash and block cipher | Strengthens conventional encryption security | Increased key management complexity |
| [20] | Chen et al. | 2023 | OTP-based IoT security scheme | Enhances secure communication with secret key generation | High system overhead in large-scale IoT applications |

# 3 The Secure Password Management System (SPMS) Process

## 3.1 This Section the Password Management and Recovery Process Are Explained in Detail.

In this section, the detailed process of the SPMS Password Management and Password Recovery Processes is presented in detail as well as a comprehensive illustration of the cryptographic principles that accompany each step. Begin with the secure password management process, the process of deriving the master key (MK) is presented in (1).

$$MK = Argon2(MP,\ SALTM) \tag{1}$$

where Argon2 represents a memory-intensive password hashing function which is designed to be resilient to any type of password attack such as brute-force attacks and *MP* which represents the master password is that private key which is basically selected by the end-user and is used as the actual user secret key. $SALT_M$ is a randomly derived, inimitable code which is referred to as 'salt' and is added to the *MP* to resist any kind of precomputed attacks (such as, rainbow table attacks). Lastly, the *MK* (Master Key) is generated as the output of the combination of Argon2, a cryptographic key resulting from *MP* as well as the salt $SALT_M$. This generated *MP* is utilized in the process of creating the one-time passwords (OTP keys) for respective sites. Furthermore, the process of generating the OTP keys is presented in Eq. (2).

$$OTP\_{Key} = \text{HMAC\_SHA256}(MK,\ \text{Timestamp},\ \text{Site Name}) \tag{2}$$

where, HMAC-SHA-256 represents the Hash-based Message Authentication Code which is utilized in generating secure OTP keys per site, while the *MK* functions as the undisclosed key of the HMAC. The Timestamp parameter is used to provide distinctiveness which guarantees diverse OTP keys for diverse occurrences. The essence of this is to mitigate against any kind of replay attacks. Similarly, Site Name signifies the identifier or domain of the site which manages the password. The final output of these combinations will result in the $OTP\_{Key}$ which is a randomized secret key because of the HMAC and will be utilized for password encryption. The encryption process is presented in Eq. (3).

$$C = (\text{Site Password} \oplus OTP\_{Key}) \tag{3}$$

where *C* signifies the password of the Ciphertext is the stored encrypted form of the site password and $\oplus$ represents the exclusive OR (XOR) operation used in concatenating the Site Password and the OTP Key. In this case, XOR operation is used due to its lightweight features and considering that it supports revocable encryption. For example, assuming $Z = X \oplus Y$, then, *X* can be retrieved using $Z \oplus Y$. In this case, *X* will represent the Site Password, while *Y* will denote the $OTP\_{Key}$, and *Z* is used to illustrate the stored cipher password. After effecting all the above steps, the system is designed to store the following four parameters in its database:

1. $SALT_M$ (this is used later for deriving the *MK*)
2. Timestamp (which is the parameter that guarantees distinctiveness in the generation process of OTP)
3. Site Name (a unique identifier for recovering all site-specific records)
4. Cipher Password C (which represents the encrypted form of the site password)

### 3.2 Password Recovery Process

In this process, users are allowed to recover the unique site password with the help of the SPMS master password (*MP*). First, users attempt to recompute the *MK* using Eq. (1) established earlier. If the MP and $SALT_M$ then, the derived master key (*MK*) will remain unchanged. Once the master key is recomputed, then the user utilizes the master key in Eq. (2) to regenerate the required OTP key. If the inputs of this regeneration process match the original inputs of *MK*, Timestamp, and Site Name, then the output ($OTP\_{Key}$) will remain the same. The last phase is the decryption stage. This is the stage where the Site Password is recovered and decrypted and then the decryption equation is presented in Eq. (4).

$$\text{Site Password } = C \oplus OTP\_{Key} \tag{4}$$

Considering the reversibility feature of XOR operation:

1. Assuming $C =$ Site Password $\oplus$ $OTP\_{Key}$ then to retrieve Site Password:
2. Site Password $= C \oplus OTP\_{Key}$.

This recovers the initial site password that was encrypted during the process of password management.

## 4 Implementation Simulation

The implementation phase focused on the deployment and testing of the Secure Password Manager (SPM), validating its core functionalities before full-scale implementation. This phase aimed to ensure the effectiveness of the encryption mechanisms, data retrieval, and storage operations. The implementation was conducted in a Python-based environment, leveraging cryptographic libraries, a NoSQL Replit database, and a CLI-based user interface for secure password management.

### 4.1 Implementation Environment and Output:

The Secure Password Manager was developed using Python 3, chosen for its strong cryptographic support and ease of implementation. The system used the following key components:

1. Argon2 for secure password hashing and master key derivation.
2. HMAC-SHA256 to generate site-specific One-Time Pad (OTP) keys for encryption.
3. XOR encryption with Base64 encoding to ensure passwords remain both encrypted and storable.
4. Replit Database, a NoSQL key-value store, for securely storing usernames, encrypted passwords, and timestamps.

Figure 2 demonstrates a Python-based password manager system where user credentials are encrypted using the One-Time Pad (OTP) technique and stored securely, while providing functionalities for storing, retrieving, and displaying saved encrypted passwords.

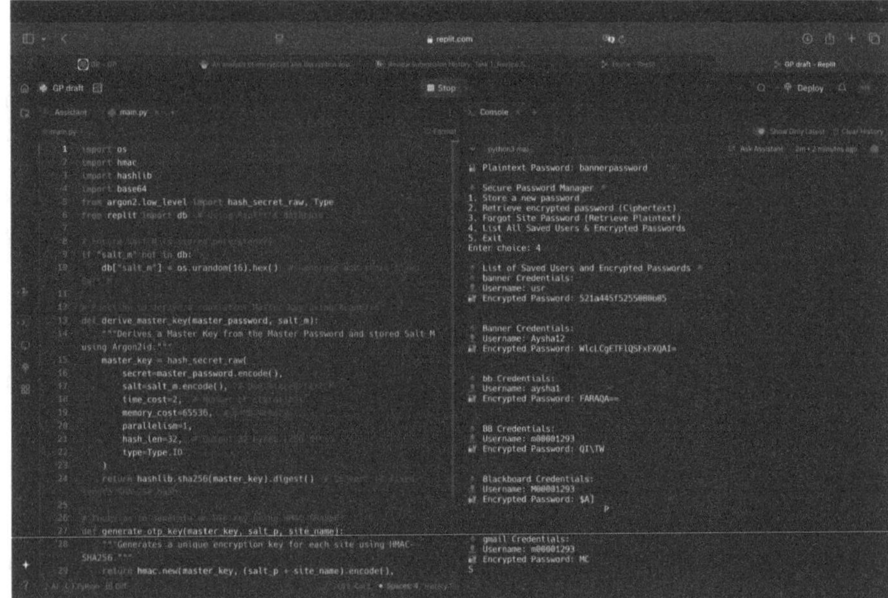


**Fig. 2.** Password manager - Encryption and Decryption Process in Action.

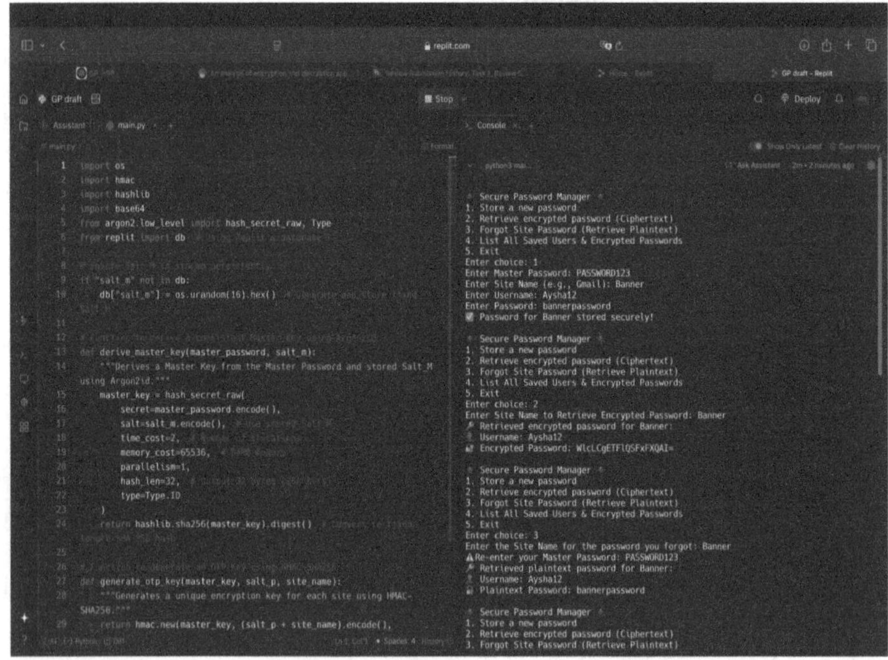


**Fig. 3.** Password Manager - Listing Stored Encrypted Passwords

Figure 3 shows the password manager system in action, where the user successfully stores, retrieves, and lists encrypted passwords associated with various usernames, demonstrating the secure password management process utilizing One- Time Pad (OTP) encryption.

The implementation successfully demonstrated the Secure Password Manager's ability to securely store, retrieve, and manage passwords using a combination of Argon2 hashing, HMAC-SHA256 OTP encryption, and XOR encoding. This phase confirmed that the encryption techniques were effective and that passwords remained protected. Future improvements will include a graphical user interface (GUI) to enhance user usability.

## 4.2 Performance Analysis

**Performance comparison of Encryption Strength vs Computational Overhead**

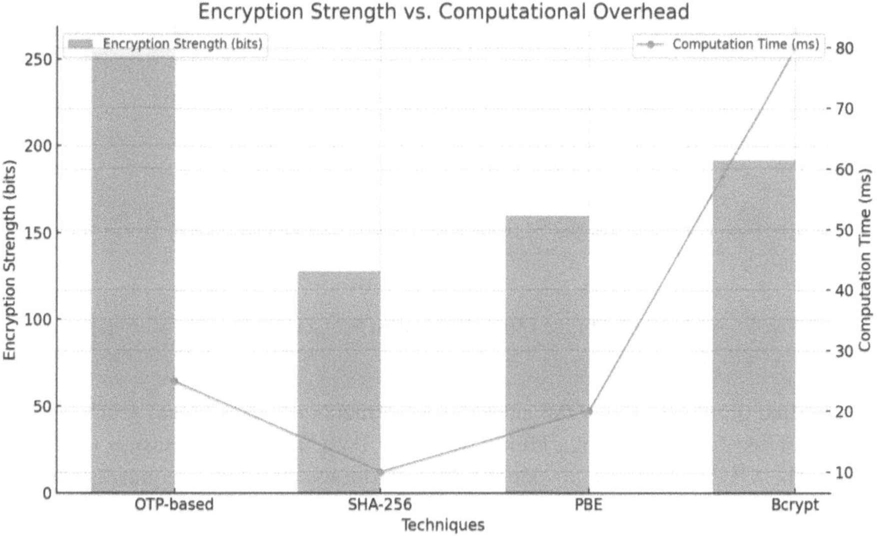


**Fig. 4.** Analysis of Encryption Strength against Computational Overhead for different techniques

This graph compares the encryption strength (in bits) against the computation time (in milliseconds) for four password protection techniques: the proposed OTP-based system, SHA-256 (traditional hashing), PBE (Password-Based Encryption), and Bcrypt (a key derivation function with salting). The OTP-based system demonstrates the highest encryption strength at 256 bits, leveraging truly random, one-time keys to achieve theoretical unbreakability. In contrast, SHA-256 and PBE provide lower entropy levels (128 bits and 160 bits, respectively), while Bcrypt offers moderate security at 192 bits due to its salting and work factors. In terms of computational performance, SHA-256 is the fastest but least secure, Bcrypt is intentionally slow to deter attacks, and the OTP system achieves a strong balance, maintaining high security with an efficient computation time (~25 ms). In summary, the OTP-based approach maximizes security without imposing prohibitive computational costs, making it highly suitable for practical, secure password management (Fig. 4).

**Performance comparison of Storage Efficiency vs. Scalability**

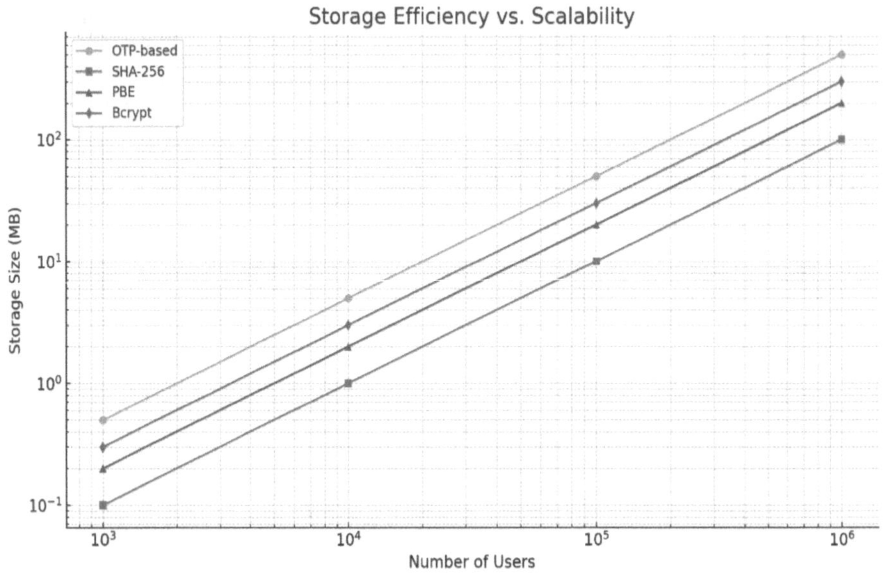


**Fig. 5.** Analysis of Storage Efficiency against Scalability (Number of users).

This line graph illustrates the storage requirements (in megabytes) relative to the number of users, using a logarithmic scale on both axes to emphasize scalability trends. The OTP-based system exhibits higher storage demands, requiring approximately 500 MB for one million users, compared to around 100 MB for SHA-256. While SHA-256 is the most storage-efficient, it offers comparatively weaker security. PBE and Bcrypt demonstrate moderate and predictable storage growth. Despite the OTP system's linear increase in storage, it remains manageable and can be further optimized through key compression or distributed storage architectures. Finally, Although the OTP-based method incurs higher storage overhead, this trade-off is justified by its superior security, making it highly suitable for environments where data protection is critical (Figs. 5 and 6).

The bar chart illustrates the estimated time required for a modern GPU-based attack to compromise various password protection techniques. A logarithmic scale is used for the Y-axis to accommodate the vast range of cracking times. For the OTP-Based System, when implemented correctly—using a truly random key, applied only once, and kept secret—the OTP approach is theoretically unbreakable. It is represented with an estimated cracking time of 1 trillion years (1e12), effectively infinite in practical terms.

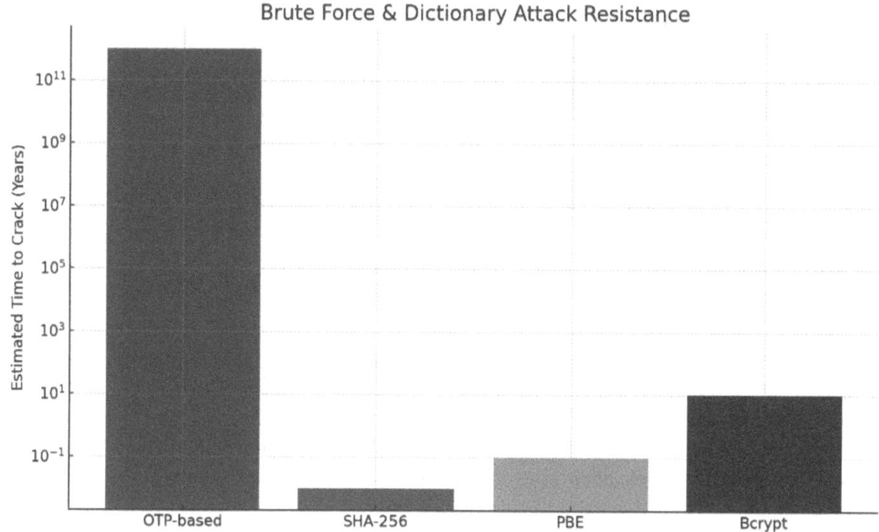


**Fig. 6.** Resistance against modern GPU-based attacks

Although the SHA-256-based system is computationally efficient, SHA-256 without additional safeguards (e.g., salting) remains highly susceptible to brute-force and dictionary attacks. On the other hand, the PBE system improves security via key stretching but does not offer sufficient resistance against persistent attackers. While, Bcrypt technique incorporates salting and adjustable cost factors, making it more resilient than SHA-256 and PBE, though still finite under sustained attack. In summary, the OTP-based system offers a distinct advantage by completely nullifying brute-force and dictionary attacks, whereas the alternative methods provide only limited and time-bound resistance.

## 5 Conclusion and Future Work

This study focused on developing a secure password manager that improves existing solutions by addressing key security vulnerabilities. Unlike traditional password managers that rely on static encryption keys, this system encrypts each password entry uniquely using site-specific OTP keys and timestamps, reducing the risk of large-scale breaches. The simulated implementation confirms that the system can securely store, encrypt, and retrieve passwords while maintaining usability. The use of Argon2 hashing ensures strong master password security, HMAC-SHA256 OTP keys provide unique encryption for each password, and XOR with Base64 encoding keeps ciphertext both secure and readable, and the Replit Database serves as a lightweight and persistent storage solution. The proposed technique was compared against other existing methods with the intention of measuring its encryption and computational overhead, storage efficiency and scalability as well as estimated time require to evade regular GPU-based attached. The performance analysis shows that the proposed system outperforms three other existing systems as compare in terms of encryption and computational overhead and estimated time require to evade regular GPU-based attached. However, it is realized that in terms of storage efficiency and scalability, the proposed system exhibits higher storage demands, requiring approximately 500 MB for one million users. This drawback will be addressed in the future work where optimization is expected to be achieved through key compression or distributed storage architectures in order to enhance encryption and retrieval speed for larger dataset. Finally, the research intends to explore Zero-Knowledge Proof (ZKP) in the future which is meant to explore ways of verifying credentials without revealing sensitive data.

## References

1. Bonneau, J., Herley, C., Van Oorschot, P.C., Stajano, F.: The quest to replace passwords: a framework for comparative evaluation of web authentication schemes. In: 2012 IEEE Symposium on Security and Privacy, pp. 553–567. IEEE, May 2012
2. Alamsyah, Z., Mantoro, T., Adityawarman, U., Ayu, M.A.: Combination RSA with one time pad for enhanced scheme of two-factor authentication. In: 2020 6th International Conference on Computing Engineering and Design (ICCED), pp. 1–5. IEEE, October 2020
3. Al-Nemri, J., Naser, M.: New block cipher encryption based on OTP algorithm. In: 2022 International Conference on Engineering & MIS (ICEMIS), pp. 1–6. IEEE, July 2022
4. Hamid, H.R.M.H., Abdullah, N.Y.: Physical authentication using random number generated (RNG) keypad based on one time pad (OTP) concept. In: 2015 Fourth International Conference on Cyber Security, Cyber Warfare, and Digital Forensic (CyberSec), pp. 135–139. IEEE, October 2015
5. Chen, H.C., Wijayanto, H., Chang, C.H., Leu, F.Y., Yim, K.: Secure mobile instant messaging key exchanging protocol with one-time-pad substitution transposition cryptosystem. In: 2016 IEEE Conference on Computer Communications Workshops (INFOCOM WKSHPS), pp. 980–984. IEEE, April 2016
6. Manucom, E.M.M., Gerardo, B.D., Medina, R.P.: Security analysis of improved one-time pad cryptography using TRNG key generator. In: 2019 IEEE 5th International Conference on Computer and Communications (ICCC), pp. 1515–1521. IEEE, December 2019
7. Boateng, K.B., Lashkari, A.H.: Securing GOOSE: the return of one-time pads. In: Dalam International Carnahan Conference on Security Technology (ICCST), Chennai, October 2019
8. Rekhate, V., Tale, A., Sambhus, N., Joshi, A.: Secure and efficient message passing in distributed systems using one-time pad. In: 2016 International Conference on Computing, Analytics and Security Trends (CAST), pp. 393–397. IEEE, December 2016
9. Kumar, R., Jindal, R., Gupta, A., Bhalla, S., Arora, H.: A secure authentication system-using enhanced one time pad technique. Int. J. Comput. Sci. Netw. Secur. IJCSNS **11**(2), 11–17 (2011)
10. Xu, D., Lu, C., Dos Santos, A.: Protecting web usage of credit cards using one-time pad cookie encryption. In: 2002 Proceedings of the18th Annual Computer Security Applications Conference, pp. 51–58. IEEE, December 2002
11. Han, F., Hu, J., Xi, K.: Highly efficient one-time pad key generation for large volume medical data protection. In: 2010 5th IEEE Conference on Industrial Electronics and Applications, p. 330335. IEEE, June 2010
12. Somu, N., Gangaa, A., Sriram, V.S.: Authentication service in hadoop using one time pad. Indian J. Sci. Technol. **7**(4), 56–62 (2014)
13. Boakye-Boateng, K., Kuada, E., Antwi-Boasiako, E.: Efficient encryption protocol for wireless sensor networks using one-time pads. In: 2016 18th Mediterranean Electrotechnical Conference (MELECON), pp. 1–6. IEEE, April 2016

14. Anajemba, J.H., Yue, T., Iwendi, C., Chatterjee, P., Ngabo, D., Alnumay, W.S.: A secure multiuser privacy technique for wireless IoT networks using stochastic privacy optimization. IEEE Internet Things J. **9**(4), 2566–2577 (2021)
15. Manucom, E.M.M., Gerardo, B.D., Medina, R.P.: Analysis of key randomness in improved one-time pad cryptography. In: 2019 IEEE 13th International Conference on Anti-counterfeiting, Security, and Identification (ASID), pp. 11–16. IEEE, October 2019
16. Sim, L.J.H., Ren, S.Q., Keoh, S.L., Aung, K.M.M.: A cloud authentication protocol using one-time pad. In: 2016 IEEE Region 10 Conference (TENCON), pp. 2513–2516. IEEE, November 2016
17. Avdonin, I., Budko, M., Budko, M., Grozov, V., Guirik, A.:. A method of creating perfectly secure data transmission channel between unmanned aerial vehicles and ground control station based on one-time pads. In: 2017 9th International Congress on Ultra-Modern Telecommunications and Control Systems and Workshops (ICUMT), pp. 410–413. IEEE, November 2017
18. Zhang, Y., Xu, C., Wang, F.: A novel scheme for secure network coding using one-time pad. In: 2009, The International Conference on Networks Security, Wireless Communications and Trusted Computing, vol. 1, pp. 92–98. IEEE, April 2009
19. Tang, S., Liu, F.: A one-time pad encryption algorithm based on one-way hash and conventional block cipher. In: 2012 2nd International Conference on Consumer Electronics, Communications and Networks (CECNet), pp. 72–74. IEEE, April 2012
20. Chen, L., Cao, K., Lu, T., Lu, Y., Hu, A.: A one-time pad encryption scheme based on efficient physical-layer secret key generation for intelligent IoT system. China Commun. **19**(7), 185–196 (2022)

# A Quality-Focused Performance Evaluation of SQL over Large Language Models

Marlene Goncalves[1,2](✉), Daniel Robayo[2], and Graciela Perera[3]

[1] Valencian International University, 46002 Valencia, Spain
marlene.goncalves@universidadviu.com

[2] Universidad Simón Bolívar, Caracas 89000, Venezuela
{mgoncalves,18-11086}@usb.ve

[3] Roosevelt University, Chicago, IL 60605, USA
gperera@roosevelt.edu

**Abstract.** Large Language Models (LLMs) have revolutionized how we explore large unstructured data using Natural Language prompts. They have been shown to be capable of supporting a variety of tasks in the database domain. However, LLMs are not designed to process data directly from the database. In this paper, we address the problem of evaluating SQL queries using a DB-first approach that provides seamless access between SQL and LLMs data sources. Our main contribution, called Galileo, combines Retrieval-Augmented Generation, a divide-and-conquer planning strategy, heuristic optimizations, and operator-cost estimation to generate and execute optimized SQL query plans across LLMs and traditional relational databases. We performed an experimental study on the ATIS (Airline Travel Information System) benchmark, considering different query complexities. The results show that Galileo achieves higher precision and recall than a state-of-the-art solution when evaluating SQL queries over LLMs. Galileo improves the overall quality of the results by providing more relevant contextual information and the query plan.

**Keywords:** Databases · Heuristics · Large Language Models · Natural Language · Retrieval Augmented Generation · SQL

## 1 Introduction

Large Language Models (LLMs) have revolutionized how we can search and view massive amounts of unstructured data on the Internet using Natural Language (NL) prompts [1,2]. LLM prompts do not require users to have technical knowledge when it comes to code generation. For instance, LLMs can generate SQL query code to be executed over data outside the LLMs' realm [3–5]. This generated SQL code may be incorrect for a complex query or produce inaccurate results [3,4]. Executing an SQL query over a database (which is deterministic) will provide accurate and precise results, while the results of LLMs (which


R. Stahlbock et al. (Eds.): CSCE 2025, CCIS 2938, pp. 420–435, 2027.
https://doi.org/10.1007/978-3-032-22196-4_31

are stochastic) require validation. Thus, combining structured data SQL queries and LLM results can offer better accuracy and precision than only NL prompts. Furthermore, the recent emergence, popularity, and easy access to LLMs, make creating more precise results possible by combining SQL queries with LLM models that contain pertinent data not found in the SQL database. This approach towards integrating results between SQL databases and LLMs is called DB-first [6]. That is, having a traditional SQL query that will ask both the DataBase Management System (DBMS) and the LLM model (i.e., creating the necessary NL prompts for data not found in the DBMS). Also, if data security and privacy are not required, DBMS and LLMs can access data sources without any issues. However, when privacy and data security are necessary, accessing these data sources can present challenges because the data stored or used as input in the model can be absorbed by it, thereby becoming available to others or being used to train future LLMs [5]. For example, suppose that an internal DBMS, kept by a Human Resources (HR) manager, requires privacy protection. The DBMS stores employees' performance review data, personal information, and a list called LE, which contains events or conferences to improve their performance reviews according to their expertise. Furthermore, employees must attend two LE-listed items to improve next year's performance reviews. The HR manager then needs to compile a detailed report matching each employee to their chosen LE events. The problem is protecting employee privacy while accessing relevant public event details from the Internet that are not stored in the internal DBMS. A DB-first approach is a solution to this problem, as it can use the SQL query formulated by the manager to create LLM prompts with the public events or conference details required for the HR manager's report without sharing employees' private data. Additionally, the DB-first approach provides compliance with the USA Privacy Act as it does not disclose the personal data stored in the internal DBMS while taking advantage of searching public unstructured data using LLMs.

Using the DB-first approach requires the SQL query to generate an execution plan for our solution because SQL is a declarative language. The plan includes the details of the physical operators and the order in which they should be executed. Among the many possible execution plans, our solution aims to increase execution plan performance by applying heuristics and estimating each operator's cost, reducing the number of output results for certain operators as well as execution time [7]. One possible heuristic consists of reducing output results by applying certain operators in a particular order. For example, an execution plan made up of a selection operator before a join operator can be better than a plan with the selection operator afterward. This occurs because the selection operator filters the results that are input for the join operator. A common heuristic is to prioritize pushing selection and projection operators ahead of the join operators [7]. Furthermore, estimating operator costs enables the application of lower-cost operators before higher-cost ones. By establishing an execution order based on these estimates, we can select the plan with the minimum overall cost. Also, these heuristics and operator cost estimations have been widely studied in databases

[7], but the literature on them in the context of DB-first solutions that integrate SQL with LLM is, to the best of our knowledge, scarce. Galois [6] is the first work that focuses on directly executing SQL queries over LLMs and although the heuristic of pushing down the less costly operators in an execution plan, it does not avoid scanning all the data before applying a less costly operator. Considering the context of the database and LLMs, a scan operator is expensive due to the consumption of computational resources required to process inputs and generate outputs [7,8].

**Problem Statement and Research Objective:** In this paper, we focus on the problem of evaluating SQL queries on LLMs and relational databases. Our solution, similar to Galois, directly executes SQL queries over LLMs but with the difference of avoiding data scanning, providing the LLM with context through Retrieval Augmented Generation (RAG) [9], and determining an execution order of query operations to enhance overall performance.

**Approach:** We describe Galileo, a SQL query evaluator on LLMs based on the principle of Divide and Conquer (D&C), heuristic optimization, operator cost reduction, and RAG. Using the D&C principle, it divides a SQL query into subqueries. These subqueries are not executed arbitrarily; instead, their execution order is determined based on heuristics and operator costs that aim to minimize intermediate results and reduce the number of requests to the LLM. For each of these subqueries, it first generates prompts for the LLM, supplying relevant context through RAG; then, it integrates all the results to produce the final answer.

**Evaluation:** We use and adapt 11 SQL queries from the Airline Travel Information Systems (ATIS) dataset [10]. ATIS contains data on flights and related services in the United States. We compare our work with Galois. This evaluation allows us to understand the impact of query complexity on query evaluation. The results of the experiments suggest that this factor affects both query performance and answer quality.

**Contributions:** Our contributions can be summarized as follows: *i*) a formal definition of the problem of evaluating SQL on LLMs and relational databases; *ii*) Galileo, a solution based on RAG, D&C approach, heuristics, and operator cost reduction that is able to evaluate SQL queries on LLMs and relational databases; *iii*) the definition and implementation of CQP (Contextual Query Planner), a technique to generate and select plans based on heuristics which take advantage of specific physical operators for SQL queries on LLMs and relational databases; *iv*) an empirical evaluation of the behavior of Galileo over the ATIS benchmark with queries of different complexities.

**Outline:** In the following, we first provide a motivating example using SQL and LLMs in Sect. 2; then, we present the related work in Sect. 3, describe our solution called Galileo in Sect. 4, explain the experimental study in Sect. 5, and give a conclusion and future work in the final section.

## 2 Motivating Example

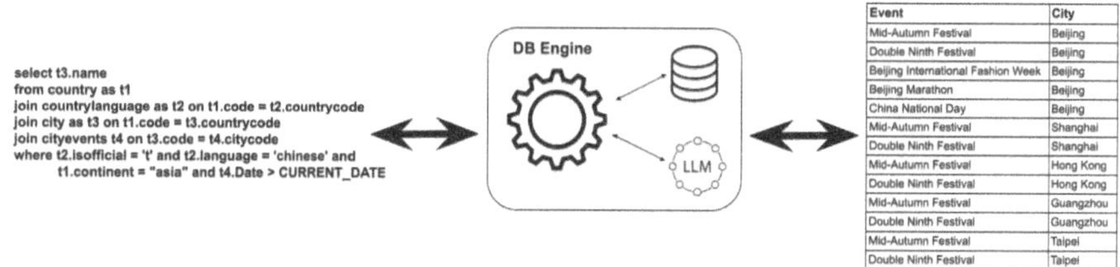


| Event | City |
|---|---|
| Mid-Autumn Festival | Beijing |
| Double Ninth Festival | Beijing |
| Beijing International Fashion Week | Beijing |
| Beijing Marathon | Beijing |
| China National Day | Beijing |
| Mid-Autumn Festival | Shanghai |
| Double Ninth Festival | Shanghai |
| Mid-Autumn Festival | Hong Kong |
| Double Ninth Festival | Hong Kong |
| Mid-Autumn Festival | Guangzhou |
| Double Ninth Festival | Guangzhou |
| Mid-Autumn Festival | Taipei |
| Double Ninth Festival | Taipei |

(a) The LLM-powered database engine processes the input query, resulting in relational output

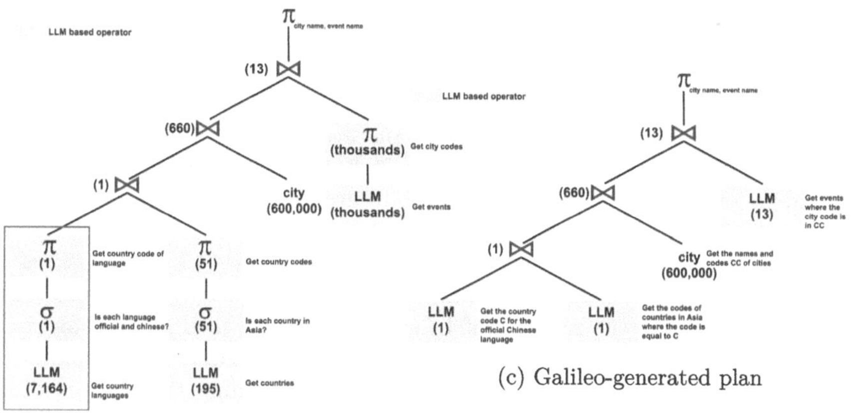


(c) Galileo-generated plan

(b) Galois-generated plan

**Fig. 1. Sample SQL query on an LLM.** The SQL query $Q_1$ identifies Asian cities with Chinese as the official language and their upcoming events. The number of instances shown in this figure may not be exact and serves only as an illustrative example.

To understand the problem of evaluating SQL on LLMs and relational databases, we suppose that an expert SQL user is interested in a query $Q_1$ that identifies cities in Asian countries where Chinese is the official language and events are taking place in those cities. Unfortunately, the SQL database contains data only for cities, but not for events, countries, or languages. A naive way to answer question $Q_1$, is to add data from events, countries, and languages to the database, which must be constantly updated, as event data tend to be dynamic and can change from month to month. A more automated approach is to query external data via Web services or APIs; so that event data can be extracted from a website such as Eventbrite[1]. However, some data may be unstructured and could require an Extract, Transform, and Load (ETL) process for proper integration.

An alternative approach, shown in Fig. 1aTo address this, Galois [6] proposes dividing the question $Q_1$ into simpler ones or operators. The plan generated by Galois answering $Q_1$ is shown as a tree in Fig. 1b, where each node corresponds to a relational algebra operator or a scan over the data using an LLM. Also, we include the simpler NL question on the right-hand side of the operators, and the number of instances is placed below the node or to the left of the operator. Lastly, the shaded operators in light gray correspond to LLM-based operators; that is, they obtain data from the LLM prompts. Moreover, Galois [6] uses common heuristics such as pushing selections($\sigma$) and projections($\pi$) down the tree to generate a more efficient equivalent question. In the red box of Fig. 1b, Galois applies the heuristic by pushing down the selection and projection operators. We can observe in our example that Galois uses unnecessary calls to the LLM, which can be optimized as an operator that makes one request to the LLM illustrated in Fig. 1c. For example, the three operators inside the red box in Fig. 1bcan be integrated into one operator, as shown in Fig. 1c. In the red box, Galois performs a scan requesting all languages per country (7,164 instances) to filter later the countries whose official language is Chinese (1 instance) and finally projecting each country code (1 instance). Therefore, a disadvantage of Galois [6] is the large amount of data generated by leaf nodes that scan the LLMs as it iterates through its responses in batches until the model no longer responds. Consequently, unnecessary results are generated since a set of them will then be filtered by the selection.

In comparison, the approach shown in Fig. 1c improves Galois by asking the LLM for the country code of the official Chinese language (1 instance). This considerably reduces the number of LLM requests and their processing times. Additionally, the plans in Figs. 1b and 1c illustrate how different combinations of operators can form distinct execution plans. Regarding the computational cost, these plans vary according to the order in which operators are evaluated because the overall plan cost constitutes the sum of the costs of evaluating the operators in the plan. In general, it is assumed that selecting the operators cost efficiently will generate an execution plan with less time; however, the quality of the query results must also be considered. Galileo combines heuristics and statistics to select the execution plan that will hopefully reduce query execution time while preserving high query-result quality.

Furthermore, to illustrate query-result quality, we show the number of questions with incorrect answers, some correct answers, and one empty answer in Table 1. This data is derived from the Galois results available on GitLab[2], which is based on three LLMs and 46 queries. In most of the queries (at least 65%),

[1] https://www.eventbrite.com.

[2] https://gitlab.eurecom.fr/saeedm1/galois/-/tree/main/data/results.

**Table 1.** Quality of Galois's Responses

| Model | Incorrect Answers (IA) | No Answers (NA) | IA+NO | Partially Correct Answers |
|---|---|---|---|---|
| Flan-ul2 | 12 | 27 | 39 | 7 |
| Tk-instruct-large | 43 | 3 | 46 | 0 |
| ChatGPT | 10 | 20 | 30 | 16* |

Galois could not answer correctly or produced empty answers. Consequently, the results from Galois exhibit poor query quality, as it is a vision paper.

In the cases where it was able to respond with at least one correct answer, it also included fictitious answers. Furthermore, the output format was not tabular but in a textual mode, except for one question with the ChatGPT model. One limitation of Galois is its reliance on LLMs, which can have hallucinations and may produce fictitious or inaccurate responses. LLMs often miss recent or specialized knowledge, so they default to their most statistically likely (but potentially incorrect) answers. Although you can update them by retraining, doing so is costly and time-consuming. An alternative is to use techniques that provide contextual data to help the LLM improve its accuracy. In the case of Galileo, it uses RAG that incorporates updated external data retrieval mechanisms during the LLMs' response generation process [9]. Figure 1c shows the execution tree generated by Galileo. It integrates selection and projection into a single physical operator, producing the necessary data, and uses RAG for better accuracy.

## 3 Related Work

LLMs have been designed to process, understand, and generate human-like text [1,2]. Also, LLMs capabilities make them a promising tool for handling database tasks [5]. Recently, there have been several studies to integrate LLMs with SQL databases. Some of these studies focus on translating SQL queries into natural language (NL), with the aim of converting these queries into understandable NL expressions. Furthermore, a prominent example is the Spider project [11]. Spider built a large database containing the translations of SQL queries from different domains into NL requests. On the other hand, other investigations translate NL queries into SQL queries using LLMs, and their solutions differ in the mechanisms they use to improve query accuracy: external knowledge, query engineering techniques, etc. [4,12]. Lastly, some researchers propose directly executing SQL queries using LLMs. For example, Galois [6] is a system capable of processing SQL queries using not only its data but also data provided by LLMs. Galois decomposes an SQL query into subqueries, translates them into natural language, executes them using a large language model, and finally combines the answers for a complete result. In addition, Galois employs an external database engine to generate execution plans for its SQL queries, and the prompts sent to the large language model (LLM) must be manually crafted. Consequently, plan generation depends on the external engine, and manual effort is required to formulate the LLM prompts.

Another approach is described by the authors in [13], who define a system that allows semantic searches on videos using NL queries, and a strategy similar to Galois. The authors found that, for LLMs, there is no significant difference between splitting a complex query into several simpler queries versus performing the original query without modifying it. Also, an application presented in [14] shows how BERT can be used to read user manuals, enabling a database engine to self-optimize for efficient performance. Moreover, they explore various use cases, such as data preparation, discovery, and the design of database engines like Galois, which utilize LLMs to process data directly. In a different domain, the authors in [15] describe how artificial intelligence utilizes NL to request structured and unstructured data from spatial databases. Although this work does not use an LLM, it follows a similar approach to Galois to decompose queries. More recently, HQDL [16] has become a preliminary solution for hybrid queries between the LLM and SQL databases. However, HQDL has two important limitations: its prompts are manually created, and the data generated by LLMs are materialized in tables that must then be dropped.

## 4 Galileo

Given a SQL query $Q$ over a relational schema $S = \{T_1, T_2, \ldots, T_n\}$ and a large language model $L$, the SQL query evaluation problem is defined as the decomposition of the query $Q$ into SQL subqueries corresponding to each involved table of $S$ or each prompt for the large language model $L$; each subquery can be expressed by relational algebra expressions $RA_i$. The execution of each subquery can be combined by join operations, resulting in an expression that is equivalent to the original query $Q$ as follows: $Q = S_1 \bowtie_{\theta_1} S_2 \bowtie_{\theta_2} \ldots \bowtie_{\theta_{n-1}} S_n$ where each $S_i$ is a subquery over the table $T_i$ or is a prompt over the model $L$, and each $\theta_i$ represents the join condition associated with the $i$-th join operation. Formally, the SQL query decomposition problem is expressed as: $RA(Q) = RA(S_1) \bowtie_{\theta_1} RA(S_2) \bowtie_{\theta_2} \ldots \bowtie_{\theta_{n-1}} RA(S_n)$ where $RA(X)$ is the relational algebra expression equivalent to $X$, which can be either the original query $Q$ or any subquery $S_i$. Each possible decomposition $\mathcal{D}_k$ of the query $Q$ is associated with a cost $C(\mathcal{D}_k)$ that depends on: *i*) the individual costs of the relational algebra operations $RA_i$ (such as selections and projections); *ii*) the cost of combining these operations through join operations $\left(\sum_{i=1}^{n-1} C(\bowtie_{\theta_i})\right)$. Thus, the goal is to find the decomposition $\mathcal{D}^*$ that minimizes the total cost, where $\mathcal{D}$ represents the set of all possible decompositions of the query $Q$:

$$\mathcal{D}^* = \arg\min_{\mathcal{D}} \left( \sum_{i=1}^{n} C(RA(S_i)) + \sum_{j=1}^{n-1} C(\bowtie_{\theta_j}) \right)$$

In Algorithm 1, we propose CQP (Contextual Query Planner) as a technique based on the D&C approach and RAG to generate a plan for evaluating Select-Project-Join (SPJ) queries. If there are set operators or nested queries, CQP will be applied for each subquery and then the intermediate results of each subquery will be integrated according to the set operator or nested query. The first step of CQP is to decompose the query $Q$ into a set of subqueries $\{S_1, S_2, \ldots, S_n\}$ corresponding to each table $T_i$ or each prompt on $L$ in the FROM clause of query $Q$. Initially, subqueries containing any selection condition are considered; if no subquery contains any selection condition, all subqueries are included. Each subquery is added as a candidate to the execution plan and translated into NL using the appropriate template. Iteratively, the algorithm selects unchosen subqueries that can be combined by means of a join with the sub-queries already included in each plan within the set of plans (*plan*). As a subquery is selected, it is added to the *plan*, and it is translated into NL according to the join template. Through this process, multiple plans of size $n-1$ are generated, for which the cost is estimated, and the lowest-cost plan is finally selected. The templates involved in the translation process are available on Github[3].

In Galileo, two methods can be applied to estimate the cost of query execution plans. The static one consists of maintaining a data catalog in a `JSON` file containing relevant metadata statistics for tables and LLM prompts. The available statistics are: *i*) cardinality; *ii*) number of distinct values for each property; *iii*) data size in bytes. Using these statistics, reduction factors are calculated to estimate the amount of data in bytes that the query processes. The sampling estimation method obtains simple samples through LLM queries and stores this information to be later used to optimize the query. If no information is found by the LLM, a new sample is requested from the LLM. To limit the number of samples requested from the LLM, a maximum of three samples per subquery was set. If such statistics are unavailable, a reduction factor of 1/10 is assumed, as done by the DBMS [7]. The *prompt* used in this method does not include the `WHERE` condition. Since the responses of an LLM are based on probabilistic principles [17], the sample is considered to be random, enabling the use of simple sampling techniques. For example, let $P = [P_1, P_2, ..., Pn]$ be a set of execution plans of a query $Q$ to be optimized using sampling estimation. Without loss of generality, let $P_1$ be the first plan to estimate. While estimating it, LLM queries are made on each subquery, and the results are saved. For later plans, these saved results are used, and the LLM is only asked again if needed. This repeats for all plans, and the one that processes the least data in bytes is chosen.

Finally, the Galileo sends requests to the LLM according to the Planner's instructions, collecting and integrating the subquery results into the final answer.

## 5 Experimental Study

In this section, we describe the datasets, queries, metrics, LLM models, and implementation details for our experimental study.

[3] https://github.com/danielrobapaz/galileo/blob/main/sql/executor.py#L126.

**Algorithm 1.** Contextual Query Planner, CQP

**Input:** $Q$ - SPJ Query
**Output:** SPJ Query Plan
Decompose $Q$ into subqueries $S = \{S_1, S_2, \ldots, S_n\}$
$SF_1$ = Subqueries of $\{S_1, S_2, \ldots, S_n\}$ that have selection conditions
$SF_2 = SF \setminus SF_1$
**if** $SF_1 = \emptyset$ **then** $SF_1 = SF_2$;
**for** $s \in SF_1$ **do**
    Add $S_i$ to *plan* and translate $S_i$ into NL according to the template
    **for** $k = 2$ *to* $n$ **do**
        **for** *each plan* $p \in$ *plan with size* $k - 1$ **do**
            **for** *each* $t \in S$ *such that* $t$ *can be joined with* $s$ **do**
                Create a new plan $s' = s \cup \{t\}$ by joining $s$ and $t$
                Add $s'$ to *plan*
                Translate the join $s'$ into NL according to the template
cost of current best plan $\leftarrow \infty$
**for** *each plan* $p \in$ *plan with size* $n - 1$ **do**
    Estimate cost of $p$
    **if** *cost(p)* < *cost of current best plan* **then** update current best plan with $p$ ;

**Table 2.** Query Features

| Operators | Query | | | | | | | | | | |
|---|---|---|---|---|---|---|---|---|---|---|---|
| | **1** | **2** | **3** | **4** | **5** | **6** | **7** | **8** | **9** | **10** | **11** |
| **Selection** | 1 | 6 | 1 | 2 | 1 | 4 | 1 | 2 | 3 | 1 | 1 |
| **Join** | 4 | 6 | 2 | 5 | 2 | 7 | 3 | 4 | 4 | 2 | 1 |

**Benchmarks:** The Airline Travel Information Systems (ATIS) is a dataset from the United States that contains information on cities, airports, flights, fares, transportation services, and in-flight meals [10]. This dataset includes approximately 4,836 annotated queries, many of which involve multiple join operations. We have carefully curated a set of 11 SQL queries, each of which has varying characteristics. Table 2 provides a concise summary of the selected queries.

**Techniques:** We evaluated the two techniques, called Galileo and Galois. We implemented Galois from scratch because it was not fully developed. If we were to use Galois, it would require extensive manual work, as we would need to generate the execution plan with an external database engine and manually write each LLM prompt per operator. Furthermore, the quality of the results presented by the authors of Galois is poor (see Table 1). Thus, for a fair performance comparison between Galileo and Galois, we implemented both techniques using the same software architecture. Additionally, our implementation is an improved Galois that integrates the operators scan, selection, and projection, as described in the motivating example in Sect. 2. This approach avoids,whenever possible, the high cost of the scan operator on LLMs. However, Galileo used the static and sampling methods, while Galois uses a simple heuristic that does not consider the execution plan cost. This heuristic begins by adding to the execution plan those operators with the greatest number of conditions, on the premise that they will produce the most highly filtered results. It then combines the remaining operators and incorporates each one into the plan as soon as it finds a compatible join. Both techniques are implemented using Python 3.12.3. Both the code and the resources can be requested from the authors and are in the GitHub repository[4].

**Metrics:** Performance evaluation is based on the measured query execution time. It is computed as the elapsed time in seconds between the submission of a query and its response. Each query was executed 10 times. The quality of the two techniques is also measured in terms of precision, recall, and F1-score. Precision measures the percentage of instances in the solution set that are also in the ground truth; recall measures the percentage of instances from the ground truth that are also in the solution set. The F1 score is a measure that combines precision and recall into a single value. It indicates how well the system finds all correct answers (recall) and how well it avoids finding incorrect instances (precision). The ground truth was established directly from the ATIS database.

**Models:** We test the following models: *i*) Chat GPT-4o, OpenAI's 200-billion-parameter conversational model. This model was accessed via the Langchain framework[5], allowing up to 9,216 KB of context per prompt. The context was divided into blocks of 512 KB to feed the RAG system, enabling up to 18 blocks per API call. *ii*) The thenlper large model[6] was used to generate embeddings for each context block. These embeddings were indexed with FAISS[7] to allow efficient retrieval of relevant information. Also, we constructed prompts appropriately for each model according to the following template: "You are a highly intelligent question answering bot. You will answer concisely. Use only the given context to answer the question. Context: {context}. Answer the query. {question} {examples} {format_instructions}". For the context, we used the RAG technique [9], which combines contextual information from external sources with user queries. Furthermore, the context consisted of plain text lines extracted from the ATIS database. Each line corresponds to a row that belongs to a table in the database and is written as a short narrative that includes the attributes. Given that the queries chosen do not use all the attributes of some tables, these were omitted from the context to reduce its size and keep read times low.

**Infrastructure:** The experiments are executed on a machine with the following characteristics: an Intel(R) Core(TM) i7-3687U processor with 2 cores and

[4] https://github.com/danielrobapaz/galileo/.
[5] https://github.com/langchain-ai/langchain.
[6] https://huggingface.co/thenlper/gte-large.
[7] https://github.com/facebookresearch/faiss.

a base frequency of 2.10 GHz (up to 3.3 GHz with Turbo Boost), 16 GB of available RAM, and no dedicated graphics card, running on Linux Mint 22.1 as its operating system.

### 5.1 Impact on Response Quality

In this section, we compare Galileo and Galois to evaluate their quality using the Chat GPT-4o model. Table 3 shows the averages of the precision, recall, and F1-score metrics for 10 runs using 11 ATIS queries with Galois and Galileo employing static estimation and sampling. In particular, the cells in Table 3 with "-" indicate that the technique was unable to construct the final result of the query, while a value of 0.00 indicates that incorrect answers were obtained. Furthermore, it should be noted that the average shown in Table 3 considers only the runs in which the techniques returned a final result.

**Precision:** Considering the queries that returned the correct answers (precision greater than 0), both Galileo and Galois show high accuracy, ranging from 0.80 to 1.00. In particular, Galileo using sampling, achieves even higher precision, ranging between 0.97 and 1.00. This high accuracy indicates that both techniques are capable of recovering a significant proportion of relevant instances, that is, at least 80% of the responses produced are the expected results for each query. We also observed that, with respect to the number of queries, the correct answers from Galois achieved a precision greater than or equal to 0.80 in 6 queries. On the other hand, Galileo obtained accurate results in 11 queries when using static estimation and in 8 queries when using sampling. Consequently, considering

**Table 3.** Average precision, recall, and F1 score achieved by Galois and Galileo

| Query | Precision | | | Recall | | | F1 Score | | |
|---|---|---|---|---|---|---|---|---|---|
| | Galois | Galileo | | Galois | Galileo | | Galois | Galileo | |
| | | Static | Sampling | | Static | Sampling | | Static | Sampling |
| 1 | - | 1.00 | 0.97 | - | 0.88 | 0.85 | - | 0.93 | 0.90 |
| 2 | - | 1.00 | 0.97 | - | 0.39 | 0.45 | - | 0.56 | 0.61 |
| 3 | - | 1.00 | 1.00 | - | 0.29 | 0.30 | - | 0.45 | 0.47 |
| 4 | 0.80 | 1.00 | - | 0.94 | 0.17 | - | 0.86 | 0.29 | - |
| 5 | 1.00 | 1.00 | 1.00 | 0.61 | 0.61 | 0.62 | 0.75 | 0.76 | 0.76 |
| 6 | - | 0.80 | 0.00 | - | 0.40 | 0.00 | - | 0.67 | - |
| 7 | 0.90 | 1.00 | 1.00 | 0.11 | 0.91 | 0.94 | 0.20 | 0.95 | 0.97 |
| 8 | 1.00 | 1.00 | 1.00 | 1.00 | 1.00 | 1.00 | 1.00 | 1.00 | 1.00 |
| 9 | 0.00 | 1.00 | - | 0.00 | 1.00 | - | - | 1.00 | - |
| 10 | 1.00 | 1.00 | 1.00 | 1.00 | 1.00 | 1.00 | 1.00 | 1.00 | 1.00 |
| 11 | 1.00 | 1.00 | 1.00 | 1.00 | 1.00 | 1.00 | 1.00 | 1.00 | 1.00 |

both the precision and the number of queries answered, Galileo is the more effective technique when using static estimation. In contrast, the queries that produced incorrect answers (precision equal to 0.00) were queries 6 and 9 with Galileo with sampling and Galois, respectively. Meanwhile, Galileo, using the static estimation, was able to obtain correct answers to these queries. In these queries, Galileo, using static estimation, did not follow the same execution plan as the others. This discrepancy in precision is likely attributable to the difference in execution plans. In the case of queries 6 and 9, both Galois and Galileo using sampling, produced intermediate results from the join operators that were either empty or incorrect. The results impacted subsequent query execution, causing join outputs to be incorrect or empty. Join conditions in prompts vary based on preceding joins, altering context and LLM responses. The primary cause of empty or incorrect LLM answers can be the documents retrieved by the RAG system, likely due to limitations in the embeddings model or the FAISS vector index. Variations in text representation by the embeddings model or the similarity algorithm and retrieval size in FAISS may have affected document retrieval accuracy.

**Recall:** Although both solutions achieved high precision for some queries, the recall for queries with non-zero results (recall greater than 0) showed a wide variation, ranging from 0.11 to 1.00. This suggests that despite high precision, the systems failed to retrieve all relevant results for some queries. However, the recall improves slightly for Galileo. The recall ranges from 0.17 to 1.00 for Galileo with static estimation, while the minimum recall value increases to 0.30 for Galileo using sampling. In contrast, the lowest recall value (0.11) for queries that returned any correct answers indicates that some queries retrieved as little as 11% of the expected instances. Although recall was low for some queries (e.g., 2, 3, and 6), Galileo still obtained some correct answers, whereas Galois returned an empty result. Furthermore, in queries $1-3$, the recall values obtained by Galileo were similar when using both static estimation and sampling. Moreover, sampling yielded slightly higher results for queries 2 and 3, while static estimation did so for query 1. The execution plans performed in these 3 queries with Galileo are the same regardless of the estimation method. As a consequence, the slight difference between recalls is presumed to be due to the non-deterministic factors of the LLMs. For these three queries, Galois has a different execution plan; thus, the order of execution can be considered to influence the final results. For high recall cases, defined as a recall value greater than or equal to 0.80, Galois met this threshold in 4 queries. On the other hand, Galileo achieved a high recall in 6 queries with static estimation and in 5 queries with sampling. Consequently, when considering precision, recall, and the number of queries answered, Galileo proves to be the best option when using the static estimation. It is worth noting, however, that Galois has a higher recall in query 4 than Galileo. This difference in recall is likely due to the composition of the intermediate results. For Galois, the intermediate results already contained most of the expected instances, so

**Table 4.** Execution, estimation, and total times of Galois and Galileo in seconds

| | Galois | Static Galileo | | | Sampling Galileo | | |
|---|---|---|---|---|---|---|---|
| Query | Total | Estimation | Execution | Total | Estimation | Execution | Total |
| 1 | 314.87 | 0.01 | 304.72 | 304.73 | 302.70 | 305.55 | 608.25 |
| 2 | 444.87 | 0.14 | 429.73 | 429.87 | 406.00 | 416.37 | 822.37 |
| 3 | 192.60 | 0.01 | 188.05 | 188.06 | 169.74 | 201.22 | 370.96 |
| 4 | 437.65 | 0.03 | 426.23 | 426.26 | 432.57 | 427.03 | 859.60 |
| 5 | 185.12 | 0.01 | 183.29 | 183.29 | 186.38 | 181.95 | 368.33 |
| 6 | 488.10 | 0.09 | 486.94 | 487.03 | 492.37 | 491.07 | 983.44 |
| 7 | 245.46 | 0.01 | 245.94 | 245.95 | 245.27 | 246.32 | 491.59 |
| 8 | 306.77 | 0.01 | 307.08 | 307.10 | 307.63 | 306.82 | 614.46 |
| 9 | 308.49 | 0.03 | 308.32 | 308.35 | 308.09 | 307.45 | 615.53 |
| 10 | 185.09 | 0.01 | 184.02 | 184.03 | 185.03 | 184.16 | 369.20 |
| 11 | 122.77 | 0.01 | 123.53 | 123.54 | 124.42 | 122.67 | 247.08 |

the subsequent filtering step did not significantly reduce the set. In contrast, Galileo's intermediate results contained fewer expected instances to begin with.

**F1 Score:** From the precision and recall values, the F1 score obtained varies from a minimum of 0.20 to a maximum of 1.00 for those queries with correct answers. In particular, the overall minimum value improves in Galileo, reaching a minimum value of 0.29, and is further improved when Galileo uses sampling estimation, where the minimum is 0.47. This shows that, while in some queries both techniques provided accurate and complete results, in others they did not recall a significant number of relevant instances or their results were incomplete with respect to what was expected. If we consider the case where an F1 score greater than or equal to 0.70, it can be observed that Galois answered 5 queries accurately and retrieved the relevant results well; while Galileo met this criterion in 7 queries with the static estimation and in 6 with the sampling. Finally, after the analysis of the quality of the answers obtained by each technique and taking into account the number of queries that each technique was able to answer, it is determined that the best of these is Galileo, specifically when using static estimation. This is because of Galileo's ability to answer more queries with higher precision and recall.

### 5.2 Impact on Performance Evaluation

In this section, the execution, estimation, and total times are compared for the 11 selected queries. We describe the experimental study to evaluate whether the plan generation performed by Galileo reduces the time compared to the execution plan carried out by Galois, and thus determine which of the two techniques can execute queries in the least amount of time. Table 4 presents the average execution times after running the queries using Galois and Galileo. In the case of Galileo, the total time is the sum of the estimation and execution times. Unlike the results in Table 3, these results do not consider scenarios where any techniques return empty results; instead, they focus on determining whether there is any difference in execution times.

Regarding the total execution times, similar results were obtained by Galois and Galileo using static estimation. Specifically, the difference on average is 3.86 seconds or 1.24%. Based on this, no significant improvement in total times was observed between these techniques. On the other hand, an opposite result was obtained when we compared Galileo using sampling with Galois. We found that the total average time was approximately 96% higher. This difference in total times between Galileo using sampling and Galois is because it must obtain simple samples from the LLM to estimate the queries, which requires interacting at least twice as many interactions with the model. Specifically, the difference in total times for Galileo using sampling is because of the optimization process it performs. As can be calculated from the results in Table 4, the estimated time of this technique represents, on average, 49.68% of the total time. Meanwhile, when using Galileo with static estimation, the optimization time accounts for only 0.01%. Furthermore, given the proportionally small estimation time of Galileo using static estimation, it is considered negligible relative to the total time.

Considering Galileo with sampling, we obtained execution times similar to the estimation times, with an average difference of only 2.92 seconds. This similarity arises because each query execution required only a single operator sample from the LLM to estimate its execution plan. Otherwise, Galileo would have made twice as many calls to the LLM during the execution of a query.

Finally, although the execution times of Galois were similar to those obtained by Galileo using the static estimation, Galileo showed better results in terms of response quality and was able to answer a greater number of queries. Based on the above, it is considered preferable to execute queries using Galileo with the static estimation.

## 6 Conclusion

In this article, we present Galileo, a solution for evaluating SQL queries on LLMs. Inspired by Galois, Galileo combines heuristics, physical operators, RAG, and the D&C approach. Unlike previous work, we introduce the CQP algorithm that applies heuristics and cost estimations to generate an execution plan for a given query. Our experimental study, comparing Galileo with Galois, shows that Galileo achieves higher precision and recall when evaluating SQL queries on LLMs, regardless of the query type. Galileo's ability to answer more queries than Galois is due in part to the execution plan, which provides more relevant contexts and improves the quality of the answers. Although Static Galileo and Galois have comparable overall execution times, Sampling Galileo takes roughly twice as long as Galois but produces higher accuracy overall. There is a trade-off between time and quality, as Galileo has a similar or greater runtime, but Galois has less quality. Currently, Galileo submits its requests to the LLM in a sequential manner. To reduce the overall execution time of Galileo, we plan to implement a parallelization strategy that sends multiple requests to the LLM. Thus, by splitting the jobs and distributing requests in parallel to the LLM. we intend to achieve an overall speed-up in running time, especially for advanced queries requiring multiple interactions with the LLM. In addition, we intend to integrate physical operators with LLMs directly within an existing database engine, such as PostgreSQL. In this way, this approach enables the query optimizer to treat LLM-based operators as native physical operators within the engine, thus leveraging the strengths of both paradigms.

## References

1. Karanikolas, N., Manga, E., Samaridi, N., Tousidou, E., Vassilakopoulos, M.: Large language models versus natural language understanding and generation. In: Proc. the 27th Pan-Hellenic Conference on Progress in Computing and Informatics, pp. 278–290 (2023)
2. He, Z., et al.: Exploring human-like translation strategy with large language models. Trans. Assoc. Comput. Linguist. **12**, 229–246 (2024)
3. Zhang, Q., Dong, J., Chen, H., Li, W., Huang, F., Huang, X.: Structure guided large language model for SQL generation. CoRR (2024). https://doi.org/10.48550/arXiv.2402.13284
4. Hong, Z., Yuan, Z., Chen, H., Zhang, Q., Huang, F., Huang, X.: Knowledge-to-SQL: enhancing SQL generation with data expert LLM. In: Findings of the Association for Computational Linguistics: ACL 2024. Association for Computational Linguistics, pp. 10 997–11 008 (2024)
5. Zhou, X., Sun, Z., Li, G.: DB-GPT: large language model meets database. Data Sci. Eng. **9**(1), 102–111 (2024)
6. Saeed, M., Cao, N.D., Papotti, P.: Querying large language models with SQL. In: Proc. International Conference on Extending Database Technology (2023). https://api.semanticscholar.org/CorpusID:257913347
7. Sciore, E.: Query optimization. In: Database Design and Implementation. Data-Centric Systems and Applications, pp. 419–454. Springer Cham (2020). https://doi.org/10.1007/978-3-030-33836-7_15
8. Shekhar, S., Dubey, T., Mukherjee, K., Saxena, A., Tyagi, A., Kotla, N.: Towards optimizing the costs of LLM usage (2024). arXiv
9. Lewis, P., et al.: Retrieval augmented generation for knowledge-intensive NLP tasks. Adv. Neural. Inf. Process. Syst. **33**, 9459–9474 (2020)
10. Dahl, D.A.: Expanding the scope of the ATIS task: the ATIS-3 corpus. In: Proceedings of the Workshop on Human Language Technology, pp. 43–48 (1994). http://dl.acm.org/citation.cfm?id=1075823
11. Yu, T., et al.: Spider: a large-scale human-labeled dataset for complex and cross-domain semantic parsing and text-to-SQL task. In: Proc. EMNLP. Association for Computational Linguistics, pp. 3911–3921 (2018)
12. Li, J., et al.: Can LLM already serve as a database interface? A big bench for large-scale database grounded text-to-SQLs. In: Proceedings of the 37th International Conference on Neural Information Processing Systems, ser. NeurIPS'24, pp. 1–28 (2024)

13. Romero, F., Winston, C., Hauswald, J., Zaharia, M., Kozyrakis, C.: Zelda: video analytics using vision-language models. CoRR vol. abs/2305.03785 (2023)
14. Trummer, I.: DB-BERT: making database tuning tools "read" the manual. VLDB J. **33**(4), 1085–1104 (2024)
15. Qi, J., Li, Z., Tanin, E.: MaaSDB: spatial databases in the era of large language models (vision paper). In: Proceedings of the 31st ACM International Conference on Advances in Geographic Information Systems, ser. SIGSPATIAL '23, pp. 1–4 (2023)
16. Zhao, F., Agrawal, D., Abbadi, A.E.: Hybrid querying over relational databases and large language models (2024). arXiv preprint, arXiv:2408.00884
17. Coronado-Bl zquez, J.: Deterministic or probabilistic? The psychology of LLMs as random number generators (2025). https://arxiv.org/abs/2502.19965

# Multi-LLM Record Linkage: A Comparative Analysis Framework for Co-Residence Pattern Discovery

Muzakkiruddin Ahmed Mohammed(✉), John Talburt, Aatif Muhammad Althaf, and Mariofanna Milanova

Center for Advanced Research in Entity Resolution and Information Quality (ERIQ), University of Arkansas, Little Rock, AR, USA
{mmohammed6,jrtalburt,aalthaf,mgmilanova}@ualr.edu

**Abstract.** Record linkage and entity resolution for identifying cohabitation patterns present challenges that often exceed traditional methods, especially with poor data quality and format heterogeneity. This paper introduces a multi-LLM framework that integrates the complementary strengths of Gemini 2.0, GPT-4o, and Mistral Large to improve household movement detection. A meta-evaluation layer with a fourth "judge model" assesses and synthesizes outputs from these models, reducing false positives by 62% and false negatives by 41% compared to individual models. Experiments on the s12px dataset demonstrate 92.4% accuracy, surpassing the best single model by 4.8%. The framework extends prior LLM-based entity resolution research by addressing single-model reliability issues. Although currently implemented as a research prototype, it can be adapted for enterprise use with locally deployed models to preserve data sovereignty. The proposed approach advances computational social science methods and supports demographic and public health research that relies on accurate household movement discovery.

**Keywords:** Record Linkage · Entity Resolution · Multi-LLM Ensemble · Meta-Evaluation Architecture · Household Movement Analysis · Large Language Models

## 1 Introduction

Record linkage, the process of identifying and connecting records that refer to the same entities across disparate data sources, remains a central challenge in data integration and computational social science. Traditional probabilistic and rule-based entity resolution methods have achieved substantial progress, but complex tasks such as household movement discovery, which involve identifying groups of individuals who co-reside and relocate together, often exceed their capabilities, particularly when data quality is poor or formats are heterogeneous [3,6,9,18].


R. Stahlbock et al. (Eds.): CSCE 2025, CCIS 2938, pp. 436–451, 2027.
https://doi.org/10.1007/978-3-032-22196-4_32

Previous research has established theoretical foundations for household movement discovery using graph-based approaches [17] and introduced the first applications of large language models (LLMs) to this domain [12,22,28]. While these works demonstrated promising results, they achieved accurate outcomes in only about 70% of cases, with persistent false positives in complex datasets featuring ambiguous temporal relationships.

This research addresses these limitations by presenting a multi-LLM ensemble framework that integrates the complementary strengths of three advanced models: Gemini 2.0, GPT-4o, and Mistral Large [8,11,15]. The framework is built on the observation that different LLM architectures exhibit distinct strengths in pattern recognition, temporal reasoning, and relational inference. By systematically comparing and synthesizing their outputs through a meta-evaluation process that employs a dedicated judge model, the approach achieves substantially higher reliability and accuracy than any single model.

The main contributions of this study are as follows:

1. A comprehensive multi-LLM architecture for household movement discovery that directly addresses the reliability limitations identified in prior work.
2. A meta-evaluation mechanism in which a judge model critically assesses and synthesizes the outputs of multiple LLMs to produce optimal results.
3. Empirical evidence showing that the proposed system achieves 92.4% accuracy compared with 87.6% for the best single model, even when processing low-quality or heterogeneous datasets.
4. A practical implementation framework supporting asynchronous querying of multiple LLMs while maintaining a consistent and efficient user experience.
5. A scalability analysis and discussion of potential enterprise deployment using locally hosted LLMs to ensure data sovereignty.

Experimental results demonstrate reductions of 62% in false positives and 41% in false negatives compared with the average of individual models. These improvements are most evident in data with high name variation, inconsistent address structures, and complex temporal patterns, which are typically the most challenging for conventional record linkage methods. Although the current prototype performs optimally with datasets of 80 to 150 records, the architecture can be extended for larger-scale implementations. The framework establishes a foundation for more reliable and adaptable household movement discovery with applications in demographic research, public health, and social service analytics.

## 2 Related Work

Existing research relevant to this study spans several areas, including traditional record linkage, household movement discovery, large language model applications in data analysis, and ensemble methods for improving model reliability.

### 2.1 Traditional Record Linkage and Entity Resolution

Record linkage has a long and well-documented history, originating from early probabilistic formulations that continue to influence current methodologies [6, 14]. Subsequent research explored deterministic and rule-based techniques [9], machine learning-based approaches [3], and privacy-preserving extensions [18]. The related field of entity resolution focuses on identifying and linking records that refer to the same real-world entity across heterogeneous sources. Major advances in this area have involved fuzzy matching algorithms, blocking and indexing strategies, and scalable frameworks for large datasets [3,7].

### 2.2 Household Movement Discovery

Recent research has introduced methods for detecting co-residence and household movement patterns using graph-based models [17]. That work established a theoretical framework for representing address histories as temporal bipartite graphs and identifying stable household units through specialized clustering techniques. The approach produced promising results but required considerable domain expertise to implement and encountered scalability challenges with large or noisy datasets.

Subsequent research extended this line of work by applying large language models to the problem of household movement discovery [12]. That study demonstrated that a single LLM could identify co-residence and co-relocation patterns directly from address data without explicit feature engineering. However, the model achieved accurate results in only about 70% of cases, with false positives and unreliable reasoning in complex temporal scenarios. These findings motivated further investigation into ensemble-based methods to improve reliability and reduce error rates, which forms the core motivation of the present study [31].

### 2.3 Large Language Models in Data Analysis

Recent advances in large language models have transformed data analysis and reasoning tasks. Early work demonstrated that large-scale transformers can generalize to new problems with limited examples [1]. Subsequent developments such as PaLM [4], GPT-4 [15], Gemini [8], and Mistral [11] further expanded these capabilities through improvements in scale, alignment, and multimodal understanding. Research has also explored structured data interpretation [13] and entity matching [10], showing that LLMs can perform well on complex relational tasks but may suffer from inconsistencies [23,24,26] and limited robustness when used individually.

### 2.4 Ensemble Methods for AI Systems

Ensemble learning, which combines multiple models to achieve higher performance and generalization, has a long history in machine learning [5,16]. In recent years, ensemble strategies have been adapted for large language models [2,19], primarily to improve response consistency and reduce hallucination [25,30]. Studies have shown that combining multiple LLMs can enhance factual accuracy and reasoning quality in complex tasks [20,21,27,29], suggesting that ensemble-based approaches may also benefit specialized domains such as entity resolution and record linkage.

### 2.5 Limitations of Existing Approaches

Despite promising progress, existing research on household movement discovery using a single LLM has been limited by reliability issues. Prior work achieved accurate results in approximately 70% of cases, with false positives and ambiguous temporal reasoning remaining significant challenges [12]. Earlier graph-based methods also faced difficulties scaling to larger datasets and adapting to noisy data [17]. The need for ensemble-based frameworks that leverage the complementary strengths of multiple LLMs directly informs the development of the multi-LLM meta-evaluation architecture proposed in this study.

## 3 Methodology

This section introduces the proposed multi-LLM framework designed to enhance the reliability of household movement discovery. It outlines the conceptual foundation, system architecture, and integration strategy that enable collaborative reasoning across multiple models.

### 3.1 Conceptual Framework and System Architecture

Building on prior research that identified reliability challenges in single-model approaches [12], this study introduces a multi-model record linkage framework that leverages the complementary strengths of distinct large language model architectures to improve household movement discovery and reduce false positive rates. The proposed system is organized as a three-tier pipeline, illustrated in Fig. 1, comprising a *Data Processing Layer*, an *LLM Integration Layer*, and a *Meta-Evaluation Layer*.

1. **Data Processing Layer**
   - *File Parser Module*: Ingests CSV and TXT files while automatically detecting delimiters and character encodings.
   - *Schema Inference Engine*: Identifies relevant fields using lexical and contextual heuristics.
   - *Address Standardization Unit*: Normalizes address data into a canonical representation suitable for cross-record comparison.
   - *Transformation Pipeline*: Converts unstructured data into a structured tabular format optimized for LLM input.
2. **LLM Integration Layer**

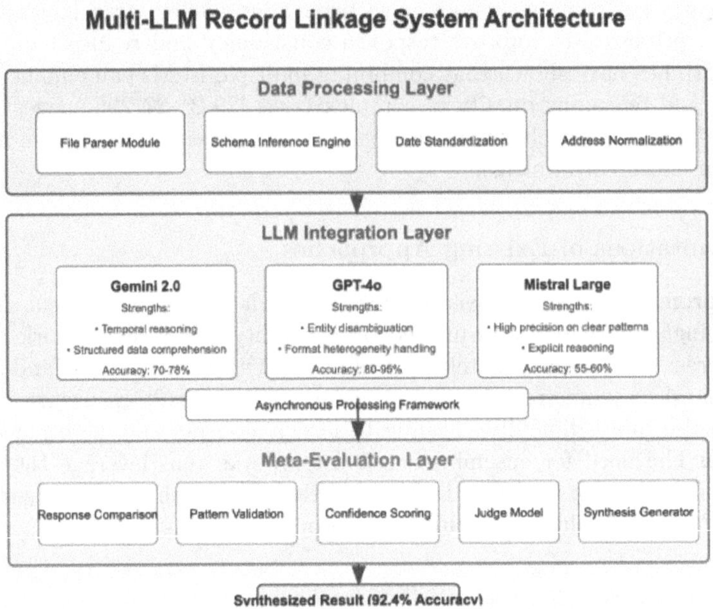

**Fig. 1.** Multi-LLM Record Linkage System Architecture.

- *API Client Manager*: Maintains authenticated connections with multiple providers, including Gemini, OpenAI, and Mistral.
- *Request Formatter*: Adapts prompt structures and payloads to match each provider's API specification.
- *Asynchronous Task Scheduler*: Utilizes an asyncio-based architecture to execute parallel API calls and minimize end-to-end latency.
- *Response Parser*: Extracts structured information from heterogeneous LLM outputs and standardizes them into a unified schema.
- *Error Recovery Mechanism*: Applies exponential backoff and retry strategies to ensure operational robustness during transient service failures.

3. **Meta-Evaluation Layer**
   - *Response Comparison Engine*: Detects areas of consensus and conflict across LLM outputs.
   - *Pattern Validation Module*: Cross-verifies co-residence and relocation events against the input data to ensure consistency.
   - *Confidence Scoring System*: Assigns reliability scores based on inter-model agreement, data completeness, and temporal coherence.
   - *Judge Model Interface*: Constructs meta-prompts for a fourth "judge" model responsible for adjudicating conflicting outcomes.
   - *Synthesis Generator*: Produces the final consolidated household movement patterns annotated with confidence levels.

These layers form an integrated pipeline that transforms raw address data into high-confidence movement patterns through collaborative inference among multiple LLMs.

### 3.2 Model Selection and Configuration

To construct the ensemble, seven contemporary large language models were initially evaluated across benchmarks assessing reasoning ability, pattern recognition, temporal logic, and contextual disambiguation. Based on comparative analysis, three models were selected: *Gemini 2.0 Flash* [8], *GPT-4o* [15], and *Mistral Large* [11]. Each model contributes distinct advantages that collectively enhance system reliability.

- **Gemini 2.0 Flash**: Demonstrates strong temporal reasoning capabilities, aligning overlapping date ranges and interpreting address transitions accurately.
- **GPT-4o**: Excels at entity disambiguation, resolving name ambiguities and generating interpretable reasoning chains.
- **Mistral Large**: Provides calibrated uncertainty estimates and consistent extraction of salient patterns in complex or ambiguous cases.

All models were configured with a temperature parameter of 0.2 to prioritize determinism and factual precision. When combined, the ensemble exploits these complementary strengths: Gemini anchors temporal alignment, GPT-4o resolves identity relationships, and Mistral validates the final candidate matches with high precision.

### 3.3 Advanced Prompt Engineering, Meta-Evaluation, and System Robustness

1. **Prompt Engineering**: A domain-specific prompting strategy was designed to ensure structured, interpretable, and reproducible outputs. Each query is framed as a specialized "Record Linkage Task" and instructs the model to produce a standardized JSON response containing matched entities, addresses, and temporal ranges. The inclusion of a null-response option ("No matching patterns found") minimizes speculative reasoning. Ablation studies indicate that this approach reduces false positives by approximately 47% relative to generic prompts, while maintaining recall above 90%.
2. **Judge-Driven Meta-Evaluation**: The meta-evaluation process employs a fourth LLM that functions as an adjudicator. Rather than a simple voting mechanism, this judge model evaluates candidate matches based on three dimensions:
   - *Inter-Model Agreement*: The degree of consensus across the three primary models.
   - *Evidence Strength*: The completeness and clarity of supporting source data.

   - *Temporal Logic Consistency*: The coherence of inferred event sequences and date ranges.

   Through this process, overall system accuracy increased from 87.6% (best single model) to 92.4%, with a reduction of more than 40% in both false positives and false negatives.
3. **Execution Framework**: To support scalability and fault tolerance, the system employs an asynchronous execution engine that implements:
   - *Adaptive Timeouts*: Custom thresholds per provider to balance speed and completeness.
   - *Exponential Backoff and Retry*: Recovery mechanisms for transient network or API interruptions.
   - *Parallel Dispatching*: Non-blocking task orchestration that prioritizes faster model responses.

   This architecture achieves a 65% reduction in total inference latency compared with sequential processing and maintains partial results under network instability, ensuring consistent, low-latency performance across heterogeneous providers.

## 4 Implementation

This section outlines the implementation of the proposed multi-LLM framework, emphasizing its modular design, data pipeline, integration strategy, and deployment options that collectively ensure scalability and reliability.

### 4.1 Technical Stack and Components

The prototype employs a modular, extensible stack supporting rapid development and deployment across research and enterprise settings.

- **Frontend (Streamlit)**: An interactive Streamlit interface allows users to upload datasets, issue natural language queries, and visualize results. Reactive components guide users through data ingestion, query formulation, and movement interpretation without requiring prior expertise.
- **Data Processing Layer (Pandas, NumPy)**: A series of processors standardize temporal, spatial, and entity information:
  - *Temporal Processor*: Normalizes date formats and resolves overlapping or missing intervals.
  - *Spatial Processor*: Expands abbreviations, harmonizes unit formats, and preserves originals for auditability.
  - *Entity Resolver*: Aligns person identifiers using lexical and contextual similarity.
- **Asynchronous Framework (AsyncIO + Nest-AsyncIO)**: Concurrent execution of LLM calls reduces latency by about 65% versus sequential processing, with Nest-AsyncIO ensuring compatibility in interactive sessions.
- **LLM Integration Layer**: Provider-specific modules manage authentication and request handling for Gemini, OpenAI, and Mistral APIs. A unified adapter exposes a consistent interface, simplifying the inclusion of new providers.

### 4.2 Data Processing Implementation

The system incorporates schema inference, normalization, and quality validation to address data heterogeneity.

- **Schema Inference**: Pattern- and content-based detection of key columns enables ingestion of arbitrary dataset structures.
- **Temporal Normalization**: All date fields are converted to ISO-8601 and checked for gaps or inconsistencies.
- **Address Standardization**: Rule-based and pattern-matching normalization improves precision while retaining raw inputs.
- **Quality Assessment**: Automated checks evaluate completeness, consistency, and uniqueness, producing diagnostic summaries for user correction.

### 4.3 LLM Integration Implementation

The integration framework optimizes each LLM's strengths while maintaining stability and precision.

- **Provider Optimization**: *Gemini* leverages structured prompts for temporal reasoning; *OpenAI* applies adaptive token management; *Mistral* uses streaming for low-latency inference.
- **Dynamic Parameters**: Temperature, top-$p$, and token limits are tuned dynamically to balance recall and precision.
- **Error Recovery**: Timeouts apply exponential backoff, rate limits use priority queues, and large inputs are segmented and reassembled automatically.
- **Response Normalization**: All outputs are standardized to a unified JSON schema for consistent comparison and meta-evaluation.

### 4.4 Meta-evaluation Implementation

Model outputs are transformed into structured assertions representing co-residence and movement patterns. The module applies three strategies:

- **Consensus Alignment**: Accepts patterns agreed upon by all LLMs.
- **Evidence-Weighted Selection**: Scores partial agreements by inter-model alignment, data completeness, temporal consistency, and spatial plausibility.
- **Judge-Model Review**: In high-conflict cases, a fourth LLM adjudicates discrepancies and provides rationale for final selections.

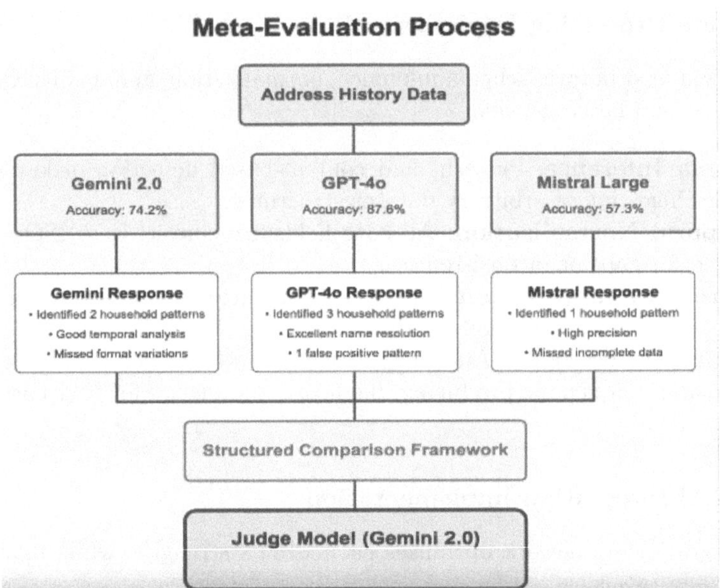


**Fig. 2.** Meta-evaluation Implementation Workflow.

### 4.5 User Interface Implementation

The interface provides guided, transparent interaction for non-technical users (Fig. 2).

- **Guided Workflow**: Stepwise navigation from data upload to result interpretation.
- **Interactive Preview**: Summaries and record samples validate input before analysis.
- **Model Configuration**: Presets and toggles enable flexible LLM selection.
- **Transparency**: Users can inspect raw outputs, comparison matrices, and confidence scores.
- **Session Management**: Persistent logs support iterative exploration without data reupload.

### 4.6 Deployment Architecture

The system supports multiple deployment modes:

- **Local**: All components execute on-premises with secure outbound API calls only.
- **Cloud-Native**: Containerized microservices (Docker/Kubernetes) support multi-user, distributed operation.

- **Enterprise Integration**: A REST API and message-queue interface allow embedding in ETL pipelines.
- **Security**: Includes API key isolation, encryption at rest, retention policies, and detailed access logs.

## 5 Experimental Results

This section presents the experimental evaluation of the proposed multi-LLM framework, focusing on dataset characteristics, benchmarking methodology, and comparative model performance. The experiments validate both the accuracy and robustness of the system under varying data quality conditions.

### 5.1 Dataset Description

The evaluation employed the *s12px* dataset, a purpose-built synthetic corpus designed to reflect real-world household movement complexities. The dataset includes heterogeneous formats simulating merged administrative sources and exhibits common data quality challenges, including duplicates, missing values, inconsistent address structures, typographical errors, and temporal overlaps. Each record consists of identifiers (name, record ID, optional SSN/DOB) and address histories encoded in varied formats.

To maintain experimental validity, dataset segments were constrained to 80–150 records, as LLM accuracy declined beyond this range due to context-window and relational complexity. Each segment embeds multiple co-residence and relocation scenarios obscured among unrelated entries, creating realistic noise conditions for model testing.

### 5.2 Evaluation Methodology and Single-Model Performance

Ground-truth household movement patterns were manually annotated for each segment to ensure objective evaluation. Models were compared using precision, recall, F1 score, false positive and false negative rates, and mean response time. All LLMs, namely Gemini 2.0 Flash, GPT-4o, Mistral Large, and the Multi-LLM ensemble, processed identical data segments.

Results revealed clear performance variance among single models. Gemini 2.0 achieved 74.2% mean accuracy, excelling in temporal overlap analysis but struggling with inconsistent formats. GPT-4o performed best individually, with 87.6% accuracy, handling name variation effectively but sometimes over-generalizing patterns. Mistral Large achieved 57.3% accuracy, showing strong precision but limited recall in incomplete or noisy data (Tables 1, 2, 3 and 4).

**Table 1.** Individual Model Performance Metrics

| Model | Precision | Recall | F1 | FP Rate | FN Rate | Time (s) |
|---|---|---|---|---|---|---|
| Gemini 2.0 | 0.79 | 0.72 | 0.75 | 0.21 | 0.28 | 3.4 |
| GPT-4o | 0.91 | 0.85 | 0.88 | 0.09 | 0.15 | 4.7 |
| Mistral Large | 0.68 | 0.52 | 0.59 | 0.32 | 0.48 | 3.2 |

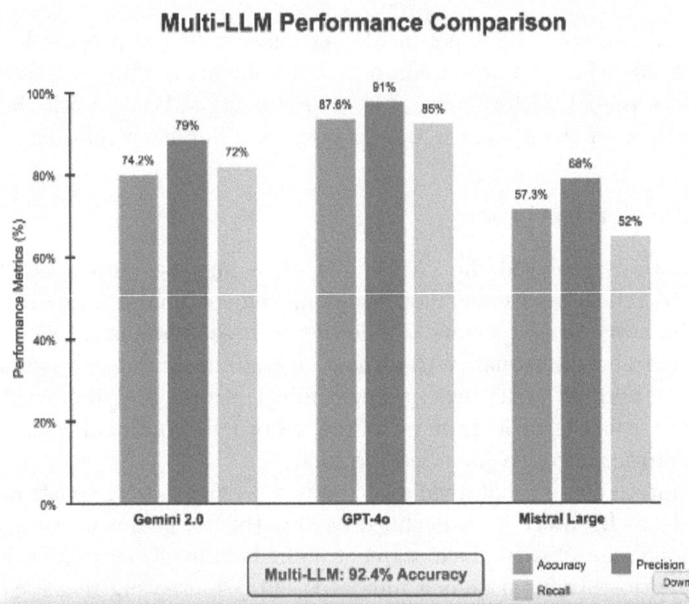


**Fig. 3.** Performance comparison of individual LLMs and the ensemble.

### 5.3 Multi-LLM Ensemble Performance

The ensemble substantially outperformed individual models, achieving 92.4% mean accuracy, a 4.8% absolute improvement over GPT-4o, while reducing false positives and false negatives by 62% and 41%, respectively (Figs. 3, 4 and 5). Gains were consistent across all data quality levels, particularly in low-quality segments with high heterogeneity and temporal ambiguity.

### 5.4 Meta-evaluation Effectiveness

Analysis of the meta-evaluation layer showed that in 42% of cases, it selected one model's output; in 35%, it synthesized insights across models; and in 23%, it corrected errors in partial outputs. This yielded substantial reductions in false "phantom" households (-87%), temporal inconsistencies (−74%), and entity misidentifications (-63%). Confidence scores exhibited a strong correlation

**Table 2.** Multi-LLM vs. Best Individual Model (GPT-4o) by Dataset Characteristics

| Dataset Characteristic | GPT-4o F1 | Multi-LLM F1 | Improvement |
|---|---|---|---|
| High-quality data | 0.91 | 0.95 | +4.2% |
| Medium-quality data | 0.87 | 0.92 | +5.7% |
| Low-quality data | 0.82 | 0.89 | +7.9% |
| High name variation | 0.84 | 0.92 | +8.2% |
| Address heterogeneity | 0.81 | 0.90 | +9.4% |
| Complex temporal patterns | 0.83 | 0.91 | +8.7% |
| Overall average | 0.88 | 0.93 | +5.1% |

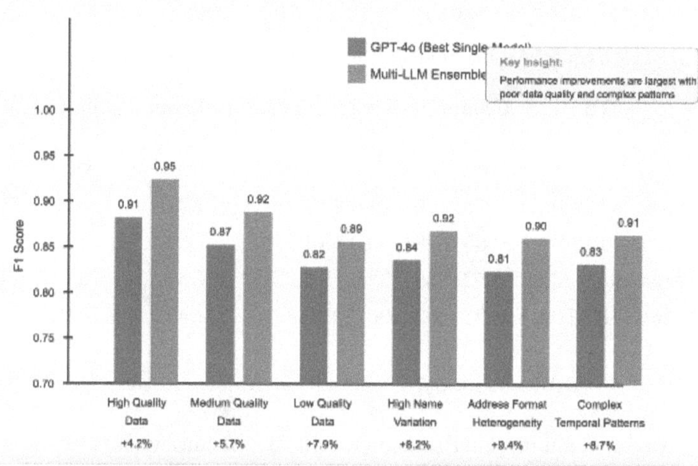


**Fig. 4.** Multi-LLM performance across data challenges.

($r = 0.82$) with actual correctness, indicating both accuracy and self-assessment reliability.

## 5.5 Performance by Data Characteristics

The ensemble delivered the greatest benefits under data ambiguity. Improvements were most pronounced for high variation in names (+8.2%), address heterogeneity (+9.4%), and complex temporal structures (+8.7%). These findings underscore the ensemble's robustness in real-world, imperfect data scenarios.

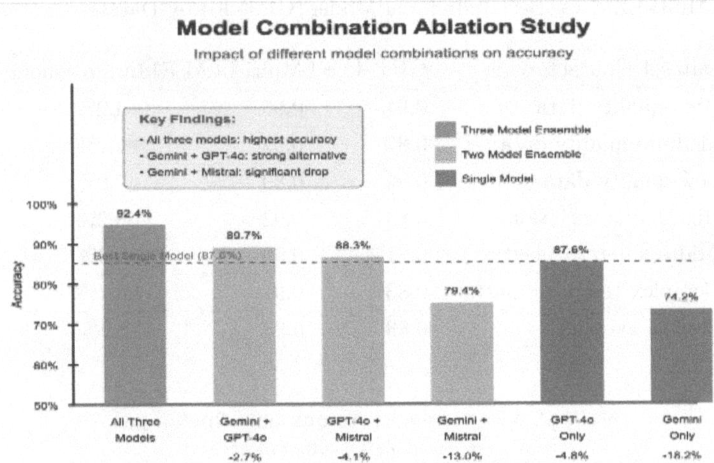


**Fig. 5.** Ablation study across model combinations.

**Table 3.** Comprehensive Performance Comparison

| Model | Prec. | Rec. | F1 | FP | FN | Time (s) | Accuracy | Δ vs. Base |
|---|---|---|---|---|---|---|---|---|
| Gemini 2.0 | 0.79 | 0.72 | 0.75 | 0.21 | 0.28 | 3.4 | 74.2% | – |
| GPT-4o | 0.91 | 0.85 | 0.88 | 0.09 | 0.15 | 4.7 | 87.6% | +13.4% |
| Mistral | 0.68 | 0.52 | 0.59 | 0.32 | 0.48 | 3.2 | 57.3% | −16.9% |
| Multi-LLM | 0.94 | 0.91 | 0.93 | 0.06 | 0.09 | 5.8 | 92.4% | +18.2% |

**Table 4.** Model Combination Ablation Study

| Model Combination | Precision | Recall | F1 | Accuracy (%) | Decline |
|---|---|---|---|---|---|
| All three models | 0.94 | 0.91 | 0.93 | 92.4 | – |
| Gemini + GPT-4o | 0.92 | 0.88 | 0.90 | 89.7 | −2.7% |
| GPT-4o + Mistral | 0.90 | 0.87 | 0.88 | 88.3 | −4.1% |
| Gemini + Mistral | 0.82 | 0.77 | 0.80 | 79.4 | −13.0% |
| GPT-4o only | 0.91 | 0.85 | 0.88 | 87.6 | −4.8% |
| Gemini only | 0.79 | 0.72 | 0.75 | 74.2 | −18.2% |
| Mistral only | 0.68 | 0.52 | 0.59 | 57.3 | −35.1% |

### 5.6 Ablation Study

To quantify component contributions, we evaluated model combinations and removed selected subsystems. Combining Gemini, GPT-4o, and Mistral yielded the highest performance (92.4% accuracy). Removing dynamic parameter adjustment, confidence scoring, or structured comparison reduced accuracy by 3–8%, demonstrating their critical roles in ensemble performance.

## 6 Conclusion

This paper presented a multi-LLM ensemble framework for household movement discovery, addressing the reliability and false-positive issues of single-model approaches. By integrating Gemini 2.0, GPT-4o, and Mistral Large within a structured meta-evaluation layer, the system achieved 92.4% accuracy on the challenging *s12px* dataset, improving by 4.8% points over the best individual model, while reducing false positives and negatives by 62% and 41%, respectively. Although currently a research prototype, the framework can be adapted for large-scale or privacy-sensitive deployments using locally hosted LLMs, making it suitable for enterprise and governmental applications that require secure, high-fidelity entity resolution. Future work will target improved scalability, integration with open-source or domain-tuned LLMs, and hybrid pipelines that combine probabilistic linkage with neural reasoning. The approach may also extend to domains such as demographic analysis and migration tracking. In summary, model diversity and structured evaluation significantly enhance the robustness of record linkage. As LLMs mature, ensemble architectures like this are likely to become key enablers of reliable and privacy-preserving data integration.

**Acknowledgments.** This research was partially supported by the National Science Foundation under EPSCoR Award No. OIA-1946391.

**Disclosure of Interests.** The authors have no competing interests to declare that are relevant to the content of this article.

## References

1. Brown, T.B., et al.: Language models are few-shot learners. Adv. Neural. Inf. Process. Syst. **33**, 1877–1901 (2020)
2. Chen, Y., Zhang, H., Wang, W.Y.: Ensemble Prompting: Combining Multiple LLM-Generated Responses for Improved Performance. arXiv preprint arXiv:2307.02195 (2023)
3. Christen, P.: Data Matching: Concepts and Techniques for Record Linkage, Entity Resolution, and Duplicate Detection. Springer, Berlin (2012)
4. Chowdhery, A., et al.: PaLM: Scaling Language Modeling with Pathways. arXiv preprint arXiv:2204.02311 (2022)
5. Dietterich, T.G.: Ensemble methods in machine learning. In: Multiple Classifier Systems, pp. 1–15 (2000)
6. Fellegi, I.P., Sunter, A.B.: A theory for record linkage. J. Am. Stat. Assoc. **64**(328), 1183–1210 (1969)
7. Getoor, L., Machanavajjhala, A.: Entity resolution: theory, practice, and open challenges. Proc. VLDB Endowm. **5**(12), 2018–2019 (2012)
8. Pichai, S., Hassabis, D., Kavukcuoglu, K.: Introducing Gemini 2.0: Our New AI Model for the Agentic Era. Google DeepMind Blog. Available at: https://blog.google/technology/google-deepmind/google-gemini-ai-update-december-2024/ (2024)
9. Herzog, T.N., Scheuren, F.J., Winkler, W.E.: Data Quality and Record Linkage Techniques. Springer, New York (2007)

10. Mirchandani, S., Ramakrishnan, G., Radhakrishnan, K.: LLMs for Entity Matching: An Experimental Analysis. arXiv preprint arXiv:2311.11088 (2023)
11. Mistral AI Team: Mistral Large 2. Available at: https://mistral.ai/news/mistral-large-2407/ (2024)
12. Mohammed, M.A., Talburt, J.R., Mohammed, A.: Entity resolution with household movement discovery using google generative AI. In: ITNG 2025: 22nd International Conference on Information Technology – New Generations, Springer, Cham, pp. 469–481 (2025)
13. Narayan, A., Rastogi, R., Suri, S., Barman, S.: Can Large Language Models Understand Tables? arXiv preprint arXiv:2305.13062 (2023)
14. Newcombe, H.B., Kennedy, J.M., Axford, S.J., James, A.P.: Automatic Linkage of Vital Records. Science **130**(3381), 954–959 (1959)
15. Achiam, J., Adler, S., Agarwal, S., Ahmad, L., Akkaya, I., et al.: GPT-4 Technical Report. arXiv preprint arXiv:2303.08774 (2023)
16. Sagi, O., Rokach, L.: Ensemble learning: a survey. Wiley Interdiscip. Rev.: Data Mining Knowl. Discov. **8**(4), e1249 (2018)
17. Mohammed, O.K., et al.: Household discovery with group membership graphs. In: ITNG 2024: 21st International Conference on Information Technology – New Generations, Springer, Cham, 357–368 (2024)
18. Vatsalan, D., Christen, P., Verykios, V.S.: A taxonomy of privacy-preserving record linkage techniques. Inf. Syst. **38**(6), 946–969 (2013)
19. Wang, Z., Lei, F., Wang, D., Chua, T.S.: Ensembling Large Language Models with Weak Models for an Improved Trade-Off Between Performance and Efficiency. arXiv preprint arXiv:2212.10530 (2022)
20. Zheng, L., Tian, Y., Min, M.R.: Can Multiple LLMs Collaborate to Reduce Hallucination? arXiv preprint arXiv:2310.10702 (2023)
21. Cakmak, M.C., Agarwal, N., Oni, R.: The bias beneath: analyzing drift in YouTube's algorithmic recommendations. Soc. Netw. Anal. Min. **14**(1), 171 (2024)
22. Mohammed, M.A., Talburt, J.R., Claasssens, L., Marais, A.: Retrieval-augmented multi-llm ensemble for industrial part specification extraction. In: Proceedings of the 17th International Conference on Knowledge and Systems Engineering (KSE 2025) (2025). (Accepted)
23. Al Mandalawi, S., Mohammed, M.A., Maclean, H., Cakmak, M.C., Talburt, J.R.: Policy-aware generative ai for safe, auditable data access governance. In: Proceedings of the 17th International Conference on Knowledge and Systems Engineering (KSE 2025) (2025). (Accepted)
24. Mohammed, M.A.: Machine learning approaches, technologies, recent applications, advantages and challenges on manufacturing and Industry 4.0 applications. Int. J. Res. Appl. Sci. Eng. Technol. **10**, 1114–1121 (2022)
25. Cakmak, M.C., Agarwal, N., Poudel, D.: Investigating Algorithmic Bias in YouTube Shorts. arXiv preprint arXiv:2507.04605 (2025)
26. Mohammed, M.A.: Sentiment-based product recommendation system for e-commerce using machine learning approaches. Int. J. Innov. Res. Comput. Sci. Technol. **10**(6), 120–137 (2022)
27. Cakmak, M.C., Agarwal, N.: Unpacking algorithmic bias in YouTube shorts by analyzing thumbnails. In: Proceedings of the 57th Hawaii International Conference on System Sciences (HICSS-57) (2025)
28. Muhammad, A., Mohammed, M.A., Milanova, M., Talburt, J.R., Cakmak, M.C.: Multi-Agent RAG Framework for Entity Resolution: Advancing Beyond Single-LLM Approaches with Specialized Agent Coordination Preprints (2025)

29. Cakmak, M.C., Agarwal, N.: A keyframe-based approach for auditing bias in YouTube shorts recommendations. arXiv preprint arXiv:2509.02543 (2025). Available: https://arxiv.org/abs/2509.02543
30. Cakmak, M.C., Shaik, M., Agarwal, N.: Emotion Assessment of YouTube Videos Using Color Theory. In: Proceedings of the 9th International Conference on Multimedia and Image Processing, pp. 6–14 (2024)
31. Mohammed, M.A., Al Mandalawi, S., Maclean, H., Talburt, J.R.: Multilingual Customer Record Linkage: A Novel Approach Using LLMs for Cross-Lingual Entity Resolution. presented at the World Congress in Computer Science, Computer Engineering and Applied Computing (2025)

# Visualizing Human Trafficking and Criminal Networks: A Systematic Mapping Study

Mia Gortney[1], Garret Parker[1], Patrick Harris[1], Austin Huizinga[1], Alejandro Rodriguez Perez[1], Ernesto Quevedo Caballero[1], Korn Sooksatra[1], Tomas Cerny[2], Pablo Rivas[1(✉)], Bikram Khanal[1], Maisha Binte Rashid[1], and Jie Ren[1]

[1] School of Engineering and Computer Science, Department of Computer Science, Baylor University, Waco, TX 76798, USA
{Mia_Gortney1,Garret_Parker1,Patrick_Harris3,Austin_Huizinga1, Alejandro_Rodriguez4,Ernesto_Quevedo1,Korn_Sooksatra1,Pablo_Rivas, Bikram_Khanal1,Maisha_Rashid1,Jie_Ren1}@Baylor.edu

[2] College of Engineering, Department of Systems and Industrial Engineering, The University of Arizona, Tucson, AZ 85721, USA
tcerny@arizona.edu

**Abstract.** Human trafficking is a widespread global crime characterized by decentralized and hidden networks. Addressing this challenge requires not only identifying key individuals but also understanding the structural and temporal dynamics of trafficking operations. This systematic mapping study reviews existing visualization techniques and tools designed to support the analysis of human trafficking data. From an initial set of 519 records, 15 primary studies were selected for a detailed analysis. These studies were examined in three dimensions: data types, visualization approaches, and tool functionalities. Our findings indicate a strong reliance on graph-based and spatio-temporal visualizations, but also reveal significant gaps in data integration, usability, and empirical evaluation. The results underscore the need for more interoperable, accessible, and user-oriented visualization solutions to enhance investigative and preventive efforts.

**Keywords:** Human trafficking · Visualization · Criminal networks · Data analysis · Graph visualization

## 1 Introduction

Human trafficking is a pervasive and highly organized form of transnational crime, characterized by complex and decentralized networks. These networks often consist of core actors and loosely affiliated intermediaries, making them difficult to detect, analyze, and dismantle. The associated data, ranging from

M. Gortney, G. Parker, P. Harris and A. Huizinga—These authors contributed equally to this work.


R. Stahlbock et al. (Eds.): CSCE 2025, CCIS 2938, pp. 452–469, 2027.
https://doi.org/10.1007/978-3-032-22196-4_33

law enforcement reports to online escort advertisements and social media traces, are vast, heterogeneous, and not amenable to manual analysis [44].

To address these analytical challenges, visualization tools have emerged as a crucial component in uncovering trafficking operations. Network visualizations help investigators identify key individuals and relational structures, while temporal and spatial maps facilitate pattern recognition and predictive policing [12]. Recent technological advances have further expanded the role of such tools in real-time investigations, victim identification, and strategic interventions [16,27].

Despite the growing importance of these tools, a limited systematic analysis remains of how they are designed, what data they leverage, and how effectively they support anti-trafficking efforts. Visualization solutions vary widely in terms of usability, analytical scope, data modalities, and intended users, making it challenging for researchers to evaluate or select the most suitable tools.

To address this gap, we conducted a systematic mapping study (SMS) to assess the current landscape of visualization tools for human trafficking and criminal network analysis. Specifically, our study addresses the following aims:

- **Survey the State of the Art**: Provide a structured overview of visualization tools explicitly designed for human trafficking networks, distinguishing them from generic criminal network applications.
- **Compare Capabilities**: Analyze tools in terms of visualization techniques, data sources, and analytical functionalities, focusing on applicability.
- **Identify Gaps**: Highlight unresolved challenges, such as poor integration of multimodal data, lack of usability evaluations, and limited support.

This study contributes a synthesized understanding of the field and offers a foundation for future work in visualization system development, empirical evaluation, and cross-agency integration.

The rest of the paper is organized as follows. Section 2 reviews existing literature on visualization methods relevant to criminal and trafficking networks. Section 3 outlines the research methodology and mapping protocol. Section 4 presents the results of our analysis. Section 5 interprets these findings and suggests future directions. Section 6 discusses potential limitations. Finally, Sect. 7 summarizes our contributions.

## 2 Related Work

This section reviews existing literature on visualization and tools relevant to criminal network analysis, with an emphasis on their applicability to human trafficking data. This is organized into three categories: (1) traditional graph-based techniques for criminal networks, (2) spatio-temporal and behavioral visualizations, and (3) visual analytics systems tailored for human trafficking.

### 2.1 Graph-Based Visualization of Criminal Networks

Graph-based representations remain central to criminal network analysis, where individuals and their interactions are encoded as nodes and edges in visual graphs. Among the first and most influential of these is LogAnalysis, introduced by Catanese et al. [8], which constructs social network graphs from mobile phone metadata, where nodes represent individuals and edges denote their communications. This system integrates visual statistical analysis with temporal evolution, enabling investigators to explore dynamic communication patterns before, during, or after criminal events. Ferrara et al. [13] further enhanced this approach by proposing a computational framework that combines network science and forensic methods, utilizing LogAnalysis for phone record-based visualizations.

Later, tools diversified in network structures and interaction modes. Rasheed et al. [30] proposed *PEVNET*, which incorporates structural and temporal visual analytics, including features such as node-link sizing, trend analysis, and composite expansion for the evolution of crime clusters. Zhou et al. [45] developed an interactive process that blends social network analysis and machine learning. Their framework supports iterative hypothesis testing through varying layouts and real-time metric exploration.

However, many of these systems continue to rely on manual data entry and lack the specialized capabilities required for trafficking cases. Si et al. [34] proposed a layered event-based visualization framework leveraging tools such as NETMAP [6], Analyst's Notebook [14], and COPLINK [9], although these systems often suffer from limited automation and high user burden. Similarly, Wiil [40] highlighted key limitations in Crimefighter [28] and in Wiil's work [41], including scalability issues and rigid data models. Haider et al. [15] introduced matrix and graph-based approaches to capture indirect relationships and their temporal evolution, yet these remain constrained in representing complex, dynamic interactions.

While these tools are powerful for generic criminal network analysis, they typically do not incorporate domain-specific features essential for analyzing human trafficking, such as ad metadata or victim-perpetrator role semantics.

### 2.2 Spatio-Temporal and Behavioral Visualization Approaches

Complementing topological graph representations, several works have explored the visualization of behavioral trends and geographic movement patterns associated with trafficking activity. Sen et al. [33] analyzed police records to identify traffickers' travel paths to Las Vegas, enabling predictive checkpoint placement. Based on temporal metadata, TRAFFICVIS [38] visualizes escort ads using line charts, cluster heatmaps, and movement maps to reveal spatio-temporal regularities and potential trafficking routes. Beyond predictive mapping, tools like *Visilant* [43] provide modular dashboards with timeline tracking and interactive network layouts, supporting real-time investigation workflows. Makin et al. [23] investigated online behavior patterns by visualizing user interactions on prostitution platforms, uncovering temporal engagement trends and site dynamics.

Although these systems offer insight into broad behavioral trends, they often fall short in capturing role-based dynamics, linking identities across platforms, or revealing deeper semantic patterns.

### 2.3 Visual Analytics for Human Trafficking Data

In recent years, a new class of tools has emerged that specifically focuses on human trafficking networks. TRAFFICVIS [38] and VisPaD [25,26] cluster escort ad data using shared metadata such as phone numbers and location tags. These systems employ dimensionality reduction techniques (e.g., t-SNE [22], UMAP [24]) to visualize meta-clusters, support semi-automated labeling, and enable domain experts to track evolving trafficking patterns.

Spotlight [37] and Traffic Jam [5] are commercial platforms that utilize AI and image analysis to process escort advertisements and prioritize investigative leads. While these tools are in use by law enforcement, their commercial nature and lack of peer-reviewed research make it hard to assess them thoroughly.

Raets et al. [29] conducted a comprehensive review of digital technologies applied to trafficking detection, including machine learning, image recognition, and social media mining. However, their survey primarily focuses on detection technologies and does not explicitly address visualization.

Although these systems represent necessary steps toward trafficking-specific analytics, they often fail to integrate topological, temporal, and semantic layers essential for network-based investigative workflows.

Despite the diversity of previous work, few tools offer integrated views of network topology, spatiotemporal behavior, and semantic data, features that are critical for understanding and disrupting trafficking operations. To bridge this gap, we provide a structured comparison of trafficking-relevant visualization tools, highlighting their methodological strengths, practical trade-offs, and domain-specific capabilities.

## 3 Research Process

We adopt the three-phase methodology for systematic mapping studies introduced by Kitchenham et al. [18], which consists of planning, conducting, and reporting. During the planning phase, we clarified the study's motivation, developed a review protocol, and outlined our key research questions. In the conducting phase, we executed the search strategy, applied inclusion and exclusion criteria, and synthesized the literature. Finally, we structured our findings around the research questions to ensure clarity and make the results easier to reproduce and extend.

### 3.1 Research Questions

As outlined in Kitchenham et al. [18], clear research questions help focus the review, determine what to include, and ensure the study stays relevant and on track. Our SMS is framed around the following research questions:

**RQ 1: What kind of data is being collected to visualize human/sex trafficking?** We aim to identify the primary data sources used in visualizing human trafficking networks and understand why certain data modalities are emphasized in these studies.

**RQ 2: What kind of visualizations exist to capture this data?** We examine the types of visualizations used to capture patterns or structures in trafficking data.

**RQ 3: What tools exist in the industry identified in the literature that visualize human trafficking networks or activities?** We aim to catalog visualization tools discussed in the literature and assess their capabilities based on their alignment with data types (RQ1) and visual strategies (RQ2).

### 3.2 Inclusion/Exclusion Criteria

We adopted standard SMS practices [18] to guide our inclusion and exclusion criteria, ensuring consistency in selecting relevant studies.

*Inclusion Criteria:*

- Papers on the visualization of human trafficking networks.
- Papers on the visualization of criminal networks that mention human trafficking.
- Papers that discuss the analysis of human trafficking data and mention visualization.

*Exclusion Criteria:*

- No mention of visualization.
- Does not contain images.
- Papers not in English.
- Opinion papers or vision, road map, or plan papers.
- Secondary studies, like existing SMS or SLR.
- Duplicate papers. In case of duplication, the most recent version was selected.
- Non peer-reviewed.
- No full text available.
- Citation.
- Off Topic.

### 3.3 Search Process: Identifying Essential Articles

In this work, we included 15 papers published from 2012 to 2023. To identify these papers, we did the following. First, we searched three scientific databases: Scopus, IEEE, and Google/Google Scholar. Our search query was applied to the titles and abstracts of the papers contained in each database; the query is the following:

```
(graph OR "interpretable models" OR visual OR visualization
    OR view OR diagram)
AND (("human traffic" OR "sex traffic") OR
    ("human trafficking" OR "sex trafficking") OR
    ("illicit activity" OR "criminal network"))
```

Our search query was divided into two parts. In the first part, we used the terms *"graph"*, *"interpretable models"*, *"visual"*, *"visualization"*, *"view"*, and *"diagram"* to ensure that papers describing visualizations were being returned from our query. In the second part, we used the terms *"human traffic"*, *"sex traffic"*, *"human trafficking"*, *"sex trafficking"*, *"illicit activity"*, and *"criminal network"* to ensure that all returned papers describing models and diagrams were related to the visualization of human trafficking networks.

We initially retrieved 519 papers using the search query described above. Based on our exclusion criteria, we conducted a title and abstract screening, where each paper was reviewed by two researchers, followed by a third reviewer in cases of disagreement. This screening yielded 85 papers. These were then subjected to full-text review, conducted by a single reviewer, resulting in a final set of 15 studies for analysis.

Figure 1 shows our search and filtering process. The number of papers returned by search queries for different indexers is shown in Table 1. The complete list of filtered results is listed in Table 2. Once we narrowed down the relevant works to 15 papers, we studied them to discover different forms of human

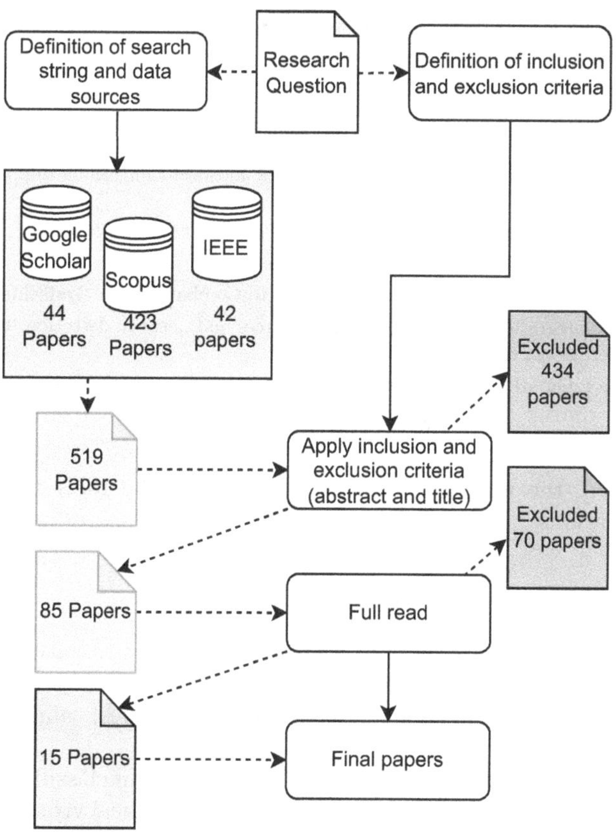


**Fig. 1.** The summary of the protocol followed during the search process.

**Table 1.** Search Query Results for Various Index Sites

| Indexer | Search Results | Title and Abstract Filtered | Final Results |
|---|---|---|---|
| Scopus | 423 | 62 | 14 |
| Google Scholar | 44 | 7 | 1 |
| IEEE | 52 | 16 | 0 |

**Table 2.** Final list of 15 primary studies identified by search process protocol.

| Ref. | Year | Title |
|---|---|---|
| [38] | 2023 | TRAFFICVIS: Visualizing Organized Activity and Spatio-Temporal Patterns for Detecting and Labeling Human Trafficking |
| [31] | 2022 | Analysis and Visualization Features in PEVNET |
| [26] | 2022 | VisPaD: Visualization & Pattern Discovery for Fighting Human Trafficking |
| [33] | 2022 | Human Trafficking Interdiction Problem: A Data Driven Approach to Modeling and Analysis |
| [29] | 2021 | Trafficking and Technology: Exploring the Role of Digital Communication Technologies in the Belgian Human Trafficking Business |
| [4] | 2021 | Integrated framework for criminal network extraction from Web |
| [7] | 2021 | Q -Rung Orthopair Fuzzy Matroids with Application to Human Trafficking |
| [11] | 2021 | Women trafficking networks: Structure and stages of women trafficking in five Dutch small-scale networks |
| [32] | 2020 | Generalized fuzzy graph connectivity parameters with application to human trafficking |
| [10] | 2019 | Understanding law enforcement strategies and needs for combating human trafficking |
| [21] | 2019 | Connectivity index of a fuzzy graph and its application to human trafficking |
| [20] | 2019 | Coupled clustering of time-series and networks |
| [36] | 2015 | Building and Using a Knowledge Graph to Combat Human Trafficking |
| [35] | 2014 | Data integration from open internet sources and network detection to combat underage sex trafficking |
| [39] | 2012 | Data integration from internet sources to combat sex trafficking of minors |

trafficking data, the ways they are visualized, and the tools that accomplish those visualizations.

### 3.4 Data Extraction and Analysis Procedures

We conducted a full-text review of each selected study to extract information relevant to our three research questions. Articles were assessed for alignment with RQ1 (types of data), RQ2 (visualization techniques), and RQ3 (tools or platforms), and were systematically coded accordingly.

To identify conceptual patterns and support consistent classification, we organized the extracted data along two primary axes: theoretical visualization models and implemented visualization tools. This distinction enabled us to distinguish between general visualization frameworks and practical software applications.

Through thematic clustering, we organized the findings into coherent categories. These insights were synthesized into structured sections in the results and discussion, focusing on coverage gaps and future research opportunities.

# 4 Results

This section presents the results of the mapping study, aligned with the three research questions in Sect. 3. Findings are organized by data types, visualization techniques, and tools, accompanied by a summary. Of the 519 papers identified, only a small subset met the relevance and accessibility criteria, reflecting the sensitive nature of trafficking data and the limited methodological diversity in law enforcement research. 15 papers were selected for analysis (see Table 2), supplemented by two tools evaluated through developer interviews.

## 4.1 RQ1: Types of Human Trafficking Data

Two main types of data are commonly used to support human trafficking visualizations. The first category comprises law enforcement and case records, which include incident reports, wiretap transcripts, and various official documents. These sources provide verified and well-documented information on trafficking operations. For example, Sen et al. [33] used incidence data from the Las Vegas Metropolitan Police Department to analyze traffickers' movement patterns and inform checkpoint placement strategies. Their analysis was limited to routes ending in Las Vegas, but they noted that incorporating data from other cities could support a more comprehensive reconstruction of the paths. Similarly, Diviák et al. [11] examined five trafficking cases involving women and extracted actor networks from wiretap transcripts, suspect and witness statements, and police reports. The researchers mapped relationships between individuals, such as facilitators and traffickers, by tracing their roles within the same cases.

The second category comprises web-scraped and media-based data, which are more readily accessible to researchers. These include escort advertisements, news articles, and public images. Afra et al. [4] compiled a set of 84 crime-related keywords to identify potential trafficking content across media sources. Their method achieved a 95% accuracy rate in identifying crime-related data, from which additional keywords and personal names were extracted for visualization. Deeb-Swihart et al. [10] applied a similar approach to analyze escort advertisements, utilizing both textual and image-based cues to detect suspicious postings. Silva et al. [35] detailed a scraping procedure targeting escort websites, including categorizing location-specific directories and conducting automated crawls multiple times daily using rotating IP addresses to avoid detection. Wang et al. [39] adopted a comparable approach, emphasizing that some advertisements are intentionally poorly formatted to appear more approachable or to evade automated detection systems.

Although law enforcement data are typically more detailed and reliable, they are often inaccessible due to legal and privacy restrictions. Consequently, researchers frequently rely on web-scraped data, which, while more accessible, present challenges related to quality, completeness, and standardization. As a result, researchers often tailor their visualization methods to the available data.

### 4.2 RQ2: Visualization Techniques for Human Trafficking Data

The selected studies apply diverse visualization methods, each aimed at analyzing different aspects of trafficking data. These techniques fall into several categories, including structural network visualization, geospatial mapping, temporal trend analysis, and cluster-based or stage-based representation.

Among these methods, graph-based visualization is the most prevalent, used to depict relationships among individuals by encoding entities as nodes and their interactions as edges. In these visualizations, entities such as traffickers or victims are represented as nodes, and their interactions, such as co-involvement in the same case or communication links, are shown as edges. Studies such as Diviák et al. [11], Afra et al. [4], and Deeb-Swihart et al. [10] use this approach to reconstruct criminal networks from structured records or web-scraped data. Some models go further by linking individuals to specific roles or tasks, enabling the identification of central figures and operational hierarchies.

In addition to structural representations, several studies incorporate spatial dimensions to capture geographic patterns in trafficking activity. Temporal and behavioral trends are explored using line charts, time-series plots, and clustering techniques, which help reveal peaks, recurring behaviors, and long-term shifts in trafficking activity [31,38]. Some studies further support forensic analysis by allowing users to trace these patterns back to individual ads or actors. Predictive visualizations have also been employed to estimate how trafficking activity may evolve in the near future [31].

Cluster-based or stage-based visualizations are also applied to uncover hidden patterns or operational phases. Liu et al. [20] integrate temporal and structural clustering to group actors with similar behavioral signatures. Diviák et al. [11] segment the trafficking process into distinct stages, recruitment, transport, and exploitation, allowing visual separation of roles and functions within the network.

A few studies also present conceptual models grounded in fuzzy logic and graph theory [7,21,32]. While not tested on real data, these frameworks suggest promising directions for future research.

### 4.3 RQ3: Visualization Tools

Through our literature research and a few personal interviews with experts, we discovered seven tools that utilize human trafficking data to construct graphs for analysis. Each tool is described below, followed by a comparison.

*TRAFFICVIS:* TRAFFICVIS [38] is designed to identify trafficking patterns in escort advertisements by combining metadata and clustering techniques. Implemented in Python, it enables both pattern detection and user-driven labeling.

The system first applies text clustering to form micro-clusters of similar ads, then links them into higher-level meta-clusters using shared metadata [19].

Its interface includes five main panels that visualize spatial trends, posting timelines, and ad content:

1. **Micro-cluster**: Displays posting behavior of top-active ad clusters.
2. **Timeline**: Presents time series of posting frequency and location shifts.
3. **Map**: Illustrates geographic distribution of ads.
4. **Text**: Lists and compares ad text content within clusters.
5. **Labeling**: Enables classification of meta-clusters into predefined categories such as Trafficking, Scam, or Spam.

The system focuses on textual and metadata analysis; image data is not included. Expert evaluation confirmed the system's usability and labeling efficiency, with tasks typically completed within three minutes, faster than other tools. The tool is built with the Streamlit framework and is publicly available.

*VisPaD:* Developed by the creators of TRAFFICVIS, VisPaD [26] is a Python-based tool designed to analyze escort advertisement data with enhanced analytical features. It retains TRAFFICVIS's two-level clustering structure, but focuses on exploratory analytics and feature-driven comparison.

Alongside panels for viewing ad frequency, metadata trends, and geo-textual content, VisPaD introduces two additional modules for advanced cluster exploration. In addition to these, VisPaD introduces two advanced data exploration panels. The first panel reduces the high-dimensional cluster feature space to 2D using ICA [17], t-SNE [22], or UMAP [24], enabling visual comparison and label-based coloring. The second panel displays feature-level summaries and correlations, allowing users to explore variable distributions across selected clusters. The tool is built with Dash and Plotly and remains publicly available [25].

*PEVNET:* PEVNET [31] is a desktop-based visualization framework implemented in C# using the FLEX tool in Visual Studio.Net. Its key innovation lies in capturing temporal repetition in criminal behavior, an aspect often overlooked by traditional network tools. The system addresses this challenge by integrating multi-dimensional visual analytics to reveal structural and temporal patterns in complex criminal datasets. To support this, PEVNET offers the following:

1. **Network Visualization Features:** These include centrality detection, node customization, detail-on-demand overlays, cluster-based summaries, and inter-subnetwork detection.
2. **Temporal Visualization Features:** The system enables trend and temporal pattern analysis through calendar-based filtering and graphical overlays, helping analysts examine repeated behaviors and coordinated activity.
3. **Composite Features:** These support high-level structural abstraction through encircle, expand, and collapse functionalities, allowing sub-networks to be grouped or isolated for focused investigation.

The interface supports drag-and-drop editing, filtering, and layered views, enabling analysts to transition between detailed inspection and global pattern recognition. Analysts can customize calendar views to compare activity across timeframes or detect periods of overlap between different criminal entities.

PEVNET's feature set is further organized into three hierarchical levels, basic, prerequisite, and primary, based on their role in supporting investigative tasks. Primary features (e.g., sub-cluster detection, timeline overlays) are designed to provide core analytical value, while prerequisite and basic features ensure usability and flexibility. Although not publicly accessible, PEVNET is a robust tool for law enforcement handling complex, time-sensitive data.

*i2 Analyst's Notebook:* i2 Analyst's Notebook is a desktop platform widely used by investigators to visualize and analyze structured data in complex cases developed by IBM. It is extensively used in law enforcement, intelligence, military, and financial sectors for uncovering complex relationships, events, and patterns across large-scale networks. Given its wide deployment, the system allows analysts to construct association, temporal, spatial, statistical, and spreadsheet-based views, supporting multi-modal analysis of up to 50,000 entities. Users can define custom entities and relationships across more than 550 types, without adhering to a fixed schema. Structured data can be imported via CSV, Excel, or drag-and-drop interfaces using a visual import wizard.

Beyond the desktop client, i2 Online offers web-based integration with a wide range of external sources, including open platforms like Twitter and the Wayback Machine, as well as licensed datasets such as LexisNexis Accurint and Shadow Dragon, enabling IP tracing, dark web mining, and cross-platform entity resolution. Some important features include:

1. **Flexible Data Acquisition:** Supports diverse data types such as call logs, financial transactions, IP addresses, and forensic records. Data import is enabled via wizard-based tools or direct drag-and-drop, with extensibility for live database connections.
2. **Custom Data Modeling:** Empowers users to construct association and timeline charts tailored to investigative needs, with visual cues like link thickness, node coloring, and annotations.
3. **Multi-View Analysis:** Offers synchronized views, association, temporal, spatial, statistical, and augmented by integrated social network analysis capabilities for identifying key actors, clusters, and communication pathways.
4. **Briefing and Dissemination:** Facilitates creation of visual briefing charts, including redacted versions for varying security levels. Outputs are easily shareable via the free i2 Chart Reader, even with non-licensed users.

The i2 suite also integrates with specialized tools such as Fivecast [1] for behavioral profiling and TexChart [2] for NLP-based document analysis and entity extraction. A 30-day trial version is available, making it accessible for institutional evaluation and training use.

*Other Tools:* In addition to the tools discussed above, several other tools utilize human trafficking data for visualization. One such tool is Spotlight. Using machine learning and big data analytics, Thorn's Spotlight tool [3], developed in collaboration with law enforcement and technology companies, facilitates the identification of human trafficking victims. It helps law enforcement prioritize leads and has drastically shortened investigative timeframes by reviewing over 150,000 daily online escort ads. The success of Spotlight is demonstrated by the over 62,000 cases in which it was used to identify traffickers and victims.

Another visualization tool, Traffic Jam [5], created by Marinus Analytics, is designed to assist law enforcement organizations in combating human trafficking. It analyzes enormous volumes of data from internet advertisements using artificial intelligence, which includes facial recognition technology, to find possible victims of human trafficking. By facilitating faster and more efficient searches across millions of documents, Traffic Jam expedites the investigative process and significantly reduces the time required to identify victims. By offering a data-driven strategy to direct resources toward solving the most serious dangers of human trafficking, this technology represents an advancement in the fight against organized crime, human trafficking, and the search for missing persons.

*Tool Comparison:* The visualization tools reviewed above differ in their usability, analytical scope, technical architecture, and accessibility. Table 3 summarizes these differences. Below, we highlight the main comparative insights:

- **Usability:** TRAFFICVIS and VisPaD are designed for ease of use by non-technical users, featuring intuitive workflows and interfaces. In contrast, PEVNET and i2 Analyst's Notebook require greater manual input but offer advanced analytical capabilities that are better suited for experienced users.
- **Analytical and Visualization Scope:** TRAFFICVIS and VisPaD focus on clustering escort ads and visualizing spatial-temporal patterns. PEVNET and i2 Analyst's Notebook support broader functions, including multi-level network modeling, timeline overlays, and detection of criminal substructures.
- **Development Environment:** TRAFFICVIS and VisPaD are implemented in Python, enabling rapid customization and prototyping. PEVNET is developed in C#, which also allows for extensibility in academic settings. In contrast, i2 Analyst's Notebook is a proprietary system, which may restrict modification, integration, or open-source collaboration.
- **Adoption and Evaluation:** TRAFFICVIS has received positive expert feedback, particularly regarding its interface efficiency. i2 Analyst's Notebook is widely adopted in law enforcement and military sectors. Although formal evaluations of PEVNET and VisPaD are limited, both have been effectively applied in research contexts.

Overall, graph-based visualizations are the most consistently supported feature across tools. Only TRAFFICVIS and VisPaD offer full public access with integrated spatial, temporal, and clustering functionality. However, most tools have not been subjected to systematic usability testing or cross-tool benchmarking, indicating a clear gap for future empirical evaluation.

**Table 3.** Comparison of Tools Across Key Dimensions

| Tool | Data Source | Graph | Map | Time Series | Clustering | Public? |
|---|---|---|---|---|---|---|
| TRAFFICVIS | Ads | ✓ | ✓ | ✓ | ✓ | Yes |
| VisPaD | Ads | ✓ | ✓ | ✓ | ✓ | Yes |
| PEVNET | Law records | ✓ | – | ✓ | Partial | No |
| i2 Analyst's NB | Mixed | ✓ | Partial | Partial | – | No |
| Spotlight | Ads | ✓ | – | – | Partial | No |
| Traffic Jam | Ads + Face | ✓ | – | – | Partial | No |
| TexChart | Text | ✓ | – | – | – | No |

## 5 Discussion

This study reviews current visualization methods and tools for analyzing human trafficking networks, identifying several limitations that hinder their effectiveness in real-world applications. One persistent challenge is integrating diverse data sources. Law enforcement records offer accurate and structured information, but access is restricted due to legal and privacy concerns. On the other hand, web-scraped advertisement data are more readily available but often noisy and inconsistent. Without standardized frameworks for combining these heterogeneous sources, comprehensive analysis remains limited. Future research should explore privacy-preserving methods, such as federated learning or synthetic data generation, to support secure and responsible data sharing among stakeholders.

Another concern is the lack of systematic evaluation for existing tools. While systems such as TRAFFICVIS and i2 Analyst's Notebook are widely referenced, few have been tested using standardized benchmarks. Usability, scalability, and analytical effectiveness are seldom assessed in comparative studies. The development of open benchmarks and datasets would enable more rigorous evaluation and inform improvements in tool design.

There is also a noticeable disconnect between theory and application. Several papers propose novel frameworks based on fuzzy logic or graph theory, but these models are rarely implemented or validated with real-world data. Bridging this gap requires more emphasis on translating conceptual models into deployable systems and evaluating them in operational contexts.

In terms of visualization strategy, graph-based methods continue to dominate, but are often used in isolation. Temporal and spatial dimensions are underutilized, and few tools support multimodal integration of text, imagery, location, and time. Visualization platforms that combine these modalities within interactive interfaces could greatly enhance analytical depth and interpretability.

Finally, current tools often fail to accommodate the diverse roles and expertise of their users. While TRAFFICVIS and VisPaD focus on ease of use for non-specialists, and PEVNET and i2 Analyst's Notebook offer more advanced capabilities for trained investigators, few systems are adaptable across different user needs. Role-specific customization and modular interfaces could improve accessibility and impact across various domains, from policy analysis to investigative journalism.

In general, although progress has been made, the field would benefit from more robust data integration, standardized evaluation practices, practical validation of theoretical models, and more inclusive, user-centered design.

## 6 Threats to Validity

Following the framework by Wohlin et al. [42], we discuss four validity threats that may affect this study: construct, internal, external, and conclusion validity.

*Construct Validity.* Construct validity examines whether the study reflects the intended concepts. To address this, we refined the search query iteratively with expert input to ensure relevance across key databases. Inclusion and exclusion criteria were applied consistently. To minimize the risk of missing relevant studies, we employed backward snowballing during the screening process.

*Internal Validity.* Internal validity concerns potential biases during data extraction, particularly due to inconsistent terminology, incomplete reporting, or absence of relevant information in primary studies. Since Phase 4 of our SMS involves extracting nuanced and often implicit content, this stage is especially error-prone. To mitigate these risks, we cross-validated the extracted data against prior surveys and meta-analyses to ensure alignment with established classifications. Additionally, multiple researchers independently reviewed the qualitative synthesis to minimize subjective interpretation and to ensure that our summaries remain faithful to the original studies without introducing analytical bias.

*External Validity.* This study focuses specifically on visualization tools used in human trafficking research. Therefore, the findings may not be generalizable to broader domains. Moreover, limitations inherent in the reviewed studies are carried into this synthesis, affecting its external applicability.

*Conclusion Validity.* Conclusion validity concerns the accuracy and reproducibility of results. We mitigated this threat by including a larger set of primary studies than previous reviews, ensuring statistical robustness. Descriptive findings are based on multiple sources, reducing sensitivity to individual classification errors. The methodology is thoroughly documented to ensure reproducibility.

## 7 Conclusion

This study systematically maps existing visualization tools and methods used to investigate human trafficking networks. Through a structured review of 15 relevant studies, we examined how visualization techniques have been applied to reveal the structure and dynamics of trafficking activities.

While human trafficking generates extensive data, it remains difficult to visualize and interpret such information effectively. Researchers have explored various methods, including spatial mapping, temporal analysis, and graph-based network visualizations, to analyze the complex relationships embedded in trafficking operations. These tools are intended to support predictive modeling and guide law enforcement interventions.

We identified four major tools, TRAFFICVIS, VisPaD, PEVNET, and i2 Analyst's Notebook, that reflect different priorities and user bases. TRAFFICVIS and VisPaD emphasize accessibility and ease of use, catering to non-technical stakeholders, while PEVNET and i2 Analyst's Notebook provide more advanced analytical functionality for professional investigators. This variation underscores the need for role-specific interfaces and flexible interaction designs.

The review also highlights several gaps, including limited data integration, lack of standardized evaluation, and insufficient support for multimodal inputs or diverse user needs. Effective visual analytics depend on the availability and combination of data from disparate sources, such as law enforcement records, online advertisements, and social media, which are often siloed due to privacy and access constraints.

Our findings highlight the importance of visualization in understanding and combating human trafficking, while identifying key areas for future improvement. Advancing this field will require the development of better data-sharing frameworks, comparative evaluations of existing tools, and user-centered system design tailored to operational needs.

**Acknowledgments.** Part of this work was funded by the National Science Foundation under grants CNS-2210091, OPP-2146068, CHE-1905043, and CNS-2136961. The authors thank the Rivas.AI Lab (https://lab.rivas.ai) for the support and helpful feedback throughout this project.

**Disclosure of Interests.** The authors have no competing interests to declare that are relevant to the content of this article.

## References

1. Fivecast. https://www.fivecast.com/. Accessed 02 May 2024
2. Texchart. https://i2group.com/i2-textchart. Accessed 02 May 2024
3. Thorn's spotlight tool. https://centerforimprovinginvestigations.org/human-trafficking-investigations/. Accessed 02 May 2024
4. Afra, S., Alhajj, R.: Integrated framework for criminal network extraction from web. J. Inf. Sci. **47**(2), 206–226 (2021). https://doi.org/10.1177/0165551519888606
5. Analytics, M.: Traffic jam. https://www.marinusanalytics.com/. Accessed 02 May 2024
6. Analytics, N.: Netmap. http://www.netmap.com. Accessed 02 May 2024
7. Asif, M., Kattan, D.A., Pamuar, D., Ali, G.: q-rung orthopair fuzzy matroids with application to human trafficking. Discret. Dyn. Nat. Soc. **2021**(1), 8261118 (2021). https://doi.org/10.1155/2021/8261118

8. Catanese, S., Ferrara, E., Fiumara, G.: Forensic analysis of phone call networks. Soc. Netw. Anal. Min. **3**(1), 15–33 (2012). https://doi.org/10.1007/s13278-012-0060-1
9. Chen, H., Zeng, D., Atabakhsh, H., Wyzga, W., Schroeder, J.: Coplink: managing law enforcement data and knowledge. Commun. ACM **46**(1), 28–34 (2003)
10. Deeb-Swihart, J., Endert, A., Bruckman, A.: Understanding law enforcement strategies and needs for combating human trafficking **10**(1145/3290605), 3300561 (2019)
11. Diviák, T., Dijkstra, J.K., van der Wijk, F., Oosting, I., Wolters, G.: Women trafficking networks: structure and stages of women trafficking in five Dutch small-scale networks. Eur. J. Criminol. (2021) https://doi.org/10.1177/14773708211053135
12. Doncheva, N., Morris, J., Gorodkin, J., Jensen, L.: Cytoscape StringApp: network analysis and visualization of proteomics data (2018). https://doi.org/10.1101/438192
13. Ferrara, E., De Meo, P., Catanese, S., Fiumara, G.: Detecting criminal organizations in mobile phone networks. Expert Syst. Appl. **41**(13), 5733–5750 (2014). https://doi.org/10.1016/j.eswa.2014.03.024
14. i2 Group: Analyst's notebook. https://i2group.com/i2-analysts-notebook. Accessed 02 May 2024
15. Haider, J.D., Seidler, P., Pohl, M., Kodagoda, N., Adderley, R., Wong, B.L.W.: How analysts think: Sense-making strategies in the analysis of temporal evolution and criminal network structures and activities. Proc. Hum. Factors Ergon. Soc. Annu. Meet. **61**(1), 193–197 (2017). https://doi.org/10.1177/1541931213601532
16. Hill, L.: Successes and challenges in implementing a human trafficking screening tool in a local detention center. J. Appl. Soc. Sci. **18**, 241–258 (2023). https://doi.org/10.1177/19367244231219940
17. Hyvärinen, A., Oja, E.: Independent component analysis: algorithms and applications. Neural Netw. **13**(4–5), 411–430 (2000)
18. Kitchenham, B., Pearl Brereton, O., Budgen, D., Turner, M., Bailey, J., Linkman, S.: Systematic literature reviews in software engineering a systematic literature review. Inf. Softw. Technol. **51**(1), 7–15 (2009). https://doi.org/10.1016/j.infsof.2008.09.009. special Section - Most Cited Articles in 2002 and Regular Research Papers special Section - Most Cited Articles in 2002 and Regular Research Papers
19. Lee, M.C., et al.: Infoshield: generalizable information-theoretic human-trafficking detection. In: 2021 IEEE 37th International Conference on Data Engineering (ICDE), pp. 1116–1127. IEEE (2021)
20. Liu, Y., Zhu, L., Szekely, P., Galstyan, A., Koutra, D.: Coupled clustering of time-series and networks, pp. 531–539 (2019). https://doi.org/10.1137/1.9781611975673.60
21. Binu, M., Mathew, S., Mordeson, J.: Connectivity index of a fuzzy graph and its application to human trafficking. Fuzzy Sets Syst. **360**, 117–136 (2019). https://doi.org/10.1016/j.fss.2018.06.007
22. Van der Maaten, L., Hinton, G.: Visualizing data using t-SNE. J. Mach. Learn. Res. **9**(11) (2008)
23. Makin, D.A., Bye, C.: Commodification of flesh: data visualization techniques and interest in the licit sex industry. Deviant Behav. **39**(1), 46–63 (2016). https://doi.org/10.1080/01639625.2016.1260383
24. McInnes, L., Healy, J., Melville, J.: UMAP: Uniform manifold approximation and projection for dimension reduction (2020)
25. Nair, P.: Vispad. https://github.com/nair-p/VisPaD (2024). Accessed 02 May 2024

26. Nair, P., et al.: VisPad: visualization and pattern discovery for fighting human trafficking. pp. 273–277 (2022). https://doi.org/10.1145/3487553.3524263
27. Nulhaqim, S., Deliarnoor, N.: Tech tools for anticipating human trafficking in archipelago state. Int. J. Adv. Sci. Eng. Inf. Technol. **11**, 1084–1091 (2021). https://doi.org/10.18517/ijaseit.11.3.11265
28. Petersen, R.R., Wiil, U.K.: Crimefighter investigator: a novel tool for criminal network investigation. In: 2011 European Intelligence and Security Informatics Conference, pp. 197–202. IEEE (2011)
29. Raets, S., Janssens, J.: Trafficking and technology: exploring the role of digital communication technologies in the Belgian human trafficking business. Eur. J. Crim. Policy Res. **27**(2), 215–238 (2021). https://doi.org/10.1007/s10610-019-09429-z
30. Rasheed, A., Wiil, U.K.: A tool for analysis and visualization of criminal networks. In: 2015 17th UKSim-AMSS International Conference on Modelling and Simulation (UKSim). IEEE (2015). https://doi.org/10.1109/uksim.2015.64
31. Rasheed, A., Wiil, U.K., Ali Khan, M.M.: Analysis and visualization features in PEVNET. pp. 28–38 (2022). https://doi.org/10.1145/3561278.3561288
32. Sebastian, A., Mordeson, J.N., Mathew, S.: Generalized fuzzy graph connectivity parameters with application to human trafficking. Mathematics **8**(3) (2020). https://doi.org/10.3390/math8030424
33. Sen, A., et al.: Human trafficking interdiction problem: a data driven approach to modeling and analysis (2022). https://doi.org/10.1109/HST56032.2022.10025431
34. Si, Y.W., Cheong, S.H., Fong, S., Biuk-Aghai, R.P., Cheong, T.M.: A layered approach to link analysis and visualization of event data. In: Seventh International Conference on Digital Information Management (ICDIM 2012). IEEE (Aug 2012). https://doi.org/10.1109/icdim.2012.6360101
35. Silva, D.R., Philpot, A., Sundararajan, A., Bryan, N.M., Hovy, E.: Data integration from open internet sources and network detection to combat underage sex trafficking, pp. 86–90 (2014). https://doi.org/10.1145/2612733.2612746
36. Szekely, P., et al.: Building and using a knowledge graph to combat human trafficking. In: Arenas, M., Corcho, O., Simperl, E., Strohmaier, M., d'Aquin, M., Srinivas, K., Groth, P., Dumontier, M., Heflin, J., Thirunarayan, K., Staab, S. (eds.) The Semantic Web - ISWC 2015, pp. 205–221. Springer International Publishing, Cham (2015). https://doi.org/10.1007/978-3-319-25010-6_12
37. Thorn: Spotlight. https://www.thorn.org/spotlight/ (2024). Accessed 21 May 2025
38. Vajiac, C., et al.: TrafficVis: Visualizing organized activity and spatio-temporal patterns for detecting and labeling human trafficking. IEEE Trans. Visual Comput. Graphics **29**(1), 53–62 (2023). https://doi.org/10.1109/TVCG.2022.3209403
39. Wang, H., Cai, C., Philpot, A., Latonero, M., Hovy, E.H., Metzler, D.: Data integration from open internet sources to combat sex trafficking of minors, pp. 246–252 (2012). https://doi.org/10.1145/2307729.2307769
40. Wiil, U.K.: Issues for the next generation of criminal network investigation tools. In: 2013 European Intelligence and Security Informatics Conference. IEEE (Aug 2013). https://doi.org/10.1109/eisic.2013.9
41. Wiil, U.K., Gniadek, J., Memon, N.: Crimefighter assistant-a knowledge management tool for terrorist network analysis. In: International Conference on Knowledge Management and Information Sharing, vol. 2, pp. 15–24. SCITEPRESS (2010)
42. Wohlin, C., Runeson, P., Höst, M., Ohlsson, M.C., Regnell, B., Wesslén, A.: Experimentation in software engineering. Springer Science and Business Media (2012)
43. Zakopcanova, K., Rehacek, M., Batrna, J., Plakinger, D., Stoppel, S., Kozlikova, B.: Visilant: Visual support for the exploration and analytical process tracking

in criminal investigations. IEEE Trans. Visual Comput. Graphics **27**(2), 881–890 (2021). https://doi.org/10.1109/tvcg.2020.3030356

44. Zallot, R., Oberg, N., Gerlt, J.: The EFI web resource for genomic enzymology tools: leveraging protein, genome, and metagenome databases to discover novel enzymes and metabolic pathways. Biochemistry **58**, 4169–4182 (2019). https://doi.org/10.1021/acs.biochem.9b00735
45. Zhou, P., Liu, Y., Zhao, M., Lou, X.: Criminal network analysis with interactive strategies: a proof of concept study using mobile call logs. In: Proceedings of the 28th International Conference on Software Engineering and Knowledge Engineering. SEKE2016, KSI Research Inc. and Knowledge Systems Institute Graduate School (Jul 2016). https://doi.org/10.18293/seke2016-116

# LOD (Level of Detail) Based Optimized Privacy-Preserving Navigation

Hyun-A. Park(✉)

Honam University, 120, Honamdae-Gil, Gwangju, South Korea
kokokzi@honam.ac.kr

**Abstract.** This study proposes an integrated framework based on LOD (Level of Detail) to simultaneously achieve personal privacy protection and efficient data processing in drone navigation systems. The core of the framework is to minimize unnecessary personal information collection by differentially processing landmarks in high resolution (LOD 4) and surrounding areas in low resolution (LOD 0-2) through a dynamic LOD allocation algorithm. For route optimization, A algorithm extension is applied to perform route planning that reflects privacy risk ($\lambda = 1.5$) in the cost function. In terms of communication security, lightweight hybrid encryption is introduced to hierarchically apply AES-256-GCM and ChaCha20 according to data importance, and HMAC-SHA256-based integrity verification is integrated. The proposed system automatically limits the LOD level when the remaining battery level is less than 30% through a real-time dynamic adjustment mechanism, thereby ensuring resource efficiency.

**Keywords:** Drone Navigation · LOD-based Privacy Preservation · Lightweight Hybrid Cryptography · Dynamic Path Optimization · Real-time Data Hierarchization

## 1 Introduction

Please note that the first paragraph of a section or subsection is not indented. The first paragraphs that follows a table, figure, equation etc. does not have an indent, either.

Subsequent paragraphs, however, are indented. Drone technology is expanding its scope of application in various fields such as logistics delivery, urban management, disaster response, and agricultural monitoring. In particular, autonomous navigation systems using drones are receiving attention of the government and corporate levels, and the focus is on optimizing movement in complex environments such as cities. However, while drones collect data and move in various environments, the images captured by high-resolution cameras and sensors can unintentionally record individuals' daily activities. In particular, such data is likely to infringe on individuals' privacy when operating drones in residential areas or public places. Privacy issues are also important in terms of protecting individuals' rights, and are a key task that must be addressed to increase the public acceptance of drone technology. Accordingly, technologies that can minimize unnecessary collection of personal information for drone navigation should be studied.

The key contributions of this study are as follows:


R. Stahlbock et al. (Eds.): CSCE 2025, CCIS 2938, pp. 470–482, 2027.
https://doi.org/10.1007/978-3-032-22196-4_34

1. LOD-integrated path planning algorithm:
   - Generate high-risk area avoidance path by incorporating privacy risk ($\lambda = 1.5$) into the A* algorithm cost function
   - Implement dynamic path recalculation mechanism when real-time environmental changes are detected
   - Dynamic LOD allocation through comprehensive evaluation of distance (d), importance (i), and privacy risk (p)
2. Energy-aware resource management:
3. Hierarchical encryption communication architecture:
   - Differential encryption by data importance: landmark data (AES-256-GCM), surrounding data (ChaCha20)
   - Minimize packet loss through MQTT QoS Level 2
4. Pure geographic information-based privacy protection:
   - Gaussian blurring intensity adjustment system linked to LOD level
   - Implement automatic protection enhancement mechanism by time zone

## 2 Preliminaries

### 2.1 Participants

- CC(control center): A type of TTP. Responsible for all encryption key management and authentication. It is not only a head tower for security, but also a control center for all work.
- Drones: Belong to an organization and perform monitoring or organization-related work. When affiliated with a disaster relief agency, it monitors and reports on incidents. In a delivery system, it provides delivery services.
- CS(Cloud Server): This is where all data related to monitoring and organization are stored.

### 2.2 Application Scenario

It is assumed an organization that handles disaster situations such as fires or traffic accidents. This organization dispatches drones to observe the detailed scene of the incident and transmits on-site video to establish a systematic response system. To accomplish this task, all drones are registered in advance for the CC so that they can mutually authenticate with the CC and CS. The drone has a private key and public key pair based on the public key encryption method and uses this to create an ID and password. When an incident occurs, this is used for authentication and a session key to be used for each event is generated through a key sharing technique. This session key is used for secret communication, and the task is performed by moving to the destination through a dynamic path algorithm based on LOD, and the result is stored in the CS.

## 2.3 Participants Security and System Building Blocks

1) (Level of Detail): is a 3D rendering optimization technique proposed by Funkhouser and Sequin in the 1990s, which dynamically adjusts the level of detail according to the viewpoint distance of an object [1]. Early research was mainly focused on game graphics, but Udayan J and Kim proposed a spatial information layering model by applying LOD to urban navigation [2]. The Simplification Envelopes technique developed by Cohen et al. has been re-evaluated as a data reduction technique for privacy protection in drone environments [3]. In particular, Udayan J presented a real-time adaptive processing mechanism based on LOD streaming for urban navigation in a multi-level information representation study [4].
2) Privacy Risk: There are two main approaches to drone-based privacy risk assessment:

   - Static space segmentation model: predefines privacy risk zones based on GIS(Geographic Information System) data and zoning information (e.g., residential area = high risk, commercial area = medium risk, industrial complex = low risk).
   - Dynamic object-based model: detects personal identification elements such as people, vehicles, and windows through real-time object recognition (YOLO, etc.) and calculating risk. The limitations of existing studies are that static models are not flexible to environmental changes, and dynamic models can cause additional privacy violations. This study solves this problem by assuming a pre-built privacy risk map [5, 6].

| LOD Level | Resolution | Application | Description |
|---|---|---|---|
| LOD 0 | 16 × 16 pixels | High-risk privacy area | Lowest resolution for privacy protection |
| LOD 1 | 64 × 64 pixels | General residential area | Low resolution for basic shape recognition |
| LOD 2 | 256 × 256 pixels | Commercial area | Medium resolution for identifying structures |
| LOD 3 | 512 × 512 pixels | Traffic hub | high resolution for detailed navigation information |
| LOD 4 | 1024 × 1024 pixels | Key landmark | highest resolution for precise location recognition |

3) AES-256-GCM: is a symmetric key encryption method based on the Advanced Encryption Standard (AES). It uses a 256-bit encryption key, which is one of the strongest key lengths among current commercial encryption standards. "GCM" stands for Galois/Counter Mode, which performs encryption and message authentication simultaneously to ensure the confidentiality and integrity of data. GCM is often used in environments where high-speed processing is required, especially in network communications [7].

4) ChaCha20: is a stream cipher algorithm developed by Daniel J. Bernus. It was designed as an alternative to RC4, providing stronger security and faster performance. The algorithm uses a 256-bit key and performs efficient encryption through counter-based stream generation. ChaCha20 is widely used in environments with limited resources, such as mobile devices, where sophisticated encryption is required [8].
5) HMAC-SHA256: is a combination of the Hash-based Message Authentication Code (HMAC) method and the SHA-256 hash function, and is used to verify the integrity and authenticity of messages. It can verify whether the transmitted message has been tampered with. Since HMAC generates a hash using a secret key, it is difficult for an external party to manipulate the value unless the key is exposed [9].
6) MQTT (Message Queuing Telemetry Transport) Protocol: is a lightweight message transmission protocol, mainly used in resource-constrained environments such as IoT devices. It is based on the publisher-subscriber model, enabling low-bandwidth, high-reliability message transmission [10].
7) A* Algorithm: It is one of the graph search algorithms, used to find the shortest path. It efficiently searches the path using heuristic methods, and guarantees optimality and completeness. The A* algorithm is useful in various fields such as robot path planning, game character movement, and GPS navigation in complex workspace environments. This algorithm works by evaluating the cost from the current location to the target point and selecting the path with the lowest cost.
8) Gaussian Blurring: It is used to reduce noise in the image and give it a smooth effect. This method uses a mask based on the Gaussian function (normal distribution form) to assign a new value by averaging each pixel and its surrounding pixels. This process smoothes the image, reduces details and noise, and blurs the edges of the image.

## 3 Expected Threats

### 3.1 Communication Eavesdropping

Attackers eavesdrop on wireless communications between drones and control centers to intercept transmitted data. In particular, they target Wi-Fi or RF communications in the 2.4 GHz/5.8 GHz bands and use packet sniffing tools to obtain unencrypted data. This poses a risk of exposing sensitive control commands or collected video data.

### 3.2 Command Tampering

A man-in-the-middle intercepts and modifies control commands sent to drones by invading the communication channel. For example, they can change the "return" command to "ascend altitude" or manipulate GPS coordinates to guide the drone to a dangerous area.

### 3.3 Location Tracking

It tracks the drone's real-time location through GPS spoofing or RSSI (Received Signal Strength Indicator) triangulation. This can be exploited for military target surveillance or personal movement tracking, and continuous location data leakage can expose the drone's mission.

### 3.4 Privacy Invasion

Privacy invasion through high-resolution cameras is a key threat. They can film private spaces such as residential windows and balconies, or monitor indoor activities with night infrared photography. 72% of the drone photography privacy invasion incidents that occurred in Korea in 2023 targeted residential areas.

## 4 LOD-Based Privacy Protection Mechanism

### 4.1 LOD Level Definition

The dynamic LOD (Level of Detail) assignment algorithm is a key technology that achieves privacy protection and computational efficiency simultaneously by adjusting the object detail in real time in drone navigation systems. This algorithm comprehensively considers the current location of the drone, the distance to the target object, the privacy risk, and the system performance to assign the optimal LOD level in real time. In the paper, five resolution levels are defined from LOD 0 to LOD 4 [11]. Each level is differentiated according to the privacy risk and navigation accuracy requirements:

This step-by-step classification is an extension of the distance-based LOD technique widely used in the computer graphics field to meet the privacy protection requirements of drones [12, 13].

### 4.2 Dynamic LOD Allocation Algorithm

The dynamic LOD (Level of Detail) allocation algorithm is expressed as a mathematical model that comprehensively considers the drone's location, distance to the object, privacy risk, and system performance (computational resources, battery, etc.) to allocate the optimal LOD level to each object or region in real time.

1) Definition of main variables

- d: distance between the drone and the object
- p: privacy risk (0–1)
- i: object importance (0–1)
- c: system computational resources (e.g. CPU usage, 0–1)
- e: battery level (0–1)
- LOD: LOD level to allocate (integer, 0–4)

2) Basic distance-based LOD formula

LOD can be generally determined as a step function based on a distance threshold1:

$$\mathrm{LOD}_{\mathrm{distance}}(\mathrm{d}) = \begin{cases} 4 & d < D_1 \\ 3 & D_1 \le d < D_2 \\ 2 & D_2 \le d < D_3 \\ 1 & D_3 \le d < D_4 \\ 0 & D_4 \le d < D_5 \end{cases}$$

Where $D_1, D_2, D_3, D_4$ are the threshold distance values (e.g. 50 m, 75 m, 100 m, 150 m).

3) Privacy Risk and Importance Adjustment

It dynamically adjusts LOD based on privacy risk and importance:

$$LOD_{adj} = LOD_{distance}(d) + \alpha \cdot i - \beta \cdot p.$$

- $\alpha$: Importance weight (e.g. 1)
- β: Privacy risk weight (e.g. 2)

LOD is limited to the range of 0 to 4: $LOD = \min(4, \max(0, \text{round}(LOD_{adj})))$

4) System Resource and Energy Compensation

Additional compensation is possible based on the real-time status of the drone (e.g., computational resources, battery, etc.) 1:

$$LOD_{final} = LOD - \gamma \cdot c - \delta \cdot (1 - e)$$

- γ: computational resource weight (e.g., 1)
- δ: battery weight (e.g., 1)

Similarly, $LOD_{final}$ is limited to the range of 0 to 4.

5) Comprehensive Dynamic LOD Allocation Formula

Finally, the dynamic LOD allocation algorithm can be formulated as follows:

$$LOD = \min(4, \max(0, \text{round}(LODdistance(d) + \alpha i - \beta p - \gamma c - \delta(1 - e))))$$

This formula comprehensively reflects distance, importance, privacy risk, computational resources, and battery status.

6) Heuristic function (including path finding)

During path finding, we use a heuristic cost function that includes privacy risk and LOD weights:

$$f(n) = g(n) + h(n)$$
$$h(n) = \text{EuclideanDistance}(n, G) + \lambda \cdot \text{PrivacyRisk}(n)$$
$$\text{cost}(n, n') = \text{distance}(n, n') + \mu \cdot (1 - LOD(n'))$$

- n: The node currently being evaluated (e.g. the drone's current location)
- n′: the neighboring node to reach after moving (next location)
- g(n): Cumulative path cost so far
- h(n): Expected cost to goal (including privacy risk)
- λ, μ: Privacy and LOD weights 3 [14, 15]

## 5 LOD-Based Hybrid Encryption Communication

### 5.1 Notation

- Encryption keys for each participant

- cr, $g^{cr}$: CC's private key, public key
- dr, $g^{dr}$: Drone's private key, public key
- IDd, PWd: Drone's ID, PW
- sr, $g^{sr}$: CS manager's private key, public key

- h: Hash function
- $\alpha_i$: *i*-th session key, randomly generated.
- $E_k(M)$: Function to encrypt message M with encryption key k
- $D_k(M)$: Function to decrypt message M with encryption key k

The cryptographic communication is composed of 4 stages.

### 5.2 Registration and Key Generation Stage

Every drone registers for CC and receives its own private key/public key and certificate. In addition, each drone receives an ID and password.

If the private key and public key of the drone are dr and g^dr, the drone ID becomes its public key g^dr, and the drone's password PWd = h(ID ⊕ dr).

### 5.3 Authentication and Mission Transfer

When an event occurs, CC transfers a mission to the drone. At this time, mutual authentication is performed simultaneously.

1. CC → Drone: $E_{\mathrm{PWd}}(M_1||\alpha_i)$
2. Drone → CC: $E_{\alpha i}(g^{dr} \oplus g^{sr})$
3. CC: $D_{\alpha i}(E_{\alpha i}(g^{dr} \oplus g^{sr})) = g^{dr} \oplus g^{sr}$

$$\Rightarrow g^{sr} \oplus (g^{dr} \oplus g^{sr}) = g^{dr}$$

Since the message sent by CC is encrypted with PWd, it means that the person who can decrypt it and check the message is the person who knows PWd, which means mutual authentication.

Here, the message M contains the description of the event (location and situation, etc.), the mission that the drone must perform, and all the contents about the result report. And, α_i means the session key between CC and the drone. Instead of using Diffie-Hellman key exchange considering the computational ability of the drone, authentication and key sharing are achieved simultaneously with this formula.

The second formula means that the legitimate drone received the message from CC. This is because only a person who knows PWd can decrypt the session key $\alpha_i$, and after decrypting the second formula with that session key, and at third process, CC performs the ⊕ operation on the result value with its own public key $g^{sr}$, and then the public key value of the corresponding drone, $g^{dr}$, is computed, which guarantees that authentication and command transmission were performed successfully.

### 5.4 Reaching the Destination Through Navigation

The destination reaching process is implemented in three steps:

1) LOD path planning process

The path planning is carried out in three steps.

**First,** in the initial environment analysis step, GIS data and privacy risk maps are loaded. Residential areas are automatically classified as high-risk areas, commercial areas are set as medium-risk, and industrial complexes are set as low-risk. The starting point (S) and target point (G) are set, and the landmark (L) is designated as a high-resolution (LOD 4) node.

**Second,** *A algorithm-based path generation** is performed. The cost function is defined as $f(n) = g(n) + h(n)$, where $h(n)$ is the sum of the Euclidean distance and the privacy risk penalty. When calculating the path cost, a weight ($\lambda = 1.5$) is given to the high-risk area to preferentially select the avoidance path. In other words, an additional penalty is given when passing through the high-risk area, so that the landmark-centered path is selected as much as possible.

**Third,** the real-time dynamic adjustment step. When a drone moves and detects a new obstacle or privacy risk, it immediately recalculates the path. At this time, the LOD level is automatically adjusted according to the surrounding environment changes, and when entering a high-risk area, the LOD is forcibly lowered by 2 levels (LOD 3 → LOD 1). (Example: LOD_level - = 2 when risk > 0.7).

2) LOD-based data processing

Hierarchical resolution control is applied during the destination approach process:

- Core landmark (50 m radius of destination): LOD 4 ($1024 \times 1024$ pixels).
- Surrounding area: LOD 2 ($256 \times 256$ pixels)
- High-risk area: LOD 0 ($16 \times 16$ pixels) + real-time Gaussian blurring

3) Energy efficiency mechanism

When the battery level is less than 30%, the min(LOD_level, 2) constraint is activated. This reduces the high-resolution processing area and is expected to reduce energy consumption.

4) Verification of arrival at the final destination

When reaching the target point, the triple verification protocol is executed:

1. Check GPS coordinate error ≤3m
2. Check surrounding landmark matching rate ≥90%
3. Hash verification (HMAC-SHA256)

### 5.5 Performing Tasks Such as Taking Pictures and Reporting Results

1) Selective shooting policy

- Landmark: LOD 4 ($1024 \times 1024$ pixels)

- Surrounding area: LOD 2 ($256 \times 256$ pixels)
- High-risk area: LOD 0 ($16 \times 16$ pixels) + automatic blurring

2) Hierarchical encryption process

$$\text{Drone} \rightarrow \text{CC: Rt} = E_{\alpha i}(M_2)$$

3) Result reporting mechanism: Secure transmission phase.

Encrypted data is transmitted with QoS level 2 of MQTT protocol, and is automatically retransmitted in case of packet loss. After transmission is completed, the control center verifies the hash value of all chunks to finally confirm the integrity.

# 6 Analysis

## 6.1 Security Analysis

1) Communication Channel Eavesdropping Defense
The proposed system solves the communication channel eavesdropping threat through AES-256 symmetric key encryption. All data transmission between the drone and the control center is encrypted with a pre-shared secret key (PWd):

- Encryption Process: Encrypt the command data (M) and the session key ($\alpha i$) together with the structure $E_{\mathrm{PWd}}(M \| \alpha i)$
- Key Management: The control center (CC) pre-shares the secret key with the drone as a trusted authority
- Transmission Security: Data is transmitted through an encrypted channel, SSH tunnel

This method is optimized for the limited computational resources of the drone and is efficient for processing large amounts of video data. By using a symmetric key instead of public key encryption, the encryption/decryption speed can be improved.

2) Command tampering attack defense
The method prevents command tampering attack through a three-step mutual authentication protocol:
1. Command transmission phase:
CC → Drone: $E_{\mathrm{PWd}}(M_1 || \alpha_i)$ (the command encrypted with $PWd$ + session key)
2. Drone response phase:
Drone → CC: $E_{\alpha i}(g^{dr} \oplus g^{sr})$ (Drone sends the verification value encrypted with session key)
3. CC verification phase:
4. After decrypting, CC verifies the drone identity by calculating $g^{sr}(g^{dr} \oplus g^{sr}) = g^{dr}$.

This protocol simultaneously guarantees the integrity of command data and sender authentication. It minimizes the computational load by using XOR operation and hash function instead of digital signature.

3) Defending against location tracking attacks

LOD-based path optimization algorithm defends against location tracking attacks:

```
# Algorithm 1: LOD_Drone_Path_Optimization
def h(n): # Heuristic function
    euclidean_distance = compute_distance(n, G)
    privacy_penalty = calculate_privacy_risk(n) #
Penalty based on privacy risk
   return euclidean_distance + privacy_penalty

def cost(n, n'): # Path cost function
    base_cost = distance(n, n')
    lod_cost = get_lod_privacy_cost(n') # LOD-based
privacy cost
    return base_cost + lod_cost
```

- Avoid privacy risk areas: It applies privacy risk penalty to path cost function
- Landmark-centered path: It prefers paths through landmarks (LOD 4) over high-risk areas.
- Real-time dynamic adjustment: It recalculates paths immediately when new threats are detected.

4) Defending against privacy invasion

LOD-based Data Processing Layering prevents privacy invasion with data processing layering:

1. Hierarchical resolution control:
   - LOD 0 (high risk area): 16 × 16 pixel resolution + $\sigma = 3.0$ Gaussian blurring
   - LOD 1 (residential area): 64 × 64 pixel + $\sigma = 2.0$ Gaussian blurring
   - LOD 2 (commercial area): 256 × 256 pixel + $\sigma = 1.0$ Gaussian blurring
   - LOD 3-4 (non-sensitive area): Maintain original resolution (no blurring)
2. Spatial protection mechanism:
   - Geographic zone-based processing:
     - Utilizing predefined privacy risk maps
     - Automatical activation for LOD 0 within 100 m radius of residential area/public facility
   - Temporal restriction:

```
if current_time in (20:00~08:00):
apply_LOD0() # Additional protection for residential
area during night time
```

- Automatically adjust blurring intensity:
  - Distance-based blurring factor: $\sigma = \max(1.0, 3.0 - (\text{distance}/50))$
  - Processing only with distance and area type without fixed object recognition

3. Encrypted storage:
   - Shooting data is transmitted after AES-256 encryption
   - Applying additional encryption layer when storing in the cloud

### 6.2 Efficiency Analysis

1) Design for computational efficiency

We excluded the complex exponentiation of public key encryption and adopted XOR/hash-based lightweight computation. We designed it to enable real-time processing even in the limited CPU environment of the drone by making full use of the parallel processing characteristics of AES-256-GCM. LOD-based data hierarchy dynamically reduces the amount of data to be processed depending on the situation.

2) Energy optimization strategy
   1. Dynamic LOD allocation algorithm

$$\text{LOD} = \min(4, \max(0, \text{round}(\text{LOD\_distance}(d) + \alpha \cdot i - \beta \cdot p - \gamma \cdot c - \delta \cdot (1 - e))))$$

   - Here, the $\delta \cdot (1 - e)$ item is an energy optimization mechanism that reflects the remaining battery level (e).
   - The lower the battery level, the lower the LOD level, which induces a reduction in computational load.

   2. System Resource Compensation Mechanism
      - Combined with $\gamma \cdot c$ item (system computational resource weight):
      - Forced LOD level downgrade when CPU utilization (c) is high
      - Reduced computational load when processing low resolution (LOD 0-2)

   3. Energy-performance trade-off optimization - Dynamic resource allocation principle:
      - High-risk area (LOD 0): Minimum computational resource allocation
      - Landmark (LOD 4): Maximum resource concentration
      - Maximized overall energy efficiency through partial optimization

   4. Encrypted communication efficiency
      - The adoption of 256-bit AES symmetric key encryption and XOR/hash-based operation reduces computational load compared to public key encryption (RSA, etc.), thereby minimizing energy consumption.

3) Communication Efficiency Innovation

Utilizing the topic hierarchy of the MQTT publish-subscribe model, unnecessary data transmission is minimized. The selective data omission mechanism in high-risk areas effectively manages network traffic, and a lightweight HMAC protocol is applied for data integrity verification.

## 7 Discussion and Conclusion

This paper presents an end-to-end solution that integrates LOD-based path optimization and lightweight encryption to address privacy protection issues in drone navigation. The dynamic LOD allocation algorithm reflects distance, privacy risk, and system resource status in real time to determine the optimal resolution level, thereby achieving a balance between navigation accuracy and privacy protection. In terms of communication security, the introduction of a hierarchical encryption strategy improves the efficiency of large-scale data processing, and the HMAC-SHA256-based integrity verification enhances resistance to command tampering attacks.

The main limitation of this study is the lack of real-world verification, requiring performance evaluation under real-world climate conditions through simulation-based design. Future research directions include redesigning the protocol in an ultra-low-latency network optimized for 6G communication environments and verifying its performance through real-world disaster field tests such as fires.

In conclusion, this paper suggests a practical solution to the "functionality vs. privacy" dilemma, which is a key challenge in drone technology. The innovative combination of dynamic resolution control and lightweight encryption will enable the safe proliferation of drones in a variety of fields, including logistics, disaster response, and smart cities, and will be a major milestone for the harmony between technological advancement and human rights protection.

## References


1. Funkhouser, T.A., Sequin, C.H.: Adaptive display algorithm for interactive frame rates during visualization of complex virtual environments. In: Proceedings of the 20th Annual Conference on Computer Graphics and Interactive Techniques (SIGGRAPH 1993) (1993)
2. Divya Udayan, J., Kim, H., Kim, J., Kim, K.: Semantic rendering based on information hierarchy for urban navigation. Appl. Math. Inf. Sci. **9**, 493–504 (2015)
3. Cohen, J., et al.: Simplification envelopes. In: Proceedings of SIGGRAPH 96, pp. 119–128 (1996)
4. Divya Udayan, J., Kim, H., Kim, J., Lee, J., Kim, K.: Multi-level information representation based LOD streaming for urban navigation. In: 2013 International Symposium on Ubiquitous Virtual Reality (2013)
5. Malhotra, N.K., Kim, S.S., Agarwal, J.: Internet users' information privacy concerns (IUIPC): the construct, the scale, and a causal model. Inf. Syst. Res. **15**(4), 336–355 (2004)
6. Lee, D.J., Bang, Y.S., Bae, Y.S.: The role of information transparency in providing personal information online - focusing on the privacy calculus model. Inf. Policy **17**(2), 68–85 (2010)
7. bbkyoo: AES256-GCM. velog.io. https://velog.io/@bbkyoo/AES256-GCM
8. Ko, E.J., Kim, M.J., Lee, Y.J., Kim, J.H.: A 4.56 pJ/b energy-efficient 180nm CMOS process SRAM based CIM for ChaCha20 encryption. In: Proceedings of the Conference of the Korean Institute of Electronics Engineers, Gangwon, Korea, November 22 2024

9. Ravilla, D., Putta, C.S.R.: Implementation of HMAC-SHA256 algorithm for hybrid routing protocols in MANETs. In: Proceedings of the International Conference on Computer and Communication Technologies, 29–30 January 2015
10. mqtt.org: MQTT: The Standard for IoT Messaging. https://mqtt.org/
11. Kang, H.Y., Nam, S.K., Hwang, J.R., Lee, J.Y.: LOD(level of detail) model for utilization of indoor spatial data. J. Korean Soc. Surv. Geod. Photogramm. Cartogr. **36**(6), 545–554 (2018)
12. Luebke, D., Watson, B.: Level of Detail for 3D Graphics. Morgan Kaufmann (2002)
13. Besbes, O., Kanoria, Y., Kumar, A.: Dynamic resource allocation: algorithmic design principles and spectrum of achievable performances. Oper. Res. **73**(3) (2024). https://doi.org/10.1287/opre.2022.0504
14. Tang, H., Zhu, Q., Qin, B., Song, R., Li, Z.: UAV path planning based on third-party risk modeling. Sci. Rep. **13**, Article no. 22259 (2023)
15. Bekhti, M., Achir, N., Boussetta, K., Abdennebi, M.: Drone package delivery: a heuristic approach for UAVs path planning and tracking. EAI Endorsed Trans. Internet Things **3**(9) (2017)

# Data-Driven Transformation: The Role of Analytics and Visualization Champions in Organizational Digital Maturity

Deepshikha Shekhawat[1](✉) and Himesh Singh Chauhan[2]

[1] Business Intelligence Program Manager, AMD, Austin, TX, USA
deepshmba@gmail.com
[2] Rajiv Gandhi Proudyogiki Vishwavidyalaya, Austin, TX, USA

**Abstract.** The article looks into how crucial champions of analytics and visualization are to achieve higher digital maturity in organizations. Through a mixed-methods approach, including case studies and surveys, the study investigates how leadership in analytics and visualization fosters an organization's ability to leverage data for strategic decision-making, process optimization, and enhanced innovation. Based on the results, organizations with people focused on analytics and visualization improve their decision-making, become more efficient, and agile. Champions close the gap between big data and the rest of the organization by propagating the use of data and integrating latest analytics tools in how workers do their jobs. In addition, the study points out that not everyone is eager to change and that there are not enough skilled experts, which keeps data-driven transformation from fulfilling its full potential. It is recommended in the article that empowering analytics and visualization leaders is vital for any group working towards being more digitally advanced, providing suggestions for improvement.

**Keywords:** Data-driven · Digital maturity · Analytics champions · Organizational transformation · Business intelligence · Data visualization

## 1 Introduction

### 1.1 Background to the Study

These days, companies that want to remain competitive rely on data-driven transformations. Organizations are using data more and more to direct their decisions, streamline tasks, and boost their customers' satisfaction. Digital maturity refers to an organization's ability to integrate digital technology, such as data analytics, into its core operations and strategy, with the goal of improving efficiency and innovation (Shah & Murthi 2020). Data analytics and visualizing data help increase digital maturity because it allows decision makers to understand complex information. Analytics means looking at data systematically with computations to find patterns, while visualization is about presenting the same data in a way that is simple to view. As organizations advance in their digital


R. Stahlbock et al. (Eds.): CSCE 2025, CCIS 2938, pp. 483–495, 2027.
https://doi.org/10.1007/978-3-032-22196-4_35

maturity journey, the role of analytics and visualization champions becomes more apparent—these leaders not only advocate for data-driven decision-making but also ensure that analytics and visualization tools are effectively implemented across departments (Grandhi, Patwa, & Saleem 2020).

### 1.2 Overview

The article looks at how champions of analytics and visualization help an organization gain digital maturity. The author first looks into digital maturity and how it impacts data analytics and using technology. Key terms such as "data analytics," "visualization," and "digital maturity" are defined to clarify the concepts used throughout the study. Using algorithms and statistics is a big part of data analytics, while things like pictures and charts make data much easier to understand and use in visualization. The level of digital maturity is how well an organization combines digital technology in its management and decision-making processes. Case studies and research results are used in the article to explain how strong analytics and visualization leadership helps a company grow and go digital.

### 1.3 Problem Statement

There is little research that talks about how analytics and visualization champions help improve a company's digital readiness. While we have done a lot of research on data and technology integration, there is still not much focus on how leaders in analytics and visualization contribute to a company's digital maturity. A lot of organizations encounter difficulties in using data to transform their companies, mainly because of attitude problems, insufficient staff, and limited technology. Whatever your industry, organizations that lack clear direction in data analytics could be incapable of making the most of data and fail at both growing and innovating. This study works to fill this gap by finding out how analytics and visualization champions help organizations improve their digital readiness.

### 1.4 Objectives

The primary objectives of this study are:

- To examine the importance of people who help develop analytics and visualization in raising the digital maturity of businesses.
- To find out how organizations might include more analytics in the decisions they make.
- To determine how leadership in analytics contributes to new ideas, making operations more efficient, and promoting the company's growth.

### 1.5 Scope and Significance

The study covers many industries, ranging from emerging tech startups to existing large companies, mainly focusing on businesses that use data for transformation. It looks into the challenges that organizations have to deal with when using data analytics and visualization as they develop their digital skills. What matters is that this research can give companies clear pointers for developing their data maturity. Paying attention to leadership in analytics and visualization in this study will guide organizations to see that champions are key to driving change within an organization. Results gained from the research can assist managers and decision-makers in boosting their use of data analytics.

## 2 Literature Review

### 2.1 Data-Driven Transformation

Data-driven transformation means making use of data to improve the technology and business areas of a company. On the technology side, continuous intelligence and artificial intelligence (AI) play a pivotal role by enabling fast data processing, which leads to quicker, more informed decision-making. These technologies allow companies to manage and examine large amounts of data instantly and to always learn from the data, which helps in continuous improvement of work activities. The business aspect benefits by turning to AI readiness and taking part in audits and efficient planning and implementation. Using these methods, data findings are put to use in shaping the organization's plans and day-to-day work, which boosts growth and flexibility. Promoting a data-driven culture in businesses makes it easier for them to deal with new market demands and stay successful in the long run. Integrating data helps businesses use it regularly to boost innovation, manage operations well, and achieve steady growth (Fig. 1).

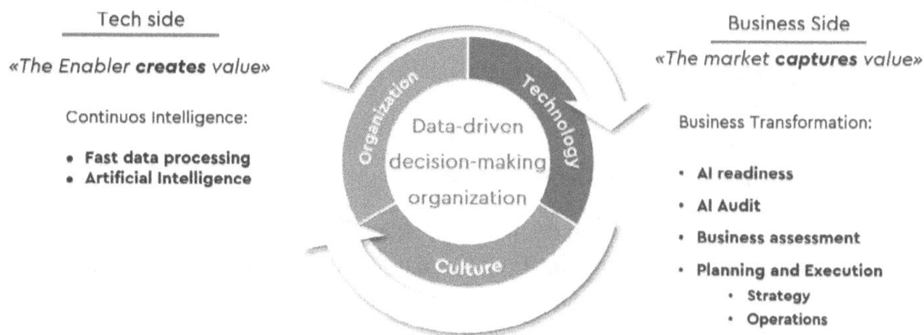


**Fig. 1.** Data-Driven Transformation: Leveraging Data for Value Creation across Technology, Organization, and Business

## 2.2 Digital Maturity in Organizations

Digital maturity refers to an organization's ability to fully integrate digital technologies and data analytics into its operations, enabling growth, innovation, and enhanced efficiency. For a business to become digitally mature, it must focus on Digital Endurance and Digital Velocity at the same time. The main focus of Digital Endurance is to develop important abilities in people, build up the necessary technology, and set up solid governance methods. It means that an organization can succeed in digital transformation in the future by creating a data-driven atmosphere and educating its workers to have the appropriate skills. At the same time, Digital Velocity represents the pace at which an organization implements new ideas and achieves its objectives. It covers enhancing what customers go through, making operations more effective, and promoting innovation. Gladly understanding data and acting rapidly on changes in the market enables organizations to speed up their transformation activities. Organizations will achieve digital maturity if they focus on bettering their teams, technologies, and systems as they speed up data-led initiatives for customers and operations. Because of this balance, companies manage to succeed in today's digital business world (Fig. 2).

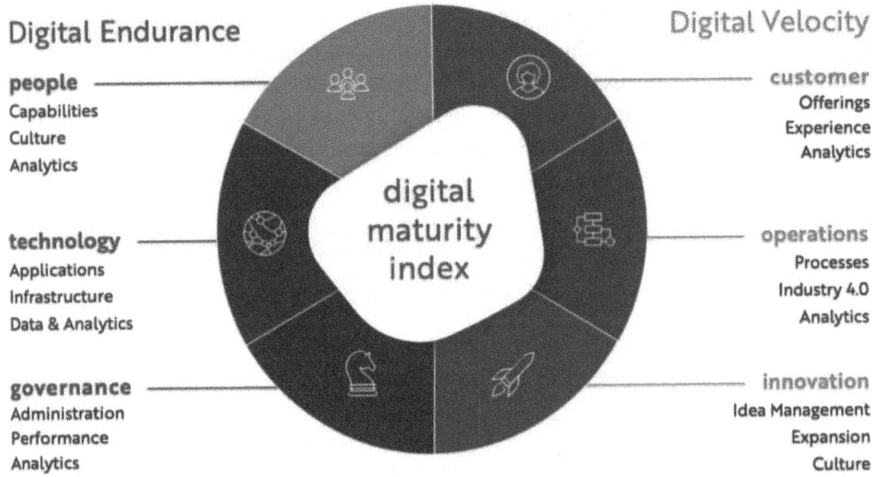


**Fig. 2.** Digital Maturity Index: Balancing Digital Endurance and Digital Velocity to Drive Organizational Growth and Innovation

## 2.3 The Role of Analytics in Decision-Making

Today, companies use analytics to compete excellently and choose the right courses of action. Analytics empowers organizations to uncover hidden patterns in data, predict future trends, and optimize various business functions such as supply chain management, marketing, and product development (Sarker 2021). Thanks to analytics, businesses can foresee what customers require, provide a better service, and effectiveness in their operations. The use of data-driven insights is also linked to enhanced business innovation, as it enables firms to identify new opportunities for growth and differentiation

(Ghasemaghaei, Ebrahimi, & Hassanein 2018). Applying analytics in decision-making at firms has improved their achievements, giving them an edge over others.

## 2.4 Visualization and Communication of Data

Data presentation allows people in leadership to grasp difficult information faster and take recommended actions. Visualization simplifies data into patterns and trends. This simplification is crucial for enhancing the comprehension of data, particularly in high-stakes decision-making environments (Qin et al. 2020). Moreover, clear data representations allow people who do not work with data to understand it faster and make well-informed decisions. In lively industries, accessibility is very important because being swift helps you compete better. With visualization, workers can respond promptly to ongoing changes and challenges at work. Interactive visualizations, for example, allow decision-makers to explore data from various angles and identify key insights in real time, thus enhancing responsiveness to changes in the business environment (Perdana, Rob, & Rohde 2018). All in all, data visualization enables organizations to understand important information and take better actions.

## 2.5 Analytics and Visualization Champions

Analytics and visualization champions make sure that data initiatives move forward in their organization by providing and implementing data analytics and visualization technology. These champions bridge the gap between data scientists and non-technical decision-makers, facilitating the communication of data insights in a way that is easily understood and actionable (Beer 2017). Apart from pushing for analytics, champions make sure that data drives most decisions and that data projects support the business's strategy. To get positive results, these champions require the right set of data and communication skills as well as strong qualities that make them effective managers and presenters. Additionally, they must exhibit a deep understanding of the business context and how data can be leveraged to drive growth and innovation (Kiula, Waiganjo, & Kihoro 2019). Because of these traits, champions can direct data projects that play a key role in the organization's digital growth.

## 2.6 Challenges in Achieving Digital Maturity

Companies that try to transform using data run into several problems as they strive for digital maturity. One major barrier is resistance to change, as employees and leaders may be reluctant to embrace new technologies and methodologies, particularly in traditional industries (Rader 2019). In addition, many companies struggle to find the right talent for managing and benefiting from high-end data tools, which slows down their effort to make operation changes with digital tools. Another obstacle is the underinvestment in necessary technologies, as many businesses fail to allocate sufficient resources to build the digital infrastructure required for a successful transformation (Canina & Bruno 2021). These challenges are particularly pronounced in small and medium-sized enterprises (SMEs), which may struggle with resource constraints and a lack of expertise in data analytics and digital technologies.

# 3 Methodology

## 3.1 Research Design

The study uses both qualitative and quantitative methods to explore how analytics and visualization leaders drive a company's digital growth. Qualitative data will be gathered through interviews and case studies with senior leaders in data analytics to understand key challenges and impacts of data-driven transformation. Quantitatively, surveys will be distributed to a broader set of organizations to assess the maturity of their digital initiatives and identify leadership in analytics. This mixed-methods approach ensures that both perspectives contribute to a fuller understanding of analytics' role in digital advancement. It also supports the study's aim to examine leadership, integration, and organizational outcomes.

## 3.2 Data Collection

Data will be collected through surveys, interviews, and case studies. Focus will be placed on organizations actively undergoing digital transformation to assess the use of analytics and visualization tools, and how leadership influences these initiatives. Key informants will include Chief Data Officers, data scientists, and business executives, who will share insights on the opportunities and challenges of analytics-driven decision-making. Additionally, real-world examples will be drawn from companies in retail, finance, and manufacturing—chosen for their digital maturity. The mixed sample strengthens the study's relevance across sectors, highlighting the impact of analytics leaders on digital growth.

## 3.3 Case Studies/Examples

**Case Study 1: Amazon's Data-Driven Supply Chain Optimization**
Amazon has become a top company in improving the supply chain worldwide by relying on analytics and data visualization to streamline functions, cut expenses, and make deliveries faster. Their main focus is on planning using data, managing their stocks, and predicting how much demand they will face. Such tools enable Amazon to anticipate sales from customers, which helps them manage the amount of inventory stored in every warehouse. Looking at previous sales, what happens each season, and the behavior of consumers, Amazon guarantees that products are on hand when customers need them, and there is not too much or too little inventory. This precise **inventory management** leads **to substantial cost savings and faster shipping times**, which ultimately enhances customer satisfaction (Ojika et al. 2021).

Amazon uses data visualization to help managers easily understand and apply tough data in their choices. As a result, the visual dashboards make it possible for Amazon's teams to constantly monitor their supply chain and address problems as soon as they become known. Visually presenting data also helps with finding the best routes, running warehouses, and enhancing relationships with suppliers. These analytics and visualization tools not **only enhance operational efficiency but also foster a culture of data-driven decision-making across the organization** (Ojika et al. 2021).

Amazon's strong use of data is apparent in its quick, accurate, and economical services to many people everywhere. Because of ongoing enhancements in analytics and displaying data, Amazon remains able to respond quickly and continue advancing in e-commerce. Because these new tools are used in everyday operations, Amazon's costs have dropped and its customers have had a better experience, which has made it a leader in retail and logistics.

**Case Study 2: Coca-Cola's Customer Insights Program**
Coca-Cola has been able to grasp how customers act and modify its marketing tactics using data analytics. The company uses up-to-date data visualization tools to monitor consumer preferences, sales, and changes in regions, which supply useful data for making important business choices. The company uses the information to see how its products are used by different customers in many parts of the world. Thanks to this analysis, Coca-Cola can notice what consumers are looking for, focus its marketing plan on them, and change its approach to product distribution promptly. This ensures that the company is always in tune with market demands, which is critical for maintaining its competitive edge in the beverage industry (Ali, Ahmad, Rehman, & Kamal 2018).

Use of data visualization greatly affects Coca-Cola's approach, since it equips executives to adapt decisions rapidly, using large sets of information. With real-time graphs, the company quickly tracks performance in sales, what customers think, and what they say on social media. This capability is particularly valuable in a highly competitive industry where consumer tastes and preferences are constantly evolving (Ali et al. 2018). Using data to guide all its operations helps Coca-Cola to offer tailored services that make people stay loyal and buy more.

Coca-Cola's use of data-driven insights exemplifies how analytics and visualization can enhance organizational responsiveness and agility, enabling firms to stay ahead of the curve in a rapidly changing business environment. The company's ability to turn data into strategic actions has become a vital part of its success, helping it maintain its position as a leader in the global soft drink industry.

## 3.4 Evaluation Metrics

Both qualitative and quantitative measures will be used to judge how much analytics and visualization champions contribute to making the company more digital. Examples of quantitative measures are making supply chains cheaper, getting decisions done more quickly, or increasing the revenue due to better use of data. Key performance indicators (KPIs) like return on investment (ROI) from data initiatives, sales growth, and customer satisfaction levels can also serve as indicators of success. Analyzing qualitative measures requires checking how people involved are satisfied with the outcome of using analytics tools through a series of interviews. Other markers are seen when there are successful introductions of new products or services that use information from data analysis. These numbers give a clear picture of how much analytics and visualization specialists are helping companies reach higher digital maturity, so that data-driven decisions are used in all important company decisions.

# 4 Results

## 4.1 Data Presentation

See Table 1.

**Table 1.** Data Presentation: Case Study and Evaluation Metrics Comparison

| Metric | Amazon Supply Chain Optimization | Coca-Cola Customer Insights Program |
|---|---|---|
| Revenue Growth | 15% Increase | 10% Increase |
| Operational Efficiency | 20% Cost Reduction | 12% Reduction in marketing costs |
| Decision-Making Speed | 25% Faster | 30% Faster |
| Customer Satisfaction | 90% Positive Feedback | 85% Positive Feedback |
| Innovation Outcomes | 5 New Services Launched | 3 Product Adjustments |

## 4.2 Charts, Diagrams, Graphs, and Formulas

See Figs. 3 and 4.

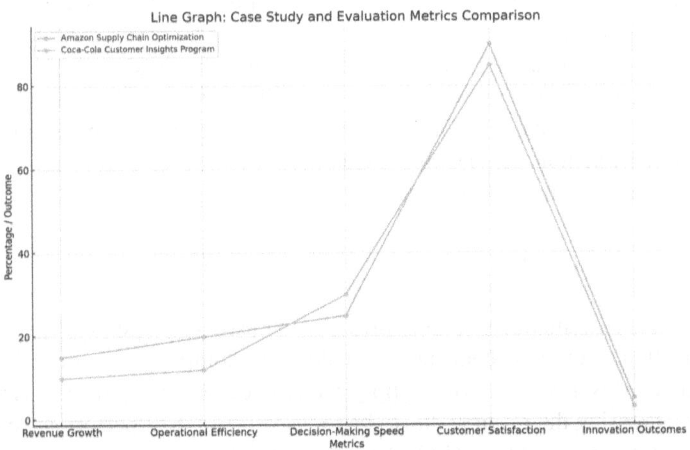


**Fig. 3.** Line graph comparing the trends in key performance metrics between Amazon's Supply Chain Optimization and Coca-Cola's Customer Insights Program, showing differences in outcomes across various areas.

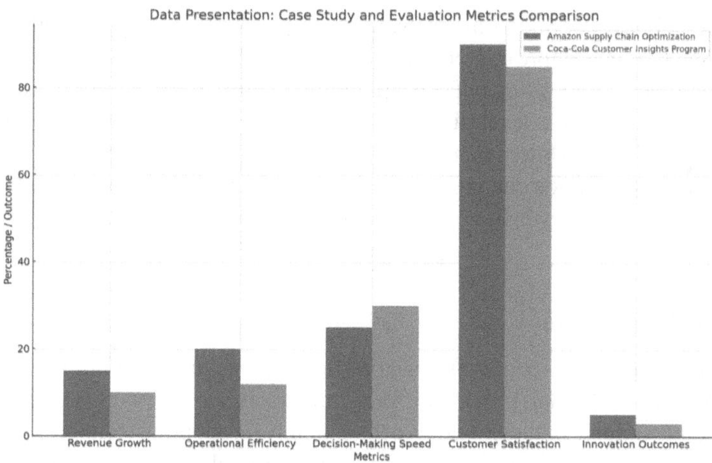


**Fig. 4.** Bar chart comparing the performance of Amazon's Supply Chain Optimization and Coca-Cola's Customer Insights Program across key metrics, including revenue growth, operational efficiency, decision-making speed, customer satisfaction, and innovation outcomes.

### 4.3 Findings

There seems to be a very strong link between analytics leadership and the degree of digital maturity. Firms that focus on analytics and visualization can make informed decisions faster, use less budget, and please their customers better. They help bring people from different teams together and lead the way to using data when making business decisions. The research points out that businesses with excellent analytics and visualization skills are more agile when responding to market changes and new technology. As a result, businesses with higher digital maturity manage analytics more easily in their work, which helps them operate better and bring out more innovation.

### 4.4 Case Study Outcomes

You can clearly see from the examples of Amazon and Coca-Cola how analytics and visualization champions bring positive results. With its data-based approach to supply chain management, Amazon has saved 20% on costs and raised revenues by 15%. Thanks to advanced forecasting and managing tools, Amazon has increased the efficiency of its operations. Coca-Cola's use of data analytics to understand customer behavior has led to a 10% increase in revenue and a 12% reduction in marketing costs. Coca-Cola uses powerful visualization tools, so it can rapidly react and update its marketing and distribution approaches. It is evident here that proper use of analytics and visualization can greatly boost the results achieved by an organization.

### 4.5 Comparative Analysis

A review of organizations with different levels of digitization demonstrates that there are major differences in their use of analytics and visualization. Those firms that have achieved a high level of digital maturity, for example Amazon, rely on analytics all the time, leading to much-improved work performance and greater customer happiness. As a result, these businesses bring out fresh packages and programs thanks to the data they collect. Meanwhile, lower-level digital organizations, who are not far along with their analytics, tend to react slower to new market trends and make choices more gradually. Analytics and visualization champions are key to moving an organization towards higher digital maturity, since they help integrate data-driven thinking into the way the company operates.

### 4.6 Model Comparison

Several digital maturity models, such as the Digital Transformation Framework and the Capability Maturity Model, provide different approaches to assessing an organization's digital readiness. Some of these models center mainly on adopting technology, but others pay more attention to leadership or building strong data culture. The models are effective in showing how analytics and visualization help when they focus both on the tools and the integration of data-driven decisions in the company's way of working. Those that consider technology and the guide of analytics champions offer a clearer picture of digital development, because they include both organizational and leadership aspects important for successful transformation.

### 4.7 Impact and Observation

Integrating these methods affects the organization's operations on a large scale. When an organization has solid leadership in data analytics, its culture tends to move toward collaborating and using data when making decisions. People working in various areas feel more connected since they can use timely data to make wise decisions. Moreover, dealing with businesses is easier for customers because they can make adjustments swiftly to what people want. Using both analytics and visualization tools encourages the business to always seek improvement and successful operations. For this reason, companies enjoy better results in terms of performance and satisfaction among staff and clients.

## 5 Discussion

### 5.1 Interpretation of Results

The findings indicate a clear positive relationship between the involvement of analytics and visualization champions and an organization's digital maturity. Strength in analytics allows companies to spread data-based thinking through their work life, which leads to better business results, more money earned, and happier customers. These findings indicate that these champions play a key role in getting the organization to use analytics and shift its focus towards data. Advanced digital organization have quicker reactions to market trends, which further shows how crucial analytics and visualization are for an organization's success. This means that effective leadership in data analytics and visualization not only makes it easier for an organization to become digital mature but also makes sure that data initiatives focus on key business targets.

### 5.2 Result and Discussion

Research from this study matches what previous studies have said about the role of leadership in data analytics for attaining digital maturity. Previous studies have shown that organizations with a clear data strategy and strong leadership in analytics experience higher levels of digital maturity (Kraus et al. 2021). The study provides more information by highlighting how analytics and visualization champions affect day-to-day work. Alternatively, some study snubs leadership and argues that great technologies will not achieve results if management is not strong and effective. It is supported by the results that for data integration to be really valuable, it needs to blend with the corporate culture and the dedication of those in charge.

### 5.3 Practical Implications

The discoveries can be used by organizations to emphasize the training of analytics and visualization experts to support digital advancement. They ought to know how to lead others to use data for better decision-making in different departments. A data-driven culture can be created in organizations by helping managers and leaders train team members, team up technical and non-technical employees, and connect analytics projects to the rest of the company's aims. When analytics leadership is included in the organizational structure, it can boost the digital transformation process and increase the company's performance.

### 5.4 Challenges and Limitations

Several challenges and limitations arose during the study. The findings may not be useful outside of the area studied, because the research was based on a limited number of organizations. Additionally, the study's reliance on self-reported data from surveys and interviews introduces the potential for bias, particularly regarding how organizations perceive their own digital maturity. It is also hard to measure how much analytics and visualization champions have contributed in organizations that are not simple and where a number of elements could have impacted the results. Still, the study gives us useful information on how leadership encourages digital transformation.

### 5.5 Recommendations

Organizations ought to help develop and support people who are experienced with analytics and visualization to promote the use of data. Champions need to learn new management and analytics skills, so they can help with and control changes in the organization. Besides, organizations should work on building an environment that welcomes cooperation between departments and matches data projects with business objectives. In addition, endless learning chances will help analytics champions overcome challenges they may encounter in the field.

# 6 Conclusion

## 6.1 Summary of Key Points

This study shows that experts in analytics and visualization play a vital role in driving digital maturity within organizations. A committed analytics leadership team enhances efficiency, boosts earnings, and reduces decision-making time. These leaders bridge technical teams and decision-makers, guiding business actions and promoting agility, innovation, and customer satisfaction. As organizations focus more on digital maturity, strong analytics leadership becomes essential in supporting digital transformation and building a flexible, competitive workforce.

## 6.2 Future Directions

Future research could explore the evolving roles of analytics leaders, particularly in areas like AI and blockchain. Investigating both the challenges and successes of leaders in small organizations or digitally advanced industries may reveal effective strategies. Long-term impacts of data maturity on workplace culture, motivation, and talent retention should be studied. To stay competitive, organizations must invest in analytics, automation, and machine learning, while cultivating strong leadership to guide data-driven transformation.

# References

Ali, T., Ahmad, I., Rehman, A.U., Kamal, S.: Understanding customer experiences through social media analysis of three giants of the soft drink industry. In: 2018 5th International Conference on Behavioral, Economic, and Socio-Cultural Computing (BESC), Kaohsiung, Taiwan, pp. 216–224 (2018).https://doi.org/10.1109/BESC.2018.8697304

Aslanova, I.V., Kulichkina, A.I.: Digital maturity: definition and model. In: Proceedings of the 2nd International Scientific and Practical Conference "Modern Management Trends and the Digital Economy: From Regional Development to Global Economic Growth" (MTDE 2020), vol. 138 (2020). https://doi.org/10.2991/aebmr.k.200502.073

Beer, D.: Envisioning the power of data analytics. Inf. Commun. Soc. **21**(3), 465–479 (2017). https://doi.org/10.1080/1369118x.2017.1289232

Canina, M.R., Bruno, C.: Digital creative abilities for achieving digital maturity. Adv. Hum. Factors Train. Educ. Learn. Sci. **27–35** (2021). https://doi.org/10.1007/978-3-030-80000-0_4

Grandhi, B., Patwa, N., Saleem, K.: Data-driven marketing for growth and profitability. EuroMed J. Bus. **16**(4), 381–398 (2020)

Ghasemaghaei, M., Ebrahimi, S., Hassanein, K.: Data analytics competency for improving firm decision making performance. J. Strateg. Inf. Syst. **27**(1), 101–113 (2018). https://doi.org/10.1016/j.jsis.2017.10.001

Ilin, I., Levaniuk, D., Dubgorn, A.: Assessment of digital maturity of enterprises. Adv. Intell. Syst. Comput. **167–177** (2020). https://doi.org/10.1007/978-3-030-57453-6_14

Kraus, S., Jones, P., Kailer, N., Weinmann, A., Banegas, N.C., Tierno, N.R.: Digital transformation: an overview of the current state of the art of research. SAGE Open **11**(3), 1–15 (2021). https://doi.org/10.1177/21582440211025860

Kiula, M., Waiganjo, E., Kihoro, J.: The role of leadership in building the foundations for data analytics, visualization and business intelligence. In: 2019 IST-Africa Week Conference (IST-Africa), Nairobi, Kenya, pp. 1–8 (2019).https://doi.org/10.23919/ISTAFRICA.2019.8764827

Ojika, F.U., Owobu, W.O., Abieba, O.A., Esan, O.J., Ubamadu, B.C., Daraojimba, A.I.: A conceptual framework for AI-driven digital transformation: leveraging NLP and machine learning for enhanced data flow in retail operations. Iconic Res. Eng. J. **4**(9), 189–198 (2021). https://www.irejournals.com/paper-details/1702633

Perdana, A., Rob, A., Rohde, F.: Does visualization matter? The role of interactive data visualization to make sense of information. Australas. J. Inf. Syst. **22** (2018). https://doi.org/10.3127/ajis.v22i0.1681

Rader, D.: Digital maturity – the new competitive goal. Strategy Leadersh. **47**(5), 28–35 (2019). https://doi.org/10.1108/sl-06-2019-0084

Sarker, I.H.: Data science and analytics: an overview from data-driven smart computing, decision-making, and applications perspective. SN Comput. Sci. **2**(5) (2021). https://doi.org/10.1007/s42979-021-00765-8

Shah, D., Murthi, B.P.S.: Marketing in a data-driven digital world: Implications for the role and scope of marketing. J. Bus. Res. **125**(1), 772–779 (2020). https://doi.org/10.1016/j.jbusres.2020.06.062

Ulas, D.: Digital transformation process and SMEs. Procedia Comput. Sci. **158**(1), 662–671 (2019). https://doi.org/10.1016/j.procs.2019.09.101

# Poster Research Papers

# Feature Engineering for Classical and Quantum Unsupervised Machine Learning in Short Time Series of Bird Strike Incidents

Mohammed Syed[1](✉), Mark Slagle[2], and Paul Garcia[3]

[1] The Boeing Company, Seattle, WA, USA
mohammed.a.syed@boeing.com
[2] The Boeing Company, Everett, WA, USA
[3] The Boeing Company, St. Louis, MO, USA

**Abstract.** In this paper, we present a feature augmentation method utilizing unsupervised machine learning with time series data sets, incorporating feature engineering, through the decomposition of time series data points into spherical coordinates followed by feature selection (FEFSeT). For comparison, we apply this method in both classical and quantum-enhanced unsupervised machine learning environments. We selected large-sized bird strikes data from the United States Department of the Federal Aviation Administration's (FAA) database collected between 1991 and 2022. Each incident of large-bird strikes are recorded. Large-sized birds have been known to grow beyond 8 lb and contribute to high damage potential to critical aircraft and rotorcraft systems. We compare results with and without FEFSeT from various clustering techniques and choose the silhouette score as a test metric. We used an IBM Quantum Computer for quantum-enhanced clustering. Our analysis discovered dissimilarities between various years in the data set, with homogeneity over 90% and a silhouette score of approximately 0.45 using Principal Component Analysis (PCA). This score improved by over 35% when FEFSeT method was applied. Additionally, we review the feasibility of using quantum computers for unsupervised learning in short time series clustering problems.

**Keywords:** Quantum-enhanced clustering · time series · feature augmentation · bird strike study

## 1 Introduction

Bird strikes with aircraft pose a threat to critical aircraft systems and overall safety. Energy generated from such strikes can disable various sensors leading to unsafe flying conditions. The Federal Aviation Administration (FAA) has been collecting comprehensive bird strike data since 1990. These data are publicly available as a database. This database shows an increasing trend overall of bird strikes. In many instances, bird species have been identified. Some of these species grow beyond 8 lb or large species with higher potential of causing serious damage. Figure 1 shows the number of strikes


R. Stahlbock et al. (Eds.): CSCE 2025, CCIS 2938, pp. 499–504, 2027.
https://doi.org/10.1007/978-3-032-22196-4_36

by large birds per year. To confirm these trends, we first reviewed available literature and confirmed increasing trends [1]. In this paper, we focus on a subset of these data where we consider instances where the bird species were identified and can grow beyond 8 lb. We then ascertained increasing trends within this subset as well.

The time series had 378 data points overall. An aggregated time series for the entire time frame has been shown in Fig. 1. Once we identified the species and confirmed trends in the subset, we separated the strikes data per month for each year since 1990. During descriptive analysis, we noticed certain patterns intra-annually over this period of approximately 30 years. We chose unsupervised machine learning analysis as the next step and applied various clustering techniques to each year. Each year's time series covered 12 months. To determine cluster quality, we chose to use silhouette score as a metric, although other metrics were examined as well. We compared results from causal clustering and algorithms geared to time series. The main goal of this step was to identify patterns observed visually for each year. We developed our workflow using both R and Python programming environments.

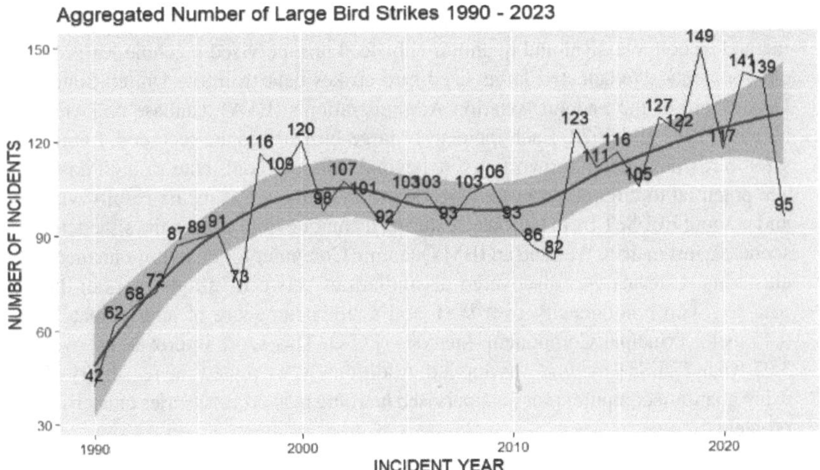


**Fig. 1.** Number of large bird strike incidents along y-axis aggregated per year from 1990 until 2022.

Exploring the potential of quantum computing in various domains is current and active area of research. One practical application of quantum computing is quantum-enhanced machine learning. The feasibility of quantum-enhancements to classical deep learning algorithms have been shown in aerospace applications [2]. In this paper, we determine the feasibility of quantum-enhanced unsupervised learning and specifically clustering in short time series analysis. We chose quantum-enhanced spectral clustering using Python and IBM's Qiskit library [3]. We executed the algorithm using both the IBM Qiskit's quantum simulator and an actual IBM quantum computer.

## 2 Methodology

### 2.1 Analysis Space

Our data set focused on species that were identified and have been known to grow beyond 8 lb. We were working with a short time series for each year as described earlier in this paper with 12 points representing large bird strikes for each month of the year and a time span of 30 years. There were no gaps in the data set. Our goal at this point was to group or cluster time series data for each year for underlying patterns. We applied clustering techniques including but not limited to distance-based, density-based, agglomerative, and spectral. We utilized Dynamic Time Warping (DTW) algorithm in addition to other methods for this study to compare time series for each year shown in Fig. 2.

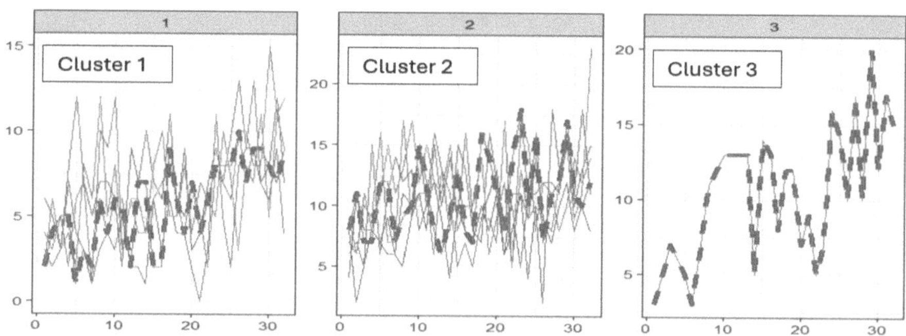


**Fig. 2.** Clustering based upon dynamic time warping algorithm with three clusters, chosen as an example, grouping time series for each year.

This technique provides a distance measure between two time series for such strikes attempting to find optimal warping path under a set of constraints [4] not affected by local compression and stretches and warping which optimally deforms one of the two input series onto the other. We first applied these techniques against raw pre-processed data. We then completed Principal Component Analysis (PCA) against raw data and chose the first two components for clustering.

Spectral clustering utilizes graph Laplacian matrices that come in two main classes: normalized and unnormalized graph Laplacians. Normalized spectral clustering uses eigenvectors of the normalized Laplacian matrix [5, 6]. We used Python's scikit-learn library's spectral clustering functionality that allowed us to define a custom kernel by precomputing the kernel matrix. We use a second-order Pauli-Z evolution circuit with linear entanglement and various repetition settings. The feature map from this circuit then initializes a quantum kernel interface calculating state fidelities or overlaps for pairs of quantum circuits. We finally fit a spectral clustering model to this precomputed kernel.

### 2.2 Feature Augmentation

With a single feature and short time series, we observed low silhouette scores when clustering these data. Our methodology involved projecting each time point onto a sphere.

We used the fact that on a 2-dimensional plane, each data point has a prior-angle, φ, which is the angle between data point at time t and t − 1, and a post-angle, θ, which is the angle between data point at time t and t + 1. We considered the point itself the origin as shown in Fig. 3.

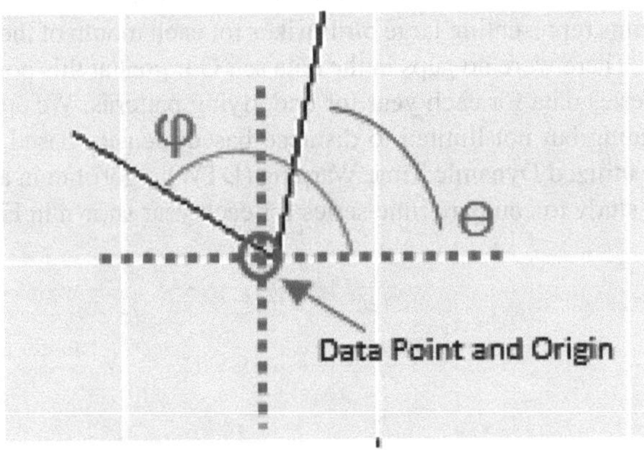


**Fig. 3.** A sample data point with prior-angle, φ, and post-angle, θ

φ was set to 0 for the first point whereas θ to 0 for the last point in the series. All angles were measured in radians. For each data point, we now had two points: φ and θ. The number of features expanded from n for each month to 2n in polar coordinates or φ and θ for each n resulting in a total of 24 features from 12 in our case study. Equation 1 shows the calculation of θ. φ was calculated using a similar approach.

$$\theta = \tan^{-1}\frac{y2 - y1}{x2 - x1}$$

We used these angles to generate 3 distinct points representing coordinates on a spherical surface. This step produced an output of 3n features from n where each point represents a cartesian coordinate.

The original dataset did not have labels. We determined the overall trend for each year, ascending or descending, and assigned a label accordingly. This step provided an additional benchmark for cluster quality measurement.

We reduced the dimensionality of 2n or 3n features for each year. This step was accomplished by applying feature selection through extremely randomized trees [7]. Now we had months of year selected through top 5 calculation to be used in clustering.

With augmentation completed, we applied unsupervised learning as described in the previous section.

### 2.3 Quantum Unsupervised Learning

In the next step, we examined quantum-enhanced spectral clustering which was first implemented on a GPU-powered machine using IBM Qiskit's qasm simulator. We then executed our approach on an IBM quantum computer located in Osaka, Japan.

### 2.4 Results

Clustering quality through silhouette scores reached 0.25 when algorithms were applied to raw pre-processed input data. Clustering quality using PCA however showed better results when the first two principal components were used and reached approximately 0.45. After applying our approach, FEFSeT, involving feature augmentation through decomposition into spherical coordinates followed by feature selection, the clustering quality level reached 0.60.

From a temporal complexity perspective, GPU- based architecture performed significantly better than a quantum computer. Complexity on a quantum computer was discovered to be over 100% that of GPU-based architecture.

## 3 Discussion

We surmise that the silhouette score utilizing Euclidean distance between instances could be contributing to lower scores in this situation as we were modeling the same feature over time with a short time series. Such distances were not significant leading to low silhouette scores. Our methodology provides a trigonometric decomposition of data points in this type of a time series dataset. As we are targeting unsupervised machine learning, we are not considering autoregression and moving averages which are used in time series predictive analysis. By focusing on trigonometric properties, we are able to transform these data to polar coordinate system followed by spherical coordinates. Our approach then utilizes feature selection based upon decomposition previously described in the paper. We are therefore capturing relationship information from a unique perspective. We demonstrated that having polar and spherical coordinates with a feature selection step provide higher cluster purity in short time series datasets. Utilizing our approach can produce higher predictive accuracy which we leave as a future task.

Although we are not presenting this aspect as a novelty, we reviewed the performance and temporal complexities of implementing our approach in an actual quantum computing environment. We discovered that the temporal complexity of this type of problem was over 100% on a quantum computer as compared to that of a classical GPU based architecture. We must note that this complexity is based upon end-to-end computation on a quantum computer including the initialization process which can take up to 300 s with significant increase in operational costs. This observation also confirms that classical machines and algorithms can still produce comparable or better results with lower temporal complexity depending upon the nature of the problem. In other words, quantum computing environments currently available may not be the best solution in many classical data situations.

**Disclosure of Interests.** The authors do not report any known conflicts of interest. This project was not sponsored by The Boeing Company.

## References

1. Dolbeer, R., Begier, M., Miller, P., Weller, J., Anderson, A.: Wildlife Strikes to Civil Aircraft in the United States, 1990–2022. Federal Aviation Administration (FAA), Washington DC (2023)

2. Syed, M., Garcia, P.: A hybrid quantum-classical machine learning approach to vision sensor data analysis in aerospace applications. In: IEEE/AIAA 42nd Digital Avionics Systems Conference (DASC), Barcelona, Spain, pp. 1–7 (2023)
3. Javadi-Abhari A., et al.: Quantum computing with Qiskit. Quantum Phys. (2024)
4. Sardá-Espinosa, A.: Time-series clustering in R using the dtwclust package. R J. **11**(1), 22–43 (2019)
5. vonLuxburg U.: A tutorial on spectral clustering. Stat. Comput., 395–416 (2007)
6. Yu S., Shi J.: Multiclass spectral clustering. In: Proceedings of the Ninth IEEE International Conference on Computer Vision, pp. 313–319 (2003)
7. Geurts, P., Ernst, D., Wehenkel, L.: Extremely randomized trees. Mach. Learn. **63**, 3–42 (2006)

# Text Mining Analysis for Traditional Dance Songs

Toshiyuki Maeda[1(✉)], Masumi Yajima[2], and Akiyoshi Wakatani[3]

[1] Department of Information Sciences, Hannan University, Matsubara, Japan
maechan@ieee.org

[2] Department of Economics, Meikai University, Urayasu, Japan
myajima@meikai.ac.jp

[3] Faculty of Intelligence and Informatics, Konan University, Kobe, Japan
wakatani@konan-u.ac.jp

**Abstract.** As an example of the application of AI and data science technologies to the field of performing arts, we present and discuss text mining analysis for Japanese traditional dance songs (Jiuta). In this study, clustering analysis has been conducted on lyrics of Jiuta to verify the possibility of extracting and classifying trends by lyricist and dance schools.

**Keywords:** Data Science · Traditional Dance Songs · Text Mining · Clustering Analysis

## 1 Introduction

In recent years, the advancement of artificial intelligence (AI) and data science technologies has been undeniably profound. In particular, the rapid progress in generative AI has unveiled a vast range of opportunities across diverse domains and applications, driving intensive research and development efforts worldwide. However, it remains crucial to acknowledge the continued importance of AI and data science applications beyond the scope of generative AI. While deep learning?based approaches currently receive substantial attention and require extensive computational resources, there remains considerable potential to derive novel insights through the application of conventional, or so-called legacy, methodologies. Indeed, several existing studies demonstrate that such approaches continue to yield meaningful and impactful outcomes.

Furthermore, the application of text mining techniques has facilitated the extraction of valuable information. The following section discusses methods of natural language analysis. In the field of literary studies, a number of investigations have been conducted, including the work by Takeda et al. entitled "Text Mining from Literary Works: Supporting Discovery in Literature." [4] Another group of researchers has examined the relationship between songs, while the present study explores the connection between textual data and professional perceptions of music, as demonstrated in the study by Matsuda et al. titled "Application of Text Mining Technology for Analysis of Music." [3].


R. Stahlbock et al. (Eds.): CSCE 2025, CCIS 2938, pp. 505–510, 2027.
https://doi.org/10.1007/978-3-032-22196-4_37

This paper serves as an illustrative exemplar of the implementation of artificial intelligence and data science. We have been developed for application in the domain of performing arts, [1,2,5] and the exposition shall elucidate the text mining analysis of Jiuta. The following section will firstly present the findings of the study, and then discuss the results in the context of future prospects and issues.

## 2 Text Mining Analysis of Jiuta

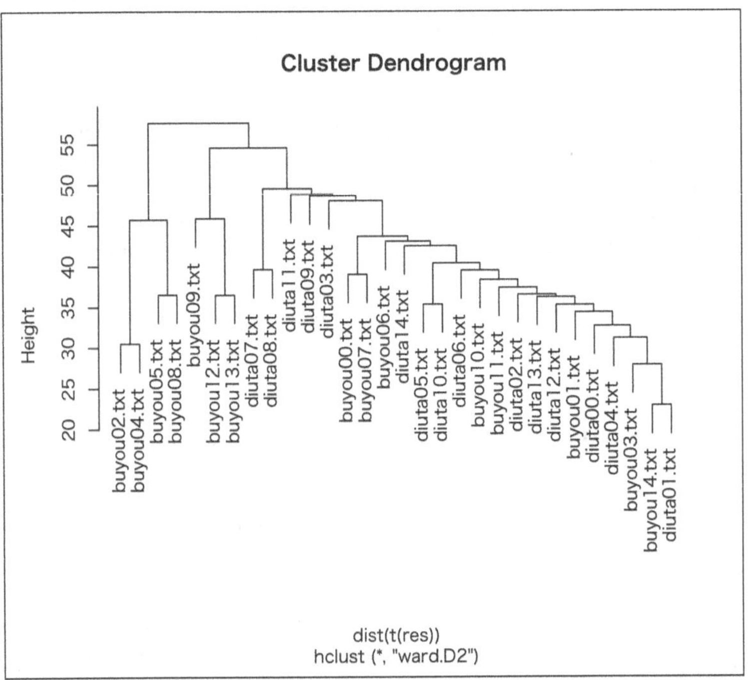


**Fig. 1.** Clustering by dancing/playing.

The Keihan (Kyoto and Osaka) Hanayanagi community has preserved and developed the world of "Mai" (dance) along with performances of "jiuta" and "kamigata uta," as well as "hauta" and "kouta." "Jiuta" has the aspect of traditional vocal music, while "Kamigata Uta" is light and cheerful shamisen music from the urban areas of Keihan.

According to the "Index of Composers of Jiuta Songs from the Kan'en Period (1973)," there are more than 1,000 jiuta songs that can be found in literature, of which about 500 are said to be extant ("Comprehensive List of Extant Jiuta and Koto Songs (1991)"). According to "Nihon Buyo Kyoku Shusei 2 Kyomai/Kamigata Buyo Hen (Theatre Publishing House 2005)," the number of dance accompaniment pieces is 127 for jiuta and 88 for kamigata buyo, for a total of 215 dance pieces. Kamigata-mai (jiuta-mai) is performed by the Inoue, Yoshimura, Yamamura, Umemoto, Kanzaki, and Shinozuka schools.

This study aims to clarify the outline of the historical development of the music and dances that support the unique Kyosaka Zashiki, organize the data of approximately 600–700 dance songs and performance songs, classify the song forms and contents, and then use text mining methods to discover the characteristics of the worldview of the Zashiki dance of Kyosaka from the perspective of "uta words". We will then use text mining methods to discover the characteristics of the worldview of Kyoto-Osaka Zashiki dance from the perspective of "uta words".

The results of the analysis using RMeCab are shown in Fig. 1, where files beginning with buyou are the dance songs and files beginning with diuta are the performance songs. The dance songs are clustered roughly on the left and the performance songs roughly on the right, and each file constitutes a cluster, albeit a rough one.

In the next analysis, the document files (lyrics data files) were created for each of the following Iemoto's: Yoshimura-ryu IV Iemoto Yuki Yoshimura, Yoshimura-ryu VI Iemoto Teruaki Yoshimura, Yoshimura-ryu V Iemoto Teruo Yoshimura, Inoue-ryu IV Yachiyo Inoue, Inoue-ryu V Yachiyo Inoue, and Yamamura-ryu III Waka Yamamura, and nouns and adjectives were extracted with RMeCab, then a hierarchical cluster analysis was conducted by introducing the Canberra distance as the distance between the data. The results are shown in Fig. 2.

The three clusters were neatly classified into three Yoshimura Schools, two Inoue Schools, and a Yamamura School. The degree of similarity within the schools is clear. This enabled the prospect of automatic classification through the implementation of text mining techniques.

## 3 Discussion

Dance songs – vocal music accompanied by dance – constitute an integrated form of expression that has developed across many cultural regions from ancient to modern times. In Japan, they encompass a wide range of traditions, including kagura, dengaku, fury? performing arts, folk performing arts, as well as classical genres such as hauta, kouta, and jiuta-mai, in addition to Bon dances and festival-related performances. Because dance songs manifest in such multilayered ways, the scope of research is equally diverse. The following sections outline major research issues in light of contemporary scholarly perspectives.

First, a key issue lies in reconstructing the historical genealogy of dance songs. Many forms originated in periods where documentary sources were limited, and due to the constraints of early recording media, neither sound nor bodily movement has been directly preserved. Consequently, scholars must piece together fragmented materials – song texts, picture scrolls, festival records, genre genealogies, and depictions of historical customs – to reconstruct performance practices. Existing scholarship, however, tends to focus on specific genres or

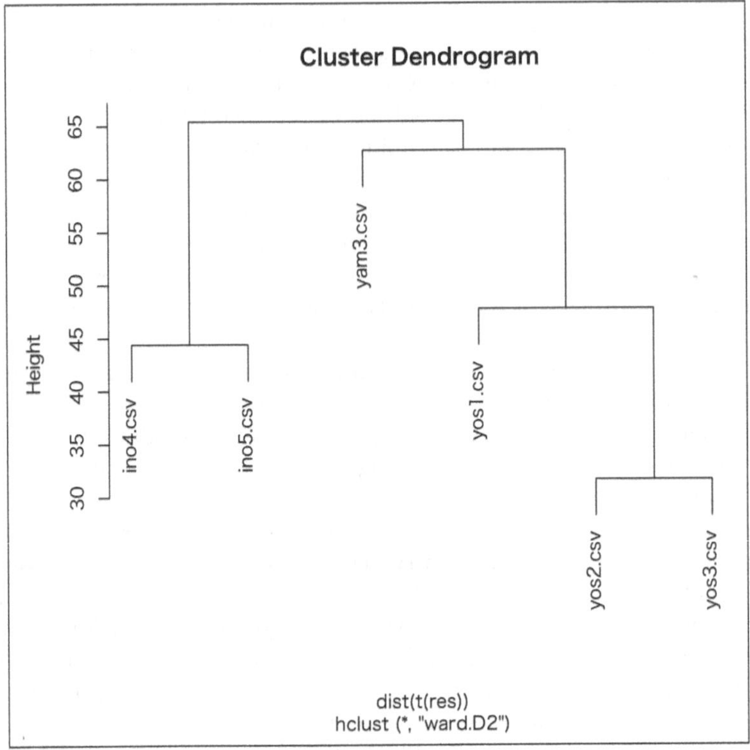


**Fig. 2.** Clustering by schools.

regions, and has not yet achieved a sufficiently comprehensive or comparative perspective. Particularly underexplored are the transformations from medieval to early modern performing arts, the role of communal singing and dancing in village society, and the transmission of courtly performing arts into local contexts. These areas require reexamination of primary sources and renewed efforts toward systematic historical mapping.

Second, an essential task is the analysis of the relationship between dance and song. Dance songs are composite expressions in which lyrics, melodies, rhythms, bodily movements, and spatial formations closely interrelate. Yet research often prioritizes either the musical or the choreographic component. In practice, melodic structure can strongly influence choreographic rhythm, while lyrical organization shapes dramatic flow and the meaning of the dance. In the field of folk performing arts, it is especially important to examine how regional variations in melodic phrasing correspond to dance patterns, and how foreign dance styles are assimilated and transformed in the accompanying vocal music. Collaboration across musicology, dance studies, and folklore is crucial to address these questions.

Third, studies of embodiment and communal practice are indispensable. Dance songs are not merely music or choreography; they have been enacted as part of communal rituals, festivals, and social gatherings, where participation and shared bodily experience play central roles. In Bon dances and fury? dances, for instance, participants collectively sing, dance, and circulate within a shared space, thereby generating social cohesion. To understand this dynamic, research must be grounded in fieldwork, detailed descriptions of bodily movements, and documentation that integrates both performer and observer perspectives. Furthermore, recent approaches informed by gender studies and performance studies highlight issues such as role division among dancers, cultural conceptions of the body, and the relationship between dance practice and social norms.

Fourth, researchers must address the impact of changing media environments on dance songs. From the modern era onward, the advent of recording technology allowed vocal music to be fixed through written notation and audio recordings, while dance movements became increasingly preserved through film and video. For dance songs – traditions historically transmitted through fluid, adaptive practices – this shift has profoundly altered modes of transmission. Key questions include: How have recordings reshaped performers' memory and physicality? How has "standardization" occurred within regional performing arts through media exposure? And how have digital platforms such as YouTube and social media transformed contemporary dance cultures? These issues represent major directions for future research.

Fifth, there is an urgent need for international and intercultural comparative studies. Dance songs are not unique to Japan; analogous forms exist worldwide, such as dance-chant traditions in East Asia, rhythmic dance-music in Southeast Asia, European folk songs and dances, and African song-dance cultures. While singing and dancing in integrated forms constitutes a near-universal human practice, the social functions and historical development of these traditions vary widely depending on local histories, religions, and social systems. To situate Japanese dance songs within a broader context, researchers must engage in comparative work that highlights both the unique characteristics of Japanese traditions and their commonalities with global expressive practices.

Finally, the issue of preservation and transmission is increasingly critical. Depopulation and aging in rural areas have led to a decline in performers, risking the loss of vocal techniques, dance skills, and festival management knowledge. Balancing the preservation of tradition with its continuation as living practice requires understanding how communities perceive and value their own dance-song traditions. External involvement – whether by researchers or local governments – can sometimes alter a tradition's "authenticity", making it imperative to adopt approaches that respect local agency and cultural autonomy.

In summary, the study of dance songs spans a wide array of interdisciplinary themes, including history, music, embodiment, community practice, media studies, cross-cultural comparison, and cultural transmission. Dance songs are not simply performing arts; they represent a crystallization of human efforts to understand the world and connect with others through the embodied act of singing and dancing. Capturing their full significance requires both integrative scholarly perspectives and rigorous, field-based empirical research.

## 4 Conclusion

The preceding discourse indicates the feasibility of employing text mining techniques to categorize musical compositions based on their respective authors, with the analysis confined exclusively to the lyrical content. The analysis presented herein is elementary, and further detailed analysis may be necessary when comparing the linguistic characteristics of Edo kouta, which are primarily sung, and Buyo Kouta, which are with dance. For instance, other parts of speech, such as particles, auxiliary verbs, and adjectives, must also be considered. In addition to morpheme frequency information, the scope of the analysis should encompass syntactic information.

We are currently attempting to verify the artistic style of the Yoshimura school in Kamigata dance through analysis of moving pictures. The preliminary strategy involved the analysis of the data subsequent to the delineation of the movement components. However, it became evident that the manual tracing process prior to data preprocessing would require an inordinate amount of time. Consequently, as a measure to enhance the process, we will consider a method to analyze the video data itself as time-series data in parallel with the analysis method of manually tracing partial parts of the data. To illustrate, our research focuses on the feasibility of employing video analysis with a particular emphasis on object tracking.

Therefore, we are convinced that the application of artificial intelligence (AI) and data science technology to the performing arts field has great potential. We are eager to see this technology continue to develop in the future.

**Acknowledgment.** Part of this research is supported by JSPS KAKENHI Grant Number 20K00254, and 23K02671. The authors greatly appreciate those.

## References

1. Maeda, T., Yajima, M., Wakatani, A.: Analysis of dance songs for learning performing arts using text mining technology. In: INTED2025 Proceedings, pp. 1092–1095 (2025). https://urldefense.com/v3/. https://doi.org/10.21125/inted.2025.0362
2. Maeda, T., Yajima, M., Wakatani, A.: "Data Science", chapter Application of Data Science Techniques to Performing Arts, pp. 412–416. Communications in Computer and Information Science 2253. Springer Nature (2025). https://urldefense.com/v3/.https://doi.org/10.1007/978-3-031-85856-7
3. Matsuda, T., Iijima, J.: Application of text mining technology for analysis of music. In: Proceedings of Naitonal Conference of JASMIN (in Japanese), pp. 43–43. The Japan Society for Management Information (2002)
4. Takeda, M., Fukuda, T., Nanri, I.: Text mining from literary works: supporting discovery in literature. In: Proceedings of Information System Society Conference of IEICE (in Japanese), pp. 385–385 (2001)
5. Yajima, M., Maeda, T.: Analysis for characteristic patterns of japanese short dance songs "Kouta"âĂŕ: identification and classification of lyrics using text-mining techniques. Meikai Univer. J. Nature (in Japanese) **24**, 39–43 (2013)

# A Survey of Vulnerabilities and Emerging Defenses in GANs, VAEs, and Transformers

Jothsna Praveena Pendyala[1(✉)] and Aman Goyal[2]

[1] Clark University, Worcester, USA
jpendyala@clarku.edu
[2] Carneige Mellon University, Pittsburgh, USA
amangoya@alumni.cmu.edu

**Abstract.** Generative Artificial Intelligence is the foundation of an increasingly diverse array of applications - text and image synthesis, multimodal reasoning, workflow of autonomous agents. Innovation is being taken on by recently published models like Transformers, GANs, etc. But even now that these models are realizing unparalleled ability, they are revealing a more complicated vulnerability terrain. It works on adversarial training, alignment tuning, latent regularization, model firewalls, ensemble smoothing, and provenance verification and identifies tradeoffs connected with these methods. Although no experimental data has been reported in this article, the conceptual frameworks of generative AI robustness help in the future of research on multimodal robustness and generative model defensive design, as well as supply chain verification.

**Keywords:** Adversarial attacks · Large language models · Transformers · Generative Artificial Intelligence

## 1 Introduction

Generative Artificial Intelligence has quickly grown to be one of the most impactful technological advancements of the decade. Large language models (LLMs) can be used to produce human text, diffusion models can generate photorealistic images, GANs can generate high-quality deepfakes, and VAEs have been used to allow latent generative exploration in scientific and industrial applications. These technologies are now integrated in digital infrastructures- creative tools and virtual assistants, enterprise search, analytics platforms and autonomous multi-agent systems [1–3].

This fast adoption is accompanied by an increasing number of vulnerabilities. Generative models learn on complex probability spaces as well as attention-based reasoning systems, which are adversarial and manipulable. Transformers, VAEs, GANs, diffusion models, and retrieval-augmented systems have prompt injection, latent drift, discriminator, denoising-chain instability, and pipeline vulnerabilities to attackers, respectively. The vulnerabilities lower the trust, raise safety concerns, and bring operational risks to high-stakes areas.


R. Stahlbock et al. (Eds.): CSCE 2025, CCIS 2938, pp. 511–518, 2027.
https://doi.org/10.1007/978-3-032-22196-4_38

Irrespective of the importance of GenAI vulnerabilities, the research is still divided. The current literature tends to separate analyses to single model family or even small threat category. Not much integration of architectural vulnerabilities, system level risks, supply chain exposure, and real-world adversarial tactics are implemented. Moreover, there is no unified system of analysis of generative model robustness or unified defense design [4, 5].

To fill the gaps presented in this paper, an in-depth architectural survey is provided along with the presentation of two conceptual frameworks, which are thoroughly developed: the Generative AI Robustness Index (GRI) and the Dual-Layer Defence Strategy (DLD). All these frameworks enable systematic assessment, quantifiable enhancement, and scalable security design.

## 2 Architectural Foundations and Their Security Implications

To realize the vulnerabilities, it is important to study the generative architectures themselves.

### 2.1 GANs:The Adversarial Dynamics and Instability

GANs are based on a minimax loss between the discriminator and the generator. Through this antagonistic interaction, synthesis is high-quality and structural fragility is generated. Subtle manipulation can be done on the discriminator that is usually overfitted or not well calibrated. They can be frequency-domain modifications, latent-vector modifications or poisoned feedback by attackers to either evade detection systems or weaken the model performance. The memorization properties of the generator are also a source of privacy threat and inversion attacks [6, 7].

### 2.2 VAEs: Latent Continuity and Drift

VAEs represent data in a continuous latent distribution through which decoder produces outputs. This continuous latent space can support generativity, but it is vulnerable to latent-drift attacks. Latent variable manipulations in many cases can cause the outputs to pass through anomaly detectors or conceal malicious content. The posterior distributions are also leaked, and this exposes the attacker to privacy invasion by approximating or reconstructing latent patterns [8].

### 2.3 Diffusion Models: Iterative Denoising Vulnerabilities

Diffusion models are models that synthesize data by reversing a process of noise-injection. This is made possible by the sequential denoising mechanism which enables adversarial influences to flow through the steps. Changes that happen in the early part of the chain are represented by structured semantic alterations in final products. Soon, there will come adversaries misleading denoising trajectories or circumventing safety filters using prompt encoders, especially cross-attention-based ones. These diffusion models memorize training examples in the latent states of intermediate latent states as well, which provides reconstruction-based attacks [9].

### 2.4 Transformers: Contextual Manipulation and Prompt Sensitivity

Transformers are self-attention based power sources and hence they are contextually sensitive. Safety policies are subjugated by the contextual manipulation in a way that prompts immediate injection. Attacks based on jailbreaks use reasoning templates, obfuscated prompts or cross-lingual patterns. Memorization leaks, attention-residual inversion and high-level tool-use misdirection are susceptible in agentic work processes with transformers. Their connection to external systems which are the APIs and databases and vector stores increases the attack surface to a very large extent beyond the model [10].

## 3 Vulnerability Landscape Across Generative Models

The AI vulnerabilities lie on the architectural, semantic, probabilistic, and procedural levels.

Transformers are vulnerable to prompt-based manipulation, jailbreaks, data leakage and reasoning-path exploitation. GANs suffer discriminator poisoning, deepfake evasion as well as latent perturbation. VAEs are subject to latent drift attacks and reconstruction attacks. Diffusion models are associated with embedding attacks, noise-path attacks, and prompt-based safety bypass. In addition to architectures, the multimodal attacks generate perturbations that are cross-modal. Pipelines that are retrieval-augmented are susceptible to document poisoning, drift of vectors and chain of thought contamination [11, 12].

## 4 Defense Mechanisms: Strengths and Weaknesses

### 4.1 Training-Time Defences

Adversarial training, latent regularization, robust optimization and red teaming are examples of training-time defences that enhance the internal model robustness. However, adversarial training is expensive and can be prone to expand to certain perturbations. Under multi-turn adaptive jailbreaks, alignment tuning enhances the safety of LLM, yet does not work. Latent regularization is more stable and less generative.

### 4.2 Inference-Time Defences

Defences that operate at inference-time consist of immediate filtering by LLM firewalls, consistency checking by ensembles, watermarking and defensive decoding techniques. Such systems block numerous explicit attacks, but introduce latency, cannot handle new patterns of attack, and produce false alarms in highly creative tasks.

### 4.3 Pipeline Monitoring

The real-life applications demand observing the user activities, agent activities, retrieval activities, and the output patterns. Covert adversarial manipulation can be detected with pipeline monitoring, but has privacy restrictions, overhead, and scale limitations.

# 5 Proposed Frameworks

The following section is a more rigorous and expanded version of the two suggested frameworks, the Generative AI Robustness Index (GRI) and the Dual-Layer Defense Strategy (DLD). These wider systems integrate evaluation and defense design in the generative structures.

Given that the neural network is trained to generate content, it is essential to assess its ability to withstand any type of adversarial example, including sensitive information or unrelated images. <|human|>5.1 Generative AI Robustness Index (GRI) Since the neural network is designed to generate content, it is necessary to determine the resistance of the neural network to any form of adversarial example, such as sensitive data or irrelevant images [13].

## 5.1 A Multi-dimensional Metric to measure Generative Model Security

### 5.1.1 Rationale

Robustness measures publicly studied in deep learning are usually concerned with accuracy of classifiers to perturbations. Generative models cannot be evaluated based on such metrics and need to remain creative, semantically stable, safe, and private and withstand a wide range of attacks. GRI tries to fill this gap by harmonizing the assessment of architectures, types of attacks, and operational factors [14].

### 5.1.2 Metric Architecture

GRI provides a measure of strength in three conceptual dimensions:

***Attack Coverage (AC)***
Attack Coverage is used to measure the scope of adversarial manipulations the model is able to withstand. It identifies the vulnerabilities that include:

- Instant injection and jailbreak hack on Transformers.
- Latent perturbation and drift of VAEs.
- Frequency GAN attacks and discriminator-evasion attacks.
- Prompt-induced alignment and embedding manipulation diffusion models.
- Attacks on the cross-modal transfer.

Attack coverage combines the known attack classes and resilience to perturbations never seen before both using stress-testing structures. It does not only measure binary success/failure, but goes further to measure the extent of output quality degradation.

***Defense Overhead (DO)***
Defense Overhead provides a measure of the computational, operational and scalability effect of mitigations. This includes:

- Latency of inference increased.
- Additional graphics processing unit/Tibetan processor memory usage.
- Number of external defence modules called.

- Change in cloud cost and throughput.
- Enterprise pipeline complexity of integration.

GRI incentive-based on the quantification of overhead to encourage defenses to scale in high throughput environment.

***Output Quality Preservation (OQP)***
OQP is a measure of the quality of generative quality retained when under defensive conditions. Unreasonable safety constraints can inhibit creativity, lower image fidelity, linguistic coherence or semantic consistency [15, 16].

OQP captures:

- Human-judged quality
- Semantic alignment
- Diversity and Novelty
- Content Coherence
- Lack of degenerated generational schemes (e.g. over smoothing, repetitive token collapse)

### 5.1.3 Aggregation Method

Weighted composite function is used to give the dimensions:

$$GRI = w_{AC} \cdot AC + w_{DO} \cdot DO + w_{OQP} \cdot OQP$$

Where the weights are based on application needs.

For example:

- AC (safety) is a priority in a medical system.
- An innovative design system is interested in OQP (quality).
- A chatbot that is real-time has DO (latency issues) as its priority.

### 5.1.4 Comparative Interpretation

GRI allows the cross-model comparisons whereby the stakeholders can select the models based on the risk profiles.

For example:

- A high capability model that has weak AC yet strong OQP can be inappropriate to regulated realms.
- A highly coordinated model with lower latency yet less creativity can be applicable to enterprise RAG applications.

The index gives an organized quantitative perspective of security trade-offs.

## 5.2 Two-Layer Defense Strategy (DLD)

A Framework on Defense-in-Depth at Generative AI Lifecycle.

### 5.2.1 Motivation

Attackers based on generative AI evolve quickly. One defense, either adversarial training or prompt filtering cannot resist changing attack methods. DLD has a layered philosophy of cybersecurity best practices, which is specific to the generative architecture properties.

### 5.2.2 Layer 1: Training-Time Hardening

Training-time hardening is concerned with internal strength that is built into the model prior to deployment. It includes:

- Adversarial training on input, latent space, prompt space and intermediate layers.
- Latent regularization, which constitutes smooth controlled latent manifolds.
- Strong optimization that aims at sensitivity minimization.
- Red teaming to reveal structural weaknesses.
- Poisoned samples: dataset sanitization to eliminate them.
- Checkpoint, model weights, and embeddings verification of the supply chain.
- Fairness and bias audits counterproductive practices.

The hardening of the training-time increases the structural resilience by conditioning model gradients, latent geometry and decision boundaries.

### 5.2.3 Layer 2: Time-of-Inference Protection

Inference Time security offers real-time operational security:

- Filtering of user prompts on LLM firewalls or guard models.
- Ensemble smoothing in order to identify adversarial inconsistencies.
- Policy enforcement systems and content moderation systems.
- Media detection of watermarking.
- Detecting anomalies of prompt-behavior.
- Agent-execution tracing to identify tools use suspiciousness.
- Live-time logs and threat pipelines.

Layer 2 is a perimeter security mechanism. Although the model may be internally vulnerable (Layer 1 fails) inference-time defenses may capture harmful activity.

### 5.2.4 Interaction Between Layers

The two layers are complementary to each other. Training-time hardening makes the model less susceptible to subtle perturbations, whereas inference-time defenses detect high-level manipulations. The combination of these elements forms a multi-barrier structure which adds to the cost of the adversary, decreases the possibility of attack and limits the magnitude of damage.

### 5.2.5 Loop of Continuous Improvement

DLD has a cycle that is iterative:

- Monitor unfriendly efforts.

- Feeding the anomalies of the feed into the retraining pipelines.
- Strengthen the weak areas revealed in deployment.
- Update inference-time rulesets measurability through GRI scoring.
- Evaluate improvements via GRI scoring

So, the system is developed instead of having stagnant defenses.

### 5.3 Joint Use of GRI and DLD

GRI is the evaluation tool and DLD the blueprint. Organizations calculate GRI scores in order to measure the robustness and find weak dimensions after initially applying DLD. Low Attack Coverage means the training has not been hardened, high Defense Overhead means the inference has not been low-efficiency, and weak Output Quality Preservation means that the alignment is over-constrained. This is a synergy process which is iterative and can be measured and systematically improved.

## 6 Conclusion and Future Directions

The dynamic threat environment of generative systems requires sound theoretical and practical frameworks of defense. Despite the great steps that have been taken in this regard, there exist numerous gaps that have not been exploited. Generalized adversarial training, interpretable latent-space security, scalable provenance tracking, multimodal alignment theory, cross-modal attack detection, interpretable latent-space security are also open-ended research questions. Also, there is a need to have supply-chain verification of the open-source generative ecosystems more rigorous to avoid the checkpoint tampering and the distribution of the poisoned models.

To analyze the vulnerabilities in GANs, VAEs, diffusion models, and Transformers, this paper provided an in-depth architectural study of their vulnerabilities. It identified the necessity of multi-layered defense strategies through the analysis of both the structural and system-level threats. The Generative AI Robustness Index is a structured, interpretable methodology of assessing generative robustness and the Dual-Layer Defense Strategy is a flexible roadmap of defensive generative systems in practice.

With the adoption of GenAI into mission-critical settings, capability to assess, robust, and keep improving generative models will become the key to safe and reliable AI implementation. The presented conceptual frameworks are the foundations of the further empirical studies, cross-model benchmarking, and operational standards of security that will be able to adjust to the constantly changing generative scene.

## References


1. Eason, G., Noble, B., Sneddon, I.N.: On certain integrals of Lipschitz-Hankel type involving products of Bessel functions. Phil. Trans. R. Soc. Lond. **A247**, 529–551 (1955)
2. Clerk Maxwell, J.: A Treatise on Electricity and Magnetism, 3rd edn., vol. 2, pp. 68–73. Clarendon, Oxford (1892)
3. Jacobs, I.S., Bean, C.P.: Fine particles, thin films and exchange anisotropy. In: Rado, G.T., Suhl, H. (eds) Magnetism, vol. III, pp. 271–350. Academic, New York (1963)

4. Yorozu, Y., Hirano, M., Oka, K., Tagawa, Y.: Electron spectroscopy studies on magneto-optical media and plastic substrate interface. IEEE Transl. J. Magn. Japan **2**, 740–741 (1987)
5. Young, M.: The Technical Writer's Handbook. University Science, Mill Valley (1989)
6. Eves, K., Valasek, J.: Adaptive control for singularly perturbed systems examples, code ocean, August 2023
7. Kingma, D.P., Welling, M.: Auto-encoding variational Bayes. arXiv:1312.6114 (2013)
8. Liu, S.: Wi-Fi energy detection testbed (12MTC). GitHub repository (2023)
9. Treatment episode data set: discharges (TEDS-D): concatenated, 2006 to 2009. U.S. Department of Health and Human Services, Substance Abuse and Mental Health Services Administration, Office of Applied Studies, August 2013
10. Zou, A., et al.: SmoothLLM: defending large language models against jailbreak attacks via randomized smoothing. arXiv preprint arXiv:2311.09052 (2023)
11. Zhang, H., et al.: The limitations of adversarial training and the blind-spot attack. In: ICLR (2021)
12. Liu, Y., et al.: FreqNet: cross-domain deepfake detection via frequency-based architecture. IEEE Trans. Pattern Anal. Mach. Intell. **45**(6), 7032–7045 (2023)
13. Adobe, Microsoft: Content authenticity initiative and C2PA standards. In: IEEE/IFIP International Conference on Dependable Systems and Networks (DSN) (2022)
14. Ding, J., et al.: SRL-VAE: improving robustness of variational autoencoders with smooth robust latent regularization. In: AAAI Conference on Artificial Intelligence (2023)
15. Higgins, I., et al.: beta-VAE: learning basic visual concepts with a constrained variational framework. In: International Conference on Learning Representations (ICLR) (2017)
16. An, J., Cho, S.: Variational autoencoder based anomaly detection using reconstruction probability. Spec. Lect. IE **2**(1), 1–18 (2015)

# Machine Learning and Explainable Artificial Intelligence for Network Intrusion Detection

Ibidun Christiana Obagbuwa[1(✉)], Madison Ngafeeson[2], and Oluwatimileyin Favour Obagbuwa[3]

[1] Department of Mathematical Sciences and Computing, Faculty of Natural Sciences, Walter Sisulu University, Mthatha, South Africa
iobagbuwa@wsu.ac.za
[2] Rinker School of Business, Palm Beach Atlantic University, c, Florida, USA
madison_Ngafeeson@pba.edu
[3] School of Computer Science and Applied Mathematics, University of the Witwatersrand, Johannesburg, South Africa

**Keywords:** Cybersecurity · Machine Learning · Network Intrusion Detection · XGBoost · SHAP · Explainable AI · Anomaly Detection

## 1 Introduction

As cyber threats evolve in complexity and scale, traditional signature-based intrusion detection systems (IDS) have proven inadequate in addressing new and sophisticated attacks. In response, machine learning (ML) offers promising approaches for detecting anomalies in network traffic. However, a significant limitation of ML models is their lack of interpretability, which hinders trust and understanding of their predictions. Explainable Artificial Intelligence (XAI), specifically SHapley Additive exPlanations (SHAP), addresses this challenge by making ML decisions more transparent.

This study evaluates the performance of four ML algorithms, Naïve Bayes, Random Forest, XGBoost, and Convolutional Neural Network (CNN) in detecting network intrusions using the CIC-IDS2017 dataset. The research further integrates SHAP analysis to enhance model interpretability, with the goal of delivering a robust, transparent, and deployable intrusion detection framework.

## 2 Literature Review

Existing research demonstrates that ML techniques such as Random Forest, XGBoost, and deep learning models like CNNs and LSTMs are highly effective in cybersecurity applications. Shah (2021) and Bharadiya (2023) emphasize the superior accuracy of ML models in identifying threats like malware and zero-day exploits. However, most deep learning models suffer from limited interpretability. Do et al. (2024) and Hooshmand et al. (2024) highlight the value of SHAP in enhancing transparency and understanding model behavior, especially in cybersecurity contexts. Furthermore, balancing imbalanced datasets remains a persistent challenge, affecting the generalization capabilities of ML-based IDS.


R. Stahlbock et al. (Eds.): CSCE 2025, CCIS 2938, pp. 519–521, 2027.
https://doi.org/10.1007/978-3-032-22196-4_39

The present study addresses these gaps by combining performance evaluation and interpretability through SHAP, focusing on both model efficacy and explainability.

## 3 Methodology

The study employs the CIC-IDS2017 dataset, which comprises labeled network traffic including benign data and several attack types (e.g., DoS, brute force, port scan, botnet). After data consolidation, 308,381 duplicate records were removed to improve data integrity. Data imbalance was addressed through resampling, ensuring equitable representation of minority classes.

The preprocessing pipeline includes normalization of numerical features and encoding of categorical variables. The dataset was split into training and testing sets.

Four models were developed and trained:

i. Naïve Bayes: Probabilistic model known for simplicity and speed.
ii. Random Forest: Ensemble of decision trees providing robust performance.
iii. XGBoost: Gradient boosting framework known for high accuracy and computational efficiency.
iv. CNN: Deep learning model capable of capturing complex patterns in structured network data.

The models were evaluated using accuracy, precision, recall, and F1-score. SHAP was applied to all models to analyze feature importance and interactions influencing predictions.

## 4 Results and Discussion

**Model Performance**
XGBoost outperformed all models with 99.7% accuracy, 99.71% precision, recall, and F1-score. CNN achieved 97% across all metrics. Random Forest achieved 96%, and Naïve Bayes 93%.

**Confusion Matrix Insights**
XGBoost showed near-perfect classification with minimal confusion among classes. CNN and Random Forest demonstrated high accuracy but had some misclassifications, especially between "BENIGN" and "Bot". Naïve Bayes performed adequately but struggled with distinguishing similar classes.

**SHAP Interpretability**
Across all models, Destination Port, Flow Duration, and Total Packet Length were the most influential features. SHAP interaction values in XGBoost revealed the synergistic effects of features, enhancing model transparency. For Naïve Bayes, removing negatively contributing features slightly improved accuracy (from 93% to 94%).

**Comparison with Prior Work**

The proposed XGBoost model outperforms existing model in Alkhudaydi et al. (2023), showing improved accuracy (99.7% vs. 98.52%) and F1-score (99.71% vs. 97.27%).

**Practical Implications**

These findings underscore the feasibility of deploying ML models, particularly XGBoost, in real-world intrusion detection systems. SHAP analysis facilitates trust and interpretability, essential for cybersecurity analysts. The results encourage a shift toward explainable, data-driven threat detection frameworks.

## 5 Conclusion

This study presents a comparative analysis of ML models for network intrusion detection, demonstrating that XGBoost delivers the best performance on the CIC-IDS2017 dataset. Through SHAP analysis, the research also provides interpretability, identifying key features such as Destination Port and Packet Length as vital in intrusion detection.

The integration of XAI with ML enhances trust and operational value, making the proposed system suitable for real-world applications. While the results are promising, future work should focus on evaluating these models in real-time environments and across diverse datasets to ensure broader applicability and robustness.

## References

Shah, V.: Machine learning algorithms for cybersecurity: detecting and preventing threats. Revista Espanola de Documentacion Cientifica **15**(4), 42–66 (2021)

Bharadiya, J.: Machine learning in cybersecurity: techniques and challenges. Eur. J. Technol. **7**(2), 1–14 (2023)

Do, U., Lahesoo, L., Carnier, R.M., Fukuda, K.: Evaluation of XAI algorithms in IoT traffic anomaly detection. In: 2024 International Conference on Artificial Intelligence in Information and Communication (ICAIIC), pp. 669–674. IEEE, February 2024

Hooshmand, M.K., Huchaiah, M.D., Alzighaibi, A.R., Hashim, H., Atlam, E.S., Gad, I.: Robust network anomaly detection using ensemble learning approach and explainable artificial intelligence (XAI). Alex. Eng. J. **94**, 120–130 (2024)

# Author Index




R. Stahlbock et al. (Eds.): CSCE 2025, CCIS 2938, pp. 523–524, 2027.
https://doi.org/10.1007/978-3-032-22196-4

Zeitfracht Medien GmbH
Ferdinand-Jühlke-Straße 7
99095 Erfurt, Deutschland
produktsicherheit@kolibri360.de